Thomas Power O'Connor

The Cabinet of Irish Literature

Selections From the Works of the Chief Poets, Orators, and Prose Writers of Ireland

Thomas Power O'Connor

The Cabinet of Irish Literature
Selections From the Works of the Chief Poets, Orators, and Prose Writers of Ireland

ISBN/EAN: 9783744689717

Printed in Europe, USA, Canada, Australia, Japan

Cover: Foto ©Thomas Meinert / pixelio.de

More available books at **www.hansebooks.com**

THE CABINET

OF

IRISH LITERATURE.

OF

IRISH LITERATURE:

SELECTIONS FROM THE WORKS OF THE

CHIEF POETS, ORATORS, AND PROSE WRITERS
OF IRELAND.

WITH BIOGRAPHICAL SKETCHES AND LITERARY NOTICES,

BY

CHARLES A. READ, F.R.H.S.,

Author of "Tales and Stories of Irish Life," "Stories from the Ancient Classics," &c.

VOL. IV.

By T. P. O'CONNOR, M.A.

LONDON: BLACKIE & SON, OLD BAILEY;
GLASGOW, EDINBURGH, AND DUBLIN.
SAMUEL L. HALL, 757 BROADWAY, NEW YORK.
1884.

CONTENTS OF VOLUME IV.

		PAGE
Portrait—CHARLES JAMES LEVER—From a photograph by Chancellor, Dublin,	...frontispiece.	
,, MRS. S. C. HALL—From a photograph by Frankland, London,	to face	34
,, THE RIGHT HON. JAMES WHITESIDE—From a photograph by Mayall, London,	,,	64
,, SIR CHARLES GAVAN DUFFY—From a photograph by Lesage, Dublin,	,,	108
,, ISAAC BUTT, M.P.—From a photograph by O'Shea, Limerick,	,,	164
,, THE RIGHT HON. EARL CAIRNS—From a photograph by Russell, Chichester,	,,	202
,, THE RIGHT HON. EARL DUFFERIN, K.C.B.—From a photo. by Notman, Montreal,	,,	246
,, JUSTIN MCCARTHY, M.P.—From a photograph by the London Stereoscopic Co.,	,,	306

	PAGE
CHARLES JAMES LEVER (1806–1872),	1
An Irish Legislator of the Olden Time (from "Charles O'Malley"),	4
A Father and Son (from "Luttrell of Arran"),	9
Song—The Irish Dragoon,	12
,, Mickey Free's Ancestry,	13
,, The "Man for Galway,"	13
,, The Widow Malone,	13
,, Bad Luck to this Marching,	14
ARCHBISHOP M'HALE (b. 1791),	14
An Irish Parliament and an Irish Famine (from "Letters"),	15
SIR JOSEPH NAPIER (b. 1804),	17
Character of Burke,	18
JAMES GODKIN (b. 1806),	19
Ulster in Eighteenth Century (from "The Land-war in Ireland"),	19
ARCHBISHOP TRENCH (b. 1807),	22
The Poetry of Words (from "The Study of Words"),	22
The Evening Hymn,	24
Some Murmur,	24
JOHN PATRICK PRENDERGAST (b. 1807),	24
The Clearing of Galway (from "The Cromwellian Settlement"),	24
HON. MRS. CAROLINE NORTON (1807–1877),	26
The Gipsy Girl in Prison (from "The Child of the Islands"),	28
The Child of Earth,	29
The Blind Man to his Bride,	30
The Arab's Farewell to his Steed,	30
JOHN EDWARD WALSH (1816–1869),	31
A Tragic Case of Abduction (from "Ireland Ninety Years Ago"),	32
MRS. S. C. HALL (1805–1881),	34
An Irish Tragedy (from "Lights and Shadows of Irish Life"),	36
AUBREY T. DE VERE (b. 1814),	40
Florence MacCarthy's Farewell to his English Love,	41
The March to Kinsale,	41
The Intercession,	42
Dirge of Rory O'More,	42
O Woods!	43
The Long Dying,	43
Grattan,	43
The "Old Land,"	43
The Little Black Rose,	44
JOSEPH SHERIDAN LE FANU (1814–1873),	44
A Narrow Escape from Murder,	45
Shemus O'Brien,	48
MARMION W. SAVAGE (1823–1872),	51
An Adventurous Couple (from "The Falcon Family,"	51
THOMAS FRANCIS MEAGHER (1823–1867),	54
Speech from the Dock,	55
Nash and the Dragoons (from "Recollections of Ireland and the Irish"),	56
SIR SAMUEL FERGUSON (b. 1810),	58
The Forging of the Anchor,	58
Una Phelimy,	60
The Fairy Thorn,	61
Willy Gilliland,	62
Pastheen Fion,	64
JAMES WHITESIDE (1806–1876),	64
Speech on the Yelverton Case,	66
Speech in Defence of Charles Gavan Duffy,	68
THOMAS D'ARCY M'GEE (1825–1868),	71
The Celts,	72
Memories,	73
Am I Remembered?	73
My Irish Wife,	73
Death of the Homeward Bound,	74
Home Thoughts,	74
The Death of O'Carolan,	74
WILLIAM M'CULLAGH TORRENS (b. 1813),	75
Byron and Lady Caroline Lamb (from Biography of Lord Melbourne),	75

CONTENTS OF VOLUME IV.

	PAGE
LADY WILDE ("Speranza"),	79
To Ireland,	80
The Year of Revolutions,	81
The Famine Year,	81
The Exodus,	82
Related Souls,	83
MEADOWS TAYLOR (1808–1876),	84
How the Mutiny was Prepared (from "Seeta"),	84
THOMAS CAULFIELD IRWIN (b. 1823),	90
Lucy's Attire,	90
Hymn to Eurydice,	91
Hearth Song,	91
L'Angelo,	92
An Urn,	92
England,	92
Summer Wanderings,	93
Sonnet,	93
RICHARD FRANCIS BURTON (b. 1821),	93
Female Influence and Poetry among the Arabs (from "Pilgrimages to Mecca," &c.),	94
JAMES RODERICK O'FLANAGAN (b. 1814),	97
Harry Deane Grady (from "The Irish Bar"),	97
WILLIAM CONNOR MAGEE, D.D. (b. 1821),	99
Christianity and Scepticism,	100
WILLIAM HOWARD RUSSELL (b. 1821),	104
After the Fall of Sebastopol (from "Letters from the Crimea"),	105
SIR CHARLES GAVAN DUFFY (b. 1816),	108
A Lay Sermon,	109
The Irish Chiefs,	110
Innishowen,	111
The Patriot's Bride,	112
JULIA KAVANAGH (1824–1877),	113
The Sisters (from "Nathalie"),	113
RICHARD DALTON WILLIAMS (1822–1862),	117
Ben-Heder,	117
Adieu to Innisfail,	118
My Cousin,	119
FRANCES POWER COBBE (b. 1822),	121
Chivalry of the Period (from "Re-echoes"),	121
JOHN FRANCIS WALLER (b. 1810),	123
The Spinning-wheel Song,	123
A Plea for Irish Song,	124
The Song of the Glass,	124
Welcome as Flowers in May,	125
Kitty Neil,	125
JOHN TYNDALL (b. 1820),	126
Scientific Limit of the Imagination,	126
JOHN CRAWFORD WILSON (b. 1825),	130
The Death of Lily,	130
How Cæsar was Driven from Ireland,	131
ANNIE KEARY (1825–1879),	132
A Scene in the Famine (from "Castle Daly"),	133
WILLIAM ALLINGHAM,	137
Ballytullagh (from "Laurence Bloomfield"),	138
Going to the Fair (do.),	138

	PAGE
Lovely Mary Donnelly,	139
Abbey Asaroe,	139
Across the Sea,	140
MAYNE REID (b. 1819),	140
The Wild West (from "The Scalp-hunters"),	141
Capture of an Indian Chief (do.),	143
EVA MARY KELLY,	145
The People's Chief,	146
Tipperary,	146
Murmurs of Love,	147
ELLEN DOWNING,	145
Past and Present,	147
Talk by the Blackwater,	148
CHARLES JOSEPH KICKHAM (b. 1830),	148
The Schoolmaster's Story (from "Sally Cavanagh"),	149
Patrick Sheehan,	153
The Irish Peasant Girl,	153
DENIS FLORENCE MACCARTHY (b. 1817),	154
The Pillar Towers of Ireland,	154
The Clan of Mac Caura,	155
The Seasons of the Heart,	156
Centenary Ode on Thomas Moore,	157
MARTIN HAVERTY (b. 1809),	158
The Elopement of Hugh O'Neill (from "History of Ireland"),	159
CHARLES GRAHAM HALPINE (1829–1868),	159
A Vesper Hymn,	160
Not a Star from the Flag,	160
Irish Astronomy,	161
Adieu,	161
JOHN FRANCIS O'DONNELL (1837–1874),	162
Where?	162
Tombs in the Church of Montorio,	163
Guesses,	163
ISAAC BUTT (1813–1879),	164
Speech on Land Tenure,	165
Lecture on Bishop Berkeley's Theory,	167
WILLIAM ALEXANDER, D.D. (b. 1824),	170
Death of an Arctic Hero,	171
Below and Above,	172
MRS. ALEXANDER,	170
The Burial of Moses,	172
FRANCIS DAVIS (b. 1810),	173
Caste and Creed,	174
My Kallagh Dhu Asthore,	175
Only a Fancy,	175
DION BOUCICAULT (b. 1822),	176
The Man of Fashion in the Country (from "London Assurance"),	176
Origin of "The Shaughraun,"	179
FRANCES BROWNE (b. 1816),	182
The Returning Janissary,	182
The Last Friends,	183
What hath Time taken?	184

CONTENTS OF VOLUME IV.

	PAGE
SIR GARNET JOSEPH WOLSELEY (b. 1833),	184
Sack of the Summer Palace (from "Narrative of the War with China"),	185
The City of Nankin (do.),	186
With the Rebels at Nankin (do.),	187
JOHN KEEGAN CASEY (1846–1870),	188
Song of Golden-headed Niamh,	188
My Cailín Ruadh,	188
Donal Kenny,	189
WILLIAM E. H. LECKY (b. 1838),	189
Dublin in the Eighteenth Century (from "History of England"),	190
Influence of the Elder Pitt (do.),	193
Character of Marcus Aurelius (from "History of European Morals"),	196
BARTHOLOMEW SIMMONS (d. 1850),	198
Napoleon's Last Look,	198
The Flight to Cyprus,	199
EARL CAIRNS (b. 1819),	201
Speech—On the Oude Proclamation,	201
" The Empress of India,	204
J. L. PORTER (b. 1823),	207
Lydda (from "The Giant Cities of Bashan"),	207
The Druses (do.),	208
Eastern Politeness (from "Handbook for Syria and Palestine"),	209
ALFRED PERCEVAL GRAVES (b. 1846),	211
Irish Spinning-wheel Song,	211
Irish Lullaby,	212
Father O'Flynn,	212
Love's Wishes,	212
The Banks of the Daisies,	213
I Once Loved a Boy,	213
Irish Lamentation to the Ulster Goll,	213
THOMAS N. BURKE (b. 1830),	213
A Nation's History,	214
The Curse of Ignorance,	215
National Music,	216
WILLIAM FRANCIS BUTLER (b. 1838),	218
A View of the Prairie (from "The Wild North Land"),	218
My Shipmates (from "The Great Lone Land"),	219
First Sight of the Rocky Mountains (do.),	220
An African Queen (from "Akim-foo"),	221
A Forest Scene in Africa (do.),	222
TIMOTHY DANIEL SULLIVAN (b. 1827),	223
O'Neill in Rome,	224
The Little Wife,	225
Song from the Backwoods,	225
To my Brother,	226
Donal of Beara (from "Dunboy"),	226
The Farmer's Son,	226
A Letter,	227
You and I,	227
ALEXANDER MARTIN SULLIVAN (b. 1830),	228
"Forty Eight" (from "New Ireland"),	228
PATRICK WESTON JOYCE (b. 1827),	233
Fairies and the Names of Places,	233
Connla of the Golden Hair (from "Old Celtic Romances"),	235
ROBERT DWYER JOYCE (b. 1830),	237
Naisi receives his Sword (from "Deirdrè"),	237
The Exploits of Curoi (from "Blanid"),	238
The Blacksmith of Limerick,	239
WILLIAM JOHN FITZPATRICK (b. 1830),	240
Anecdotes of Keogh, the Irish Massillon (from "Irish Wits and Worthies"),	241
Finglas Churchyard (do.),	243
EARL OF DUFFERIN (b. 1826),	245
An Icelandic Dinner (from "Letters from High Latitudes"),	246
On Irishmen as Rulers,	248
A Plea for Toleration,	250
JOHN CASHEL HOEY (b. 1828),	251
Origin of O'Connell,	251
The Coast of Clare,	253
MRS. CASHEL HOEY (b. 1830),	253
A Terrible Interview (from "No Sign"),	253
WILLIAM GORMAN WILLS (b. 1828),	258
The Queen and Cromwell (from "Charles the First"),	259
WILLIAM ARTHUR (b. 1819),	260
Commercial Biography (from "The Successful Merchant"),	261
Position and Mind (do.),	262
SIR WILLIAM THOMSON (b. 1824),	264
The Origin of Life,	264
JOHN TODHUNTER (b. 1839),	266
The Daughter of Hippocrates,	267
Song—Hither, O Love!	269
Chorale—Where shall Freedom's banner,	269
Lost,	269
Found,	269
ROSA MULHOLLAND,	270
The Pursuit of a Rebel (from "Hester's History"),	270
J. A. MACGAHAN (1845–1878),	273
The Russian Officer (from "Campaigning on the Oxus"),	273
MISS CASEY (E. OWENS BLACKBURNE) (b. 1848),	277
Biddy Brady's Banshee (from "A Bunch of Shamrocks"),	277
JOHN BOYLE O'REILLY,	280
Chunder Ali's Wife,	280
My Native Land,	281
My Mother's Memory,	281
Unspoken Words,	281
JOHN PETTLAND MAHAFFY (b. 1839),	282
Thoughts on Nearing Greece (from "Rambles and Studies in Greece"),	282
Marathon (do.),	283
The Acropolis of Athens and the Rock of Cashel (do.),	284
RICHARD DOWLING (b. 1846),	285
The Deaf-Mute casts off his Son (from "The Mystery of Killard"),	286

CONTENTS OF VOLUME IV.

	PAGE
ARTHUR O'SHAUGHNESSY (1840–1881),	289
Supreme Summer,	289
Song—In the long enchanted Weather,	290
" Has Summer come without the Rose,	291
The Fountain of Tears,	291
HON. LEWIS WINGFIELD (b. 1842),	292
Strogue Abbey (from "My Lords of Strogue")	292
Ennishowen (do.),	294
MISS LAFFAN,	296
Three Dublin Arabs (from "Flitters, Tatters, and the Counsellor"),	297
The Death of Flitters (do.),	298
EDWARD DOWDEN (b. 1843),	301
The Growth of Shakspere's Mind and Art,	301
The Singer,	302
MARGARET STOKES,	303
The Northmen in Ireland (from "Early Christian Architecture in Ireland"),	303
JUSTIN MCCARTHY (b. 1830),	305
The Afghan Tragedy (from "A History of our own Times"),	306
EDMUND JOHN ARMSTRONG (1841–1865)	312
Mary of Clorah,	312
A Journey in Woe (from "The Prisoner of Mount St. Michael"),	314
Pilgrims,	315
GEORGE FRANCIS ARMSTRONG (b. 1845),	316
Ugone's Last Hours,	316
STANDISH O'GRADY (b. 1846),	318
Fight of Cuculain and Fardia (from "History of Ireland"),	318
MRS. J. H. RIDDELL,	321
Not Proven (from "A Life's Assize"),	322
JOHN T. GILBERT,	324
The Limits of the Pale (from "History of the Viceroys of Ireland"),	325
EARL OF DUNRAVEN (b. 1841),	327
Canoe Travelling (from "The Great Divide"),	327
A City in the Great West (do.),	328
CHARLES A. READ (1841–1878),	330
An Irish Mistake,	331
Beyond the River,	334
LIST OF AUTHORS IN THE WORK,	335

THE CABINET

OF

IRISH LITERATURE.

PERIOD A.D. 1800—1880.

CHARLES LEVER.

BORN 1806—DIED 1872.

[Charles Lever belongs to the class of authors whom readers regard with a personal love. The kindness of heart, the sunniness of temper, the high spirit, and pure feeling that are found in his books naturally suggest the idea that the author himself possessed the virtues he portrayed; and the assumption is correct. Charles Lever was, indeed, like one of those Irish gentlemen whom his pen has made as familiar figures to us as beings of real life; and his character and career were, like theirs, full of light and shade, of virtues and foibles. His generosity often degenerated into recklessness and display; he did an immense deal of work, but his work was desultory, and often careless; and a stout heart occasionally broke down, and a sanguine temperament turned to despair, before small obstacles and trifling sorrows. But, take him with all his faults, Lever was a true man—a true Irishman; proud, courageous, high-minded; a faithful husband, a devoted father, an affectionate friend, and a passionate lover of his country and countrymen.

Curiously enough, this singularly Celtic character was only half Irish. His father, James Lever, was an Englishman, and the descendant of an old Lancashire family. Emigrating to Ireland James Lever found his nationality a considerable recommendation to the government of the day: for those were the times when, in the words of the old song, "'Twas treason to be a Milesian." He was a carpenter and builder by trade, and he obtained profitable employment in erecting the spacious Custom House, whose lofty halls now resound, not with the joyful voice of bustling trade, but with the melancholy echoes of officials or tourists. When the Bank of Ireland, too, was removed from Mary's Abbey to the seat of the old Parliament in College Green, Lever officiated as clerk of the works while the necessary alterations were being made. He was also engaged in building the new college at Maynooth. In 1795 he married Julia, daughter of Mathew Chandler, and descendant of an old Cromwellian family. The issue of this marriage were two sons—James, born in 1796, and Charles James, who first saw the light ten years later, namely, on August 31, 1806. Charles went to various schools before he was ripe for Trinity College, and numerous stories are, of course, told to show that, like so many other great men, he gave indications of future greatness while learning the three R's, and graduating in the pains and penalties of the birch. It is said, for instance, that he displayed a wonderful power of story-telling; that he had a strong inclination for getting up amateur and Lilliputian theatricals; and there is a tale—which is, we fear, apocryphal—of his having, while still a boy, confounded and convinced a police magistrate who was inquiring into the circumstances of a school-fight. In the October of 1822 he entered Trinity College, not having yet reached his seventeenth year. His course was undistinguished so far as letters went; but he acquired distinction of another kind. Robust in health, stout of frame, and joyous in temperament, he naturally joined in the wild fun that the gay young student loves; drank, stopped up o' nights, drove furiously, rode madly, played jokes on the dons, sang ballads in the streets, and did all the other wild things which are chronicled in his earlier works. Before he had completed his medical studies he went on a trip to America, and if all that tradition says be correct, passed a very adventurous time there. It is said, among other things, that he went among the Red Indians, adopted their dress and customs, and became so indispensable to them that he had finally to make his escape by stratagem and at great risk to his life. Several of his tales certainly—notably *O'Leary*—contain accounts of life among the Indians, which are full of striking adventures and apparently faithful to life; and an intimate friend of Lever's quotes a statement of his to the effect that he walked through the streets of Quebec "in the mocassins, and with the head feathers." He also in those early years took a tour on the Continent, and studied medicine for some time at the university of Göttingen. He spent some time at Heidelberg and Vienna; and at Weimar he made the acquaintance of the greatest of German poets—Goethe. Returning to Dublin he introduced some of the features of student life he had learned in Germany; establishing a Burschenschaft, of which he was elected Grand Llama, and wherein were enrolled Samuel Lover, and many other young Irishmen who afterwards rose to celebrity. In midsummer, 1831, Lever graduated as Bachelor of Medicine; for some reason or other he never took the higher degree at his *alma mater*, but, like Goldsmith, was content with the M.D. of Louvain.

For a while Lever practised his profession without any very distinguished success in his father's house in Talbot Street, Dublin. The outbreak of cholera brought him sterner and more laborious employment; he was sent by the Board of Health to Clare, where the terrible epidemic raged with great fierceness. The daily tasks of Lever during this period were enough to try the nerve and break the health of almost any man; and, indeed, during this time there was a holocaust of medical men. A cheery temper, a stout heart, and a robust constitution saved Lever. While he was passing through these painful scenes he was gleaning other than medical knowledge; he was storing up material for the description of tragic incident and humorous character. The *Martins* and *St. Patrick's Eve* contain many of the most painful pictures which presented themselves before the young doctor's eyes; while a coterie of gay and witty acquaintances sat unconsciously for some of the portraits in *Harry Lorrequer* and *Jack Hinton*; "Father Malachy Brennan" in the former, and "Father Tom Loftus" in the latter, are both drawn from two Roman Catholic clergymen with whom Lever at this period came in contact; and not only the priests themselves, but some of their ecclesiastical superiors and friends, were rather annoyed at the somewhat unclerical freedom of manners with which they were credited. The next scene of his medical labours was Portstewart, where he practised as dispensary doctor, holding at the same time an appointment in connection with a hospital at Derry. While thus occupied he made the acquaintance of W. H. Maxwell, who, perhaps, more than any other man, influenced him in entering upon a literary career. It was while he was in Portstewart also that he married. The story of Lever's love and conjugal life is in itself a touching romance, and one of the finest traits in his whole career. He was one of the few men who had a first and only love; and who retained through long years of married life the fresh feelings and keen affection of the wooer. It is related that while he was still a school-boy, he used to make presents of flowers to Kate Baker as love-tokens. In course of time she left Dublin, as he did, her father having been appointed master of the endowed school at Navan. Thither followed Lever from his northern home, and soon was accepted. It is believed that in order to avoid the anger of old James Lever, who was anxious that his son should make a wealthy match, the marriage was kept secret for some time.

The life of a dispensary doctor, subject to the caprices, the vulgarities, and the petty tyrannies of poor-law guardians, in the end wore out Lever, who was not of a very patient temper, and who, besides, was subject to periodical fits of nomadic restlessness. It struck him that he might find in Brussels a pleasant home, and that the English population there would be large enough to give him sufficient practice. He was taken up by Sir H. Seymour, the English minister, though he never received the official rank which so many biographers have given him; he was not physician to the embassy, for no such office existed. Lever's experiences in Brussels were pleasant, and he had every prospect of attaining greater success there as a medical man than even he had anticipated. But again he was transferred just as he had begun to take root.

It was a considerable period before Lever could be convinced that he had literary genius, and that he should adopt the literary career, but he had shown traces of his inclinations at an early age. While still a student he had contributed humorous sketches to the daily papers and to a short-lived periodical called the *Irish National Magazine*. It was not, however, till the foundation of the *Dublin University Magazine*—a literary event destined to deeply influence the lives of so many intellectual Irishmen—that he attempted anything on an extended scale. The first instalment of the *Confessions of Harry Lorrequer* appeared in the February number of the magazine in 1837. This production at once gained the favour of the people and the publisher; and Lever was surprised to find it proposed that the series should be transferred from the magazine to the more dignified and lasting form of a three-volume work. The book did not attract much notice in the London press; but it had caught the vigilant eye of Mr. Richard Bentley, and a keen competition arose between the London publisher and M℅Glashan of Dublin, who had accepted *Harry Lorrequer* for the *Dublin University*, of which he was then part proprietor. The final result was that *Charles O'Malley* appeared under Irish auspices. It is unnecessary for us to expatiate on the merits of a story that has proved its popularity by having run through innumerable editions, nor to eulogize characters which have become as familiar as real persons. Suffice it to say, *O'Malley* was highly successful, and strengthened greatly Lever's position.

The connection with M℅Glashan which the publication of those stories created, led to a desire to make the connection still closer. An article of Lever in defence of Lord Eliot, then chief-secretary for Ireland, gained him some favour in official quarters; and Lever formed hopes that, if he returned to his native country, he might receive a public appointment that would be easy and remunerative. M℅Glashan at the same time offered him the editorship of the *University Magazine* at a liberal salary, the condition being that he should contribute some portion of a story every month, and that for this he should receive £1200 a year.

In January, 1842, Lever entered upon his duties; and *Jack Hinton*, which had been begun in the previous year, appeared month after month. It may be here said that the materials for the graphic pictures of Galway and Galway society, which appear in so many of Lever's works, were gathered during periodical visits made in youth to his brother, the Rev. John Lever, who had a cure in the county. It may also be added that he always felt a deep liking for that part of the country. During the greater part of his tenure of editorial office, Lever lived at Templeogue House. There he kept open house after a style more Irish and generous than prudent; and he had visits from all the Irish, and many of the English celebrities of his time. Isaac Butt was one of his most frequent guests; and Thackeray there collected some of the materials for his *Irish Sketch Book*. *O'Leary*—a work which others highly praised, and the author himself rather disliked—*Tom Burke*, in which he utilized military incidents he had collected in a number of French works; the *O'Donoghue* —the idea of which was suggested by a tour in Killarney—appeared in rapid succession. It may be well to notice that Lever was involved in other than literary troubles during his editorial career; a violent attack by one of the contributors brought him into collision with the well-known *littérateur*, Mr. S. C. Hall: an angry correspondence was followed by a challenge; but after all the preliminaries were arranged, a reconciliation on terms honourable to both parties was arranged.

Three years of residence and hard work in Dublin produced once more the desire for change; and Lever left Dublin for the Continent, never again to be a resident in his native land. His life from this period onward is that of a wanderer in strange lands—a cosmopolitan to a great extent in languages and in residence, in sympathies and experiences; but his heart always yearned after the old country, for whose people and feelings and customs he felt an enduring love. Amid the blaze of literary fame he often longed to be a doctor in Ireland; and in the course of his after-life he made more than one attempt to get a settled position again there; and when that failed, consoled himself by taking a hurried glimpse at it in the course of occasional tours. Before he left Dublin he had made arrangements with Messrs. Chapman and Hall for the production of *St. Patrick's Eve*—a short story founded on his experiences as a cholera doctor, and the *Knight of Gwynne*. The first of these the public received somewhat coldly, for it was considered that a master of farce had no right to intrude on the domain of pathos; but it is a work which found considerable favour with more appreciative critics. The *Knight of Gwynne* is also pitched in a much more serious key than previous works. Lever's idea was to create a character in which there might be the "same unswerving fidelity of friendship, the same courageous devotion to a cause, the same haughty contempt for all that was mean or unworthy," which were the traits of an "educated and travelled Irishman of the period." To these he wished to add "the lighter accessories of genial temperament, forgiving disposition, a chivalrous respect for women." The story, as is well known, relates to the period when the Act of Union was passed, and there are portraits of Castlereagh, a prime mover in that business, and Bagenal Daly, a type of the member of parliament which Sir Jonah Barrington has immortalized. The picture of Castlereagh is perhaps more favourable than would be expected by those who regret the departure of the legislative independence of Ireland; but this is partly accounted for by the fact that Lever's views of that statesman were very much softened by his intercourse at Brussels with Sir H. Seymour, who had been one of Castlereagh's subordinates and friends.

During the next few years Lever passed most of his time at Florence, where he attracted a large amount of attention by the splendour of his equipage and his stud. It was his habit to drive about the streets with his children dressed in rather theatrical style; but in extenuation of this offence it may be remembered that Alfieri, the great Italian poet, was not free from a similar desire to display the beauties of his stables and his equestrian skill. During this period were written *Roland Cashel*, *Maurice Tiernay*, *Con Cregan*, and *Sir Jasper Carew*. *The Fortunes of Glencore*, which came next, marks the beginning of a new and completely different era in Lever's career. Here we have that mixture of Irish life in its simplicity, and the intrigues of small courts, and the follies of continental society. It may be said that every work produced by Lever after this period contained the same mixture of characters and scenes. We do not intend to go over each work at any length. *Glencore* was followed by the *Martins of Cro' Martin*, in which is told one of the most romantic and most poetical tales of the wreck of an old Irish family; *The Daltons*; *Davenport Dunn*, where John Sadleir the member of parliament and forger figures; *One of Them*, in which we find alternately described the dispensary at Portstewart and the salon at Florence; *Gerald Fitzgerald*; *Tony Butler*, published anonymously; *Sir Brooke Fosbrooke*, which he described as the "most carefully written" of his works, and where Chief-justice Lefroy is painted. *The Bramleys* appeared in the *Cornhill Magazine*, and is remarkable for an elaborate plot, the mystery of which was preserved to the end,—an unusual occurrence with Lever. This was followed by *That Boy of Northcott's*, in which the story is irresolute, and the end hurried. *The Rent in the Cloud* is also rather a poor work; and *A Day's Ride*, which Dickens accepted for *Household Words*, proved so unattractive that the editor took the extreme step of announcing the end of the work by a certain date. The last work which Lever produced was *Lord Kilgobbin*, and in this there was no sign of a failing hand. It was received with unanimous praise by the press, and was regarded more as the work of a writer in his full vigour than of an elderly man who was finishing a prolonged literary career. From time to time for several years before his death, Lever was in the habit of contributing a series of articles to *Blackwood* on current topics under the *nom de plume* of Cornelius O'Dowd.

In 1858 he was appointed by his friends in the Tory administration vice-consul at Spezzia, and in 1867 he was promoted to the consulship at Trieste. The latter years of his life were darkened by the necessity for continual work in consequence of somewhat embarrassed circumstances, and he also chafed much under the necessity of living away in comparative exile in a Dalmatian seaport. He also suffered from ill health. He paid his last visit to Ireland a short time before his death, and on the 1st June, 1872, he passed away painlessly in sleep.]

AN IRISH LEGISLATOR OF THE OLDEN TIME.

(FROM "CHARLES O'MALLEY."[1])

The rain was dashing in torrents against the window-panes, and the wind sweeping in heavy and fitful gusts along the dreary and deserted streets, as a party of three persons sat over their wine in that stately old pile which once formed the resort of the Irish members, in College Green, Dublin, and went by the name of Daly's Club House. The clatter of falling tiles and chimney-pots—the jarring of the window-frames and howling of the storm without, seemed little to affect the spirits of those within, as they drew closer to a blazing fire, before which stood a small table covered with the remains of a dessert, and an

---

[1] By permission of Messrs. W. H. Smith & Son.

abundant supply of bottles, whose characteristic length of neck indicated the rarest wines of France and Germany; while the portly magnum of claret—the wine *par excellence* of every Irish gentleman of the day—passed rapidly from hand to hand, the conversation did not languish, and many a deep and hearty laugh followed the stories which every now and then were told, as some reminiscence of early days was recalled, or some trait of a former companion remembered.

One of the party, however, was apparently engrossed by other thoughts than those of the mirth and merriment around; for in the midst of all he would turn suddenly from the others, and devote himself to a number of scattered sheets of paper upon which he had written some lines, but whose crossed and blotted sentences attested how little success had waited upon his literary labours. This individual was a short, plethoric-looking, white-haired man of about fifty, with a deep, round voice, and a chuckling, smothering laugh, which, whenever he indulged, not only shook his own ample person, but generally created a petty earthquake on every side of him. For the present I shall not stop to particularize him more closely; but when I add that the person in question was a well-known member of the Irish House of Commons, whose acute understanding and practical good sense were veiled under an affected and well-dissembled habit of blundering that did far more for his party than the most violent and pointed attacks of his more accurate associates, some of my readers may anticipate me in pronouncing him to be Sir Harry Boyle. Upon his left sat a figure the most unlike him possible; he was a tall, thin, bony man, with a bolt-upright air and a most saturnine expression; his eyes were covered by a deep green shade, which fell far over his face, but failed to conceal a blue scar that, crossing his cheek, ended in the angle of his mouth, and imparted to that feature, when he spoke, an apparently abortive attempt to extend towards his eyebrow; his upper lip was covered with a grizzly and ill-trimmed moustache, which added much to the ferocity of his look, while a thin and pointed beard on his chin gave an apparent length to the whole face that completed its rueful character. His dress was a single-breasted, tightly-buttoned frock, in one button-hole of which a yellow ribbon was fastened, the decoration of a foreign service, which conferred upon its wearer the title of count; and though Billy Considine, as he was familiarly called by his friends, was a thorough Irishman in all his feelings and affections, yet he had no objection to the designation he had gained in the Austrian army. The count was certainly no beauty, but, somehow, very few men of his day had a fancy for telling him so; a deadlier hand and a steadier eye never covered his man in the Phœnix; and though he never had a seat in the House, he was always regarded as one of the government party, who more than once had damped the ardour of an opposition member, by the very significant threat of "setting Billy at him." The third figure of the group was a large, powerfully-built, and handsome man, older than either of the others, but not betraying in his voice or carriage any touch of time. He was attired in the green coat and buff vest which formed the livery of the club; and in his tall, ample forehead, clear, well-set eye, and still handsome mouth, bore evidence that no great flattery was necessary at the time which called Godfrey O'Malley the handsomest man in Ireland.

"Upon my conscience," said Sir Harry, throwing down his pen with an air of ill-temper, "I can make nothing of it; I have got into such an infernal habit of making bulls, that I can't write sense when I want it."

"Come, come," said O'Malley, "try again, my dear fellow. If you can't succeed, I'm sure Billy and I have no chance."

"What have you written? Let us see," said Considine, drawing the paper towards him, and holding it to the light. "Why, what the devil is all this? you have made him 'drop down dead after dinner of a lingering illness brought on by the debate of yesterday.'"

"Oh, impossible!"

"Well, read it yourself; there it is; and, as if to make the thing less credible, you talk of his 'Bill for the Better Recovery of Small Debts.' I'm sure, O'Malley, your last moments were not employed in that manner."

"Come, now," said Sir Harry, "I'll set all to rights with a postscript. 'Any one who questions the above statement, is politely requested to call on Mr. Considine, 16 Kildare Street, who will feel happy to afford him every satisfaction upon Mr. O'Malley's decease, or upon miscellaneous matters.'"

"Worse and worse," said O'Malley. "Killing another man will never persuade the world that I'm dead."

"But we'll wake you, and have a glorious funeral."

"And if any man doubt the statement, I'll call him out," said the count.

"Or, better still," said Sir Harry, "O'Malley has his action at law for defamation."

"I see I'll never get down to Galway at this rate," said O'Malley; "and as the new election takes place on Tuesday week, time presses. There are more writs flying after me this instant, than for all the government boroughs."

"And there will be fewer returns, I fear," said Sir Harry.

"Who is the chief creditor?" asked the count.

"Old Stapleton, the attorney in Fleet Street, has most of the mortgages."

"Nothing to be done with him in this way?" said Considine, balancing the cork-screw like a hair-trigger.

"No chance of it."

"May be," said Sir Harry, "he might come to terms if I were to call and say—You are anxious to close accounts, as your death has just taken place. You know what I mean."

"I fear so should he, were you to say so. No, no, Boyle, just try a plain, straightforward paragraph about my death. We'll have it in Falkner's paper to-morrow; on Friday the funeral can take place, and, with the blessing o' God, I'll come to life on Saturday at Athlone, in time to canvass the market."

"I think it wouldn't be bad if your ghost were to appear to old Timins the tanner, in Naas, on your way down; you know he arrested you once before."

"I prefer a night's sleep," said O'Malley; "but come, finish the squib for the paper."

"Stay a little," said Sir Harry, musing; "it just strikes me that, if ever the matter gets out, I may be in some confounded scrape. Who knows if it is not a breach of privilege to report the death of a member? And to tell you truth, I dread the serjeant and the speaker's warrant with a very lively fear."

"Why, when did you make his acquaintance?" said the count.

"Is it possible you never heard of Boyle's committal?" said O'Malley; "you surely must have been abroad at the time; but it's not too late to tell it yet.

"Well, it's about two years since old Townsend brought in his Enlistment Bill, and the whole country was scoured for all our voters, who were scattered here and there, never anticipating another call of the House, and supposing that the session was just over. Among others, up came our friend Harry, here, and, the night he arrived, they made him a 'Monk of the Screw,' and very soon made him forget his senatorial dignities.

"On the evening after his reaching town the bill was brought in, and at two in the morning the division took place—a vote was of too much consequence not to look after it closely—and a castle messenger was in waiting in Exchequer Street, who, when the debate was closing, put Harry, with three others, into a coach, and brought them down to the House. Unfortunately, however, they mistook their friends, voted against the bill, and, amid the loudest cheering of the opposition, the government party were defeated. The rage of the ministers knew no bounds, and looks of defiance and even threats were exchanged between the ministers and the deserters. Amid all this poor Harry fell fast asleep, and dreamed that he was once more in Exchequer Street, presiding among the monks, and mixing another tumbler. At length he awoke and looked about him—the clerk was just at the instant reading out, in his usual routine manner, a clause of the new bill, and the remainder of the House was in dead silence. Harry looked again around on every side, wondering where was the hot water, and what had become of the whisky-bottle, and above all, why the company were so extremely dull and ungenial. At length, with a half shake, he roused up a little, and giving a look of unequivocal contempt on every side, called out, 'Upon my soul, you're pleasant companions —but I'll give you a chant to enliven you.' So saying, he cleared his throat with a couple of short coughs, and struck up, with the voice of a Stentor, the following verse of a popular ballad:—

"'And they nibbled away, both night and day,
    Like mice in a round of Glo'ster;
Great rogues they were all, both great and small;
    From Flood to Leslie Foster.
                        "'Great rogues all.'

"'Chorus, boys!'

If he was not joined by the voices of his friends in the song, it was probably because such a roar of laughing never was heard since the walls were roofed over. The whole house rose in a mass, and my friend Harry was hurried over the benches by the serjeant-at-arms, and left for three weeks in Newgate to practise his melody."

"All true," said Sir Harry, "and worse luck to them for not liking music; but come now, will this do?—'It is our melancholy duty to announce the death of Godfrey O'Malley, Esq., late member for the county of Galway, which took place on Friday evening at Daly's Club House. This esteemed gentleman's family—

one of the oldest in Ireland, and among whom it was hereditary not to have any children——'"

Here a burst of laughter from Considine and O'Malley interrupted the reader, who with the greatest difficulty could be persuaded that he was again bulling it.

"The devil fly away with it," said he, "I'll never succeed."

"Never mind," said O'Malley; "the first part will do admirably; and let us now turn our attention to other matters."

A fresh magnum was called for, and over its inspiring contents all the details of the funeral were planned; and as the clock struck four, the party separated for the *night*, well satisfied with the result of their labours.

When the dissolution of parliament was announced the following morning in Dublin its interest in certain circles was manifestly increased by the fact that Godfrey O'Malley was at last open to arrest; for as, in olden times, certain gifted individuals possessed some happy immunity against death by fire or sword, so the worthy O'Malley seemed to enjoy a no less valuable privilege, and for many a year had passed, among the myrmidons of the law, as writ-proof. Now, however, the charm seemed to have yielded, and pretty much with the same feeling as a storming party may be supposed to experience on the day that a breach is reported as practicable, did the honest attorneys, retained in the various suits against him, rally round each other that morning in the Four Courts.

Bonds, mortgages, post-obits, promissory notes—in fact, every imaginable species of invention for raising the O'Malley exchequer for the preceding thirty years—were handed about on all sides, suggesting to the mind of an uninterested observer the notion that, had the aforesaid O'Malley been an independent and absolute monarch, instead of merely being the member for Galway, the kingdom over whose destinies he had been called to preside would have suffered not a little from a depreciated currency and an extravagant issue of paper. Be that as it might, one thing was clear: the whole estates of the family could not possibly pay one-fourth of the debt, and the only question was one which occasionally arises at a scanty dinner on a mail-coach road—who was to be the lucky individual to carve the joint, where so many were sure to go off hungry.

It was now a trial of address between these various and highly-gifted gentlemen who should first pounce upon the victim, and when the skill of their caste is taken into consideration, who will doubt that every feasible expedient for securing him was resorted to? While writs were struck against him in Dublin, emissaries were despatched to the various surrounding counties to procure others in the event of his escape. *Ne exeats* were sworn, and water-bailiffs engaged to follow him on the high seas; and, as the great Nassau balloon did not exist in those days, no imaginable mode of escape appeared possible, and bets were offered at long odds that, within twenty-four hours, the late member would be enjoying his *otium cum dignitate* in his majesty's jail of Newgate.

Expectation was at the highest—confidence hourly increasing—success all but certain—when, in the midst of all this high-bounding hope, the dreadful rumour spread that O'Malley was no more. One had seen it just five minutes before in the evening edition of Falkner's paper—another heard it in the courts—a third overheard the chief-justice stating it to the master of the rolls—and lastly, a breathless witness arrived from College Green with the news that Daly's Club House was shut up, and the shutters closed. To describe the consternation the intelligence caused on every side is impossible; nothing in history equals it, except, perhaps, the entrance of the French army into Moscow, deserted and forsaken by its former inhabitants. While terror and dismay, therefore, spread amid that wide and respectable body who formed O'Malley's creditors, the preparations for his funeral were going on with every rapidity; relays of horses were ordered at every stage of the journey, and it was announced that, in testimony of his worth, a large party of his friends were to accompany his remains to Portumna Abbey—a test much more indicative of resistance in the event of any attempt to arrest the body, than of anything like reverence for their departed friend.

Such was the state of matters in Dublin, when a letter reached me one morning at O'Malley Castle, whose contents will at once explain the writer's intention, and also serve to introduce my unworthy self to my reader. It ran thus:—

"DEAR CHARLEY,—Your uncle Godfrey, whose debts [God pardon him] are more numerous than the hairs of his wig, was obliged to die here last night. We did the thing for him completely; and all doubts as to the reality of the event are silenced by the circumstantial detail of the newspaper 'that he was confined six weeks to his bed from a cold he caught ten days ago, while on guard.' Repeat this, for it's better we had all the same story till he comes to life again, which, maybe, will not take place before Tuesday or Wednesday. At the same time canvass the county for him, and say he'll be with his friends next week, and up in Woodford and the Scariff barony: say he died a true Catholic; it will serve him on the hustings. Meet us in Athlone on Saturday, and bring your uncle's mare with you—he says he'd rather ride home; and tell Father Mac Shane to have a bit of dinner ready about four o'clock, for the corpse can get nothing after he leaves Mountmellick.—No more now, from yours, ever,

"HARRY BOYLE.

"Daly's, about eight in the evening.

"To Charles O'Malley, Esq., O'Malley Castle, Galway."

When this not over clear document reached me I was the sole inhabitant of O'Malley Castle, a very ruinous pile of incongruous masonry, that stood in a wild and dreary part of the county of Galway, bordering on the Shannon. On every side stretched the property of my uncle, or at least what had once been so; and, indeed, so numerous were its present claimants, that he would have been a subtle lawyer who could have pronounced upon the rightful owner. The demesne around the castle contained some well-grown and handsome timber, and, as the soil was undulating and fertile, presented many features of beauty; beyond it all was sterile, bleak, and barren. Long tracts of brown heath-clad mountain, or not less unprofitable valleys of tall and waving fern, were all that the eye could discern, except where the broad Shannon, expanding into a tranquil and glassy lake, lay still and motionless beneath the dark mountains, a few islands, with some ruined churches and a round tower, alone breaking the dreary waste of water.

Here it was that I had passed my infancy and my youth, and here I now stood, at the age of seventeen, quite unconscious that the world contained aught fairer and brighter than that gloomy valley with its rugged frame of mountains.

When a mere child I was left an orphan to the care of my worthy uncle. My father, whose extravagance had well sustained the family reputation, had squandered a large and handsome property in contesting elections for his native county, and in keeping up that system of unlimited hospitality for which Ireland in general, and Galway more especially, was renowned. The result was, as might be expected, ruin and beggary. He died, leaving every one of his estates encumbered with heavy debts, and the only legacy he left to his brother was a boy of four years of age, entreating him, with his last breath, "Be anything you like to him, Godfrey, but a father, or at least such a one as I have proved."

Godfrey O'Malley, some short time previous, had lost his wife, and when this new trust was committed to him, he resolved never to remarry, but to rear me up as his own child, and the inheritor of his estates. How weighty and onerous an obligation this latter might prove, the reader can form some idea. The intention was, however, a kind one; and to do my uncle justice, he loved me with all the affection of a warm and open heart.

From my earliest years his whole anxiety was to fit me for the part of a country gentleman, as he regarded that character—viz. I rode boldly with fox-hounds; I was about the best shot within twenty miles of us; I could swim the Shannon at Holy Island; I drove four-in-hand better than the coachman himself; and from finding a hare to hooking a salmon, my equal could not be found from Killaloe to Banagher. These were the staple of my endowments. Besides which, the parish priest had taught me a little Latin, a little French, and a little geometry, and a great deal of the life and opinions of St. Jago, who presided over a holy well in the neighbourhood, and was held in very considerable repute.

When I add to this portraiture of my accomplishments that I was nearly six feet high, with more than a common share of activity and strength for my years, and no inconsiderable portion of good looks, I have finished my sketch, and stand before my reader.

It is now time I should return to Sir Harry's letter, which so completely bewildered me, that, but for the assistance of Father Roach, I should have been totally unable to make out the writer's intentions. By his advice I immediately set out for Athlone, where, when I arrived, I found my uncle addressing the mob from the top of the hearse, and recounting his miraculous escapes as a new claim upon their gratitude.

"There was nothing else for it, boys; the Dublin people insisted on my being their member, and besieged the club-house. I refused—they threatened—I grew obstinate—they furious. 'I'll die first,' said I. 'Galway or nothing!'" "Hurrah!" from the mob. "O'Malley for ever!" "And ye see, I kept my word, boys—I did die; I died that evening at a quarter-past eight. There, read it for yourselves; there's the paper; was waked and carried out, and here I am after all, ready to die in earnest for you—but never to desert you."

The cheers here were deafening, and my uncle was carried through the market down to the mayor's house, who, being a friend of the opposite party, was complimented with three groans; then up the Mall to the chapel, beside which Father Mac Shane resided. He was then suffered to touch the earth once more, when, having shaken hands with all of his constituency within reach, he entered the house to partake of the kindest welcome and best reception the good priest could afford him.

My uncle's progress homeward was a triumph; the real secret of his escape had somehow come out, and his popularity rose to a white heat. "An it's little O'Malley cares for the law—bad luck to it; it's himself can laugh at judge and jury. Arrest him—nabocklish—catch a weasel asleep," &c. Such were the encomiums that greeted him as he passed on towards home; while shouts of joy and blazing bonfires attested that his success was regarded as a national triumph.

A FATHER AND SON.

(FROM "LUTTRELL OF ARRAN."[1])

[Luttrell, a disappointed man, lives in one of the islands of Arran, off the coast of county Galway, away from all society. He has an only son, named Harry, whom he loves and yet keeps at a distance; and whom he would almost sacrifice to his pride. The necessity for sending two letters to the mainland gives him an opportunity of gratifying his morbid feelings: the extract that follows tells how. The scene opens with a conversation between Luttrell and a fisherman of the island.]

"How is the wind, Hennesy?" asked he of his boatman.

"Strong from the east, sir, and comin' on harder."

"Could you beat up to Westport, think you? I have two letters of importance to send."

"We might, sir," said the man, doubtingly, "but it's more likely we'd be blown out to sea."

"How long is this gale likely to last?"

---

[1] This extract is somewhat abridged.

"It's the season of these winds, your honour, and we'll have, maybe, three weeks or a month of them, now."

"In that case you must try it. Take three men with you, and the large yawl; put some provisions and water on board; perhaps a little ballast, too."

"That we will, sir. She'll take a ton more, at least, to carry sail in this weather."

"Are you afraid to go?" asked Luttrell, and his voice was harsh and his manner stern.

"Afraid! devil a bit afraid!" said the man, boldly, and as though the imputation had made him forget his natural respect.

"I'd not ask you to do what I'd not venture on myself."

"We all know that well, sir," said the boatman, recovering his former manner.... "You bade me remind you, sir, that the next time the boat went over to Westport that I was to take Master Harry, and get him measured for some clothes; but of course you'd not like to send him in this weather."

"I think not; I think there can be no doubt of that," cried Luttrell, half angrily. "It's not when the strong easterly gales have set in, and a heavy sea is coming up from the south'ard, that I'd tell you to take a boy——" He stopped suddenly, and turning fiercely on the sailor, said, "You think I have courage enough to send you and a boat's crew out, and not to send my son. Speak out and say it. Isn't that what you mean?"

"It is not, sir. If you towld me to take the child, I wouldn't do it."

"You wouldn't do it?" cried Luttrell, passionately.

"I would not, sir, if you never gave me another day's pay."

"Leave the room—leave the house, and prepare to give up your holding. I'll want that cabin of yours this day month. Do you hear me?"

"I do, sir," said the man, with a lip pale and quivering.

"Send Sam Joyce here."

"He's only up out of the fever since Monday, sir."

"Tell Maher I want him, then; and mind me, sir," added he, as the man was leaving the room, "no story-telling, no conspiring, for if Dan Maher refuses to obey my orders, whatever they are, he'll follow you, and so shall every man of you, if I leave the island without a family except my own."

"Don't send your child out, anyways," said the man.

"Leave the room, sir," said Luttrell, imperiously; and the man, cowed and crestfallen, closed the door and withdrew.

As though to carry corroboration to the sailor's warning, a fierce blast struck the window at the moment, making the old woodwork rattle, and threatening to smash it in, while the dark sky grew darker, and seemed to blend with the leaden-coloured sea.

"I want you to go over to Westport, Maher," said Luttrell to a hard-featured, weather-beaten man of about fifty, who now stood wet and dripping at the door.

"Very well, sir," was the answer.

"Take the big yawl, and any crew you please. Whenever all is ready come up here for your orders."

"Very well, sir," said the man, and retired.

"Where's Master Harry, Molly?" cried Luttrell, advancing into the passage that led towards the kitchen.

"He's out on the rocks, watching the sea."

"Call him in here. I want to speak to him. What are you doing here, sir? I told you to leave this." This stern speech was addressed to Hennesy, who, with evident signs of sorrow on his face, stood half hid beside the door.

"I was hopin' your honour wouldn't turn me out after nine years' sarvice, when I never did or said one word to displaze you."

"Away with you—be off—I have no time to parley with fellows like you. Come in here, Harry," and he laid his hand on the boy's shoulder, and led him into his room. "I'm sending a boat over to Westport, would you like to go in her?"

"Wouldn't I?" said the boy, as his eyes flashed wildly.

. . . . . .

The day—a dark and stormy one—was drawing to a close as the yawl got under weigh. She was manned by a stout crew of five hardy islanders; for although Maher had selected but three to accompany him, Tim Hennesy volunteered, and, indeed, jumped on board as the boat sheered off, without leave asked or given. Luttrell had parted with his boy in his habitual impassive way—reminded him that he was under Tom Maher's orders, equally on shore as on board—that he trusted to hear a good account of him on his return, and then said a cold "good-bye," and turned away.

When Harry, who rarely had so long an interview with his father, left the room, he felt a sort of relief to think it was over; he had been neither punished nor scolded; even the warning that was given was very slight, and uttered in no unkindness.

A wild cry, half yell, half cheer, broke from the fishermen on the shore; a squall had struck the boat just as she got under weigh, and though she lay over, reeling under the shock, she righted nobly again, and stood out boldly to sea.

At first from the window of his lonely room, and then, when the boat had rounded the point of land, and could be no more seen, from a little loopholed slit in the tower above him, Luttrell watched her course. Even with his naked eye he could mark the sheets of spray as they broke over the bow and flew across her, and see how the strong mast bent like a whip, although she was reduced to her very shortest sail, and was standing under a double-reefed mainsail and a small storm-jib. Not another boat, not another sail of any kind, was to be seen; and there seemed something heroically daring in that little barque, that one dark speck, as it rose and plunged, seen and lost alternately in the rolling sea.

It was only when he tried to look through the telescope and found that his hand shook so much that he could not fix the object, that he himself knew how agitated he was. He drew his hand across his brow and found it clammy with a profuse and cold perspiration. By this time it was so dark that he had to grope his way down the narrow stairs to the room below. He called for Molly. "Who was that you were talking to? I heard a strange voice without there."

"Old Moriarty, the pilot, your honour; I brought him in out of the wet to dry himself."

"Send him in here to me," said Luttrell, who, throwing a root of oak on the fire, sat down with his back to the door, and where no light should fall upon his face.

"It's blowing fresh, Moriarty," said he, with an affected ease of manner, as the old man entered and stood nigh to the door.

"More than fresh, your honour. It's blowin' hard."

"You say that because you haven't been at sea these five-and-twenty years; but it's not blowing as it blew the night I came up from Clew, no, nor the day that we rounded Tory Island."

"Maybe not; but it's not at its worst yet," said the old fellow, who was ill-pleased at the sneer at his seamanship.

"I don't know what the fellows here think of such weather, but a crew of Norway fishermen—ay, or a set of Deal boatmen—would laugh at it."

"Listen to that now, then," said the other, "and it's no laughing matter;" and as he spoke a fierce gust of wind tore past, carrying the spray in great sheets, and striking against the walls and windows with a clap like thunder. "That was a squall to try any boat!"

"Not a boat like the large yawl!"

"If it didn't throw two tons of water aboard of her my name isn't Moriarty."

"Master Harry is enjoying it, I'm certain," said Luttrell, trying to seem at ease.

"Well! It's too much for a child," said the old man, sorrowfully.

"And you are frightened by a night like this?"

"I'm not frightened, sir; but I'd not send a child out in it, just for——" He stopped and tried to fall back behind the door.

"Just for what?" said Luttrell, with a calm and even gentle voice—"just for what?"

"How do I know, your honour. I was saying more than I could tell."

"Yes; but let me hear it. What was the reason that you supposed—why do you think I did it?"

Deceived and even lured on to frankness by the insinuating softness of his manner, the old man answered: "Well it was just your honour's pride, the ould Luttrell pride, that said, 'We'll never send a man where we won't go ourselves,' and it was out of that you'd risk your child's life!"

The leaden gray of morning began to break at last, and the wind seemed somewhat to abate, although the sea still rolled in such enormous waves, and the spray rose over the rocks and fell in showers over the shingle before the windows. Luttrell strained his eyes through the half-murky light, but could descry nothing like a sail seaward. He mounted the stairs of the tower, and stationing himself at the loopholed window, gazed long and earnestly at the sea. Nothing but waves—a wild, disordered stretch of rolling water—whose rocking motion almost at last made his head reel.

The wind had greatly abated, and the sea also gone down, but there was still the heavy roll and the deafening crash upon the shore that follow a storm. "The hurricane is passing westward," muttered Luttrell; "it has done its work here!" And a bitter scorn curled his lips as he spoke. He was calling upon his pride to sustain him. It was a hollow ally in his time of trouble; for as he gazed and gazed, his eyes *would* grow dim with tears, and his heavy heart would sigh, as though to bursting.

As the day wore on and the hour came when he was habitually about, he strolled down to the beach, pretending to pick up shells, or gather sea anemones, as he was wont. The fishermen saluted him respectfully as he passed, and his heart throbbed painfully as he saw, or fancied he saw, a something of compassionate meaning in their faces. "Do they believe, can they think that it is all over, and that I am childless?" thought he. "Do they know that I am desolate?" A pang shot through him at this that made him grasp his heart with his hand to suppress the agony.

He rallied after a minute or so, and walked on. He had just reached the summit of the little bay, when a sort of cheer or cry from those behind startled him. He turned and saw that the fishermen were gathered in a group upon one of the rocks, all looking and pointing seaward; with seeming indolence of gait, while his anxiety was almost suffocating him, he lounged lazily towards them.

"What are the fellows looking at?" said he to the old pilot, who, with some difficulty, had just scrambled down from the rock.

"A large lugger, your honour, coming up broad?"

"And is a fishing-boat so strange a thing in these waters?"

"She's out of the fishin' grounds altogether, your honour; for she's one of the Westport boats. I know her by the dip of her bowsprit."

"And if she is, what does it signify to us?" asked Luttrell, sternly.

"Only that she's bearin' up for the island, your honour, and it's not often one of them comes here."

"The seldomer the better," said Luttrell, gloomily. "When the fellows find there are no grog-shops here they turn to mischief, break down our fences, lop our trees, and make free with our potatoes. I'll have to do one of these days what I have so often threatened—warn all these fellows off, and suffer none to land here."

Perhaps the old pilot thought that other and very different feelings might at that moment have had the sway over him, for he looked away, and shook his head mournfully.

"She has a flag at the peak," cried one of the men from the rock.

"She has what?" asked Luttrell impatiently.

"She has the half-black, half-white ensign, your honour."

"Your own flag at the peak," said the pilot.

"More of their insolence, I suppose," said Luttrell; "because they have a hamper or a parcel on board for me, perhaps."

"I don't think it's that, sir," said the other moodily.

"What is it, then?" cried he harshly.

"'Tis, maybe, your honour, that they have some news of——" he was going to say "Master Harry," but the ghastly paleness of Luttrell's face appalled and stopped him.

"News of what did you say?"

"Of the big yawl, sir; they maybe saw her at sea."

"And if they had, would that give them a right to hoist the Luttrell flag? We are low enough in the world, Heaven knows!" he cried, "but we are not come to that pass yet when every grocer of Westport can carry our crest or our colours." This burst of mock anger was but to cover a rush of real terror; for he was trembling from head to foot, his sight was dimmed, and his brain turning. He felt the coward, too, in his heart, and did not dare to face the old man again. So, turning abruptly away, he went back to the house.

"My fate will soon be decided now," said he, as he tottered into his room and sat down, burying his face in his hands.

The group of fishermen on the rock grew larger and larger, till at last above thirty were clustered on the point all eagerly watching and as earnestly discussing every motion of the lugger. It was soon clear that her course was guided by some one who knew the navigation well, for instead of holding on straight for the bay, where she was to cast anchor, she headed to a point far above it, thus showing that her steersman was aware of the strong shore current that had force enough to sweep her considerably out of her course. Meanwhile they had ample time to discuss her tonnage, her build, her qualities for freight and speed, and her goodness as a sea-boat. "I wonder did she see the yawl?" said one at length, for, with a strange and scarcely accountable terror, none would approach the theme that was uppermost in every heart. The word once uttered all burst in at once, "'Tis with news of her she's come! She saw her 'put in' to Belmullet or to Westport, or she saw her sheltering, perhaps, under the high cliffs of the coast, 'lying-to,' till the gale lightened." None would say more than this.

"Hurrah!" cried one at last, with a joyful cheer, that made every heart bound, "I see Master Harry; he's steerin'!"

"So he is!" shouted another; "he's settin' up on the weather gunwale, and his head bare too. I see his hair flyin' wild about him."

"Go up and tell the master."

"Faix, I'm afeerd; I never spoke to him in my life."

"Will you, Owen Riley?"

"Sorra step I'll go; he turned me out of the place for saying that the cobble wanted a coat of pitch, and she sank under me after. Let ould Moriarty go."

"So I will. 'Tis good news I'll have to bring him, and that never hurt the messenger." And so saying the old pilot hastened, as fast as his strength would permit, to the house.

The door was open, and he passed in. He sought for Molly in the kitchen, but poor Molly was away on the beach, following the course the lugger seemed to take, and hoping to be up at the point she might select to anchor at. The old man drew cautiously nigh Luttrell's door, and tapped at it respectfully.

"Who's there? Come in; come in at once," cried Luttrell in a harsh voice. "What have you to say? Say it out."

"'Tis to tell your honour that Master Harry——"

"What of him? What of him?" screamed Luttrell; and he seized the old man by the shoulders and shook him violently.

"He's steerin' the lugger, your honour, and all safe."

A cry, and a wild burst of laughter, broke from the overburdened heart, and Luttrell threw himself across the table and sobbed aloud.

THE IRISH DRAGOON.[1]

Oh love is the soul of an Irish dragoon,
In battle, in bivouac, or in saloon—
 From the tip of his spur to his bright sabretasche.
With his soldierly gait and his bearing so high,
His gay laughing look, and his light speaking eye,
He frowns at his rival, he ogles his wench,
He springs in his saddle and chasses the French—
 With his jingling spur and his bright sabretasche.

His spirits are high, and he little knows care,
Whether sipping his claret, or charging a square—
 With his jingling spur and his bright sabretasche.
As ready to sing or to skirmish he's found,

---

[1] This and the following four songs are from *Charles O'Malley*.

To take off his wine, or to take up his ground;
When the bugle may call him, how little he fears,
To charge forth in column, and beat the Mounseers—
    With his jingling spur and his bright sabretasche.

When the battle is over, he gaily rides back
To cheer every soul in the night bivouac—
    With his jingling spur and his bright sabretasche.
Oh! there you may see him in full glory crown'd,
As he sits 'mid his friends on the hardly won ground,
And hear with what feeling the toast he will give,
As he drinks to the land where all Irishmen live—
    With his jingling spur and his bright sabretasche.

MICKEY FREE'S ANCESTRY.

Air—"Na Guilloch y' Goulen."

Oh! once we were illigint people,
    Though we now live in cabins of mud;
And the land that ye see from the steeple
    Belonged to us all from the Flood.
My father was then King of Connaught,
    My grand-aunt Viceroy of Tralee;
But the Sassenach came, and, signs on it!
    The devil an acre have we.

The least of us then were all earls,
    And jewels we wore without name;
We drank punch out of rubies and pearls—
    Mr. Petrie can tell you the same.
But, except some turf mould and potatoes,
    There's nothing our own we can call;
And the English—bad luck to them!—hate us,
    Because we've more fun than them all!

My grand-aunt was niece to St. Kevin,
    That's the reason my name's Mickey Free!
Priest's nieces—but sure he's in heaven,
    And his failins is nothin' to me.
And we still might get on without doctors,
    If they'd let the ould Island alone;
And if purple men, priests, and tithe-proctors,
    Were crammed down the great gun of Athlone.

THE "MAN FOR GALWAY."

To drink a toast,
A proctor roast,
    Or bailiff as the case is,
To kiss your wife
Or take your life
    At ten or fifteen paces;
To keep game-cocks—to hunt the fox,
    To drink in punch the Solway,
With debts galore, but fun far more;
    Oh! that's "the man for Galway."
        Chorus—With debts, &c.

The King of Oude
Is mighty proud,
    And so were onst the *Caysars*—(Cæsars)
But ould Giles Eyre
Would make them stare,
    Av he had them with the Blazers.
To the devil I fling—ould Runjeet Sing,
    He's only a prince in a small way,
And knows nothing at all of a six-foot wall;
    Oh! he'd never "do for Galway."
        Chorus—With debts, &c.

Ye think the Blakes
Are no "great shakes;"
    They're all his blood relations,
And the Bodkins sneeze
At the grim Chinese,
    For they come from the *Phenaycians:*
So fill the brim, and here's to him
    Who'd drink in punch the Solway;
With debts galore, but fun far more;
    Oh! that's "the man for Galway."
        Chorus—With debts, &c.

THE WIDOW MALONE.

Did ye hear of the Widow Malone,
    Ohone!
Who lived in the town of Athlone
    Alone?
Oh! she melted the hearts
Of the swains in them parts,
So lovely the Widow Malone,
    Ohone!
So lovely the Widow Malone.

Of lovers she had a full score,
    Or more,
And fortunes they all had galore,
    In store;
From the minister down
To the clerk of the crown,
All were courting the Widow Malone,
    Ohone!
All were courting the Widow Malone.

But so modest was Mrs. Malone,
    'Twas known
No one ever could see her alone,
    Ohone!
Let them ogle and sigh,
They could ne'er catch her eye,
So bashful the Widow Malone,
    Ohone!
So bashful the Widow Malone.

Till one Mister O'Brien from Clare,
    How quare!

It's little for blushin' they care
   Down there;
Put his arm round her waist,
Gave ten kisses at laste,
"Oh," says he, "you're my Molly Malone,
   My own;"
"Oh," says he, "you're my Molly Malone."

And the Widow they all thought so shy—
   My eye—
Ne'er thought of a simper or sigh,
   For why?
But "Lucius," says she,
"Since you've made now so free,
You may marry your Mary Malone,
   Ohone!
You may marry your Mary Malone."

There's a moral contained in my song
   Not wrong,
And one comfort it's not very long,
   But strong:
If for widows you die,
Larn to *kiss, not to sigh*,
For they're all like sweet Mistress Malone,
   Ohone!
Oh! they're very like Mistress Malone."

BAD LUCK TO THIS MARCHING.

Air—"Paddy O'Carroll."

Bad luck to this marching,
Pipeclaying and starching,
How neat one must be to be killed by the French!
I'm sick of parading,
Through wet and cowld wading,
Or standing all night to be shot in a trench.
   To the tune of a fife
   They dispose of your life,
You surrender your soul to some illigant lilt;
   Now I like Garryowen,
   When I hear it at home,
But it's not half so sweet when you're going to be kilt.

   Then though up late and early,
   Our pay comes so rarely,
The devil a farthing we've ever to spare;
   They say some disaster
   Befel the paymaster;
On my conscience I think that the money's not there.
   And, just think, what a blunder,
   They won't let us plunder,
While the convents invite us to rob them, 'tis clear,
   Though there isn't a village,
   But cries, "Come and pillage,"
Yet we leave all the mutton behind for Mounseer.

Like a sailor that's nigh land,
I long for that island
Where even the kisses we steal if we please;
   Where it is no disgrace
   If you don't wash your face,
And you've nothing to do but to stand at your ease.
   With no sergeant t' abuse us,
   We fight to amuse us,
Sure it's better bate Christians than kick a baboon;
   How I'd dance like a fairy
   To see ould Dunleary,
And think twice ere I'd leave it to be a dragoon!

ARCHBISHOP M'HALE.

[Archbishop M'Hale has played an important part in the political history of Ireland for over half a century, and may be regarded as the man who next to O'Connell has exercised the deepest and most prolonged influence on the Roman Catholic population of the country. Though his views are decidedly pronounced and have been expressed in emphatic language, the consistency of his career, the independence of his character, and his strong love of country have procured for him considerable respect even among those who most strongly oppose him. John M'Hale was born as far back as 1791, at Tubbernavine, in Mayo. Having acquired the rudiments of learning in Castlebar, he entered at Maynooth, and after a distinguished career there was made professor of dogmatic theology. After he had held this place for eleven years he was raised to episcopal rank, being appointed coadjutor-bishop of Killala with the title of the Bishop of Maronia. During this period his pen was constantly busy. He wrote a series of letters under the signature of "Hierophilus," which were mostly concerned with controversial questions and Catholic emancipation. Indeed, during the greater part of his life there has scarcely been an occasion of public interest on which he has not expressed his views. His letters are remarkable for great vigour of style, and it was this fact, together with the masculine energy of his eloquence and character, that procured for him the title of "the Lion of the Fold of Juda" from O'Connell. On the death of Dr. Kelly he was promoted to the archiepiscopal see of Tuam. In his new position he continued to issue public pronouncements at intervals on such questions as "church establishment," "education," and the like. All his letters up to 1847 have been collected into one volume. Some sermons which were preached in Ireland, England, and Italy have been translated into Italian by the Abate de Lucca, apostolic nuncio at Vienna. He is also the author of a work published in 1827 entitled *Evidences and Doctrines of the Catholic Church*. Another department of literature to which he has devoted a large amount of time, and in which he has accomplished great things, is the attempt to revive an interest in the Irish language and literature. He has published translations into Irish of more than sixty of Moore's melodies in the same metre as the original, and in 1861 he produced a large octavo volume containing six books of the *Iliad* in an Irish translation. He has also published translations into the Celtic tongue of several portions of the Bible.]

AN IRISH PARLIAMENT AND AN IRISH FAMINE.

(FROM "LETTERS."[1])

TO THE RIGHT HONOURABLE LORD JOHN RUSSELL.

St. Jarlath's, Tuam, December 15, 1846.

"*Dignus imperio . . . si non imperasset.*"—*Tacitus.*—"Had he not the misfortune to rule, he would have been deemed deserving of empire.")

My Lord—This sententious contrast between the hopes of the aspiring Cæsar and the disappointment inflicted by the reigning emperor, is but too applicable to those statesmen whose talents, so hopeful in opposition, seem to be blighted on their attainment of political power. Within the brief interval of twelve months, two remarkable letters have appeared, bearing your lordship's signature. The one boldly promulgated the sound doctrine of free trade, and expressed a generous sympathy with the destitution of the Irish people, which was but light, compared to the famine with which they are now afflicted. The other was so chilling, as to have filled those with despair whom it would have been wisdom to console—among whom hunger now

[1] By permission of the author.

rages with such terrible activity, that it is consigning to the grave its daily victims. The one was the studied essay of a popular candidate for the distinctions of office—the other was the cold and conventional language which was borrowed from the political ritual of preceding prime ministers. It was on the buoyant hopes inspired by the language of the first, your lordship was borne to your present responsible position; and should you persevere in a line of policy, towards a suffering nation, accordant with the cold-hearted sentiments contained in your second letter, it requires no extraordinary prescience to predict that it will assuredly prove the precursor of your political fall.

By one of those awful calamities with which Providence sometimes visits states and nations, five millions of people, forming an integral portion of a flourishing and mighty empire, are entirely deprived of food, and consigned to all the horrors of famine. The prime minister is naturally and rightfully appealed to, to relieve the suffering part with an equitable application of the wealth of the entire body, and he replies to them, to look to themselves, and rely on their own resources. Self-reliance is a fine theme when sufficient for any crisis; but to tell a people to supply themselves with food, when both food and means of procuring it are gone, appears like the requisition of the Hebrews to make bricks without materials. And does your lordship, too, advocate, by this singular letter, the nullity of the imperial union? For forty-six years the people of Ireland have been feeding those of England with the choicest produce of their agriculture and pasture; and while they thus exported their wheat and their beef in profusion, their own food became gradually deteriorated in each successive year, until the mass of the peasantry was exclusively thrown on the potato. New improvements in agriculture were projected—scientific reforms in the rearing and feeding of cattle were discussed and adopted; but to the mass of the people the practical fruit of those improvements was a fresh interdict of the use of flesh-meat or of flour, and a further extension of the dominion of a less nutritive kind of that same vegetable, to the exclusive use of which they were inexorably doomed!

No matter—a cry of Irish prosperity was raised by those who were enabled to subject the growers of corn to the uniform consumption of an inferior quality of food; and the same cry was re-echoed from the shores of

England, gladdened with the abundance with which its inhabitants were supplied, careless of the misery of which that abundance was productive in Ireland, and losing sight altogether of the dietary destitution which, during the spring and summer months, its people were uniformly fated to endure. The English legislature was not ungrateful to the Irish landlords for those exporting services, so beneficial to the English population, and in return for the increased quantity of the nobler food, which alone they would condescend to make use of, it furnished them with facilities of seizure of crops and ejectment of tenantry never known before the Union; so that if any of the peasantry should become too fastidious for the use of potatoes, or aspire to the interdicted food of flesh-meat or flour, destined to swell the rent-rolls of the one, and feed the petted population of the other, they were sure to be summarily driven from their tenements, for not raising further food for export, and reproached with utter ignorance of the very elements of agriculture. On the expulsion of the tenantry to the skirtings of the moor, cattle-shows became all the rage in Ireland, and meetings were held to witness and applaud the successful zeal with which Irish graziers could supply with still larger quantities of beef, and pork, and mutton, the increasing demands of the English people. The animals were exhibited—not such an exhibition, however, as when the animals passed in review before him, who was constituted by their common Creator, the owner of the earth, as well as all its animal productions. In these exhibitions this order appeared reversed, and whilst the neglected condition of the poor peasantry showed the estimation in which they were held, the unnatural dimensions of those pampered brutes would indicate that they were looked on as the beings which shared, to the greatest extent, the kindred sympathies of their owners. Such, with a few benevolent exceptions, was the spirit that guided those cattle exhibitions.

As long as the people of Ireland were thus draining it of its necessary food into England, and enriching the landed proprietors with its price, the blessings of the Union became a theme of their joint commendation. Any allusion to the solicitude which an Irish parliament would naturally exhibit for the Irish people, was treated as a topic that indicated folly or sedition. More produce and finer stock, according to these speculators in money, were the only wants of Ireland; at the same time that it was certain, if the prudence and stock were fourfold, the millions of the people, irrevocably doomed to the potato, would be equally debarred from their participation.

At length their cries have reached to heaven; and He who has created the poor and the rich has answered: "Now I will hear; the time of retribution is come; vengeance is already sweeping the land," verifying the words of the inspired writings: "By reason of the misery of the needy, and the groans of the poor, now will I arise, saith the Lord." In a great national chastisement all must in some degree be involved; and though many of the poor are made victims, perhaps from their want of due resignation, and to teach them that there can be still deeper misery than that which they endured, the entire destruction of the potato crop reads an awful lesson of the cruelty of which that aliment has been made the instrument. It was intended by the Almighty as a valuable adjunct of human sustenance to his creatures—it has been abused by man as an instrument of rapacious wealth—of dire oppression, and of national degradation. Its destruction shows what some seemed ignorant of—that the interests of all are identified; that one class cannot permanently flourish, and another be abandoned to decay, and that the people cannot be pushed to the verge of starvation, without landlords and rulers sharing in all the perils of their position. The perishing potato is the most formidable agitator, the oppressors of the people had ever yet to wrestle with. But though the transition to the full harvest will be severe, it will become in the hands of Providence, that caused the decay, the fructifying seed of our national regeneration.

Such is now the frightful state of this country, brought on, as it were, by a systematic collusion between the Irish landlords and the English legislature, and to which Ireland never would have been reduced, had she the protection of a native parliament. The famine has not, it is true, directly sprung from the Union. But severe as it is, it would not be so fatal, if Ireland had not been rendered too feeble to cope with the calamity, by the emaciating process to which it had been previously subjected. In the year 1800, the first year of the disastrous Union, the potatoes sold for 18d. a stone, and meal brought even a larger price than it is now sold for. Yet there was no starvation in Ireland, nor any necessity to appeal for relief to the imperial exchequer. No; because the constitution of the country was yet sound. It was not exhausted by the drainage of near half a century; and the vitality and vigour which it received from the free-trade of 1782, not only sustained it through that trying crisis, but were felt to a far remoter period. Let any dispassionate person contrast those two years—the people during the former calamity sustaining themselves, notwithstanding the pressure of higher prices—and the people now as feeble and powerless as children, faltering on the public ways, and many of them sinking beneath a lighter scourge—and he must come to the conclusion, that the only safety for the Irish people is the restoration of their own legislature. Had we not, preceding this disaster, three or four seasons of unprecedented plenty and prosperity? Where are their fruits now to meet the present exigency? The temperate habits of the people refute the slander that they were improvidently wasted. No: the fruits of the first seasons were forced from the tenantry in lieu of the arrears which preceding years of distress had accumulated; and allow me to tell you, that though, in all equity, the loss of a crop should be proportionably sustained by the proprietor and the tenant, there is not a farthing of arrears which might grow during the famine, that would not hang over the poor tenants, even for ten years, to be rigorously exacted, when Heaven might bless them with a more plentiful harvest.

SIR JOSEPH NAPIER.

[Sir Joseph Napier is the youngest son of William Napier, a descendant of the Merchiston branch of the Napier family, and was born at Belfast in December, 1804. In youth he had the advantage of several able teachers, one of these being the afterwards famous dramatist J. Sheridan Knowles. He entered Trinity College in 1820, and his undergraduate career was remarkable for proficiency in classics. In 1825 he graduated B.A., and at first intended to read for a fellowship, but he afterwards resolved to devote himself to the profession of the law. During his stay at college he took part in reviving the old Historical Society, one of his colleagues in this work being Chief-justice Whiteside. Many years after (in 1856) Mr. Napier was chosen president of the society. After a time spent in London qualifying himself more fully for his profession, he returned to his native country and became a member of the Irish bar. In 1831 he was called, and before long became one of the most sought-after juniors. In 1843 he made his appearance before the House of Lords, in the once celebrated appeal case of Samuel Gray, which involved the accused's right of challenging a juror, and he succeeded in having the conviction of his client reversed. On his return to Ireland he was made a Q.C., and for many years afterwards was employed in most of the cases of importance that were appealed for final decision to the House of Lords.

In 1847 Mr. Napier contested with Sir Frederick Shaw the seat for Dublin University. He was defeated, but was elected on the resignation of Sir Frederick in the following year. For a long period he took a prominent part in discussing the more important questions before the House of Commons, always supporting the Conservative party. This support received recognition on Lord Derby's accession to office in 1852, when he was appointed attorney-general for Ireland, and held the office until the fall of his chief. When Lord Derby came into power a second time in 1858, Mr. Napier received still higher distinction, being promoted to the post of Irish lord-chancellor, which he held till his party left office the following year. In 1867 Lord Derby again showed his appreciation of Mr. Napier's abilities and public services by creating him a baronet. In the same year he became vice-chancellor of Trinity College, Dublin, and in 1868 was made privy-councillor of Great Britain, being shortly afterwards constituted a member of the judicial committee of the privy-council. He also bears the honorary degrees of LL.D. of Dublin University and D.C.L. of Oxford.

The labours of his profession have not prevented Sir Joseph Napier from taking a large share in various important public movements. He has been twice elected president of the jurisprudence section of the Social Science Association, and in connection therewith has published several able addresses on law reform. After the Irish disestablishment act was passed he took an active part in the reconstruction of the Church. Amongst his literary productions we may notice, Lectures on "The Increase of Knowledge," "Richard Baxter and his Times," "Edmund Burke" (from which we quote), " Facts and Fallacies of the Sabbath Question," "Things New and Old," a pamphlet on "The Education Question," "Lectures on Butler's Analogy," besides many others.]

CHARACTER OF BURKE.

Notwithstanding the honourable motives, the wise and liberal policy of the Rockingham cabinet, the ambition of Pitt and the intrigues of the mercenaries of the court party brought about another change of administration. The Duke of Grafton, who had served with Lord Rockingham, was the nominal chief of a new cabinet on a plan arranged by Pitt, who was now made lord privy-seal and Earl of Chatham. In a small publication entitled *A Short Account of a Short Administration*, Burke placed before the public a summary of the measures which had been carried by the Rockingham party in the year and twenty days in which they held office.

The marquis was desirous to get employment for Burke in the new administration; and the Duke of Grafton strongly urged Pitt, now Lord Chatham, to seek the services of Burke. The duke said that he had the means of knowing his integrity—that he might thoroughly be trusted. And in a letter of October 17, 1774, to Lord Chatham, he says; "Of those whom I should wish, and Mr. Conway also wishes, to see to support him is Mr. Burke, the readiest man upon all points, perhaps, in the whole house." Lord Chatham replied: "The gentleman your grace points out as a necessary recruit, I think a man of parts and an ingenious speaker. *As to his notions and maxims of trade, they never can be mine.*" He had promised the first open place at the board of trade to Lord Lisburne — there was no room for the Irish commoner—the young Irishman of whom General Lee had then written to the Prince Royal of Poland, that he "had astonished everybody by the power of his eloquence, and his comprehensive knowledge in all our exterior and internal politics and commercial interests. He wants nothing but that sort of dignity annexed to rank and property in England to make him the most considerable man in the lower house." He was distanced by Lord Lisburne. Chatham, who in the House of Commons had congratulated Burke on his first success, and his friends on the value of the acquisition they had made (as we learn from the excellent Earl of Charlemont), Chatham, at this crisis of the American question, turned aside from Burke as a basilisk. With a view to complete a job for his brother-in-law, James Grenville, he made Charles Townsend his chancellor of the exchequer—Townsend, whose character Burke has so inimitably sketched—who treated Chatham's distinction of internal and external taxation as simply ridiculous, but pledged himself to find a revenue nearly sufficient to meet the expense properly required for the colonies. And of this Chatham was apprised. Despising the wisdom of Burke, and enduring the folly of Townsend, Chatham and his composite cabinet, which Burke had painted in colours that have not yet faded, inaugurated a system of taxation affecting British manufactures, and therefore not properly within trade regulations; duties were imposed and to be collected in America, in a way which marked their imperial origin and purpose; thus inflicting indirectly on the colonies, against the soundest principles of commercial policy, what Chatham had so strenuously contended to be against the constitutional right directly to impose. With such a ministry Burke could have no communion.

He had been one of a party with a creed of enlightened policy, and a purpose of promoting the best interests of England. He was comparatively a poor man, he had not the influence of social position, but he had so far won his way by the self-elevating power of industry and virtue, under the blessing and guidance of God. His nature was earnest and artless, he had not the finesse that is often miscalled sagacity, nor the cunning which (as Bacon says) is but the counterfeit of wisdom. Lord Charlemont has described him as amiable and excellent, but sometimes allowing his zeal to carry him beyond the bounds of prudence. Horace Walpole says, that of all the eminent men he ever met, Burke had the least political art. This exactly squares with what we might collect from his own admissions. He had no reserve—no kind of concealment—whatever the subject was he poured forth the affluence of his thoughts and feelings. Sir Philip Francis happily remarked, "You always see both the best and the worst of him."

JAMES GODKIN.

[This gentleman, who holds a pension for "literary merit" from the state, was born in the year 1806, at Gorey, county Wexford. He began life as a Dissenting minister in Armagh, and was a missionary in connection with the Irish Evangelical Society. In consequence of having written a prize essay on Federalism, entitled "The Rights of Ireland," this connection ceased, and he then turned his attention to journalism. In the year 1847 he found himself in London, and became the correspondent of several Irish and Scotch papers, besides contributing to several magazines. Returning to Ireland he established in Belfast the *Christian Patriot*. He afterwards became editor of the *Derry Standard*, and then removing to the capital, he for several years held the chief post on the *Daily Express*. While engaged on this paper he acted as the Dublin correspondent of the *Times*. It may here be remarked that his letters to this journal were remarkable for their keen and comprehensive knowledge of Irish affairs. He is the author of *Ireland and her Churches, The Land-War in Ireland, The Religious History of Ireland*, &c. The second of these works is a most interesting compilation of all that has been written on the much-vexed question of the relations between the owners and the tillers of the soil in Ireland. Some of his writings on ecclesiastical and land questions had a large influence in bringing about the disestablishment of the Irish Church and the new Lands Acts. We may also mention that early in life Mr. Godkin wrote several controversial works.]

ULSTER IN EIGHTEENTH CENTURY.

(FROM "THE LAND-WAR IN IRELAND."[1])

[Mr. Godkin's book, *The Land-war in Ireland*, gives several most interesting pictures of the social condition of the country at different periods. Many of his descriptions will convey information that will be novel even to Irishmen. From the extract, for instance, which follows, it will be seen that during part of the eighteenth century what we are accustomed to regard as the prosperous North was really the poorest part of Ireland. It will be also observed that the perpetual struggle between the landlord and the tenant went on at that period quite as fiercely when the two classes were of the same, as when they were of different creeds.]

Let us then endeavour to get rid of the pernicious delusions about race and religion in dealing with this Irish land question. Identity of race and substantial agreement in religion did not prevent the Ulster landlords from uprooting their tenants when they fancied it was their interest to banish them—to substitute grazing for tillage, and cattle for a most industrious and orderly peasantry.

The letters of Primate Boulter contain much valuable information on the state of Ulster in the last century, and furnish apt illustrations of the land question, which, I fancy, will be new and startling to many readers. Boulter was Lord-primate of Ireland from 1724 to 1738. He was thirteen times one of the lords justices. As an Englishman and a good churchman he took care of the English interests and of the Establishment. The letters were written in confidence to Sir Robert Walpole and other ministers of state, and were evidently not intended for publication. An address "to the reader" from some friend states truly that they give among other things an impartial account of "the distressed state of the kingdom for want of *tillage*, the vast sums of money sent out of the nation for corn, flour, &c., the dismal calamities thereon, the want of trade, and the regulation of the English and other coins to the very great distress of all the manufacturers, &c. They show that he was a man of sound judgment, public-spirited, and very moderate and impartial for the times in which he lived. His evidence with regard to the relations of landlord and tenant in Ulster is exceedingly valuable at the present moment. . . .

Primate Boulter repeatedly complained to Walpole, the Duke of Newcastle, and other ministers, that the Ulster farmers were deserting the country in large numbers, emigrating to the United States, then British colonies, to the West Indies, or to any country where they hoped to get the means of living, in many cases binding themselves to work for a number of years *as slaves* in payment of

---

[1] By permission of Messrs. Macmillan & Co.

their passage out. The desire to quit the country of their birth is described by the primate as a mania. Writing to the Archbishop of Canterbury in 1728, he says:—"We are under great trouble here about a frenzy that has taken hold of very great numbers to leave this country for the West Indies, and we are endeavouring to learn what may be the reasons of it, and the proper remedies." Two or three weeks later he reported to the Duke of Newcastle that for several years past some agents from the colonies in America, and several masters of ships, had gone about the country "and deluded the people with stories of great plenty and estates to be had for going for in those parts of the world." During the previous summer more than 3000 men, women, and children had been shipped for the West Indies. Of these not more than one in ten were men of substance. The rest hired themselves for their passage, or contracted with masters of ships for four years' servitude, "selling themselves as servants for their subsistence." The whole north was in a ferment, people every day engaging one another to go next year to the West Indies. "The humour," says the primate, "has spread like a contagious distemper, and the people will hardly hear anybody that tries to cure them of their madness. The worst is that it affects only *Protestants*, and reigns chiefly in the north, which is the seat of our linen manufacture."

As the Protestant people, the descendants of the English and Scotch who had settled in the country in the full assurance that they were building homes for their posterity, were thus deserting those homes in such multitudes, their pastors sent a memorial to the lord-lieutenant, setting forth the grievances which they believed to be the cause of the desertion. On this memorial the primate wrote comments to the English government, and in doing so he stated some astounding facts as to the treatment of the people by their landlords. He was a cautious man, thoroughly acquainted with the facts, and writing under a sense of great responsibility. In order to understand some of those facts we should bear in mind that the landlords had laid down large portions of their estates in pasture to avoid the payment of tithes, and that this burden was thrown entirely upon the tenants who tilled the land. Now, let my readers mark what the primate states as to their condition. He says:—"If a landlord takes too great a portion of the profits of a farm for his share by way of rent (as the tithe will light on the tenant's share), the tenant will be impoverished; but then it is not the tithe, but the increased rent that undoes the farmer; and, indeed, in this country, where I fear the tenant hardly ever has more than one-third of the profits he makes of his farm for his share, and too often but a *fourth*, or, perhaps, a *fifth part*, as the tenant's share, is charged with the tithe, his case is no doubt hard, but it is plain from what side the hardship arises." What the gentlemen wanted to be at, according to the primate, was, that they might go on raising their rents, and that the clergy should receive their old payments. He admits, however, that the tenants were sometimes cited to the ecclesiastical courts, and if they failed to appear there they stood excommunicated; and he adds, "possibly when a writ *de excommunicato capiendo* is taken out, and they find they have £7 or £8 to pay, *they run away*, for the greatest part of the occupiers of the land here are so poor, that an extraordinary stroke of £8 or £10 falling on them is certain ruin to them." He further states that, to his own knowledge, many of the clergy had chosen rather to lose their "small dues" than to be at a certain great expense in getting them, "and at an uncertainty whether the farmer would not at last *run away without paying anything*."

Such was the condition of the Protestants of Ulster during the era of the penal code; and it is a curious fact that it was the Presbyterians and not the Catholics that were forced by the exactions of the Protestant landlords and the clergy to run away from the country which their forefathers had been brought over to civilize. But there was another fact connected with the condition of Ulster which I dare say will be almost incredible to many readers. The tenantry, so cruelly rack-rented and impoverished, were reduced by two or three bad seasons to a state bordering upon famine. There was little or no corn in the province. The primate set on foot a subscription in Dublin, to which he himself contributed very liberally. The object was to buy food to supply the necessities of the north, and to put a stop to "the great desertion" they had been threatened with. He hoped that the landlords would "do *their* part by remitting some arrears, or making some abatement of their rents." As many of the tenants had eaten the oats they should have sowed their lands with, he expected the landlords would have the good sense to furnish them with seed; if not, a great deal of land would lie waste that year. And where were the provisions got? Partly in

Munster, where corn was very cheap and abundant. But the people of Cork, Limerick, Waterford, and Clonmel objected to have their provisions sent away, although they were in some places "as cheap again as in the north; but where dearest, at least one-third part cheaper." Riotous mobs broke open the storehouses and cellars, setting what price they pleased upon the provisions; and, what between those riots and the prevalence of easterly winds, three weeks elapsed before the £3000 worth of oats, oatmeal, and potatoes could be got down to relieve the famishing people of the north, which then seemed black enough even to its own inhabitants. Hence the humane primate was obliged to write: "The humour of going to America still continues, and the scarcity of provisions certainly makes many quit us. There are now seven ships at Belfast that are carrying off 1000 passengers thither, and if we knew how to stop them, as most of them can neither get victuals nor work at home, it would be cruel to do it."

The Presbyterian clergy suffered greatly from the impoverishment of their people. Several of them who had been receiving a stipend of £50 a year, had their incomes reduced to less than £15. In their distress they appealed to the primate, and, staunch churchman as he was, they found in him a kind and earnest advocate. Writing to Sir Robert Walpole, on March 31, 1729, he pleaded for the restoration of £400 a year, which had been given to the nonconforming clergy of Ireland from the privy purse in addition to the £1200 royal bounty, which, it appears, had been suspended for two years, owing to the death of the late king. "They are sensible," said his grace, "there is nothing due to them, nor do they make any such claim; but as the calamities of this kingdom are at present very great, and by the desertion of many of their people to America, and the poverty of the greatest part of the rest, their contributions, particularly in the north, are very much fallen off, it would be a great instance of his majesty's goodness if he would consider their present distress." In our own days a Presbyterian minister would be considered to deserve well of his country if he emigrated to America, and took with him as many of the people as he could induce to forsake their native land. But what was the great plea which Primate Boulter urged on the English minister on behalf of the Presbyterian clergy of his day? It was that they had exerted their influence to prevent emigration. "It is," he said, "but doing them justice to affirm that they are very well affected to his majesty and his royal family, and by the best inquiries I could make, do their best endeavours to keep their congregations from deserting the country, not more than one or two of the younger ministers having anyways encouraged the humour now prevailing here; and his majesty's goodness in giving them some extraordinary relief on this occasion of their present great distress would undoubtedly make them *more active to retain their people here*. I cannot help mentioning on this occasion that, what with scarceness of corn in the north, *and the loss of all credit there*, and by the numbers that go, or talk of going, to America, and with the disturbances in the south, this kingdom is at present in a deplorable condition." . . .

From the pictures of the times he presents we should not be surprised at his statement to the Duke of Newcastle, that the people who went to America made great complaints of the oppressions they suffered, and said that those oppressions were one reason of their going. When he went on his visitation in 1726 he "met all the roads full of whole families that had left their homes to beg abroad," having consumed their stock of potatoes two months before the usual time. During the previous year many hundreds had perished of famine. What was the cause of this misery, this desolating process going on over the plains of Ulster? The archbishop accounts for it by stating that many persons had let large tracts of land from 3000 to 4000 acres, which were stocked with cattle, and had no other inhabitants on their land than so many cottiers as were necessary to look after their sheep and black cattle, "*so that, in some of the finest counties, in many places there is neither house nor corn-field to be seen in ten or fifteen miles' travelling*, and daily in some counties many gentlemen, as their leases fall into their hands, tie up their tenants from tillage; and this is one of the main causes why so many venture to go into foreign service at the hazard of their lives if taken, because they cannot get land to till at home."

My readers should remember that the industrious, law-abiding, Bible-loving, God-fearing people, who were thus driven by oppression from the fair fields of Ulster, which they had cultivated, and the dwellings which they had erected, to make way for sheep and cattle—because it was supposed by the landlords that sheep and cattle paid better—were the descendants of British settlers who came to the country under a royal guarantee of *freeholds and permanent tenures.* Let them picture to their minds this fine race of honest, godly people, rack-rented, crushed, evicted, heart-broken—men, women, and children—Protestants, Saxons, cast out to perish as the refuse of the earth, by a set of landed proprietors of their own race and creed; and learn from this most instructive fact that if any body of men has the power of making laws to promote its own interest, no instincts of humanity, no dictates of religion, no restraints of conscience can be **relied** upon to keep them from acting with ruthless barbarity, and doing more to ruin their country **than** a foreign invader could accomplish **by letting** loose upon it his brutal soldiers.

ARCHBISHOP TRENCH.

Some writers have thought it necessary to justify the admission of Archbishop Trench into a gallery of Irish worthies, pointing out that, wherever he might have been born himself, his ancestors were all unmistakably Irish. There is no necessity whatever for this apology, the fact being that Dr. Trench is Irish by birth as well as by descent; he was born in Dublin, and not in England, as has been often asserted. Richard Chenevix Trench is the second son of the late Mr. Richard Trench, brother of the first Lord Ashtown. His mother, a woman of remarkable endowments, of whom her son has left a graceful memoir, was the grand-daughter of Dr. Chevenix, Bishop of Waterford. He was born on September 9, 1807. Having graduated in Trinity College, Cambridge, in 1829, he became perpetual curate of Curdridge Chapel; thence he passed to other cures, the most important of which, in its consequences on his after-life, was that of Alverstoke, near Gosport. Here he was under Dr. Wilberforce, afterwards the famous Bishop of Winchester. The friendship which was thus formed lasted throughout life, and joined the two men in many undertakings. When Dr. Wilberforce ceased to be Dean of Westminster Dr. Trench stepped into the vacant place; and in his new episcopal dignity as Bishop of Oxford, Dr. Wilberforce had his old friend beside him as examining chaplain.

While Dr. Trench had thus been ascending the ladder of ecclesiastical promotion, he had been acquiring reputation in other directions. In 1835 he published *Justin Martyr and other Poems*, a work which was highly eulogized by such competent authorities as *Blackwood's Magazine* and the *Athenæum*, and which has passed through numerous editions. *Sabbation, Honor Neale, and other Poems*, followed in 1838, and further enhanced the reputation of the author, *Blackwood* declaring that he was "among the foremost of our young poets." At intervals followed *Elegiac Poems, Poems from Eastern Sources, Genoveva and other Poems*. Dr. Trench has also published *Sacred Poems for* **Mourners***, Sacred Latin Poetry*, and *Life's a Dream* from the Spanish of Calderon. He has also written a considerable number of prose works. The greater part of those are devoted to theological subjects, and need not be recapitulated here. Besides these, he has published a series of books on philological subjects which are very widely known. *The Study of Words*, the most popular of the series, is a charming volume. The pedigree of our vocabulary is so traced as to make the reader appreciate the delight of following the history of an ancient and romantic family; and a subject which in most writers is dry, is enlivened with poetic feeling, anecdote, and a charming style.

Dr. Trench was consecrated Archbishop of Dublin on January 1, 1864, on the decease of Dr. Whately. He took a prominent part in the agitation caused by the proposal to disestablish the Irish Church, and was afterwards engaged in some of the animated controversies that were involved in the reconstruction of that Church

THE POETRY OF WORDS.

(FROM "THE STUDY OF WORDS.")[1]

Language is fossil poetry; in other words, we are not to look for the poetry which a people may possess only in its poems, or its poetical customs, traditions, and beliefs. Many a single word also is itself a concentrated poem,

---

[1] By permission of the author.

having stores of poetical thought and imagery laid up in it. Examine it, and it will be found to rest on some deep analogy of things natural and things spiritual; bringing those to illustrate and to give an abiding form and body to these. The image may have grown trite and ordinary now; perhaps through the help of this very word may have become so entirely the heritage of all, as to seem little better than a commonplace; yet not the less he who first discerned the relation, and devised the new word which should express it, or gave to an old, never before but literally used, this new and figurative sense, this man was in his degree a poet—a maker, that is, of things which were not before, which would not have existed, but for him, or for some other gifted with equal powers. He who spake first of a "dilapidated" fortune, what an image must have risen up before his mind's eye of some falling house or palace, stone detaching itself from stone, till all had gradually sunk into desolation and ruin. Or he who to that Greek word which signifies "that which will endure to be held up to and judged by the sunlight," gave first its ethical signification of "sincere," "truthful," or as we sometimes say, "transparent," can we deny to him the poet's feeling and eye? Many a man had gazed, we are sure, at the jagged and indented mountain ridges of Spain before one called them "sierras" or "saws," the name by which now they are known, as *Sierra* Morena, *Sierra* Nevada; but that man coined his imagination into a word, which will endure as long as the everlasting hills which he named. . . .

"Iliads without a Homer," some one has called, with a little exaggeration, the beautiful but anonymous ballad poetry of Spain. One may be permitted, perhaps, to push the exaggeration a little further in the same direction, and to apply the same language not merely to a ballad but to a word. . . . Let me illustrate that which I have been here saying somewhat more at length by the word "tribulation." We all know in a general way that this word, which occurs not seldom in Scripture and in the Liturgy, means affliction, sorrow, anguish; but it is quite worth our while to know *how* it means this, and to question the word a little closer. It is derived from the Latin "tribulum"—which was the threshing instrument or harrow, whereby the Roman husbandman separated the corn from the husks; and "tribulatio" in its primary significance was the act of this separation. But some Latin writer of the Christian church appropriated the word and image for the setting forth of a higher truth; and sorrow, distress, and adversity being the appointed means for the separating in men of whatever in them was light, trivial, and poor, from the solid and the true, their chaff from their wheat, he therefore called these sorrows and trials "tribulations," threshings, that is, of the inner spiritual man, without which there could be no fitting him for the heavenly garner. Now in proof of my assertion that a single word is often a concentrated poem, a little grain of pure gold capable of being beaten out into a broad extent of gold-leaf, I will quote, in reference to this very word "tribulation," a graceful composition by George Wither, a poet of the seventeenth century. You will at once perceive that it is all wrapped up in this word, being from first to last only the expanding of the image and thought which this word has implicitly given; it is as follows:—

"Till from the straw, the flail the corn doth beat,
Until the chaff be purged from the wheat,
Yea, till the mill the grains in pieces tear,
The richness of the flour will scarce appear.
So, till men's persons great afflictions touch,
If worth be found, their worth is not so much,
Because, like wheat in straw, they have not yet
That value which in threshing they may get.
For till the bruising flails of God's corrections
Have threshèd out of us our vain affections;
Till those corruptions which do misbecome us
Are by thy sacred Spirit winnowed from us;
Until from us the straw of worldly treasures,
Till all the dusty chaff of empty pleasures,
Yea, till his flail upon us he doth lay,
To thresh the husk of this our flesh away;
And leave the soul uncovered; nay, yet more,
Till God shall make our very spirit poor,
We shall not up to highest wealth aspire;
But then we shall; and that is my desire."

This deeper religious use of the word "tribulation" was unknown to classical antiquity, belonging exclusively to the Christian writers: and the fact that the same deepening and elevating of the use of words recurs in a multitude of other, and many of them far more signal instances, is one well deserving to be followed up. Nothing, I am persuaded, would more mightily convince us of the new power which Christianity proved in the world than to compare the meaning which so many words possessed before its rise, and the deeper meaning which they obtained so soon as they were assumed as the vehicles of its life, the new thought and feeling enlarging, purifying, and ennobling the very words which they employed.

THE EVENING HYMN.

To the sound of evening bells
    All that lives to rest repairs,
Birds unto their leafy dells,
    Beasts unto their forest lairs.

All things wear a home-bound look,
    From the weary hind that plods
Through the corn-fields, to the rook
    Sailing toward the glimmering woods.

'Tis the time with power to bring
    Tearful memories of home
To the sailor wandering
    On the far-off barren foam.

What a still and holy time!
    Yonder glowing sunset seems
Like the pathway to a clime
    Only seen till now in dreams.

Pilgrim! here compelled to roam,
    Nor allowed that path to tread,
Now, when sweetest sense of home
    On all living hearts is shed,

Doth not yearning sad, sublime,
    At this season stir thy breast,
That thou canst not at this time
    Seek thy home and happy rest?

SOME MURMUR.

Some murmur, when their sky is clear
    And wholly bright to view,
If one small speck of dark appear
    In their great heaven of blue.
And some with thankful love are filled,
    If but one streak of light,
One ray of God's good mercy gild
    The darkness of their night.

In palaces are hearts that ask,
    In discontent and pride,
Why life is such a dreary task,
    And all good things denied.
And hearts in poorest huts admire
    How love has in their aid
(Love that not ever seems to tire)
    Such rich provision made.

JOHN PATRICK PRENDERGAST.

[Mr. Prendergast was born in Dublin in 1807, and was educated at Reading, England, under the Rev. Dr. Valpy. He graduated at Trinity College, Dublin, and was called to the bar in 1830. In conjunction with the Very Rev. Dr. Russell, the president of Maynooth College, he was appointed by Lord Romilly to select state papers relating to Ireland from the Carte Collection of Papers in the Bodleian Library, Oxford. Mr. Prendergast was afterwards engaged in cataloguing the state papers (Ireland) of James I. He is the author of *The Cromwellian Settlement of Ireland*, a second edition of which appeared in 1870. This is a very remarkable product of industry, informed by zeal. It is the first work that has thrown full light on a dark period in Irish history. In its pages we have an account of that terrible tragedy in Irish history—the displacement of the old Irish and Anglo-Irish families by the retainers of Cromwell; and the story is told with great dramatic skill. Every student of Irish history—and especially of the history of the Irish land—should make himself familiar with this excellent book. Mr. Prendergast is at present engaged on a new work on "The Scandinavians." He is an honorary member of the Royal Historical Society of Great Britain.]

THE CLEARING OF GALWAY.

(FROM "THE CROMWELLIAN SETTLEMENT."[1])

[One of the measures of the English parliament during the Protectorate was to sell several of the Irish towns in order to satisfy the demands of the soldiery and public creditors. The results of this step was that the old inhabitants were "cleared out" in order to make way for the new immigrants from England. In most cases the persons displaced were themselves originally of the English race. The following extract describes this process in the capital of Connaught.]

Galway seems to have been, even before the English conquest, the seat of foreign traders; and some time after the invasion of Henry II.

[1] By permission of the author.

the town is found inhabited by a number of families, all of French and English blood, who refused to intermarry with the Irish. Their relations with the native race may best be understood by one of the corporation by-laws, which enacts (A.D. 1518) that none of the inhabitants should admit any of the Burkes, M'Williams, Kellys, or any other sept into their houses, to the end "that neither O ne Mac should strutte ne swagger throughe the streets of Gallway." In 1641 the townsmen were all English. Richard Martin, one of the principal inhabitants, in announcing from Galway the outbreak of the Irish in the neighbourhood to Lord Ormond, informs him (December, 1641) that the town is disfurnished with arms and munitions, so that to defend those maiden walls they had but naked bodies; and in allusion to a rumour current that they would be allowed none, he says, God forbid it should be true. "If it be (said he) we are very unfortunate to be hated by some powerful neighbours for being all English; and to have our four hundred years' constant and unsuspected loyalty without the help of a garrison (until the last year, when there was no need for it) forgotten and buried."

Galway was the last fortress of the Irish in the war of 1641, and surrendered to Ludlow on the 20th March, 1652, on articles, securing the inhabitants their residences within the town, and the enjoyment of their houses and estates. The taxation was soon so great, that many of the townspeople quitted their habitations, and removed their cattle, unable to endure it. Consequently the contribution fell the heavier on the remaining inhabitants. This tax was collected from them every Saturday by sound of trumpet; and if not instantly paid, the soldiery rushed into the house, and seized what they could lay hands on. The sound of this trumpet every returning Saturday shook their souls with terror like the trumpet of the day of judgment. On the 15th March, 1653, the commissioners for Ireland, remarking upon the disaffection thus exhibited, confiscated the houses of those that had deserted the town. Those that fled were wise in time. On 23d July, 1655, all the Irish were directed to quit the town by the 1st of November following, the owners of houses, however, to receive compensation at eight years' purchase; in default the soldiers were to drive them out. On 30th October this order was executed. All the inhabitants, except the sick and bedrid, were at once banished, to provide accommodation for such English Protestants whose integrity to the state should entitle them to be trusted in a place of such importance; and Sir Charles Coote on the 7th November received the thanks of the government for clearing the town, with a request that he would remove the sick and bedrid as soon as the season might permit, and take care that the houses while empty were not spoiled by the soldiery. Among the sick and bedrid was not counted Robert French, a cripple, though not able to stand or sit without the assistance of another. He was helped out of the town by George French, and they betook themselves to a village in the country. They had converted all their little substance into money, in hopes to bestow the same in some bargain of advantage to them. But their banishment was peculiarly unfortunate. On the 10th June, 1664, in the dead time of the night, they were plundered of £44, 12s. in money, and of gold rings, spoons, and other things to the value of £20, and of their evidences, and writings of great value, by four unknown and disguised horsemen, who, upon fresh pursuit, could not be discovered in the country—only of late one of them was hanged in Galway. Ever since they were in a miserable condition, living on the charity of friends. They accordingly asked liberty of the lord-lieutenant and council to live again and abide in Galway, out of the danger of further plundering.

Mathew Quin and Mary Quin (otherwise Butler) his wife, asked liberty of the lord-lieutenant to clear the graveyard of Saint Francis's Abbey, without the walls in the north Franchises of the town of Galway, of the stones laid in heaps upon the graves by the late usurped power. It was the burial place of the petitioners and their ancestors since the reign of James I., and of very many inhabiting the town and country near it. The late Abbey was demolished by the usurpers, and the monuments defaced and taken away, and the stones laid down in great heaps upon the graves. So that the inhabitants who ought to be buried there cannot be interred in their ancestral vaults and graves without great charge and trouble. By such desolation the town was made ready for newer English to inhabit.

On 22d July, 1656, the commissioners for Ireland moved his highness, the lord-protector, and council of state, that some considerable merchants of London might be urged to occupy it, to revive its trade and repair the town, which was falling into ruin, being almost depopulated, and the houses falling down for want of inhabitants. But the city of London had known enough of Ireland. Star-chambered in 1637 for their neglect at Derry, and "censured in" £70,000, and their charter suspended, and their whole plantation effaced by the Irish war in 1641, they would venture no more. The lord-protector and council therefore turned to two less experienced cities.

There was a large debt of £10,000 due to Liverpool for their loss and suffering for the good cause. The eminent deservings and losses of the city of Gloucester also had induced the parliament to order them £10,000, to be satisfied in forfeited lands in Ireland. The commissioners for Ireland now offered forfeited houses in Galway, rated at ten years' purchase, to the inhabitants of Liverpool and Gloucester, to satisfy their respective debts, and they were both to arrange about the planting of it with English Protestants. To induce them to accept the proposal, the commissioners enlarged upon the advantages of Galway. It lay open for trade with Spain, the Straits, the West Indies, and other places; no town or port in the three nations, London excepted, was more considerable. It had many noble uniform buildings of marble, though many of the houses had become ruinous by reason of the war, and the waste done by the impoverished English dwelling there. No Irish were permitted to live in the city, nor within three miles of it. If it were only properly inhabited by English, it might have a more hopeful gain by trade than when it was in the hands of the Irish that lived there. There was never a better opportunity of undertaking a plantation and settling manufactures there than the present, and they suggested that it might become another Derry.

The bait took. On 17th February, 1657-58, the houses in Flood Street, Key Street, Middle Street, Little Gate Street, south side of High Street, and other parts adjoining, valued to £1518, 8s. 9d. by the year, were set out to the well-affected inhabitants of Gloucester. Others of like value were set out to those of Liverpool. But no new Gloucester or Liverpool arose at Galway. Nor did her ancient crowds of shipping return to her bay.

For it is a comparatively easy thing to unsettle a nation or ruin a town, but not so easy to resettle the one, or to restore the other to prosperity, when ruined; and Galway, once frequented by ships with cargoes of French and Spanish wines, to supply the wassailings of the O'Neils and O'Donels, the O'Garas and the O'Kanes, her marble palaces handed over to strangers, and her gallant sons and dark-eyed daughters banished, remains for 200 years a ruin; her splendid port empty, while her "hungry air" in 1862 becomes the mock of the official stranger.

HON. MRS. CAROLINE NORTON.

Born 1807 — Died 1877.

[It is true of literary characters as, perhaps, of countries, that those have been happiest who have had no history—whose lives may be summed up by giving the date of their birth, their marriage, and their death, and whose fortunes are only concerned with the publication of their works and their reception by the public. The biographer of the Hon. Mrs. Norton must tell an interesting and checkered but sad story. She was the grand-daughter of Richard Brinsley Sheridan, and the daughter of his son Thomas. She inherited that wit which is proverbially regarded as the heritage of the whole Sheridan family. She was born in 1807, and while still in her girlhood she had begun to wield her pen and pencil. We are almost afraid to mention the age at which she is said to have produced—in conjunction with her sister, Lady Dufferin—the *Dandies' Rout*, with illustrations from her own designs; but it is certain she had published by 1829 the *Sorrows of Rosalie*—that is to say at a time when she was but twenty-two years of age. Before she had passed from the years of tutelage she had entered into an engagement rather more serious, and destined to influence her much more calamitously than the writing of premature poems.

The Hon. George Chapple Norton, a brother of Lord Grantley, became a suitor for her hand; and—probably with the readiness of girls who neither know their own character nor that of others—she consented to be betrothed, and in 1829 was married. It did not take long to convince her that the choice she had made was a most unhappy one. Her husband is described as indolent and conceited, devoid of talent, and devoted to pleasure, and sometimes so brutal as to resort to physical violence. Being a younger son he was almost wholly without means, and in order to gratify his extravagant tastes, he called in the aid of his wife in every case. She was compelled to toil night and day at literary work, so that in one year she claimed to have bestowed on her husband no less a sum than £1400. Next Mr. Norton demanded that his wife should exercise her influence with Lord Melbourne, then a minister, to procure him a situation under the crown. On Lord Melbourne Mrs. Norton had several claims. She could point to the fact that her grandfather had been one of the pillars of the Whigs, and by them been allowed to die in poverty and misery; and she might add that her father had been a contemporary and a friend of the minister himself. It was unfortunate for both Lord Melbourne and Mrs. Norton that they should have ever come together. The circumstances of both were alike in many respects. Of an affectionate and ardent nature, they, one and the other, found themselves deprived of home sympathies. Lady Caroline Lamb, the wife of Mr. Lamb, as Lord Melbourne was once called, is known to have been one of the most afflicting wives that ever destroyed domestic happiness. Capricious, uncertain-tempered, and partially insane, she persecuted her husband and all her acquaintances by the wildest freaks—the best known of these being her ostentatiously expressed, and as ostentatiously rejected, love for Lord Byron. Mrs. Norton and Lord Melbourne had also the similar gifts of high conversational powers, amiability of manner, geniality of temper, and the other qualities which constitute social talent. Mrs. Norton, it should be added, was, like her two sisters, very beautiful.

Mr. Norton took advantage of the admiration and respect which the minister manifested towards his wife, and obtained a situation as police-magistrate in London. He is said to have greatly neglected his duties, to have quarrelled with his colleagues, and to have indulged in undignified correspondence with the newspapers; and the result was that his official superior was obliged to express dissatisfaction with his conduct. He was, besides, exasperated against Lord Melbourne by his refusal to lend him money. He took his revenge by bringing an action for divorce against the minister and Mrs. Norton, laying the damages at £10,000; but the jury found the charge so entirely unsupported that they gave a verdict for the defendants without leaving the box. This led to the final separation of Mrs. Norton and her husband; but the public was reminded occasionally of the unhappy relations between the two by some disagreeable law case, in which the wife found herself compelled to engage in defence of her rights, and by occasional references from her pen to her hapless lot.

During the greater part of her life Mrs. Norton was one of the idols and the chief ornaments of society; for her vivacious intellect, fine powers of repartee, and distinguished and varied talents made her everywhere a welcome guest. Towards the end of her days, however, she lived in retirement, and for a short space before her death she was confined to her room. Her career had a somewhat romantic close. Her first husband's death left her a widow in 1869. Eight years afterwards she was again married, her husband being Sir W. Stirling-Maxwell, between whom and her there had existed a friendship of many years. The marriage was purely platonic. Mrs. Norton was married in her own drawing-room in the spring of 1877, and in the June following she was dead. It was a singular coincidence that her sister, the Countess of Gifford, as has been said in her memoir, should have been married for the second time under somewhat similar circumstances. Lady Dufferin married Lord Gifford when he was on his death-bed; Mrs. Norton was united to Sir W. Stirling-Maxwell when she had almost entered into the valley of the shadow of death.

The list of Mrs. Norton's works is a long one. The *Sorrows of Rosalie*, which we have already mentioned, was praised enthusiastically by Christopher North in the *Noctes Ambrosianæ*, and found an eulogist also in James Hogg; and Miss E. Owens Blackburne has declared in her *Illustrious Irishwomen*, that Mrs. Norton never produced, "even in more matured literary career," "anything fuller of the blended fire and pathos with which all her poetry is characterized, than this her first important poem." The *Undying One* followed in 1830. This is a version of the legend of the Wandering Jew, and was received with somewhat contradictory critical judgment. The *London Monthly Review* was cuttingly severe; while the *New Monthly Magazine* declared that if one or two poems of equal grace and originality were produced, the public would be roused from the apathy into which it had fallen into with regard to poetry. Her next work dealt with a blot on English society,—the condition of the persons employed in factories—the women and children especially. Her feelings found expression in a poem, "A Voice from the Factories," published in 1836; and in 1841 her letters in the *Times* on the same subject were issued in a collected form.

The *Dream*, published in 1840, is one of the most ambitious and finest of Mrs. Norton's poems. It describes a dialogue between a mother and daughter. The daughter dreams, and when awaked, tells her dream. She "depicts the bliss of a first love and an early union, which is followed by the mother's admonitory comment, imparting the many accidents to which wedded happiness is liable, and exhorting to moderation of hope, and preparation for severer duties." In dealing with such a theme, Mrs. Norton, of course, had to allude to several of the circumstances of her own troubled life; and the consequence is that the poem is remarkable for many passages of splendid passion. *The Child of the Islands* describes with much vehement eloquence the condition of the poor in England. "The Child of the Islands" is the Prince of Wales, who was then in infancy. The poem is remarkable for a realism in the pictures of our social ills which was then uncommon in our literature. Among her other poems we may mention *The Lady of La Garaye*, which is considered the most polished and classic of all Mrs. Norton's longer poems. Among her fugitive pieces we may also mention the well-known "The Arab's Farewell to his Horse," "We have been Friends together," "The Blind Man to his Bride," and "The Child of the Earth." Mrs. Norton also produced three novels—*Stuart of Dunleath*, *Lost and Saved*, and *Old Sir Douglas*, in most of which the wrongs of women in circumstances similar to her own form a chief theme. On the same subject she also issued pamphlets on several occasions. She is the authoress besides of the *Martyr*, a tragedy, and of several tales and sketches, and she edited a lively book on society in Sierra Leone. Her prose is inferior to her poetry; and we limit our extracts accordingly to quotations from her poetic works.]

THE GIPSY GIRL IN PRISON.[1]

Wild Nomades of our civilized calm land!
Whose Eastern origin is still betrayed

---

[1] From "Summer," in *The Child of the Islands.*

By the swart beauty of the slender hand,—
Eyes flashing forth from overarching shade,—
And supple limbs for active movement made;
How oft, beguiled by you, the maiden looks,
For love her fancy ne'er before portrayed,
And, slighting village swains and shepherd-crooks,
Dreams of proud youths, dark spells, and wondrous magic books!

Lo! in the confines of a dungeon cell,
(Sore weary of its silence and its gloom!)
One of this race: who yet deserveth well
The close imprisonment which is her doom:
Lawless she was, ere infancy's first bloom
Left the round outline of her sunny cheek;
Vagrant and prowling Thief;—no chance, no room
To bring that wild heart to obedience meek;
Therefore th' avenging law its punishment must wreak.

She lies, crouched up upon her pallet bed,
Her slight limbs starting in unquiet sleep;
And oft she turns her feverish, restless head,
Moans, frets, and murmurs, or begins to weep:
Anon, a calmer hour of slumber deep
Sinks on her lids, some happier thought hath come;
Some jubilee unknown she thinks to keep,
With liberated steps, that wander home
Once more with gipsy tribes a gipsy life to roam.

But no, her pale lips quiver as they moan:
What whisper they? A name, and nothing more;
But with such passionate tenderness of tone,
As shows how much those lips that name adore,
She dreams of one who shall her loss deplore
With the unbridled anguish of despair!
Whose forest-wanderings by her side are o'er,
But to whose heart one braid of her black hair
Were worth the world's best throne, and all its treasures rare.

The shadow of his eyes is on her soul—
His passionate eyes, that held her in such love!
Which love she answered, scorning all control
Of reasoning thoughts, which tranquil bosoms move,
No lengthened courtship it was his to prove,
(Gleaning capricious smiles by fits and starts)
Nor feared her simple faith lest he should rove:
Rapid and subtle as the flame that darts
To meet its fellow flame, shot passion through their hearts.

And though no holy priest that union blessed,
By gipsy laws and customs made his bride;
The love her looks avowed, in words confessed,
She shared his tent, she wandered by his side,

His glance her morning-star, his will her guide.
Animal beauty and intelligence
 Were her sole gifts—his heart they satisfied,—
Himself could claim no higher, better sense,
So loved her with a love, wild, passionate, intense!

And oft, where flowers lay spangled round about,
 And to the dying twilight incense shed,
They sat to watch heaven's glittering stars come
 out,
 Her cheek down-leaning on his cherished
 head—
That head upon her heart's soft pillow laid
In fulness of content; and such deep spell
Of loving silence, that the word first said
With startling sweetness on their senses fell,
Like silver coins dropped down a many-fathomed
 well.

Look! her brows darken with a sudden frown—
 She dreams of Rescue by his angry aid—
She dreams he strikes the Law's vile minions
 down,
And bears her swiftly to the wild-wood shade!
There, where their bower of bliss at first was
 made,
Safe in his sheltering arms once more she sleeps:
 Ah happy dream! She wakes; amazed, afraid,
Like a young panther from her couch she leaps,
Gazes bewildered round, then madly shrieks and
 weeps!

For, far above her head, the prison-bars
 Mock her with narrow sections of that sky
She knew so wide, and blue, and full of stars,
 When gazing upward through the branches
 high
 Of the free forest! Is she then to die?
Where is he—where—the strong-armed and the
 brave,
Who in that vision answered her wild cry?
Where is he—where—the lover who could save
And snatch her from her fate—an ignominious
 grave?

Oh, pity her, all sinful though she be,
 While thus the transient dreams of freedom
 rise,
Contrasted with her waking destiny!
 Scorn is for devils; soft compassion lies
In angel hearts, and beams from angel eyes.
Pity her! Never more, with wild embrace,
 Those flexile arms shall clasp him ere she dies;
Never the fierce sad beauty of her face
Be lit with gentler hope, or love's triumphant grace!

Lonely she perishes; like some wild bird
 That strains its wing against opposing wires;
Her heart's tumultuous panting may be heard,
 While to the thought of rescue she aspires;
Then, of its own deep strength it faints and
 tires:

The frenzy of her mood begins to cease;
 Her varying pulse with fluttering stroke ex-
 pires,
And the sick weariness that is not peace
Creeps slowly through her blood, and promises
 release.

Alas, dark shadows, press not on her so!
 Stand off, and let her hear the linnet sing!
Crumble, ye walls, that sunshine may come
 through
 Each crevice of your ruins! Rise, clear spring.
Bubbling from hidden fountain-depths, and
 bring
Water, the death-thirst of her pain to slake!
 Come from the forest, breeze with wandering
 wing!
There dwelt a heart would perish for her sake—
Oh, save her! No! Death stands prepared his prey
 to take.

But, because youth and health are very strong,
 And all her veins were full of freshest life,
The deadly struggle must continue long
 Ere the freed heart lie still, that was so rife
With passion's mad excess. The jailer's wife
Bends, with revolted pity on her brow,
 To watch the working of that fearful strife,
Till the last quivering spark is out. And now
All's dark, all's cold, all's lost, that loved and
 mourned below.

THE CHILD OF EARTH.

Fainter her slow step falls from day to day,
 Death's hand is heavy on her darkening brow;
Yet doth she fondly cling to earth and say:
 "I am content to die, but oh! not now!
Not while the blossoms of the joyous spring
 Make the warm air such luxury to breathe;
Not while the birds such lays of gladness sing;
 Not while bright flowers around my footsteps
 wreathe.
Spare me, great God, lift up my drooping brow!
I am content to die—but, oh! not now!"

The spring hath ripened into summer time,
 The season's viewless boundary is past;
The glorious sun hath reached his burning prime—
 Oh! must this glimpse of beauty be the last!
"Let me not perish while o'er land and lea,
 With silent steps the lord of light moves on;
Nor while the murmur of the mountain bee
 Greets my dull ear with music in its tone!
Pale sickness dims my eye, and clouds my brow;
I am content to die—but, oh! not now!"

Summer is gone, and autumn's soberer hues
 Tint the ripe fruits, and gild the waving corn;

The huntsman swift the flying game pursues,
  Shouts the halloo, and winds his eager horn.
"Spare me awhile to wander forth and gaze
  On the broad meadows and the quiet stream,
To watch in silence while the evening rays
  Slant through the fading trees with ruddy gleam!
Cooler the breezes play around my brow;
I am content to die—but, oh! not now!"

The bleak wind whistles, snow showers, far and near,
  Drift without echo to the whitening ground;
Autumn hath passed away, and cold and drear
  Winter stalks on, with frozen mantle bound.
Yet still that prayer ascends:—"Oh! laughingly
  My little brothers round the warm hearth crowd,
Our home-fire blazes broad, and bright, and high,
  And the roof rings with voices glad and loud;
Spare me awhile, lift up my drooping brow!
I am content to die—but, oh! not now!"

The spring is come again—the joyful spring!
  Again the banks with clustering flowers are
    spread;
The wild bird dips upon its wanton wing—
  The child of earth is numbered with the dead!
"Thee never more the sunshine shall awake,
  Beaming all readily through the lattice-pane;
The steps of friends thy slumbers may not break,
  Nor fond familiar voice arouse again!
Death's silent shadow veils thy darkened brow;
Why didst thou linger?—thou art happier now!"

THE BLIND MAN TO HIS BRIDE.

When first, beloved, in vanished hours
  The blind man sought thy hand to gain,
They said thy cheek was bright as flowers
  New freshened by the summer's rain.
The beauty which made them rejoice
  My darkened eyes might never see;
But well I knew thy gentle voice,
  And that was all in all to me.

At length, as years rolled swiftly on,
  They talked to me of time's decay,
Of roses from thy soft cheek gone,
  Of ebon tresses turned to grey.
I heard them, but I heeded not;
  The withering change I could not see;
Thy voice still cheered my darkened lot,
  And that was all in all to me.

And still, beloved, till life grows cold,
  We'll wander 'neath the genial sky,
And only know that we are old
  By counting happy hours gone by;

Thy cheek may lose its blushing hue,
  Thy brow less beautiful may be,
But oh, the voice which first I knew,
  Still keeps the same sweet tone to me.

THE ARAB'S FAREWELL TO HIS STEED.

My beautiful, my beautiful! that standest meekly
  by,
With thy proudly-arched and glossy neck, and dark
  and fiery eye!
Fret not to roam the desert now with all thy wingèd
  speed;
I may not mount on thee again!—thou'rt sold, my
  Arab steed!

Fret not with that impatient hoof—snuff not the
  breezy wind;
The farther that thou fliest now, so far am I behind;
The stranger hath thy bridle-rein, thy master hath
  his gold;—
Fleet-limbed and beautiful, farewell!—thou'rt
  sold, my steed, thou'rt sold!

Farewell!—Those free untired limbs full many a
  mile must roam,
To reach the chill and wintry clime that clouds the
  stranger's home;
Some other hand, less kind, must now thy corn
  and bed prepare;
That silky mane I braided once, must be another's
  care.

The morning sun shall dawn again—but never
  more with thee
Shall I gallop o'er the desert paths where we were
  wont to be—
Evening shall darken on the earth; and, o'er the
  sandy plain,
Some other steed, with slower pace, shall bear me
  home again.

Only in sleep shall I behold that dark eye glancing
  bright—
Only in sleep shall hear again that step so firm
  and light;
And when I raise my dreaming arms to check or
  cheer thy speed,
Then must I startling wake, to feel thou'rt sold!
  my Arab steed.

Ah! rudely then, unseen by me, some cruel hand
  may chide,
Till foam-wreaths lie, like crested waves, along
  thy panting side,
And the rich blood that's in thee swells, in thy
  indignant pain,
Till careless eyes that on thee gaze may count each
  starting vein!

Will they ill use thee?—if I thought—but no,—
it cannot be;
Thou art so swift, yet easy curbed, so gentle, yet
so free;—
And yet if haply when thou'rt gone, this lonely
heart should yearn,
Can the hand that casts thee from it now, command thee to return?

"Return!"—alas! my Arab steed! what will thy
master do,
When thou, that wast his all of joy, hast vanished
from his view?
When the dim distance greets mine eyes, and
through the gathering tears
Thy bright form for a moment, like the false
mirage, appears?

Slow and unmounted will I roam, with wearied
foot, alone,
Where, with fleet step, and joyous bound, thou oft
hast borne me on;

And sitting down by the green well, I'll pause,
and sadly think,—
"'Twas here he bowed his glossy neck when last
I saw him drink."

When last I saw thee drink!—Away! the fevered
dream is o'er!
I could not live a day, and know that we should
meet no more;
They tempted me, my beautiful! for hunger's
power is strong—
They tempted me, my beautiful! but I have loved
too long.

Who said that I had given thee up? Who said
that thou wert sold?
'Tis false! 'tis false! my Arab steed! I fling them
back their gold!
Thus—thus, I leap upon thy back, and scour the
distant plains!
Away! who overtakes us now shall claim thee for
his pains.

JOHN EDWARD WALSH.

BORN 1816 — DIED 1869.

[Mr. Walsh was well known as a keen but moderate politician, a sound lawyer, and a profound judge; but it will be new to most people that he was in early life an ardent *littérateur*.

John Edward Walsh was the son of the Rev. Dr. Walsh, vicar of Finglass, and was born in the parish of his father on November 12, 1816. He had a distinguished career in college, and was one of the most prominent members of the College Historical Society. He was called to the bar in 1839. For some years, however, he had scarcely any practice, and thus was afforded leisure for literary exertion. He produced a work on the duties of justices of the peace, which became a text-book. In the *Dublin University Magazine* he found a medium for articles on subjects of more general interest; and his sketches of Irish life in the olden time are among the most interesting articles in the earlier years of the periodical. Those essays were collected, and published in 1847 under the title *Ireland Sixty Years Ago*. The work is very entertaining, and gives an excellent idea of the strange manners and customs of our countrymen about the time when Castlereagh was passing the Union, and Sir Jonah Barrington was collecting the materials for his memoirs. It has passed through several editions, and its title, owing to the lapse of time, has had to undergo an alteration. It is now known as *Ireland Ninety Years Ago*.

As the years went on business began to come in on Mr. Walsh, and in the end he was one of the most largely employed counsel at the equity bar. Legal occupation excluded literary activity; and from this time forward his career belongs no longer to the literary chronicler. Suffice it to say, that in 1857 he became a queen's counsel; in 1866, attorney-general; and towards the close of the same year was raised to the bench as Master of the Rolls. In his new position he acquired the reputation of being an excellent judge; and, still in the prime of life, he had the right to look forward to many years' enjoyment of his dignified position. But while returning from a continental tour he was suddenly taken ill in Paris, and after a few days' suffering passed away on Oct. 17, 1869, in his fifty-second year. This sudden termination to the promising career of a man so universally respected and so deeply liked caused regret among all classes. For some time before his death he had been contemplating a biography of Lord-chancellor Clare; but he had not got beyond the collection of the materials.]

A TRAGIC CASE OF ABDUCTION.

(FROM "IRELAND NINETY YEARS AGO."[1])

Abduction, or forcibly carrying off heiresses, was another of those crying evils which formerly afflicted Ireland; but it was an outrage so agreeable to the spirit of the times, and so congenial to the ardent and romantic character of the natives, that it was considered an achievement creditable to the man, and a matter of boast and exultation to the woman. From the time that the King of Leinster abducted the frail Dervogle, and royalty set an example of carrying off ladies, it was a constant practice. When once it went abroad that a woman in any station in life had money, she became the immediate object of some enterprising fellow, who readily collected about him adherents to assist in his attempt. No gentleman or farmer felt himself safe who had a daughter entitled to a fortune; she was sure to be carried off with or without her consent, and he lived in a constant state of alarm till she was happily disposed of in marriage. It was generally the wildest, most "devil-may-care" fellow who undertook the enterprise, and unfortunately such a character was found to have most attractions in the eyes of a young and romantic girl.

On the Derry side of the Foyle, and about two miles from the city, is Prehen, the seat of the Knoxes. It is highly wooded, and covers a considerable tract, descending to the river, and overhanging the broad expanse of water in this place with its dark shade. The circumstance which marked its ancient owners with affliction is of such a character as to correspond with the gloom that pervades its aspect; and no traveller passes it without many reflections on the sad event which happened there.

John M'Naghtan was a native of Derry. His father was an opulent merchant, and gave his son all the advantages of a most liberal education. He graduated in Trinity College, Dublin; but having inherited from his uncle a large estate, which precluded the necessity of engaging in any profession, he commenced a career of dissipation, then too common in Ireland. He married early, but his extravagance soon involved him in such distress that he was arrested by the sheriff in his own parlour for a considerable debt, in the presence of his pregnant wife. The shock was fatal. She was seized with premature labour, and both wife and child perished. Being a man of address and ability, he was appointed to a lucrative situation in the revenue by the then Irish government, and in the course of his duty contracted an intimacy with the family of Mr. Knox, of Prehen, whose daughter, a lovely and amiable girl, was entitled to a large fortune, independent of her father. To her M'Naghtan paid assiduous court, and as she was too young at the time to marry, he obtained a promise from her to become his bride in two years. When the circumstance was made known to her father, he interdicted it in the most decided manner, and forbade M'Naghtan's visits to his house. This was represented as so injurious to M'Naghtan's character, that the good-natured old man was persuaded again to permit his intimacy with his family, under the express stipulation that he should think no more of his daughter. One day the lovers found themselves alone, with no companion but a little boy, when M'Naghtan took from his pocket a prayer-book, and read himself the marriage ceremony, prevailing on Miss Knox to answer the responses, which she did, adding to each, "provided my father consent." Of this ceremony M'Naghtan immediately availed himself; and, when he next met her at the house of a mutual friend, openly claimed her as his wife. Again he was forbidden the house by the indignant father. He then published an advertisement in all the newspapers, declaring the young lady was married to him. By a process, however, in the spiritual court, the pretended marriage was entirely set aside.

In the course of these proceedings M'Naghtan wrote a threatening letter to one of the judges of the court of delegates, and, it was said, lay in wait to have him murdered when he came on circuit, but fortunately missed him in consequence of the judges taking a different road. The result was, that M'Naghtan was obliged to fly to England. But here his whole mind was bent on obtaining possession of his wife; so at all hazards he returned, and lay concealed in the woods of Prehen. Warning of this circumstance had been communicated to her father, but he seemed to despise it. There was, however, a blacksmith, whose wife had nursed Miss Knox, and he, with the known attachment of such a connection in Ireland, always followed his foster-daughter, as her protector, whenever she ventured abroad.

To detach his daughter from this unfor-

---

[1] By permission of Messrs. M. H. Gill & Son, Dublin.

tunate connection, Mr. Knox resolved to leave the country, and introduce her to the society of the metropolis; and in the beginning of November, 1761, prepared to set out for Dublin. M'Naghtan and a party of his friends having intimation of his intention, repaired to a cabin a little distance from the road, with a sack full of fire-arms. From hence one of the party was despatched to the house of an old woman who lived by the way-side, under the pretence of buying some yarn, to wait for the coming up of Mr. Knox's carriage. When it did arrive, the woman pointed it out, named the travellers it contained, and described the position in which they sat. They were Mr. Knox, his wife, his daughter, and a maid-servant. It was attended by but one servant, and the smith before mentioned. The scout immediately ran before, and communicated to M'Naghtan the information he received. The carriage was instantly surrounded by him and three other men. M'Naghtan and one of his accomplices fired at the smith, whom they did not kill, but totally disabled. The blinds were now close drawn, that the persons inside might not be recognized. M'Naghtan rode up to it, and either by accident or design discharged a heavily-loaded blunderbuss into it at random. A shriek was heard inside. The blind was let down, and Mr. Knox discharged his pistol at the assassin. At the same moment another was fired from behind a stack of turf, by the servant who had concealed himself there. Both the shots took effect in the body of M'Naghtan. He was, however, held on his horse by his associates, who rode off with him. The carriage was then examined. Miss Knox was found dead, weltering in her blood. On the first alarm she had thrown her arms about her father's neck to protect him, and so received the contents of the murderer's fire-arms. Five balls of the blunderbuss had entered her body, leaving the other three persons in the carriage with her unhurt and untouched by this random shot.

The country was soon alarmed, and a reward of five hundred pounds offered for the apprehension of the murderers. A company of light horse scoured the district, and amongst other places were led to search the house of a farmer named Wenslow. The family denied all knowledge of M'Naghtan, and the party were leaving the house when the corporal said to one of his companions, in the hearing of a countryman who was digging potatoes, that the discoverer would be entitled to a reward of three hundred pounds. The countryman immediately pointed to a hay-loft, and the corporal running up a ladder, burst open the door, and discovered M'Naghtan lying in the hay. Notwithstanding his miserably wounded state, he made a desperate resistance, but was ultimately taken and lodged in Lifford gaol. Some of his accomplices were arrested soon after. They were tried before a special commission at Lifford, and one of them received as king's evidence. M'Naghtan was brought into court wrapped in a blanket, and laid on a table in the dock, not being able to support himself in any other position. Notwithstanding acute pain and exceeding debility, he defended himself with astonishing energy and acuteness. A singular trait of Irish feeling occurred in the course of the trial. One of his followers implicated in the outrage, named Dunlap, was a faithful and attached fellow, and his master evinced more anxiety to save his life than his own. As a means of doing so, he disclaimed all knowledge of his person: "Oh, master dear," said the poor fellow in the dock, "is this the way you are going to disown me after all?"

On the day of execution M'Naghtan was so weak as to be supported in the arms of attendants. He evinced the last testimony of his regard to the unfortunate young lady he had murdered, of whom he was passionately fond, and whom he mourned as his wife. The cap which covered his face was bound with black, his jacket was trimmed with black, having jet buttons, and he wore large black buckles in his shoes. When lifted up the ladder, he exerted all his remaining strength to throw himself off, and with such force that the rope broke, and he fell gasping to the ground. As he was a man of daring enterprise and profuse bounty, he was highly popular, and the crowd made a lane for him to escape, and attempted to assist him. He fiercely declined their aid, declaring, in a manner characteristic of the impetuous pride of his nature, that "he would not live to be pointed at as the half-hanged man." He called to his follower, Dunlap, for the rope which was round his neck, the knot of which was slipped and placed round his own. Again he was assisted up the ladder, and collecting all his energies, he flung himself off, and died without a struggle. His unfortunate but faithful follower stood by wringing his hands as he witnessed the sufferings of his dear master, and earnestly desired that his own execution might be hastened, that he might soon follow him and die by the same rope.

This murder and execution took place on the road between Strabane and Derry; and as the memory of them still lives among the peasantry, the spot is pointed out to passengers, and recalls traits of what Ireland was about one hundred years ago, even in the most civilized county. Abduction was then a common mode of courtship in the north as well as in the south, and a man was deemed a man of spirit if he so effected his marriage. Any fatal accident resulting to resisting friends was considered a venial offence, and the natural effect of their unreasonable obstinacy.

The circumstances and character of the parties in this affair rendered it one of the deepest interest. The young lady was but fifteen, gentle, accomplished, and beautiful, greatly attached to the unhappy man, devotedly fond of her father, and, with the strongest sense of rectitude and propriety, entangled in an unfortunate engagement from simplicity and inexperience. The gentleman was thirty-eight, a man of the most engaging person, and a model of manly beauty. His manners were soft, gentle, and insinuating, and his disposition naturally generous and humane; but when roused by strong excitement, his passions were most fierce and uncontrollable. His efforts on his trial were not to preserve his life, which became a burden to him after the loss of her he loved, but to save from a like fate a faithful follower, and to exculpate his own memory from a charge of intended cruelty and deliberate murder.

MRS. S. C. HALL.

[Anna Maria Fielding was born in Dublin not long after the century had commenced. While still an infant she was taken to Bannow, in county Wexford, where her maternal grandfather and grandmother lived. Her family on the mother's side was of illustrious Huguenot descent, tracing back its lineage partly to French and partly to Swiss sources. In her early home at Bannow the future authoress drank in the vivid impressions of Irish scenery and life, which she was destined to so finely reproduce afterwards. She lived, as she herself tells us, in a locality rich in the picturesque, and amid a people whose strong individuality offered abundant materials for the student of character. The young Irish girl was not, however, given any lengthened opportunity of studying her country and countrymen; for she was but fifteen when she left Ireland and settled in London. In September, 1824, she was married to Mr. Samuel Carter Hall. To this event we probably owe her accession to the ranks of *littérateurs;* and she herself gained through it the blessing of a devoted companion, alike in tastes, in sympathies, and in aims.

Mr. Hall, during the early years of his married life, was engaged in the production of an illustrated "annual" called the *Amulet;* and here Mrs. Hall's first sketches appeared. Those sketches a publisher — much to the astonishment of the young writer, who was modestly unconscious of her own power — offered to produce in a collected form; and thus in 1829 appeared Mrs. Hall's first work, *Sketches of Irish Character.* The volume met with immediate and deserved success; for the stories were distinguished by fidelity to life, pathos without exaggeration, bright but never ill-natured humour, and absolute freedom from political or religious bigotry. Mrs. Hall's next work was one intended for the young — *The Chronicles of a Schoolroom* — a volume in which, while things are treated with the necessary simplicity, there is a complete absence of the goody-goody tone and wishy-washy sentiment of so many books with a like purpose. *The Buccaneer,* published in 1829, was Mrs. Hall's first attempt at a regular novel. The scene is laid in England, and the time chosen is the protectorate of Oliver Cromwell. *The Outlaw,* which followed in 1832, also belonged to the department of the historical novel; the Revolution of 1688 being the period described, and James II. the chief character. Though many of the scenes described in those stories bear a strong impress of truth and give a good idea of the times, the passages which will be read with most pleasure are those descriptive of domestic life.

Mrs. Hall was probably more at home in a work which appeared in the interval between the two historical novels. *Tales of Woman's Trials* is a delightful volume, full of touching stories, told with delicacy, poetic feeling, and truth. Two of the tales are especially beauti-

Mrs S. C. HALL.
FROM A PHOTOGRAPH BY FRANKLAND

ful—"Marian Raymond," and "The Trials of Lady Montague." In both the moral is the sad one that loving and noble natures are powerless to check the follies or elevate the characters of worthless and weak beings to whom their fate has strongly attached them. In the first a proud, beautiful, high-minded woman finds that the lover of whom she had dreamed as perfection, and to whom she was united after years of separation and the death of a first and worthless husband, has been transformed by a soldier's life and bad surroundings to a dissipated, sensual, unprincipled fellow; and the end of her girlish dreams of perfect happiness is early death from a broken heart. In the second story the loving sufferer is a mother; and the worthless persecutor a son, who ends a life of follies and vices in a street row. *Uncle Horace* came next, and then followed, perhaps, Mrs. Hall's most powerful work. This was *Lights and Shadows of Irish Life* (published in 1838). The tales here told are—as the title implies—descriptive of the brighter and the darker sides of Irish life—of the passionate affections of home, the gay hearts, and also the dark passions of Irish men and women. There is a story in the chapter headed "Ruins,"—it is the story we quote—of the desolation brought on an Irish home by the seduction of a peasant girl by the squire, which is very powerful, and cannot be read without keen excitement. The character of the seducer, too, is delineated with great skill, and is one of the best descriptions in Irish literature of the bad and good sides of the Irish squire. Foolish, improvident, and vicious, Terence O'Toole yet attracts by his kindliness of heart, his high spirit, his unbending pride; and the story of the heavy retribution he paid for the sin of his youth is deeply moving. The tale is also remarkable for giving a picture of the extraordinary relations which used to exist between the Irish tenant and landlord. Another story in this series was produced on the stage under the title of *The Groves of Blarney*, and proved highly successful. The *French Refugee*, a shorter piece, had been brought out in 1837, and was received with much favour.

Marian, or a Young Maid's Fortune, was published in 1840, and at once became popular. It has passed through several editions, and has been translated into German and Dutch. Meantime, the literary fortunes of Mr. Hall had been influencing strongly those of his wife. In 1830 he had succeeded the poet Campbell as the editor of the *New Monthly Magazine*; and in 1840 he entered upon a more serious undertaking—founding the *Art Union*, a title afterwards changed to the *Art Journal*. Of this periodical Mr. Hall has continued to be the chief spirit for now nearly forty years, and, in its pages, has done incalculable service to the cause of art in the United Kingdom. To her husband's journal Mrs. Hall contributed "Midsummer Eve," a fairy tale (republished in 1847), in which there is a skilful mingling of the picturesque legendary lore and the comicalities of real life in Ireland. In the same journal also appeared "Pilgrimages to English Shrines," a series of "pleasant illustrated sketches of the homes and haunts of genius and virtue in our own land." This work was published in its collected form in 1850. Mrs. Hall's pen had meantime been busy in other works. In 1840 appeared a new series of Irish portraits under the title *Tales of the Irish Peasantry*. In 1841-43 was produced from the combined pens of herself and her husband an interesting work, *Ireland: its Scenery, Character, &c*. In 1845 appeared a novel, *The White Boy*; in 1857, *A Woman's Story; Can Wrong be Right?* in 1862; *The Fight of Faith, a story of Ireland*, in 1868-9.

Long as is this list, it gives but a faint idea of the indefatigable industry of Mr. and Mrs. Hall. A writer has recently calculated that the two have had some share in the production of no less than 500 volumes! We have mentioned already several of their joint productions: to those we may add, *The Book of the Thames* and *The Book of South Wales*.

It is much to the credit of both Mr. and Mrs. Hall, that, notwithstanding their severe literary labours, they have found time to take an active part in the chief philanthropic movements of the time. Mrs. Hall was the originator of the fund in honour of Miss Florence Nightingale; it was in her drawing-room that the first subscription was commenced; and the result of the labours of herself and her husband was a fund amounting to £45,000. They have also assisted in founding the Hospital for Consumption, and other useful institutions. The cause of temperance has found most earnest and untiring advocates in Mr. and Mrs. Hall; and they have written many tales and sketches in which the evils of intemperance have been graphically portrayed. In 1874 came the fiftieth anniversary of the marriage of Mr. and Mrs. Hall; and the "golden wedding" was made the occasion of a remarkable testimony to the esteem in which they are held. Subscriptions amounting to £1500 were quickly raised, and presented to the veteran writers; as was also an album, containing five hundred letters from persons of all ranks and nations testifying to their worth. Mrs. Hall was in the receipt of £100 a year from the civil list, and the Queen expressed her esteem for our gifted countrywoman by presenting her with portraits of herself and the Prince Consort. One of the most recent acts of Mr. and Mrs. Hall was to help in celebrating the centenary of Moore, of whom they were in their early days intimate friends. They also paid further honour to his memory in erecting by subscription a window in Bromham Church, where he is buried. Mrs. Hall died Jan. 30, 1881.]

AN IRISH TRAGEDY.

(FROM "LIGHTS AND SHADOWS OF IRISH LIFE."[1])

[This is the story of an old man whom Mr. and Mrs. S. C. Hall during a tour found wandering about in Ireland.]

"The four winds of heaven have been blowing upon my head these sixty years," said an old beggar to me, "until they have hardly left a gray hair to cover it." Clooney Blaney passed his latter years in migrating from parish to parish, and from ruin to ruin; he was fond of the "ould places;" though, unlike the "Old Mortality" of the great master spirit of our age, he had no desire to restore inscriptions or preserve monuments, he took much pleasure in patching up holes in crumbling walls, and spent the long days of summer, bareheaded, as indeed he always was, within their precincts.

Of all the ruins in my neighbourhood he seemed most to delight in those of the seven castles of Clomines. Whether it was that they afforded him more extensive wandering room, being scattered some on the very brink of the Scar, some far in the green and beautiful meadow, I know not; but I have often seen Clooney's bald head peeping above the gigantic trees of ivy that waved their sombre shining leaves in the gay sun, and heard the clatter of his trowel in the gray twilight of evening, as he pattered with the mortar or wet clay to "steady," as he used to say, "the stones—poor things!" Clooney could not bear to see the stone of a ruin displaced.

"It was weary work for those who put them there, and why should their spirits be bothered by letting go to destruction what we'll never build the like of again?"

I met him, or rather saw him once, seated on the bridge of Tintern—not the Monmouthshire Tintern, but its Irish namesake.

"I'm lookin at that fine ould place with a glad heart, lady," said Clooney: "I've been outside every taste of that beautiful abbey this morning, and sorra as much as the paring of your nail out of place: all the stones firm, and the ould ancient mortar as firm as the stones; my eyes never ache looking at a fine even wall, and it's a good thing to see so holy a building so looked after; the pigs and the rooks are the worst enemies I have: the pigs do be always rooting at my walls, and the crows—ah! it's they're the bad stone-masons—it takes all the little thriffle I begs, and all the lime I gathers, to stop up the holes of them big black birds. It's a fine thing to keep a vow."

"Is it true, as I have heard, that you have taken an obligation on yourself never to wear a hat, and to wander over Ireland until your death, repairing the ruins of your country?"

"It is, ma'am," replied Clooney, "every word of it true: but if you plaze I'd rather not tell it to you here, for the people do be passing: so we'll go across the bohreen and into the meadow by the strame, and there, if you wish, I'll tell you every word of my history: not that there's much in the differ between it and any Irish history going, they're too much alike, that's the worst of them."

I followed Clooney, and as the old man trudged on before, I could not avoid registering in my memory the picture he presented; the few hairs which, according to his own observation, "the winds had left to cover his bare head," when unmoved by the air, fell over his shoulders in two or three long thin tresses, now floating around him like a halo, and then twisting into elfin locks at either side of his bald crown: slung across his shoulder was his begging bag, patched with pieces of blue, red, or gray stuff; and his sturdy staff, from the top of which, suspended by a string, hung his trowel, was a genuine shillala, armed with a ferule, so that it might serve either for climbing or fighting: he was firm and erect in his carriage, and as he wended his way, first removing a car which was turned up upon its wheels to stop a gap, then striking his staff firmly into the ground, as if he delighted to see how deep it would go, as a specimen of the strength of his arm—it was impossible not to see in him the wreck of much bodily and mental power; and I called to mind sundry stories of

---

[1] By permission of the authoress.

poor Clooney which represented him at once eccentric and superior to his associates, if indeed the peasants, among whom he only passed occasionally, deserved to be so called.

The very air seemed weighed nearer to the earth by sadness. As I looked upon the sky its blue clear canopy grew gray and dim, and the stream murmured hoarsely amongst the sedges. Clooney was seated on a block of red granite, probably one that had not been needed for the completion of the bridge; he had unslung his wallet, and placed it by his side on the ground, his staff and trowel resting on it. I could hardly tell what made old "Gray Jacket," his sobriquet amongst the peasantry, so interesting to me at that moment: I suppose it was his being so admirably in keeping with the scene—the turrets of Tintern Abbey to the right just peering amid the trees; one arch of the old bridge we had stood upon seen above the swelling hill, and looking more calmly beautiful than ever it had looked before—at least to me—with its fringe of blossoming wall-flowers, and its patches of moss, green, gray, and brown, Nature's own cunning embroidery: then, from far away, the boom of the fearful ocean came upon the ear, and I saw over the cliffs which skirted its shores the wavering and shining wings of the snowy seagulls, as they hovered for a moment in mid air, and then disappeared into the bay. So still, so calmly still was the scene, that I felt startled when Clooney's voice exclaimed, "There's a soft seat for you, lady dear, upon the stump of that ould tree, and you have no occasion to fear toads or sarpints, or anything of that sort; I dare say you know why yourself;" and the old man smiled half in jest, half in earnest, at the allusion the Irish are so fond of making to the powers of Saint Patrick.

"Were you ever in Connamara, Dick Martin's kingdom, as I've heard it called lately, though that same gentleman's dead this good while?"

"Never."

"An more's the shame an' the pity," he replied, "for Connamara flogs the Lakes, and the Giant's Causeway, and the caves of Mitchelstown, for bare grandeur; it's a wonderful place entirely; so desolate, so lonely-looking, with nothing to disturb the clouds but an eagle flying through them; and the '*sough*' of the wind among the rocks is like the moaning of dead thousands: it's a wonderful distric' intirely—and forrinners, to look at it, would think there could be but small pleasure in living in such a place: but it's very quare to see how people take delight in what they're used to. To my thinking it used to be the joysomest place in the wide world. Well, lady, I was born and bred up just on the borders of Connamara, and had the run of the house of one Terence O'Toole."

"O'Toole of Mount Brandon!" I exclaimed.

"Mount Brandon was its English name, to be sure; but the gentleman was beyond your memory, died before your time."

"He did; but I have often heard of both his talents and eccentricities. So you were really brought up by Terence O'Toole—by a man whose ancestral property extended to thousands upon thousands of green and fertile acres, whose power was that of a despot over his tenantry, and who died——Do, Clooney, tell me how he died!"

"Avich! how fond people are to know how people die, and yet, to my thinking, people's deaths have a sort of relationship with their lives; your quiet careful men die in their beds, while others, great, good, and of high blood, maybe have no bed to die on. Well, lady, I have heard tell that Terence O'Toole was in his youth the handsomest man ever born in Ireland, and that's saying a bould word: he carried everything before him in college with his head, and everything out of it with his sword or pistol, for he had a dead thrust with the one, and a dead bullet with the other; he never put up with an affront, nor ever gave the wall to an inferior—or a superior; he was the devil for making love, which gave him some trouble in Ireland, but in far countries none at all, for there, I heard say, it's the ladies make love to the gentlemen: he was always the finest-bred man in the company, mighty civil and courteous, and Christian-like too, for whenever he shot a man in a *jewel*[1] he would always kneel down by the side of the corpse and ax its forgiveness, which the whole country considered very condescending in the same gentleman: he was also the finest dancer in France, and the best singer in Rome, when he was there—one who knew, said that a French queen, who was afterwards beheaded, was deeply in love with him. In the thick of his young days his father died, and left him a power of land and a power of debts, but he didn't think it behouldin' him to mind either the one or the other, though, like a thrue patriot, he gave up all foreign company-keeping, and resolved to spend his money like a prince in his own counthry. So fond was he

---

[1] Duel.

of Mount Brandon, that he wouldn't be in Parliament, and was quite satisfied with returning the members without thinking of being a member himself: he made it a boast too that not a member should ever spend a farthing in trating the men, only all at his expense. A six weeks' election was nothing in those times, open house for all comers and goers, whisky on draft for the poor, and claret on draft for the rich; nothing but feasting and fighting. Ah! Ireland will never see such times again!"

"I hope not!" I ejaculated, as the vision of duels and shillalas rose before me, "I hope not!" I think Clooney looked at me reproachfully; I am not quite certain, but I think he did.

"Those were his young days," he continued, "and I suppose he thought they could never have an end; and, to be sure, every one in the counthry thought it high time for him to marry, but he did not think so himself, for his eye was set on a farmer's daughter on the estate, a young and beautiful girl, who loved him as no one ever loved him before or since. She proved that—by bearing shame for his sake; and God knows, the memory of that poor girl's love is tould by the ould people of Connamara to this day, the same as they'd tell of a ghost, to warn their daughters from danger. Her father was a could, proud man, of an ancient family, and she was the only *dote*, and proud he was of the admiration bestowed upon her by high and low; though little he thought what was to follow: but when it was made plain to him, he said no hard word to her, but he took her hand, and walked her out of their house, and took the key out of the door, and nine straws out of the thatch, and he left her weeping in a neighbour's house, and went up to the Mount, which was *thronged* with company, and walked straight into the hall, where they were at their wine after dinner; and *the masther* never saw him till he stood at the foot of his table, white as a sheet, and his teeth chattering. And the ould man laid the key of the farm and the nine straws upon the table without a word; and, having done that, he knelt down upon his bended knees, and he riz his long lean arms above his white head, and he cursed Terence O'Toole, with a curse that came slow and heavy from his lips, and that no one in all that grand company had power to stop; and when he had finished cursing, he turned his back upon them all, and stalked right away without another word or a sign. It struck the masther, that if he acted so, he might ill use the poor girl, upon whom his heart had been set; and as soon as he could he got away to see after her. He heard that she had been taken suddenly in her trouble in the neigbour's house, and that now she had a babby on her bosom. Well, to be sure, he ordered everything for her like a lady, and went home, consoling himself for the sin, with thinking of all the good he would do for her, and for every one else; and how he would get her proud father over. But before the morning broke he was waked by the small cry of a babby under his window, and he called up the ould housekeeper, for his heart mistrusted, and she took it in; and there was a taste of a note from the grandfather pinned on its breast; and when he read the note (no one ever saw that scrap from that day to this) he flew to the cabin she'd been in, and there was the woe of the world; for the ould man had first stole away the babby, coaxed the stupid woman that had charge of it to let him have it to show its father; come back in no time, and, while the nurse slept, rolled his poor, feeble, helpless girl up in the blanket as she lay, and carried her, God knows where. Well, to be sure, O'Toole roused the counthry, and, for that the snow lay deep on the ground, they tracked the old man's steps to the border of a broad lake, and there, lady, the mark of the feet ended; but the ice of the water was broken, and destroyed at the edge, and under it——!"

"Good God!" I exclaimed, petrified with horror.

"Ay, sure enough, lady, the proud ould man had buried his own and his child's dishonour under that ice!" He paused, and then continued. "The gentleman took no pains to hide his sorrow; and the monument to *her* memory was put up of beautiful white marvel; and some talked of her end, *but more talked of O'Toole's generosity*."

The world, I thought to myself, was the same then as it is now.

"I have heard tell," recommenced Clooney, "that the masther was never to say like himself afther that day; he took on more than ever with the fighting and the drinking, and seemed for a time to love nothing but the hounds. But a talk of great trouble came over the place, and the great gentleman was afraid to go off his own land for fear of being took; and then came a dissolate of Parliament, and he was advised to go in, and so he did; and promised the gentleman he had got in before, a situation. Well, he went off in great grand style to Dublin, where the Parliament was then; and some English lady at the castle, with thousands, fell in love with him and married him, though he never held up his head like a man afther. She was a weakly, conceited little lady, and was never to say asy till she got him to London; and I've seen a deal in my life, but I never yet saw the Irish fortune, to say nothing of the remnants of one, that could stand London.

"The master, when he would come home, was not like himself, but chuff and rough; and the expenses at the Mount made less, and many retainers turned off, and ancient residenters cast away, and the family seldom in it, and the masther high and up like with the gentry. I remember once he went as foreman to the grand-jury with padlocks on his pockets, and when asked why, he made answer, he was afraid to go among such a pickpocketing set without them; and so they challenged him to fight, and it was a fine sight to see them all go out one afther the other, and he flinging away, winging one, laming another, and so on; but he behaved mighty like a gentleman all through, for he did not shoot one of them dead. Another election came on, and who should start against the masther, but the very gentleman that he had brought in so often—set up against him upon his own ground out of revenge for his forgetting the situation he promised—and such a contest!—the ouldest people in the counthry never remembered the like. The luck of the O'Tooles turned; he fought—was wounded—and lost the election. This was not long before the rebellion; and sure any one then would know that throubles were coming, both to the ould residenters and the country itself. 'Where's your mistress?' said the masther to the ould housekeeper, and she handing him a drink of whey out of a silver pint. 'My lady's in her own room, very bad with the narvous disorder,' replied the ould woman. 'And my sons, where are they?' 'Indeed, then, they are just amusing themselves with shooting each other for divarshun, now the bother of an election is over.' 'This is not wine-whey,' said the poor gentleman. 'My grief, no, sir; but it's good two milk,' she made answer. 'Sorra a drop of wine in the cellars; and the devil of a marchant has sent in an execution over eleven hundred for his bill, and no one here strong enough to keep it out; only I oughtn't to be telling you the throubles, my darlint masther, while the weakness is on you.' She might well think of the wakeness, and he almost fainting. 'Where's the boy?' said he again; and by 'the boy,' he meant me. 'He's below,' she said, 'afther hiding some of the plate under the turf-rick, for fear of them vagabonds seeing it.' 'Send him up,' says the master; and though I'd the run of the house all my life, it was the first time I was ever had up before him. He called me to his bedside, he put his hand upon my head, and looked for full five minutes in my face; he then sighed out from the deep of his heart, and turned upon the bed. 'May I go, your honour?' I said. 'Aye,' he made answer, 'do; why should you not go, poor boy? those I trusted in are all gone.' 'Maybe your honour would let me try to turn the luck, by staying,' I made answer. He held his hand over the side of the bed; I fell on my knees and kissed it; and I never left him from that day to the day of his death."

The old man, overcome by the full gush of remembrance, laid his head on his hands, and continued silent for some minutes.

"The young gentlemen (he had but the two) were fine, proud, wilful boys; that on the tip-top of an English education had been learnt what faults their father had done; and indeed they did pretty much the same themselves, only in a different way, siding with their mother against him: and she had none of the great love for her husband which makes people cling to the throuble sooner than lave the throubled. I'm not going to set up but what the masther was hard to bear with; he certainly was. Yet any way, she soon took herself and her children off to England, to her relations—poor wake lady! The best property that could be sould was sould; and at last, if it wasn't for the tenants who had been made over with the land to the new proprietors, the house of Mount Brandon would have been badly kept; but they were ever and always sending a pig, or a fat sheep, or something on the sly, to the housekeeper, who knew they war for the masther's use, and he none the wiser. Oh! 'tis untold what I've seen him suffer; trying, in his gray-headed years, to swallow the pride: and when at last we found that some, though they knew he had nothing but his body to give, wanted *that* to rot in a jail, we were night and day on the watch to keep them out; and one night the masther says, in his strange way that there was no gainsaying, 'It's a fine clear night, and I should like to walk to the ruin by the side of the monument.' I couldn't tell you how his health had gone and his strength along with it; everything but *his pride*. And the ould housekeeper and myself went along with him;

and he romanced so much as we went, first about one thing and then about the other, that I thought the throuble had turned his brain. It was a clear, moonshiny night, and the stars were beaming along the sky, now in, now out; and he sat down upon an ancient stone, as this might be, and he says,—I remember the very words—

"'Boy,' says he, 'the time will be, and that not long off, when what little respect belongs to ould families and ould ruins will be done away entirely; and the world will hear tell of ould customs and the like; but they will look round upon the earth for them in vain—they will be clean gone! If I had my life to begin over again I'd take great delight in restoring all them things. It's no wonder I should have sympathy with ruins; I, who have ruined, and am ruined.'

"'Sir,' said the old housekeeper, who was hard of hearing, and stupid when she did hear, 'Sir,' said she, 'sure Michelawn and the boys might mend the ruins up of this ould chapel, if it's any fancy for it you have.' So he looked at me, and smiled a sort of a smile, could and chilly, without anything happy in it; like the smile you see sometimes upon the lips of a corpse when the mouth falls a little—a gasping smile. 'Sir,' keeps on the ould silly craythur, 'come away home, for it isn't safe for you to be anything like out of the house, which you haven't been for many a long month before.'

"'True,' said he, 'true, just let me look here;' and he turned to where the little monument stood to the poor girl's remembrance, and he laid his hand on the marble urn which was at the top, and drew it back on a suddent, as if he had not thought that it would have been so could. He then rooted with his stick among the buttercups and daisies that grew about it; and with a quick thought flung off his hat, and fell on his knees upon the grass. As he fell, so four men, vagabonds of the law, sprung on him. Whether he felt their hould or not is between him an' Heaven; but this I do know, that when I looked in his face, as they held him up off the grass, he was dead."

"And that was the end of the most beautiful and most accomplished Irishman of the last century!"

"It was his end, God help us! And the murdering villians kept possession of the body for debt. The neighbouring gentry would not suffer it, and offered to pay the money; but his ould tenants would not hear of that; they rose to a man over the estates which had once belonged to him and his, battled the limbs of the law out of possession, and gave the masther the finest wake and funeral that the counthry had seen for fifty years. There was a hard fight betwixt them and the constables when the body was moving, but they bet them off. And then—whew!—who would follow them into the Connamara hills!"

"What became of his sons?"

"They are both dead: nor is there one stone upon another of Mount Brandon."

"But about *your* obligation?"

"Ay! didn't you hear that he wished the ould ruins of ould Ireland looked to?"

"True; but why do you wear no hat?"

"Didn't he, who was so high, so great, die that bitter night, bareheaded?"

The old man's eyes were moist with tears.

"One other question, Clooney; the poor girl's child—the baby who wailed beneath his window?"

"Didn't he call me 'boy,' and give me his hand to kiss; and don't I do pilgrimage through the world for the sins of my father and my mother! The poor girl's babby was the only child that loved him!"

AUBREY T. DE VERE.

[Poetic genius has, in the case of the De Vere family, proved hereditary. In a preceding volume we gave extracts from Sir Aubrey de Vere; in this the same duty devolves with regard to Aubrey T. de Vere, his third son.

Aubrey Thomas de Vere was born in 1814 at the paternal mansion, Curragh Chase, county Limerick, and he was educated at Trinity College. He has written both in prose and verse, and the list of his works is lengthy. In 1842 appeared *The Waldenses, or the Fall of Rora*, a lyrical tale; in 1843, *The Search after Proserpine, Recollections of Greece, and other Poems*; in 1856, *Poems, Miscellaneous and Sacred*; in 1857, *May Carols*; in 1861, *The Sisters, Inisfail, and other Poems*; in 1864, *The Infant Bridal, and other Poems*; in 1869, *Irish Odes, and other Poems*; in 1872,

The Legends of St. Patrick; in 1874, *Alexander the Great,* a dramatic poem; and in 1879, *Legends of the Saxon Saints.* Besides the above-mentioned drama he has written *St. Thomas of Canterbury.* His prose works are *English Misrule and Irish Misdeeds* (1848); *Picturesque Sketches of Greece and Turkey* (1850); *The Church Settlement of Ireland, or Hibernia Pacanda* (1866); *Ireland's Church Property and the right use of it* (1867); and *Pleas for Secularization* (1867). A volume of correspondence entitled *Proteus and Amadeus,* in which the chief religious and philosophical questions in controversy at the present day were reviewed, and published in 1878, was edited by Mr. De Vere.

Of the volumes of poetry enumerated, that which possesses the greatest interest for Irish readers is *Inisfail,* from which the following extracts are taken. The idea is very original; it is to convey in a series of poems a picture of the chief events in certain great cycles of Irish history. "Its aim," writes the poet himself, "is to embody the *essence* of a nation's history." "Contemporary historic poems," he proceeds, "touch us with a magical hand; but they often pass by the most important events, and linger beside the most trivial. Looking back upon history, as from a vantage ground, its general proportions become palpable; and the themes to which poetry attaches herself are either those critical junctures upon which the fortunes of a nation turn, or such accidents of a lighter sort as illustrate the character of a race. A historic series of poems thus becomes possible, the interest of which is continuous, and the course of which reveals an increasing significance." In accordance with this plan the writer illustrates each epoch by some representative poem and event. At one time he celebrates a great victory in the joyous swing of the ballad; at another an elegy depicts the darkness of a nation's defeat. A great religious epoch is celebrated in stately rhyme; and at another moment the poet has to resort to a lighter measure when individual love plays an important part in fashioning the history of the future. In this way the history of Ireland is presented in a series of tableaux. It is impossible to speak too highly of the skill with which the poet performs his task: he gives, from the nature of the work, specimens of his mastery over all forms of poetry—the martial, the sacred, the passionate, the sad, and over a large variety of measures. The volume published under the title of *The Infant Bridal,* also contains many exquisite gems from his various works. Of his prose that which we most prefer is to be found in the introductions he has written to his own and his father's works. The style combines the two qualities of simplicity and cultured grace. His *English Misrule and Irish Misdeeds* is a generous defence of his countrymen against the scurrilous attacks of some English writers and public speakers.]

FLORENCE MACCARTHY'S FAREWELL TO HIS ENGLISH LOVE.

My pensive-brow'd Evangeline!
What says to thee old Windsor's pine,
  Whose shadow o'er the pleasance sways?
It says, "Ere long the evening star
Will pierce my darkness from afar:
  I grieve as one with grief who plays."

Evangeline! Evangeline!
In that far distant land of mine
  There stands a yew-tree among tombs!
For ages there that tree has stood,
A black pall dash'd with drops of blood;
  O'er all my world it breathes its glooms.

England's fair child, Evangeline!
Because my yew-tree is not thine,
  Because thy gods on mine wage war,
Farewell! Back fall the gates of brass;
The exile to his own must pass:
  I seek the land of tombs once more.

TO THE SAME.

We seem to tread the self-same street,
  To pace the self-same courts or grass;
Parting, our hands appear to meet:
  O vanitatum vanitas!

Distant as earth from heaven or hell,
  From thee the things to me most dear:
Ghost-throng'd Cocytus and thy will
  Between us rush. We might be near.

Thy world is fair: my thoughts refuse
  To dance its dance or drink its wine;
Nor canst thou hear the reeds and yews
  That sigh to me from lands not thine.

THE MARCH TO KINSALE.
DECEMBER, A.D. 1601.

O'er many a river bridged with ice,
  Through many a vale with snow-drifts dumb,
Past quaking fen and precipice
  The Princes of the North are come!

Lo, these are they that year by year
  Roll'd back the tide of England's war;—
Rejoice, Kinsale! thy help is near!
  That wondrous winter march is o'er.
    And thus they sang, "To-morrow morn
      Our eyes shall rest upon the foe:
    Roll on, swift night, in silence borne,
      And blow, thou breeze of sunrise, blow!"

Blithe as a boy on march'd the host,
  With droning pipe and clear-voiced harp;
At last above that southern coast
  Rang out their war-steeds' whinny sharp;
And up the sea-salt slopes they wound,
  And airs once more of ocean quaff'd;
Those frosty woods the rocks that crown'd
  As though May touch'd them waved and laugh'd.
    And thus they sang, "To-morrow morn
      Our eyes shall rest upon our foe:
    Roll on, swift night, in silence borne,
      And blow, thou breeze of sunrise, blow!"

Beside their watch-fires couch'd all night
  Some slept, some laugh'd, at cards some play'd,
While, chaunting on a central height
  Of moonlit crag, the priesthood pray'd:
And some to sweetheart, some to wife
  Sent message kind; while others told
Triumphant tales of recent fight,
  Or legends of their sires of old.
    And thus they sang, "To-morrow morn
      Our eyes at last shall see the foe:
    Roll on, swift night, in silence borne,
      And blow, thou breeze of sunrise, blow!"

THE INTERCESSION.[1]

ULSTER, A.D. 1641.

Iriel, the priest, arose and said,
  "The just cause never shall prosper by wrong!
The ill cause battens on blood ill shed;
  'Tis Virtue only makes Justice strong.

"I have hidden the Saxon's wife and child
  Beneath the altar; behind the porch;
O'er them that believe not these hands have piled
  The stoles and the vestments of holy Church!

"I have hid three men in a hollow oak;
  I have hid three maids in an ocean cave:"
As though he were lord of the thunder stroke,
  The old priest lifted his hand—to save.

But the people loved not the words he spake;
  And their face was changed for their heart was sore:
They answer'd nought; but their brows grew black,
  And the hoarse halls roar'd like a torrent's roar.

"Has the stranger robb'd you of house and land?
  In battle meet him and smite him down!
Has he sharpen'd the dagger? Lift ye the brand!
  Has he trapp'd your princes? Set free the clown!

"Has the stranger his country and knighthood shamed?
  Though he 'scape God's vengeance, so shall not ye!
His own God chastens! Be never named
  With the Mullaghmast slaughter! Be just and free!"

But the people received not the words he spake,
  For the wrong on their heart had made it sore;
And their brows grew black like the stormy rack,
  And the hoarse halls roar'd like the wave-wash'd shore.

Then Iriel the priest put forth a curse;
  And horror crept o'er them from vein to vein;—
A curse upon man and a curse upon horse,
  As forth they rode to the battle plain.

And there never came to them luck nor grace,
  No saint in the battle-field help'd them more,
Till O'Neill, who hated the warfare base,
  Had landed at Doe on Tirconnell's shore.

True Knight, true Christian, true Prince was he!
  He lived for Erin; for Erin died:
Had Charles proved true and the faith set free,
  O'Neill had triumph'd at Charles's side.

DIRGE OF RORY O'MORE.

A.D. 1642.

Up the sea-sadden'd valley at evening's decline
A heifer walks lowing; "the Silk of the Kine;"[2]
From the deep to the mountain she roams, and again
From the mountains' green urn to the purple-rimm'd main.

Whom seek'st thou, sad mother? Thine own is not thine!
He dropp'd from the headland; he sank in the brine!

---

[1] Dr. Leland and other historians relate that the Catholic clergy frequently interfered for the protection of the victims of that massacre which took place at an early period of the Ulster rising of 1641. They hid them beneath their altars. From the landing of Owen Roe O'Neill all such crimes ceased.—*De Vere.*

[2] One of the mystical names for Ireland used by the bards.

'Twas a dream! but in dream at thy foot did he
  follow
Through the meadow-sweet on by the marish and
  mallow!

Was he thine? Have they slain him? Thou
  seek'st him, not knowing
Thyself too art theirs, thy sweet breath and sad
  lowing!
Thy gold horn is theirs; thy dark eye and thy
  silk!
And that which torments thee, thy milk, is their
  milk!

'Twas no dream, mother land! 'Twas no dream,
  Inisfail!
Hope dreams, but grief dreams not—the grief of
  the Gael!
From Leix and Ikerren to Donegal's shore
Rolls the dirge of thy last and thy bravest—
  O'More!

O WOODS!

O woods, that o'er the waters breathe
  A sigh that grows from morn till night!
O waters, with your voice like death,
  And yet consoling in your might;
Ye draw, ye drag me with a charm,
  As when a river draws a leaf,
From silken court and citied swarm,
  To your cold homes of peace in grief.

In boyhood's flush I trod the shore
  When slowly sank a crimson sun,
Revealed at moments, bid once more
  By rolling mountains, gold or dun:
But now I haunt its marge when day
  Has laid his fulgent sceptre by,
And tremble over waters gray
  Long windows of a hueless sky.

THE LONG DYING.

The dying tree no pang sustains;
  But, by degrees relinquishing
Companionship of beams and rains,
  Forgets the balmy breath of spring.

From off th' enringèd trunk that keeps
  His annual count of ages gone,
Th' embrace of summer slowly slips;—
  Still stands the giant in the sun.

His myriad lips, that suck'd of old
  The dewy breasts of heaven, are dry;
His roots remit the crag and mould;
  Yet painless is his latest sigh.

He falls; the forests round him roar;—
  Ere long on quiet bank and copse
Untrembling moonbeams rest; once more
  The startled babe his head down drops.

But ah for one who never drew
  From age to age a painless breath!
And ah the old wrong ever new!
  And ah the many-centuried death!

GRATTAN.

God works through man, not hills or snows!
  In man, not men, is the godlike power;
The man, God's potentate, God foreknows;
  He sends him strength at the destined hour.
His Spirit he breathes into one deep heart:
His cloud he bids from one mind depart:
A Saint!—and a race is to God re-born!
A Man!—One man makes a nation's morn!

A man, and the blind land by slow degrees
  Gains sight! A man, and the deaf land hears!
A man, and the dumb land like wakening seas
  Thunders low dirges in proud, dull ears!
One man, and the People, a three days' corse,
Stands up, and the grave-bands fall off perforce;
One man, and the nation in height a span
To the measure ascends of the perfect man.

Thus wept unto God the land of Eire:
  Yet there rose no man and her hope was dead:
In the ashes she sat of a burn'd-out fire;
  And sackcloth was over her queenly head.
But a man in her latter days arose;
A deliverer stepp'd from the camp of her foes:
He spake; the great and the proud gave way,
And the dawn began which shall end in day!

THE "OLD LAND."

Ah, kindly and sweet, we must love thee perforce!
  The disloyal, the coward alone would not love
    thee:
Ah mother of heroes! strong mother! soft nurse!
  We are thine while the large cloud swims on-
    ward above thee!
By thy hills ever blue that draw heaven so near;
  By thy cliffs, by thy lakes, by thine ocean-lull'd
    highlands;
And more—by thy records disastrous and dear,
  The shrines on thy headlands, the cells in thine
    islands!

Ah, well sings the thrush by Lixnau and Traigh-li!
Ah, well breaks the wave upon Umbhall and
  Brandon!

Thy breeze o'er the upland blows clement and free,
  And o'er fields, once his own, which the hind must abandon.
A caitiff the noble who draws from thy plains
  His all, yet reveres not the source of his greatness;
A clown and a serf, 'mid his boundless domains
  His spirit consumes in the prison of his straightness!

Through the cloud of its pathos thy face is more fair:
  In old time thou wert sun-clad; the gold robe thou worest!
To thee the heart turns as the deer to her lair,
  Ere she dies, her first bed in the gloom of the forest.
Our glory, our sorrow, our mother! Thy God
  In thy worst dereliction forsook but to prove thee:—

Blind, blind as the blindworm; cold, cold as the clod;
  Who, seeing thee, see not, possess but not love thee!

THE LITTLE BLACK ROSE.[1]

The little Black Rose shall be red at last!
  What made it black but the East wind dry,
And the tear of the widow that fell on it fast?
  It shall redden the hills when June is nigh!

The Silk of the Kine shall rest at last!
  What drave her forth but the dragon-fly?
In the golden vale she shall feed full fast
  With her mild gold horn, and her slow dark eye.

The wounded wood-dove lies dead at last:
  The pine long bleeding, it shall not die!
—This song is secret. Mine ear it pass'd
  In a wind o'er the stone plain of Athenry.[2]

JOSEPH SHERIDAN LE FANU.

BORN 1814 — DIED 1873.

[The subject of our memoir is yet another member of the large family of wits that sprung from the stock of the Sheridans. Joseph Sheridan Le Fanu was the grandson of Alicia Le Fanu, the favourite sister of Richard Brinsley Sheridan, and an authoress herself, like nearly every member of her family. His father was the Rev. Thomas P. Le Fanu. Joseph was born in Dublin on the 28th of August, 1814. He graduated with honours in Trinity College, and at an early age he began writing for the newspapers. Ultimately he became part proprietor of the *Dublin Evening Mail*, with its weekly issue the *Warder;* and a few years before his death he was also the owner of the *Dublin University Magazine.*

To the last-named periodical he began to contribute shortly after its start. His first great success was with his poetry, two of his pieces, "Shemus O'Brien," and "Phadrig Crohoore" being excellent specimens of the half humorous, half pathetic composition, which best depicts Irish life. One of these we quote. Le Fanu was also the author of a considerable number of novels. His chief power was in describing scenes of a mysterious or grotesque character, and the mystery in some of his series is kept up with considerable skill to the end. Some of the best things, however, he wrote were shorter sketches in the old numbers of the *Dublin University Magazine*, an extract from one of which we give. In 1850 he published *The Cock and Anchor, a Chronicle of Old Dublin*. This was followed in 1863 by the *House by the Churchyard*. He is also the author of *Uncle Silas, Tenants of Malory, Willing to Die,* and other stories. In most of these later productions there is the skilfulness in contriving a plot of which we have spoken; there are also frequently fine scenes; but some of the stories are weakened by the want of condensation so common in tales that appear in serial form.

Mr. Le Fanu, who had retired from social life several years previously, owing to the death of his wife, died in his house in Merrion Square, Dublin, on February 7, 1873. His friends, according to a magazine article, "admired him for his learning, his sparkling wit, and pleasant conversation, and loved him for his manly virtues . . . and his loving affectionate nature."]

---

[1] Ireland is spoken of in this little poem in the mystical terms commonly employed among the older Irish bards: the moral is that Ireland should hope for a bright future in spite of its gloomy past.—ED.

[2] The scene of a great Irish defeat.

A NARROW ESCAPE FROM MURDER.

[The tale from which the following passage is an extract appeared under the title, "Passage in the Secret History of an Irish Countess," in the November number (1838) of the *Dublin University Magazine*. The same facts supplied the chief incident in *Uncle Silas*. A young girl—she is the countess—is left by her father as the ward of her uncle. This uncle wishes her to marry his son, "Edward T⸺n." She refuses, and one night the events described in the following extract took place. The Emily mentioned is daughter of the uncle of the countess.]

I went to my room early that night, but I was too miserable to sleep. At about twelve o'clock, feeling very nervous, I determined to call my cousin Emily, who slept, you will remember, in the next room, which communicated with mine by a second door. By this private entrance I found my way into her chamber, and without difficulty persuaded her to return to my room and sleep with me. We accordingly lay down together—she undressed, and I with my clothes on—for I was every moment walking up and down the room, and felt too nervous and miserable to think of rest or comfort. Emily was soon fast asleep, and I lay awake, fervently longing for the first pale gleam of morning, reckoning every stroke of the old clock with an impatience which made every hour appear like six. It must have been about one o'clock when I thought I heard a slight noise at the partition door between Emily's room and mine, as if caused by somebody's turning the key in the lock. I held my breath, and the same sound was repeated at the second door of my room—that which opened upon the lobby—the sound was here distinctly caused by the revolution of the bolt in the lock, and it was followed by a slight pressure upon the door itself, as if to ascertain the security of the lock. The person, whoever it might be, was probably satisfied, for I heard the old boards of the lobby creak and strain, as if under the weight of somebody moving cautiously over them. My sense of hearing became unnaturally, almost painfully acute. I suppose the imagination added distinctness to sounds vague in themselves. I thought that I could actually hear the breathing of the person who was slowly returning down the lobby; at the head of the staircase there appeared to occur a pause; and I could distinctly hear two or three sentences hastily whispered; the steps then descended the stairs with apparently less caution. I now ventured to walk quickly and lightly to the lobby door, and attempted to open it; it was indeed fast locked upon the outside, as was also the other. I now felt that the dreadful hour was come; but one desperate expedient remained—it was to awaken Emily, and by our united strength, to attempt to force the partition door, which was slighter than the other, and through this to pass to the lower part of the house, whence it might be possible to escape to the grounds, and forth to the village. I returned to the bedside, and shook Emily, but in vain; nothing that I could do availed to produce from her more than a few incoherent words—it was a death-like sleep. She had certainly drank of some narcotic, as had I probably also, spite of all the caution with which I had examined everything presented to us to eat or drink. I now attempted, with as little noise as possible, to force first one door, then the other—but all in vain. I believe no strength could have effected my object, for both doors opened inwards. I therefore collected whatever movables I could carry thither, and piled them against the doors, so as to assist me in whatever attempts I should make to resist the entrance of those without. I then returned to the bed and endeavoured again, but fruitlessly, to awaken my cousin. It was not sleep, it was torpor, lethargy, death. I knelt down and prayed with an agony of earnestness; and then seating myself upon the bed, I awaited my fate with a kind of terrible tranquillity.

I heard a faint clanking sound from the narrow court which I have already mentioned, as if caused by the scraping of some iron instrument against stones or rubbish. I at first determined not to disturb the calmness which I now felt, by uselessly watching the proceedings of those who sought my life; but as the sounds continued, the horrible curiosity which I felt overcame every other emotion, and I determined, at all hazards, to gratify it. I therefore crawled upon my knees to the window, so as to let the smallest portion of my head appear above the sill. The moon was shining with an uncertain radiance upon the antique gray buildings, and obliquely upon the narrow court beneath, one side of which was therefore clearly illuminated, while the other was lost in obscurity, the sharp outlines of the old gables, with their nodding clusters of ivy, being at first alone visible. Whoever or whatever occasioned the noise which had excited my curiosity, was concealed under the shadow of the dark side of the quadrangle. I placed my hand over my eyes to shade them from the moonlight, which was so bright as to be almost dazzling, and, peering into the darkness, I first dimly, but afterwards gradually, almost with full distinctness, beheld the form of a man engaged in digging what appeared to be a rude hole close under the wall. Some implements, probably a shovel and pickaxe, lay beside him, and to these he every now and then applied himself as the nature of the ground required. He pursued his task rapidly, and with as little noise as possible. "So," thought I, as shovelful after shovelful the dislodged rubbish mounted into a heap, "they are digging the grave in which, before two hours pass, I must lie, a cold, mangled corpse. I am *theirs*—I cannot escape." I felt as if my reason was leaving me. I started to my feet, and in mere despair I applied myself again to each of the two doors alternately. I strained every nerve and sinew, but I might as well have attempted, with my single strength, to force the building itself from its foundation. I threw myself madly upon the ground, and clasped my hands over my eyes as if to shut out the horrible images which crowded upon me. The paroxysm passed away. I prayed once more with the bitter, agonized fervour of one who feels that the hour of death is present and inevitable. When I arose I went once more to the window and looked out, just in time to see a shadowy figure glide stealthily along the wall. The task was finished. The catastrophe of the tragedy must soon be accomplished. I determined now to defend my life to the last; and that I might be able to do so with some effect, I searched the room for something which might serve as a weapon; but either through accident, or from an anticipation of such a possibility, everything which might have been made available for such a purpose had been carefully removed. I must thus die tamely and without an effort to defend myself. A thought suddenly struck me—might it not be possible to escape through the door, which the assassin must open in order to enter the room? I resolved to make the attempt. I felt assured that the door through which ingress to the room would be effected was that which opened upon the lobby. It was the more direct way, besides being, for obvious reasons, less liable to interruption than the other. I resolved then to place myself behind a projection of the wall, whose shadow would serve fully to conceal me, and when the door should be opened, and before they should have discovered the identity of the occupant of the bed, to creep noiselessly from the room, and then to trust to Providence for escape. In order to facilitate this scheme, I removed all the lumber which I had heaped against the door; and I had nearly completed my arrangements, when I perceived the room suddenly darkened by the close approach of some shadowy object to the window. On turning my eyes in that direction, I observed at the top of the casement, as if suspended from above, first the feet, then the legs, then the body, and at length the whole figure of a man present itself. It was Edward T——n. He appeared to be guiding his descent so as to bring his feet upon the centre of the stone block which occupied the lower part of the window; and having secured his footing upon this, he kneeled down and began to gaze into the room. As the moon was gleaming into the chamber, and the bed curtains were drawn, he was able to distinguish the bed itself and its contents. He appeared satisfied with his scrutiny, for he looked up and made a sign with his hand, upon which the rope by which his descent had been effected was slackened from above, and he proceeded to disengage it from his waist: this accomplished, he applied his hands to the window-frame, which must have been ingeniously contrived for the purpose, for with apparently no resistance the whole frame, containing casement and all, slipped from its position in the wall, and was by him lowered into the room. The cold night waved the bed-curtains, and he paused for a moment—all was still again—and he stepped in upon the floor of the room. He held in his hand what appeared to be a steel instrument, shaped something like a hammer, but larger and sharper at the extremities. This he held rather behind him, while, with three long *tip-toe* strides, he brought himself to the bedside. I felt that the discovery must now be made, and held my breath in momentary expectation of the execration in which he would vent his surprise and disappointment. I closed my eyes—there was a pause—but it was a short one. I heard two dull blows, given in rapid succession: a quivering sigh, and the long-drawn, heavy breathing of the sleeper was for ever suspended. I unclosed my eyes, and saw the murderer fling the quilt across the head of his victim: he then, with the instrument of death still in his hand, proceeded to the lobby door, upon which he tapped sharply twice or thrice—a quick step was then heard approaching, and a voice whispered something from without—Edward answered, with a kind of chuckle, "Her ladyship is past complaining; unlock the door, in the devil's name, unless you're afraid to come in, and help me to lift the body out of the window." The key was turned in the lock—the door opened —and my uncle entered the room. I have told you already that I had placed myself under the shade of a projection of the wall, close to the door. I had instinctively shrunk down cowering towards the ground on the entrance of Edward through the window. When my uncle entered the room, he and his son both stood so very close to me that his hand was every moment upon the point of touching my face. I held my breath, and remained motionless as death.

"You had no interruption from the next room?" said my uncle.

"No," was the brief reply.

"Secure the jewels, Ned; the French harpy must not lay her claws upon them. You're a steady hand, by G—; not much blood—eh?"

"Not twenty drops," replied his son, "and those on the quilt."

"I'm glad it's over," whispered my uncle again; "we must lift the—the *thing* through the window, and lay the rubbish over it."

They then turned to the bedside, and, winding the bed-clothes round the body, carried it between them slowly to the window, and, exchanging a few brief words with some one below, they shoved it over the window sill, and I heard it fall heavily on the ground underneath.

"I'll take the jewels," said my uncle; "there are two caskets in the lower drawer."

He proceeded, with an accuracy which, had I been more at ease, would have furnished me with matter of astonishment, to lay his hand upon the very spot where my jewels lay; and having possessed himself of them, he called to his son—

"Is the rope made fast above?"

"I'm not a fool—to be sure it is," replied he.

They then lowered themselves from the window. I now rose lightly and cautiously, scarcely daring to breathe, from my place of concealment, and was creeping towards the door, when I heard my cousin's voice, in a sharp whisper, exclaim, "Scramble up again; G—d d—n you, you've forgot to lock the door;" and I perceived, by the straining of the rope which hung from above, that the mandate was instantly obeyed. Not a second was to be lost. I passed through the door, which was only closed, and moved as rapidly as I could, consistently with stillness, along the lobby. Before I had gone many yards I heard the door through which I had just passed double locked on the inside. I glided down the stairs in terror, lest, at every corner, I should meet the murderer or one of his accomplices. I reached the hall, and listened for a moment to ascertain whether all was silent around; no sound was audible; the parlour windows opened on the park, and through one of them I might, I thought, easily effect my escape. Accordingly, I hastily entered; but, to my consternation, a candle was burning in the room, and by its light I saw a figure seated at the dinner-table, upon which lay glasses, bottles, and the other accompaniments of a drinking party. There was no other means of escape, so I advanced with a firm step and collected mind to the window. I noiselessly withdrew the bars and unclosed the shutters—I pushed open the casement, and, without waiting to look behind me, I ran with my utmost speed, scarcely feeling the ground under me, down the avenue, taking care to keep upon the grass which bordered it. I did not for a moment slack my speed, and I had now gained the centre point between the park gate and the mansion-house—here the avenue made a wider circuit, and in order to avoid delay, I directed my way across the smooth sward round which the pathway wound, intending, at the opposite side of the flat, at a point which I distinguished by a group of old birch trees, to enter again upon the beaten track, which was from thence tolerably direct to the gate. I had, with my utmost speed, got about half-way across this broad flat when the rapid treading of a horse's hoofs struck upon my ear. My heart swelled in my bosom, as though I would smother. The clattering of galloping hoofs approached —I was pursued—they were now upon the sward on which I was running—there was not a bush or a bramble to shelter me—and, as if to render escape altogether desperate, the moon, which had hitherto been obscured, at this moment shone forth with a broad clear light, which made every object distinctly visible. The sounds were now close behind me. I felt my knees bending under me, with the sensation which torments one in dreams. I reeled —I stumbled—I fell—and at the same instant the cause of my alarm wheeled past me at full gallop. It was one of the young fillies which pastured loose about the park, whose frolics had thus all but maddened me with terror. I scrambled to my feet, and rushed on with weak but rapid steps, my sportive companion still galloping round and round me with many a frisk and fling, until, at length, more dead than alive, I reached the avenue gate and crossed the stile, I scarce knew how. I ran through the village, in which all was silent as the grave, until my progress was arrested by the hoarse voice of a sentinel, who cried, "Who goes there?" I felt that I was now safe. I turned in the direction of the voice, and fell fainting at the soldier's feet. When I came to myself I was sitting in a miserable hovel, surrounded by strange faces, all bespeaking curiosity and compassion. Many soldiers were in it also; indeed, as I afterwards found, it was employed as a guard-room by a detachment of troops quartered for that night in the town. In a few words I informed their officer of the circumstances which had occurred, describing also the appearance of the persons engaged in the murder; and he, without loss of time, proceeded to the mansion-house of Carrickleigh, taking with him a number of his men. But the villains had discovered their mistake, and had effected their escape, before the arrival of the military.

Deep and fervent as must always be my gratitude to Heaven for my deliverance, effected by a chain of providential occurrences, the failing of a single link of which must have insured my destruction, I was long before I could look back upon it with other feelings than those of bitterness, almost of agony. The only being that had ever really loved me, my nearest and dearest friend, ever ready to sympathize, to counsel, and to assist—the gayest, the gentlest, the warmest heart—the only creature on earth that cared for me—*her* life had been the price of my deliverance; and I then uttered the wish—which no event of my long and sorrowful life has taught me to recall—that she had been spared, and that in her stead *I* were mouldering in the grave forgotten and at rest.

SHEMUS O'BRIEN.

PART I.

Jist after the war, in the year 'Ninety-Eight,
As soon as the boys were all scattered an' bate,
'Twas the custom, whenever a peasant was got,
To hang him by trial—barrin' such as was shot.
There was trial by jury goin' on by daylight,
An' the martial-law hangin' the lavings by night.
It's them was hard times for an honest gossoon;
If he missed in the judges he'd meet the dragoon;
An' whether the sojers or judges gave sentence,
The divil a much time they allowed for repentance;
An' many a fine boy was then on his keepin',
With small share of restin', or sittin', or sleepin';
An' because they loved Erinn, an' scorned to sell it,
A prey for the bloodhound—a mark for the bullet—
Unsheltered by night and unrested by day,
With the heath for their barrack, revenge for their pay.

An' the bravest an' honestest boy of thim all
Was Shemus O'Brien, from the town of Glingall;
His limbs wor well set, an' his body was light,
An' the keen-fangèd hound had not teeth half as white;
But his face was as pale as the face of the dead,
An' his cheek never warmed with the blush of the red;
An' for all that, he wasn't an ugly young boy,
For the divil himself couldn't blaze with his eye—
So droll an' so wicked, so dark an' so bright,
Like a fire-flash that crosses the depth of the night;
An' he was the best mower that ever has been,
An' the elegantest hurler that ever was seen:
In fencin' he gave Patrick Mooney a cut,
An' in jumpin' he bate Tom Molony a foot;
An' for lightness of foot there was not his peer,
For, by heavens, he'd almost outrun the red deer;
Au' his dancin' was such that the men used to stare,
An' the women turn crazy, he did it so quare;
An' sure the whole world gave in to him there!

An' it's he was the boy that was hard to be caught,
An' it's often he ran, an' it's often he fought,
An' it's many's the one can remember right well
The quare things he did; an' it's oft I heerd tell
How he frightened the magistrates in Cahirbally,
An' escaped through the sojers in Aherloe valley,
An' leathered the yeomen, himself agin four,
An' stretched the four strongest on old Galtimore.

But the fox must sleep sometimes, the wild deer must rest,
An' treachery prey on the blood of the best:
Afther many an action of power an' of pride,
An' many a night on the mountain's blake side,
An' a thousand great dangers an' toils overpast,
In the darkness of night he was taken at last.

Now, Shemus! look back on the beautiful moon,
For the door of the prison must close on you soon;
And take your last look at her dim, misty light,
That falls on the mountain an' valley to-night—
One look at the village, one look at the flood,
An' one at the sheltering, far-distant wood:

Farewell to the forest, farewell to the hill,
An' farewell to the friends that will think of you still,
Farewell to the patthern, the hurlin', an' wake,
An' farewell to the girl that would die for your sake!

An' twelve sojers brought him to Maryborough jail,
An' with irons secured him, refusin' all bail.
The fleet limbs wor chained and the sthrong hands wor bound,
An' he lay down his length on the cold prison ground;
An' the dhrames of his childhood kem over him there,
As gentle and soft as the sweet summer air;
An' happy remimbrances crowdin' on ever,
As fast as the foam-flakes dhrift down on the river,
Bringin' fresh to his heart merry days long gone by,
Till the tears gathered heavy and thick in his eye.
But the tears didn't fall, for the pride iv his heart
Wouldn't suffer one dhrop down his pale cheek to start;
An' he sprang to his feet in the dark prison cave,
An' he swore with a fierceness that misery gave,
By the hopes iv the good an' the cause iv the brave,
That when he was mouldering in the cowld grave,
His inimies never should have it to boast
His scorn iv their vengeance one moment was lost.
His bosom might bleed, but his cheek should be dhry,
For undaunted he lived, and undaunted he'd die.

PART II.

Well, as soon as a few weeks were over an' gone,
The terrible day of the trial came on;
There was such a great crowd, there was scarce room to stand,
An' sojers on guard, an' dragoons sword in hand;
An' the court-house so full that the people were bothered,
An' attorneys and criers on the point of being smothered,
An' counsellors almost gave over for dead,
An' the jury sittin' up in the box overhead;
An' the judge settled out so determined an' big,
With the gown on his back, an' an elegant wig;
An' silence was called, an' the minit 'twas said,
The court was as still as the heart of the dead.
An' they heard but the opening of one prison lock,
An' Shemus O'Brien kem into the dock.

For one minute he turned his eyes round on the throng,
An' then looked on the bars, so firm and so strong;
An' he saw that he had not a hope nor a friend,
A chance to escape nor a word to defend;
An' he folded his arms as he stood there alone,
As calm and as cold as a statue of stone.

An' they read a big writin', a yard long at laste,
An' Shemus didn't see it, nor mind it a taste.
An' the judge took a big pinch of snuff, an' he says:
"Are you guilty or not, Jim O'Brien, if you plaise?"
An' all held their breath in the silence of dread,
An' Shemus O'Brien made answer an' said:
"My lord, if you ask me if in my lifetime
I thought any treason, or did any crime,
That should call to my cheek, as I stand alone here,
The hot blush of shame or the coldness of fear,
Though I stood by the grave to receive my death-blow,
Before God an' the world I would answer you No!
But if you would ask me, as I think it like,
If in the rebellion I carried a pike,
An' fought for ould Ireland, from the first to the close,
An' shed the heart's blood of her bitterest foes—
I answer you Yes; an' I tell you again,
Though I stand here to perish, it's my glory that then
In her cause I was willin' my veins should run dry,
An' now for her sake I am ready to die."

Then the silence was great, and the jury smiled bright,
An' the judge wasn't sorry the job was made light;
By my soul, it's himself was the crabbed ould chap!
In a twinkling he pulled on his ugly black cap.

Then Shemus's mother, in the crowd standin' by,
Called out to the judge with a pitiful cry:
"O Judge, darlin', don't—oh! don't say the word!
The crathur is young—have mercy, my lord!
You don't know him, my lord; oh! don't give him to ruin!
He was foolish—he didn't know what he was doin'!
He's the kindliest crathur, the tinderest-hearted;
Don't part us for ever, we that's so long parted!
Judge mavourneen, forgive him—forgive him, my lord!
An' God will forgive you—oh! don't say the word!"

That was the first minit O'Brien was shaken,
When he saw he was not quite forgot or forsaken!
An' down his pale cheek, at the word of his mother,
The big tears were running, one after the other,
An' two or three times he endeavoured to spake,
But the strong manly voice used to falter an' break.
But at last, by the strength of his high-mounting pride,
He conquered an' mastered his grief as swelling tide;
An' says he: "Mother, don't—don't break your poor heart!
Sure, sooner or later, the dearest must part.
An' God knows it's better than wand'ring in fear

On the bleak trackless mountain among the wild
 deer,
To be in the grave, where the heart, head, an'
 breast
From labour an' sorrow for ever shall rest.
Then mother, my darlin', don't cry any more—
Don't make me seem broken in this my last hour;
For I wish, when my heart's lyin' under the raven,
No true man can say that I died like a craven."
Then towards the judge Shemus bent down his
 head,
An' that minit the solemn death-sentence was said.

PART III.

The mornin' was bright, an' the mists rose on high,
An' the lark whistled merrily in the clear sky—
But why are the men standing idle so late?
An' why do the crowd gather fast in the street?
What come they to talk of?—what come they to
 see?
An' why does the long rope hang from the cross-
 tree?
O Shemus O'Brien, pray fervent an' fast!
May the saints take your soul, for this day is your
 last.
Pray fast an' pray strong, for the moment is nigh,
When strong, proud, an' great as you are, you
 must die!—
At last they drew open the big prison gate,
An' out came the sheriffs an' sojers in state;
An' a cart in the middle, an' Shemus was in it—
Not paler, but prouder than ever that minit;
An' as soon as the people saw Shemus O'Brien,
Wid prayin' and blessin', an' all the girls cryin',
A wild wailin' sound kem on all by degrees,
Like the sound of the lonesome wind blowin'
 through trees.
On, on to the gallows the sheriffs are gone,
An' the car an' the sojers go steadily on.
An' at every side swellin' around iv the cart,
A wild sorrowful sound that would open your
 heart.
Now under the gallows the car takes its stand,
And the hangman gets up with a rope in his hand.
An' the priest havin' blest him, gets down on the
 ground;
An' Shemus O'Brien throws one look around.
Then the hangman drew near, and the people grew
 still,
Young faces turn sickly, an' warm hearts turn chill;
An' the rope bein' ready, his neck was made bare,
For the gripe of the life-strangling cords to
 prepare;
And the good priest has left him, havin' said his
 last prayer.
But the good priest did more—for his hands he
 unbound,
An' with one daring spring Jim has leaped on the
 ground!

Bang! bang! go the carbines, an' clash go the
 sabres;
He's not down! he's alive! now attend to him,
 neighbours!

By one shout from the people the heavens are
 shaken—
One shout that the dead of the world might awaken.
Your swords they may glitter, your carbines go
 bang,
But if you want hangin' 'tis yourselves you must
 hang!
To-night he'll be sleepin' in Aherloe glin,
An' the divil's in the dice if you catch him agin.
The sojers run this way, the sheriffs run that,
An' Father Malone lost his new Sunday hat;
An' the sheriffs were, both of them, punished
 severely,
An' fined like the divil, because Jim done them
 fairly.
A week after this time, without firin' a cannon,
A sharp Yankee schooner sailed out of the Shannon;
An' the captain left word he was going to Cork,
But the devil a bit—he was bound for New York.

The very next spring—a bright mornin' in May,
An' just six months after the great hangin' day—
A letter was brought to the town of Kildare,
An' on the outside was written out fair:—
"To ould Mrs. O'Brien, in Ireland, or elsewhere."
An' the inside began—"My dear good ould Mother,
I'm safe, and I'm happy; an' not wishin' to bother
You in the radin'—with the help of the priest—
I send you inclosed in this letter at least
Enough to pay him an' to fetch you away
To the land of the free an' the brave—Amerikay!
Here you'll be happy, an' never made cryin',
As long as you're mother of Shemus O'Brien.
Give my love to sweet Biddy, an' tell her beware
Of that spalpeen who calls himself 'Lord of Kildare;'
An' just say to the judge, I don't now care a rap
For him, or his wig, or his dirty black cap.
An' as for the dragoons—them paid men of
 slaughter—
Say I love them as well as the devil loves holy
 water.
An' now, my good mother, one word of advice—
Fill your bag with potatoes, an' bacon, an' rice.
An' tell my sweet Biddy, the best way of all
Is now an' for ever to leave ould Glengall,
An' come with you, takin' a snug cabin berth,
An' bring us a sod of the ould Shamrock earth.
An' when you start from ould Ireland, take
 passage at Cork,
An' come straight across to the town of New York;
An' there ask the mayor the best way to go
To the town of Cincinnati—the state Ohio:
An' there you will find me, without much tryin',
At the 'Harp an' the Eagle,' kept by Shemus
 O'Brien."

MARMION W. SAVAGE.

Born 1823 — Died 1872.

[The novels of Marmion W. Savage were very popular in their day. They belong for the most part to that era in romance inaugurated by the late Charles Kingsley, in which a connection was preached between a firm belief in the truths of Christianity and the possession of well-developed muscles. Savage was born in Dublin in 1823 or 1824, and spent there the greater part of his life, holding an official position. Removing to London in 1856 he gave himself up to the literary profession, and produced in rapid succession a series of stories, *The Bachelor of the Albany*, *My Uncle the Curate*, *Reuben Medlicott*, and the *Woman of Business*. The first and third were highly popular, and have been reprinted in New York. The *Falcon Family*, produced at an earlier date, is on the whole the best known and the choicest of his stories. It is intended as a satire on the leaders of the Young Ireland party; and some of the sarcasm is very keen and amusing, but, as political pictures, his sketches are no better than caricature. Savage is happier in his description of Cockney adventurers than Irish extravagances; and his portraits of two social parasites are intensely amusing. He was the editor for some years of the *Examiner*; and he also brought out an edition with notes of Sheil's *Political and Social Sketches*. He died in Torquay, whither he had retired for his health, on May 1, 1872. He was married twice; his first wife was a niece of Lady Morgan. Savage would probably have been better known, but that the restraints of official life compelled him to veil the authorship of his early works. His novels fully make up for their want of constructive skill by their sketches of contemporary character—sketches not the less amusing because the standpoint of the author is that of good-humoured cynicism.]

AN ADVENTUROUS COUPLE.

(FROM THE "FALCON FAMILY.")

Mrs. Falcon was a woman in the August of her days; brisk and blooming, with black hair and brown complexion, her nose slightly aquiline, her lips small and compressed; her eyes dark, piercing, bold, practical; her features in general regular and massive, with a free and daring expression which had a charm of its own for those who like what the French call *une beauté insolente*. She was above the middle height, and looked even taller than she actually was, in consequence of her remarkably stately and commanding carriage, a point to which, perhaps, she paid the more attention, as it was the only carriage she could call her own. All the developments of her person were on a large scale; she wanted no milliner's assistance to help her to bustle through the world.

Falcon was very tall and meagre; his nose was red and hooked; his eyes twinkling and intelligent; his forehead high, narrow, receding, bald, garnished on each side with an upright tuft of reddish hair. . . . .

Mr. Falcon was an immense favourite with little England; he was the school-boy's architect and ship-builder, and Master of the Ordnance to the British Nursery; incomparable at making cannon with quills, mortars of trotter-bones, armadas of old corks, and armies out of visiting-tickets. Then, for children who were sager than to play with anything but the toys of philosophy, he could suffocate canaries in exhausted receivers, develop electric sparks from the bristling backs of reluctant kittens, exhibit the laws of refraction with a slop-basin and a tea-spoon, and seduce needles out of work-boxes with a magnet of amazing virtue, which he always carried in his waistcoat pocket. In a word, he was the darling of the darlings; secured the nurseries first, and there planted the artillery with which he often carried the dining-room; which was, of course, the main point.

Mrs. Falcon had the usual success that follows the steps of a fine and a clever woman, where she had not the sharpness or the jealousy of her own sex to cope with. Wherever male influence was ascendant, the gypsy was seldom repulsed, and often received with hearty welcome. What man, who had either the eye of a Rubens for florid beauty, or the taste of a Borrow for Zingaree adventure, could contemplate either her person or her character without admiration! In houses where petticoat government was established she had a more difficult card to play; and she relied, of course, upon her intellectual resources and diplomatic abilities altogether.

Mrs. Falcon had been, in her maiden estate, a Miss Georgina Hawke, the daughter of a dissipated clergyman, and the niece of a profligate peer, who had passed from the House of Lords into the bankrupts' calendar in consequence of his patrician propensity to deal in horse-flesh. Lively and handsome, indifferently educated, and loosely principled (having lost her mother at a very early age), the brown Georgina passed the first twenty years of her life wandering up and down the British dominions, in a sort of aristocratic vagrancy, transmitted from house to house, forwarded from uncle to aunt, tossed from one cousin to another, generally received with welcome, because, beside being a relative, she was pretty and entertaining, but as commonly parted with (when she was not unceremoniously packed off) with equal or greater alacrity, in consequence of an amiable, and, in her case, a pardonable tendency to overtax the hospitalities of her friends and relations. Under these unfavourable circumstances, leading this vagabond life, the deficiences she laboured under in the refinements and accomplishments of ladies of her social rank were anything but surprising. A tomboy at twelve, she was an Amazon at twenty; and those free, rollicking manners, which made her popular enough with country gentlemen, rendered her proportionably formidable to her own sex, particularly to mothers who had daughters to bring up and out, of an age to be influenced by bad example. However, she managed to pick up as she jogged along a scrap of an accomplishment here, and a sprig of useful knowledge there. She could never remember where she got her music; and Heaven only knew where she acquired the little French she possessed, and of which she was apt to make an adventurous and amusing display. But she was accused of picking up other things, as well as information, on her rambles; and in truth she was from the outset a little predatory, as well as migratory, in her habits; that is to say, she did not participate in all the respect that judges and lawyers express for the rights of property; or perhaps she inclined to the primitive Christian system of community of goods. Her moral delinquencies, however, were generally taken in good part; her relatives and connections were as often entertained as annoyed by her petty larcenies; and sometimes they even laughed heartily as they screamed, "*À la voleuse! À la voleuse!*" when the daughter of the parson and niece of the lord trooped off in their satin boots, or marched away in their Cashmere shawls. Considering that, amongst other houses, she had occasionally sojourned in those of dignitaries of the Church, and even in episcopal palaces, it was marvellous that Georgina Hawke's organ of conscientiousness had not been better developed, and very curious, too, that she should evince, as she always did, a particular fancy for matters of gold and silver. But never could she resist the temptations of loose *bijouterie;* and numerous were the occasions when vanished thimbles, missing pencil-cases, and rings or bracelets supposed to be in the crucible or in the moon, were accidentally discovered in the recesses of her reticule, or the *oubliette* of some still more roguish privy pocket.

Miss Hawke, in fact, was an Autolycus in petticoats, "littered under Mercury," a "snapper-up of unconsidered trifles;" for, having a shrewd gift of observation, she had remarked in her tenderest years the thousand "waifs and strays" (as lawyers phrase it) in the forms of combs, caps, aprons, chains, fans, feathers, veils, garters, flowers—the accumulations of bygone seasons, and the *débris* of fashions out of date—which strew and encumber the bed-rooms and boudoirs of her sex, as leaves do the brooks in autumn; and perhaps she observed, too, that the hands of the lady's-maid are unequal in every case to the clearing away of all this gay rubbish. At any rate she was a match for any lady's-maid in the land at this species of Augean labour; but even when she pounced upon articles of greater value, a diamond brooch or a braid of pearls, how often did she redeem the act of temporary felony (in the opinion of all but the party plundered) by the transfer to a very pretty neck of what was destined to deck a very plain one!

Upon the whole, it was a question whether our hawk, turned "*la pie voleuse*" (for her girlhood was so nicknamed), was more admired than feared. She certainly did produce more or less alarm wherever she showed her handsome brazen face; and ere she attained her seventeenth year there was a desire very generally felt and expressed to see her married and settled in the world.

At length she was thrown, by one of the changes and chances of a roving life, into a mercantile circle in some town in the north of England; and from that hour she may be said to have become the undisputed property of the middle classes. Then, for the first time, she found herself a personage, and discovered the importance in England of being allied even to nobility under a cloud. Could she have minced herself into twenty pieces there would not have been enough of the lord's niece for the excellent people into whose society she was now cast. Cotton and hardware fought for her: she was the desire of the potteries, the idol of the power-looms, and the goddess of those who dealt in crockery. Now an iron-master carried her off to Birmingham; now the stocking-weavers of Nottingham possessed her; she was the pride of Kidderminster, the mania of Manchester, and the love of Leeds. There came matrimonial offers in the course of things;—indigos proposed; teas paid their addresses; wine wooed, and cutlery courted her. It ended as such matters end frequently, in her intermarrying neither with china, cutlery, teas, wine, nor indigo. Suddenly—marvellously, mysteriously—she committed matrimony one foggy morning with a moss-trooping adventurer like herself. In short, never was there a more suitable union in point of character, or a more hazardous one in point of prudence, than that of Georgina Hawke to the ingenious Mr. Peregrine Falcon.

To the dismay of her patrician kindred she now reappeared at their houses in town, and their halls in the country, presenting them with her straggling, eccentric husband. His picture has been already drawn; it is only necessary to add here, that his nose was not uniformly pink, but changed colour with the seasons;—pink in spring, red in summer, purple in autumn, and in winter something between blue and crimson. The feature was the more important, because his nose was the only thing about Mr. Falcon that seemed to flourish. His person was a precise antithesis to his wife's: a shilling pamphlet on Poor Laws by Ridgway beside a thumping quarto Book of Beauty, by Heath.

Falcon, however, resembled his spouse in being equally self-educated. Whatever were his intellectual deficiences he did not owe them to the systems of Eton and Harrow. He was a living proof that a man may be shallow without being indebted to Cambridge or under the slightest obligation to Oxford. Busy rather than industrious; volatile rather than active; cleverish rather than clever;—he had been in fifty different offices in half that number of years; for all through life he was "the gentleman in search of a situation." He remembered the time when he had been a clerk at Somerset House; he had once superintended a copper-mine; he had managed a lunatic asylum; controlled the accounts of a national cow-pock institution, supervised port duties, been secretary to a horticultural association, and acted as deputy librarian to the British Museum; and he had now just resigned the place of inspector of works to a new railway company, which he had only filled for three weeks, with a view to obtain the appointment of secretary to the Irish Branch Society for the Conversion of Polish Jews. His employers had generally a high opinion of his talents for a month or so, but they usually got tired of him before the end of a second; and if they did not, he got weary of them before the expiration of a third; and thus the engagement very rarely lasted for half a year. The consequence, however, of this multifarious life was that he knew a little of everything knowable, and something of everybody in England. He passed, upon twenty subjects, for a very learned man amongst people who knew nothing at all about them; in mathematics he had crossed the ass's bridge, peeped into the angles of a parallelogram, and nibbled a little at square roots; he was geologist enough to talk of conglomerate, and to be up to *trap;* his botany qualified him to speak of the petals of a rose, the stamina of a tulip, and the nectary of a snap-dragon; he knew the alphabets of several languages, and had "a little Latin and less Greek," like his illustrious countryman William Shakspeare; so that, upon the whole, he was not one of the least accomplished smatterers of the smattering age we live in.

In the course of his many-coloured life he had numerous opportunities of conferring little official favours and obligations on a variety of people, and he had used these opportunities with tolerable dexterity and effect (if not always with the strictest regard to probity), so as to make a considerable number of friends, not in the sentimental sense of the word, but in its most practical, economical, and fiscal signification.

Such was the pair which had now roamed the world, without certain income or fixed residence, with various fortunes and few misfortunes, not always hand in hand, but still conjugally united, for nearly twenty years; living none knew how, yet living tolerably well; dwelling none knew where, yet never very badly housed; eating, drinking, and sleeping better than nine-tenths of her majesty's subjects, yet seldom paying a butcher's bill, very rarely a wine-merchant's, and never a landlord or a tax-collector. Meanwhile, they had scrupulously obeyed the first rule of Nature's arithmetic—the law of multiplication. Besides the two daughters and the son already mentioned, they had another girl named Paulina, and an elder boy, Pickever Falcon, who was heir to the family estates in Airshire, and the patrimonial castle in the isle of Sky.

THOMAS FRANCIS MEAGHER.

Born 1823 — Died 1867.

[Meagher was the orator of the Young Ireland party; and his speeches—fiery, brilliant, and highly finished—contributed as much as the writings of the *Nation* to stir the people to insurrection.

Thomas Francis Meagher was born on August 3, 1823, in Waterford, which his father had represented for some time. He left the colleges of Clongowes-Wood and Stonyhurst, where he had been educated, with a brilliant reputation. When he returned to Ireland in 1843, after a tour on the Continent, he found the country in the full fever of the repeal agitation; and he ultimately gave to the movement the benefit of his eloquent tongue. As time went on he joined the more fiery spirits of the Young Ireland party. He was one of the deputation to Paris in 1848 to congratulate France on the establishment of the Republic; and on his return he presented with a glowing speech an Irish tricolor flag to the citizens of Dublin. In May of the same year he was arrested for seditious language; but the jury being unable to agree, he was discharged. Soon after, when the passage of the treason felony act drove the Young Ireland leaders into open insurrection, Meagher was among those who took the field. He was arrested, tried, and sentenced to death. We quote his speech on this occasion. The sentence was afterwards commuted to transportation, and he was sent to Tasmania with O'Brien and Macmanus.

In 1852 he made his escape and landed in America, where he was enthusiastically received. For a time he became public lecturer; in 1855 he was admitted to the bar. The outbreak of the American civil war opened up to Meagher another career. From the beginning he was an enthusiastic supporter of the cause of the North. First he raised a body of Zouaves, who were incorporated in the famous 69th New York Regiment under the command of Colonel Corcoran. He was present and distinguished himself at the battle of Bull's Run, where his horse was shot under him. Afterwards he raised the famous Irish Brigade, of which he was elected first general. The services which this gallant force rendered to the arms of the Union are well known, and have been admitted by all the historians of the civil war. The brigade especially distinguished itself in the seven days' fighting around Richmond; and its conduct at Antietam was made the subject of flattering notice in an order of the day by General M'Clellan. The terrible battle of Fredericksburg gave the general and his troops an opportunity of still further adding to their laurels. Seven times they charged up to the crest of the enemy's breastworks; and the best proof of their desperate courage was that out of 1200 men whom the general led into battle, only 280 appeared next day on parade. In this engagement Meagher himself was wounded in the leg, and for a while had to retire from active service. In the May following, however, he was able once more to lead his forces; and at Chancellorsville the destruction of the broken brigade was completed. Meagher now came to the conclusion that it was no longer desirable to drag the phantom regiment into action, and resigned. Criticism was freely passed on Meagher's skill as a general, but there was complete agreement of opinion that he had proved himself a gallant soldier, of a courage at once cool and reckless. After he had resigned his command he was appointed by President Lincoln brigadier-general of volunteers, and also had charge of the district of Etowah, where he had under his orders a force of 12,000 infantry, 200 guns, and also some cavalry.

At the conclusion of the war he was made acting governor of the territory of Montana. He had a tragic end. While travelling in a steamer on the Mississippi, he fell overboard, and was drowned. His body was never recovered. At the time of his death, July 1,

1867, he was but forty-three years of age. He published a volume of his speeches and some essays under the title *Recollections of Ireland and the Irish*. The latter display a keen sense of humour, and some powers of description; but his work as a writer was far inferior to his achievements as an orator. He was at his best when he was the youthful mouthpiece of the passions and dreams of the "Young Irelanders;" his speeches in America, though brilliant, were not unfairly, though somewhat contemptuously, characterized by his friend and admirer John Mitchel as "rhetorical exercitations."]

SPEECH FROM THE DOCK.

My Lords,—It is my intention to say only a few words. I desire that the last act of a proceeding which has occupied so much of the public time, shall be of short duration. Nor have I the indelicate wish to close the dreary ceremony of a state prosecution with a vain display of words. Did I fear that hereafter, when I shall be no more, the country which I have tried to serve would think ill of me, I might, indeed, avail myself of this solemn moment to vindicate my sentiments and my conduct. But I have no such fear. The country will judge of those sentiments and that conduct in a light far different from that in which the jury by which I have been convicted have viewed them; and by the country, the sentence which you, my lords, are about to pronounce, will be remembered only as the severe and solemn attestation of my rectitude and truth. Whatever be the language in which that sentence be spoken, I know that my fate will meet with sympathy, and that my memory will be honoured. In speaking thus accuse me not, my lords, of an indecorous presumption. To the efforts I have made in a just and noble cause, I ascribe no vain importance, nor do I claim for those efforts any high reward. But it so happens, and it will ever happen, that they who have tried to serve their country—no matter how weak their efforts may have been—are sure to receive the thanks and blessings of its people.

With my country, then, I leave my memory —my sentiments—my acts,—proudly feeling that they require no vindication from me this day. A jury of my countrymen, it is true, have found me guilty of the crime of which I stood indicted. For this I feel not the slightest feeling of resentment towards them. Influenced as they must have been by the charge of the lord chief-justice, they could have found no other verdict. What of that charge? Any strong observations on it I feel sincerely would ill befit the solemnity of the scene; but I earnestly beseech of you, my lord—you who preside on that bench—when the passion and the prejudices of this hour have passed away, to appeal to your own conscience, and ask of it, Was your charge as it ought to have been, impartial and indifferent between the subject and the crown?

My lords, you may deem this language unbecoming in me, and perhaps it might seal my fate. But I am here to speak the truth, whatever it may cost. I am here to regret nothing I have ever done, to retract nothing I have ever said. I am here to crave with no lying lips the life I consecrate to the liberty of my country. Far from it. Even here—here, where the thief, the libertine, the murderer, have left their foot-prints in the dust—here, on this spot, where the shadows of death surround me, and from which I see my early grave, in an unanointed soil open to receive me—even here, encircled by these terrors, that hope which first beckoned me to the perilous sea upon which I have been wrecked, still consoles, animates, and enraptures me. No, I do not despair of my old country— her peace, her glory, her liberty! For that country I can do no more than bid her hope. To lift this island up, to make her a benefactor to humanity, instead of being the meanest beggar in the world—to restore her to her native power and her ancient constitution—this has been my ambition, and my ambition has been my crime. Judged by the law of England, I know this crime entails the penalty of death; but the history of Ireland explains this crime and justifies it. Judged by that history I am no criminal, you (addressing Mr. Macmanus) are no criminal, you (addressing Mr. O'Donoghue) are no criminal. Judged by that history, the treason of which I stand convicted loses all its guilt, is sanctified as a duty, and will be ennobled as a sacrifice!

With these sentiments, my lords, I await the sentence of the court. Having done what I felt to be my duty, having spoken what I felt to be the truth, as I have done on every other occasion of my short career, I now bid farewell to the country of my birth, my passion, and my death,—a country whose misfortunes have invoked my sympathies—whose factions I sought to quell—whose intelligence I prompted to a lofty aim—whose freedom has been my fatal dream. To that country I now offer as a pledge of the love I bore her, and of the sincerity with which I thought and spoke and struggled for her freedom, the life of a young heart; and with that life, the hopes, the honours, the endearments of a happy, a prosperous, and honourable home. Pronounce then, my lords, the sentence which the law directs. I trust I shall be prepared to meet its execution. I shall go, I think, with a pure heart and perfect composure to appear before a higher tribunal—a tribunal where a Judge of infinite goodness, as well as of justice, will preside, and where, my lords, many many of the judgments of this world will be reversed.

NASH AND THE DRAGOONS.

(FROM "RECOLLECTIONS.")

The day after I had arrived at Waterford from Stonyhurst, the trades of the city held a public meeting to petition Parliament for the repeal of the union. The meeting took place at the town-hall. There was a dense crowd. The enthusiasm was vehement—the rhetoric still more so. The speakers rose with the occasion, and from the loftiest clouds flung hail and lightning on the listeners. Two of these soared far above the rest. Strikingly different in their "physique" and speech, the one impersonated the Iron age, the other the age of Gold. The one was an alderman and draper. The other was a schoolmaster, and earned his bread by dispensing the fruit of knowledge. James Delahunty was the alderman's name. James Nash was the schoolmaster's name.

The schoolmaster was full of humour, full of poetry, full of gentleness and goodness; he was a patriot from the heart and an orator by nature. Uncultivated, luxuriant, wild, his imagination produced in profusion the strangest metaphors, running riot in tropes, allegories, analogies, and visions. Of ancient history and books of ancient fable he had read much, but digested little. He was a Sheil in the rough. Less pretentious than Phillips, he was equally fruitful in imagery and diction, and more condensed in expression. His appearance was in keeping with the irregularity and strangeness of his rhetoric. That he had a blind eye, was a circumstance which, at first sight, forcibly struck one. The other was crooked, but evidently gifted with a wonderful ubiquity of vision. It was everywhere. In a crowd it took in every visible point; and, though revolving on an eccentric axis, impartially diffused its radiance all round. He had a comical face. Every conceivable emotion and mood was blended there in an amusing enigma, the exact meaning of which it was most difficult, if not impossible, to solve. Addressing an audience, his attitude excited the highest merriment, whilst his sound sentiments and capital hits called forth the loudest cheers. His usual attire was an old claret-coloured coat, buttoned to the neck. What his trousers consisted of, or looked like, I nearly forget; but it would be no great mistake to say they were of drab cloth, hung very voluminously about the ankles, and were deeply stained. The hat—as comical an affair as the face—was cocked on one side of his head, and suggested a devil-may-care defiance of the world.

"Mr. Mayor and fellow-citizens"—it was thus he addressed the meeting the morning I returned to Waterford—"I came to attend this meeting, driving Irish *tandem*—that is, one foot before the other." With exuberant adjectives, he then went on to compliment the distinguished people who were present at the meeting. The Right Worshipful the Mayor of the city was in the chair. The Right Rev. Dr. Foran, the Catholic bishop, was on the platform. "Patriotism," exclaimed Nash, "flashes from the mitre of the one, and burns in the civic bosom of the other." Then he proceeded, in an amazing medley of facts, and metaphors, and figures of arithmetic, to enumerate the evils which the legislative union had produced. "What has been the upshot of it all?" he asked. "Why, it comes to this, they haven't left us a pewter spoon to run a railroad with through a plate of stirabout." The threats of coercion uttered by the government next claimed his notice. He despised them; repelled them; haughtily flung them back. He defied the government; he defied them to come on. "Let them come on," he exclaimed, "let them come on; let them draw the sword; and then woe to the conquered! Every potato field shall be a Marathon, and every boreen a Thermopylæ."

I have often thought of delivering a lecture on Nash. Of a class now almost extinct in Ireland—the Irish schoolmasters—he was the finest specimen I ever saw. Had Carleton seen him he would have immortalized him in type. As it is, he is dead, buried in some potter's field. Like all the poor, honest, gifted men—the rude, bright chivalry of the towns and fields—who thought infinitely more of their country than of themselves—he died in utter poverty, companionless and nameless. Yet, should anyone give me a file of the *Waterford Chronicle* from 1826 to 1847, there would be in my possession the materials of an epic, of which poor Nash, with his headlong honesty and reckless genius, should be the hero. He was a conspicuous figure in the political action of Waterford for more than twenty years. During the days of the Catholic Rent he was conspicuous. In Stuart's election, which broke down the prestige and power of the Beresfords, he was conspicuous. In the elections of 1830 and 1832 he was equally so. In 1843 he emerged from his classic seclusion—for a season gave over flogging his boys and making them Spartans—and appeared once more as a Demosthenes on the hill of Ballybricken, the Acropolis of Waterford.

The last time I saw Nash was the day of my father's election as representative of Waterford, in the month of July, 1847. It was about five o'clock in the evening. The polling was nearly at a close. Sir Henry Winston Barron and Mr. Wyse were sadly beaten. The excitement of the people was intense. For years they had longed for this victory; and at last, in a fuller measure and with a more precipitous speed than they expected, it had come. They hated these gentlemen, for these gentlemen were aristocrats in social life and imperialists in politics. They were not of the people, nor among them, nor for them. Both would lord it over them—the one from vulgar affection; the other instigated by the haughtiness of superior intellect. For a long time they had kept their seats, not with the assent of the people, but favoured by circumstances and a temporizing policy, dictated by the leaders of the people. Circumstances were changed—radically changed—and the temporizing policy, before the breath of the national spirit, was impetuously swept away. Hence the defeat of these Whigs—both of them respectable men, and one of them an eminent scholar—who had so long misrepresented in the supreme political convention of the empire the heart and mind of the chief city of the Suir.

A huge crowd was before the town-hall. The Mall was impassable. The windows on both sides of the thoroughfare were filled with eager and excited gazers. The doorsteps, the lamp-posts, the leads and skylights of every house within sight or hearing of the town-hall, were densely thronged. A troop of dragoon guards, coming down Beresford Street in double file, pushed their way through the enormous crowd, and suddenly facing about, formed line in front of the town-hall, in the centre of the Mall, thereby cutting the crowd in two. At this moment Nash made his appearance in one of the front windows of the town-hall immediately facing and looking down on the dragoons. His queer eye played through the multitude for a moment. Then giving his hat, as was usual with him on all such occasions, a jerk to one side, he turned up the cuffs of his coat, unbuttoned his shirt sleeves, took a bite of an orange, and commenced his harangue.

"Men of Waterford! the day is ours. Barron is beaten. Wyse is beaten. The boys are with us. The girls are with us. The soldiers are with us—aren't ye, boys?"

There was a tremendous cheer at this. Many of the dragoons seemed pleased. Their captain, however, became highly incensed. Banners, and green boughs, and scarfs, and handkerchiefs, and hats, and bonnets were flung out and shaken to and fro, up and down, in tumultuous delight. The horses of the dragoons became restless. They champed their bits impatiently, flinging flakes of froth here and there upon the crowd. They pranced a little, and shied a little, and backed a little. The cheering still went on. In the midst of all, at that window in the town-hall, with his crooked eye in full play, and his hat still on one side, stood Nash, with the most comical complacency, waiting for the excitement to subside. It did subside a little, and he went on to say that he loved a soldier's life, and would be a dragoon before long. The only objection he had to the service was the red jacket. Why shouldn't it be green?

"Why shouldn't it, boys?" he exclaimed, addressing himself to the dragoons, "why shouldn't it be green—our own immortal green?"

There was another tremendous cheer when this was asked, and the dragoons gave way to the good-nature and enthusiasm of the crowd. They laughed out aloud, and some of them cheered, and not a few of them waved their swords.

"Do you see that?" cried Nash, and he dashed his hat about, and tore his coat wide open, and hurrahed with all his might. But the captain, a handsome young snob, with sleepy eyelashes and the daintiest moustaches, looking down the line, gave his men the order to move off, which they did amidst the loudest cheers—poor Nash all the time twisting his eye, and shouting as before with all his might. That was the last time I saw him.

His object was to remove the dragoons; and the speediest way to do so was to appeal to their patriotism. He thought so, and his calculations were right. The dragoons were ordered off, and Nash and his audience had it all to themselves. The day was their own.

SIR SAMUEL FERGUSON.

[Sir Samuel Ferguson belongs to a class of literary Irishmen not too common in the history of the present century. Irish writers have as a rule belonged to either of two kinds; they have been active political workers on the national side, their literary efforts being the complement of their public struggles, or, abandoning national sympathies altogether, they have neglected Irish subjects entirely, or have written of them only to deride. The place of Sir Samuel Ferguson is in neither of these two divisions. Holding aloof from political organizations, he has nevertheless maintained the full ardour of Irish feeling; and all his writings tend in some form or other to advance the cause of Irish literature.

He was born in Belfast in 1810, and having passed his first years of education at the well-known academical institution there, entered Trinity College. In 1838 he was called to the bar; in 1859 he became a queen's counsel, and in 1867 he finally retired from his profession. He had been appointed in the latter year to a position which eminently suited him, and for which he was most fitted. He has been throughout his life an ardent student of Celtic archæology; and it was therefore singularly appropriate that he should have, as deputy-keeper of the records, the duty of exploring the muniments of ancient Irish history, and arranging the results. Let us finish our record of his professional career by saying that he received some recognition of his labours in 1878 by having the honour of knighthood conferred upon him.

Ferguson's literary life began when he was almost a boy; and his first attempt was a triumph. The "Forging of the Anchor," which he offered to *Blackwood*, was not only received, but was honoured with a special and highly eulogistic notice from the mighty editor "Christopher North." The verdict of Wilson has been affirmed by the public; for the ballad remains to the present day one of the most widely popular among contemporary verses. The poem established Ferguson as a contributor to the great northern magazine; and for some years he was one of its most welcome writers. The best known of his articles is "Father Tom and the Pope," a sketch of quaint and often brilliant humour, which immediately attracted, and has permanently retained great popularity, and which was for years supposed to be from the bright pen of Dr. Maginn. The *Dublin University* next offered a market nearer home; and from the first Ferguson contributed largely. In its pages will be found compositions of various kinds: poems original and translated, tales and reviews. In the "Hibernian Nights' Entertainments" he dealt some well-deserved blows at the caricatures of Irish character which used to pass, and to some extent still do duty, for portraits of Irish life. Those sketches have been republished in a volume. Sir Samuel has also written a remarkable epic, *Congal*, and an excellent volume of translations from the Irish entitled *Lays of the Western Gael*.]

THE FORGING OF THE ANCHOR.[1]

Come, see the *Dolphin's* anchor forged: 'tis at a white heat now:
The bellows ceased, the flames decreased; tho' on the forge's brow
The little flames still fitfully play thro' the sable mound;
And fitfully you still may see the grim smiths ranking round,
All clad in leathern panoply, their broad hands only bare;
Some rest upon their sledges here, some work the windlass there.

The windlass strains the tackle chains, the black mound heaves below;

---

[1] This and the following extracts are by permission of the author.

And red and deep, a hundred veins burst out at every throe:
It rises, roars, rends all outright—O, Vulcan, what a glow!
'Tis blinding white, 'tis blasting bright; the high sun shines not so!
The high sun sees not, on the earth, such fiery fearful show;
The roof-ribs swarth, the candent hearth, the ruddy lurid row
Of smiths that stand, an ardent band, like men before the foe;
As, quivering thro' his fleece of flame, the sailing monster, slow
Sinks on the anvil—all about, the faces fiery grow—
"Hurrah!" they shout, "leap out—leap out;" bang, bang, the sledges go:
Hurrah! the jetted lightnings are hissing high and low;
A hailing fount of fire is struck at every squashing blow;
The leathern mail rebounds the hail; the rattling cinders strow
The ground around; at every bound the sweltering fountains flow,
And thick and loud the swinking crowd at every stroke pant "ho!"

Leap out, leap out, my masters; leap out and lay on load!
Let's forge a goodly anchor—a bower thick and broad;
For a heart of oak is hanging on every blow, I bode;
And I see the good ship riding, all in a perilous road—
The low reef roaring on her lee—the roll of ocean pour'd
From stem to stern, sea after sea; the mainmast by the board;
The bulwarks down, the rudder gone, the boats stove at the chains!
But courage still, brave mariners—the Bower yet remains,
And not an inch to flinch he deigns, save when ye pitch sky high,
Then moves his head, as tho' he said, "Fear nothing—here am I!"

Swing in your strokes in order, let foot and hand keep time;
Your blows make music sweeter far than any steeple's chime;
But, while ye sling your sledges, sing—and let the burden be,
The anchor is the anvil king, and royal craftsmen we!

Strike in, strike in—the sparks begin to dull their rustling red;
Our hammers ring with sharper din, our work will soon be sped;
Our anchor soon must change its bed of fiery rich array,
For a hammock at the roaring bows, or an oozy couch of clay;
Our anchor soon must change the lay of merry craftsmen here,
For the yeo-heave-o', and the heave-away, and the sighing seaman's cheer;
When, weighing slow, at eve they go—far, far from love and home;
And sobbing sweethearts, in a row, wail o'er the ocean foam.

In livid and obdurate gloom he darkens down at last;
A shapely one he is, and strong, as e'er from cat was cast.—
O trusted and trustworthy guard, if thou hadst life like me,
What pleasures would thy toils reward beneath the deep green sea!
O deep-sea Diver, who might then behold such sights as thou?
The hoary-monster's palaces! methinks what joy 'twere now
To go plumb plunging down amid the assembly of the whales,
And feel the churn'd sea round me boil beneath their scourging tails!
Then deep in tangle-woods to fight the fierce sea unicorn,
And send him foiled and bellowing back, for all his ivory horn;
To leave the subtle sworder-fish of bony blade forlorn;
And for the ghastly-grinning shark to laugh his jaws to scorn:—
To leap down on the kraken's back, where 'mid Norwegian isles
He lies, a lubber anchorage for sudden shallow'd miles,
Till, snorting, like an under-sea volcano, off he rolls;
Meanwhile to swing, a-buffeting the far astonished shoals
Of his back-browsing ocean-calves; or, haply in a cove,
Shell-strown, and consecrate of old to some Undine's love,
To find the long-hair'd mermaidens; or, hard-by icy lands,
To wrestle with the sea-serpent, upon cerulean sands.

O broad-armed Fisher of the deep, whose sports can equal thine?
The *Dolphin* weighs a thousand tons, that tugs thy cable line;
And night by night 'tis thy delight, thy glory day by day,

Through sable sea and breaker white, the giant
  game to play—
But shamer of our little sports! forgive the name
  I gave—
A fisher's joy is to destroy—thine office is to save.

O lodger in the sea-kings' halls, couldst thou but
  understand
Whose be the white bones by thy side, or who that
  dripping band,
Slow swaying in the heaving wave, that round
  about thee bend,
With sounds like breakers in a dream blessing
  their ancient friend—
Oh, couldst thou know what heroes glide with
  larger steps round thee,
Thine iron side would swell with pride; thou'dst
  leap within the sea!

Give honour to their memories who left the pleasant strand,
To shed their blood so freely for the love of Fatherland—
Who left their chance of quiet age and grassy
  church-yard grave,
So freely, for a restless bed amid the tossing wave—
Oh, though our anchor may not be all I have fondly
  sung,
Honour him for their memory, whose bones he
  goes among!

UNA PHELIMY.

AN ULSTER BALLAD, 1641.

"Awaken, Una Phelimy,
  How canst thou slumber so?
How canst thou dream so quietly
  Through such a night of woe?
Through such a night of woe," he said,
  "How canst thou dreaming lie,
When the kindred of thy love lie dead,
  And he must fall or fly?"

She rose and to the casement came;
  "Oh, William dear, speak low;
For I should bear my brother's blame
  Did Hugh or Angus know."
"Did Hugh or Angus know, Una?
  Ah, little dreamest thou
On what a bloody errand bent
  Are Hugh and Angus now."

"Oh, what has chanced my brothers dear?
  My William, tell me true!
Our God forbode that what I fear
  Be that they're gone to do!"
"They're gone on bloody work, Una,
  The worst we feared is done;

They've taken to the knife at last,
  The massacre's begun!

"They came upon us while we slept
  Fast by the sedgy Bann;
In darkness to our beds they crept,
  And left me not a man!
Bann rolls my comrades even now
  Through all his pools and fords;
And their hearts' best blood is warm, Una,
  Upon thy brothers' swords!

"And mine had borne them company,
  Or the good blade I wore,
Which ne'er left foe in victory
  Or friend in need before,
In theirs as in their fellows' hearts
  Also had dimmed its shine,
But for these tangling curls, Una,
  And witching eyes of thine!

"I've borne the brand of flight for these,
  For these, the scornful cries
Of loud insulting enemies;
  But busk thee, love, and rise;
For Ireland's now no place for us;
  'Tis time to take our flight,
When neighbour steals on neighbour thus,
  And stabbers strike by night.

"And black and bloody the revenge
  For this dark midnight's sake,
The kindred of my murdered friends
  On thine and thee will take,
Unless thou rise and fly betimes,
  Unless thou fly with me,
Sweet Una, from this land of crimes
  To peace beyond the sea.

"For trustful pillows wait us there,
  And loyal friends beside,
Where the broad lands of my father are,
  Upon the banks of Clyde;
In five days hence a ship will be
  Bound for that happy home;
Till then we'll make our sanctuary
  In sea-cave's sparry dome:
Then busk thee, Una Phelimy,
  And o'er the waters come!"

. . . .

The midnight moon is wading deep;
  The land sends off the gale;
The boat beneath the sheltering steep
  Hangs on a seaward sail;
And, leaning o'er the weather-rail,
  The lovers, hand in hand,
Take their last look of Innisfail;
  "Farewell, doomed Ireland!"

"And art thou doomed to discord still?
  And shall thy sons ne'er cease

To search and struggle for thine ill,
  Ne'er share thy good in peace?
Already do thy mountains feel
  Avenging Heaven's ire?
Hark—hark—this is no thunder peal,
  That was no lightning fire!"

It was no fire from heaven he saw,
  For, far from hill and dell,
O'er Gobbin's brow the mountain flaw
  Bears musquet-shot and yell,
And shouts of brutal glee, that tell
  A foul and fearful tale,
While over blast and breaker swell
  Thin shrieks and woman's wail.

Now fill they far the upper sky,
  Now down mid air they go,
The frantic scream, the piteous cry,
  The groan of rage and woe;
And wilder in their agony
  And shriller still they grow—
Now cease they, choking suddenly,
  The waves boom on below.

"A bloody and a black revenge!
  Oh, Una, blest are we
Who this sore-troubled land can change
  For peace beyond the sea;
But for the manly hearts and true
  That Antrim still retain,
Or be their banner green or blue,
  For all that there remain,
God grant them quiet freedom too,
  And blithe homes soon again!"

THE FAIRY THORN.

AN ULSTER BALLAD.

"Get up, our Anna dear, from the weary spinning wheel;
  For your father's on the hill and your mother is asleep:
Come up above the crags, and we'll dance a highland reel
  Around the Fairy Thorn on the steep."

At Anna Grace's door 'twas thus the maidens cried,
  Three merry maidens fair in kirtles of the green;
And Anna laid the rock and the weary wheel aside,
  The fairest of the four, I ween.

They're glancing through the glimmer of the quiet eve,
  Away in milky wavings of neck and ankle bare;
The heavy-sliding stream in its sleepy song they leave,
  And the crags in the ghostly air:

And linking hand in hand, and singing as they go,
  The maids along the hill-side have ta'en their fearless way,
Till they come to where the rowan-trees in lonely beauty grow
  Beside the Fairy Hawthorn gray.

The Hawthorn stands between the ashes tall and slim,
  Like matron with her twin grand-daughters at her knee;
The rowan berries cluster o'er her low head gray and dim
  In ruddy kisses sweet to see.

The merry maidens four have ranged them in a row,
  Between each lovely couple a stately rowan stem,
And away in mazes wavy, like skimming birds they go,
  Oh, never carolled bird like them!

But solemn is the silence of the silvery haze
  That drinks away their voices in echoless repose,
And dreamily the evening has stilled the haunted braes,
  And dreamier the gloaming grows.

And sinking one by one, like lark-notes from the sky,
  When the falcon's shadow saileth across the open shaw,
Are hushed the maiden's voices, as cowering down they lie
  In the flutter of their sudden awe.

For, from the air above, and the grassy ground beneath,
  And from the mountain-ashes and the old White-thorn between,
A power of faint enchantment doth through their beings breathe,
  And they sink down together on the green.

They sink together silent, and stealing side to side,
  They fling their lovely arms o'er their drooping necks so fair,
Then vainly strive again their naked arms to hide,
  For their shrinking necks again are bare.

Thus clasped and prostrate all, with their heads together bowed,
  Soft o'er their bosoms beating—the only human sound—
They hear the silky footsteps of the silent fairy crowd,
  Like a river in the air, gliding round.

Nor scream can any raise, nor prayer can any say,
  But wild, wild the terror of the speechless three—
For they feel fair Anna Grace drawn silently away,
  By whom they dare not look to see.

They feel their tresses twine with her parting locks
    of gold,
  And the curls elastic falling, as her head with-
    draws;
They feel her sliding arms from their tranced arms
    unfold,
  But they dare not look to see the cause:

For heavy on their senses the faint enchantment
    lies
  Through all that night of anguish and perilous
    amaze;
And neither fear nor wonder can ope their quiver-
    ing eyes
  Or their limbs from the cold ground raise.

Till out of Night the Earth has rolled her dewy side,
  With every haunted mountain and streamy vale
    below;
When, as the mist dissolves in the yellow morning
    tide,
  The maidens' trance dissolveth so.

Then fly the ghastly three as swiftly as they may,
  And tell their tale of sorrow to anxious friends
    in vain—
They pined away and died within the year and day,
  And ne'er was Anna Grace seen again.

WILLY GILLILAND.

AN ULSTER BALLAD.

Up in the mountain solitudes, and in a rebel ring,
He has worshipped God upon the hill, in spite of
    church and king;
And sealed his treason with his blood on Bothwell
    Bridge he hath;
So he must fly his father's land, or he must die the
    death;
For comely Claverhouse has come along with grim
    Dalzell,
And his smoking rooftree testifies they've done
    their errand well.

In vain to fly his enemies he fled his native land;
Hot persecution waited him upon the Carrick
    strand;
His name was on the Carrick cross, a price was on
    his head,
A fortune to the man that brings him in, alive or
    dead!
And so on moor and mountain, from the Laggan to
    the Bann,
From house to house, and hill to hill, he lurked
    an outlawed man.

At last, when in false company he might no longer
    bide,

He staid his houseless wanderings upon the Collon
    side,
There in a cave all under ground he laired his
    heathy den,
Ah, many a gentleman was fain to earth like hill-
    fox then.
With hound and fishing-rod he lived on hill and
    stream by day,
At night, betwixt his fleet greyhound and his
    bonny mare he lay.

It was a summer evening, and, mellowing and still,
Glenwhirry to the setting sun lay bare from hill to
    hill;
For all that valley pastoral held neither house nor
    tree,
But spread abroad and open all, a full fair sight
    to see,
From Slemish foot to Collon top lay one unbroken
    green;
Save where in many a silver coil the river glanced
    between.

And on the river's grassy bank, even from the
    morning gray,
He at the angler's pleasant sport had spent the
    summer day:
Ah! many a time and oft I've spent the summer
    day from dawn,
And wondered, when the sunset came, where time
    and care had gone,
Along the reaches curling fresh, the wimpling
    pools and streams,
Where he that day his cares forgot in these delight-
    ful dreams.

His blythe work done, upon a bank the outlaw
    rested now,
And laid the basket from his back, the bonnet from
    his brow,
And there, his hand upon the Book, his knee upon
    the sod,
He filled the lonely valley with the gladsome word
    of God;
And for a persecuted kirk, and for her martyrs dear,
And against a godless church and king, he spoke
    up loud and clear.

And now, upon his homeward way he crossed the
    Collon high,
And over bush and bank and brae he sent abroad
    his eye,
But all was darkening peacefully in gray and
    purple haze,
The thrush was silent in the banks, the lark upon
    the braes—
When suddenly shot up a blaze—from the cave's
    mouth it came;
And troopers' steeds and troopers' caps are glancing
    in the same!

He couched among the heather, and he saw them,
    as he lay,
With three long yells at parting, ride lightly east
    away;
Then down with heavy heart he came, to sorry
    cheer came he,
For ashes black were crackling where the green
    whins used to be,
And stretched among the prickly coomb, his heart's
    blood smoking round,
From slender nose to breast-bone cleft, lay dead
    his good greyhound!

"They've slain my dog, the Philistines! they've
    ta'en my bonny mare!"—
He plunged into the smoky hole; no bonny beast
    was there—
He groped beneath his burning bed, (it burned him
    to the bone,)
Where his good weapon used to be, but broadsword
    there was none;
He reeled out of the stifling den, and sat down on
    a stone,
And in the shadows of the night 'twas thus he made
    his moan—

"I am a houseless outcast; I have neither bed nor
    board,
Nor living thing to look upon, nor comfort save the
    Lord:
Yet was the good Elijah once in worse extremity;
Who succoured him in his distress, He now will
    succour me;
He now will succour me, I know; and, by His
    holy name,
I'll make the doers of this deed right dearly rue
    the same!

"My bonny mare! I've ridden you when Claver'se
    rode behind,
And from the thumbscrew and the boot you bore
    me like the wind;
And, while I have the life you saved, on your sleek
    flank, I swear,
Episcopalian rowel shall never ruffle hair!
Though sword to wield they've left me none—yet
    Wallace wight, I wis,
Good battle did on Irvine side wi' waur weapon
    than this."—

His fishing-rod with both his hands he griped it as
    he spoke,
And, where the butt and top were spliced, in pieces
    twain he broke;
The limber top he cast away, with all its gear abroad,
But, grasping the tough hickory butt, with spike
    of iron shod,
He ground the sharp spear to a point; then pulled
    his bonnet down,
And meditating black revenge, set forth for Carrick
    town.

The sun shines bright on Carrick wall and Carrick
    Castle gray,
And up thine aisle, Saint Nicholas, has ta'en his
    morning way;
And to the North-gate sentinel displayeth far and
    near
Sea, hill, and tower, and all thereon, in dewy fresh-
    ness clear,
Save where, behind a ruined wall, himself alone to
    view,
Is peering from the ivy green a bonnet of the blue.

The sun shines red on Carrick wall and Carrick
    Castle old,
And all the western buttresses have changed their
    gray for gold;
And from thy shrine, Saint Nicholas, the pilgrim
    of the sky
Hath gone in rich farewell, as fits such royal votary;
But, as his last red glance he takes down past black
    Slieve-a-true,
He leaveth where he found it first, the bonnet of
    the blue.

Again he makes the turrets gray stand out before
    the hill,
Constant as their foundation rock, there is the
    bonnet still!
And now the gates are opened, and forth in gallant
    show
Prick jeering grooms and burghers blythe, and
    troopers in a row;
But one has little care for jest, so hard bested is he
To ride the outlaw's bonny mare, for this at last
    is she!

Down comes her master with a roar, her rider with
    a groan,
The iron and the hickory are thro' and thro' him
    gone!
He lies a corpse; and where he sat the outlaw sits
    again,
And once more to his bonny mare he gives the
    spur and rein;
Then some with sword and some with gun, they
    ride and run amain;
But sword and gun, and whip and spur, that day
    they plied in vain!

Ah! little thought Willy Gilliland, when he on
    Skerry side
Drew bridle first, and wiped his brow after that
    weary ride,
That where he lay like hunted brute, a caverned
    outlaw lone,
Broad lands and yeomen tenantry should yet be
    there his own;
Yet so it was; and still from him descendants not
    a few
Draw birth and lands, and, let me trust, draw love
    of Freedom too.

PASTHEEN FION.[1]

(FROM THE IRISH.)

Oh, my fair Pastheen is my heart's delight;
Her gay heart laughs in her blue eye bright;
Like the apple blossom her bosom white,
And her neck like the swan's on a March morn bright!
   Then, Oro, come with me! come with me! come with me!
   Oro, come with me! brown girl, sweet!
   And, oh! I would go through snow and sleet
   If you would come with me, my brown girl, sweet!

Love of my heart, my fair Pastheen!
Her cheeks are as red as the rose's sheen,
But my lips have tasted no more, I ween,
Than the glass I drank to the health of my queen!
   Then, Oro, come with me! come with me! &c.

Were I in the town, where's mirth and glee,
Or 'twixt two barrels of barley bree,
With my fair Pastheen upon my knee,
'Tis I would drink to her pleasantly!
   Then, Oro, come with me! come with me! &c.

Nine nights I lay in longing and pain,
Betwixt two bushes, beneath the rain,
Thinking to see you, love, once again;
But whistle and call were all in vain!
   Then, Oro, come with me! come with me! &c.

I'll leave my people, both friend and foe;
From all the girls in the world I'll go;
But from you, sweetheart, oh, never! oh, no!
Till I lie in the coffin stretched, cold and low!
   Then, Oro, come with me! come with me! &c.

JAMES WHITESIDE.

Born 1806 — Died 1876.

[Chief-justice Whiteside has shared the fate of the majority of great orators. His contemporaries speak of him with enthusiasm: there are proofs that he exercised marvellous influence on his audiences; yet when you come to examine the specimens of his oratory left behind, you find their quality far out of proportion to the effect they produced. It is a trite observation that the physical qualities of the man contribute almost as much as the intellectual to the success of the orator; and so, when the man has passed away, the oration he leaves behind loses half its force. Let the speeches, however, of Whiteside read now as they will, there is convincing proof, not only in the recollections of those who heard him, but in the records of scenes in which he moved, that he was one of the greatest orators Ireland ever produced, or the English parliament ever heard.

James Whiteside was born on the 12th August, 1806, in Delgany, county Wicklow, and was the son of the Rev. Wm. Whiteside, the rector of the parish. His undergraduate career in Trinity College was distinguished: and he took his degree with honours. Perhaps, however, the success he attained in the Debating Society was dearer and ultimately more valuable to him. During his residence in London, while taking out his law terms, he was also fond of appearing in some of those arenas—not always, perhaps, too reputable—which the metropolis affords to those who desire to enter the oratorical lists. In 1830 he was called to the Irish bar; and before long had a large practice and a high reputation. In 1842 he was made a Q.C.; and from that time onwards there was scarcely a case of great importance at Nisi Prius in which he was not employed. He, however, received a higher honour than that of arguing in civil trials, however important; he was sought as counsel in the most momentous state prosecutions of our century; and particularly in that which, whether from the position of the defendant, or the magnitude of the issues, is perhaps the most remarkable in the history of our country. When O'Connell, Charles Gavan Duffy, and their colleagues, were put on trial in 1844, Whiteside was one of the counsel for their defence. This was an honour which might well weigh down even a great orator and lawyer; for not only had Whiteside to rise to the height of a sublime occasion, but to stand in rivalry with such orators of genius as Sheil and Isaac Butt. The accounts which we receive of the speech prove that he was equal to his trust. At the end of the first day of the speech there rose enthusiastic cheers from all parts of the court—from lawyers accustomed to control their feelings—from men and from women, from Catholic and Protestant; and his peroration is said to have

---

[1] "Fair youth" or "fair maiden."

THE RIGHT HON JAMES WHITESIDE
LORD CHIEF JUSTICE OF IRELAND

FROM A PHOTOGRAPH BY MAYALL LONDON

BLACKIE & SON LONDON GLASGOW & EDINBURGH

moved to tears even the judges, who assuredly were not easily impressed by appeals in favour of O'Connell and his friends. Again in 1848, he was the counsel at a great state trial, his client on this occasion being Smith O'Brien. Of course he could not save the prisoner, whose deeds had been proclaimed in the light of day; but he made a splendid speech, and his cross-examination of the informer Dobbyn is described as a most exciting scene. A few years after this he had an opportunity of displaying his eloquence in a more conspicuous place—in 1851 he was returned as member for Enniskillen. It is notorious that the most eloquent orator at the bar is frequently the most ineffective speaker in parliament. With Whiteside this was not the case, and before long he had established a position at St. Stephen's equal to that he had so long held in his own country and his own profession. Just as in the Four Courts, he used to draw the loungers from the hall, and even the busy from the surrounding courts, when he was addressing a jury, so in parliament the news that he was on his feet brought to the house a rush of members from the library, or dining-room, or lobby. He attained soon the position of being one of the chief spokesmen of the Conservative party, and on several most important occasions was considered an equal antagonist to such eminent Liberal orators as Gladstone or Bright. More than once, too, when a great question arose he was put forward as the mover of the Conservative resolution. During the debates on the Crimean war he had a vigorous encounter with Mr. Gladstone, in which he certainly proved himself fully equal to the occasion. Among his other more remarkable speeches may be mentioned that on the Kars debate in April 1856, on Italy in July 1859, on America in 1861, and on the Irish Church Bill in 1863, and several subsequent occasions.

When his party came into power, he was, of course, raised to office, becoming in 1852 solicitor-general, and in 1858 attorney-general for Ireland. During this period he was still actively engaged in his profession, and in 1861 he added another to his many forensic triumphs. He was one of the counsel for Miss Longworth in the famous Yelverton trial. It is not necessary to dilate here on the enormous excitement which that case everywhere produced, and nowhere to such an extent as in Ireland, where sympathy with the sex, the religion, and the wrongs of the lady evoked an extraordinary amount of popular enthusiasm in her favour. The interest with which the speech of Whiteside was looked forward to was intensified by the news that a near relative was ill, and that he would be unable to speak. This apprehension, however, proved to be incorrect. He appeared at the proper time, and made, perhaps the greatest, certainly the most exciting of all the speeches he had yet delivered. It is impossible to adequately describe the effect which it produced, and the peroration, which may still be read with delight, caused extraordinary emotion. Nor was the admiration with which it was regarded confined to those who heard him, for when Mr. Whiteside returned to take his place in the House of Commons, that critical and perhaps not very emotional assembly paid him the compliment of rising *en masse* in token of their respect.

In 1866, with the return of the Conservative party to office, Mr. Whiteside once more became attorney-general. He held this post for but a few weeks, the resignation of Mr. Lefroy leaving a vacancy in the lord chief-justiceship of the Queen's Bench. It was almost a necessity of his position, perhaps also of his years, that he should have accepted this office. But it added nothing to his fame, and perhaps little to his comfort. His mind was not of the judicial cast, and his legal learning was not supposed to be profound. He, therefore, could not hope to add to his fame as an orator that of a great judge. He seemed himself to be scarcely ever comfortable in his new position. The wild humour, with which he had been accustomed to set both the bar and the House of Commons in a roar, had to be replaced by an ill-assumed gravity, and might be said to degenerate in the end into mopishness. He dropped almost entirely out of public sight, a thing that must have been particularly galling to a man who had lived so conspicuously for the greater part of his life in the eye of the public. On the 25th November, 1876, he died at Brighton, whither he had gone for the good of his health.

In addition to his speeches he has left behind some literary productions, but none of these are equal to his great abilities. A tour for the benefit of his health produced *Italy in the Nineteenth Century*—a work sketchy, disconnected, commonplace; and only remarkable by raising controversies of doubtful utility. This, first published in 1848, passed through six editions. *Vicissitudes of the Eternal City*, published in 1849, consists almost entirely of translation from a sort of guide-book by Signor Canini, and is not of any particular importance. Of higher interest are his lectures, delivered on various occasions; two of them especially, entitled "Life and Death of the Irish Parliament." A volume of his essays and lectures, historical and literary, was published in 1869.]

THE YELVERTON CASE.

EXTRACT FROM THE SPEECH.

I wish I could bring you into the solitary chamber of Teresa Longworth, when he [Major Yelverton] impressed on her religious mind that he sympathized with her and her religion —when he stood beside her at the mass, when he argued with her upon the nature of the sacrament that contracting parties might confer upon themselves—when he went with her, at Warrenpoint and Rostrevor, to the service of the Church—when he seemed to understand as well as herself, when he prayed with her in the ritual of the Church after he gained her by the marriage at Rostrevor—and, above all, when he heard of his sister's letter, in which she asked him if it was true he had embraced the Roman Catholic religion, which was distinctly stated in his presence, and admitted by his own conduct. After all these facts you have the crowning act of his entering a Roman Catholic church to be married by a Roman Catholic priest, whose questions, even on his own evidence, he answered in a prevaricating way that he was a Roman Catholic, but, upon the evidence of the woman who stood beside him, and whose fate in life depended upon the validity of the marriage, he answered that he was a Catholic, and no Protestant. Combine these facts together—unite them all. I submit they are not contravened by the doubtful evidence given on the other side—of sergeants and corporals—who go to church only to go to sleep — of them who saw him in church once in three years, and that evidence, unaccompanied with the performance of any one solemn rite, such as the acceptance of the sacrament, which, in a sense, binds a man to his religion. Lastly, I submit that if you come to the conclusion that the day he knelt down before priest Mooney, and clasped the hand of the woman who knelt by his side, he then and there represented by his language, conduct, and demeanour that he was of the Roman Catholic religion, — law, reason, justice, morality, and that religion which has been degraded by the argument on the part of the defendant—all unite to induce you to find a verdict that will bind him by the marriage—a marriage good according to the argument of his own counsel, as good as if performed by the Archbishop of Canterbury, good in conscience, good in the sight of God, good in the face of the Church, good in the face of the world, if it were not for a penal statute of the time of George II., that in my opinion was never passed to meet such a case as this.

The great question in the case is whether you believe Teresa Longworth. In order to damage her character, to assail her virtue, in order to destroy her love for truth, they say that before she was wedded to this defendant she spoiled herself of the rich jewel of her virtue. How is that proved? Look at the reason of the thing. First look at the facts. He says he admired her, he says she was agreeable—he says, in this evidence of his, which I cannot stop to read—indignation, if I did, might prevent my proceeding—that, as he sat beholding her, young and beautiful, in the convent of Galeta, then it was he formed the design of making her his mistress. If that was his design—it was not her design that she should be so. He wishes still to be near her. He is found with her at Edinburgh and Rostrevor. I ask you, do you believe that if he had attained the grand object of his desires, if he had gained possession of her person, was master of the great secret of her life—do you believe he would have gone to that church and put himself into the predicament in which he stands to-day, by becoming her wedded husband? Do you believe that this man, who has been represented to you by his counsel as a skilful seducer—do you believe that this man, who planned her ruin, who pursued his object persistently for a long period of time, who travelled with her from Waterford to Rostrevor, and who has studied and learned the various degrees of the great crime of seduction, that he, if he had gained his object, would ever have married her in the church of Kilone? Impossible! To weaken the force of her testimony, he tells you of occurrences at Edinburgh, and in the Hull steamer, which you will not believe, which are contradicted by everything in the case, by all his own acts. He got the bill from Cummins's Hotel at Waterford, and would not produce it, nor allow us to give evidence about it. He went everywhere to get every bit and scrap of evidence upon which he could rely. He produces from the Rostrevor Hotel a bill dated the 15th, the fact being that he was married on the 15th, and did not leave the hotel till the 18th; and with all this inquiring and searching there is not a solitary fact established against her. But, says the defendant—" You artful woman, you temptress, you enchantress, why did you dare to send anybody round the different hotels to ascertain what could be proved against you?" Who is it puts that question? The defendant. And what is he detected in having done? He cut a lock of hair from the head of a child seven years old, that he thought was like the hair on the head of the woman he had deceived, and that he intended to marry, and not to marry, and that he wants now to unmarry. He gets a piece of a gown he says she wore, and he places before his witnesses what is not the hair of his wife, and a piece of a dress that may not have been the dress of that injured woman, and endeavours to fabricate evidence to destroy her character as he had destroyed her happiness; and when, by accident, we learned it,—for we knew it not, I aver, until the lady in the box told you the story of the lock of hair, which her counsel heard then for the first time,—we asked how it was discovered, the young woman, Miss Crabbe, was telegraphed for, and now that she has arrived, why are you not to believe her? Sergeant Armstrong talked of murder. What would be your feelings if you had been on the point of sending to the gallows a fellow-being upon the evidence of Bridget Cole and Rose Fagan that the woman who sat in the witness-box was the woman who called on them,—a statement falsified before your own eyes? Would you ever enjoy a happy hour?—would you ever fail to deplore the rash act you had done as jurors in being persuaded by rash evidence of identity to take away the life of your innocent fellow-creature? Honour and virtue are as dear to woman as life. Why should you rob her of her honour, all that is left her, upon the rotten testimony that has been concocted against her?

Why did we do what we did in this respect? Because we found what was being fabricated against us. That young woman told you the truth, the whole truth, and nothing but the truth, and she has demonstrated that what was sworn by Cole and the other woman is entirely and absolutely false. What, therefore, becomes of that portion of the case? It has vanished. It is gone. What is the remainder of this case on the correspondence? I pray attention to it. The correspondence read by my learned friend (Sergeant Sullivan), who, like a lawyer, commenced where he ought to commence, and gave it from the date of the marriage to the closing awful scene that took place at Leith, is all through, I say, the correspondence of married people. Love and anxiety on his part. On her part a statement of all the difficulties and embarrassments to which, as his wife, she was subjected in a distant country—letters addressed to her as his wife, letters from her to him as her husband—all things clear, intelligent, and distinct, until, at last, there is a letter—glided over by Sergeant Armstrong, which I call the Christmas-day letter, and if there is one of you who has a doubt that there was a secret lawful marriage, I beg of you to hear what Major Yelverton himself has written on the subject. "I have every reason," he says, "to believe that next June will see you through the scrape." No one denies that tallies with the date of the marriage. He writes:—"Carrissima mia—I fear it is not a reservation of *bon bons* that has caused my silence this time, but what you wrote in your last letter but one. You say I told you my resolution in case certain events did occur. You were very angry, but it would be my duty, and if I love I must do it. Your resolution is founded on false views. Where is your duty of keeping faith with me? I have never intentionally deceived you, and have done more than I promised at great risk." Was that a voyage up the Rhine, gentlemen? No. I call on you to believe that what he there refers to was the marriage ceremony in the church at Rostrevor. "I told you the event we fear could be avoided, and you certainly cannot doubt that it is equally unwelcome to me as it can be to you; but, if the future proves that I have been deceived by others, that will not absolve you from your faith, the which, if you break with me, you will never from that moment have even one of tolerable content during the rest of your life. If you do feel any love for me you must change that resolution. If I depart this life you may speak; or, if you do, you may leave a legacy of the facts; but whilst we both live you must trust me and I must trust you. When I find my trust misplaced, if you have any affection for me, I do not envy you the future. Your duty lies this way, not that." Gentlemen of the jury, what does that mean? What, I again ask, does it mean? It means this—I, your inexorable master, warn you that you must not disclose our marriage. I care not for the birth of a child. Secrecy is the bond. No matter how you are exposed, no matter how you are degraded, I have made a sacrifice for you, and whatever may be your feelings as a gentlewoman, a wife, and a mother, you must endure the disgrace, or else you shall never have one happy hour for the rest of your life. What is the argument of his counsel? That from the day he was at Galeta he was her deliberate, skilful, scientific, and unconscionable seducer.

Though, says the defendant (by his argument), I have added hypocrisy, profanity, deception, and blasphemy, I am not bound to pay for the sustenance of this woman. I am not her wedded husband, I stand before you her profligate and unprincipled seducer. I found her young, I found her virtuous, I found her beautiful. What is she now? Innocence defiled, virtue lost, beauty spoiled, and hopes of life fled for ever. Better the hand of death had swept her to an early grave; it would have been consecrated by the tears of maternal affection—gentle tears, recalling happy memories of the past, assuaged and checked by blessed hopes of a bright immortal future. He has blasted her happiness in this life, he has endangered it in the life to come, according to his own argument. Save him from the consequences of that argument, and do not brand him, as his counsel do, as a scientific, deliberate, unprincipled seducer. How stands the question, now that the whole of this great trial is before you—now that you have all these facts—and I cannot dwell at this hour minutely upon each particular circumstance, as I might have done if I had gained you at an earlier hour of the day, in endeavouring to reason it step by step? I ask you to judge of that woman as she has appeared before you; and then say, Do you believe her? Trace her life up from the first hour that she stood within the wall of the convent until the day she sat in that box to tell the story of her multitudinous sorrows. Ask yourselves what fact has been proved against her with any living man save the defendant. Her crime is she loved him too dearly, and too well. Had she possessed millions, she would have flung them at his feet. Had she a throne to bestow, she would have placed him on that throne. She gave him the kingdom of her heart, and made him sovereign of her affections. There he reigned with undisputed sway. Great the gift! Our affections were by an Almighty hand planted in the human heart. They have survived the fall, and repaired the ravages of sin and death. They dignify, exalt, and inspire our existence here below, which, without them, were cold, monotonous, and dull. They unite heart to heart by adamantine links. Nor are their uses limited to this life. We may well believe that when the mysterious union between soul and body is dissolved, the high affections of our nature, purified, spiritualized, immortalized, may add to the felicity unspeakable reserved for the spirits of the just made perfect through the countless ages of eternity. She gave him her affections—she gave him her love —a woman's love! Who can fathom its depths? Who can measure its intensity? Who can describe its devotion? She told you herself what that love was when she wrote to him, "If you were to be executed as a convict I would stand below the gallows." If he had taken that woman for his wife misery would have endeared him to her, poverty she would have shared, from sickness or misfortune she would never have fled; she would have been his constant companion, his guide, his friend—his polluted mistress, never! Therefore, I now call on you to do justice to that injured woman. You cannot restore her to the husband she adored or the happiness she enjoyed. You cannot give colour to that faded cheek, or lustre to that eye that has been dimmed by many a tear. You cannot relieve the sorrows of her bursting heart, but you may restore her to her place in society. You may, by your verdict, enable her to say, "Rash I have been, indiscreet I may have been through excess of my affection for you, but guilty, never!" You may replace her in the rank which she would never disgrace— you may restore her to that society in which she is qualified to shine, and has ever adorned! To you I commit this great cause. I am not able longer to address you. Would to God I had talents or physical energy to exert either or both longer on the part of this injured, insulted woman. She finds an advocate in you— she finds it in the respected judge on the bench—she finds it in every heart that beats within this court, and in every honest man throughout the country.

IN DEFENCE OF C. G. DUFFY.[1]

I have told you what constitutes the great crime of conspiracy; it is one of combination, and it is fearfully set forth in books, so often quoted in the history of the state trials of England, where there are terrible examples given of wrong verdicts, by which men were deprived of their liberty, their lives, and by which innocence was struck down. But, on the other hand, there were in those state trials

[1] For a notice of Charles Gavan Duffy, see page 114.

great and glorious examples of triumphs over power, over the crown, and over kings—as in the case of Hardy on parliamentary reform, and in the case of Horne Tooke, who saved public opinion so far from being extinguished in England, and which would have been the case had not the jury interfered. In earlier days, in the days of the Second James, the seven bishops were charged with a conspiracy for asserting the opinion of freedom; but then a jury also interfered, and those bishops were acquitted, and acquitted amidst those shouts which proclaimed universal freedom. In darker periods of history—in the times of Cromwell, who usurped the monarchy and all under the sacred name of religion, yet dared not to abolish the forms of public justice, they so prevailed and subsisted—that when, in the plenitude of his power, he prosecuted for a libel, there were twelve honest men who had the courage not to pronounce the defendant guilty, thus proving that the unconquerable love of liberty still survived in the hearts of Englishmen. I will say that the true object of this unprecedented prosecution is to stifle the discussion of a great public question. Reviewed in this light, all other considerations sink into insignificance; its importance becomes vast indeed. A nation's rights are involved in the issue—a nation's liberties are at stake—that won—what preserves the precious privileges you possess? The exercise of the right of political discussion—free, untrammelled, bold. The laws which wisdom framed —the institutions struck out by patriotism, learning, or genius—can they preserve the springs of freedom fresh and pure? No; destroy the right of free discussion, and you dry up the sources of freedom. By the same means by which your liberties were won, can they be increased or defended. Do not quarrel with the partial evils free discussion creates, nor seek to contract the enjoyment of the greatest privilege within the narrow limit timid men prescribe. With the passing mischiefs of its extravagance, contrast the prodigious blessings it has heaped on man.

Free discussion aroused the human mind from the torpor of ages—taught it to think, and shook the thrones of ignorance and darkness. Free discussion gave to Europe the Reformation, which I have been taught to believe the mightiest event in the history of the human race—illuminated the world with the radiant light of spiritual truth. May it shine with steady and increasing splendour! Free discussion gave to England the Revolution, abolished tyranny, swept away the monstrous abuses it rears, and established the liberties under which we live. Free discussion, since that glorious epoch, has not only preserved but purified our constitution, reformed our laws, reduced our punishments, and extended its wholesome influence to every portion of our political system. The spirit of inquiry it creates has revealed the secrets of nature—explained the wonders of creation, teaching the knowledge of the stupendous works of God. Arts, science, civilization, freedom, pure religion, are its noble realities. Would you undo the labours of science, extinguish literature, stop the efforts of genius, restore ignorance, bigotry, barbarism,—then put down free discussion, and you have accomplished all. Savage conquerors, in the blindness of their ignorance, have scattered and destroyed the intellectual treasures of a great antiquity. Those who make war on the sacred rights of free discussion, without their ignorance imitate their fury. They may check the expression of some thought which, if uttered, might redeem the liberties or increase the happiness of man. The insidious assailants of this great prerogative of intellectual beings, by the cover under which they advance, conceal the character of their assault upon the liberties of the human race. They seem to admit the liberty to discuss—blame only its extravagance, pronounce hollow praises on the value of freedom of speech, and straightway begin a prosecution to cripple or destroy it. The open despot avows his object is to oppress or enslave—resistance is certain to encounter his tyranny, and perhaps subvert it. Not so the artful assailant of a nation's rights—he declares friendship while he wages war, and professes affection for the thing he hates.

State prosecutions, if you believe them, are ever the fastest friends of freedom. They tell you peace is disturbed, order broken by the excesses of turbulent and seditious demagogues. No doubt there might be a seeming peace—a death-like stillness—by repressing the feelings and passions of men. So in the fairest portions of Europe this day, there is peace, and order, and submission, under paternal despotism, ecclesiastical and civil. That peace springs from terror, that submission from ignorance, that silence from despair. Who dares discuss, when with discussion and by discussion tyranny must perish? Compare the stillness of despotism with the healthful animation, the natural warmth, the bold language, the proud bearing, which spring from freedom, and the consciousness of its possession. Which will you prefer? Insult not the dignity of manhood by supposing that contentment of the heart can exist under despotism. There may be degrees in its severity, and so degrees in the sufferings of its victims. Terrible the dangers which lurk beneath the calm surface of despotic power. The movements of the oppressed will at times disturb the tyrant's tranquillity, and warn him, that their day of vengeance or of triumph may be nigh. But in these happy countries the very safety of the state consists in freedom of discussion. Partial evils in all systems of political governments there must be; but their worst effects are obviated when their cause is sought for, discovered, considered, discussed. Milton has taught a great political truth, in language as instructive as his sublimest verse: —"For this is not the liberty which we can hope, that no grievances ever should arise in the commonwealth—that let no man in this world expect; but when complaints are freely heard, deeply considered, and speedily reformed—then is the utmost bound of civil liberty obtained that wise men look for." Suffer the complaints of the Irish people to be freely heard. You want the power to have them speedily reformed. Their case to-day may be yours to-morrow. Preserve the right of free discussion as you would cling to life. Combat error with argument, misrepresentation by fact, falsehood with truth. "For who knows not," saith the same great writer, "that truth is strong—next to the Almighty? One needs no policies nor stratagems to make her victorious—these are the shifts error uses against her power."

If this demand for a native parliament rest on a delusion, dispel that delusion by the omnipotence of truth. Why do you love—why do other nations honour England? Are you—are they dazzled by her naval or military glories, the splendour of her literature, her sublime discoveries in science, her boundless wealth, her almost incredible labours in every work of art and skill? No; you love her—you cling to England because she has been for ages past the seat of free discussion, and therefore, the home of rational freedom, and the hope of oppressed men throughout the world. Under the laws of England it is our happiness to live. They breathe the spirit of liberty and reason. Emulate this day the great virtues of Englishmen—their love of fairness—their immovable independence, and the sense of justice rooted in their nature—these are the virtues which qualify jurors to decide the rights of their fellow-men. Deserted by these, of what avail is the tribunal of a jury? It is worthless as the human body when the living soul has fled. Prove to the accused, from whom, perchance, you widely differ in opinion—whose liberties and fortunes are in your hands—that you are there not to persecute, but to save. Believe me, you will not secure the true interests of England by leaning too severely on your countrymen. They say to their English brethren, and with truth—We have been at your side whenever danger was to be faced or honour won. The scorching sun of the east and the pestilence of the west, we have endured to spread your commerce—to extend your empire—to uphold your glory. The bones of our countrymen whitened the fields of Portugal, of Spain, of France. Fighting your battles they fell—in a nobler cause they could not. We have helped to gather your imperishable laurels. We have helped to win your immortal triumphs. Now, in time of peace, we ask you to restore that parliament you planted here with your laws and language, uprooted in a dismal period of our history, in the moment of our terror, our divisions, our weakness, it may be our crime. Re-establish the commons on the broad foundation of the people's choice—replace the peerage, the corinthian pillars of the capitol, secured and adorned with the strength and splendour of the crown —and let the monarch of England, as in ages past, rule a brilliant and united empire in solidity, magnificence, and power.

When the privileges of the English parliament were invaded, that people took the field, struck down the ministry, and dragged their sovereign to the block. We shall not imitate English precedent, while we struggle for a parliament. That institution you prize so highly, which fosters your wealth, adds to your prosperity, and guards your freedom, was ours for six hundred years. Restore the blessing and we shall be content. This prosecution is not essential for the maintenance of the authority and prerogative of the crown. Our gracious sovereign needs not state prosecutions to secure her prerogatives or preserve her power. She has the unbought loyalty of a chivalrous and gallant people. The arm of authority she requires not to raise. The glory of her gentle reign will be— she will have ruled, not by the sword, but by the affections; that the true source of her power has been, not in terrors of the law, but in the hearts of her people. Your patience is exhausted. If I have spoken suitably to the subject, I have spoken as I could have wished; but if, as you may think, deficiently, I have spoken as I could. Do you, from what has been said, and from the better arguments omitted, which may be well suggested by your manly understandings and your honest hearts, give a verdict consistent with justice, yet leaning to liberty—dictated by truth, yet inclining to the side of the accused men, struggling against the weight, and power, and influence of the crown, and prejudice more overwhelming still—a verdict undesired by any party, but to be applauded by the impartial monitor within your breasts, becoming the high spirit of Irish gentlemen, and the intrepid guardians of the rights and liberties of a free people.

THOMAS D'ARCY M'GEE.

BORN 1825 — DIED 1868.

[The history of the majority of the brilliant men who took part in the insurrectionary movement in 1848 is one of failure. Meagher was drowned, Williams died young and in poverty, Mitchel's brief triumph of a few days was the close of a bitter struggle through life against ever-recurring failure. Two of the '48 men, however, are conspicuous exceptions to the darker fate of their companions, for, in other countries, and amid happier surroundings, they attained to the high political position for which their talents fitted them; we mean, M'Gee and Duffy.

Thomas D'Arcy M'Gee was born on April 13, 1825. His ancestors on both the paternal and maternal sides were remarkable for their devotion to the national cause. His father was in the coast-guard service. When he was eight, young M'Gee was removed to Wexford, where he lost his mother—a gifted woman, well versed in Irish literature, and the first inspirer in her son of the sentiments which formed the basis of his character. When but seventeen he went to America, on a visit to an aunt in Providence, Rhode Island. The advent of the anniversary of American independence gave the lad an opportunity of displaying his great oratorical powers. His speech on the then absorbing subject of repeal proved highly successful, and in consequence he was offered employment on the *Boston Pilot*, which he accepted. Two years after the beginning of this connection he was advanced to the post of editor, an important position for one just nineteen years old. This, however, was not his only triumph; the fame of his speeches crossed the Atlantic, and, attracting the attention of O'Connell, were characterized by him as "the inspired utterances of a young exiled Irish boy in America."

An offer of a situation on the *Freeman's Journal* brought him back to Ireland; but he soon abandoned that journal for the more congenial *Nation*, which, under the editorship of Gavan Duffy, was at this period preaching those extreme doctrines which gave rise to the Young Ireland school. M'Gee soon became involved in the political movements, and figured as one of the leaders of the revolutionary party, being elected secretary of the Confederation. He was imprisoned for a short time in consequence of a violent speech which he made in county Wicklow.

When the insurrection broke out he was travelling in Scotland, whither he had been sent on a mission to arouse his fellow-countrymen. Although a price was set upon his head, he could not resist the desire to see his wife, to whom he had just been married, and, protected by Dr. Maguire, the Roman Catholic Bishop of Derry, he paid her a visit, afterwards escaping in the disguise of a priest to America. He started in New York a paper called the *Nation*. His articles therein, being strongly condemnatory of the action of the Roman Catholic priesthood during 1848, brought him into collision with that body. He afterwards went to Boston, where he established the *American Celt*.

As time went on his views underwent great modification, and he regretted the articles which led him to wield his pen in controversy with Bishop Hughes of the diocese of New York. He changed his place of residence several times, and finally, in 1858, left the United States to settle down in Canada. He had not been long resident in Montreal when he was elected to the Canadian parliament, in the debates of which assembly he soon distinguished himself. In 1862 he was rewarded by being chosen president of the executive council, afterwards holding the office of minister of agriculture.

His political views had by this time changed very considerably. He abandoned all the revolutionary doctrines of his youth, and became the loyal adherent of the British connection. He also gained notoriety by some imprudent and vehement attacks upon those of his countrymen who still persisted in revolutionary ways. In 1865 he visited Ireland as representative of Canada at the Dublin Industrial Exhibition, and, during a visit to his father's home at Wexford, he delivered a lecture in which he bitterly denounced the then rising portent of Fenianism. The result of this, naturally, was to make him still more obnoxious to the revolutionary party.

In 1867 he was again in Europe, this time as commissioner to the Paris Exhibition. He was busied at this period with the important work of confederating the various Canadian colonies—a large and wise measure which was greatly due to his initiative. The raids which had been made on Canada provoked him to still more bitter attacks on the Fenians, and further estranged from him the sympathies of certain classes of his countrymen. A large number of his fellow-citizens entertained for him, on the other hand, feelings of deep respect, and on St. Patrick's Day, 1868, this feeling found expression in one of the most successful banquets ever given in Canada to a public man. This, as we have said, was on March 17. On the night of April 7 following, M'Gee was assassinated by a man supposed to be connected with some revolutionary organization. He had spoken that very evening, and with his usual vigour, in the legislative assembly, and had only just parted from one of his colleagues. His assassin was captured and executed shortly afterwards. This tragic end evoked deep expressions of feeling; and his funeral was made the occasion of a great demonstration of public esteem.

The best known and most favourable results of M'Gee's literary activity are his poems—a volume of which was published after his death. Many of these are of a very high order of merit, full of passion and eloquence, tenderness and melody. He wrote besides an excellent *History of Ireland*, *Lives of Irish Writers* (published 1846), *History of the Irish Settlers in North America* (1851), *Catholic History of North America* (1854), and other works. His speeches are also marked by great vigour and eloquence.]

THE CELTS.

Long, long ago, beyond the misty space
　Of twice a thousand years,
In Erin old there dwelt a mighty race,
　Taller than Roman spears;
Like oaks and towers they had a giant grace,
　Were fleet as deers,
With winds and waves they made their 'biding place,
　These western shepherd seers.

Their ocean-god was Mân-â-nân, M'Lir,
　Whose angry lips,
In their white foam, full often would inter
　Whole fleets of ships;
Cromah their day-god, and their thunderer,
　Made morning and eclipse;
Bride was their queen of song, and unto her
　They prayed with fire-touched lips.

Great were their deeds, their passions, and their sports;
　With clay and stone
They piled on strath and shore those mystic forts,
　Not yet o'erthrown;
On cairn-crown'd hills they held their council-courts;
　While youths alone,
With giant dogs, explored the elk resorts,
　And brought them down.

Of these was Fin, the father of the Bard,
　Whose ancient song
Over the clamour of all change is heard,
　Sweet-voic'd and strong.
Fin once o'ertook Granee, the golden-hair'd,
　The fleet and young;
From her the lovely, and from him the fear'd,
　The primal poet sprung.

Ossian! two thousand years of mist and change
　Surround thy name—
Thy Finian heroes now no longer range
　The hills of fame.
The very name of Fin and Gaul sound strange—
　Yet thine the same—
By miscalled lake and desecrated grange—
　Remains, and shall remain!

The Druid's altar and the Druid's creed
　We scarce can trace.
There is not left an undisputed deed
　Of all your race,
Save your majestic song, which hath their speed,
　And strength, and grace;
In that sole song, they live and love, and bleed—
　It bears them on thro' space.

Oh, inspir'd giant! shall we e'er behold,
　In our own time,

One fit to speak your spirit on the wold,
  Or seize your rhyme?
One pupil of the past, as mighty soul'd
  As in the prime,
Were the fond, fair, and beautiful, and bold—
  They, of your song sublime!

MEMORIES.

I left two loves on a distant strand,
One young, and fond, and fair, and bland;
One fair, and old, and sadly grand,—
My wedded wife and my native land.

One tarrieth sad and seriously
Beneath the roof that mine should be;
One sitteth sibyl-like, by the sea,
Chanting a grave song mournfully.

A little life I have not seen
Lies by the heart that mine hath been;
A cypress wreath darkles now, I ween,
Upon the brow of my love in green.

The mother and wife shall pass away,
Her hands be dust, her lips be clay;
But my other love on earth shall stay,
And live in the life of a better day.

Ere we were born my first love was,
My sires were heirs to her holy cause;
And she yet shall sit in the world's applause,
A mother of men and blessed laws.

I hope and strive the while I sigh,
For I know my first love cannot die:
From the chain of woes that loom so high
Her reign shall reach to eternity.

AM I REMEMBERED?

Am I remember'd in Erin
I charge you, speak me true—
Has my name a sound, a meaning
In the scenes my boyhood knew?
Does the heart of the mother ever
Recall her exile's name?
For to be forgot in Erin,
And on earth, is all the same.

O mother! mother Erin!
Many sons your age hath seen—
Many gifted, constant lovers
Since your mantle first was green.
Then how may I hope to cherish
The dream that I could be
In your crowded memory number'd
With that palm-crown'd companie?

Yet faint and far, my mother,
As the hope shines on my sight,
I cannot choose but watch it
Till my eyes have lost their light ;
For never among your brightest,
And never among your best,
Was heart more true to Erin
Than beats within my breast.

MY IRISH WIFE.

I would not give my Irish wife
  For all the dames of the Saxon land—
I would not give my Irish wife
  For the Queen of France's hand.
For she to me is dearer
  Than castles strong, or lands, or life—
An outlaw—so I'm near her
  To love till death my Irish wife.

Oh, what would be this home of mine—
  A ruined, hermit-haunted place,
But for the light that nightly shines,
  Upon its walls from Kathleen's face?
What comfort in a mine of gold—
  What pleasure in a royal life,
If the heart within lay dead and cold,
  If I could not wed my Irish wife?

I knew the law forbade the banns—
  I knew my king abhorred her race—
Who never bent before their clans,
  Must bow before their ladies' grace.
Take all my forfeited domain,
  I cannot wage with kinsmen strife—
Take knightly gear and noble name,
  And I will keep my Irish wife.

My Irish wife has clear blue eyes,
  My heaven by day, my stars by night—
And twinlike truth and fondness lie
  Within her swelling bosom white.
My Irish wife has golden hair—
  Apollo's harp had once such strings—
Apollo's self might pause to hear
  Her bird-like carol when she sings.

I would not give my Irish wife
  For all the dames of the Saxon land—
I would not give my Irish wife
  For the Queen of France's hand.
For she to me is dearer
  Than castles strong, or lands, or life,—
In death I would be near her,
  And rise beside my Irish wife!

DEATH OF THE HOMEWARD BOUND.

Paler and thinner the morning moon grew,
Colder and sterner the rising wind blew—
The pole-star had set in a forest of cloud,
And the icicles crackled on spar and on shroud,
When a voice from below we heard feebly cry,
"Let me see—let me see—my own Land ere I
    die.

"Ah, dear sailor, say, have we sighted Cape Clear?
Can you see any sign? Is the morning light near?
You are young, my brave boy; thanks, thanks, for
    your hand,
Help me up, till I get a last glimpse of the land—
Thank God, 'tis the sun that now reddens the sky,
I shall see—I shall see—my own Land ere I die.

"Let me lean on your strength, I am feeble and old,
And one half of my heart is already stone cold—
Forty years work a change! when I first crossed
    the sea
There were few on the deck that could grapple
    with me;
But my prime and my youth in Ohio went by,
And I'm come back to see the old spot ere I die."

'Twas a feeble old man, and he stood on the deck,
His arm round a kindly young mariner's neck,
His ghastly gaze fixed on the tints of the east,
As a starvling might stare at the sound of a feast;—
The morn quickly rose, and revealed to his eye
The Land he had prayed to behold, and then die!

Green, green was the shore, though the year was
    near done—
High and haughty the capes the white surf dash'd
    upon—
A grey ruined convent was down by the strand,
And the sheep fed afar, on the hills of the land!
"God be with you, dear Ireland," he gasped with
    a sigh,
"I have lived to behold you—I'm ready to die."

He sunk by the hour, and his pulse 'gan to fail,
As we swept by the headland of storied Kinsale—
Off Ardigna bay, it came slower and slower,
And his corpse was clay cold as we sighted Tramore.
At Passage we waked him, and now he doth lie,
In the lap of the Land, he beheld but to die.

HOME THOUGHTS.

If will had wings, how fast I'd flee
To the home of my heart o'er the seething sea!
If wishes were power—if words were spells,
I'd be this hour where my own love dwells.

My own love dwells in the storied land,
Where the Holy Wells sleep in yellow sand;
And the emerald lustre of Paradise beams
Over homes that cluster round singing streams.

I, sighing alas! exist alone—
My youth is as grass on an unsunn'd stone,
Bright to the eye, but unfelt below—
As sunbeams that lie over Arctic snow.

My heart is a lamp that love must relight,
Or the world's fire-damp will quench it quite.
In the breast of my dear my life-tide springs—
Oh! I'd tarry none here, if will had wings.

For she never was weary of blessing me,
When morn rose dreary on thatch and tree;
She evermore chanted her song of faith,
When darkness daunted on hill and heath.

If will had wings, how fast I'd flee
To the home of my heart o'er the seething sea!
If wishes were power—if words were spells,
I'd be this hour where my own love dwells.

THE DEATH OF O'CAROLAN.[1]

There is an empty seat by many a board,
    A guest is missed in hostelry and hall—
There is a harp hung up in Alderford
    That was in Ireland sweetest harp of all.
The hand that made it speak, woe's me, is cold,
    The darkened eyeballs roll inspired no more;
The lips—the potent lips—gape like a mould,
    Where late the golden torrent floated o'er.

In vain the watchman looks from Mayo's towers
    For him whose presence filled all hearts with
    mirth;
In vain the gathered guests outsit the hours,
    The honoured chair is vacant by the hearth.
From Castle-Archdall, Moneyglass, and Trim,
    The courteous messages go forth in vain,
Kind words no longer have a joy for him
    Whose lowly lodge is in death's dark demesne.

Kilronan Abbey is his castle now,
    And there till doomsday peacefully he'll stay;
In vain they weave new garlands for his brow,
    In vain they go to meet him by the way;
In kindred company he does not tire,
    The native dead and noble lie around,
His life-long song has ceased, his wood and wire
    Rest, a sweet harp unstrung, in holy ground.

Last of our ancient Minstrels! thou who lent
    A buoyant motive to a foundering race—
Whose saving song, into their being blent,
    Sustained them by its passion and its grace,—
God rest you! May your judgment dues be light,
    Dear Turlogh! and the purgatorial days
Be few and short, till clothed in holy white,
    Your soul may come before the throne of rays.

[1] For a notice of this bard, see vol. l. p. 156.

WILLIAM M'CULLAGH TORRENS.

[Mr. William M'Cullagh Torrens was born in Dublin in October, 1813, being the eldest son of Mr. James M'Cullagh, of Greenfield. In 1863 he assumed his maternal name for family reasons. He began his distinguished public career many years back. Having graduated in Trinity College, Dublin, he was admitted to the Irish and afterwards to the English bar; and for several years he practised with success, especially before parliamentary committees. After he had held office as a commissioner of inquiry into the operation of the poor-law in Ireland, and as private secretary to Lord Taunton (then Mr. Henry Labouchere), he represented Dundalk from 1848 to 1852. In the latter year he unsuccessfully contested Yarmouth, and he was equally unfortunate in 1857, for, having been returned, he was afterwards unseated on petition. In 1865 he was elected for Finsbury. The parliamentary career of Mr. Torrens has been active, and he has succeeded on more than one occasion in making important and even vital changes in the measures brought forward by ministers. For instance, it was on his proposal that the lodger franchise was granted on the household suffrage bill of Lord Beaconsfield (then Mr. Disraeli), and an amendment of his to the education measure of Mr. Forster led to the establishment of the London School Board. He also passed the measure which has done so much to improve the dwellings of the poor. To the pen of Mr. Torrens we owe several valuable contributions to political history. He has written biographies of Sheil, Sir James Graham, and, quite recently, Lord Melbourne, a most interesting and brightly written volume, from which we make our quotation. He is also the author of *Lectures on the Study of History*, *Industrial History of Free Nations*, and a scathing review of British action in India, under the title, *Empire in Asia, How we came by it; a Book of Confessions*. The active pen of Mr. Torrens is now engaged in a political study, which ought to prove extremely instructive. It is a contrast in the form of two biographies between "Proconsul and Tribune"—the proconsul being the Marquis of Wellesley, and the tribune Daniel O'Connell. The first volume (the "Life of Lord Wellesley") has been published.]

BYRON AND LADY CAROLINE LAMB.[1]

[Lady Caroline Lamb was the wife of the Hon. Mr. Lamb, afterwards Lord Melbourne, and prime minister. Her love escapade with Byron is well known, and has been referred to in the memoir of the Hon. Mrs. Norton. It may be necessary to explain that "William" in the following passage from the biography is Lord Melbourne, at that period the Hon. William Lamb: Lady Melbourne is his mother.]

Whatever may have been the effects of life passed in the whirl of distraction and indulgence which characterized the early days of the regency, they were nowhere more traceable perhaps than upon the young and impressionable dwellers at Melbourne House. Lady Melbourne had ceased, indeed, to be more than casually amused by whims or novelties; and she moved on in her own diplomatic way, observant of all that was going on around her in looks and spirits, less brilliant than she once had been, though still not a bit like sixty-two: in artifices of dress and arts of manner more consummate than ever. Like Lady Holland at Kensington and Lady Spencer at St. James's Place, her ascendency in the household was supreme; yet there were some things her influence could not control, some energies she could not fire. William would do anything to please her when asked; but she knew it was no use always asking him to work as others worked for political advancement. Disenchantment seemed to have spread its insidious spell over him; and though weary enough of *ennui*, she could not bring him, and he could not bring himself, to set about any undertaking requiring effort or toil. His wife, unceasingly active, spent her existence with as little concentration of aim. Painting, music, reading, writing verses, patronizing plays, taking part in private theatricals, dreaming romantically, and talking in a way to make people stare; riding on horseback, often coquetting, sometimes quarrelling (she hardly knew about what) with her husband, trying to please her father-in-law, who thought her a fidget; and

---

[1] Extracted by permission of the author.

trying to please her child, whose wistful gaze of incurious wonder made her for the moment staid and sad:—these and a world of intermingling trifles filled up her time. But her versatility found no resting-place, and the fatal habit of mentally looking into the glass grew upon her day by day. Her quick powers of appreciation were thrown away upon a glittering crowd of forms and faces, but few of which she paused to look at long enough to be able to caricature. None of the remarkable persons whom she met in society fixed her attention or riveted her fancy. It was not a profitable condition of mind, but it had been well for her and all who loved her had her butterflyhood continued longer. Out of the unknown a new influence was about to break forth on English society, and especially upon that portion of it wherein she moved, compared with which all other talents, genius, and originality seemed to her but as so many dull and motionless lamps, while the lightning was flashing in at the window. An instinctive sense of misgiving impelled her at first to turn away; but when this new element of dazzling and resistless power came so gently as not even to cause a start, and in its vivid and seemingly harmless beauty lingered and played all the summer evening round her, her imagination was led captive to its will.

Up to this time the name of Byron, save to a comparative few, may be said to have been unknown. Lord Carlisle, though one of his guardians, had seldom inquired after him during his college days; and on his coming of age forgot to ask him to dinner. When he took the oaths and his seat at Westminster he was not recognized by any one of his peers; and on the chancellor offering his hand in welcome, as a new member of the House, he mistook the courtesy for the form of party enlistment, and took it so ungraciously that Lord Eldon turned away with a frown. Morbidly sensitive to neglect, and attributing it to a slight deformity of which nobody but himself thought or cared, and fevered with an insatiable thirst for distinction, he published in 1809 a satire in which he attacked nearly every critic and poet of the day, in order to be revenged for the ridicule cast by Brougham on his *Hours of Idleness* in the *Edinburgh Review*. With his Cambridge class-fellow, Mr. Hobhouse, he spent two years abroad, and returned full of aspirations as a poet and a politician. Through Samuel Rogers, his only acquaintance of note, he was introduced to Lord Holland, who, *more suo*, forgetting the petulance of his 'prentice rhymes, aided him cheerfully with information and advice for his maiden speech in the Lords. It was an undoubted success, and he was forthwith enrolled as a promising recruit in the ranks of the Liberal party. But in the crowd of celebrities and competitors for notice at Holland House his vanity might have eaten its heart out with scant pity or heed, had he not been able to lay the world under tribute in a very different sphere. His speech, he thought, would prove a good advertisement for *Childe Harold*, which appeared a few days afterwards. Rogers and Moore had seen it in the proof, and foretold the triumph which awaited him. The former told Lady Caroline Lamb that she ought to know the new poet, and lent her his copy to read before the work came out. Soon afterwards Lady Westmoreland introduced him to her. Her first impression was unfavourable, and she wrote in her diary, "Mad, bad, and dangerous to know." But the *éclat* of his poem made him in a few weeks the star without rival of society. Wherever he went, and he soon went everywhere, to use his own expression, " the women suffocated him." His air of abstraction and look of melancholy, and the rumours put about of his eccentric life, all contributed to fan the flame. Emulation for his favour became fierce, and the wiles spread for his bewitchment were innumerable. Lady Caroline avers that she spread none. She had called at Holland House after a morning ride through wind and rain; he was unexpectedly announced, and she owns that she ran away to readjust her toilet before they met. His grave attention pleased her; the interview ended in his asking leave to call, and the acquaintance thus begun quickly ripened into friendship.

He lived much at Melbourne House, where he was received on terms of the utmost familiarity. For the talents of society, in which Lady Melbourne had probably no equal in her day, his admiration was unbounded. The world she knew by long and keen observation, and whose scenes she had the rare faculty of picturing by a few graphic touches, was all a new world to him. There was hardly a person of note among courtiers, politicians, artists, or men of letters, from the time of Garrick and Chatham, whom she had not known; and there was not a prominent character living whom she did not weigh in the balance of her own judgment, and whose idiosyncrasy she could not, when she would, accurately tell. This, with casual acquaintances, was not often.

Experience had taught her the thanklessness of those who delight in another's unguarded candour. She used to say that few men were to be trusted with their neighbours' secrets, and hardly any woman with her own. But she found Byron better worth gossiping with than other young men of his years. He asked her questions which it really interested her to answer; and, notwithstanding her habitual wariness and reserve, a remarkable degree of confidence sprang up between them.

With Lady Caroline it was hero-worship. The fascination wrought upon her susceptible and credulous fancy by his account of his youth and foreign adventures; his dark hints at the hidden griefs, the sorrows of his loneliness, the pain of early disappointments, and his real or pretended indifference to passing success; the ever-changing beauty of his features, and the glittering splendour of his verse; and all these laid with a look and tone of ineffable gallantry at her feet by one whose nobility dated from the Conquest, fairly bewildered her. It is all very well for those who have never been brought within the perilous circle of such a spell to talk pharisaically of the ease with which it might have been resisted. But to be just, one must estimate antecedents and surroundings; the enervating atmosphere of dissipation, and the *furore* about a picturesque poet of high degree. If these things are not taken into account, what really is left but the mingled echo of two names of whose brief association and subsequent severance the world has heard too much and understands too little. It was impossible that such intimacy should not be remarked, but this was exactly what his vanity wanted. With all his profession of democratic enthusiasm, he was habitually swayed by aristocratic feeling; with all his romance in rhyme about devotion to nameless and secluded beauty, he was vain as any coxcomb of being greeted by smiles of quality, and to be known as the favourite of supreme fashion. In the best set Lady Caroline was just then one of the fair and fickle rulers. Melbourne House was the centre of gaiety and revel.

"My cousin Hartington wanted to have waltzes and quadrilles; and at Devonshire House it would not be allowed, so we had them in the great drawing-room at Whitehall. All the *bon ton* assembled there continually. There was nothing so fashionable. But after a time Byron contrived to sweep them all away."

For his overweening egotism, gratified by special recognition in the glittering throng, chafed at devotion to the pastime in which he could not participate. He preferred sentimental talk with a clever and wayward woman, whose self-idolatry, already too mature, ripened into fruit as bitter as his own. One who knew her long and well, and who was more than others lenient to her errors, has said of her that her conversation had all the charm of intellect, fancy, culture, and a low, musical voice: it had but one fault, that it was all about herself. There was an affinity in this respect between them which in itself became gradually the cause of disappointment and vexation. Craving on the one side encountered exaction on the other; and as neither knew how to stifle ill-humour or chagrin, he would grow moody and she fretful when their rival egotisms jarred.

For the sensitive plant which could yield small fruit
Of the love that it felt from the leaf to the root
Desired more than all, it loved more than ever,
Where none wanted but it could belong to the giver.

She brought him fresh verses on which she had spent half the sleepless night in an agony of hope that his eye would kindle and his lips respond to emotions she had thus endeavoured to express. But though he failed not to praise the well-chosen epithet and flowing rhythm, he was far too full of his own greater thoughts to be able, had he tried, to affect enthusiasm at the tinkling of her lyric bells. In her mortification she would inwardly upbraid him with being, like the rest of his sex, too self-engrossed; and the time was to come when she would tell him so in no measured terms. But with *Childe Harold* she could not thus make free.

At a reception one evening Lord Holland took an antique censer from a cabinet to show it to some learned guest; as he passed Byron and Lady Caroline he turned and said gallantly to her, "You see I bear you incense." "Offer it to Lord Byron," she replied; "he is accustomed to it." How soon the poet began to tire of the confidential iteration of morbid fancies, which were not redeemed by grandeur of outline or depth of colouring that marked those drawn from the dark chamber of his imagery—who can tell? But he loved being conspicuous in everything; and above the admiration of women he coveted the envy of men, and liked being spoken of as a favoured intimate at Melbourne House.

Throughout the year 1813 Byron continued to visit constantly at Whitehall and Kensington. The *Giaour* and *Bride of Abydos* kept his name before the public, and, in the estimation of his female critics, maintained his reputation. Lord Holland was too good-natured, and too loyal in everything to the taste of his wife, to be niggardly in his praise. Other men more fastidious and outspoken in their criticisms tried to induce the poet to take more serious interest in politics, but without effect; his letters and journals evince hardly a trace of sympathy or regard for the great events which were stirring the heart of Christendom; and it seems to have been for him too great a sacrifice of pleasure to attend frequently even as a listener any long debate in the House of Lords. His second speech did not attract much notice; and with all his pretentious vows of zeal for liberty, he was a soldier that, without encouragement of fife and drum, could not be got to march. His time was spent for the most part in flattering pretty women, or being flattered by them; and by his own account he was not sure with which of them he was most in love. Lamb grew tired of his airs of self-importance, and laughed at his wife's exaggerated estimate of his perfections. If sometimes provoked at her misplaced friendship, he anticipated that it would soon wear out; and sighed only at the illusion he was unable to dispel. He knew better what Byron was than she could ever know, and felt secure that ere very long he would declare himself bored, and betake himself to other company. There was another circumstance which no doubt influenced him, but of which few were aware. Byron had in confidence told Lady Melbourne his intention and desire to form a matrimonial alliance, in order that he might settle down at Newstead and take the part that became him in public life. Would she advise him? Did she not know every one worth knowing in the sphere out of which he did not care to wed? Would she not save him from the daughters of Heth? To the mind of the old lady thus consulted no connection seemed more suitable than one with her young relative, the daughter of Sir Noel Milbanke, who, besides many other attractions, possessed a considerable fortune, and was heiress to the barony of Wentworth in her own right. Without professing to fall in love the poet offered her his hand. It was refused, but with so much kindness, and even compliment, that he readily agreed that they should continue friends, and upon indifferent subjects correspond.

At Cheltenham, then in highest vogue, many of those with whom he was most intimate—the Hollands, Cowpers, Jerseys, Oxfords, and Melbournes—passed September pleasantly. Lady Melbourne had more leisure there; she listened to his wandering talk and gave him good advice. Whatever it was, he believed it sound and wise. On receipt of a letter from her not long afterwards he wrote,—"I have had a letter from Lady Melbourne, the best friend I ever had in my life, and the cleverest of women. I write with most pleasure to her, and her answers are so sensible, so *tactique*. I never met with half her talent. If she had been a few years younger what a fool she would have made of me, had she thought it worth her while, and I should have lost a valuable and most agreeable *friend*."[1]

The *Corsair* was followed by *Lara*. The hero of the latter, writes Ward, "is just the same sort of gloomy, haughty, mysterious villain as Childe Harold, the Giaour, the Corsair, and all the rest. There is a strange mixture of fertility and barrenness. One would think it was easier to invent a new character than to describe the old one over and over again."[2]

On the 20th of April, 1814, the King of France entered London accompanied by the prince regent, who went to meet him at Stanmore. The Duke of Montrose, master of the horse, and Viscount Melbourne, were in attendance. A vast concourse of all classes awaited their arrival in town, and the populace, they scarce knew why (except that they had a certain notion that the end of the weary war was near), vociferously bade the Bourbon god-speed on his way back to Paris. Later on, the allied sovereigns came to thank in person the royal representative of England's constancy and courage, which had stood fast for them and theirs when all else in Europe quailed. For weeks London was in carnival. Rejoicings and festivities never ceased; and those who, through evil report and good report, had helped to sustain the policy thus crowned at last with triumph, could not but feel, as Lamb confessed he did, historic exultation. He was very proud of his country, and not a little proud of having never despaired of its success. When all their other visits were paid the czar and the King of Prussia went with the regent to inspect the great naval arsenals, and were entertained by the officers of the fleet.

---

[1] Byron's diary, Nov. 13th and 17th, 1813.
[2] Letter to Bishop of Llandaff, July 7th, 1814.

On leaving Portsmouth for Goodwood, early on the 25th of June, their majesties were received at breakfast by the Duke of Richmond. In the afternoon they visited Lord Egremont at Petworth, where a brilliant company, including Lord and Lady Melbourne and William Lamb, awaited them. Thence they proceeded to Dover, and embarked next day.

By letters patent of the 11th of August, 1815, Lord Melbourne was created a peer of the United Kingdom, as Baron Melbourne of Melbourne in the county of Derby. He took the oaths and his seat on the 5th of February, 1816. Early in this year Lord Byron had married Miss Milbanke with the advice and approval of Lady Melbourne, and in spite of many petulant warnings of evil to come from Lady Caroline. Her cousin might be learned, and pious, and philosophical, but she was quite unsuited for a soul that was all sensibility and romance. It would never do; she was quite sure of that. A woman that went to church *punctually*, understood statistics, and had a bad figure; how could Conrad find any real community of sentiment with such a being! But the real grievance was that Byron could no longer be a lord-in-waiting to her majesty expectant of Whitehall. Ere long he heard of her complainings at his absence and alienation; and he had the effrontery to address to his peevish and hypochondriacal friend the lines beginning—

"And sayest thou, Cara," &c.,

in which, to excuse the discontinuance of his visits, he tells her that in fact he is thinking of nobody else, and apologizes for conjugal perfidy by the assurance that "falsehood to all else is truth to thee." The only palliation that can be suggested for all the inconsistent, exaggerated, and indefensible freaks in rhyme of which poor Lady Caroline was the theme, is the poetic license Byron gave himself of treating esthetically the impulse of the hour without the least regard to what had gone before or was to follow after, and with entire indifference to the obligations of delicacy and of truth. The world has already heard too much of his ill-starred union, and how, during its brief continuance, he was willing to have it believed that he still valued the society of Lady Caroline more than that of his wife. During Lady Caroline's temporary stay in Ireland a correspondence was kept up between them in prose and verse. At length, on learning that she was about returning to England, Byron resolved to put an end to all future communication; and did so in a letter which bore on its seal the coronet and initials of Lady Oxford, whom he knew she disliked. Before she recovered from the illness that ensued he had quitted England, and they met no more.

LADY WILDE (SPERANZA).

[In the course of the year 1847 Gavan Duffy received at the *Nation* office a copy of verses which were signed by the *nom de plume* "Speranza," but which gave no indication of the real name of the author. From time to time other verses came from the same hand in the same mysterious manner. These poems by a new writer attracted a vast amount of attention even in the pages which were then made bright by so many brilliant poets, and the verses of "Speranza" became more welcome than those of any other writer of the time. "Speranza," moreover, was not only a maker of poems, but there also came from her hand some of the most daring, effective, and vehement prose articles of the *Nation*. One of the articles, attributed to "Speranza's" pen, was the well-known one, headed *Jacta alea est*, which created more sensation than anything that had previously appeared in the *Nation*, and was one of those produced on the trial of Gavan Duffy. After some months of mystification Mr. Duffy was invited by Speranza to pay a visit to a house in Leeson Street, and there the editor of the *Nation*, brought face to face with the contributor, found to his surprise that "Speranza" was not a man but a lady in her early youth.

Jane Francesca Elgee—such was "Speranza's" name—had been brought up amid surroundings of intense Conservatism,—and indeed, when the immense funeral procession that marked the admiration in which Thomas Davis was held, passed by her window, she did not know who that great poet was. Some time after this she got hold of *The Spirit of the Nation*, containing poems by Dalton Williams; her imagination was fired; her patriotic feelings aroused, and thus she became a national poetess.

Miss Elgee comes of a family which is well known, and had already obtained high distinction in several paths of Irish life. The Elgees were originally an Italian race, descended, it is said, from the *Algiati* of Florence. The first of the family that came to Ireland was the great-grandfather of the poetess, and the name, which had undergone many mutations up to that period, finally settled into its present form. Her grandfather, Archdeacon Elgee, rector of Wexford, played a remarkable part in the days of the rebellion, and on account of his popularity was left scatheless by the rebels of his time. Her mother, Sara Kingsbury, was the daughter of Dr. Thomas Kingsbury, Commissioner of Bankrupts, who in his day was the owner of the well-known mansion Lisle House, Dublin. Her uncle Sir Charles Ormsby, Baronet, was a member of the last Irish parliament; Sir Robert M'Clure, the discoverer of the North-west passage, of whose exploits an account has been given in another part of this work, was a first cousin; and she is also a relative of Maturin, the author of *Bertram*. Her only brother, Judge Elgee, was one of the most distinguished members of the American bar. In 1851 Miss Elgee became the wife of Dr. Wilde, afterwards Sir William Wilde, who died a few years ago in Dublin, after he had held for many years an eminent position in his profession.

Lady Wilde has been a contributor to literature constantly throughout her life, and her later as well as her earlier poems have been almost exclusively devoted to the noble theme of national regeneration. A volume of her poetry has been published by Duffy, and in addition to her original verses, the book contains translations from nearly every European language. Unfortunately up to the present there has been no collection of her essays, which are scattered in rich abundance over periodical literature; but this neglect is about to be remedied, for a volume of her prose writings is in preparation. By Irishmen at home and abroad she is acknowledged as the national poetess of her time, and the specimens of her verses that we give below will easily explain the strong influence they wielded in days of political excitement, and which they still retain wherever the Irish people are to be found.

Lady Wilde recently published a pamphlet on the *Irish in America*, which has attracted great attention on both sides of the Atlantic. She has also published several translations of French and German works, amongst others, *Sidonia the Sorceress*, from the German, which has been reprinted in America; and a very remarkable philosophical novel from the German, entitled *The First Temptation, or Eritis sicut Deus*, in three volumes.]

TO IRELAND.[1]

My country, wounded to the heart,
  Could I but flash along thy soul
Electric power to rive apart
  The thunder-clouds that round thee roll,
And, by my burning words, uplift
Thy life from out Death's icy drift,
Till the full splendours of our age
Shone round thee for thy heritage—
As Miriam's, by the Red Sea strand
Clashing proud cymbals, so my hand
    Would strike thy harp,
    Loved Ireland!

She flung her triumphs to the stars
  In glorious chants for freedom won,
While over Pharaoh's gilded cars
  The fierce, death-bearing waves rolled on;
I can but look in God's great face,
And pray him for our fated race,
To come in Sinai thunders down,
And, with his mystic radiance, crown
Some prophet-leader, with command
To break the strength of Egypt's band,
    And set thee free,
    Loved Ireland!

New energies, from higher source,
  Must make the strong life-currents flow,
As Alpine glaciers in their course
  Stir the deep torrents 'neath the snow.
The woman's voice dies in the strife
Of Liberty's awakening life;
We wait the hero heart to lead,
The hero, who can guide at need,
And strike with bolder, stronger hand,
Though towering hosts his path withstand,
    Thy golden harp,
    Loved Ireland!

For I can breathe no trumpet call,
  To make the slumb'ring soul arise;
I only lift the funeral-pall,
  That so God's light might touch thine eyes,

---

[1] This and the following extracts are made by permission of the authoress.

And ring the silver prayer-bell clear,
To rouse thee from thy trance of fear;
Yet, if thy mighty heart has stirred,
Even with one pulse-throb at my word,
Then not in vain my woman's hand
Has struck the gold harp while I stand,
   Waiting thy rise
    Loved Ireland!

THE YEAR OF REVOLUTIONS.

Lift up your pale faces, ye children of sorrow,
The night passes on to a glorious to-morrow!
Hark! hear you not sounding glad liberty's pæan,
From the Alps to the isles of the tideless Ægean?
And the rhythmical march of the gathering nations,
And the crashing of thrones 'neath their fierce exultations,
And the cry of humanity cleaving the ether,
With hymns of the conquering rising together—
God, Liberty, Truth! How they burn heart and brain—
These words shall they burn—shall they waken in vain?

No! soul answers soul, steel flashes on steel,
And land wakens land with a grand thunder-peal.
Shall we, oh! my brothers, but weep, pray, and groan,
When France reads her rights by the flames of a throne?
Shall we fear and falter to join the grand chorus,
When Europe has trod the dark pathway before us?
Oh, courage! and we, too, will trample them down,
The minions of power, the serfs of a crown.
Oh, courage! but courage, if once to the winds
Ye fling freedom's banner, no tyranny binds.

At the voice of the people the weak symbols fall,
And humanity marches o'er purple and pall,
O'er sceptre and crown, with a glorious disdain,
For the symbol must fall and humanity reign.
Onward! then onward! ye brave to the vanguard,
Gather in glory round liberty's standard!
Like France, lordly France, we shall sweep from their station
All, all who oppose the stern will of a nation;
Like Prussia's brave children will stoop to no lord,
But demand our just rights at the point of the sword.

We'll conquer! we'll conquer! No tears for the dying,
The portal to Heaven be the field where they're lying.
We'll conquer! we'll conquer! No tears for the slain,

God's angels will smile on their death-hour of pain.
On, on in your masses dense, resolute, strong
To war against treason, oppression, and wrong;
On, on with your chieftains, and him we adore most,
Who strikes with the bravest and leads with the foremost,
Who brings the proud light of a name great in story,
To guide us through danger unconquered to glory.

With faith like the Hebrew's we'll stem the Red Sea—
God! smite down the Pharaohs—our trust is in thee;
Be it blood of the tyrant or blood of the slave,
We'll cross it to freedom, or find there a grave.
Lo! a throne for each worker, a crown for each brow,
The palm for each martyr that dies for us now;
Spite the flash of their muskets, the roar of their cannon,
The assassins of Freedom shall lower their pennon;
For the will of a nation what foe dare withstand?
Then patriots, heroes, strike! God for our Land!

THE FAMINE YEAR.

Weary men, what reap ye?—Golden corn for the stranger.
What sow ye?—Human corses that wait for the avenger.
Fainting forms, hunger-stricken, what see you in the offing?
Stately ships to bear our food away, amid the stranger's scoffing.
There's a proud array of soldiers—what do they round your door?
They guard our masters' granaries from the thin hands of the poor.
Pale mothers, wherefore weeping?—Would to God that we were dead—
Our children swoon before us, and we cannot give them bread.

Little children, tears are strange upon your infant faces,
God meant you but to smile within your mothers' soft embraces.
Oh! we know not what is smiling, and we know not what is dying;
But we're hungry, very hungry, and we cannot stop our crying.
And some of us grow cold and white—we know not what it means;
But, as they lie beside us, we tremble in our dreams.

There's a gaunt crowd on the highway—are ye
    come to pray to man,
With hollow eyes that cannot weep, and for words
    your faces wan?

No; the blood is dead within our veins—we care
    not now for life;
Let us die hid in the ditches, far from children
    and from wife;
We cannot stay and listen to their raving, famished
    cries—
Bread! Bread! Bread! and none to still their
    agonies.
We left our infants playing with their dead
    mother's hand;
We left our maidens maddened by the fever's
    scorching brand;
Better, maiden, thou wert strangled in thy own
    dark-twisted tresses—
Better, infant, thou wert smothered in thy mo-
    ther's first caresses.

We are fainting in our misery, but God will hear
    our groan;
Yet, if fellow-men desert us, will He hearken
    from his throne?
Accursed are we in our own land, yet toil we still
    and toil;
But the stranger reaps our harvest—the alien owns
    our soil.
O Christ! how have we sinned, that on our native
    plains
We perish houseless, naked, starved, with branded
    brow, like Cain's?
Dying, dying wearily, with a torture sure and
    slow—
Dying, as a dog would die, by the wayside as we go.

One by one they're falling round us, their pale
    faces to the sky;
We've no strength left to dig them graves—there
    let them lie.
The wild bird, if he's stricken, is mourned by the
    others,
But we—we die in Christian land—we die amid
    our brothers,
In the land which God has given, like a wild beast
    in his cave,
Without a tear, a prayer, a shroud, a coffin, or a
    grave.
Ha! but think ye the contortions on each livid
    face ye see,
Will not be read on judgment-day by eyes of Deity?

We are wretches, famished, scorned, human tools
    to build your pride,
But God will yet take vengeance for the souls for
    whom Christ died.
Now is your hour of pleasure—bask ye in the
    world's caress;

But our whitening bones against ye will rise as
    witnesses,
From the cabins and the ditches, in their charred,
    uncoffin'd masses,
For the Angel of the Trumpet will know them as
    he passes.
A ghastly, spectral army, before the great God
    we'll stand,
And arraign ye as our murderers, the spoilers of
    our land.

THE EXODUS.

"A million a decade!" Calmly and cold
    The units are read by our statesmen sage;
Little they think of a nation old,
    Fading away from history's page;
        Outcast weeds by a desolate sea—
        Fallen leaves of humanity.

"A million a decade!"—of human wrecks,
    Corpses lying in fever sheds—
Corpses huddled on foundering decks,
    And shroudless dead on their rocky beds;
        Nerve and muscle, and heart and brain,
        Lost to Ireland—lost in vain.

"A million a decade!" Count ten by ten,
    Column and line of the record fair;
Each unit stands for ten thousand men,
    Staring with blank, dead eye-balls there;
        Strewn like blasted trees on the sod,
        Men that were made in the image of God.

"A million a decade!"—and nothing done;
    The Cæsars had less to conquer a world;
And the war for the right not yet begun,
    The banner of freedom not yet unfurled:
        The soil is fed by the weed that dies;
        If forest leaves fall, yet they fertilize.

But ye—dead, dead, not climbing the height,
    Not clearing a path for the future to tread;
Not opening the golden portals of light,
    Ere the gate was choked by your piled-up dead:
        Martyrs ye, yet never a name
        Shines on the golden roll of fame.

Had ye rent one gyve of the festering chain,
    Strangling the life of the nation's soul;
Poured your life-blood by river and plain,
    Yet touched with your dead hand freedom's goal;
        Left of heroes one footprint more
        On our soil, tho' stamped in your gore—

We could triumph while mourning the brave,
    Dead for all that was holy and just,

And write, through our tears, on the grave,
  As we flung down the dust to dust—
    "They died for their country, but led
    Her up from the sleep of the dead."

"A million a decade!" What does it mean?
  A nation dying of inner decay—
A churchyard silence where life has been—
  The base of the pyramid crumbling away:
    A drift of men gone over the sea,
    A drift of the dead where men should be.

Was it for this ye plighted your word,
  Crowned and crownless rulers of men?
Have ye kept faith with your crucified Lord,
  And fed his sheep till he comes again?
    Or fled like hireling shepherds away,
    Leaving the fold the gaunt wolf's prey?

Have ye given of your purple to cover,
  Have ye given of your gold to cheer,
Have ye given of your love, as a lover
  Might cherish the bride he held dear,
    Broken the sacrament-bread to feed
    Souls and bodies in uttermost need?

Ye stand at the judgment-bar to-day—
  The angels are counting the dead-roll, too;
Have ye trod in the pure and perfect way,
  And ruled for God as the crowned should do?
    Count our dead—before angels and men,
    Ye're judged and doomed by the statist's pen.

RELATED SOULS.

Between us may roll the severing ocean
  That girdles the land where the red suns set,
But the spell and thrill of that strange emotion
  Which touched us once is upon us yet.
Ever your soul shadows mine, o'erleaning
  The deepest depths of my inmost thought;
And still on my heart comes back the meaning
  Of all your eloquent lips have taught.
    Time was not made for spirits like ours,
    Nor the changing light of the changing hours;
    For the life eternal still lies below
    The drifted leaves and the fallen snow.

Chords struck clear from our human nature
  Will vibrate still to that past delight
When our genius sprang to its highest stature,
  And we walked like gods on the spirit-height.
Can we forget—while these memories waken,
  Like golden strings 'neath the player's hands,
Or as palms that quiver, by night-winds shaken,
  Warm with the breath of the perfumed lands?
    Philosophy lifted her torch on high,

And we read the deep things of the spirit thereby,
  And I stood in the strength your teaching gave,
  As under Truth's mighty architrave.

Royally crowned were those moments of feeling,
  Or sad with the softness of twilight skies,
While silent tears came mournfully stealing
  Up through the purple depths of our eyes!
I think of you now—while ocean is dashing
  The foam in a thunder of silver spray,
And the glittering gleams of the white oars flashing
  Die in the sunset flush of the day.
    For all things beautiful, free, divine,
    The music that floats through the waving pine,
    The starry night, or the infinite sea,
    Speak with the breath of your spirit to me.

All my soul's unfulfilled aspiration—
  Founts that flow from eternal streams—
Awoke to life, like a new creation,
  In the paradise light of your glowing dreams.
As gold refined in a threefold fire,
  As the Talith robe of the sainted dead,
Were the pure, high aims of our hearts' desire,
  The words we uttered, the thoughts half said.
    We spoke of the grave with a voice unmoved,
    Of love that could die as a thing disproved,
    And we poured the rich wine, and drank, at our pleasure,
    Of the higher life, without stint or measure.

Time fled onward without our noting,
  Soft as the fall of the summer rain,
While thoughts in starry cascades came floating
  Down from the living fount of the brain.
Yet—better apart! Without human aidance
  I cross the River of Life and Fate—
Wake me no more with that voice, whose cadence
  Could lure me back from the Golden Gate;
    For my spirit would answer your spirit's call,
    Though life lay hid where the death-shadows fall,
    And the mystic joys of the world unseen
    Would be less to me than the days that have been.

Life may be fair in that new existence
  Where saints are crowned and the saved rejoice,
But over the depth of the infinite distance
  I'll lean and listen to hear your voice.
For never on earth, though the tempest rages,
  And never in heaven, if God be just,
Never through all the unnumbered ages
  Can souls be parted that love and trust.
    Wait—there are worlds diviner than this,
    Worlds of splendour, of knowledge, and bliss!
    Across the death-river—the victory won—
    We shall meet in the light of a changeless sun.

MEADOWS TAYLOR.

BORN 1808 — DIED 1876.

[Colonel Meadows Taylor was born in Slater Street, Liverpool, Sept. 25, 1808. Both his father and grandfather were Irish, and he himself spent the last years of his life in the family house in Ireland, Old Court, Harold's Cross, Dublin. He was sent out to India when quite a boy, to what promised to be a lucrative situation in a mercantile house in Bombay. The merchant, however, proved to be an embarrassed tradesman; and the disappointed lad had to look for other employment. In this difficulty a kinsman came to his aid, and obtained him a commission as one of the military contingent of the Nizam of Hyderabad.

The connection which thus opened between the young officer and the native ruler lasted, in one form or another, for the thirty-eight years which Taylor spent in India. His career was most useful and distinguished. Appointed after he had passed through some minor positions to be the administrator of the province of Shorapoor, he succeeded by his courage and tact in reducing thousands of hitherto unsubdued warriors to tranquillity; increased the revenue, while reducing the taxation; and, in short, changed a most turbulent and ill-governed, into an orderly and comparatively prosperous state. He also distinguished himself several times during his career by the astuteness with which he tracked out the crimes which were perpetrated by the murderous Thugs; and he was one of the first Europeans to suspect the existence of that fell organization. During the mutiny he rendered great services to the English forces by keeping the portions of the North-west quiet, and by supplying stores to the British forces. In 1860 he left India amid the deep regrets of the native population, to whom he had endeared himself by his sense of justice, his evenness of temper, combined with strength of will, and his evident anxiety for their interest and respect for their feelings.

On his first visit to England on vacation he offered to a publisher a work he had written in India, *Confessions of a Thug*. The encouraging reception which this met turned his thoughts to literature; and, as a result, he produced at intervals a series of stories illustrative of great epochs in Indian history. *Tippoo Sultaun, a Ta'e*, the first, was published in 1840, *Tara* followed in 1863, *Ralph Darnell* in 1865, and *Seeta* in 1872. The last mentioned, from which our quotation is taken, deals with the period of the Indian mutiny; and, like all the books of the author, gives a lifelike and picturesque description of the strange people, curious customs and ideas, and wild scenes in India, that land of wonders. Colonel Taylor also wrote a *Manual of Indian History*, *A Noble Queen*, and the *Story of my Life*, published by his daughter after his death, in which his strange and adventurous career is told in a simple and unpretentious style. Most of his works are now being republished in a cheap form by Messrs. C. Kegan Paul & Co.

He paid a visit to India in 1875, and on his way home died at Mentone, May 13, 1876.]

HOW THE MUTINY WAS PREPARED.

(FROM "SEETA."[1])

[Azráel Pandé, the chief personage in the following scene, is a leader of the Dacoits, or murderous robbers of India, who formed one of the revolutionary elements that led to the Indian mutiny. The passage quoted describes one of the secret meetings, in which this emissary prepared the way for the outbreak.]

After the close of the Afghan war much discontent was manifested in the Bengal native army. The massacre of the Khyber Pass was bitterly remembered, and the English government was held, by the men of Oudh and Bahar, to be responsible for the loss and desolation which had fallen upon the thousands of families of those who had perished in the miserable retreat from Kabool. If this did not affect the majority of the men in actual service, so as to form a ground for complaint or mutiny, there was another subject which every day became, in their minds, one of paramount importance; one which grew with the times, and the increasing dominion of the British power. The Bengal Sepoys had hitherto been employed, with a few trifling exceptions, in India only, and chiefly in those provinces wherein their

---

[1] By permission of Messrs. C. Kegan Paul & Co.

homes lay. True, they had marched as cheerfully into Afghanistan as the Rajpoots had in the times of the Moghul emperor Akhbar, and that tradition was not dead; but it had been as a temporary and exceptional service, it was well paid while it lasted, and, it was believed, would not recur again. Sinde, however, had become British in 1843, and, it was at first determined, should be garrisoned by native troops from Bengal. So, therefore, regiments were told off for the duty from among those which lay on the frontier of the Punjab; and one, the Sixty-fourth, when on its march southwards, mutinied for war-pay. It seemed to the men that it was no part of their contract to serve in, to them, a foreign land, without the substantial reward of increased pay; and under the sympathy of the whole of their comrades throughout the army, the Sixty-fourth refused to proceed. Eventually, and relying on an unwarrantable promise made to them by their colonel, they did march, and arrived in Sinde, where the truth was made known to them. Then they mutinied again; but subsequently became penitent at Lukhnow, and only the leading men of the mutiny were punished.

Similar in spirit and design was the mutiny, in the same year, of the Thirty-fourth Regiment, then stationed on the Punjab frontier. Disaffected to the core, it presented no feature or chance of redemption to loyalty: and it was marched to Meerut, where native officers and men, guilty and innocent alike, were at a public parade stripped of their uniforms and cast adrift, with every accompaniment of disgrace, to become the leaven of much further mischief than that which had prevailed. The wisdom of the act was questioned by many then, as it came to be in subsequent years; but the authorities had decided that an overwhelming necessity existed for the enforcement of discipline in the native army, and for a time the fate of the Thirty-fourth seemed to have effected the desired end. What became of the regiment no one knew, or perhaps cared to know very much; the men were neither watched nor traced, and seemed to have disappeared among the vast population to which they belonged.

Of one, however, we know—a restless, vindictive spirit, who for twelve years had roamed through the country, disseminating the leaven of his own regiment, wherever he went, with a skill and pertinacity which were worthy of a better cause. Immediately after the scene at Meerut Azráel Pandé had betaken himself to the jungles of Bundelkhund. He had become a leader in the local insurrection that followed; had narrowly escaped capture; and though ever welcomed by Sepoys, and supported by his rare talent of recitation, became, under a vow to Kalee, the Dacoit leader of whom this tale has had experience. This man had traversed the Punjab, where, in 1849 and 1850, a spirit of mutiny prevailed, which was suppressed with difficulty, and was similar to that of 1844. He had passed then from station to station, from regiment to regiment, carrying messages and letters, urging, instigating, and exhorting all. He went too to Dehly, and Amballa, and Meerut, finding everywhere existence of the same spirit; but, while many were like-minded, the majority hesitated and hung back. There was no general combination, and no settled purpose anywhere.

The question among all was merely mercenary; whether, in fact, they should serve in the Punjab on ordinary pay, or demand and exact the war allowances. If he urged a combined movement of mutiny, the elders wagged their heads, told him that the salt of the Koompanee Bahadoor was still sweet, and till it became bitter in their mouths they would bide their time. Most of the petty intrigues of the Dehly Court were known to him; but they excited no interest or sympathy among his comrades, and so the Punjab excitement gradually appeared to die out. Regiments in their turn came and went in ordinary course; and, after the example of the disbandment of the Sixty-sixth the idea of further mutiny seemed to have passed away.

When Azráel Pandé escaped from Noorpoor he betook himself to his old courses; for he was practically safer among Sepoys than in the country at large. Again he made his way to Meerut, Dehly, and other large stations, and heard from his friends, with exultation, that the discontent, which had seemed to slumber for a while, existed in deeper force than ever; and he soon learned also, that the smouldering fire needed but a breath to be blown into a fierce conflagration which should cover the land.

Was he singular in this? Indeed, no. Wherever he went he found others as active and earnest as himself; working, if not exactly to the same end, at least in the same direction. He found that the ordinary Brahmin priesthood were rapidly becoming aroused to the dangers that threatened their faith, and had become active missionaries of sedition. He heard of Mahomedans who, with bolder views, were organizing means for the overthrow of English power, the restitution of Mahomedan sovereignty, and a pure profession of their faith; but there could be no real help from such sources. Brahmins might preach sedition, but they could not arouse the people; Mahomedans might aim at the re-establishment of the throne of Dehly, but that would bring no relief to Hindoos; indeed, perhaps the reverse. Even if both combined, of which there was no possibility, and succeeded in exciting rebellion, what could be effected by rude mobs, bent on the plunder of their own countrymen? So long as his old comrades were faithful to the salt they had hitherto eaten, he knew that any rising would be crushed out before it could attain a head. Any destruction of the English, therefore, must depend on the united efforts of the men to whom he belonged, who now, as he believed, were everywhere coming to the resolution which should place the result beyond doubt. Everywhere, too, agents of the new movement seemed to be swarming. Hundreds—nay, there might have been thousands—busy like himself. Some, his old comrades of the Thirty-fourth, others, men of the Sixty-sixth, the last disbanded; again, discontented spirits who had taken their discharge from the army and public service, and agents of traitorous Rajahs and Nawabs, jogees, bairagees, pedlars—all such forming a vast host. Was it possible that the seed they sowed broadcast should not bear fruit? Old grievances had, indeed, died out, and their interest had passed away; but others, far more powerful and exciting, now existed in their stead.

As he travelled eastwards he met a wave of more than discontent, for it amounted to absolute terror, surging up from Bengal, and spreading far and wide over the land. He heard but one cry, "Pollution!" not only among Hindoos but Mahomedans. True, nothing was definite as yet, but the dread existed, and was increasing at every step of his progress. Priests, merchants, artisans, farmers, and soldiers were alike affected. It was a terrible engine; but none could be more effective for his purpose. The terror of pollution came home with fearful force alike to every Hindoo of every caste, and to all Mahomedans. Pollution could not be escaped: it could not be remedied. It concerned both the bold and the timid; and even the most timid grew bold under the influence of the new and possible danger. The excitement which now prevailed was different from any that had ever preceded it, and more intense. Had the time, then, come when the English, the authors and contrivers of this new tyranny, were to perish—to be destroyed in one huge popular commotion, from which none could escape? Not come exactly, and yet perhaps was very near; and the now venerable prediction of the terrible Sumbut 1914,[1] to which all alike looked, and in which all believed, might be fulfilled.

On the night of the 10th November, 1856, there was a meeting in the "lines" of the Thirty-fourth Native Infantry, then stationed at Barrackpoor, near Calcutta. The old Thirty-fourth had been disbanded at Meerut in 1844; and the present regiment, which had been raised a few years afterwards, retained, in no small degree, the traditions of its predecessor. Azráel Pandé knew most of the men; he had met their delegates in many stations of the army. He had visited them on several previous occasions, and he knew that they were faithful to the new cause in which so many had embarked. He had reached Calcutta after a rapid journey, and had brought with him letters and messages from many regiments, which had already been read with interest. That night he was to leave Calcutta again: and a final meeting had been arranged to bid him farewell, and to hear his last injunctions and counsel.

The "lines" of Sepoy Regiments in India form, as it were, villages, with broad streets between the houses, or cabins, which are all of one pattern. They contain a well-sized room, which can be divided by a partition, when necessary; the walls are built of clay, or sundried brick, and the roofs thatched. Each company has its separate row or street; and each man a house to himself, except when two of the same caste may desire to live together. These "lines" are generally planted with trees, and have a pretty and comfortable appearance. The houses of the native commissioned and non-commissioned officers are superior to those of the privates; and in some instances have separate inclosures or gardens.

One of these separate houses in the —— company of the Thirty-fourth, now the scene of the meeting, belonged to a jemadar, or

---

[1] The Sumbut or Eastern Year 1914 corresponded to the interval between March 25, 1857, and March 19, 1858, in the Christian Calendar. In every Hindoo almanac for a century, it had been foretold that the power of the English would be destroyed in that year; and the belief in that prophecy was one of the causes that led to the mutiny.

native lieutenant of the regiment, with whom Mungul Pandé, his cousin and Azráel's nephew, a private in the regiment, lived. He had applied for leave to hold a recitation of religious books at night, and to be allowed "lights and singing," which was not unusual, and had attracted no particular attention.

Azráel Pandé was the reciter, and the reading had continued late into the night. One by one the listeners had departed, and those who had come for a special purpose alone remained. The jemadar looked closely round the room to see if any one not in the secret were present, and went out to ascertain that all was safe; and on entering again he carefully put out the lights, except one small lamp which burned in a niche, and even were it noticed from without, would attract no particular attention. Then he barred the door, and said, "We may speak freely now, brothers; let Azráel Pandé tell us what he has heard, and what he would have us do. Gather close to him, that he may not need to raise his voice."

There were about twenty men, tall and strong, as men of Oudh and Bahar always are; men with handsome, regular features, and fair skins, descendants of the Aryan warriors of past ages. They were not all of the Thirty-fourth, for there were other regiments at the station who had sent delegates to hear counsel, and make arrangements. These men now huddled together on the earthen floor; and Azráel Pandé, their teacher, naked to the waist, his head bare, his long, soft, wavy hair thrown back over his shoulders, and his forehead, breast and arms painted with the sacred marks of their faith, sat in a raised seat above them, on which his host generally slept. The light from the lamp flickered, and cast weird, varying shadows about the room, and now and again rested brightly upon him, shewing his broad, muscular frame, and lighting up his stern, savage features; but the faces of the men before him were in deep shadow; and all that could be seen of them, closely muffled as they were, was their gleaming eyes, as one turned to another in the most exciting portions of their teacher's address.

"Brothers!" he said, when all were silent and still, "I am not one unknown to ye. What part I played in the old Thirty-fourth ye know well, and I need not remind you of it. What I have done since, ye do not know; but for twelve years, wherever I could strike a blow against the Feringee power, I have not failed to do so. Wherever I saw hesitation, doubt, or cupidity among our people, I have preached, I have urged, I have entreated them not to forget the past, but to cling together for their honour and their caste, in a time which the holy mother, Kalee, told me was to come. I have borne hunger and thirst, poverty and weariness, in my wanderings from place to place. I have been tried and sentenced to die: and I should have been hanged in pollution, but for that poor fellow who sits among ye, who saved my life at the risk of his own. As a Gosain, as a Bairagee, as a Jogee, as a pilgrim carrying Ganges water on his shoulders for hundreds of miles—as a Brahmin expounding these holy books before me, I have travelled throughout the length and breadth of the country. I have attended fairs, and markets, and holy shrines. I have been the honoured guest of great Rajahs, and even of Nawabs; and—O listen, brothers!—I have heard but one cry—a cry that came from the very souls of the people—deliverance from the English!

"Why is this? Listen, and I will tell you. Which of us on the march, as he stepped into any one of the holy rivers, has not cried out, 'Jey Gunga Mata!' and then, 'Jey Koompanee Bahadoor!' With such cries our fathers went to battle, and won a thousand victories. But that is past. The 'Koompanee' is not as it used to be; it is no longer an incarnation of our gods. It has changed into a mean, cheating robber, who farms this great Hind of ours from the government of England, and robs it of all it can carry away. Where do those great ships yonder take the cotton, and the indigo, and the silk which the poor ryots have produced, but to England? Do they bring us anything in return? No! nothing but what we have to buy, and very dearly; and even the old Moghuls did not tax our salt and our opium. When the 'Koompanee' was as a prince we served them; and shed our blood for them in faith and honour. They were our fathers and our mothers. But now!—listen to what they have done.

"Three years ago I was in Nagpoor. The Rajah, who had been kind to me, died. No adoption to perform his obsequies was allowed, and his soul now wanders in hell. Then the Feringees seized his kingdom, confiscated his wealth, and even the clothes and jewels of his wives; and these, and their horses and elephants, their bullocks, were sold by auction, and the Koompanee took the money. Listen further. In the same year the Rajah of Jhansy died, a man who flew the English flag over his fort with his own. He left his little kingdom to be taken care of by the English for his descendants; but they seized it themselves, and keep it fast. In the west they took Sattara, and the family of Sivajee are beggars. Well, all these were state acts, and concern distant people. You have not heard their groans and cries as I have; and let them pass.

"But the greed of dominion has come nearer to you. It has come at last to our homesteads in Oudh, where our people have lived free for thousands of years; and Oudh has become Feringee, like Nagpoor and Jhansy. Is not all this true, and need it not be avenged?

"Do not murmur," he continued, stretching out his hands over the now excited men. "The time comes—nay, it is near,—when you may shout 'Jey Kalee' with me, and bathe your hands in the hot English blood. Do not murmur, my sons, but listen. Have I told you all? Nay, if it were so, the loss of these kingdoms need not concern you. Those that lost them might cry and wail, but that would not affect one rupee of your pay, or one yard of the land ye possess. The English are too wise to interfere with them. But is there no more? What did I hear the people in the meeting of the Dhurma Subha say, only two days ago? What did I hear the Brahmins in the temple of Kalee, when I worshipped there to-day, say among themselves, and to us strangers: 'Come here no more!' they cried. 'The order is gone out from the new Lord Sahib, that all Hindoos must become Christians, for the Queen of England has so determined. Come no more!' they cried, beating their mouths and their breasts; 'this day—any day—the holy temple of the mother whom we serve, may be defiled with cow's blood!' Ah yes; they believed this, those wise old priests, and why should not we, my sons?"

Then there was a low, hoarse murmur of, "We have heard it: we believe it!"

"Yes," he continued, "you believe that, because the wrong comes home to yourselves. But listen further. We soldiers used to feel that we were safe against going over the sea. Now I hear on every hand a groan of despair that you are no longer safe; that when the order comes you must go over the black water, which washes out all trace of caste. You, every one of you that hear me now—every Brahmin and Rajpoot who heard me to-night —every one of the tens of thousands who serve in the army—must go—go to-morrow, if the Lord Sahib wills it—over the sea. If you by chance escape this fate your sons cannot. Every man who enlists now must swear on the Ganges water, and holy Toolsee, to ensure the destruction of his own caste! What horrible mockery is this! Yet they will require you all, young and old, to go, or they will blow you away from their guns.

"Why are you quiet? Why have you borne this? This order is nearly half a year old, yet you have done nothing! Where is your honour, where is your caste? Do I speak to Brahmins and Rajpoots, or to outcast Mléchas and leather-dressers? Does not this come home to your hearts? When you return from the sea, will your wives embrace you? will they put your children into your arms? will your stalwart sons admit you into your homes? I tell you they will not, they dare not! They will say to you, 'Begone! ye are polluted.' They will not give you a cup of water were you even dying of thirst at your door. They cannot look upon you; they will shout to you, 'Ye were cowards to lose your caste, and had better died!'

"Ah, yes!" he cried, as he wiped the foam from his lips; "you may writhe there, and murmur, and weep; but you, who are Brahmins, know that this is true, as well as I, a Brahmin, who tells it to you. But listen, I have yet more to say. Am I inventing tales to frighten you with? Not I. What the English do, they spread abroad that all may know it; and look you, my sons, how hellish are their contrivances to sap the very foundations of Hindoo faith and purity. Now the law is gone forth, that Hindoo widows may marry again—Brahmins, Kshettrees, Soodras alike!—Think, anyone of you, where your honour would be, if your widow married another man? Where would be the old respect and love which sealed the devotion of its life by holy suttee? Now, every woman who pleases may, like a prostitute, take a new husband. Think of the pity of this: think of the sin of it!" "Brothers!" he cried, with his hands outstretched and quivering, and his eyes flashing, "such are your own wives now, such are your mothers or sisters, for such have the English made them. I thank God that this misery is saved me, that mine died years ago, and that I have no child to endure pollution. There were times when Brahmins and Rajpoots plunged their swords and spears into their wives' hearts when there was even a suspicion or a dread of dishonour. As I traversed Rajpootana I heard many an old ballad which told of such things—for these memories never die—and I could say them to you; but no! you could not feel them: you are dead—dead to honour—dead to shame—dead to your faith! You have no caste, how should you understand the thoughts or the honour of those who still hold it? Are you silent?"

They were silent, for most were sobbing, some gnashed their teeth, and drew their breath in hard gasps and sighs.

"Another few words would I speak, my sons," he continued; "and you know this last ignominy better than I do. What are these new muskets which have been sent among you? Did not the old win all Hind for the English? win it with your fathers' blood, freely poured out. Did not thousands of our people perish in the Khyber amidst the snow and ice—whose blood cries for vengeance? Did not these men die with the old guns in their frozen hands? We, in the former times, did not want cows' and pigs' fat for them; our arms were strong enough to ram down the cartridges that we used, and our bullets then were as deadly as these; who ever withstood them? Now, the Feringees must have new cartridges and new guns, which require the fat of cows and pigs. I tell you there is no sense in this, no reason for this. Who is there in Hind left to fight? We, the men of Oudh and Bahar, have conquered all, even from the Sikhs. Ah yes, see brothers! the Sikhs and the Ghoorkhas don't mind fat, and they will be brought down on you in thousands and tens of thousands, to blow you away from guns, or to send you home to cover your faces and weep like women. So there is no need of this change of arms; but this is certain, that when you have once handled and bitten these fat-besmeared cartridges, you had better go to the Padré Sahib, and take the Baptisma at once. Poor fellows! you will have no caste left, and all the waters of Gunga Mata will not wash out your impurity. What will it then signify if you are all made to eat together in messes, as the white soldiers do? and then you will have cows' fat and pigs' fat in plenty, and Christians and Mléchas to cook your food. There is an order gone out about that in jails already, and what are you better than convicts? They have put chains on the land, these English. There are iron roads and iron wires stretching up to Dehly, and now going on to Peshàwur, upon the land and its people. When they reach the Indus, yours will follow. You with your caste who would have protected Hindoos, will no longer be Hindoos! but Christian slaves—unable to protect them.

"Do not weep, brothers! do not groan. This is no time for weeping. Arise! be resolute! Strike! for the sake of your honour, your faith and your caste. When there are no English, you will be free. Be like me, who have vowed this day before Kalee Mata, that every Feringee man, woman, or child, must die, and that she shall lick their blood. O! I will feed her with much of it, and it will be sweet—sweet!—for they are her direst enemies. Do not speak!" he continued, in the same hissing and mocking tone in which he had addressed the men. "I know your hearts, I know what you would say. But one thing I ask. If you are men, if you have still faith and caste, reach forward your hands one over another, and touch these books!" And the men rose to their feet and did as he had desired.

"Now swear," said Azráel solemnly; "by this holy Geeta, by the five products of the cow, and by my feet, that when the time comes, ye, and those ye represent, will strike in for the faith! That ye will refuse, even to the extremity of death, to take the cartridges, and to go beyond the sea!"

"We swear!" replied the men, in a hoarse whisper, "Jey Kalee Mata, we will be true to thee, even to death!"

"Good, my sons!" continued Azráel, "she, the mother, will help us all in our oaths. Now listen to her last words: 'Be cautious! wait for the signal! Do not anticipate it by any foolish haste which will bring destruction on us all. It is but for a little time; the English are in sore strait, their country is small, and they have few soldiers. They have now war in Europe with the Russians, and war in Persia, and they will soon have war in China. They have to send more of their troops from India, and already they have not half their usual number, and still they trust us. Ha! ha! ha! Well! they might have done so safely, had they kept their old faith!' Now depart: I go to Cawnpore, to Agra, to Dehly, to Amballa; Gokul will go to Dinapore with your letters. Write what has happened here to every camp in the army, but cautiously; and when Sumbut 1914 begins, the signal will not be long deferred.

"Now go! I leave my brother's son, Mungal Pandé, with you, be careful of him as one of your own."

Then the men passed him silently one by one, touching his feet reverently with their hands, and then their foreheads and breasts, and so glided out of the door into the darkness of the night. Before morning had dawned, Azráel Pandé rose and took leave of his host and his nephew, conjuring them to be faithful, and went to take his place in the northern train, on one of the iron chain roads that were to bind India and enslave its people!

"O Mother! wait, wait but a little," he murmured, stretching forth his hands towards Calcutta, "and thou shalt have the blood!"

THOMAS CAULFIELD IRWIN.

[Thomas Caulfield Irwin was born on May 4, 1823, at Warrenpoint, county Down. His father, Thomas Irwin, was a physician; his mother the daughter of Mr. Caulfield Cooke, a barrister, whose brother, the Rev. William Cooke, was, it may be mentioned, attached to St. Peter's Church, Dublin, at the same time as the Rev. Charles Maturin, the celebrated author of *Bertram*. Mr. Irwin was educated by private tutors, and acquired a thorough acquaintance with classics and several continental languages. He entered upon a literary career at an early age. By 1853 he was already so favourably known that he was employed by Mr. (now Sir) Charles Gavan Duffy to supply poetical contributions and literary essays to his journal. In 1854 he began to contribute to the *Dublin University Magazine*, and he continued to write frequently in that periodical until a recent period. Four collections of his poems have been published, *Versicles* (1856); *Poems* (1866); *Irish Historical and Legendary Poems* (1868); and *Songs and Romances* (1878). In the latter year there also appeared a selection of his prose writings under the title *Summer and Winter Stories*.

These volumes, however, represent but a small portion of what Mr. Irwin has written: 130 Tales, of various length, and essays on a vast number of subjects, have proceeded from his pen. He is the author of a romance of antique life, *From Cæsar to Christ*, in which there is a striking representation of Roman and British civilization in the reign of Nero. Many of the scenes are finely described, and some of the situations are very strong and exciting. He is also the author of a poetic drama, *Ortus and Ermia*, a versified translation of *Catullus*, and translations besides from several classical and continental poets. The verses of Mr. Irwin are fully deserving of the warm appreciation with which they have been received. He has true poetic inspiration. Picturesqueness and rich colour, a chaste and pure style, and a mastery of measure characterize all that he has written. Some of his prose reminds one of De Quincey in its picturesqueness and stately diction.]

LUCY'S ATTIRE.

(FROM "VERSICLES.")

When the Summer's sultry noon
   Flecks her chamber with its rays,
Or in arbours sweet, the moon
   Warmly waning through the haze,
Sheds along her careless hair
Languid lustres, she shall wear
Floating robes of purest white,
And perflèd scarf as airy light
As morning cloud: but when the crown
Of golden Autumn turns to brown,
And sad the wind of sunset blows
About the evening's shortened close;
When bees have settled in their hive,
And leaf-strewn gates are closed at five;
When moonlight fays in pantries flock
O'er milky pail and honey-crock,—
Oh then, in garb of russet she
Shall pace the rounds of housewifery;
   With key-bunch safe in apron fold,
     Mix with the twilight ouphs, and feast
     In morning casements, looking east,
   The bright-eyed robin puff'd with cold.

When December's leaden day
   Scarcely breaks the clasp of night,
Soft shall be her garb, and gay,
   Soft and warm in winter's spite;
Nettled caps of closest coil
Shall guard her locks in silken toil;
Bonnets blithe of darling dyes
Enshade her forehead's coquetries;
Collars crescent-shaped and white,
   Needled from the flaxen skein,
   Round her gentle throat will show
Like a wreath of crispy snow;—
   Even her finger tips shall glow
In tiny gloves that fit as tight

As pink sheaths of the perfumed bean.
But when norland tempests stir,
  Blowing o'er the frosted lands,
She must wear, without demur,
  Cosy refuges of fur
For sweetest neck, and cold white hands;
So that whosoe'er she meet
Shall deem her soft salute a treat:
And though skies are gray and dull
  Round about her, yet within
Mantle lined with warmest wool,
  Shall her heart make merry din;
As she treads the noon-day town
  Toward the costly decked bazaar;
Or, by evening forest brown
  Wanders with her favourite star.

Such shall seem her outward dress;
  As the mystic seasons roll
Seasoned with them; while no less
  Shall their image tinge her soul,
    Chaste as chill December; bright
    As starry July's summer night;
    Pure as April's gelid buds,
    Rich as August's fruited woods;
    Blending in its many moods,
    Nature's warmth with Heaven's light.

HYMN TO EURYDICE.

(FROM "ORPHEUS.")

Oh! love in life, oh! Paradise enrounded
  By weary distances of desert space,
At length I breathe amid thy bounteous regions,
  And meet at length thy spirit, face to face.
The present swims in sunlight past my vision,
  The past in dreams of darkness fades away,
And the fresh life-spring of a newer nature
  In fullest fountain rises into day.

There is love that broods like sunset o'er the ocean,
  Lapsing down content with change of shade and hue;
There is passion, proud, and conquerless, and earnest
  As the lightning-globe that cleaves the deeps of blue;
But oh! there is a worship of pure Beauty
  To whose altar turns the spirit's tranced sight,
Like a star which splendours through some magic casement,
  Misted round with urns of frankincense at night.

Oft at dawn her voice awakes my dreaming fancy,
  Like the sweet wind whispering in the rose's ear;
And her presence to my soul in trance of twilight,
  Where the first star lights the even, hovers near;

Like some purple sunset shadow in a valley,
  Girt with summer woods, by waters as they flow,
Glassing old heroic ruins on their stillness,
  Hamlet homes, and distant summits spired in snow.

Oh could sweet fancy realize its visions,
  Far, far from dusty cities would we roam,
O'er the earth in happy pilgrimage together,
  Till at length, some magic hour, we reached a home
In some golden land of noon beyond the mountains,
  In some ancient isle of sweet perfection, where
'Mid twilight temples, highest-thoughted music
  Filled with spirit round the fragrance of the air.

Where the goldened lark would set our hearts to music,
  As in jubilant communion with the sun,
We'd pace the airy mountains o'er the ocean,
  'Til the nightingale in woodland dusk begun:
Where joyously in heaven's light our spirits
  Would broaden with the glory of the hours;
And close beneath transparent dark in slumber,
  Life's odours masked in crimson folded flowers.

This were to live, to tread the world together,
  Passing on to higher lives beyond the night;
While Thought in subtle spheres illumed the future,
  And Fancy charmed the present in its flight:
Thus in loving pass the blossom of our being,
  'Mid realities of Beauty, and its dreams,
Like seraphs through some inland tract of heaven,
  Floating Godward up the glory of its streams.

HEARTH SONG.

(FROM "AN ANTIQUE DREAM.")

Spirit of the half-closed eyes,
  Pacing to a drowsy tune,
    Come to me ere midnight wanes,
    Come with all thy dreamy trains,
    Scattering o'er me poppy rains;
Dropping me 'mid weary sighs,
  Deep into a feathered swoon.
Leave thy odorous bed an hour—
Leave thy ebon-curtained bower—
  Leave thy cavern to the moon.
    Lowly burns the whitened hearth,
    Slowly turns the quiet earth.
    Now the woods and skies are dumb,
    In the dizzy midnight hum,
    Come to me, sweet phantom, come.

Hidden in the folded gray
  Of thy garment, bear the urn

Full of Lethe's unsunn'd streams;
  Bring the flowers that live in dreams,
  Bring the boy[1] who often seems
O'er the earth with me to stray,
  When the weary planets burn,
  In a cloud of shifting light,
  Through the hollow life of night
Mimicking the scene of day:
  Ye are coming nigher, nigher,
  With my song I seem to tire;
    I can hear thy pinion's hymn
    Round my faint ear's closing rim—
  Ye are coming, phantoms dim!

L'ANGELO.

(FROM "VERSICLES.")

I sit at eve within the curtain's fold,
  Where shone thy gentle face in the full moon
So many an eve; and sing some antique tune
We sung together oftentimes of old:
In that dear nook the lonely moonbeams fall,
  And touch thy empty chair with mournful light:
Thy picture gazes on me from the wall;
  I hear thy footsteps in old rooms at night.

On lonely roads beneath the darksome dawn,
  When broods upon the broad dead land the wind,
  I wander sadly, looking oft behind,
Maychance that I may see thy sceptre wan;
For still I deem thou followest me, and still
  Believe that love departs not with the clay:
Thy face looks on me from the morning hill,
  Thy smile comes sadly from the close of day.

Oft, oft by sandy ridges o'er the sea,
  Or over distant famished fields at night,
  Where sheds some low blue star its thinnest light,
I seek in earth's dim solitudes for thee:
Proud of the everlasting love I bear,
  Still mix with nature, drawing thence relief;
While, from the void of sunset's empty air,
  The stars look on the glory of my grief.

AN URN.

(FROM "SONGS AND ROMANCES.")

Mute urn, whose heart is empty now
  Of the dear ashes of a heart!
Who bearest on thy marble brow
    Nought but a name, and cry of grief,
    Memorial sad as brief;

---

[1] Morpheus was represented as a boy.

Hast thou no echo, like the ocean shell,
  Thy vague, dim history to tell,
Or in faint mystic murmurs to impart
  That of the soul invisible
    Whose form is flown?
A ruin amid ruins still thou art,
    Silent and alone.

Was it a hero whose proud dust
  Was once thy treasure, mournful urn?
A fool of battle's gloried lust,
  Death's puppet in a world where death
  Allows of life so brief a breath?
Or maiden fair, whose gentle breast
  Love filled, and sorrow laid at rest?
Or poet-brain, whose thoughts would burn
  In reverie, like the golden west?
    Or wise, bright-thoughted sage?
Or little child from tearful mother torn?
    Love's, life's last heritage.

Yon star-world shining o'er the sea,
O urn, upon thy silent form,
Though bright, may be a grave like thee;
  The symbol of a vanished past
  In yonder unimagined vast,
    Where suns and spheres, the bright abodes
    Of spirits, ranging up to gods,
Awhile in life's eternal storm
    Take shape and die. Yon senseless star,
    Ere yet through future fires it pass,
Ere yet from ruin 'tis re-born,
Bears its dim epitaph afar
    Like thine—"Alas!"

ENGLAND.

(FROM "THE LAST SIBYL.")

In sense-life lags the sunny sultaned East,
Its stationary empires, and its life
Of superstition, ignorance, and war.
But while awaiting morn, in dark it lies,
Lo! on the world's sea verge, northward away,
Shadowed by rolling cloud drifts from the pole,
An isle shall rear its navy-girdled throne,
Towering triumphant o'er the restless brine.
There shall arise the earth's progressive race.
Spirits of stubborn strength and energy,
Adventurous, daring, breathing of the sea.
Their mighty thunder-brimmed fleets shall awe
The citadelled harbours of the hoary main;
Their argosies with world-wealth laden deep,
Shall circle earth in valiant voyagings,
From summer's seas to winters of the pole,
Battling the blinding snow-drifts of the north,
Or heaving heavily on sultry sails,
Around the burning sun-belt of the earth.
A mighty land shall grow, and from its shores,

As from a sun-born, light-diffusing soul,
Shall spring a growth of nations destinied
To reign, and reigning, fill the world with peace;
Exalted o'er them that she may exalt,
And raise unto the stature of her power,
From continents of kindred west and south,
The races wandering on the skirts of night.

SUMMER WANDERINGS.

(FROM "SONGS AND ROMANCES.")

Lo! down the smoothes of water now
  Slides on some old barge travel-worn,
  And heavily heaped with yellow corn,
    From the valley's harvest lands;
    Beside the helm the steersman stands;
    While 'mid the sheaves of harvest wealth,
  Girls with cheeks as red as morn,
All autumn-bronzed on neck and brow,
  Lie in tumbles :—faint behind
The sleeky ripple gurgles slow
  Back to its level calm of glass;
  Onward as they swiftly pass,
The currents stutter round the prow;
  And as the wearied horses pause
  Beside the hedge of crimson'd haws,
    The veined water-lights waver and gleam
In dappling patches over their backs;
The boat rope whisps, and drippingly slacks
    In lisping plashes into the stream.
Blue insects on the large-leaved cool,
By starts jet o'er the quiet pool:
    Around the stalk of the hollyhock,
The yellow, lithe, thin-waisted wasp,
    Emitting sounds, now like a lisp
In the dry glare, now like a rasp,
Climbs slowlily with stealthy clasp,
    And vicious, intermittent hum;
Noses awhile each sickly bloom
    Withered round the edges crisp—
    Then headlong vanishing grows dumb.

SONNET.

In my soul's temple, sacredly enshrined
  'Mid airs the most divine, oh! still may I
  Conserve whate'er of best to beautify
The passing hours, synthetic search may find;
The truths of science, known to sense and mind,
  The singing pictures of sweet poetry;
  Ideas turned to use; all forms of art;
  High sympathies to symphony all strife;
A healthy hatred of the lies of life;
And in the holy of holies of the heart
Love for those loving me with purest faith,
  Volitioned in the future as the past,
  To guard; or, seek them through the terrorless vast,
When the earth melts beneath the touch of death.

RICHARD FRANCIS BURTON.

[Captain Burton has written some thirty volumes in description of his various wanderings throughout the globe. Other travellers have become better known, and been more highly rewarded; but there can be no doubt that the man who has never attained higher rank than a captaincy, or a more splendid office than a consulship, has more greatly dared, and won more knowledge, than any explorer of his time.

Richard Francis Burton was born in Tuam, county Galway, in 1821, and is the son of Colonel Joseph Netterville Burton. In 1842 he entered the Indian army, and continued in that service till 1861. He applied himself early to the study of eastern languages and customs; and having persisted in this labour of love during his entire life, he is now master of twenty-nine languages, European and Oriental. His first expedition was a singular proof of his knowledge of eastern ways and of his bold and enterprising spirit. He went to Mecca and Medina in the disguise of a pilgrim, and so was able to see sacred spots which had never before been beheld by the eye of the infidel. It is from his interesting work describing this expedition that our quotation is taken. He subsequently went on two exploring expeditions to Central Africa, his companion in both cases being the lamented Captain Speke. He had been employed by the government during the Crimean war on military service; in 1861 he was appointed to a consulship at Fernando Po, and he occupied his time in exploring the interior of Africa, paying a visit, among other persons, to the redoubtable and sanguinary King of Dahomey. He has held office in succession at São Paulo (Brazil), Damascus, and Trieste; and in each place he has found time to devote himself to his favourite occupation of surveying many men and various cities. He has been through North and South America, knows Syria and Iceland; has lived in almost every part of India; and in recent years has made several visits to the famous land of Midian. In the lengthy list of Captain Burton's books we may notice: *Narratives of Mission to Dahomey* (1864); *Vikram and the Vampire, or Tales of Hindu Devilry* (1869); *Two Trips to Gorilla Land* (1875); *Ultima Thule, or a Summer in Iceland* (1875); *The Gold Mines of Midian and the Ruined Midianite Cities* (1878). He is a good narrator of his adventures, and has many wondrous tales to tell. His style is not very polished, but it is usually graphic, and shows keen and humourous observation. Its chief fault is, perhaps, that Captain Burton, out of the fulness of his knowledge, enters too much into detail.]

FEMALE INFLUENCE AND POETRY AMONG THE ARABS.

There are two things which tend to soften the ferocity of Bedouin life. These are, in the first place, intercourse with citizens, who frequently visit and intrust their children to the people of the Black tents; and, secondly, the social position of the women.

The author of certain "Lectures on Poetry, addressed to Working Men," asserts that Passion became Love under the influence of Christianity, and that the idea of a virgin mother spread over the sex a sanctity unknown to the poetry or the philosophy of Greece and Rome. Passing over the objections of deified Eros and Immortal Psyche and of the virgin mother,—symbol of moral purity,—being common to all old and material faiths, I believe that all the noble tribes of savages display the principle. Thus we might expect to find, wherever the fancy, the imagination, and the ideality are strong, some traces of a sentiment innate in the human organization. It exists, says Mr. Catlin, amongst the North American Indians, and even the Gallas and the Somal of Africa are not wholly destitute of it. But when the barbarian becomes a semi-barbarian, as are the most polished Orientals, or as were the classical authors of Greece and Rome, then women fall from their proper place in society, become mere articles of luxury, and sink into the lowest moral condition. In the next state, "civilization," they rise again to be "highly accomplished," and not a little frivolous.

Were it not evident that the spiritualising of sexuality by imagination is universal among the highest orders of mankind, I should attribute the origin of love to the influence of the Arabs' poetry and chivalry upon European ideas rather than to mediæval Christianity.

In pastoral life, tribes often meet for a time, live together whilst pasturage lasts, and then separate perhaps for a generation. Under such circumstances youths, who hold with the Italian that

"Perduto e tutto il tempo
Che in amor non si spende,"

will lose heart to maidens, whom possibly, by the laws of the clan, they may not marry, and the light o' love will fly her home. The fugitives must brave every danger, for revenge, at all times the Bedouin's idol, now becomes the lode-star of his existence. But the Arab lover will dare all consequences. "Men have died and the worms have eaten them, but not for love," may be true in the West; it is false in the East. This is attested in every tale where love, and not ambition, is the groundwork of the narrative. And nothing can be more tender, more pathetic than the use made of these separations and the long absences by the old Arab poets. Whoever peruses the "Suspended Poem" of Lebid will find thoughts at once so plaintive and so noble, that even Dr. Carlyle's learned verse cannot wholly deface their charm. The author returns from afar. He looks upon the traces of hearth and home still furrowing the desert ground. In bitterness of spirit he checks himself from calling aloud upon his lovers and his friends. He melts at the remembrance of their departure, and long indulges in the absorbing theme. Then he strengthens himself by the thought of Nawara's inconstancy, how she left him and never thought of him again. He impatiently dwells upon the charms of the places which detain her, advocates flight from the changing lover and the false friend, and, in the exultation with which he feels his swift dromedary start under him upon her rapid course, he seems to find some consolation for woman's perfidy and forgetfulness. Yet he cannot abandon Nawara's name or memory. Again he dwells with yearning upon scenes of past felicity, and he boasts of his prowess,—a fresh reproach to her,—of his gentle birth, and of his hospitality. He ends with an encomium upon his clan, to which he attributes, as a noble Arab should, all the virtues of man. This is Goldsmith's deserted village in El Hejaz. But the Arab, with equal simplicity and pathos, has a fire, a force of language, and a depth of feeling, which the Irishman, admirable as his verse is, could never rival.

As the author of the *Peninsular War* well remarks, women in troublesome times, throwing off their accustomed feebleness and frivolity, become helpmates meet for man. The same is true of pastoral life. Here, between the extremes of fierceness and sensibility, the weaker sex, remedying its great want, power, raises itself by courage, physical as well as moral. In the early days of El Islam, if history be credible, Arabia had a race of heroines. Within the last century, Ghaliyah, the wife of a Wahhabi chief, opposed Mohammed Ali himself in many a bloody field. A few years ago, when Ibn Asm, popularly called Ibn Rumi, chief of the Zubayd clan about Rabigh, was treacherously slain by the Turkish general, Kurdi Usman, his sister, a fair young girl, determined to revenge him. She fixed upon the "Arafat-day" of pilgrimage for the accomplishment of her designs, disguised herself in male attire, drew her handkerchief in the form of "lisam" over the lower part of her face, and with lighted match awaited her enemy. The Turk, however, was not present, and the girl was arrested, to win for herself a local reputation equal to that of the maid of Salamanca. Thus it is that the Arab has learned to swear that great oath " by the honour of my women."

The Bedouins are not without a certain Platonic affection, which they call " Hawa (or Ishk) uzri,"—pardonable love. They draw the fine line between *amant* and *amoreux*: this is derided by the townspeople, little suspecting how much such a custom says in favour of the wild men. In the cities, however, it could not prevail. Arabs, like other Orientals, hold that, in such matters, man is saved, not by faith, but by want of faith. They have also a saying not unlike ours—

" She partly is to blame who has been tried,
He comes too near who comes to be denied."

The evil of this system is that they, like certain southerns, *pensano sempre al male*— always suspect, which may be worldly wise, and also always show their suspicions, which is assuredly foolish. For thus they demoralize their women, who might be kept in the way of right by self-respect and a sense of duty. To raise our fellow-creatures we have only to show that we think better of them than they deserve—disapprobation and suspicion draw forth the worst traits of character and conduct.

From ancient periods of the Arab's history we find him practising " knight-errantry," the wildest form of chivalry. " 'The Songs of Antar,'" says the author of the *Crescent and the Cross*, " show little of the true chivalric spirit." What thinks the reader of sentiments like these? " This valiant man," remarks Antar, (who was " ever interested for the weaker sex,") " hath defended the honour of women." We read in another place, " Mercy, my lord, is the noblest quality of the noble." Again, " It is the most ignominious of deeds to take free-born women prisoners." " Bear not malice, O Shibub!" quoth the hero, " for of malice good never came." Is there no true greatness in this sentiment?—" Birth is the boast of the *fainéant*; noble is the youth who beareth every ill, who clotheth himself in mail during the noon-tide heat, and who wandereth through the outer darkness of night." And why does the " knight of knights " love Ibla? Because " she is blooming as the sun at dawn, with hair black as the midnight shades, with Paradise in her eye, her bosom an enchantment, and a form waving like the tamarisk when the soft winds blow from the hills of Nejd?" Yes, but his chest expands also with the thoughts of her " faith, purity, and affection,"—it is her moral as well as her material excellence that makes her the hero's " hope, and hearing, and sight." Briefly, in Antar I discern

" ——A love exalted high
By all the glow of chivalry ; "

and I lament to see so many intelligent travellers misjudging the Arab after a superficial experience of a few debased Syrians or Sinaites. The true children of Antar have *not* " ceased to be gentlemen."

In the days of ignorance, it was the custom for Bedouins, when tormented by the tender passion, which seems to have attached them in the form of " possession," for long years to sigh and wail and wander, doing the most truculent deeds to melt the obdurate fair. When Arabia islamized, the practice changed its element for proselytism. The Fourth Caliph is fabled to have travelled far, redressing the injured, punishing the injurer, preaching to the infidel, and especially protecting women—the chief end and aim of knighthood. The Caliph El Mutasem heard in the assembly of his courtiers that a woman of Sayyid family had been taken prisoner by a "Greek barbarian" of Ammoria. The man on one occasion struck her, when she cried "Help me, O Mutasem!" and the clown said derisively, "Wait till he cometh upon his pied steed!" The chivalrous prince arose, sealed up the wine-cup which he held in his hand, took oath to do his knightly *devoir*, and on the morrow started for Ammoria with 70,000 men, each mounted on a piebald charger. Having taken the place, he entered it, exclaiming, "Labbayki, Labbayki!—Here am I at thy call." He struck off the caitiff's head, released the lady with his own hands, ordered the cup-bearer to bring the sealed bowl, and drank from it, exclaiming, "Now, indeed, wine is good!" To conclude this part of the subject with another far-famed instance. When El Mutanabbi, the poet, prophet, and warrior of Hams (A. H. 354), started together with his son on their last journey, the father proposed to seek a place of safety for the night. "Art thou the Mutanabbi," exclaimed his slave, "who wrote these lines,—

"'I am known to the night, and the wild, and the steed,
To the guest, and the sword, to the paper and reed?'"

The poet, in reply, lay down to sleep on Tigris' bank, in a place haunted by thieves, and, disdaining flight, lost his life during the hours of darkness.

It is the existence of this chivalry among the "Children of Antar" which makes the society of Bedouins ("damned saints," perchance, and "honourable villains,") so delightful to the traveller who, like the late Haji Wali (Dr. Wallin), understands and is understood by them. Nothing more *naïve* than his lamentations at finding himself in the "loathsome company of Persians," or among Arab townspeople, whose "filthy and cowardly minds" he contrasts with the "high and chivalrous spirit of the true Sons of the Desert." Your guide will protect you with blade and spear, even against his kindred, and he expects you to do the same for him. You may give a man the lie, but you must lose no time in baring your sword. If, involved in dispute with overwhelming numbers, you address some elder, "Dakhilak ya Shaykh!"—(I am) thy protected, O Sir,—and he will espouse your quarrel, and, indeed, with greater heat and energy than if it were his own. But why multiply instances?

The language of love and war and all excitement is poetry, and here, again, the Bedouin excels. Travellers complain that the wild men have ceased to sing. This is true if "poet" be limited to a few authors whose existence everywhere depends upon the accidents of patronage or political occurrences. A far stronger evidence of poetic feeling is afforded by the phraseology of the Arab, and the highly imaginative turn of his commonest expressions. Destitute of the poetic taste, as we define it, he certainly is: as in the Milesian, wit and fancy, vivacity and passion, are too strong for reason and judgment, the reins which guide Apollo's car. And although the Bedouins no longer boast a Lebid or a Maisunah, yet they are passionately fond of their ancient bards. A man skilful in reading "El Mutanabbi" and the "Suspended Poems" would be received by them with the honours paid by civilization to the travelling millionnaire. And their elders have a goodly store of ancient and modern war songs, legends, and love ditties, which all enjoy.

I cannot well explain the effect of Arab poetry to one who has not visited the desert. Apart from the pomp of words, and the music of the sound, there is a dreaminess of idea and a haze thrown over the object, infinitely attractive, but indescribable. Description, indeed, would rob the song of indistinctness, its essence. To borrow a simile from a sister art. The Arab poet sets before the mental eye the dim grand outlines of a picture,—which must be filled up by the reader, guided only by a few glorious touches, powerfully standing out, and the sentiment which the scene is intended to express;—whereas, we Europeans and moderns, by stippling and minute touches, produce a miniature on a large scale so objective as to exhaust rather than to arouse reflection. As the poet is a creator, the Arab's is poetry, the European's versical description. The language, "like a faithful wife, following the mind and giving birth to its offspring," and, free from that "luggage of particles" which clogs our modern tongues, leaves a mysterious vagueness between the relation of word to word, which materially assists the sentiment, not the sense, of the poem. When verbs and nouns have—each one—many different significations, only the radical or general idea suggests itself. Rich and varied synonyms, illustrating the finest shades of meaning, are artfully used; now scattered to startle us by distinctness, now to form as it were a star about which dimly seen satellites revolve. And, to cut short a disquisition which might be prolonged indefinitely, there is in the Semitic dialect a copiousness of rhyme which leaves the poet almost unfettered to choose the desired expression. Hence it is that a stranger speaking Arabic becomes poetical as naturally as he would be witty in French and philosophic in German. Truly spake Mohammed el Damiri, "Wisdom hath alighted upon three things—the brain of the Franks, the hands of the Chinese, and the tongues of the Arabs."

JAMES RODERICK O'FLANAGAN.

[James Roderick O'Flanagan is the son of Captain O'Flanagan, and was born in Fermoy barracks, September 1st, 1814. He received his early education in the principal school of his native town. After a lengthened tour on the Continent he published his first work, *Impressions at Home and Abroad*, 1837. In the following year he began practising as a barrister, and for many succeeding years his talents were known and appreciated on the Munster circuit. In 1845 Mr. O'Flanagan began contributing a series of important articles to the *Dublin University Magazine* on "Irish Rivers." For several years he was a constant writer in various leading Irish periodicals, and was editor of the *Irish National Magazine*. In 1861 *The History of Dundalk* appeared. It is a work of great local interest, and was written in conjunction with the late John D'Alton. *The Bar Life of O'Connell*, published in 1866, was well received by the public; the author wrote from personal knowledge of his subject, and his narrative thus possesses a strong and living interest. A sporting novel, *Brian O'Ryan*, was his next work, followed by his most valuable contribution to Irish literature, *The Lives of the Lord Chancellors of Ireland* (1870). These volumes embrace a period extending from the reign of Henry III. to the reign of Queen Victoria. The political and religious aspect of affairs is touched upon without bias or prejudice of any kind. The author advocates throughout what every true lover of his country would approve, "the abandoning of sectarian and political differences, and remembering their common country." The opening chapter of the first volume introduces the reader to the legal forms and tribunals of the Irish, previous to the introduction of the English laws. It is deeply interesting, and portrays to the thoughtful reader the character and history of the race more truly than many a lengthened volume. Mr. O'Flanagan's late work, *The Irish Bar* (1878-9), is written in a bright lively style, and shows no falling off either in the author's memory or powers of graphic description. The times depicted can never again return; those who have personal experience of them are fast passing away, and only such works as *The Irish Bar* remain, increasing in value year by year as links between the present and the wild, eccentric, but highly picturesque past in Irish life. His latest book, *The Munster Circuit* (1880), has been favourably reviewed in *The Times;* and the author is now engaged in preparing for the press a work entitled *Anecdotes and Sketches of Prelates and Priests of every Denomination*.]

HARRY DEANE GRADY.

(FROM "THE IRISH BAR."[1])

Among the most eminent Irish Nisi Prius lawyers of the earlier portion of the present century, was Harry Deane Grady. He was a native of the county of Limerick, and was fitted by nature as well as by profession for the bar. In stature he was short and stout, with a face indicative of shrewd wit and caustic humour. His voice was loud, and he possessed a robust sort of phraseology which smacked more of the *fortiter in modo* than *suaviter in re*. He had been elected one of the members for Limerick in the Irish House of Commons, and soon became one of the government's staunch supporters. When remonstrated with on going against the wishes of his constituents who were opposed to the Union, he very resolutely declared his ideas to be strongly in favour of that project, and hinted the government had made it worth his while to vote for that measure.

"What!" cried his indignant remonstrator, "do you mean to sell your country?"

---

[1] By permission of Messrs. Sampson Low & Co.

"Thank God," cried this pure patriot, "that I have a country to sell."

He was very coarse in his expressions, and when reminded that he owed his position to his constituents, he said, "I care nothing for my constituents, I get nothing good from them. Begad if I only shake hands with them they give me the itch."

His bullying, bustling, browbeating manner was of great use in Nisi Prius cases, when rough work was to be done, and no one at the bar could perform any sort of bullying better than Harry Deane Grady. His great delight was to encounter a really intelligent, but assumedly obtuse Irish witness, when a trial of skill would take place, the astute counsel endeavouring to extract much in favour of his client, and the witness resolved to reveal but little. Grady would give the witness his own way at first, pretend to credit his statement, nay, encourage him with such words as "exactly," "just so," and thus leading the witness to suppose he had gained the victory, and triumphed over "the counsellor," but all this time Grady was ingeniously weaving a net in which to ensnare his victim, and having obtained the requisite admissions, suddenly changed his tactics, and obliged the baffled witness to admit his story was a pure invention.

Grady exercised much influence in court by what he termed "his jury eye." His right eye was constantly used in winking at the jury when he wished them to note some particular answer from an adverse witness. Appearing in court one morning in rather depressed spirits, which, for one of his usual joyous temperament, was very unusual, a sympathizing friend said,—

"Harry, are you unwell? You are not as lively as usual."

"How can I, my dear fellow?" he answered.

"What's the matter with you?"

"My *jury eye is out of order*," was the reply.

But Harry Deane Grady's rough manner was not always successful. O'Connell could be rough when occasion required, but no one could be smoother, or use the blarney with more tact, when it was the fitter instrument to ensure success. The following anecdote illustrates the difference between these two eminent barristers in a very complete manner.

Shortly after joining the Munster Circuit, O'Connell was travelling with Harry Deane Grady. They shared in the expense of a chaise, and were posting from Cork to Dublin. Their route lay over the Kilworth mountains, then much frequented by highway-robbers. While changing horses in Fermoy, a few miles at the south side of the Kilworth mountains, both gentlemen made the disagreeable discovery that though they had pistols, they had no powder, and their balls, therefore, were useless. . . .

While Grady and O'Connell were regretting not having looked to their weapons before leaving Cork, the clatter of horses' hoofs and the martial sound of dragoons, with their long swords, saddles, and bridles attracted their attention.

"Hallo," cried O'Connell, "we're in luck. Here is the escort of the judges, and we may be able to get a supply from them."

"That's very likely," said Grady, as the corporal and four of the privates came from the stable, where they had left their chargers, and tramped as troopers do tramp into the hotel.

"I'll go at once, and see what I can get," said Harry as he passed into the hall. He walked up to the corporal, and in his blunt way said, "Soldier, will you sell me some powder?"

The corporal stood on his dignity. He eyed his interrogator very superciliously, as he replied, "I do not sell powder, sir."

"Then perhaps you'd tell me where I could get some. Or you might buy it for me!"

"I am here on duty, and, besides, I do not know this place, sir," replied the dragoon.

Grady, somewhat crestfallen, returned to his companion, who overheard what passed through the open door.

"The dragoon is a sulky fellow," he said, "he would neither sell or buy for me!"

"Harry," replied Dan O'Connell, "you offended him by calling him a soldier, when he is a corporal. I'll try my hand." O'Connell then went to the hall, and observed to the dragoon, who was looking rather ruefully at the downpour of rain then falling,—

"This is heavy rain, sergeant. 'Tis too bad, the judges do not get the yeomen or militia to escort them, without requiring the service of the regular troops."

"True enough, sir. It is harassing duty such weather as this, but duty must be done."

"I hear a bad account of the road before me—these Kilworth mountains are said to harbour robbers. My pistols are useless, for, unfortunately, I left Cork without procuring a supply of powder; could you procure me some and you'd oblige me?"

"I shall be most happy to let you have what I hope may suffice for you, sir," replied the corporal, opening his cartouch-box. O'Connell produced his pistols, and the bore exactly corresponded with the cartridges of the dragoon.

"Take half-a-dozen cartridges, sir," said the man, "and I'm glad to be able to oblige you."

"A glass of spirits and water will do you no harm this wet day," said O'Connell, and the dragoon drank his health, ere he resumed the saddle.

"Dan," cried Grady, when O'Connell displayed his plentiful store of ammunition, "you'll do—blarney for ever."

The course Harry Deane Grady had taken in supporting the Union caused him to be much censured by several influential persons in Limerick, who were opposed to that measure. They were resolved to express their disapproval, and having convened a meeting of the Limerick electors, deputed three to wait upon the place-hunting member. They consisted of a Protestant bishop, suspected of democratic leanings, Dr. Cheyne, an eminent physician, and General Burgoyne, who had served in China. Harry listened very patiently while they denounced his conduct in very severe terms, accusing him of injuring his country, deserting his duty, and betraying his constituents. These very serious charges were met by Harry with a bold denial.

"I did none of these crimes, my lord and gentlemen," he said. "I was opposed to the Union at first, but as soon as it was rightly explained to me,[1] I saw it was the greatest boon this country could receive, and I am satisfied my constituents will approve of my vote when I bring the case to their full knowledge."

"No, indeed!" was the response; "they all declare you have betrayed them."

"Nonsense, gentlemen—rank nonsense," cried the indomitable place-man; "you come between me and my constituents, and induce them to condemn me, on the *ipse dixit* of a republican parson, a quack doctor, and a battered old mandarin."—As the deputation felt Harry was getting personal they bowed and withdrew.

When it suited his purpose to abuse he spared no one. During a trial at the Limerick assizes his first cousin was a witness for the party opposed to his clients, and Harry cross-examined him in a most unsparing and savage way. He did not rest there. When addressing the jury, in alluding to the evidence of this witness, he said, "This case is supported by evidence as disgraceful as ever came before a judge or jury; the plaintiff, not content with the most outrageous statement, supports it by placing this wretched creature on the table, for whom I can find no fitter appellation than his miserable jackal."

The gentleman thus publicly vituperated was of very haughty demeanour, and we can well imagine his feelings on being thus held up to public view by his own first cousin.

During the day, after leaving court, he saw Harry in one of the principal streets of Limerick, appearing with outstretched hand. When within a short distance,—

"My dear John," cried Harry, "I'm heartily glad to see you."

"I wonder, sir," replied his cousin coldly, "you dare address me, after the gross insult you inflicted upon me this morning." He was about passing, when the cool counsel said,—

"Oh, never mind that, John; that's my trade, you know. I'll dine with you to-day."

"If you go to my house I'll take care not to dine at home," was the reply.

"All the better," responded Harry; "in that case, I shall have Mary (his cousin's wife) all to myself."

Harry Deane Grady's daughters were very lovely and most accomplished girls, and made brilliant marriages. Indeed, so many peers were attracted by their fascinations to his residence at Dublin, it was called "The House of Lords." One daughter became Lady Muskerry, another Lady Masserene, another Lady Roche. He had a beautiful place near Stillorgan, and lived to an old age.

WILLIAM CONNOR MAGEE, D.D.

[Irishmen of whatever creed cannot but feel gratified to know that thousands are willing to wait patiently for hours at St. Paul's, Westminster Abbey, or some other of our great churches, to hear the eloquence of a fellow-countryman, who is one of the greatest pulpit orators of the day. Dr. Magee, the Bishop of Peterborough, is at present beyond all question the most popular preacher in the Church of England, and has a reputation to which there has been nothing like rivalry since the death of Dr. Wilberforce.

---

[1] He was appointed a commissioner of revenue, with £1200 a year.

William Connor Magee was born at Cork in 1821, and comes from a family which is very distinguished in ecclesiastical history. His grandfather, Archbishop Magee, was, as is known, one of the most influential politicians and ablest theologians of his time. His father was the Rev. John Magee, vicar of St. John's, Drogheda. The career of Dr. Magee at Trinity College was distinguished both in the official studies prescribed, and in that unofficial but perhaps equally important arena, the College Historical Society. He there stood out for oratorical power from all his contemporaries, and heads the list of auditors in the revived Intern Society. Over his gradations in ecclesiastical office we can pass rapidly. Ordained in 1844, his first charge was that of a curate of St. Thomas's Church in Dublin. After a residence of two years in Malaga, where he was obliged to take refuge on account of his health, he was attached to St. Saviour's Church in Bath for two years, and in 1850 he was transferred to the Octagon Chapel, first as joint and afterwards as sole incumbent. His tenure of office gave opportunity for the exercise of his activity and intellectual influence. Among other results of his incumbency, it may be mentioned that when the Liberation Society started an organization in Bath, a counter association was established through the efforts of Dr. Magee under the title of "The Bath Church Defence Society;" and a brilliant lecture on "The Voluntary System and the Established Church" was so effective that several other societies of a like kind immediately arose throughout the country. Dr. Magee was afterwards attached to the Quebec Chapel in London. In 1864 he became rector of Enniskillen, in the same year was made dean of Cork, and in 1866 became dean of the Chapel Royal, Dublin. Dr. Jeune, the bishop of Peterborough, died in 1868, and Dr. Magee was raised to the vacant see. Some unflattering comment was naturally evoked by the promotion of an Irishman and a graduate of Trinity College to an English bishopric; but the commanding position which Dr. Magee has since attained in the Church, and the great abilities—of which, indeed, he had already given ample proof—have more than vindicated his right to the high position.

The published writings of Dr. Magee are almost exclusively of a religious character, and consist in the main of sermons preached upon special occasions. Long before his elevation to the episcopate he was sought after on several notable occasions on which a declaration of opinion from the English Church was particularly needful. Thus he was selected to preach before the British Association at Norwich in 1868, and it was he also who delivered the inaugural sermon at the Church Congress in Dublin. The latter discourse has since been republished under the title of "The Breaking Net," and its perusal years after its delivery will explain to a large extent the remarkable enthusiasm with which it was received at the time. The other discourses of Dr. Magee which have excited most attention are "The Gospel and the Age," preached at the ordination at Whitehall Chapel in 1860; "The Church's Fear and the Church's Hope," preached in Wells Cathedral in 1864; and "The Relation of the Atonement to the Divine Justice," an address delivered to the clergy at Radley. A series of discourses delivered at Norwich in defence and confirmation of the Christian faith have also attracted great notice, and have been translated into several continental languages. Dr. Magee has had opportunities, however, of delivering other than purely ecclesiastical addresses. As a member of the House of Lords he has occasionally taken part in discussions on subjects of a political character. His speech in vindication of the Irish Church was beyond all question the ablest defence of that institution, and at once brought him into the first rank of parliamentary debaters in the Upper House. He has since made noteworthy addresses on the Permissive Bill and other public measures.

Dr. Magee's style is the very reverse of that which is usually, but most unjustly, associated with Irish eloquence, and is also free from the most frequent vices of popular preaching. He is simple, and indeed seems to scorn ornament. Lucidity of statement and cogency of argument are the characteristics of all his writings, in which a definite object is always kept steadily in view, and is gradually brought nearer by what appears to be the easiest and most certain steps.]

CHRISTIANITY AND SCEPTICISM.

Scepticism demands certainty. Christianity offers certainty, and gives it in the end. But the certainty Christianity gives is the certainty partly of reason, partly of faith, and partly of experience, whereas the certainty that scepticism demands is the certainty of science only. Or we may state it finally thus:—Every one, even the most extreme of unbelievers, will admit that there is something to be said for Christianity. Christianity is not altogether unreasonable and unworthy of a hearing as regards its evidences; for, after all, the men who have believed in Christianity during the last eighteen hundred years have not been precisely the greatest fools of their age. Leibnitz, and Butler, and Pascal were not exactly drivellers—they were men capable of thinking, of weighing an argument, of understanding evidences; and not these only, but hundreds and thousands of the most powerful and subtle intellects that humanity has ever known, who in their day weighed the evidences of Christianity,—aye, and weighed them in spite of doubt, and fought their way through every one of those doubts that are tangling round the feet of men now as they come to Christ— were not such utter fools, that any one is entitled with a wave of his hand to dismiss Christianity altogether as an absurdity and a folly. All who are at all reasonable will admit there is something to be said for the evidences of Christianity; and, on the other hand, every reasonable Christian will admit there is something to be listened to—something at least that appears at first sight reasonable and fair—in some of the objections to Christianity.

But the real question is this:—The Christian says to the sceptic, "It is unreasonable of you to ask that every difficulty should be got rid of, and every question answered, before you believe Christianity." The sceptic says to the Christian, "It is unreasonable of you to ask me to believe Christianity until you have set at rest every doubt and answered every possible question." Now I ask you to consider which of these is right, which is the reasonable demand,—that of the Christian for faith upon sufficient, probable evidence; or that of the sceptic for assent only upon scientific demonstration? This is our question to-night.

In order to argue this question fairly and calmly, without passion or prejudice, let us pass away altogether for the moment from the subject of religion and religious doubt, and let us consider the uses and abuses of doubt in other matters than religion. We all know that men do doubt and have doubted about many subjects besides religion. Try, then, and recall to your minds your first doubt. It will be long, very long, ago in your life. Your first doubt is only a little later than your first belief. The first instinct of the child is to believe everything,—to believe that everything he sees, everything he hears, is true. All appearances for the child are realities. The sun is to him a ball of fire that climbs up the sky in the morning and sets in the evening. The stars are little specks of light set in a blue firmament. The earth is a flat space. The words of men are true words. Everything that appears to him at first *is*. Very soon, however, the child learns that what appears is not always what it appears—learns to distrust appearances,—learns that under the appearance there is often a different reality; that is to say, he learns his first lesson of doubt. And very valuable and important is this first calling out of the instinct of doubt,—this first awakening of the sceptical part of man,—of his understanding. For the nature of the understanding is ever to ask the question, "What?" and "Why?"—ever to seek under appearances for their cause or for their underlying reality. And so the mind of man—the sceptical, inquiring mind—is ever questioning of every apparent fact, "Is this what it seems?" and if it is, "Why is it so?" or if it is not, "Why is it not?" Thus doubt—precious and invaluable doubt—is ever leading man on from question to question, and every question that he asks, if he can but gain from science the true answer to it, is ever leading him a step on in knowledge. The mind of man is ever asking, and nature and science are ever furnishing answers to his questions. So man goes on from belief to doubt, from doubt to belief, from belief to greater knowledge; and thus doubt is still the cause of progress, the implement of discovery, the spur to reformation, the motive power that is specially needed for the ever-onward march of humanity in knowledge and science. Doubt! without this invaluable instinct of doubt humanity would be stagnant: with it, and by its help, humanity progresses. We do not disparage, we highly value, the uses of doubt.

But, observe! this doubt is useful upon one condition and one only,—that it start from a first belief. For what is the source of all this doubt and this thirst after knowledge? It is the supreme, instinctive belief that beneath all appearances there *is* a reality,—that something underlies and causes all being; and it is the search after this (if I may so speak of it) Essence of Existence,—the search after this I AM, —that still leads on the doubter. If he had no faith in some underlying reality beneath all these phenomena,—these appearances,— there would be no progress; and so doubt is ever seeking for that which *is*, ever seeking to get below that which appears, and yet it never reaches it. Never yet has scientific investigation, whetted and excited by sceptical inquiry, ever reached to the great Reason of all reasons; the great Cause of all causes; the great Fact that underlies all facts; and yet ever, as we seek for it, we are advancing in knowledge. We do not reach *it*, but we are ever reaching and passing on beyond that which lies between us and it. So you see the action of doubt in the human mind is just like that of the mainspring in a watch. The mainspring of a watch, as you know, is firmly attached at one end, and it is ever seeking to uncoil itself but yet never completely doing so, and the result of this is that the hands of the watch move uniformly. If you cut the attachment the hands will give one wild whirl, and then be still and useless. It is just the same with faith and doubt in the human mind. Doubt is attached to the primary belief that there is a Cause for all things, but it is ever seeking to escape from that belief; it is ever trying to detach itself, but never succeeding; and the result is, there is a constant and a measured progress of the human mind.

But we have next to consider how much further the intellect, which thus has been ruling and testing our beliefs, may go. So far we have seen the intellect, the sceptical understanding in man—that in us which asks "Why?" and "What?"—acting as supreme judge and ruler, and all evidence as yet has been submitted to it alone. Now the real question is this:—Must it indeed be the sole rule and judge of all beliefs? Are there any beliefs that cannot be submitted to it alone? Are there any domains of knowledge and of certainty which cannot be reached by the sceptical intellect, and into which some other part of man's nature must enter, to decide as to his belief? Let us go back to that early childhood of which I have been speaking, in which the child, who at first believes everything, learns his first lesson of doubt. A child, as I have said, not only believes in appearances, but he believes in testimony. He believes in human nature. His intuitive belief is in the truthfulness of humanity. Every word that is said to a child at first he believes; but he very soon learns his second great lesson of doubt and distrust; learns that every one who speaks to him is not true; learns that it is not wise for him to believe everything that is said to him. Is that as happy a discovery as that other discovery of which we spoke? Does it lead to like happy results? Does it make the discoverer feel better, wiser, happier? Would you say to the child, "Go on, my child, in this progress of doubt and distrust. Believe no one until he has proved to you that you must believe him. Doubt every one, distrust every one, refuse to accept any word of any human being until you have demonstration for it?" Would the man who grew up in that distrustful spirit be a happy man? Would he be a wise man? Is it wisdom always to distrust human nature? and yet, if it is not, I ask you what *demonstration* you can have of the truthfulness of every person whom you trust? You are always trusting. Can you prove logically that you are right in any of those trusts? The wife of your bosom may be false to you for all you can tell. The little children whose eyes look up to yours with such loving trust, and whose laughter sounds in your ears like the music of summer brooks,—you cannot prove that they are not hating you in their hearts. The friend whom you trust in business,—you cannot prove logically that he is not a traitor and a rogue. Such things have been; we know they have. Men have been deceived by their wives, hated by their children, betrayed by their friends, and robbed by their men of business. It is quite possible that this may be so in your case. Are you therefore to distrust every one? Would it be wise of you to do so? Why! you know that if a man were to act upon this principle, and were to say, "I do not trust my wife, my children, my friends; I do not trust any one until they prove to me, demonstrate to me, leave me in no doubt of their honesty, their love, or their truthfulness," you would not call him a wise man, you would call him a madman. You would put that man in a lunatic asylum. And why? Because, you would say, that he gave the surest evidence of madness; that one part of his nature had acquired a diseased intensity, which had mastered all the rest. You would say that that man had gone mad with distrust and suspicion,—had gone sceptically mad,— and you would treat him accordingly. And yet I defy any one here to show logically that the man might not be right. I defy any one to give that man such a logical and scientific demonstration as would prove to him beyond all possibility of doubt that his friends, or his wife, or his children, were not in a conspiracy to deceive and to wrong him. You see, then, that there is an absolute necessity for trust in the ordinary affairs of common life.

But I pass on to another and still more important point. I have said, and I hope you see, that life must be conducted upon the principle of faith or trust; but let us ask now, whether the rule of life, morality, can exist without faith?—whether we can get a demonstrative or scientific basis for morality itself? I ask this question, because those who are loudest in their prophecies of the destruction of religion are always loudest in their boasts of the gain to morality that would follow. They tell you, "When we have swept away every vestige of religion, then, and then only, will morality be really strong, free from the corrupting influence of religious superstition." Let us consider this. Let us ask—How will morality bear the assaults of scepticism? What is morality? Morality is that code or rule of action which you follow in questions of right or wrong. It is something different from the moral sense or the power of *feeling* right or wrong: it is the power of *knowing* what is right or wrong. Practically it is the established code or rule of right and wrong in the society in which you happen to be living. This is morality for most men. Or if not this, it is the code (or rule) of right and wrong which each man forms or adopts for himself. Let us try how this code will resist the action of the sceptical principle which, you remember, demands demonstration for everything before it believes,—asks to see before it assents. I ask the man who says he has a system of morality, "What is it? Is it your own code, or is it the code of what you call the common sense or common morality of mankind?" I will take the last first, for that is what most people do say. Very few persons are bold enough to say, "Everything that I think about morals must necessarily be right." On the whole morality means what mankind generally think is moral. But I ask you first: "Have you ever got the universal sense of humanity upon any one question of right or wrong? Do you know that all mankind agree with you? Do you know that even the greater part of mankind agree with you? Have you ever submitted this particular question to the great majority of mankind? Have you got their answer? If you have, can you prove to me logically, that the majority on any question of morals must always be right, and the minority always wrong? If men differ, and they do differ, on a great many moral questions, which is right?—the majority or the minority? Or, again, whose morality is it that you will have? That of your own day or that of the past generation? These differ very much on many points. As you know, our ancestors approved of duelling and the slave-trade. We disapprove of both. Which are in the right?—I am not asking you which you *feel* to be right; but I am asking you which you can prove logically or to demonstration to be right? Or if you cannot decide the question by majority or minority, —and I suppose very few persons would think of deciding a question of morality, as they would settle the election of a member of parliament, by majority or minority,—how are you to decide it? "By asking what the opinion of the wise and good in all ages has been." How are you to know the wise and good? Before you can know the wise and good, you must know what wisdom and goodness are, and if you know what wisdom and goodness are, what need have you to look to the wise and good to tell you? "I question the wise and good, because I want wise and good opinions." But who are the wise and good? "Why, the men who give me wise and good opinions." Is that logical? Will that stand the test of sceptical inquiry? Is that what men call demonstration about morals? This appeal to the universal verdict of humanity is simply illogical and preposterous, for the reason that you yourself are a part of that universal humanity, and that, if you differ from its verdict, it is not the verdict of universal humanity, and if you agree with it, and take it because it agrees with your own, you might as well have taken your own in the first instance. As you cannot get out of this logical difficulty, then it comes to this—that each man is to decide entirely for himself and apart from all others what is right or wrong. Is it so? What is it then in us which decides what is right and wrong? Our conscience. It is an authority, then! And what about freethought and authority? Why should man's free-thought, his sceptical intellect, submit itself to the decision of that in him which we call the conscience? Why, he knows that his conscience has been mistaken more than once —that at one time he thought that right which he now thinks wrong. Why must he submit himself, then, to these contradictory decisions of his conscience? Because we are told it is a part of his nature. But it is also part of his nature to have passion and appetite. Give me a logical proof, a demonstration that will hold water, something I can see as clearly as that two and two make four—that one part of my nature is to yield to another part? Why am I to mutilate one part of my nature at the bidding of another? And who and what am I? Have I any logical demonstration as to what I am? I have a scientific demonstration.

if you like, and what is that? Why, that I am carbon, and lime, and phosphorus, and certain other chemicals put together after a particular fashion. No dissector has ever dissected out a soul—no man of science has ever demonstrated a spirit or a conscience. Then, I ask, why am I to obey the bidding of one convolution of my brain more than that of another? Or if my interests come into collision with the interests of another man—that is to say, another mass of carbon, lime, and phosphorus—what is there in the existence of that collection of chemicals (and, mind you, science tells you no more than that) which gives it the right to give a law to that other collection of chemicals which I call myself? What is the duty that I owe to that mass of chemicals? I owe nothing to it. You cannot demonstrate it—you cannot make it as clear as that two and two make four—that I am to do to another man what I would he should do unto me. "Duty!" "Right!" These are words of the spirit, of the soul. Science never yet revealed the soul, and therefore the man who will believe nothing but what he sees and what can be demonstrated to him, will deny at last the existence of duty, in obedience to his sceptical intellect, just as he begins by denying the existence of God for the same reason.

Now, I ask you, how do you get out of this difficulty? I know that many do, and I thank God for it. I am very far indeed from saying that every man who denies Christianity must necessarily be an immoral man. We thankfully acknowledge that, as men may be worse than their principles, so they may be far better than their principles; and we do most firmly believe and thankfully acknowledge that men who are not Christians extricate themselves from this logical difficulty. But how do they do it? They do it just in the same way in which men extricate themselves from difficulty and doubt and scepticism in the affairs of life. They extricate themselves by calling up another instinct of their nature to fight the instinct of doubt: they call up the instinct of faith. How does a man in practical life fight the sceptical instinct which bids him doubt his fellows? He appeals to the instinct of faith. He says—"I *will* believe,—I *will* silence this busy devil in my heart that is ever bidding me doubt of what is holiest and best; I will to believe in human nature; I will to silence these sceptical questions of the mere understanding; I will to believe in a higher and nobler humanity."

And so it is in the matter of morality. How is it that any one can extricate himself from the logical and scientific difficulties that I have been speaking of? He does so in one way, and one only. He does it by an act of faith. He rises up to a belief in a nature and a person— in his own personality and in his own higher and better nature. He *wills* to believe that he is something more than a compound of material elements. He wills and chooses to believe that conscience in him is something supreme and divine. He wills and chooses to believe that the man in him is something above the animal. And by an exercise of faith, —of faith in himself, of faith in his own higher and better self— and by this alone, he silences the eternal "Why?" of the sceptical intellect— the serpent in him "more subtle than any beast of the field," which, if it had its way, would make of every man nothing but a beast; the sceptical understanding, which, taking its retaining fee from the passions and the appetites, ever seeks to reason away the supremacy of the conscience—to justify the revolt of man's appetites against his own higher and spiritual nature. This is the only way of escape from the difficulties which the sceptical intellect raises against morals, against society, against law, against all that makes life endurable or lovable, quite as much as it does against religion itself.

WILLIAM HOWARD RUSSELL.

[Dr. Russell is the founder of a new and most useful department in journalism. He was, to all intents and purposes, the first "special correspondent," since his letters from the Crimea first gave the English world regular and graphic accounts of the doings at the seat of war. The "special correspondent" has now become a necessity of every newspaper; and that branch of journalistic work has attracted to it picked men in point of ability, courage, and dash, but Dr. Russell may still claim a foremost place in his power of graphic, picturesque, and, at the same time, unpretentious description of war and war's alarms.

William Howard Russell was born on March 28, 1821, at Lilyvale, county Dublin. He entered Trinity College in 1838, and his first idea was to devote himself to an academical career. Events, however, decided otherwise. In 1841 he had been employed temporarily to do some work for the *Times*, and the editor, struck by the humour and the descriptive power of the young writer's pen, offered him in 1842 a permanent engagement. Russell was first employed as a parliamentary reporter; but the exciting days of Repeal supplied his editor with the opportunity of giving him more congenial work, and he was employed as a travelling correspondent to attend the meetings held by O'Connell and others. In 1846-47 he was again in Ireland, acting as a special commissioner to inquire into the state of the country; and he was a graphic and forcible describer of the famine and plague that then scourged the people.

The outbreak of the Crimean war brought him into still further prominence. The accounts he gave of the mismanagement that reigned supreme in the first disastrous months of the expedition attracted the attention both of the public and parliament; and his splendid pictures of the great events of the war were waited for with anxiety and read with intense interest. Honours were heaped upon him when he returned, his own university conferring the degree of LL.D. Whenever, after this, there came any interesting movement on the Continent or at home the employment of Dr. Russell was a matter of course. He went through the Indian mutiny; was sent to America to detail the stirring scenes in the civil war, being compelled, however, to return home on account of his free-spoken criticism; he described Bismarck's great wars in Austria and in France; was with the expedition that first tried to lay the Atlantic cable; and accompanied the Prince of Wales on his visit to India. He was called to the bar in 1850; and in 1869 unsuccessfully contested Chelsea in the Conservative interest. He is the proprietor and editor of the *Army and Navy Gazette*.]

AFTER THE FALL OF SEBASTOPOL.

(FROM "LETTERS FROM THE CRIMEA.")

The surprise throughout the camp on the Sunday morning was beyond description when the news spread that Sebastopol was on fire, and that the enemy were retreating. The tremendous explosions, which shook the very ground like so many earthquakes, failed to disturb many of our wearied soldiers.

As the rush from camp became very great, and every one sought to visit the Malakoff and the Redan, which were filled with dead and dying men, a line of English cavalry was posted across the front from our extreme left to the French right. They were stationed in all the ravines and roads to the town and trenches with orders to keep back all persons except the generals and staff, and officers and men on duty, and to stop all our men returning with plunder from the town, and to take it from them. As they did not stop the French, or Turks, or Sardinians, this order gave rise to a good deal of grumbling, particularly when a man, after lugging a heavy chair several miles, or a table, or some such article, was deprived of it by our sentries. The French complained that our dragoons let English soldiers pass with Russian muskets, and would not permit the French to carry off these trophies; but there was not any foundation for the complaint. There was assuredly no jealousy on one side or the other. It so happened that as the remnants of the French regiments engaged on the left against the Malakoff and Little Redan marched to their tents in the morning, our second division was drawn up on the parade-ground in front of their camp, and the French had to pass their lines. The instant the leading regiment of Zouaves came up to the spot where our first regiment was placed, the men, with one spontaneous burst, rent the air with an English cheer. The French officers drew their swords, their men dressed up and marched past as if at a review, while regiment after regiment of the second division caught up the cry, and at last our men presented arms to their brave comrades of France, the officers on both sides saluted with their swords, and this continued till the last man had marched by.

Mingled with the plunderers from the front were many wounded men. The ambulances never ceased,—now moving heavily and slowly with their burdens, again rattling at a trot to the front for a fresh cargo,—and the ground between the trenches and the camp was studded with cacolets or mule litters. Already the funeral parties had commenced their labours. The Russians all this time were swarming on the north side, and evinced the liveliest interest in the progress of the explosions and conflagrations. They took up ground in their old camps, and spread all over the face of the hills behind the northern forts. Their steamers cast anchor, or were moored close to the shore among the creeks, on the north side, near Fort Catherine. By degrees the generals, French and English, and the staff officers edged down upon the town, but Fort Paul had not yet gone up, and Fort Nicholas was burning, and our engineers declared the place would be unsafe for forty-eight hours. Moving down, however, on the right flank of our cavalry pickets, a small party of us managed to turn them cleverly, and to get out among the French works between the Mamelon and Malakoff. The ground was here literally paved with shot and shell, and the surface was deeply honeycombed by the explosion of the bombs at every square yard. The road was crowded by Frenchmen returning with paltry plunder from Sebastopol, and with files of Russian prisoners, many of them wounded, and all dejected, with the exception of a fine little boy in a Cossack's cap and a tiny uniform greatcoat, who seemed rather pleased with his kind captors. There was also one stout Russian soldier, who had evidently been indulging in the popularly credited sources of Dutch courage, and who danced all the way into the camp with a Zouave.

There were ghastly sights on the way, too—Russians who had died, or were dying as they lay, brought so far towards the hospitals from the fatal Malakoff. Passing through a maze of trenches, of gabionades, and of zigzags and parallels, by which the French had worked their sure and deadly way close to the heart of the Russian defence, and treading gently among the heaps of dead, where the ground bore full tokens of the bloody fray, we came at last to the head of the French sap. It was barely ten yards from that to the base of the huge sloping mound of earth which rose full twenty feet in height above the level, and showed in every direction the grinning muzzles of its guns. The tricolor waved placidly from its highest point, and the French were busy constructing a semaphore on the top. There was a ditch at one's feet some twenty or twenty-two feet deep, and ten feet broad. That was the place where the French crossed—there was their bridge of planks, and here they swarmed in upon the unsuspecting defenders of the Malakoff. They had not ten yards to go. We had two hundred, and the men were then out of breath. Were not planks better than scaling-ladders? This explains how easily the French crossed. On the right hand, as one issued from the head of the French trench, was a line of gabions on the ground running up to this bridge. That was a flying sap, which the French made the instant they got out of the trench into the Malakoff, so that they were enabled to pour a continuous stream of men into the works with comparative safety from the flank fire of the enemy. In the same way they at once dug a trench across the work inside, to see if there were any galvanic wires to fire mines. Mount the parapet and descend—of what amazing thickness are these embrasures! . . .

Inside the sight was too terrible to dwell upon. The French were carrying away their own and the Russian wounded, and four distinct piles of dead were formed to clear the way. The ground was marked by pools of blood, and the smell was noisome; swarms of flies settled on dead and dying; broken muskets, torn clothes, caps, shakos, swords, bayonets, bags of bread, canteens, and haversacks, were lying in indescribable confusion all over the place, mingled with heaps of shot, of grape, bits of shell, cartridges, case and canister, loose powder, official papers, and cooking tins. The traverses were so high and deep that it was almost impossible to get a view of the whole of the Malakoff from any one spot, and there was a high mound of earth in the middle of the work, either intended as a kind of shell-proof, or the remains of the old White Tower. The guns, which to the number of sixty were found in the work, were all ships' guns, and mounted on ships' carriages, and worked in the same way as ships' guns. There were a few old-fashioned, oddly-shaped mortars. On looking around the work one might see that the strength of the Russian was his weakness—he fell into his own bomb-proofs. In the parapet of the work might be observed several entrances—very narrow outside, but descending and enlarging downwards, and opening into rooms some four or five feet high, and eight or ten square. These were only lighted from the outside by day, and must have been pitch dark at night, unless the men were allowed lanterns. Here the garrison retired when exposed to a heavy bombardment. The odour of these narrow chambers was villainous, and the air reeked with blood and abominations unutterable. There were several of these places, and they might bid defiance to the heaviest mortars in the world: over the roof was a layer of *ships' masts*, cut into junks, and deposited carefully; then there was over them a solid layer of earth, and above that a layer of gabions, and above that a pile of earth again.

In one of these dungeons, excavated in the solid rock, and which was probably underneath the old White Tower, the officer commanding seems to have lived. It must have been a dreary residence. The floor and the entrance were littered a foot deep with reports, returns, and perhaps despatches assuring the czar that the place had sustained no damage. The garrison were in these narrow chambers enjoying their siesta, which they invariably take at twelve o'clock, when the French burst in upon them like a torrent, and, as it were, drowned them in their holes. The Malakoff was a closed work, only open at the rear to the town; and the French having once got in, threw open a passage to their own rear, and closed up the front and the lateral communications with the curtains leading to the Great Redan and to the Little Redan. Thus they were enabled to pour in their supports, in order and without loss, in a continued stream, and to resist the efforts of the Russians, which were desperate and repeated, to retake the place. They brought up their field-guns at once, and swept the Russian reserves and supports, while Strange's batteries from the Quarries carried death through their ranks in every quarter of the Karabelnaia. With the Malakoff the enemy lost Sebastopol. The ditch outside, towards the north, was full of French and Russians, piled over each other in horrid confusion. On the right, towards the Little Redan, the ground was literally strewn with bodies as thick as they could lie, and in the ditch they were piled over each other. Here the French, victorious in the Malakoff, met with a heavy loss and a series of severe repulses. The Russians lay inside the work in heaps, like carcasses in a butcher's cart; and the wounds, the blood — the sight exceeded all I had hitherto witnessed.

Descending from the Malakoff we came upon a suburb of ruined houses open to the sea — it was filled with dead. The Russians had crept away into holes and corners in every house, to die like poisoned rats; artillery horses, with their entrails torn open by shot, were stretched all over the space at the back of the Malakoff, marking the place where the Russians moved up their last column to retake it under the cover of a heavy field-battery. Every house, the church, some public buildings, sentry-boxes — all alike were broken and riddled by cannon and mortar. Turning to the left, we proceeded by a very tall snow-white wall of great length to the dockyard gateway. This wall was pierced and broken through and through with cannon. Inside were the docks, which, naval men say, were unequalled in the world. The steamer was blazing merrily in one of them. Gates and store sides were splintered and pierced by shot. There were the stately dockyard buildings on the right, which used to look so clean and white and spruce. Parts of them were knocked to atoms, and hung together in such shreds and patches that it was only wonderful they cohered. The soft white stone of which they and the walls were made was readily knocked to pieces by a cannon-shot.

Of all the pictures of the horrors of war which have ever been presented to the world, the hospital of Sebastopol offered the most horrible, heart-rending, and revolting. How the poor human body could be mutilated, and yet hold its soul within it, when every limb is shattered, and every vein and artery is pouring out the life-stream, one might study there at every step, and at the same time wonder how little will kill! The building used as an hospital was one of the noble piles inside the dockyard wall, and was situated in the centre of the row, at right angles to the line of the Redan. The whole row was peculiarly exposed to the action of shot and shell bounding over the Redan, and to the missiles directed at the Barrack Battery; and it bore, in sides, roof, windows, and doors, frequent and distinctive proofs of the severity of the cannonade.

Entering one of these doors I beheld such a sight as few men, thank God, have ever witnessed. In a long, low room, supported by square pillars, arched at the top, and dimly lighted through shattered and unglazed window-frames, lay the wounded Russians, who had been abandoned to our mercies by their general. The wounded, did I say? No, but the dead — the rotten and festering corpses of the soldiers, who were left to die in their extreme agony, untended, uncared for, packed as close as they could be stowed, some on the floor, others on wretched trestles and bedsteads, or pallets of straw, sopped and saturated with blood, which oozed and trickled through upon the floor, mingling with the droppings of corruption. With the roar of exploding fortresses in their ears — with shells and shot pouring through the roof and sides of the rooms in which they lay — with the crackling and hissing of fire around them, these poor fellows, who had served their loving friend and master the czar but too well, were consigned to their terrible fate. Many might have been saved by ordinary care. Many lay, yet alive, with maggots crawling about in their wounds. Many, nearly mad by the scene around them, or seeking escape from it in their extremest agony, had rolled away under the beds, and glared out on the heart-stricken spectator—oh! with such looks! Many, with legs and arms broken and twisted, the jagged splinters sticking through the raw flesh, implored aid, water, food, or pity, or, deprived of speech by the approach of death, or by dreadful injuries in the head or trunk, pointed to the lethal spot. Many seemed bent alone on making their peace with Heaven. The attitudes of some were so hideously fantastic as to appal and root one to the ground by a sort of dreadful fascination. Could that bloody mass of clothing and white bones ever have been a human being, or that burnt, black mass of flesh have ever held a human soul? It was fearful to think what the answer must be. The bodies of numbers of men were swollen and bloated to an incredible degree; and the features, distended to a gigantic size, with eyes protruding from the sockets, and the blackened tongue lolling out of the mouth, compressed tightly by the teeth, which had set upon it in the death-rattle, made one shudder and reel round.

In the midst of one of these "chambers of horrors"—for there were many of them—were found some dead and some living English soldiers, and among them poor Captain Vaughan, of the 90th, who afterwards died of his wounds. I confess it was impossible for me to stand the sight, which horrified our most experienced surgeons; the deadly, clammy stench, the smell of gangrened wounds, of corrupted blood, of rotting flesh, were intolerable and odious beyond endurance. But what must have the wounded felt, who were obliged to endure all this, and who passed away without a hand to give them a cup of water, or a voice to say one kindly word to them? Most of these men were wounded on Saturday—many, perhaps, on the Friday before—indeed it is impossible to say how long they might have been there. In the hurry of their retreat the Muscovites seem to have carried in dead men to get them out of the way, and to have put them on pallets in horrid mockery. So that their retreat was secured, the enemy cared but little for their wounded. On Monday only did they receive those whom we sent out to them during a brief armistice for the purpose, which was, I believe, sought by ourselves, as our overcrowded hospitals could not contain, and our overworked surgeons could not attend to any more.

The Great Redan was next visited. Such a scene of wreck and ruin!—all the houses behind it a mass of broken stones—a clock-turret, with a shot right through the clock; a pagoda in ruins; another clock-tower, with all the clock destroyed save the dial, with the words, "Barwise, London," thereon; cook-houses, where human blood was running among the utensils; in one place a shell had lodged in the boiler, and blown it and its contents, and probably its attendants, to pieces. Everywhere wreck and destruction. This evidently was a *beau quartier* once. The oldest inhabitant could not have recognized it on that fatal day. Climbing up to the Redan, which was fearfully cumbered with the dead, we witnessed the scene of the desperate attack and defence, which cost both sides so much blood. The ditch outside made one sick—it was piled up with English dead, some of them scorched and blackened by the explosion, and others lacerated beyond recognition. The quantity of broken gabions and gun-carriages here was extraordinary; the ground was covered with them. The bomb-proofs were the same as in the Malakoff, and in one of them a music-book was found, with a woman's name in it, and a canary bird and a vase of flowers were outside the entrance.

SIR CHARLES GAVAN DUFFY.

[In telling the story of the late D'Arcy M'Gee's life, we alluded to the career of Sir Charles Gavan Duffy, pointing out the close resemblance, not only in the early, but in the later fortunes of the two men. They both began life as writers in a revolutionary journal; they were both indicted as violators of the law, and they both, in later times, held high office as ministers of the crown.

Charles Gavan Duffy was born in Monaghan in 1816. His early days were not smooth, for his family, though it numbered several distin-

SIR CHARLES GAVAN DUFFY.
FROM A PHOTOGRAPH BY LESAGE DUBLIN

guished men in its past, was not well-to-do, and young Duffy had, at an early age, to rely on his own energies. He was but a lad when he went to Dublin, and obtained employment as sub-editor on the *Dublin Morning Register*. He returned soon afterwards to his native north as the editor of a paper of considerable influence in Belfast. Once more he turned his face to the metropolis, and obtained an engagement on the *Mountain*, an organ of O'Connell. It was not till 1842, however, that his career could be said to have really begun. In that year he, in conjunction with Thomas Davis and John B. Dillon, founded the *Nation*. The memoirs we have already given of several Irishmen—orators, poets, and prose writers—will have brought home to the reader what was the immense significance of this event in the literary and political world of Ireland. It will, therefore, be here but necessary to say that Duffy's new journal attracted to it all the young talent of the country, and that there grew up a literature which challenges favourable comparison with that of any other period of Irish history. Duffy was soon brought face to face with the difficulties which lay in the path of a journalist of anti-governmental politics; in 1844 he was tried with O'Connell, was defended, as we have already stated, by Whiteside, and was found guilty. The verdict, it will also be known, was quashed on an appeal to the House of Lords.

We need not here repeat the history of the breach that took place between O'Connell and the Young Ireland party. Duffy was one of the founders of the Irish Confederation, which the more ardent section set up in opposition to O'Connell's pacific organization. When the troublous days of 1848 came Duffy had to pass through the same trials as his companions; the *Nation* was suppressed; he himself arrested, and only released after the government had four times attempted, and four times failed, to obtain a conviction.

Duffy began life again, resuscitated the *Nation*, and preached the modified gospel of constitutional agitation. He also had a share in founding a Parliamentary party, having been elected for New Ross in 1852. The object of this party was to obtain legislative reforms, especially for the cultivators of the soil; and one of its principles was to hold aloof from both the English parties. The defection of the late Justice Keogh and others drove several of the "Independent opposition" party, as it was called, to despair, and destroyed for the moment all confidence in parliamentary agitation. Duffy, being one among those who had abandoned hope, left Ireland to seek brighter fortunes and more promising work in another land.

He had not been long in Australia before his talents met suitable recognition: he had left Ireland in 1856, and was minister of public works in Victoria in 1857. That office he held twice afterwards; and, in 1871, he attained to the still higher position of prime minister of the colony. Being defeated in parliament he demanded the right to dissolve; but Viscount Canterbury, for reasons which were at the time the subject of hot controversy, declined to accede to the request, and Duffy had to resign. He was offered knighthood, which he at first refused, but ultimately accepted in May, 1873. In 1876 he was elected speaker of the Legislative Assembly. He has, since his departure from Ireland, paid two visits of some duration to Europe; and during his last there was a rumour, which proved to be false, that he intended once more to re-enter public life at home.

Sir Charles Duffy is a writer of vigorous prose and an effective orator; it is on his poems, however, that his reputation rests. Those poems are few in number, but there is scarcely one among them which is not excellent. He has also published speeches made on various occasions, and is the editor of a volume of Irish ballads which has reached its fortieth edition.]

A LAY SERMON.

Brother, do you love your brother?
  Brother, are you all you seem?
Do you live for more than living?
  Has your Life a law and scheme?
Are you prompt to bear its duties,
  As a brave man may beseem?

Brother, shun the mist exhaling
  From the fen of pride and doubt,
Neither seek the house of bondage
  Walling straitened souls about;
Bats! who, from their narrow spy-hole,
  Cannot see a world without.

Anchor in no stagnant shallow—
  Trust the wide and wondrous sea,
Where the tides are fresh for ever,
  And the mighty currents free;
There, perchance, oh! young Columbus,
  Your New World of truth may be.

Favour will not make deserving—
  (Can the sunshine brighten clay?)

Slowly must it grow to blossom,
  Fed by labour and delay,
And the fairest bud of promise
  Bears the taint of quick decay.

You must strive for better guerdons;
  Strive to *be* the thing you'd seem;
Be the thing that God hath made you,
  Channel for no borrowed stream;
He hath lent you mind and conscience;
  See you travel in their beam!

See you scale life's misty highlands
  By this light of living truth!
And with bosom braced for labour,
  Breast them in your manly youth;
So when age and care have found you,
  Shall your downward path be smooth.

Fear not, on that rugged highway,
  Life may want its lawful zest;
Sunny glens are in the mountain,
  Where the weary feet may rest,
Cooled in streams that gush for ever
  From a loving mother's breast.

"Simple heart and simple pleasures,"
  So they write life's golden rule;
Honour won by supple baseness,
  State that crowns a cankered fool,
Gleam as gleam the gold and purple
  On a hot and rancid pool.

Wear no show of wit or science,
  But the gems you've won, and weighed;
Thefts, like ivy on a ruin,
  Make the rifts they seem to shade:
Are you not a thief and beggar
  In the rarest spoils arrayed?

Shadows deck a sunny landscape,
  Making brighter all the bright:
So, my brother! care and danger
  On a loving nature light,
Bringing all its latent beauties
  Out upon the common sight.

Love the things that God created,
  Make your brother's need your care;
Scorn and hate repel God's blessings,
  But where love is, *they* are there;
As the moonbeams light the waters,
  Leaving rock and sand-bank bare.

Thus, my brother, grow and flourish,
  Fearing none and loving all;
For the true man needs no patron,
  He shall climb and never crawl;
Two things fashion their own channel—
  The strong man and the waterfall.

THE IRISH CHIEFS.

Oh! to have lived like an IRISH CHIEF, when hearts
    were fresh and true,
And a manly thought, like a pealing bell, would
    quicken them through and through;
And the seed of a gen'rous hope right soon to a
    fiery action grew,
And men would have scorned to talk and talk, and
    never a deed to do.
    Oh! the iron grasp,
    And the kindly clasp,
  And the laugh so fond and gay;
    And the roaring board,
    And the ready sword,
  Were the types of that vanished day.

Oh! to have lived as Brian lived, and to die as
    Brian died;
His land to win with the sword, and smile, as a
    warrior wins his bride.
To knit its force in a kingly host, and rule it with
    kingly pride,
And still in the girt of its guardian swords over
    victor fields to ride;
    And when age was past,
    And when death came fast,
  To look with a softened eye
    On a happy race
    Who had loved his face,
  And to die as a king should die.

Oh! to have lived dear Owen's life—to live for a
    solemn end,
To strive for the ruling strength and skill God's
    saints to the Chosen send;
And to come at length with that holy strength,
    the bondage of fraud to rend,
And pour the light of God's freedom in where
    Tyrants and Slaves were denned;
    And to bear the brand
    With an equal hand,
  Like a soldier of Truth and Right,
    And, oh! Saints, to die,
    While our flag flew high,
  Nor to look on its fall or flight.

Oh! to have lived as Grattan lived, in the glow of
    his manly years,
To thunder again those iron words that thrill like
    the clash of spears;
Once more to blend for a holy end, our peasants,
    and priests, and peers,
Till England raged, like a baffled fiend, at the
    tramp of our Volunteers.
    And, oh! best of all,
    Far rather to fall
  (With a blesseder fate than he,)
    On a conqu'ring field,

Than one right to yield,
Of the Island so proud and free!

Yet, scorn to cry on the days of old, when hearts were fresh and true,
If hearts be weak, oh! chiefly *then* the Missioned their work must do;
Nor wants our day its own fit way, the want is in you and *you;*
For these eyes have seen as kingly a King as ever dear Erin knew.
    And with Brian's will,
    And with Owen's skill,
    And with glorious Grattan's love,
    He had freed us soon—
    But death darkened his noon,
And he sits with the saints above.

Oh! could you live as Davis lived—kind Heaven be his bed!
With an eye to guide, and a hand to rule, and a calm and kingly head,
And a heart from whence, like a Holy Well, the soul of his land was fed,
No need to cry on the days of old that your holiest hope be sped.
    Then scorn to pray
    For a by-past day—
    The whine of the sightless dumb!
    To the true and wise
    Let a king arise,
And a holier day is come!

INNISHOWEN.[1]

God bless the gray mountains of dark Donegal,
God bless Royal Aileach, the pride of them all;
For she sits evermore like a queen on her throne,
And smiles on the valleys of Green Innishowen.
  And fair are the valleys of Green Innishowen,
  And hardy the fishers that call them their own—
  A race that nor traitor nor coward have known
  Enjoy the fair valleys of Green Innishowen.

Oh! simple and bold are the bosoms they bear,
Like the hills that with silence and nature they share;
For our God, who hath planted their home near his own,
Breath'd His spirit abroad upon fair Innishowen.
  Then praise to our Father for wild Innishowen,
  Where fiercely for ever the surges are thrown—
  Nor weather nor fortune a tempest hath blown
  Could shake the strong bosoms of brave Innishowen.

See the bountiful Couldah[2] careering along—
A type of their manhood so stately and strong—
On the weary for ever its tide is bestown,
So they share with the stranger in fair Innishowen.
  God guard the kind homesteads of fair Innishowen,
  Which manhood and virtue have chos'n for their own;
  Not long shall that nation in slavery groan,
  That rears the tall peasants of fair Innishowen.

Like that oak of St. Bride which nor Devil nor Dane,
Nor Saxon nor Dutchman could rend from her fane,
They have clung by the creed and the cause of their own
Through the midnight of danger in true Innishowen.
  Then shout for the glories of old Innishowen.
  The stronghold that foemen have never o'erthrown—
  The soul and the spirit, the blood and the bone,
  That guard the green valleys of true Innishowen.

Nor purer of old was the tongue of the Gael,
When the charging *aboo* made the foreigner quail;
Than it gladdens the stranger in welcome's soft tone,
In the home-loving cabins of kind Innishowen.
  Oh! flourish, ye homesteads of kind Innishowen,
  Where seeds of a people's redemption are sown;
  Right soon shall the fruit of that sowing have grown,
  To bless the kind homesteads of green Innishowen.

When they tell us the tale of a spell-stricken band
All entranced, with their bridles and broadswords in hand,
Who await but the word to give Erin her own,
They can read you that riddle in proud Innishowen.

---

[1] Innishowen (pronounced Innishone) is a wild and picturesque district in the county Donegal, inhabited chiefly by the descendants of the Irish clans permitted to remain in Ulster after the plantation of James I. The native language, and the songs and legends of the country, are as universal as the people. One of the most familiar of these legends is, that a troop of Hugh O'Neill's horse lies in magic sleep in a cave under the hill of Aileach, where the princes of the country were formerly installed. These bold troopers only wait to have the spell removed to rush to the aid of their country; and a man (says the legend) who wandered accidentally into the cave, found them lying beside their horses, fully armed, and holding the bridles in their hands. One of them lifted his head, and asked, "Is the time come?" and when he received no answer—for the intruder was too much frightened to reply—dropped back into his lethargy. Some of the old folk consider the story an allegory, and interpret it as they desire.—*Edward Hayes.*

[2] The Couldah, or Culdaff, is the chief river in the Innishowen mountains.

Hurra for the Spæmen[1] of proud Innishowen!—
Long live the wild Seers of stout Innishowen!—
May Mary, our mother, be deaf to their moan
Who love not the promise of proud Innishowen!

THE PATRIOT'S BRIDE.

Oh! give me back that royal dream
    My fancy wrought,
When I have seen your sunny eyes
    Grow moist with thought;
And fondly hop'd, dear Love, your heart from mine
    Its spell had caught;
And laid me down to dream that dream divine,
    But true, methought,
Of how *my* life's long task would be, to make *yours*
    blessed as it ought.

To learn to love sweet Nature more
    For your sweet sake,
To watch with you—dear friend, with you!—
    Its wonders break;
The sparkling Spring in that bright face to see
    Its mirror make—
On summer morns to hear the sweet birds sing
    By linn and lake;
And know your voice, your magic voice, could still
    a grander music wake!

On some old shell-strewn rock to sit
    In Autumn eves,
Where gray Killiney cools the torrid air
    Hot autumn weaves;
Or by that Holy Well in mountain lone,
    Where Faith believes
(Fain would I b'lieve) its secret, darling, wish
    True love achieves.
Yet, oh! its Saint was not more pure than she to
    whom my fond heart cleaves.

To see the dank mid-winter night
    Pass like a noon,
Sultry with thought from minds that teemed,
    And glowed like June:
Whereto would pass in sculp'd and pictured train
    Art's magic boon;
And music thrill with many a haughty strain,
    And dear old tune,
Till hearts grew sad to hear the destined hour to
    part had come so soon.

---

[1] An Ulster and Scotch term signifying a person gifted with "second sight"—a prophet.

To wake the old weird world that sleeps
    In Irish lore;
The strains sweet foreign Spenser sung
    By Mulla's shore;
Dear Curran's airy thoughts, like purple birds
    That shine and soar;
Tone's fiery hopes, and all the deathless vows
    That Grattan swore;
The songs that once our own dear Davis sung—ah,
    me! to sing no more.

To search with mother-love the gifts
    Our land can boast—
Soft Erna's isles, Neagh's wooded slopes,
    Clare's iron coast;
Kildare, whose legends gray our bosoms stir
    With fay and ghost;
Gray Mourne, green Antrim, purple Glenmalur—
    Lene's fairy host;
With raids to many a foreign land to learn to love
    dear Ireland most.

And all those proud old victor-fields
    We thrill to name;
Whose mem'ries are the stars that light
    Long nights of shame;
The Cairn, the Dun, the Rath, the Tower, the Keep,
    That still proclaim
In chronicles of clay and stone, how true, how deep
    Was Eiré's fame.
Oh! we shall see them all, with her, that dear,
    dear friend we two have lov'd the same.

Yet ah! how truer, tend'rer still
    Methought did seem
That scene of tranquil joy, that happy home,
    By Dodder's stream;
The morning smile, that grew a fixèd star
    With love-lit beam,
The ringing laugh, locked hands, and all the far
    And shining stream
Of daily love, that made our daily life diviner than
    a dream.

For still to me, dear Friend, dear Love,
    Or both—dear Wife,
Your image comes with serious thoughts,
    But tender, rife;
No idle plaything to caress or chide
    In sport or strife;
But my best chosen friend, companion, guide,
    To walk through life,
Link'd hand in hand, two equal, loving friends,
    true husband and true wife.

JULIA KAVANAGH.

Born 1824 — Died 1877.

[Julia Kavanagh was the descendant of two ancient Irish families, and her father, Mr. Morgan Kavanagh, was known as the author of some curious works upon the source and science of languages. She was born at Thurles in 1824, but at an early age she accompanied her parents to London. A lengthened residence in France during her girlhood enabled her to give those graphic descriptions of French life and character in which she so greatly excelled. In her twentieth year she returned to London, and adopted literature as a profession. Her work, *The Three Paths, a Story for Young People*, appeared in 1847; *Madeleine, a Tale of Auvergne*, followed in 1848; *Women in France during the Eighteenth Century* next appeared. About 1853 she revisited France, and travelled through Switzerland and Italy,—the result of a prolonged tour being the publication in 1858 of *A Summer and Winter in the Two Sicilies*. In 1862 *French Women of Letters* appeared, and met with such a favourable reception as to induce the author to publish in the following year *English Women of Letters*, as a companion to her former work. Of the novels which flowed from her prolific pen, we may name: *Grace Lee, Rachel Gray, Beatrice, Sibyl's Second Love, Dora, Adèle*, and *Queen Mab*. She wrote also an interesting work entitled *Women of Christianity*.

All Miss Kavanagh's books have passed through several editions, and most of them have been republished in America, where she was a favourite. In a writer so voluminous we must expect a certain amount of inequality; but it can be said with truth that her French tales are exquisite,—true to life, delicate in expression, simple, and at the same time refined in style and thoroughly pure in tone. "Her writing," remarks Mr. Charles Wood, from whose interesting sketch in the *Athenæum* we take most of our statement, "was quiet and simple in style, but pure and chaste, and characterized by the same high-toned thought and morality that was part of the author's own nature." *Nathalie*, the volume from which our extract is given, is one of the best stories of French life probably ever written by an English hand. The hero, a man of strong will, of deep but controlled emotions, and of a high sense of honour, is well painted, though he has a little too much of that unpleasant sternness, and that discourteous self-assertion, with which too frequently female novelists delight to endow their favourites. The picture of the affectionate, warm-hearted heroine is without a blot. For several years before her death Miss Kavanagh had been in poor health, and she died suddenly on the morning of the 28th of October, 1877, at Nice, where she had resided for some years with her mother. *Forget-me-Nots* is the appropriate title of her last work, published after her death in 1878.]

THE SISTERS.

(FROM "NATHALIE.")

[Nathalie and Rose are sisters. Rose has been for years a confirmed invalid, and at the period when the extract opens is close upon death. Nathalie, on the other hand, has been rejected by the stern and not altogether reasonable lover who is Miss Kavanagh's hero. The contrast between the spiritual-minded sister and the earthly but delightful Nathalie is beautifully brought out in the passage.]

A few days before her end they sat together in their little room, where Rose had of late remained almost exclusively. It was a calm autumn evening, full of serenity and repose. The tower of the old abbey rose in dark and distinct outlines on the blue sky; the colony of rooks cawed and wheeled round it in circling flight, before they settled down to their night's rest. Beyond the abbey extended the abandoned cloisters, and the lonely churchyard, with low gray tomb-stones sunk into the earth, and a few dark cypresses, rising tall and motionless, in the stillness of evening. The sun had set, but a rosy flush still lingered in the west, blending softly with shades of vapoury gray, which melted in their turn into the deepening blue of the upper sky.

"It will be fine to-morrow," said Rose.

She was leaning back in her chair, which faced the window. Her look was fastened on the sky; her countenance was calm. Nathalie sat near her, looking at her sister, and holding one of her hands within her own.

"How do you know it will be fine to-morrow?" she asked.

"Look at those red streaks in the sky. Besides, the air is so clear and still. Listen, and you will hear the lowing of the distant cattle. How faint it sounds! The herds are coming back from pasture. Yes, it will surely be fine to-morrow."

The heart of Nathalie grew sad within her. She had seldom or ever heard her sister allude to the beauties of nature before her illness, but since then, the dying girl seemed to love such themes. The freshness of the summer mornings, the warmth and life of fervid noonday, the fading loveliness of eve, were for ever haunting her sick-bed. Although Rose knew well her state, and never expressed the least regret for life, Nathalie sometimes feared her sister was not quite so resigned as she had first thought her to be. When Rose spoke thus of what would so soon be lost to her for ever, the young girl gently endeavoured to divert her thoughts. She now observed,—

"Madame Lavigne wishes to know whether there is anything you would like to-night?"

"She is very kind, but I wish for nothing. Look at that large, brilliant star, Nathalie. Does it not seem to rise slowly before us, as if it knew of its own beauty? Is there not something of the spirit of life in its light, so tremulous and yet so clear?"

"It is very beautiful," answered Nathalie; "but I fear you will take cold, Rose." She rose to close the window as she spoke.

"Do not," replied Rose, arresting her with her pale thin hand; "there is no chillness in the air, and the sight of all this beauty does me good."

Nathalie resumed her seat. There was a brief silence.

"You may close the window now," at length said Rose.

"The room is almost dark; shall I get a light?"

"Not yet. My poor aunt being blind herself, cannot endure others to have light burning. I do not wish to vex her for the little while I have yet to live."

Nathalie turned her head away.

"Oh! Rose," she said, at length, "why speak thus? You cannot know."

"But you do know," gravely replied Rose, "and knowing, should not seek to deceive me."

Nathalie did not answer. Her sister continued, "You see that I am well aware of everything; we can therefore talk quite frankly; and there is a question I have long wished to ask you;—what will you do when I am gone?"

"God knows," answered Nathalie, in a low tone.

"Will you stay here with my poor aunt, who has so great a horror of being left alone with Désirée?"

Nathalie shook her head.

"You will not," pursued Rose, "and I cannot blame you; it were indeed a living death. But what will you do, my poor child?"

"Trust to Providence."

There was a pause.

"It is strange," at length said Rose, "but it seems to me as if you did not speak with your usual frankness. Answer me truly—have you any plan settled in your own mind?"

She bent forward as she spoke to look at her sister, whose troubled and averted look confirmed her suspicion.

"What is it, Nathalie?" she gravely asked.

"You talk of settled plan—I have none, Rose, but when Mademoiselle Dantin called the other day, she asked me if I would return to her school after the vacation."

"Did you consent?"

"No, I did not."

"But you wish for it. Why so?"

"It is as good a place as another, and she has offered me an increase of salary."

Rose looked at her fixedly.

"And these," she said at length, "these are your motives for going back to that school, so near that house which was once to have been yours? Oh, Nathalie! do you think me blind? Do you think me unable to read your heart and its enduring resentment? Oh! you are indeed a true daughter of the South—proud and vindictive."

A flush rose to Nathalie's brow.

"Yes, Rose," she said, with subdued vehemence, "you speak truly; I feel it is my mother's southern blood, and hers only, that flows in my veins. And in the south, if we know how to love, we also know how to hate. He once said I had energy enough for the feeling. I will show him he was a prophet. He said he would be years away: do not believe it, Rose; do not believe it. He will return soon, perchance; soon enough, at least, for my purpose. He shall see me the dependant of a tyrannical mistress, and he shall say to himself that he might have spared me that fate, for which I care not, but which, if what his aunt has told me be true, it will grieve and torment him to see. We cannot be so near without meeting; I shall neither seek nor avoid it, but I know that it will be so. He took one last look when we parted; I was pale and sorrow-stricken then; but I am not so now; pride has come to my aid, and when we meet again there will be enough left for regret, in the beauty that once pleased his eye. He will suffer, I know he will; let him; I, too, have suffered. He will feel that though thus ever near, we are for ever separated; let him; I, too, have felt it. There will arise in his heart a ceaseless regret for something lost; an unavailing wish that the past might be effaced. Let the regret and desire rise; I, too, have known them."

Her brow was knit, her looks fixed, her lips were firmly compressed, and for awhile her pale face lit up with something of the deadly beauty given to the Medusa.

"You see, Rose," she resumed, more calmly, "that I am, as you say, vindictive; but mine is the passive vengeance of mere feeling."

"What becomes of your vengeance, if he is indifferent and cold?" asked Rose.

"He cannot, he cannot," vehemently replied the young girl; "he cannot be so. Indifferent! I defy him."

"And if he repents? if he asks you to forgive the past?"

"He will not do so, Rose; but if he did I should refuse him, as inexorably as ever he uttered refusal."

Rose looked at her with gentle seriousness.

"My poor child," she said, "can you indeed hold those feelings, whilst living, as you do, in the very sight and presence of death. Look at me; think of what I am, of what I shall be ere long, and confess that the feelings of your heart belong to the perishable, not to the divine, part of your nature. You have received your sorrow as a curse, and it was sent only as a chastening trial."

"Oh! Rose, give me your faith," sadly replied Nathalie, "and I will forswear my feelings, and confess that my fate is just. But how can I, when I see you so good, so meek, so noble, condemned from childhood to passive sufferings? I was rebellious, but you, Rose, needed no trial. What has your wasted youth led to?"

Rose laid her hand lightly on her sister's arm.

"Nathalie," she said very earnestly, "know this: none, no, none have ever suffered in vain. The silent tears which the lonely night beheld were not in vain; the inward and still unknown strife was not in vain; not even the dreams of my youth or the sorrows of your love have been in vain. We are linked to one another, here below, by a chain so fine, that mortal eye can never see it; so strong, that mortal strength can never break it. If the sorrow we have known has given us a more kindly feeling towards the suffering; if it has only drawn forth one gentle word more, can it be said to have been in vain?"

"Oh! Rose," gloomily said Nathalie, "life is more than a duty, at that rate; it is an eternal sacrifice."

"And why not?" asked Rose, with a kindly look; "why not? Yes, a sacrifice. There are many paths; the goal is one. Some—they are happy—are called upon to struggle for truth and right, in the sight of God and man; to endure the weariness, the burning heat of the noonday sun, until the evening's well-earned rest is won at length. Oh! great and glorious is their fate—a fate angels might envy. Others, less known, less tried, more happy, according to human weakness, accomplish humble duties, and follow only the cool, shady paths of life. They toil and suffer, too, but the pure halo of a divine peace is around them still. To a third class, whom the Almighty knows as less gifted to act, less fit to soothe the woes and cares of others, another fate is given. Theirs," she added, and her voice grew tremulous and low, "is to pass through life in the vain longing for doing better things; in stagnant quietness when the soul's passion is action; their sacrifice is that of will, and they, too, have their reward, and enter at last into the end and consummation of all things—God."

But though the soul of Rose, long purified by faith, could rise thus high, that of Nathalie, darkened by earthly shadows, could not follow.

"And is this," she asked, looking at her sister, "the reward promised to virtue?"

"And why should virtue seek a reward?" returned the inexorable Rose. "Above all, why should it hope for what was never promised—an earthly reward? Who first invented that sinful lie? Crosses, sorrows, and untold agonies of spirit, these are its proper rewards; let it seek none other. But you look half-terrified. My child, do not misunderstand me. All is not misery: there is joy in the brave endurance of sorrow; there is happiness in adoration, not in the cold lip-worship, but in the fervent adoration of the silent heart; and there is a divine peace in prayer. For what is prayer? Communion with God and humanity: with the great Being whose infinitude is beyond mortal comprehension; with the frail finite creatures who suffer here below in their narrow space. I can see you pity me; but when I have known all these feelings, is it possible I should think myself quite unhappy?"

"Do you regret life?" asked Nathalie.

"No; that were difficult," replied Rose, with a touch of sadness; "nature is weak, and, according to her, I have not been quite happy. But my sorrows have led to this much good: that though I am young and see the light of life fading from me fast, I fear not death. Can the solitary lamp which burned unheeded through the long and weary night, see with terror the dawn which tells the coming of a purer day? We hear of the shadow of the valley of death; we should hear of the shadow of the valley of life; for life is indeed a gloomy valley, full of doubt, and still shrouded in dark mists. We descend into it we know not how; obscurity and dismay beset the path we must tread; we journey we know not whither, unless through faith; but as we ascend the air becomes more pure, the sky more clear; and when we stand on the crowning rock, light reigns above, and darkness at our feet."

She spoke with fervent earnestness.

"I envy you your living faith," said Nathalie, eyeing her mournfully; "I am not happy, I feel as if I should never again be happy in this life; but I would not leave the dark valley yet, and my whole soul would sink with terror at the prospect of death."

"But you shall not die yet, my poor child," affectionately said Rose, turning towards her sister with a faint smile; "it is natural for you to feel thus. The flesh is weak in youth. Faith comes with sorrowing years, and when we leave its early hours behind us, life grows less dear. Oh! why at any age is death made so very awful? Why were the scythe, the skeleton, the grim visage, given as attributes to this gentle deliverer? I would have him an angel, calm, pitying, and sad, but beautiful, and no king of terrors. A deliverer he is, for does he not sever the subtle yet heavy chain which links the spirit to the flesh, life to clay? Nathalie, do you remember that passage in the service of the mass, when, after the Hosanna has been sung, the choir raise their voices and sing: Benedictus qui venit in nomine Domini—'Blessed be he who cometh in the name of the Lord.' From my earliest years these words produced a strange impression on me. As a child I wondered what glorious messenger from heaven was thus solemnly greeted by those of earth. I thought of winged angels visiting patriarchs of the desert; of spirits in white robes with diadems made of the eternal stars. Oh, Nathalie! even such a pure messenger is death to me now. He comes, the bearer of glorious tidings, the herald of the Eternal, and I too say, 'Blessed be he who cometh in the name of the Lord.'"

Rose bowed her head and uttered the last words in a low tone as if it were something inward, and not mere external sense, that spoke within her. The moon had risen from behind the abbey-tower, and now threw its pale ray on her calm features and bending profile. As she sat there, in an attitude of monumental stillness, Nathalie gazed on her with an awe which is not that we feel for the dying or the dead. Rose belonged to neither; the barque was not yet bearing her away over that dark flood which leads to the better land; but she stood on the very brink of the breaking waves, and her clear glance seemed already to behold the unknown shore beyond. It was this awed Nathalie. To her that other world, of which Rose spoke so calmly, was shrouded in mists. She believed, but human faith is weak, and she had too long made her home among the dreams and hopes of earth, not to dread bidding them a last farewell.

Three days after this Rose died.

It was a calm twilight; she had laid down on her bed to rest awhile; Nathalie sat at the foot of her couch; an unconquerable sadness had been over her since the morning, when Rose had given a strange lingering look at the rising sun, and then turned away with something like sudden pain. Towards evening Nathalie had said to her,—

"Do look at that beautiful sunset."

"No," replied her sister, in a low tone, "it is better not;" and she steadily kept her look averted until the last golden gleam had faded away from the walls of the little room. Then she turned and looked at the gray sky, and smiled—perchance at this last victory. It was soon after this that she lay down; she felt drowsy, she said, and wearied, sleep would do her good. She spoke for a few minutes more to her sister, then slowly fell asleep. She woke no more, and Nathalie never knew at what moment, whilst she watched there by her sister, sleep had ceased, and death begun.

"She is sleeping," whispered Désirée, when

Nathalie, at length alarmed, called her up; "she was always quiet—very quiet, Mademoiselle Nathalie; one never heard her about the place, she is a very quiet girl."

But when she saw what sort of a repose had fallen on the quiet Rose, she hid her face in her hands, and wept by that bed of death.

Like a shadow Rose had moved through life, and like a shadow she noiselessly passed away from it when her time was come.

RICHARD DALTON WILLIAMS.

Born 1822 — Died 1862.

Richard Dalton Williams was one of the young recruits which the *Nation* drew into its ranks in the exciting days when O'Connell's agitation, after it had reached its zenith, was about to perish before a more ardent and daring movement. Early in 1842 appeared in the newly-started paper the "Lament for Owen Roe." This was the first poem which came from the pen of Thomas Davis. A few months later the *Nation* published the "Munster War Song." This was the first contribution of Williams.

At the moment when he wrote this spirit-stirring appeal Williams was still a schoolboy. He was born in Dublin; the date of his birth is uncertain, but the one usually assigned is the 8th of October, 1822. At an early age he was removed to Grenanstown, near the Devil's Bit, one of the most romantic spots in Tipperary. He was first sent to school to St. Stanislaus College, Tullabeg; and afterwards to Carlow College. It was while a pupil at the latter place that he wrote the poem in the *Nation* already referred to. His school-boy days over, he went to Dublin to prepare for the medical profession. In his leisure hours he amused himself by writing a series of poems full of grotesque humour under the title *The Misadventures of a Medical Student*. These verses may be read still with keen delight, but much of their point is lost owing to the ephemeral character of many of the allusions. Though the revolutionary tempest was passing over Dublin, Williams managed to pursue his studies with considerable diligence; but at last the time came when he could no longer escape from the maelstrom. On May 26, 1848, Mitchel was convicted, and on the following day his paper, the *United Irishman*, was suppressed. New revolutionary journals at once rose to fill the vacant place; John Martin started the *Irish Felon;* and Williams, with his friend Kevin Izod O'Doherty, established the *Irish Tribune*. Of course the new journals went the same way as the old; Martin was convicted and transported, so was O'Doherty; but against Williams the crown failed to obtain a conviction.

Williams resumed for a while his medical studies, taking his diploma in Edinburgh; but, like so many others, he felt such deep disappointment at the failure of the movement of 1848 that he longed for another land and different surroundings. In 1851 he emigrated to America, and after a while settled down in New Orleans as a medical man. After this came two flittings, his last residence being Thibodeaux in Louisiana. Here he was when the great American civil war broke out. He took advantage of the occasion to write the "Song of the Irish-American Regiments," in which the old rebel sentiments were expressed in stirring verse. While his pen thus retained its full vigour, Williams himself had begun to decay; consumption had seized hold of his frame, and on July 5, 1862, he died. A touching incident followed. His resting-place had been marked by nothing better than a rude deal board bearing his name and the date of his death. Shortly after his death some companies of Irish-American soldiers happened to pass through the locality; and, resolving that the spot of a countryman so gifted and so faithful should be properly marked, raised by subscription a monument of Carrara marble, inscribed with a brief but eloquent epitaph.

The poems of Williams have been issued in a collected form by the proprietors of the *Nation*, in whose early pages his *nom de plume* of "Shamrock" was so well known.

BEN-HEDER.

I rambled away, on a festival day,
  From vanity, glare, and noise,
To calm my soul, where the wavelets roll
  In solitude's holy joys,—
By the lonely cliffs, whence the white gull starts,
  Where the clustering sea-pinks blow,

And the Irish rose on the purple quartz
  Bends over the waves below—
Where the ramaline clings, and the samphire swings,
  And the long laminaria trails,
And the sea-bird springs on his snowy wings,
  To blend with the distant sails.
I leaned on a rock, and the cool waves there
  Plashed on the shingles round,
And the breath of Nature lifted my hair—
Dear God! how the face of thy child is fair!
And a gush of memory, tears, and pray'r,
  My spirit a moment drowned.

I bowed me down to the rippling wave—
  For a swift sail glided near—
And the spray as it fell upon pebble and shell
  Received, it may be, a tear.
For well I remember the festal days,
  On this shore, that Hy-Brassil seemed—
The friends I trusted, the dreams I dreamed,
  Hopes high as the clouds above—
Perchance 'twas a dream of a land redeemed,
  Perchance 'twas a dream of love.
When first I trod on this breezy sod,
  To me it was holy ground,
For genius and beauty, rays of God,
  Like a swarm of stars shone round.

Well! well! I have learned rude lessons since then,
  In life's disenchanted hall;
I have scanned the motives and ways of men,
  And the skeleton grins through all.
Of the great heart-treasure of hope and trust
  I exulted to feel mine own,
Remains, in that down-trod temple's dust,
  But faith in God alone.
I have seen too oft the domino torn,
  And the mask from the face of men,
To have aught but a smile of tranquil scorn
  For all believed in then.
The day is dark as the night with woes,
  And my dreams are of battles lost,
Of eclipse, phantoms, wrecks, and foes,
  And of exiles tempest-tost.

No more! no more! On the dreary shore
  I hear a *caoina*-song;
With the early dead is my lonely bed—
  You shall not call me long;
I fade away to the home of clay,
  With not one dream fulfilled;
My wreathless brow in the dust I bow,
  My heart and harp are stilled.
Oh! would I might rest, when my soul departs,
  Where the clustering sea-pinks blow,
And the Irish rose on the purple quartz
  Droops over the waves below—
Where crystals gleam in the caves about,
  Like virtue in human souls,
And the victor Sea, with a thunder-shout,
  Through the breach in the rock-wall rolls!

ADIEU TO INNISFAIL.

Adieu!—The snowy sail
Swells her bosom to the gale
And our bark from Innisfail
  Bounds away.
While we gaze upon thy shore
That we never shall see more,
And the blinding tears flow o'er,
  We pray:—

Ma vuirneen! be thou long
In peace the queen of song—
In battle proud and strong
  As the sea.
Be saints thine offspring still,
True heroes guard each hill,
And harps by every rill
  Sound free!

Though round her Indian bowers
The hand of nature showers
The brightest blooming flowers
  Of our sphere;
Yet not the richest rose
In an *alien* clime that blows,
Like the briar at home that grows
  Is dear.

Though glowing breasts may be
In soft vales beyond the sea,
Yet ever, *gra ma chree*,
  Shall I wail
For the heart of love I leave,
In the dreary hours of eve,
On thy stormy shores to grieve,
  Innisfail!

But mem'ry o'er the deep
On her dewy wing shall sweep,
When in midnight hours I weep
  O'er thy wrongs;
And bring me, steeped in tears,
The dead flowers of other years,
And waft unto my ears
  Home's songs.

When I slumber in the gloom
Of a nameless, foreign tomb,
By a distant ocean's boom,
  Innisfail!
Around thy em'rald shore
May the clasping sea adore,
And each wave in thunder roar,
  "All hail!"

And when the final sigh
Shall bear my soul on high,
And on chainless wing I fly
  Through the blue,
Earth's latest thought shall be,
As I soar above the sea,
"Green Erin, dear, to thee
  Adieu!"

MY COUSIN.

This summer my cousin came up from the South,
Just because a "strange kiss" was annoying her mouth;
And now-a-days ladies think nothing of hopping
Fifty miles after breakfast to go an hour shopping.
Sweet Mary, my cousin, from Heaven inherits
Good-nature and beauty, good sense and high spirits;
Without affectation of fashion or lore,
She is just what you see her, no less and no more;
With wit rich and brilliant as summer-dropt rain,
To the breast of the weakest she never caused pain;
Yet the passion and pride and the love of Tipp'rary
At intervals flash from my wild cousin Mary—
No prude on the one hand, nor flirt on the other,
And, in fact, I'm her cousin—thank God!—not her brother.
'Twas natural, of course, in my gladness and haste,
That somehow my arm should encircle her waist;
It stole round, and was met with such artless good will,
That I wish from my soul it were trembling there still.
Well, we chatted a long time, as cousins will chat,
Of friends and relations—of this one and that;
And between every story of that one and this,
I kissed her—as surely a cousin may kiss.
Here I can't quote the Fathers for aid, to be sure,
But I could the less nice and more musical Moore.
They say contiguity aids inflammation,
But here it spared not my complete isolation,
Who, in bachelor loneliness, all the year round
Live shut up from my kind, like a bull in a pound.
"Come, tell me," said Mary, displaying her glove
And the little hand in it, "were you ever in love?
The truth—the whole truth—no concealment should be
Between you and a friend—I mean cousin—like me."
"In love! my dear Mary! ay, dozens of times,
And I've thereupon written some acres of rhymes;
But, though arrows were fixed in my bosom as thickly
As fruit in plum-pudding, I convalesce quickly,
Unaided by aught save philosophy's pure ray
And the youthful heart's *vis medicatrix naturæ*.
When a lover is gridironed thoroughly brown,
Let him try homœopathy sooner than drown,
And with this dose of folly drive the other one down.
Talk of gunshots and stabs!—but there's nothing, by gorra, kills
A man off so sure as *hypertrophied auricles*—
That fatal derangement, so surely advancing
In the train of pic-nics, Valentining, and dancing.
Some men have their hearts, between flirts and flirtation,
In a state of perpetual acute inflammation."

But Mary liked not such a jesting reply,
And the dawn was o'ercast in the blue of her eye,
And, as cloudlets career from the summer wind's chase,
The ghost of a frown flitted over her face;
But deponent avers, on his harp, 'twas about
The most wretched attempt ever made at a pout.
Still, presto! at once to the dismal I glided;
For poets are prisms, and all many-sided.
So let us look gloomy, and classic, and blue,
And cut with the comic the anapæsts too.

"My cousin! if the poet's heart
 Unveil to human eyes
The wound of memory's poisoned dart,
 That every balm defies,
'Tis not to soothe a morbid gloom,
 Or cause thy tears to flow,
That I unbar the bosom's tomb
 And 'wake the buried woe.'
Beneath, in funeral darkness hid,
 Young Hope encharnelled lies—
Nor would I lift the coffin lid
 Except to Mary's eyes.
And yet my tale is briefly told—
 A tale of every day—
The heart in boyhood e'en made cold,
 Too early thrown away.
Some hearts there are will twine their strings
 Like tendrils of the vine,
Round all contiguous lovely things,
 And such, alas! was mine.
I worshipped all things beautiful—
 I loved the low wind's tune;
I loved at night to hear the bird
 That serenades the moon;
I loved the roaring cataract
 That thunders from the rock,
And breaks its solid prison walls
 In fragments with the shock.
I loved the bounding thunderbolt
 Among the Irish hills—
I loved to see its lurid glare
 Illume the whitened rills.
And faery minstrels round me played
 Upon the midnight breeze,
And from the founts I called up sylphs
 And syrens from the seas.
Aglaia, fair Euphrosyne,
 Thalia—Graces three—
With linkèd limbs, from Tenedos
 Came o'er the silver sea;
And all the bright Castalides,
 From cool Pierian caves,
With zoneless bosoms, sang to me,
 And Tritons from the waves.
The waves!—the waves!—the Atlantic waves!
 Like plumèd hosts that bound,
And, like thy tides, my spirit swelled,
 Dark Ocean! at thy sound.

But not the fires that flash on high,
   Nor streams beneath that roll,
Like woman's hallowed beauty made
   The music of my soul.
And her sweet smile o'er all my dreams
   Like stars on fountains played,
And in the vesper hour I heard
   Her whispers thrill the shade;
And round her graceful form I flung
   The purple clouds of song,
Until the vision dazzled me,
   Although it lived not long.
Now undeceived, no more a lover,
   Life's brightest, saddest dream is over.
I toiled up Love's Vesuvius, resolved to die or win it,
And, like *L'Homme Blasé*, find 'it only smokes, there's nothing in it.'
I only hope for friendship now,
   To cheer my lonely way,
And chase remembrance from my brow,
   With gently winning ray;
Then sun me in thy cloudless eyes,
   Be all the past forgiven,
And should remorseful mem'ries rise,
   Oh, speak of Hope and Heaven!"

(Mem.—This fusillade of pathos I have always found victorious,
If properly supported by the muscle *amatorius*.[1])

"But truce to sadness and digression.
   Voici, ma chère, the entire confession.
Thrice my shafts the Fates have parried;—
My first flame's dead, my second married—
The third (she's gone to France) one day
   In tears and sofa-cushions lay—
So, drawing innocently near her,
I tried to rally, soothe, and cheer her.
Why spin the tale? In that blest hour
Long-prisoned Love proclaimed his pow'r;
Wild words I spoke, the most sincere
That song e'er poured in Beauty's ear;
And oh! her words, remembered dearly,
Still ring within my bosom clearly—
And though the links are broken now
That bound us then with mutual vow,
I know that then her words were true—
Her feelings' springs were fresh and new—
Her melting lips, Love's very shrine,
Then ever warmly welcomed mine.
No practised airs had she t' assist her,
Sweet rose! she trembled when I kissed her—
And as the tides forth from my soul
Of love and song would mingled roll,
She clasped in tears her minstrel lover,
Like flow'rs from which the dews rill over."

Here, to make the tale impressive, my arm again stole round her.

(Mem.—This very artless gesture seemed in no way to astound her.)

'My fourth'—— "Oh! come," said Mary, "don't you think that three will do?
Now, I don't believe one-third of what you tell me can be true—
Were you ever once undoubtedly?" "Dear Mary, yes, alas!
And here behold her portrait!" and I led her to the glass.

Now, all this time, in love being a wretched tactician,
I forgot that the keyhole commands our position,
And the landlady, crouched like a cat in a passion,
And one eye closed up in the sharpshooter fashion,
Was squinting—no eye ever squinted as can hers—
At our simple endearments and primitive manners.
Till her glance, that would turn new milk into cider,
Flashed fire through the keyhole, and murdered a spider,
Who therein, like Napoleon, with gusto and skill,
Was applying geometry merely to kill.
The mine was exploded—she says, in a fume,
She wouldn't have such goings on in *her* room.
"You romp with the housemaid, you flirt with my nieces,
And have broken the peace of my daughter to pieces."

Now, reader, there's far less connection between her
And me than there is 'twixt a *carpus* and *femur*;
But this was a piece of artistical dodging
To keep Mary away evermore from my lodging.
Yet I answered her calmly and pleasantly—"Ah! so!"
Hitching up, with a smile, my retiring Tommaso,[2]
"Pray, ma'am, would you think me so very imprudent,
If a poet, a brick, and a medical student,
Received at her hands that indulgent humanity
Which, with shower-baths and time, soothes both love and insanity?
But as to her peace, Major Thunderbolt broke it.
Put that in your pipe, my dear madam, and smoke it.
And to prove that I know your pet lobster, I wager
A month's rent that I give a true sketch of the Major:
He has gooseberry eyes, and a conical head,
With an elephant's snout, but amazingly red;
Long, lank, incoherent, with swaggering pace,
Supercilious and dont-care-a-pin-for-you face,
And a nursery of whisker from dewlap to pole,
Like a garrisoned rampart defending the whole."
But here her brow flushed to a sort of a curious
Anti-teetotalish atropurpureus,

---

[1] A muscle of the orbit used in ogling.

[2] *Vulgo*, Tommy.

And she faced me full front, wheeling swiftly about on
Her—dear me!—her—thank God for Greek—*epiglouton*.[1]
Ah! woman, that tongue of thine—young ones and old—
Is worse than a scalpel, by Jove, when you scold,
And, Bellona-like, charge, in life's battle, across us
With your genio-cherito-chrondrio-glossus:[2]—
"As for Lucy, Lord knows it were better the Major,
Or a private, indeed, than a quack, should engage her.
Oh, yes! you're a doctor? but, faith, if your pill
Is all like what I got, you'll cure less than you kill;
For a fortnight I hadn't an hour to myself,
And they settled a cat that found one on the shelf.
Though you think you look wise in your specs, since you got 'em,
Had you twenty glass eyes, you're a humbug at bottom."

FRANCES POWER COBBE.

[One of the favourite subjects of Miss Cobbe's pen is that which, by a somewhat misleading synedoche, is called "woman's rights." She has maintained in many an essay the claims of her sex to have a place in the professions and a share in the political activity of her time. In her own self she is, perhaps, one of the strongest arguments in favour of her view, for she has shown in literature an activity that is paralleled by few men, and a grace of style and freshness of thought for which more than one masculine writer might vainly sigh.

Frances Power Cobbe is the daughter of Mr. Charles Cobbe of Newbridge House, county Dublin, and was born on December 4, 1822. She received her education at Brighton. For many years she has been a frequent contributor to the periodical literature of the day, and her essays republished in volume form make up a goodly list. She has published amongst other things *Essays on the Pursuits of Women*, 1863; *Broken Lives*, 1864; *Cities of the Past*, reprinted from *Fraser's Magazine*, 1864; *Italics: Brief Notes on Politics, People, and Places in Italy; Darwinism in Morals and other Essays*, 1872; *The Hopes of the Human Race Hereafter and Here*, 1874. The work from which we quote, entitled *Re-echoes*, appeared in 1876. It is a republication of essays which she contributed to the *Echo*, and which formed for many years one of the most attractive features in that journal.]

CHIVALRY OF THE PERIOD.

We have been tempted sometimes to ask whether the sentiment of chivalry were not defunct, along with revenge and remorse, and sundry other tragic passions, to be read of in books, but no longer witnessed on the real stage of life. Of course we should expect to find it modified according to the conditions of modern civilized existence. Nobody desires to see a Hercules, a Theseus, or a Perseus going about in England slaying monsters, and robbers, and dragons for the public good; nor do we expect to hear of Sir Galahad riding through a forest (shall we say St. John's Wood?) in search of distressed maidens to defend with sword and lance.

We smile, not only at classic and mediæval chivalry, but at the reflection of it in the Elizabethan age, when the gallant Lord Herbert of Cherbury solemnly debated whether his vow as a Knight of the Bath did not compel him to "succour" a small damsel of six, from whom a romping schoolboy had stolen a blue ribbon. Yet a stage further, and we find the chivalry of the eighteenth century represented by Lord Chesterfield, whose "ruling passion strong in death" manifested itself in his last expiring groan, "Give Mr. Dayrolles a chair!" That was an ebb of chivalry at all events. Has the tide turned in our day, or has it still further receded?

In more respects than one we fear the appearances are against us. The non-intervention policy, sound as it usually is, as regards nations, is certainly carried in these busy days rather too far into private life. We have time enough, alas! to spread scandalous stories; but to take the trouble to contradict and cram them down the scandal-monger's throat is a thing for which we profess to have no leisure. We give our money freely enough to men in distress; but to obey a summons for help in

---

[1] Bustle.—*epi*, upon, and *gloutos*.
[2] A muscle of the tongue.

the case of a brawl or a robbery, or to run the risk of appearing in a court of justice or in the columns of a newspaper—this is a chivalry for which we have no taste. Still more largely does the critical spirit which pervades all modern life detract from the generous enthusiasm of loyalty and admiration with which men used to look up to their leaders in the world of thought and action. So clear is this, that it is now actually startling in common discourse to hear a man speak in anything like the spirit of chivalry even of his friend and ally.

But it is especially in the treatment of women by men that chivalry is always supposed to show itself. How may this be with us now? We fear it is a very enigmatical thing, this same masculine chivalry of the nineteenth century. In the humbler ranks it never induces men to prevent women from doing the coarsest and hardest labour. They may sweep crossings, and fill coal trucks, and dance on tight ropes, and no chivalry says "Leave it for me!" But when women work so long that their small strength competes with men after the fashion of the tortoise and the hare, then chivalry limits the hours of female labour; and when women by chance discover that they can earn a good deal of money in some new way—say by painting on china—then the chivalry of their male companions induces them to seize their maul-sticks and forbid them to do any work but that for which the smallest pay is to be obtained. Chivalry is not in the least shocked at the sight of a woman dressed in male attire dancing on a public stage, but chivalry is disgusted beyond measure at the spectacle of a modest lady attending the sick as a physician in a hospital. Chivalry has not lightened any single tax, succession duty, or other burden in favour of women. There is nothing for which a woman pays less, and gets the same thing as a man. But there are a great many things for which women pay as much (or, from their ignorance, more) than a man, and obtain less in the way of accompanying rights and privileges, without chivalry being in the remotest degree concerned with the matter. All this, to our thinking, is rather unchivalrous chivalry. But, then, there is to balance it that masculine "politeness" of which we always hear so much. A woman has, indeed, generally to pick her steps with some difficulty through the mire of life, but then she is sure to be offered an arm to go down a broad carpeted staircase to dinner. Do we not always hear, whenever there is talk of admitting women to new professions, that in such case they must be prepared to forego the "chivalry" with which they have hitherto been treated, and find it exchanged for some unprecedented mode of behaviour which (it is grimly added) they "won't like"? But do men, then, really feel that it would be a luxury to treat women rudely?—an enjoyment from which this same "chivalry" somehow cruelly debars them so long as women do nothing (at least, nothing remunerative) in the way of work? Will it be a release to them from the irksome bondage of good manners when they may brush past a feeble lady with a dig of their elbows in her side, and keep a poor old woman standing while they lounge in a rocking-chair, or puff tobacco in the face of another, and bid a pretty girl "go to Jericho?" We really do not quite believe it, at least not in the case of the pretty girl, however it may be with the old women.

The truth seems to be, that though the outward forms of chivalrous courtesy are not lost, the self-sacrificing part of it, which constitutes its true beauty and value, is in some danger of being forgotten amid our modern press of business and general struggle for existence. In the leisure of the drawing-room every one is courteous; in the hurry of quitting a steamboat not one in a dozen is moderately good-mannered. The young, the well-dressed, and (of course, as nature will have it) the beautiful, are treated with a care often quite superfluous; the aged, the feeble, and the solitary are rudely pushed aside. When a train draws up at a terminus, and there is ample time for descent, many a well-bred man will offer his hand to the lady passengers to aid them to alight. When a train is going to start, and an "unprotected" seeks to take her ticket and climb into her carriage, it too often happens that one man will push before her to the ticket-window, and a second give her a poke with his umbrella; while a third, with agility quite remarkable, jumps before her into the carriage and takes the corner seat. The true spirit of chivalry was never better exemplified, though somewhat awkwardly expressed, than by a poor dull school-boy home for the holidays, amid a party where there were many pretty young girls, and one deaf, decrepid old lady. The other boys in company bore off the girls to dinner, each with many juvenile compliments. "And I," said the dull lad, offering his arm to the astonished old lady—"I'll take you, Miss D., because you are little, and because you are old!"

JOHN FRANCIS WALLER.

[Dr. Waller is an instance of the poets who preserve in age the ardour of their youth. He is still an active contributor to periodical literature; but his career began at a period which is now almost antique. He was born in Limerick in 1810; entered Trinity College when he was but sixteen, and graduated a year before the great Reform Act. He was called to the bar in 1833; in 1852 received from his university the honorary degrees of LL.B. and LL.D., and some time later was appointed one of the permanent officials of the Courts of Chancery.

Such, briefly, are some of the facts connected with the professional and less important side of Dr. Waller's career. To many it may be more interesting to know that he began to write in those early years when he was in London studying for the bar. The foundation of the *Dublin University Magazine* opened to him, as to so many other Irish *littérateurs*, a field of literary activity. For many years he was one of the most frequent of its poetic contributors, his poems appearing usually under the *nom de plume* of "Jonathan Freke Slingsby." A collection of those poems under the title of *The Slingsby Papers* was published in 1852. In 1854 Dr. Waller brought out a second volume of poems, which were highly spoken of both in the English and Irish press. In 1856 appeared the *Dead Bridal.* In addition to his poetic labours Dr. Waller has done his share of the wear-and-tear work of literature. He edited the *University Magazine* for some years after the retirement of Charles Lever from the post; wrote many of the articles in *The Imperial Dictionary of Universal Biography*, and generally supervised the production of that book; and he also published an edition of Goldsmith's works.

Dr. Waller's chief strength as a poet lies in his power of melodious versification. The rhythm and rhyme in his pieces, the shorter ones especially, are perfect. Many of his songs have accordingly become extremely popular, and have been eagerly grasped at by the musical composer in search of the fit accompaniments of words to music. The majority of Dr. Waller's poems are tender, or tranquilly fanciful; but he has a rich vein of humour as well, and some of his verses are very mirth-provoking.]

THE SPINNING-WHEEL SONG.[1]

Mellow the moonlight to shine is beginning;
Close by the window young Eileen is spinning;
Bent o'er the fire her blind grandmother, sitting,
Is croaning, and moaning, and drowsily knitting—
"Eileen, achorn, I hear some one tapping."
"'Tis the ivy, dear mother, against the glass flapping."
"Eileen, I surely hear somebody sighing."
"'Tis the sound, mother dear, of the summer wind dying."
 Merrily, cheerily, noisily whirring,
 Swings the wheel, spins the reel, while the foot's stirring;
 Sprightly, and lightly, and airily ringing,
 Thrills the sweet voice of the young maiden singing.

"What's that noise that I hear at the window, I wonder?"
"'Tis the little birds chirping the holly-bush under."
"What makes you be shoving and moving your stool on,
And singing all wrong that old song of 'The Coolun?'"
There's a form at the casement—the form of her true love—
And he whispers, with face bent, "I'm waiting for you, love;
Get up on the stool, through the lattice step lightly,
We'll rove in the grove while the moon's shining brightly."
 Merrily, cheerily, noisily whirring,
 Swings the wheel, spins the reel, while the foot's stirring;
 Sprightly, and lightly, and airily ringing,
 Thrills the sweet voice of the young maiden singing.

The maid shakes her head, on her lip lays her fingers,
Steals up from the seat—longs to go, and yet lingers,
A frightened glance turns to her drowsy grandmother,
Puts one foot on the stool, spins the wheel with the other.
Lazily, easily, swings now the wheel round;
Slowly and lowly is heard now the reel's sound;
Noiseless and light to the lattice above her
The maid steps—then leaps to the arms of her lover.

[1] This and the following pieces are quoted by permission of the author.

Slower—and slower—and slower the wheel swings;
Lower—and lower—and lower the reel rings;
Ere the reel and the wheel stopped their ringing and moving,
Thro' the grove the young lovers by moonlight are roving.

A PLEA FOR IRISH UNION.

Air—"St. Patrick's Day."

The white and the orange, the blue and the green, boys,
We'll blend them together in concord to-night;
The orange, most sweet, amid green leaves is seen, boys,
The loveliest pansy is blue and white.
    The light of the day,
    As it glides away,
Paints with orange the white clouds that float on the West;
    And the billows that roar,
    Round our own island shore,
Lay their green heads to rest on the blue Heaven's bosom,
Where sky and sea meet in the distance away.
As Nature thus shows us how well she can fuse 'm,
We'll blend them in love on St. Patrick's Day.

The hues of the prism, philosophers say, boys,
Are nought but the sunlight resolved into parts,
They're beauteous, no doubt, but I think that the ray, boys,
Unbroken, more lights up and warms our hearts.
    Each musical tone,
    Struck one by one,
Makes melody sweet, it is true, on the ear;
    But let the hand ring
    All at once every string,
And, oh! there is harmony now that is glorious,
In unison pealing to Heaven away;
For UNION is hearty, and strength, and victorious,
Of hues, tones, and hearts, on St. Patrick's Day.

Those hues in one bosom be sure to unite, boys,
Let each Irish heart wear those emblems so true;
Be fresh as the green, and be pure as the white, boys,
Be bright as the orange, sincere as the blue,
    I care not a jot
    Be your scarf white or not,
If you love as a brother each child of the soil.
    I ask not your creed,
    If you stand in her need,
To the land of your birth in the hour of her dolours,
The foe of her foes, let them be who they may.
Then, "fusion of hearts and confusion of colours,"
Be the Irishman's toast on St. Patrick's Day.

THE SONG OF THE GLASS.

Once Genius, and Beauty, and Pleasure
    Sought the goddess of Art in her shrine;
And prayed her to fashion a treasure,
    The brightest her skill could combine.
Said the goddess, well pleased at the notion,
    "Most gladly I'll work your behest;
From the margin of yonder blue ocean,
    Let each bring the gift that seems best."
    Chorus.—Then push round the flagon, each brother,
        But fill bumper-high ere it pass;
        And while we hob-nob one another,
        You'll sing us "The Song of the Glass."

Beauty fetched from her ocean-water
    The sea-wraik that lay on the strand;
And Pleasure the golden sands brought her
    That he stole from Time's tremulous hand.
But Genius went pondering and choosing,
    Where gay shells and sea-flowers shine,
Grasped a sun-lighted wave in his musing,
    And found his hand sparkling with brine.
    Chorus.—Then push round the flagon, &c.

"'Tis well," said the goddess, as smiling,
    Each offering she curiously scanned,
On her altar mysteriously piling
    The brine, and the wraik, and the sand;
Mixing up, with strange spells as she used them,
    Salt, kali, and flint in a mass,
With the flame of the lightning she fused them,
    And the marvellous compound was—GLASS!
    Chorus.—Then push round the flagon, &c.

Beauty glanced at the Crystal, half-frighted,
    For stirring with life it was seen;
Till gazing, she blushed all delighted,
    As she saw her own image within.
"Henceforth," she exclaimed, "be thou ever
    The mirror to Beauty most dear;
Not from steel, or from silver, or river,
    Is the reflex so lustrous and clear."
    Chorus.—Then push round the flagon, &c.

But Genius the while rent asunder
    A fragment, and raising it high,
Looked through it, beholding with wonder
    New stars over-clustering the sky.
With rapture he cried, "*Now* is given
    To Genius the power divine,
To draw down the planets from heaven,
    Or roam through the stars where they shine."
    Chorus.—Then push round the flagon, &c.

The rest fell to earth—Pleasure caught it—
    Plunged his bowl, ere it cooled, in the mass;
To the form of the wine-cup he wrought it,
    And cried—"*Here's the true use of Glass!*"

Then leave, boys, the mirror to women—
    Through the lens let astronomers blink—
There's no glass half so dear to a true man
    As the wine-glass when filled to the brink.

    Chorus.—Then push round the flagon, &c.

WELCOME AS FLOWERS IN MAY.

At day's declining, a maid sat twining
    A garland shining with wild-flowers gay;
But her heart it was sore, and the tears swelled o'er
    Her eye at the door on that eve in May.

"And take," she cried, to her young heart's pride,
    "From your plighted bride, on this holy day,
A true-love token of fond vows spoken
    That may not be broken—these flowers of May.

"In life and in death, if you hold to your faith,
    Keep ever this wreath, 'twill be sweet in decay;
Come poor or with wealth, come in sickness or health,
    To my heart you'll be welcome as flow'rs in May.

"Yet oh, if ever, when wide seas sever
    Our hearts, you waver in faith to me,
A true Irish maid will never upbraid
    Affection betrayed—from that hour you're free!

"I set small store upon golden ore,
    I'll not love you the more for your wealth from the sea;
The hand that will toil at our own loved soil,
    Free from crime or from spoil, is the hand for me!"

The blessing half spoke, her fast tears choke,
    And strong sobs broke the young man's pray'r;
One blending of hearts, and the youth departs—
    The maid weeps alone in the silent air.

Full many a score that lone maid counted o'er
    Of day-dawns and night-falls—a year to the day—
When sadly once more at the seat by the door,
    Stood the youth as before, on that eve in May.

For the love of that maid, wherever he strayed,
    Kept his soul from stain, and his hand from guilt;
Like an angel from God, till his feet retrod
    The cherished sod where his first-love dwelt.

"I bring you no store of the bright gold ore,
    But, poor as before, I return to decay;
For my bride I've no wealth but broken health,
    Hopes withered and dead as these flowers of May."

The maiden has prest her true love to her breast,
    Her joyful haste no doubts delay;
In his arms she sighs "'Tis *yourself* I prize,
    To my heart you are *welcome as flowers in May!*"

KITTY NEIL.

"Ah, sweet Kitty Neil, rise up from that wheel—
    Your neat little foot will be weary from spinning;
Come trip down with me to the sycamore-tree—
    Half the parish is there, and the dance is beginning.
The sun is gone down, but the full harvest-moon
    Shines sweetly and cool on the dew-whitened valley;
While all the air rings with the soft, loving things
    Each little bird sings in the green shaded alley."

With a blush and a smile, Kitty rose up the while,
    Her eye in the glass, as she bound her hair, glancing;
'Tis hard to refuse when a young lover sues—
    So she couldn't but choose to—go off to the dancing.
And now on the green, the glad groups are seen—
    Each gay-hearted lad with the lass of his choosing;
And Pat, without fail, leads out sweet Kitty Neil—
    Somehow, when he asked, she ne'er thought of refusing.

Now Felix Magee puts his pipes to his knee,
    And, with flourish so free, sets each couple in motion;
With a cheer and a bound, the lads patter the ground—
    The maids move around just like swans on the ocean.
Cheeks bright as the rose—feet light as the doe's,
    Now coyly retiring, now boldly advancing—
Search the world all round, from the sky to the ground,
    NO SUCH SIGHT CAN BE FOUND AS AN IRISH LASS DANCING!

Sweet Kate! who could view your bright eyes of deep blue,
    Beaming humidly through their dark lashes so mildly,
Your fair-turned arm, heaving breast, rounded form,
    Nor feel his heart warm, and his pulses throb wildly?
Poor Pat feels his heart, as he gazes, depart,
    Subdued by the smart of such painful yet sweet love;
The sight leaves his eye, as he cries with a sigh,
    "*Dance light, for my heart, it lies under your feet, love!*"

JOHN TYNDALL.

[Professor Tyndall is an instance of native genius and energy raising themselves to a lofty reputation in spite of early difficulties, and by nought but worthy means.

John Tyndall was born in 1820 at Leighlin-Bridge, Carlow. His parents were poor; but, with that zeal for education which is one of the best characteristics of the Irish people, they managed to have their son taught well; and he early acquired a sound knowledge of mathematics. His first employments were not of a particularly philosophic character, for he had to be content with the post of a "civil assistant" of the Ordnance Survey in his native district, and with employment in railway engineering operations in connection with a Manchester firm. In 1847 came what was, probably, much more congenial employment, when he received an appointment as a teacher in Queenwood College, Hampshire. Here he formed a friendship which was destined to deeply influence his life. The chemist of the college was Mr. (now Dr.) Frankland, and with him Tyndall began that career of physical investigation in which he has since gained such a fame. In company with his friend he went abroad and prosecuted for some time the study of chemical and other phenomena. His discoveries had been noted, and he received the fellowship of the Royal Society. In 1853 he was elected professor of natural philosophy in the Royal Institution, and was successor of Michael Faraday as superintendent. It is not our duty to speak in detail of his scientific achievements. We must content ourselves with saying that he has received those honours which are conferred on those alone who have reached the highest position in the scientific world. He has been President of the British Association, has been made an LL.D. of Cambridge and of Edinburgh, a D.C.L. of Oxford, and held office in 1877 as President of the Birmingham and Midland Institute. In 1872 he went on a lecturing tour in the United States, and the proceeds he devoted to the encouragement of original research.

Professor Tyndall is best known to the general public as a lecturer. He shares with his friend, Professor Huxley, a singular power of making the dark ways of science light to the ordinary understanding by a style of wonderful clearness, and brightened with humour and apt illustration. Indeed, he is one of the pioneers in the new era, in which a polished style has been found quite compatible with the revelation of physical truths. His published works are numerous. Most of them are on purely scientific subjects; but occasional visits to the Continent and explorations among the Alps have led to the production of pleasant volumes, in which the scientist brings into striking and sometimes amusing combination the dreamy eye of the lover of the picturesque, and the keen eye of the philosopher in search of explanations of physical phenomena.]

SCIENTIFIC LIMIT OF THE IMAGINATION.

(FROM ADDRESS TO BRITISH ASSOCIATION.[1])

If you look at the face of a watch you see the hour and minute hands, and possibly also a second-hand, moving over the graduated dial. Why do these hands move? and why are their relative motions such as they are observed to be? These questions cannot be answered without opening the watch, mastering its various parts, and ascertaining their relationship to each other. When this is done we find that the observed motion of the hands follows of necessity from the inner mechanism of the watch when acted upon by the force invested in the spring.

The motion of the hands may be called a phenomenon of art, but the case is similar with the phenomena of nature. These also have their inner mechanism, and their store of force to set that mechanism going. The ultimate problem of physical science is to reveal this mechanism, to discern this store, and to show that from the combined action of both the phenomena of which they constitute the basis must of necessity flow.

I thought that an attempt to give you even a brief and sketchy illustration of the manner in which scientific thinkers regard this problem would not be uninteresting to you on the present occasion; more especially as it will give me occasion to say a word or two on the tendencies and limits of modern science; to point out the region which men of science

---

[1] By permission of the author.

claim as their own, and where it is mere waste of time to oppose their advance, and also to define, if possible, the bourne between this and that other region to which the questionings and yearnings of the scientific intellect are directed in vain.

There have been writers who affirmed that the pyramids of Egypt were the productions of nature; and in his early youth Alexander von Humboldt wrote a learned essay with the express object of refuting this notion. We now regard the pyramids as the work of men's hands, aided probably by machinery of which no record remains. We picture to ourselves the swarming workers toiling at those vast erections, lifting the inert stones, and, guided by the volition, the skill, and possibly at times by the whip of the architect, placing them in their proper positions. The blocks in this case were moved and posited by a power external to themselves, and the final form of the pyramid expressed the thought of its human builder.

Let us pass from this illustration of constructive power to another of a different kind. When a solution of common salt is slowly evaporated, the water which holds the salt in solution disappears, but the salt itself remains behind. At a certain stage of concentration the salt can no longer retain the liquid form; its particles, or molecules, as they are called, begin to deposit themselves as minute solids, so minute, indeed, as to defy all microscopic power. As evaporation continues solidification goes on, and we finally obtain, through the clustering together of innumerable molecules, a finite crystalline mass of a definite form. What is this form? It sometimes seems a mimicry of the architecture of Egypt. We have little pyramids built by the salt, terrace above terrace from base to apex, forming a series of steps resembling those up which the Egyptian traveller is dragged by his guides. The human mind is as little disposed to look unquestioning at these pyramidal salt-crystals as to look at the pyramids of Egypt without inquiring whence they came. How, then, are these salt-pyramids built up?

Guided by analogy, you may, if you like, suppose that, swarming among the constituent molecules of the salt there is an invisible population, guided and coerced by some invisible master, and placing the atomic blocks in their positions. This, however, is not the scientific idea, nor do I think your good sense will accept it as a likely one. The scientific idea is that the molecules act upon each other without the intervention of slave labour; that they attract each other and repel each other at certain definite points, or poles, and in certain definite directions; and that the pyramidal form is the result of this play of attraction and repulsion. While, then, the blocks of Egypt were laid down by a power external to themselves, these molecular blocks of salt are self-posited, being fixed in their places by the forces with which they act upon each other.

I take common salt as an illustration because it is so familiar to us all; but any other crystalline substance would answer my purpose equally well. Everywhere, in fact, throughout inorganic nature, we have this formative power, as Fichte would call it—this structural energy ready to come into play, and build the ultimate particles of matter into definite shapes. The ice of our winters and of our polar regions is its handiwork, and so equally are the quartz, felspar, and mica of our rocks. Our chalk-beds are for the most part composed of minute shells, which are also the product of structural energy; but behind the shell, as a whole, lies a more remote and subtle formative act. These shells are built up of little crystals of calc-spar, and to form these crystals the structural force had to deal with the intangible molecules of carbonate of lime. This tendency on the part of matter to organize itself, to grow into shape, to assume definite forms in obedience to the definite action of force, is, as I have said, all-pervading. It is in the ground on which you tread, in the water you drink, in the air you breathe. Incipient life, as it were, manifests itself throughout the whole of what we call inorganic nature.

The forms of the minerals resulting from this play of polar forces are various, and exhibit different degrees of complexity. Men of science avail themselves of all possible means of exploring their molecular architecture. For this purpose they employ in turn as agents of exploration, light, heat, magnetism, electricity, and sound. Polarized light is especially useful and powerful here. A beam of such light, when sent in among the molecules of a crystal, is acted on by them, and from this action we infer with more or less of clearness the manner in which the molecules are arranged. That differences, for example, exist between the inner structure of rock-salt and crystallized sugar or sugar-candy, is thus strikingly revealed. These differences may be made to display themselves in chromatic phenomena of great splendour, the play of molecular force being so regulated as to remove some of the coloured constituents of white light, and to leave others with increased intensity behind.

And now let us pass from what we are accustomed to regard as a dead mineral to a living grain of corn. When *it* is examined by polarized light, chromatic phenomena similar to those noticed in crystals are observed. And why? Because the architecture of the grain resembles the architecture of the crystal. In the grain also the molecules are set in definite positions, and in accordance with their arrangement they act upon the light. But what has built together the molecules of the corn? I have already said regarding crystalline architecture that you may, if you please, consider the atoms and molecules to be placed in position by a power external to themselves. The same hypothesis is open to you now. But if in the case of crystals you have rejected this notion of an external architect, I think you are bound to reject it now, and to conclude that the molecules of the corn are self-posited by the forces with which they act upon each other. It would be poor philosophy to invoke an external agent in one case and to reject it in the other.

Instead of cutting our grain of corn into slices and subjecting it to the action of polarized light, let us place it in the earth and subject it to a certain degree of warmth. In other words, let the molecules, both of the corn and of the surrounding earth, be kept in that state of agitation which we call warmth. Under these circumstances the grain and the substances which surround it interact, and a definite molecular architecture is the result. A bud is formed; this bud reaches the surface, where it is exposed to the sun's rays, which are also to be regarded as a kind of vibratory motion. And as the motion of common heat with which the grain and the substances surrounding it were first endowed, enabled the grain and these substances to exercise their attractions and repulsions, and thus to coalesce in definite forms, so the specific motion of the sun's rays now enables the green bud to feed upon the carbonic acid and the aqueous vapour of the air. The bud appropriates those constituents of both for which it has an elective attraction, and permits the other constituent to resume its place in the air. Thus the architecture is carried on. Forces are active at the root, forces are active in the blade, the matter of the earth and the matter of the atmosphere are drawn towards both, and the plant augments in size. We have in succession the bud, the stalk, the ear, the full corn in the ear; the cycle of molecular action being completed by the production of grains similar to that with which the process began.

Now there is nothing in this process which necessarily eludes the conceptive or imagining power of the purely human mind. An intellect the same in kind as our own would, if only sufficiently expanded, be able to follow the whole process from beginning to end. It would see every molecule placed in its position by the specific attractions and repulsions exerted between it and other molecules, the whole process and its consummation being an instance of the play of molecular force. Given the grain and its environment, the purely human intellect might, if sufficiently expanded, trace out *à priori* every step of the process of growth, and, by the application of purely mechanical principles, demonstrate that the cycle must end, as it is seen to end, in the reproduction of forms like that with which it began. A similar necessity rules here to that which rules the planets in their circuits round the sun.

You will notice that I am stating my truth strongly... But I must go still further, and affirm that, in the eye of science, *the animal body* is just as much the product of molecular force as the stalk and ear of corn, or as the crystal of salt or sugar. Many of the parts of the body are obviously mechanical. Take the human heart, for example, with its system of valves, or take the exquisite mechanism of the eye or hand. Animal heat, moreover, is the same in kind as the heat of a fire, being produced by the same chemical process. Animal motion, too, is as directly derived from the food of the animal, as the motion of Trevethyck's walking engine from the fuel in its furnace. As regards matter, the animal body creates nothing; as regards force, it creates nothing. Which of you by taking thought can add one cubit to his stature? All that has been said, then, regarding the plant may be restated with regard to the animal. Every particle that enters into the composition of a muscle, a nerve, or a bone, has been placed in its position by molecular force. And unless the existence of law in these matters be denied, and the element of caprice introduced, we must conclude that, given the relation of any molecule of the body to its environment, its position in the body might be determined mathematically. Our difficulty is not with the *quality* of the problem, but with its *complexity;* and this difficulty might be met by the simple expansion of the faculties which we now possess. Given this expansion, with the necessary molecular data, and the chick might be deduced as rigorously and as logically from the egg as the existence of Neptune was deduced from the disturbances of Uranus, or as conical refraction was deduced from the undulatory theory of light.

You see I am not mincing matters, but avowing nakedly what many scientific thinkers more or less distinctly believe. The formation of a crystal, a plant, or an animal, is in their eyes a purely mechanical problem, which differs from the problems of ordinary mechanics in the smallness of the masses and the complexity of the processes involved. Here you have one half of our dual truth; let us now glance at the other half. Associated with this wonderful mechanism of the animal body we have phenomena no less certain than those of physics, but between which and the mechanism we discern no necessary connection. A man, for example, can say *I feel, I think, I love;* but how does *consciousness* infuse itself into the problem? The human brain is said to be the organ of thought and feeling; when we are hurt the brain feels it, when we ponder it is the brain that thinks, when our passions or affections are excited it is through the instrumentality of the brain. Let us endeavour to be a little more precise here. I hardly imagine there exists a profound scientific thinker, who has reflected upon the subject, unwilling to admit the extreme probability of the hypothesis, that for every fact of consciousness, whether in the domain of sense, of thought, or of emotion, a certain definite molecular condition is set up in the brain; who does not hold this relation of physics to consciousness to be invariable, so that, given the state of the brain, the corresponding thought or feeling might be inferred; or given the thought or feeling, the corresponding state of the brain might be inferred.

But how inferred? It is at bottom not a case of logical inference at all, but of empirical association. You may reply that many of the inferences of science are of this character; the inference, for example, that an electric current of a given direction will deflect a magnetic needle in a definite way; but the cases differ in this, that the passage from the current to the needle, if not demonstrable, is thinkable, and that we entertain no doubt as to the final mechanical solution of the problem. But the passage from the physics of the brain to the corresponding facts of consciousness is unthinkable. Granted that a definite thought, and a definite molecular action in the brain occur simultaneously; we do not possess the intellectual organ, nor apparently any rudiment of the organ, which would enable us to pass, by a process of reasoning, from the one to the other. They appear together, but we do not know why. Were our minds and senses so expanded, strengthened, and illuminated as to enable us to see and feel the very molecules of the brain; were we capable of following all their motions, all their groupings, all their electric discharges, if such there be; and were we intimately acquainted with the corresponding states of thought and feeling, we should be as far as ever from the solution of the problem, "How are these physical processes connected with the facts of consciousness?" The chasm between the two classes of phenomena would still remain intellectually impassable. Let the consciousness of *love*, for example, be associated with a right-handed spiral motion of the molecules of the brain, and the consciousness of *hate* with a left-handed spiral motion. We should then know when we love that the motion is in one direction, and when we hate that the motion is in the other; but the "WHY?" would remain as unanswerable as before.

In affirming that the growth of the body is mechanical, and that thought, as exercised by us, has its correlative in the physics of the brain, I think the position of the "Materialist" is stated, as far as that position is a tenable one. I think the materialist will be able finally to maintain this position against all attacks; but I do not think, in the present condition of the human mind, that he can pass beyond this position. I do not think he is entitled to say that his molecular groupings and his molecular motions *explain* everything. In reality they explain nothing. The utmost he can affirm is the association of two classes of phenomena, of whose real bond of union he is in absolute ignorance. The problem of the connection of body and soul is as insoluble in its modern form as it was in the prescientific ages. Phosphorus is known to enter into the composition of the human brain, and a trenchant German writer has exclaimed, "Ohne Phosphor, kein Gedanke." That may or may not be the case; but even if we knew it to be the case; the knowledge would not lighten our darkness. On both sides of the zone here assigned to the materialist he is equally helpless. If you ask him whence is this "Matter" of which we have been discoursing, who or what divided it into molecules, who or what impressed upon them this necessity of running into inorganic forms, he has no answer. Science is mute in reply to these questions. The process of things upon this earth has been one of amelioration. It is a long way from the iguanodon and his contemporaries to the president and members of the British Association. A time may, therefore, come when this ultra-scientific region by which we are now enfolded may offer itself to terrestrial, if not to human investigation. Meanwhile, the mystery is not without its uses. It certainly may be made a power in the human soul; but it is a power which has feeling, not knowledge, for its base. It may be, and will be, and we hope is turned to account, both in steadying and strengthening the intellect, and in rescuing man from that littleness to which, in the struggle for existence, or for precedence in the world, he is continually prone.

JOHN CRAWFORD WILSON.

[John Crawford Wilson was born at Mallow, county Cork, on the 20th April, 1825, but he has passed the great part of his life in London. He is favourably known as a poet, dramatist, and miscellaneous writer. His chief poetical works are, *The Village Pearl, and other Poems*, 1852; *Elise and Flights to Fairy Land*, 1863; *Lost and Found*, a pastoral, 1865. His most important dramas are *Gitanilla* and a stage version of his poem *Lost and Found*. *Jonathan Oldaker, or Leaves from the Diary of a Commercial Traveller*—a bright and amusing series of sketches and tales—has passed through several editions. For eighteen years Mr. Wilson has been a member of the Dramatic Authors' Society, and is president of the Whitefriars' Club, a literary association which he was chiefly instrumental in founding. Among his fugitive pieces, which have been highly praised, we find *Eight Hours at the Sea-side*, a sketch, and *A New Ode to St. Patrick*, a poem. "As an author," says a reviewer, "Mr. Wilson has been eminently successful, the scenes he depicts and the characters he introduces being calculated to promote a thrilling interest, nor is he wanting in that quality of pathos which invests a story, where requisite, with solemn and sober touches." "To the moral qualities which distinguish poets Mr. Wilson may lay an undoubted claim," says the *Athenæum*. "Genuine feeling is so infectious that such a writer can hardly tell a plain and pathetic story to unsympathizing readers." The greater number of the author's poems depict the pathetic and tender feelings of our nature, and among these his poem *Home* takes a high place. In *Lost and Found*, the most ambitious of his poetical efforts, he depicts a heroine in humble life who nobly sacrifices all she holds dear, her lover and her fame, to gratify a father and shield a sister from disgrace.]

THE DEATH OF LILY.

(FROM "HOME."[1])

They called her "Lily"—Lilian was her name—
But from her birth she seemed so waxen white—
So fairy slight—so gentle and so pure,
That to her father's mind she ever brought
The image of that pale and fragile flower:
And so he called her "Lily." 'Twas a term
In which endearment, tenderness, and hope
Were all wreathed up; the hope too often crossed
By jealous fears, when some untoward breath
Too roughly bent to earth the sickly flower,
Leaving it drooping on its yielding stem.

And there she lay at last,—almost in Heaven—
Of Time and of Eternity a part—
A dying, living link, uniting those
Who live to die—and die to ever live!

Her eyes were closed. Her mother thought she slept
The sleep that wakes no more: but 'twas not so.
A step was on the stair—the fading eyes
Opened again on earth—the wasted cheeks—
Dimpled once more, as round the lips a smile
Played like the shadow of a silver cloud
Upon a sunlit stream. "Mother! 'tis he—
'Tis father's footstep—and so very kind—
So thoughtful of his Lily, he has left
His heavy boots below; he pauses now—
Clings to the rail, and sobs. I hear it all!

---

[1] This and the following extract are made by the author's permission.

He fears I am gone Home. Go, mother dear!
Tell him I could not go till he returned.
I want to feel his kiss upon my lips;
And take it up to Heaven."
                       Another sob,
And then a choking whisper from without.
"May I come in? If she is gone, say 'No.'
If not, say 'Yes.' I'll tread so very light—
I shall not wake her, wife. May I come in?"

  A faltering voice said "Come!" 'Twas Lily's
      voice;
So he went in—a stalwart lusty man—
A giant, with a tiny infant's heart,
Weeping big tears that would not be controlled.
Oh! how he loved that child—how she loved him!
Yet both so opposite; her little soul
Clinging round his—a tendril round an oak—
A lily cleaving to a rugged rock.

  He sat beside her bed, and in his hands
Buried his streaming eyes. His soul rebelled:
"She had no right to die—to rive his heart;
Rob him and it, of all life's tenderest ties."
He felt as he could say, "Lily, lie there
For ever dying; but, oh! never die
'Til I die too." He thought not of his wife—
She was his other self. She was himself;
But Lily was their cherished life of life—
Of each and both a part—so grafted on,
That, if removed, they must become once more
Two bodies with two souls—no longer one,
Their living link destroyed—not loving less,
But singly loving—'twixt their hearts a gulf
Unbridged by Lily's love;—a love so pure
That not a taint of selfishness was near;
All this he felt, and on the future looked
As on a desolation.
                       Lily spoke—
Or whispered rather—but a thunder peal
Would less affect him than her sinking tones:
"Raise me, dear father; take me to your breast—
Your broad kind breast, so full of love for me—
'Twill rest me on my road—'tis half-way Home!"

  And then he rose, and round her wasted form
His brawny arms—before whose mighty strength
The massive anvil quivered, as his hands
Swung high the ponderous sledge—or in whose
      gripe
The fiery steed stood conquered and subdued—
Closed, as the breath of heaven, or God's own love,
So lightly, softly, gently, hemmed they in
The little dying child. Then there he sat,
Her face upon his breast, and on his knee
Her tearless mother's head; for all her tears
Were inly wept, dropping like molten lead
Upon her breaking heart.
                       Far in the west
Long waves of crimson clouds stretched o'er the
      hills;
And through those clouds, as in a sea of blood,
The sun sank slowly down. Ere his last ray
Glanced upwards from the earth, the father felt
His Lily lift her head—celestial light
Beamed from her eyes, as for the last embrace,
She to her mother turned, and then to him:
"They beckon me," she said; " I come! I come!"
Around his neck she twined her faded arms,
Rising obedient to her heavenly call;
Again he pressed her lips, but in the kiss
Her soul enfranchised, bounded from its thrall;
Its crumbling fetters drooped upon his heart—
The angel was at Home!

HOW CÆSAR WAS DRIVEN FROM IRELAND.

(FROM THE "NEW ODE TO ST. PATRICK.")

When Cæsar, by conquests unsated,
  On Erin's soft slopes set his eye,
His troops he debarked, and, elated,
  Strolled forth to a wake, as a spy.
That brawny barbarian, the Briton,
  In Britain he'd beaten anew,
Then furbished fresh fetters to fit on
  The Free-men of Brian Boru.

Disguised in a pair of cord "britches,"
  Frieze coat, sturdy brogues, and caubeen,
He scrambled through hedges and ditches,
  To where the wake lights could be seen.
He set out quite fearless and hearty,
  Arrived somewhat soon in the night,
And skrewdged himself in ere the party
  Was quite drunk enough for a fight.

He laughed, the big thief, and grew frisky,
  And drank with a mighty good-will
(He'd never afore tasted whisky,
  Or even "heerd tell" of a "still").
King Brian Boru sat and eyed him,
  So also did huge Fin-ma-Cool,
And a third, in a cloak, with, beside him,
  A crozier propped up by a stool.

They all seemed to relish the liquor
  (No exciseman near it had been);
The quicker they tippled, the quicker
  They puffed at the fragrant dudheen.
To Cæsar the pipe was extended
  By him with the crozier and cloak,
But Cæsar refused, and, offended,
  Said "Cities must blaze when I smoke."

"O cities?" says t'other, quite civil;
  "You'll want a big pipe for that same;—
I know ye."—"If so, you're the devil,"
  Says Cæsar, "so tell me my name."

"Your name and your fame," says the other,
  "Might both be much safer at home,—
The bogs of green Erin would smother
  Such haythens as Cæsar from Rome."

Then Cæsar jumped up in a hurry,
  And turned for to run to the door—
All laughed, for he found, in his flurry,
  His feet fixed like wax to the floor!
"Who are you? what ails me?" he muttered;
  "Why, why should I tremble and faint,
And quake at the words you have uttered!
  I fear neither Satan nor Saint.

"What are you? your glances appal me?"
  The other replied with a smile,
"Saint Patrick, my countrymen call me,
  The Guardian of Erin's green Isle.
You've *veni'd*, and *vidi'd*, *nót vici'd*—
  Embark in your fleet, and when there,
I'll send you, if you're not too nice-eyed,
  Such live-stock as Erin can spare."

Proud Cæsar fell down right afore him,
  And grovelled his length as he lay;
Then knelt to the Saint, to adore him,
  But Fin-ma-Cool dragged him away.
He rose, seemed desirous to linger,
  So Brian Boru bade him "Go!"
Saint Patrick, he lifted his finger,
  And Fin-ma-Cool lifted his toe.

He shot from the spot like a rocket,
  For Fin-ma-Cool kick'd with a will;
His men on the beach felt the shock, it
  Electrified valley and hill,
He fell with a thud on the sod, he
  Was "telescoped in," but they rose,
First pulling him out of his body,
  And secondly, out of his clothes.

Away Cæsar sailed, sore and weary,
  From Brian Boru and his rule,
From the Saint who had made him feel "skeary;"
  And the big toe of big Fin-ma-Cool.
Away o'er the billowy Biscay,
  Sea-sickened, soul-saddened, he sped,
Convulsed with a craving for whisky,
  And braved by his bullies for bread.

ANNIE KEARY.

BORN 1825 — DIED 1879.

[Annie Keary "should have died hereafter." She was not torn away in youth, nor had she but just begun to show her literary powers; but no reader—no Irish reader, at least—who studied one of her latest works, could help believing that there were yet rich stores in her imagination which had still to be drawn upon for delight and instruction, and which now are lost for ever.

She was the daughter of an Irish clergyman, who shortly before her birth had obtained a living in Bath, and there she was born about 1825. She was Irish in heart and sympathies, as well as in descent, and her father, though like her in another land, seems to have been of a similar mind, for it was from him she obtained—as she wrote to a countrywoman—much of her knowledge of Irish scenes and insight into Irish character. She published, in 1861, *Early Egyptian History;* in 1863 appeared *Janet's Home;* in 1866, *Clemency Franklyn;* in 1869, *Oldbury;* in 1870, *Nations Around,* which she contributed to the "Sunday Library;" in 1875, *Castle Daly;* and *A Doubting Heart* has been published in volume form since her death. She was also the authoress of *A York and a Lancaster Rose,* and, in collaboration with her sister, of a Scandinavian story entitled *The Heroes of Asgard.*

Of those works the most remarkable is *Castle Daly.* This is a fascinating book, and probably the best Irish story of the present generation. It sets out with the purpose of contrasting English and Irish character, and English and Irish ideas. No Irish reader can complain that the writer has not the tenderest sympathy with the feelings of her country-people, and on the other hand full justice is done to the virtues of English men and women. It is a part of the author's design to present the cases of Ireland and England, and both sides are discussed with eloquence, wit, and energy. It is a triumph of artistic skill that these discussions, however, are not introduced *apropos* of nothing, and to the interruption of the narrative. They arise naturally out of the fortunes of the character, and are inextricably mixed up with the plot; and thus the story conveys its weighty political moral while apparently employed solely in pleasing the reader's curiosity. We hesitate not to say that a careful study of this work would do more to instruct the student of Anglo-Irish politics than cart-loads of blue-books and yards of parliamentary oratory. Finally, as to the style of the work, it is such as a realistic book should be—unpretentious, lucid, and spontaneous.

Miss Keary suffered for some time before her death from a tedious and painful illness, and on March 3, 1879, she passed away at Eastbourne. At the time of her death her story, *A Doubting Heart*, was appearing, and continued for some months after, to appear in *Macmillan's Magazine*. "To the very large circle of her family and intimate friends," says a short obituary note in that periodical, " whom her talents, and still more her singular sweetness, wisdom, and unselfishness, had endeared her in no common degree, her loss will be deep and enduring."]

A SCENE IN THE FAMINE.

(FROM "CASTLE DALY."[1])

[The passage describes the visit of Ellen Daly, daughter of the Irish squire, to Dennis Malachy, who had formerly been one of the Castle Daly tenants. He had been evicted by John Thornley, an English agent of upright principles and excellent intentions, but mistaken from ignorance of Irish feelings. Malachy, in revenge, had fired at Thornley, but had in mistake killed Mr. Daly, the landlord, whom he and all the tenants loved. Finally, to understand the scene, it must be said that John Thornley is in love with Miss Ellen Daly.]

When Ellen had climbed the steep head of the ravine, and rounded the jutting-out ledge of rock that partly concealed Malachy's rude shieling, she paused to rest for an instant, and looking across the craggy wall into the hollow beneath was relieved to find that her companion had not attempted to follow her, even with his eyes. He was standing sentinel at the foot of the rock stairs she had clambered, with his face towards the opening of the ravine.

His figure was diminished in size by the distance, but Ellen wished him still further away, when she remembered the sight that would meet her eyes as soon as she pushed open the rough door at the end of the path she had entered on. From some dark corner of the rude shed the gaunt shape of a man would start up at the sound of her footstep,

[1] By permission of Messrs. Macmillan & Co.

and lift eyes full of a terrible hunger to her face.

It was now nearly a year since these two—the man she had left below and him she was about to visit—had been hunting each other, one with the hope and purpose in his mind of bringing the actors in a great crime to just punishment, the other with a deadly hunger for vengeance in his heart that the pangs of bodily hunger had scarcely had power to tame. Ellen's heart sank in fear at the thought of their discovering each other's neighbourhood, even now; but she thought it better to run this risk than to leave her errand unaccomplished. Malachy's wife and children and old mother shared the shelter of the shieling with him, and had become, since the famine, objects of almost equal dislike to the neighbours, who believed that a curse rested on the family, and who were capable of leaving them to starve unthought of—though they would not on any temptation have delivered up the man to justice.

The cabin door stood open, and there was no smoke issuing from the aperture; but Ellen was not surprised. The weather was warm, and as it was three days since any member of the household had been to Eagle's Edge to beg for food, it was only too probable that there was nothing in the cabin to cook. She pushed the door a little; it seemed to resist the pressure, as if something lay across the threshold, and it was not without considerable effort, and with a dull thud as of some heavy body thrust aside, that it yielded so far as to allow her to squeeze herself inside.

It was almost dark in the inclosure, for though the loosely-fitted stones let air and light through, the upper end of the ravine lay in deep shadow just then, and the eye had to grow accustomed to the dim light for anything to be seen distinctly.

" Molly," Ellen said, softly, " it is I come to bring you food at last. Are you all asleep? Molly! Dennis!" She called twice, and then her eyes beginning to see what was around her, grew large with horror, and a fit of cold shuddering seized her. The place was not empty, but it was very still. Just opposite to her was a figure half-seated on the ground with its back to the wall. A child's form lay motionless across its knees, the head rested on a stone in the wall, and there was light enough through a crevice above to show Ellen that the death-pale, hollow face, with dropped jaw and half-closed eyes that looked so strangely without seeing were those of Malachy's young wife. "Nora," she tried to say, but the word would not come, only a hoarse sob in her throat; then she turned and looked into the dense darkness at the end of the shed where it sloped up towards the mountain side. A heap of dead fern-leaves and moss lay along the floor there, and on it were stretched two other motionless bodies of an old woman and a child.

Ellen forced herself to stoop over them, and in desperation dragged away the tattered shawl that half hid the old woman's face, and putting her hand on her shoulder, shook her gently. "Molly, Molly, wake! I have brought you help." The figure fell back into its settled position again as soon as her hand left it, and Ellen started up horror-struck again. Her hand had come in contact with the withered cheek, and its touch stung her with cold. She felt she must struggle out into the open air before she fainted, and then, preparing to move, she perceived what the object was that had impeded the opening of the door. It lay almost over her feet; she had stepped on it in entering; the prostrate body of Dennis Malachy, who seemed to have fallen down beside the threshold as he was attempting to leave the shieling, perhaps to seek help in the last extremity of his wife and children, perhaps to escape from the chamber of death. There was something in his attitude less lifeless than in that of the others. Sick and trembling as she was Ellen could not step over him again without ascertaining whether there might not be a spark of life left. She turned the face, which was towards the floor, upwards, drew it to the opening, and rested the head on the door-sill where the air could blow upon it; then, hardly knowing whether she most dreaded to see the eyes remain shut, or that they should open on her with some look of unspeakable pain, such as she could never forget afterwards, she rushed out of the cabin and tottered down the rocky path, stumbling and dragging herself up again, but never pausing till she had reached the spot where John Thornley stood, and seized him by the arm.

"Come! come! there are people dying up there. There are dead people up there."

Her voice sounded strange and hoarse to herself, and greatly startled him, as did her pale face and horror-stricken looks.

"You must not go there again. I will go," he said. "I will see what is wanted, and fetch help."

"To stay here alone would be worse, much worse," Ellen answered, recovering her voice and calmness in a degree, now that a living fellow-creature's face was near to be looked at. "Let me go back; there is a man in the cabin up there who has some life in him still, I think; if I go back to him with you, and we can do anything for him, I shall not always have such a great horror of what I have seen."

"How near is help to be had?" John asked, as they were climbing the path, "for I cannot let you stay here if the man you speak of recovers and lingers a while. Some one else must be fetched to watch him."

"It would not be so hard as another watch we had," Ellen said, the scene of her father's death flashing on her memory as she spoke, and with it a shuddering wonder that she should be going to minister to the last moments of the man to whose thirst for revenge he had fallen a victim, and with John Thornley to aid her. She had been forgetting who it was that was dying during the last moment or two.

John could have knelt down and kissed the stone on which her foot rested at the moment, in gratitude for that *we;* but she was not thinking of him except as a strange coadjutor in the strange task. He would not let her enter the cabin till he had gone in first. When he beckoned her to follow, Dennis Malachy had been lifted from the threshold of the door, and placed on a heap of straw near the wall, with a log of wood under his head. John had opened Ellen's basket, and was attempting to put some drops of brandy between the parched lips. "He is not dead," he said, "but I don't think there is a possibility of saving him; he is so terribly wasted, he must die."

Ellen knelt down on the floor and began to bathe the temples with water. "He breathes still. I wish you would go down into the village and find a priest, and bring him here. The old woman who is lying dead there did that for papa."

"This is Dennis Malachy then, your father's murderer? I did not know him."

"The cause of his death, but not his murderer," said Ellen, quickly, withdrawing her hand instinctively at the word from the brow she was bathing. "He told me solemnly it was not his hand that sent the bullet."

"You have known where he was ever since?"

"No, only since hunger drove him to betray himself to me. I remembered then that papa forgave. Only he forgave— no one else could;

the others hunted Dennis to his death. But he was not always a bad man; I remember him when he was good and gentle, and used to meet us on our walks, and carry us home on his shoulder when we were tired. I don't know whose fault it was that he came to this, but I don't believe that it was all his own."

With the last words she slipped her arm under his head, and raised it a little. The lids that drooped over the half-closed eyes quivered, the breast heaved, and with a sudden spasm of parting strength the dying man sat half upright, and stared wildly round him. John Thornley involuntarily put up his hand to shade his eyes from the stare fixed on him.

"An orphan's curse might drag to hell
   A spirit from on high;
But, oh, more terrible than that
   Is the curse in a dead man's eye."

The lines came into John's mind, and stayed there, and could not be exorcised for long afterwards. Then the dying man's eyes were turned on Ellen, and the hands that had clutched convulsively were spread out imploringly towards her.

"Miss Eileen, Miss Eileen, save me! don't let me do it or I'll lose me soul. Why did ye bring *him* here, that I might curse him wid me last breath, and lose me soul?"

"You shall not, Dennis," Ellen said, bending over him so as to hide Mr. Thornley's face from his sight. "Look at me, and remember the words I said to you that night, when I told you my father forgave you, and that the Father in heaven forgives us when we forgive our enemies."

"Shure you bade me spare him, and I did your bidding, and I'm glad. It's all over wid us now, Miss Eileen. Praise be to God and His blessed Mother! the starving's over, and the pain wid all of us, and I'm going. Why would we any of us live any longer?—dying's a dale aisier—in peace." The head sank back again, the last words were murmured between lips that quivered, and then became convulsed in a strong spasm. There was a long, shuddering gasp, then Mr. Thornley came round and drew Ellen's arm from under the head.

"It is over," he said. "Come away with me; you must not stay here a moment longer; there is nothing more for you to do; I will take care that all is done that is right by these." He glanced round at the corpses. "We shall surely be able to persuade some one from the next village to come up and do what is necessary."

"But are you sure there is nothing more we can do? The children," said Ellen; "the little girl lying by the grandmother in the bed—little Nora—I hardly looked at her."

"But I have looked. Those two must have been dead many hours; it is a terrible sight; you must come away." Almost by force he raised her from her kneeling position on the floor, and lifted her over the threshold into the open air. Then she sat down on a stone by the wayside, and burying her face in her hands, gave way to the tears that had been choking her for so long. He stood by watching the bright drops that trickled through her fingers on to the ground, longing for the right and the power to comfort her, and almost hating himself for the excess of feeling that made it impossible to say a word that would not betray too much; and then again for not having courage even in that moment to say all.

She lifted up her head after a long time, and turned to him with one of the appealing confiding looks, free from all self-consciousness, that always touched him so deeply—so much more deeply than any consciousness would have done, even if it had given him more hope.

"Do you think," she said humbly, "that this was at all my fault?"

"Your fault! how could it be? I was thinking that there was no one on earth but yourself who, under the circumstances, would have acted towards that man as you have acted."

"But I went away last week to stay with cousin Anne, trusting that Father Peter would look after the Malachys, and you see he was not able."

"In times like these, when there is so much misery around, it will not do to waste strength in regretting what was unavoidable. It must have been a miserable death-in-life they lived up here shunned by every one."

"Cousin Anne offered to take the children, but Nora and Molly would not give them up. They said they would all hold together till the end, and so they have done."

By this time Ellen had risen from the stone, and they proceeded to descend the hill. When they reached the head of the ravine, John Thornley said,

"Which way shall we turn? Shall I take you home and get help from Eagle's Edge, or will you persevere in going to the Hollow?"

"To the Hollow, I think. We are more than half-way there, and about half a mile from this place there is a hamlet where I know a great many people are congregated to-day."

The walk was almost a silent one, for it was impossible to talk on any common topic; and the horror of the scene they had left seemed to grow instead of lessen in John's mind as they walked through the smiling green valley in the glorious autumn afternoon; the air, fragrant with the thymy scent of the thousand minute flowers that bordered the road, musical with placid country sounds—sheep-bleatings and cattle-lowings from the hill-sides, and with the plover's shrill cry as the bird skimmed across their path and darted away, rising high in the air and dipping again in search of food on the boggy surface of the valley.

"I cannot get the remembrance of that man's face out of my mind," John began abruptly, when they were near enough to the village to hear the stroke of the little chapel bell that was still tolling. "I am afraid the terrible reproach there was in it when he looked his last on me will haunt me in every miserable or weak moment of my life henceforth. Yet, looking back soberly, as I must try to do, I don't think I ought to blame myself for any part of my conduct to him. I only did what I believed to be my duty."

"It did not look like duty to him, you see, because he had grown up with notions of rights and law very different from yours. He appeared to you only a lawless robber holding on to property that did not belong to him; but in his own mind there were stubborn, blind beliefs in right that had come down to him through centuries of his ancestors, and these were too much a part of him to be thrown off at any bidding of yours. He could not have explained himself to you or any one, but the conviction that you were the robber and injurer, and not he, was strong in his thoughts and confused all his relations to you. I have often talked over these things with cousin Anne lately, when we have been trying to account for the terrible crimes this year has witnessed among people whose generosity of nature we believe in, and for the wild projects current now among Connor's friends."

"If I had gone to the appointed meeting that night, and been shot, Dennis would have been looked upon as a hero. These people would not have connected that crime with punishment. Yet I was only acting in your father's interest."

"They did not understand that, because my father was such a careless ruler, and the change was so great and sudden. My dear father blamed himself, you know, and thought that death-shot his due."

After a pause of thought, John took up the conversation again. "I begin to see where the fault lies. A few minutes ago I was saying vehemently to myself that at least I had been guilty of no injustice, yet I felt that the sting of remorse would not strike so deep if I were really blameless. Now I see how it is. I ought never to have come here, knowing so little as I did of the people I had to deal with, having scarcely glanced at the problems that rise up before me now as almost unfathomable. I know what Miss O'Flaherty thought of my presumption. If I had been less self-confident, less contemptuous of other people's doings, less full of system, perhaps—but I dare not look back in that way, the consequences are too terrible. Your father's death, the miserable end of that man and his family—it will not do to look back and trace consequences in cases of such tremendous importance; it would be giving conscience too terrible a power; the burden of life would be too heavy to carry for a day."

"Yes, indeed," said Ellen, "if we had to carry all by ourselves. We should be tempted to put off seeing our own share of responsibility in all the ill that happens, however much worse the suffering might be in the end, when we had to see the truth."

"Don't speak of yourself as if you had any share in the pain to-day has brought to me."

"But I have. I don't think any great wrong or misery can befall without more or less blame belonging to all the lookers-on. It is a circle that spreads out farther than our dull consciences can trace. Here we are in the hamlet I spoke of. That little cottage among the trees half-way up the hill is the priest's house, where you are sure to find plenty of people to-day. I think I will go into the chapel down there. Some service or other is going on now, and I shall perhaps see some one I know who will help us if your errand fails; and I shall rest there while you go up the hill."

John despatched his business more speedily than he expected, and turned his steps towards the little white-washed building that served the villagers for a place of worship. The narrow space was so crowded to-day with people thronging round the different little altars that he had some difficulty in finding Ellen. He saw her at last among a throng of women kneeling in a circle at the end of the chapel, and he made his way up to her. The women drew apart as he approached, to make room for him at her side; and almost involuntarily he knelt down a little way behind her. There was preaching going on. He had not come in at the beginning, and could not make out whether any text for the sermon had been given out; but the sentence, "Man does not live by bread alone," was repeated several times by the preacher, and each time a groan of acquiescence burst forth from the pale lips of the famine-stricken people kneeling round, who seemed to hang upon the speaker's words as if they were food indeed. Then the preacher went on to describe in glowing words, and with much metaphor and eloquence, the spirit life—nourished by the true bread—into the full enjoyment of which the good priest who had addressed his flock from that spot two days ago had now entered. At another time John might have listened critically—questioning the wisdom or the utility of such an exercise under such circumstances; but now kneeling on the mud floor among that sea of pale faces that were gradually losing their ghastliness under the illumination of hope in the Unseen, thus set forth before eyes that in every other quarter beheld only despair, he could not question. Here were needs—depths and breadths and lengths and heights of suffering—which no science or philosophy of his could reach or touch, but which seemed here in these words of childlike faith to find solution swallowed up in yet more unfathomable heights and depths and lengths and breadths of love. At the end of the sermon something was said about the new light which the dawning of that Eternal Day would cast on the perplexities and sufferings and wrongs of our lives. It would be easy, the preacher said, to forgive all wrongs, fancied or real, when all the links that had bound our lives together and to God were made clear. Ellen turned her face, radiant with a tremulous tearful smile, towards him at the words, and held out her hand. The moment he held it seemed to John Thornley to open the door for him into a new life. It might not be a life of happy human love, but one tending to higher, nobler, more self-sacrificing ends than he had yet known; he prayed low to himself that it might be. The next moment the blessing was given, there was a movement among the kneelers by the altar, and Ellen rose and they left the place together.

They met Peter Lynch in the throng outside the chapel door, who gave Ellen such a gloomy account of his mistress's state of health that she was glad to accept his offer of a seat on the three-wheeled car which had brought him to the village, and so hasten her arrival at the Hollow.

John Thornley, after placing her in the car, shook hands with her in silence. It did not seem necessary for him to say, "We shall meet to-morrow." That hand-clasp in the chapel seemed just then to have made him independent of future meetings or partings, and to have given him a spiritual hold on her presence so firm that no distance of space nor spite of circumstance could ever oblige him to let it go again. Far or near, dear to her or indifferent, he believed he should live from henceforth in its light.

WILLIAM ALLINGHAM.

[William Allingham was born at Ballyshannon,—that picturesquely situated town in the north of Ireland to which his poems have so often recurred. He early began to contribute to London periodicals, writing, among others, in the *Athenæum* and *Household Words*. In 1850 his first volume of poems was published. In 1854 a second, under the title *Day and Night Songs*, was issued; and in the following year appeared another edition of the same work, enlarged, and illustrated by Millais and several other artists. *Fifty Modern Poems* appeared in 1865. *Laurence Bloomfield in Ireland* is a picture of contemporary Ireland. It is written in decasyllabic couplets, and is divided into twelve chapters. Having originally appeared in *Fraser*, it was, in 1869, published in volume form. *Songs, Poems, and Ballads*, which appeared in 1877, is a revised collection from previous works, along with many new pieces which Mr. Allingham had contributed from time to time to periodical literature. It will not be necessary to pass any critical judgment here on a poet who has an assured position. The specimens we quote from *Laurence Bloomfield* will give a good idea of the simplicity, strength, and realistic power of that remarkable poem. We also append a few of the shorter lyrics, in which he is, perhaps, happiest. It should be added that Mr. Allingham is well known also as a prose writer. He was for many years connected with *Fraser's Magazine*, and in 1872, on Mr. Froude's resignation, became editor—a position he held till a recent period. Some of the essays written under the *nom de plume* of "Patricius Walker" have been published in volume form.]

BALLYTULLAGH.

(FROM "LAURENCE BLOOMFIELD."[1])

The hamlet Ballytullagh, small and old,
Lay negligently cluster'd in a fold
Of Tullagh Hill, amid the crags and moor;
A windy dwelling-place, rough, lonesome, poor;
So low and weather-stain'd the walls, the thatch
So dusk of hue, or spread with mossy patch,
A stranger journeying on the distant road
Might hardly guess that human hearts abode
In those wild fields, save when a smoky wreath
Distinguish'd from huge rocks, above, beneath,
Its huddled roofs. A lane goes up the hill,
Cross'd, at one elbow, by a crystal rill,
Between the stepping-stones gay tripping o'er
In shallow brightness on its gravelly floor,
From crags above, with falls and rocky urns,
Through sward below, in deep deliberate turns,
Where each fine evening brought the boys to play
At football, or with *camuns*[2] drive away
The whizzing *nagg*;[3] a crooked lane and steep,
Older than broad highways, you find it creep,
Fenced in with stooping thorn-trees, bramble-brakes,
Tall edge-stones, gleaming, gay as spotted snakes,
With gold and silver lichen; till it bends
Between two rock-based, rough-built gable ends,
To form the street, if one may call it street,
Where ducks and pigs in filthy forum meet;
A scrambling, careless, tatter'd place, no doubt;
Each cottage rude within doors as without;
All rude and poor; some wretched,—black, and bare,
And doleful as the cavern of Despair.
And yet, when crops were good, nor oatmeal high,
A famine or a fever-time gone by,
The touch of simple pleasures, even here,
In rustic sight and sound the heart could cheer.
With voice of breezes moving o'er the hills,

Wild birds and four-foot creatures, falling rills,
Mingled the hum of huswife's wheel, cock-crow,
The whetted scythe, or cattle's evening low,
Or laugh of children. Herding went the boy,
The sturdy diggers wrought with spade and *loy*,[4]
The tether'd she-goat browsed the rock's green ledge,
The clothes were spread to dry on sloping hedge,
The *colleens* did their broidery in the shade
Of leafy bush, or gown-skirt overhead,
Or wash'd and *beetled*[5] by the shallow brook,
Or sung their ballads round the chimney-nook
To speed a winter night, when song, and jest,
And dance, and talk, and social game are best;
For daily life's material good enough
Such trivial incidents and homely stuff.
Here also could those miracles befall
Of wedding, new-born babe, and funeral;
Here every thought, and mood, and fancy rise
From common earth and soar to mystic skies.

GOING TO THE FAIR.

(FROM "LAURENCE BLOOMFIELD.")

Ere yet the sun has dried on hedge and furze
Their silver veils of dewy gossamers,
Along the winding road to Lisnamoy
The drover trudges and the country boy,
With cows that fain would crop its fringe of sward,
And pigs, their hindfoot jerking in a cord,
And bleating sheep; the farmer jogs his way,
Or plies his staff and legs of woollen gray;
The basket-bearing goodwives slowly move,
White-capt, with colour'd kerchief tied above,
On foot, or in the cart-front placed on high
To jolt along in lumbering luxury;
Men, women, pigs, cows, sheep, and horses tend
One way, and to the Harvest Fair they wend.

. . . . . .

'Tis where the road-side rivulet expands,
And every stone upon its image stands,
The country maidens finish their attire,
Screen'd by the network of a tangled briar;
On grassy bank their shapely limbs indue
With milk-white stocking and the well-black'd shoe,
And court that mirror for a final grace,
The dazzling ribbons nodding round their face.
Behold our Bridget tripping to the fair;
Her shawl is splendid, but her feet are bare;
Till, quick the little bundle here untied
The shoes come forth, the skirts are shaken wide,
And Biddy enters Lisnamoy in pride;
Nor be it long ere Denis she espies,
To read her triumph in his joyful eyes.

---

[1] This and the following extracts are made by permission of the author.
[2] *Camuns*, sticks bent at one end.
[3] *Nagg*, wooden ball.
[4] *Loy*, a half-spade.
[5] *Beetling*, thumping clothes with a truncheon (beetle).

But first of all, with calm submissive face,
Beads in her hand, within the Holy Place
She kneels, among the kneelers who adore
In silent reverence on that mystic floor;
Then with a curtsey, and with symbol meet
On brow and breast, returning to the street.

LOVELY MARY DONNELLY.

Oh, lovely Mary Donnelly, it's you I love the best!
If fifty girls were round you I'd hardly see the rest.
Be what it may the time of day, the place be where it will,
Sweet looks of Mary Donnelly, they bloom before me still.

Her eyes like mountain water that's flowing on a rock,
How clear they are, how dark they are! and they give me many a shock.
Red rowans warm in sunshine and wetted with a show'r,
Could ne'er express the charming lip that has me in its pow'r.

Her nose is straight and handsome, her eyebrows lifted up,
Her chin is very neat and pert, and smooth like a china cup,
Her hair's the brag of Ireland, so weighty and so fine;
It's rolling down upon her neck, and gather'd in a twine.

The dance o' last Whit-Monday night exceeded all before,
No pretty girl for miles about was missing from the floor;
But Mary kept the belt of love, and O but she was gay!
She danced a jig, she sung a song, that took my heart away.

When she stood up for dancing, her steps were so complete,
The music nearly kill'd itself to listen to her feet;
The fiddler moan'd his blindness, he heard her so much praised,
But bless'd his luck to not be deaf when once her voice she raised.

And evermore I'm whistling or lilting what you sung,
Your smile is always in my heart, your name beside my tongue;
But you've as many sweethearts as you'd count on both your hands,
And for myself there's not a thumb or little finger stands.

Oh, you're the flower o' womankind in country or in town;
The higher I exalt you, the lower I'm cast down.
If some great lord should come this way, and see your beauty bright,
And you to be his lady, I'd own it was but right.

O might we live together in a lofty palace hall,
Where joyful music rises, and where scarlet curtains fall!
O might we live together in a cottage mean and small;
With sods of grass the only roof, and mud the only wall!

O lovely Mary Donnelly, your beauty's my distress.
It's far too beauteous to be mine, but I'll never wish it less.
The proudest place would fit your face, and I am poor and low;
But blessings be about you, dear, wherever you may go!

ABBEY ASAROE.

Gray, gray is Abbey Asaroe, by Ballyshanny town,
It has neither door nor window, the walls are broken down;
The carven stones lie scatter'd in briars and nettle-bed;
The only feet are those that come at burial of the dead.
A little rocky rivulet runs murmuring to the tide,
Singing a song of ancient days, in sorrow, not in pride;
The boor-tree and the lightsome ash across the portal grow,
And heaven itself is now the roof of Abbey Asaroe.

It looks beyond the harbour-stream to Gulban mountain blue;
It hears the voice of Erna's fall,—Atlantic breakers too;
High ships go sailing past it; the sturdy clank of oars
Brings in the salmon-boat to haul a net upon the shores;
And this way to his home-creek, when the summer day is done,
Slow sculls the weary fisherman across the setting sun;
While green with corn is Sheegus Hill, his cottage white below;
But gray at every season is Abbey Asaroe.

There stood one day a poor old man above its broken bridge;
He heard no running rivulet, he saw no mountain-ridge;

He turn'd his back on Sheegus Hill, and view'd
    with misty sight
The abbey walls, the burial-ground with crosses
    ghostly white;
Under a weary weight of years he bow'd upon his
    staff,
Perusing in the present time the former's epitaph;
For, gray and wasted like the walls, a figure full
    of woe,
This man was of the blood of them who founded
    Asaroe.

From Derry to Bundrowas Tower, Tirconnell broad
    was theirs;
Spearmen and plunder, bards and wine, and holy
    abbot's prayers;
With chanting always in the house which they had
    builded high
To God and to Saint Bernard,—whereto they came
    to die.
At worst, no workhouse grave for him! the ruins
    of his race
Shall rest among the ruin'd stones of this their
    saintly place.
The fond old man was weeping; and tremulous
    and slow
Along the rough and crooked lane he crept from
    Asaroe.

ACROSS THE SEA.

I walk'd in the lonesome evening,
    And who so sad as I,
When I saw the young men and maidens
    Merrily passing by.
    To thee, my love, to thee—
    So fain would I come to thee!
While the ripples fold upon sands of gold
    And I look across the sea.

I stretch out my hands; who will clasp them?
    I call,—thou repliest no word:
O why should heart-longing be weaker
    Than the waving wings of a bird!
    To thee, my love, to thee—
    So fain would I come to thee!
For the tide's at rest from east to west,
    And I look across the sea.

There's joy in the hopeful morning,
    There's peace in the parting day,
There's sorrow with every lover
    Whose true-love is far away.
    To thee, my love, to thee—
    So fain would I come to thee!
And the water's bright in a still moonlight,
    As I look across the sea.

MAYNE REID.

[Captain Mayne Reid was born in Kloskilt, county Down, in 1819, being a year younger than many of his biographers have made out. His father was an eminent Presbyterian clergyman, and intended his son to follow the same calling, but after studying for some time with this view, he suddenly left—some say ran away from—home. He sailed for the United States, more with the idea of seeing the world and finding adventures than with any definite plan. He landed at New Orleans, and went on several excursions on the Red River and the Missouri. During this period he traded and hunted with the Indians, and for more than five years he enjoyed the wild adventures, the strange and eccentric scenes, and the bracing freedom of the prairie. It was at this stage of his life he obtained that intimate acquaintance with the Indian character and wild scenery which he has so well reproduced in several of his works. Afterwards he went on a tour through the United States, visiting almost every part of the country. He had already begun to use his pen, but the outbreak of the war between the United States and Mexico in 1845 supplied a new and, at the moment, more attractive field of activity. He sought for and obtained a commission, and passed through some of the most exciting and dangerous scenes of the war. He was present at the capture of Vera Cruz. He led the last charge of the infantry at Cherubusco, and as one of the forlorn hope at Chapultepec he was severely wounded and reported killed. At the close of the war he resigned his commission, and his next idea was the organization of the American legion to help the Hungarians in their insurrection against the then oppressive rule of Austria. When he arrived at Paris he found that the rebellion had been suppressed. From this period forward he has been a *littérateur*, and works have come from his pen with extraordinary fertility. The popularity of his writings at home and abroad has been remarkable. Of *The Scalp-hunters* alone a million of copies are said to have been sold. The *Athenæum* says that in Russia he is more popular than even Scott or Dickens. In

France, Spain, and Italy several authors have produced different translations of his works. Of his writings we can here mention but a few of the most remarkable. *The Rifle Rangers, The Scalp-hunters, The War Trail, The Quadroon, The White Chief,* and *The Headless Horseman.* In his works there are many scenes of vivid description, and the rapidity with which he hurries the reader from scene to scene, makes his stories highly excitable.]

THE WILD WEST.[1]

Unrol the world's map and look upon the great northern continent of America. Away to the wild west, away toward the setting sun, away beyond many a far meridian let your eyes wander. Rest them where golden rivers rise among peaks that carry the eternal snow. Rest them there.

You are looking upon a land whose features are unfurrowed by human hands, still bearing the marks of the Almighty mould, as upon the morning of creation; a region whose every object wears the impress of God's image. His ambient spirit lives in the silent grandeur of its mountains, and speaks in the roar of its mighty rivers: a region redolent of romance, rich in the reality of adventure.

Follow me, with the eye of your mind, through scenes of wild beauty, of savage sublimity.

I stand in an open plain. I turn my face to the north, to the south, to the east, and to the west; and on all sides behold the blue circle of the heavens girdling around me. Nor rock nor tree breaks the ring of the horizon. What covers the broad expanse between? Wood? water? grass? No; flowers! As far as my eye can range it rests only on flowers, on beautiful flowers!

I am looking as on a tinted map, an enamelled picture brilliant with every hue of the prism.

Yonder is golden yellow, where the helianthus turns her dial-like face to the sun. Yonder, scarlet, where the malva erects its red banner. Here is a parterre of the purple monarda, there the euphorbia sheds its silver leaf. Yonder the orange predominates in the showy flowers of the asclepia; and beyond the eye roams over the pink blossoms of the cleome.

The breeze stirs them. Millions of corollas are waving their gaudy standards. The tall stalks of the helianthus bend and rise in long undulations like billows on a golden sea.

They are at rest again. The air is filled with odours sweet as the perfumes of Araby or Ind. Myriads of insects flap their gay wings: flowers of themselves. The bee-birds skirr around, glancing like stray sunbeams; or, poised on whirring wings, drink from the nectared cups; and the wild bee, with laden limbs, clings among the honeyed pistils, or leaves for his far hive with a song of joy.

Who planted these flowers? Who hath woven them into these pictured parterres? Nature. It is her richest mantle, richer in its hues than the scarfs of Cashmere.

This is the "weed prairie." It is misnamed. It is *the garden of God.*

. . . .

The scene is changed. I am in a plain as before, with the unbroken horizon circling around me. What do I behold? Flowers? No; there is not a flower in sight, but one vast expanse of living verdure! From north to south, from east to west, stretches the prairie meadow, green as an emerald, and smooth as the surface of a sleeping lake.

The wind is upon its bosom, sweeping the silken blades. They are in motion; and the verdure is dappled into lighter and darker shades, as the shadows of summer clouds flitting across the sun.

The eye wanders without resistance. Perchance it encounters the dark hirsute forms of the buffalo, or traces the tiny outlines of the antelope. Perchance it follows, in pleased wonder, the far-wild gallop of a snow-white steed.

This is the "grass prairie," the boundless pasture of the bison.

. . . .

The scene changes. The earth is no longer level, but treeless and verdant as ever. Its surface exhibits a succession of parallel undulations, here and there swelling into smooth round hills. It is covered with a soft turf of brilliant greenness. These undulations remind one of the ocean after a mighty storm, when the crisped foam has died upon the waves, and the big swell comes bowling in. They look as though they had once been such waves, that, by an omnipotent mandate, had been transformed to earth, and suddenly stood still.

This is the "rolling prairie."

. . . .

Again the scene changes. I am among green-

---

[1] This and the following extract from *The Scalp-hunters* are by permission of the author.

swards and bright flowers; but the view is broken by groves and clumps of copse-wood. The frondage is varied, its tints are vivid, its outlines soft and graceful. As I move forward new landscapes open up continuously: views park-like and picturesque. "Gangs" of buffalo, "herds" of antelope, and "droves" of wild horses, mottle the far vistas. Turkeys run into the coppice, and pheasants whirr up from the path.

Where are the owners of these lands, of these flocks and fowls? Where are the houses, the palaces that should appertain to these lordly parks? I look forward expecting to see the turrets of tall mansions spring up over the groves. But no. For hundreds of miles around no chimney sends forth its smoke. Although with a cultivated aspect, this region is only trodden by the mocassined foot of the hunter, and his enemy the red Indian.

These are the "mottes"—the "islands" of the prairie sea.

. . . . .

I am in the deep forest. It is night, and the log-fire throws out its vermilion glare, painting the objects that surround our bivouac. Huge trunks stand thickly around us; and massive limbs, gray and giant-like, stretch out and over. I notice the bark. It is cracked, and clings in broad scales crisping outward. Long snake-like parasites creep from tree to tree, coiling the trunks as though they were serpents and would crush them! There are no leaves overhead. They have ripened and fallen; but the white Spanish moss, festooned along the branches, hangs weeping down like the drapery of a death-bed. Prostrate trunks, yards in diameter and half-decayed, lie along the ground. Their ends exhibit vast cavities, where the porcupine and opossum have taken shelter from the cold.

My comrades, wrapped in their blankets, and stretched upon the dead leaves, have gone to sleep. They lie with their feet to the fire, and their heads resting in the hollow of their saddles. The horses, standing around a tree, and tied to its lower branches, seem also to sleep. I am awake and listening. The wind is high up, whistling among the twigs, and causing the long white streamers to oscillate. It utters a wild and melancholy music. There are few other sounds, for it is winter, and the tree-frog and cicada are silent. I hear the crackling knots in the fire, the rustling of dry leaves "swirled" up by a stray gust, the "coo-whoo-a" of the white owl, the bark of the racoon, and, at intervals, the dismal howling of wolves. These are the nocturnal voices of the *winter* forest. They are savage sounds; yet there is a chord in my bosom that vibrates under their influence, and my spirit is tinged with romance as I lie and listen.

. . . . .

The forest in autumn; still bearing its full frondage. The leaves resemble flowers, so bright are their hues. They are red, and yellow, and golden, and brown. The woods are warm and glorious now, and the birds flutter among the laden branches. The eye wanders delighted down long vistas and over sunlit glades. It is caught by the flashing of gaudy plumage, the golden green of the paroquet, the blue of the jay, and the orange wing of the oriole. The red-bird flutters lower down in the coppice of green pawpaws, or amidst the amber leaflets of the beechen thicket. Hundreds of tiny wings flit through the openings, twinkling in the sun like the glancing of gems.

The air is filled with music: sweet sounds of love. The bark of the squirrel, the cooing of mated doves, the "rat-ta-ta" of the pecker, and the constant and measured chirrup of the cicada, are all ringing together. High up, on a topmost twig, the mocking-bird pours forth his mimic note, as though he would shame all other songsters into silence.

. . . . .

I am in a country of brown barren earth and broken outlines. There are rocks, and clefts, and patches of sterile soil. Strange vegetable forms grow in the clefts and hang over the rocks. Others are spheroidal in shape, resting upon the surface of the parched earth. Others rise vertically to a great height like carved and fluted columns. Some throw out branches, crooked shaggy branches, with hirsute oval leaves. Yet there is a homogeneousness about all these vegetable forms, in their colour, in their fruit and flowers, that proclaims them of one family. They are cacti. It is a forest of the Mexican *nopal*. Another singular plant is here. It throws out long thorny leaves that curve downward. It is the agave, the far-famed mezcal-plant of Mexico. Here and there, mingling with the cacti, are trees of acacia and mezquite, the denizens of the desert land. No bright object relieves the eye; no bird pours its melody into the ear. The lonely owl flaps away into the impassable thicket, the rattlesnake glides under its scanty shade, and the coyote skulks through its silent glades.

. . . . .

I have climbed mountain after mountain,

and still I behold peaks soaring far above crowned with the snow that never melts. I stand upon beetling cliffs, and look into chasms that yawn beneath, sleeping in the silence of desolation. Great fragments have fallen into them, and lie piled one upon another. Others hang threatening over, as if waiting for some concussion of the atmosphere to hurl them from their balance. Dark precipices frown me into fear, and my head reels with a dizzy faintness. I hold by the pine-tree shaft, or the angle of the firmer rock.

Above, and below, and around me are mountains piled on mountains in chaotic confusion. Some are bald and bleak; others exhibit traces of vegetation in the dark needles of the pine and cedar, whose stunted forms half-grow, half-hang from the cliffs. Here a cone-shaped peak soars up till it is lost in snow and clouds. There a ridge elevates its sharp outline against the sky; while along its sides lie huge boulders of granite, as though they had been hurled from the hands of Titan giants!

A fearful monster, the grizzly bear, drags his body along the high ridges; the carcajou squats upon the projecting rock, waiting the elk that must pass to the water below; and the bighorn bounds from crag to crag in search of his shy mate. Along the pine branch the bald buzzard whets his filthy beak; and the war-eagle, soaring over all, cuts sharply against the blue field of the heavens.

These are the Rocky Mountains, the American Andes, the colossal vertebræ of the continent!

CAPTURE OF AN INDIAN CHIEF.

Our eyes rolled over the prairie together, eastward, as the speaker pointed. An object was just visible low down on the horizon, like a moving blazing star. It was not that. At a glance we all knew what it was. It was a helmet, flashing under the sunbeam, as it rose and fell to the measured gallop of a horse.

"To the willows, men! to the willows!" shouted Seguin. "Drop the bow! Leave it where it was. To your horses! Lead them! Crouch! crouch!"

We all ran to our horses, and seizing the bridles, half-led, half-dragged them within the willow thicket. We leaped into our saddles, so as to be ready for any emergency, and sat peering through the leaves that screened us.

"Shall we fire as he comes up, captain?" asked one of the men.

"No."

"We kin take him nicely, just as he stoops for the bow."

"No; not for your lives!"

"What then, captain?"

"Let him take it and go," was Seguin's reply.

"Why, captain! what's that for?"

"Fools! do you not see that the whole tribe would be back upon our trail before midnight? Are you mad? Let him go. He may not notice our tracks, as our horses are not shod. If so, let him go as he came, I tell you."

"But how, captain, if he squints yonder-away?"

Garey, as he said this, pointed to the rocks at the foot of the mountain.

"*Sac-r-r-ré Dieu!* the Digger!" exclaimed Seguin, his countenance changing expression.

The body lay on a conspicuous point, on its face, the crimson skull turned upward and outward, so that it could hardly fail to attract the eye of any one coming in from the plain. Several coyotes had already climbed up on the slab where it lay, and were smelling around it, seemingly not caring to touch the hideous morsel.

"He's bound to see it, captain," added the hunter.

"If so, we must take him with the lance, the lasso, or alive. No gun must be fired. They might still hear it, and would be on us before we could get round the mountain. No! sling your guns! Let those who have lances and lassoes get them in readiness."

"When would you have us make the dash, captain?"

"Leave that to me. Perhaps he may dismount for the bow; or, if not, he may ride into the spring to water his horse, then we can surround him. If he see the Digger's body he may pass up to examine it more closely. In that case we can intercept him without difficulty. Be patient! I shall give you the signal."

During all this time the Navajo was coming up at a regular gallop. As the dialogue ended he had got within about three hundred yards of the spring, and still pressed forward without slackening his pace. We kept our gaze fixed upon him in breathless silence, eyeing both man and horse.

It was a splendid sight. The horse was a large coal-black mustang, with fiery eyes and red open nostrils. He was foaming at the mouth, and the white flakes had clouted his throat, counter, and shoulders. He was wet all over, and glittered as he moved with the play of his proud flanks. The rider was naked from the waist up, excepting his helmet and plumes, and some ornaments that glistened on his neck, bosom, and wrists. A tunic-like skirt, bright and embroidered, covered his hips and thighs. Below the knee his legs were naked, ending in a buskined mocassin that fitted tightly around the ankle. Unlike the Apachés there was no paint upon his body, and his bronze complexion shone with the hue of health. His features were noble and warlike, his eye bold and piercing, and his long black hair swept away behind him, mingling with the tail of his horse. He rode upon a Spanish saddle with his lance poised on the stirrup, and resting lightly against his right arm. His left was thrust through the strap of a white shield, and a quiver with its feathered shafts peeped over his shoulder.

His bow was before him.

It was a splendid sight, both horse and rider, as they rose together over the green swells of the prairie; a picture more like that of some Homeric hero than of a savage of the "wild west."

"Wagh!" exclaimed one of the hunters in an undertone; "how they glitter! Look at that 'ar head-piece! it's fairly a-blazin'!"

"Ay," rejoined Garey, "we may thank the piece o' brass. We'd have been in as ugly a fix as he's in now if we hadn't sighted it in time. What!" continued the trapper, his voice rising into earnestness; "Dacoma, by the Eternal! The second chief of the Navajoes!"

I turned toward Seguin to witness the effect of this announcement. The Maricopa was leaning over to him, muttering some words in an unknown tongue, and gesticulating with energy. I recognized the name "Dacoma," and there was an expression of fierce hatred in the chief's countenance as he pointed to the advancing horseman.

"Well, then," answered Seguin, apparently assenting to the wishes of the other, "he shall not escape, whether he sees it or no. But do not use your gun: they are not ten miles off: yonder behind the swell. We can easily surround him. If not, *I* can overtake him on this horse, and here's another."

As Seguin uttered the last speech he pointed to Moro. "Silence!" he continued, lowering his voice; "Hish-sh!" The silence became death-like. Each man sat pressing his horse with his knees, as if thus to hold him at rest.

The Navajo had now reached the border of the deserted camp; and inclining to the left, he galloped down the line, scattering the wolves as he went. He sat leaning to one side, his gaze searching the ground. When nearly opposite to our ambush, he descried the object of his search, and sliding his feet out of the stirrup, guided his horse so as to shave closely past it. Then, without reining in, *or even slacking his pace*, he bent over until his plume swept the earth, and picking up the bow, swung himself back into the saddle.

"Beautiful!" exclaimed the bull-fighter.

"By gosh! it's a pity to kill him," muttered a hunter; and a low murmur of admiration was heard among the men.

After a few more springs the Indian suddenly wheeled, and was about to gallop back, when his eye was caught by the ensanguined object upon the rock. He reined in with a jerk, until the hips of his horse almost rested upon the prairie, and sat gazing upon the body with a look of surprise.

"Beautiful!" again exclaimed Sanchez; "*carrambo*, beautiful!"

It was, in effect, as fine a picture as ever the eye looked upon. The horse with his tail scattered upon the ground, with crest erect and breathing nostril, quivering under the impulse of his masterly rider; the rider himself, with his glancing helmet and waving plumes, his bronze complexion, his firm and graceful seat, and his eye fixed in the gaze of wonder.

It was, as Sanchez had said, a beautiful picture—a living statue; and all of us were filled with admiration as we looked upon it. Not one of the party, with perhaps an exception, should have liked to fire the shot that would have tumbled it from its pedestal.

Horse and man remained in this attitude for some moments. Then the expression of the rider's countenance suddenly changed. His eye wandered with an inquiring and somewhat terrified look. It rested upon the water, still muddy with the trampling of our horses.

One glance was sufficient; and, with a quick strong jerk upon the bridle, the savage horseman wheeled and struck out for the prairie.

Our charging signal had been given at the same instant; and, springing forward, we shot out of the copsewood in a body.

We had to cross the rivulet. Seguin was some paces in advance as we rode forward to it. I saw his horse suddenly baulk, stumble over the bank, and roll headlong into the water!

The rest of us went plashing through. I did not stop to look back. I knew that *now* the taking of the Indian was life or death to all of us; and I struck my spur deeply and strained forward in the pursuit.

For some time we all rode together in a dense "clump." When fairly out on the plain we saw the Indian ahead of us about a dozen lengths of his horse; and one and all felt with dismay that he was keeping his distance, if not actually increasing it.

We had forgotten the condition of our animals. They were faint with hunger, and stiff from standing so long in the ravine. Moreover, they had just drunk to a surfeit.

I soon found that I was forging ahead of my companions. The superior swiftness of Moro gave me the advantage. El Sol was still before me. I saw him circling his lasso; I saw him launch it and suddenly jerk up; I saw the loop sliding over the hips of the flying mustang. He had missed his aim. He was recoiling the rope as I shot past him, and I noticed his look of chagrin and disappointment.

My Arab had now warmed to the chase, and I was soon far ahead of my comrades. I perceived, too, that I was closing upon the Navajo. Every spring brought me nearer, until there were not a dozen lengths between us.

I knew not how to act. I held my rifle in my hands, and could have shot the Indian in the back; but I remembered the injunction of Seguin, and we were now closer to the enemy than ever. I did not know but that we might be in sight of them. I dared not fire.

I was still undecided whether to use my knife or endeavour to unhorse the Indian with my clubbed rifle, when he glanced over his shoulder and saw that I was alone.

Suddenly he wheeled, and throwing his lance to a charge, came galloping back. His horse seemed to work without the rein, obedient to his voice and the touch of his knees.

I had just time to throw up my rifle and parry the charge, which was a right point. I did not parry it successfully. The blade grazed my arm, tearing my flesh. The barrel of my rifle caught in the sling of the lance, and the piece was whipped out of my hands. The wound, the shock, and the loss of my weapon had discomposed me in the *manège* of my horse, and it was some time before I could gain the bridle to turn him. My antagonist had wheeled sooner, as I knew by the "hist" of an arrow that scattered the curls over my right ear. As I faced him again another was on the string, and the next moment it was sticking through my left arm.

I was now angry; and drawing a pistol from the holster I cocked it and galloped forward. I knew it was the only chance for my life.

The Indian, at the same time, dropped his bow, and, bringing his lance to the charge, spurred on to meet me. I was determined not to fire until near and sure of hitting.

We closed at full gallop. Our horses almost touched. I levelled and pulled trigger. The cap snapped upon my pistol!

The lance-blade glittered in my eyes; its point was at my breast. Something struck me sharply in the face. It was the ring-loop of a lasso. I saw it settle over the shoulders of the Indian, falling to his elbows. It tightened as it fell. There was a wild yell, a quick jerk of my antagonist's body, the lance flew from his hands, and the next moment he was plucked out of his saddle and lying helpless upon the prairie.

His horse met mine with a concussion that sent both of them to the earth. We rolled and scrambled about and rose again.

When I came to my feet El Sol was standing over the Navajo with his knife drawn, and his lasso looped around the arms of his captive.

"The horse! the horse! secure the horse!" shouted Seguin, as he galloped up; and the crowd dashed past me in pursuit of the mustang, which, with trailing bridle, was scouring over the prairie. In a few minutes the animal was lassoed, and led back to the spot so near being made sacred with my grave.

EVA MARY KELLY—ELLEN DOWNING.

[Some references we have already made to the poetry of the *Nation* will have told the reader that many of the most powerful poems came from the pens of women. We have already mentioned the most distinguished of those female contributors—Lady Wilde (Speranza). Two others were Eva Mary Kelly, now Mrs. Kevin Izod O'Doherty (whose *nom de plume* usually was "Eva"), and Miss Ellen Downing (known as "Mary"). Mr. A. M. Sullivan has, in his *New Ireland*, told in a very interesting manner the very different stories of those two lives. "Eva Mary Kelly," he writes, "was the daughter of a county Galway gentleman, and could have been little more than a girl when the contributions bearing her pseudonym began to attract attention. . . . . Kevin O'Doherty was at this time a young medical student in Dublin. From admiring 'Eva's' poetry he took to admiring, that is, loving herself. The outbreak of 1848, however, brought a rude interruption to Kevin's suit. He was writing unmistakably seditious prose, while 'Eva' was assailing the constituted authorities in rebel verse. Kevin was arrested and brought to trial. Twice the jury disagreed. The day before his third arraignment he was offered a virtual pardon—a merely nominal sentence—if he would plead guilty. He sent for Eva and told her of the proposition. 'It may seem as if I did not feel the certainty of losing you, perhaps for ever,' said he, 'but I don't like this idea of pleading guilty. Say, what shall I do?' 'Do!' answered the poetess; 'why, be a man and face the worst. I'll wait for you however long the sentence may be.' Next day fortune deserted Kevin. The jury found him guilty. The judge assigned him ten years' transportation. 'Eva' was allowed to see him once more in the cell to say adieu. She whispered in his ear, 'Be you faithful. *I'll wait.*' And she did. Years flew by, and the young exile was at length allowed once more to tread Irish soil. Two days after he landed at Kingstown 'Eva' was his bride.

"Less happy," goes on Mr. Sullivan, "was the romance of 'Mary's' fate. She was a Munster lady, Miss Ellen Downing by name, and, like 'Eva,' formed an attachment to one of the 'Young Ireland' writers. In 'Forty-eight' he became a fugitive. Alas! in foreign climes he learned to forget home vows. 'Mary' sank under the blow. She put by the lyre, and in utter seclusion from the world lingered for a while; but ere long the spring flowers blossomed on her grave."]

THE PEOPLE'S CHIEF.

BY MISS KELLY.

Come forth, come forth, O Man of men! to the
    cry of the gathering nations,
We watch on the tow'r, we watch on the hill, pouring our invocations—
Our souls are sick of sounds and shades, that mock
    our shame and grief,
We hurl the Dagons from their seats, and call the
    lawful Chief!

Come forth, come forth, O Man of men! to the
    frenzy of our imploring,
The winged despair that no man can bear, up to
    the Heavens soaring—
Come! faith and hope, and love and trust, upon
    their centre rock,
The wailing Millions summon thee amid the earthquake shock!

We've kept the weary watch of years, with a wild
    and heart-wrung yearning,
But the star of the Advent we sought in vain,
    calmly and purely burning;
False meteors flash'd across the sky, and falsely
    led us on;
The parting of the strife is come—the spell is o'er
    and gone!

The storms of enfranchised passions rise as the
    voice of the eagle's screaming,
And we scatter now to the earth's four winds the
    memory of our dreaming!
The clouds but veil the lightning's bolt—Sibylline
    murmurs ring,
In hollow tones from out the depths—the People
    seek their King!

Come forth, come forth, Anointed One! nor blazon
    nor honours bearing—
No "ancient line" be thy seal or sign, the crown
    of Humanity wearing—
Spring out, as lucent fountains spring exulting
    from the ground—
Arise, as Adam rose from God, with strength and
    knowledge crown'd!

The leader of the world's wide host guiding our
    aspirations,
Wear thou the seamless garb of Truth sitting
    among the nations!
Thy foot is on the empty forms around in shivers
    cast—
We crush ye with the scorn of scorn, exuviæ of
    the past!

The Future's close gates are now on their ponderous hinges jarring,
And there comes a sound as of winds and waves
    each with the other warring:
And forward bends the list'ning world, as to their
    eager ken
From out that dark and mystic land appears the
    Man of men!

TIPPERARY.

BY MISS KELLY.

Were you ever in sweet Tipperary, where the fields
    are so sunny and green,
And the heath-brown Slieve-bloom and the Galtees
    look down with so proud a mien?

'Tis there you would see more beauty than is on
    all Irish ground—
God bless you, my sweet Tipperary, for where
    could your match be found?

They say that your hand is fearful, that darkness
    is in your eye,
But I'll not let them dare to talk so black and
    bitter a lie.
Oh! no, *macushla storin!* bright, bright, and
    warm are you,
With hearts as bold as the men of old, to your-
    selves and your country true.

And when there is gloom upon you, bid them
    think who has brought it there—
Sure a frown or a word of hatred was not made for
    your face so fair;
You've a hand for the grasp of friendship—an-
    other to make them quake,
And they're welcome to whichsoever it pleases
    them most to take.

Shall our homes, like the huts of Connaught, be
    crumbled before our eyes?
Shall we fly, like a flock of wild geese, from all
    that we love and prize?
No! by those who were here before us, no churl
    shall our tyrant be;
Our land it is theirs by plunder, but, by Brigid,
    ourselves are free.

No! we do not forget the greatness did once to
    sweet Erie belong;
No treason or craven spirit was ever our race
    among;
And no frown or no word of hatred we give—but
    to pay them back;
In evil we only follow our enemies' darksome
    track.

Oh! come for a while among us, and give us the
    friendly hand;
And you'll see that old Tipperary is a loving and
    gladsome land;
From Upper to Lower Ormond, bright welcomes
    and smiles will spring,—
On the plains of Tipperary the stranger is like a
    king.

MURMURS OF LOVE.

FROM THE IRISH.—BY MISS KELLY.

The stars are watching, the winds are playing;
They see me kneeling, they see me praying;
They hear me still, through the long night saying
    Asthore machree, I love you, I love you!

And oh! with no love that is light or cheerful,
But deep'ning on in its shadow fearful;
Without a joy that is aught but tearful,
    'Tis thus I love you, I love you.

Whispering still, with those whispers broken,
Speaking on, what can ne'er be spoken,
Were all the voices of earth awoken—
    Oh! how I love you, I love you!

With all my heart's most passionate throbbing,
With wild emotion, and weary sobbing,
Love and light from all others robbing—
    So well I love you, I love you!

With the low faint murmurs of deep adoring,
And voiceless blessings for ever pouring,
And sighs that fall with a sad imploring,
    'Tis thus I love you, I love you.

With the burning beating, the inward hushing,
Ever and ever in music gushing,
Like mystic tones from the sea-shell rushing,
    Oh, thus I love you, I love you.

They pass me dancing, they pass me singing,
While night and day o'er the earth are winging;
But I sit here, to my trance still clinging—
    For oh! I love you, I love you!

PAST AND PRESENT.

BY MISS DOWNING.

True love, remembered yet through all that mist
    of years,
Clung to with such vain, vain love—wept with
    such vain tears—
On the turf I sat last night, where we two sat of
    yore,
And thought of thee till memory could bear to
    think no more.

The twilight of the young year was fading soft
    and dim;
The branches of the budding trees fell o'er the
    water's brim;
And the stars came forth in lonely light through
    all the silent skies;
I scarce could see them long ago, with looking in
    thine eyes.

For oh! thou wert my starlight, my refuge, and
    my home;
My spirit found its rest in thee, and never sought
    to roam;
All thoughts and all sensations that burn and
    thrill me through,
In those first days of happy love were calmed and
    soothed by you.

How wise thou wert—how tender—ah! but it
  seemed to be
Some glorious guardian angel that walked this
  earth with me;
And now, though hope be over, and love too much
  in vain,
What marvel if my weary heart finds naught like
  thee again?

Beloved, when thou wert near me, the happy and
  the right
Were mingled in one gentle dream of ever fresh
  delight;
But now the path of duty seems cold and dark to
  tread,
Without one radiant guide-star to light me overhead.

If there were ought my faith in thee to darken or
  remove—
One memory of unkindness—one chilling want of
  love!—
But no—thy heart still clings to me as fondly,
  warmly true,
As mine, through chance, and change, and time,
  must ever cling to you.

If thou wert aught to shrink from—to blush with
  sudden shame—
That he who won the beating heart the lips must
  fear to name!
But oh! before the whole wide world how proudly
  would I say:
"He reigned my king long years ago—he reigns
  my king to-day."

And so I turn to seek thee throughout all the mist
  of years,
And love with vain devotion, and weep with vainer
  tears;

And on the turf I sit alone, where we two sat of
  yore,
And think of thee till memory can bear to think
  no more.

TALK BY THE BLACKWATER.

BY MISS DOWNING.

Faint are the breezes, and pure is the tide,
Soft is the sunshine, and you by my side;
'Tis just such an evening to dream of in sleep;
'Tis just such a joy to remember and weep;
Never before since you called me your own
Were you, I, and nature so proudly alone—
  Cushlamachree, 'tis blessed to be
  All the long summer eve talking to thee.

Dear are the green banks we wander upon;
Dear is our own river, glancing along;
Dearer the trust that as tranquil will be
The tides of the future for you and for me;
Dearest the thought, that, come weal or come woe,
Through storm or through sunshine together they'll
  flow—
  Cushlamachree, 'tis blessed to be
  All the long summer eve thinking of thee.

Yon bark o'er the waters, how swiftly it glides!
My thoughts cannot guess to what haven it rides;
As little I know what the future brings near;
But our bark is the same, and I harbour no fear;
Whatever our fortunes, our hearts will be true;
Wherever the stream flows 'twill bear me with
  you—
  Cushlamachree, 'tis blessed to be
  Summer and winter time clinging to thee.

CHARLES JOSEPH KICKHAM.

[The revolutionary movement which came to be known as Fenianism was unlike that of 1848 in the character of its leaders. As has been seen from previous memoirs, the older political agitation was associated with a brilliant outburst of intellectual effort; and the majority of the leaders have left behind high intellectual heritage, or asserted under other skies, and in more favourable circumstances, their possession of great intellectual powers. The Fenian movement, on the other hand, was poor in its literary products; and few of its leading spirits have, since its collapse, reached to any lofty position. The best part of Fenian literature was to be found in the *Irish People*, the journalistic organ of the association; and the chief contributors to that journal were Mr. T. Clarke Luby, Mr. John O'Leary, and Mr. C. J. Kickham.

Charles Joseph Kickham was born at Mullenahone, county Tipperary, in 1830. At the age of thirteen he met with an accident, to which we probably owe the many fine productions of his pen: he was deprived of hearing. He began in about his eighteenth year to contribute poems and tales to Irish journals and magazines; and when the *Irish People* was started he became, as has been said, one of its chief leader-writers. Involved thus in the Fenian movement, he was one of those on whom the government made a descent; and having been tried and convicted he was sentenced to fourteen years' penal servitude. His comment on the conclusion of the trial was terse: "I have endeavoured," he said, "to serve Ireland, and now I am prepared to suffer for Ireland." Four years after his conviction he was released.

Mr. Kickham has published two complete stories, *Sally Cavanagh, or Untenanted Graves*, from which we give an extract, and *Knocknagow, or the Homes of Tipperary*. These stories have been read wherever there is an Irish home, and have made sad or joyous thousands of Irish hearts. They have found approval also in the columns of English and not friendly journals, which, disliking, perhaps bitterly, some of the ideas of the author, have found themselves able to meet him in friendliness on the impartial ground of literature. His books, indeed, deserve alike their popularity with the peasant and the approval of the critic. His pictures of life—especially of peasant life—are wonderfully true to nature, full of keen observation, humour, and fidelity. In his attention to minute details and homely incident he resembles in a great degree the style of MM. Erckmann-Chatrian.

Mr. Kickham's ballads are equally popular, and are just what ballads for the people should be—simple in language, direct in purpose, and in an easy and common measure. A collected edition of his works is now being published by Messrs. Duffy & Son. Two volumes containing the stories already named have appeared; two more are promised, the one consisting of a new story; the other of Mr. Kickham's songs and ballads.]

THE SCHOOLMASTER'S STORY.

(FROM "SALLY CAVANAGH."[1])

"It was necessary to have the name and age of each pupil on the roll. When I wrote down the name of Rose Mulvany I turned to her to inquire what was her age. I hardly knew why, but I could not ask the question, and put up the book without putting down her age. The next week I got two or three 'new scholars,' and when asking their ages I took courage and said: 'And how old are you, Rose?' She looked up, and smiling bashfully, replied: 'I believe I'm seventeen and a bit, sir,' and then bending her head she shook down her wavy auburn hair to hide her blushes. She found out a low seat, and always sat upon it, in order, as I saw, to make herself look small among the other girls. I remarked, too, that she always wore her cloak, for the purpose, as I guessed, of concealing her well-developed figure. All this reserve, however, was thrown aside when I was not present. How often did I watch her from the window during play-hours, bounding like a wild fawn among the children! All the children loved her; and it was so interesting to see some little creature explaining the lesson to poor Rose, who would take her tiny instructress up in her arms and kiss her as a reward for her trouble. But after a few months Rose Mulvany could read and write pretty well, and, in fact, knew as much as most girls of her age and class. Every day I felt more and more interested in her; but I was pained to observe that she became more reserved, and even appeared to stand almost in awe of me. She would check herself suddenly in the midst of her wildest glee on seeing me approach, and shake down her tresses to hide her face. I used to stand by sometimes and encourage the boys and girls at their games in the play-ground; but the moment I appeared, Rose would put on her cloak hastily and steal away.

"After a while I began to call at her father's house on Sunday evenings. How glad the kind old couple were to see me! And Rose, too, was less reserved on these occasions than at school, but she was still very timid. The thought often occurred to me that she disliked me; but I believe now the contrary was the case. It was very foolish in me to torment myself as I did; for, as I afterwards remembered, her face always lighted up on seeing me, and while I stayed, though she generally remained silent, she looked perfectly happy. I wished very much that my dear mother should see her, but I was quite afraid lest she should feel prejudiced against her. For I noticed that my mother was quite jealous of every one who she imagined might make too deep an impression on me. I believe she thought no one good enough for me.

"So matters stood, when one day John Mulvany came into the school and handed me a letter to read. I read it, and my heart died within me. A relative had paid his daughters' passage to America. Rose had an elder sister, a quiet, good, industrious girl. Her father

[1] By permission of the author.

called Rose, and told her to come home with him. She did not know what was in the letter, but I believe she guessed it; for as she went out she looked at me, and turning round her head, kept her eyes fixed upon me till her father closed the door. I never saw her look directly at me before while I was looking at her.

"On Midsummer's day she came with her father and mother to take leave of the scholars. I shall never forget the scene. The children clung to her, most of them crying passionately. Several of the boys even were obliged to brush the tears from their eyes as they looked at her. For the first time the poor girl was well dressed; and surely a creature more radiantly beautiful was never seen. When they had gone I went mechanically through the business of the day. I locked the school-room as usual, and turned my steps homeward. Before going into my little cottage I walked for an hour down by the river. I asked myself should I declare my affection for her, and ask her to stay and be my wife. But what reason had I to hope that she had cared for me? And what would my dear mother think? Was I even sure that Rose's parents would consent? For, with all their respect for me, I thought it quite possible that they would not consider me a fit match for their daughter. The schoolmaster is thought so little of in this country. No; I had not the courage to ask Rose Mulvany to be my wife.

"In the evening I went down to the bridge, where the people were assembled round a bonfire. There was a dance too. The sisters were there, with their arms twined round each other's waists. There was something touchingly sorrowful in their faces. I thought my heart would burst as I looked at Rose. She was so sad, and oh! how lovely. You, Mr. Purcell, was there. A young girl asked you to dance. After dancing with her you looked round to choose a partner, as is the custom. You asked Rose Mulvany to dance. I saw her eyes flash with pleasure. All gloom was gone in an instant. Surely the pang I felt at that moment was not caused by jealousy? But I did feel a pang; and immediately a gloomy foreboding took possession of my heart. I moved to the side of Rose's sister.

"'Mary,' said I, 'take care of Rose.'

"She looked at her sister, and then at me. She took my hand and pressed it without speaking. I knew she understood me.

"I accompanied them home. Oh! the grief of that poor father and mother! For a while it made me forget my own. I bade farewell to Mary, and kissed her. I *could* not do more than take Rose's hand. Her head drooped, and her lips parted as I did so. As I let go her cold hand she fell senseless into my arms. Oh, fool! fool! why did I not save her then?

"Mary died of fever on the voyage. Her sister landed in New York. And—oh, my God! how can I write the words? Rose Mulvany, the beautiful, the innocent, the pure, is a lost, polluted thing. My life, since I learned her fate, has been one dream of agony. I have endeavoured, but in vain, to tear her from my heart. I know she is lost to me for ever. But the thought that she is lost to virtue and to God—leading a life of sin and dragging souls to hell—is wearing away my life.

"My dear, good mother is gone to rest. I have laid her beside my father. I leave Ireland to-morrow. I go to save Rose Mulvany. If it be God's will that I shall succeed, you will hear from me. Good-bye, my true friend, and may you be happy!"

. . . .

"For the last year scarcely a day has passed that I have not determined to write to you the next day. But I always saw, or fancied I saw, some good reason for delaying the fulfilment of my promise yet another day. The monotony of my life, however, has just been varied a little by meeting accidentally with an old friend; and this has roused me to do what I have been so long thinking of doing. I am writing in my own little wooden house far away in the lonesome prairie. On last Sunday as I was returning home after having heard mass at a little village thirty miles from where I live, I saw a man lying on the ground by the side of the road. His arms were resting upon a box, and his face buried between his hands. A fine little boy lay near him asleep, with the man's coat folded under his head. I at once saw they were immigrants, and from Ireland, who had left the railway, and were proceeding on foot to some village or farmhouse in this neighbourhood.

"'God save you,' I called out, pulling up my horse at the same time.

"'God save you kindly,' he replied, raising his head and looking at me.

"'Connor Shea!' I exclaimed; 'surely you are Connor Shea?'

"'That's my name sure enough,' said he. 'But you have the advantage of me.'

"'I must be indeed altered,' I remarked, 'when my old friend Connor Shea does not know me.'

"When I told him my name he started to

his feet, and was hastening towards me. But as he advanced I saw him reel and stagger, and before I could dismount and come to his assistance, he fell heavily to the ground. The boy told me that for several days back his father had eaten nothing but a few grapes which a lady had given him; and I at once concluded that Connor Shea had fever. Fortunately my house was not far off, and after bathing his temples and getting him to swallow a cooling draught, he was able to mount my horse, and half an hour's slow walking brought us to the door. The poor fellow is now free from fever, but it will be some days before he will be strong enough to go to work. He begs that you will not let his wife know of his illness. Neddy is a fine fellow, and his father has consented to leave him under my care. This is a great boon to me, particularly during winter when all out-door work is suspended here. I hope to have Neddy sufficiently advanced to have him bound to some respectable business in the course of next year. Connor has given me a full account of 'the neighbours,' since I left home. Alas, for poor Ireland! And now, in as few words as possible, let me tell you what has happened to myself since my arrival in this country.

"First of all, I found out the person through whom I had learned Rose Mulvany's fate. He accompanied me to the house where she had lived. With what mingled feelings of rage, and grief, and loathing I passed the threshold! It was one of those places where vice is decked out in tawdry finery. But I shall not disgust you with a description of it. The poor lost creature whom I sought had left the place in ill health some months before. A dissipated-looking woman remarked with a laugh that the pace was too fast for the young 'greeny,' and she broke down. This account excited my pity for the lost one, against whom I was beginning to feel something like resentment as I looked round on her brazen companions in shame. I was informed that Rose had gone to a city in the far west, and thither I started in search of her on the following day.

"I got employment in the great western city. My days were devoted to work, and from midnight till dawn I spent amid scenes the remembrance of which makes me shudder. Well, I found her at last—found Rose Mulvany in one of the very lowest haunts of crime and debauchery. The scene has left but a confused impression on my mind; music and dancing, the fumes of alcohol and tobacco, oaths and laughter and shrill screams of anger. And in the midst of this pandemonium I saw the once innocent Irish maiden with . . .

"I was quite calm. Do you not wonder that I was so? I even felt a sort of satisfaction, not at having found her, but at seeing her degradation with my own eyes. I felt as if the spell were broken, and my sufferings at an end. The thought that she was what I now saw her had made me miserable for years; yet I felt for a moment an impulse to laugh outright at my folly. I saw before me a creature too low for contempt, too debased for pity, too loathsome to be hated. Turning away, not with disgust, but with utter indifference, I was hurrying out of the polluted atmosphere into the open air, when a thought struck me that made me pause.

"'Is it not my duty,' I asked myself—'am I not bound as a Christian to make an effort to save her?'

"My conscience whispered, that not to make the effort would be a crime. I had a message sent to her that a person wished to see her in an adjoining room. The door opened, and with a smirk on her face, Rose Mulvany approached me. For a moment she looked surprised, but this was only because her reception was different from what she expected. She soon, however, began to retreat slowly backwards, while her eyes were fixed on me with a wild stare. In this way she had reached the door, and was turning the handle behind her back, when I stepped forward and placed my hand against the door.

"'I believe,' said I, 'you remember me.'

"She moved away from me again, and asked me in a low, hoarse tone to let her out.

"'Not until I have first spoken to you, Rose,' I replied.

"'Don't speak to me,' said she.

"'I wish to speak to you for your good.'

"'Do you not see what I am?' she asked.

"'I do,' said I, 'and that is the reason I have sent for you.'

"'Am I not lost?'

"'But, Rose, you may be saved—your soul may be saved.'

"She covered her face with her hands, and the bright auburn hair fell down, as I so often saw it fall in the old school-house.

"'Rose,' said I, in a softened voice, 'I do not want to reproach you.'

"'Reproach me!' she exclaimed, looking up quickly; 'what right have you to reproach me?'

"The question took me by surprise, for I certainly thought I had the best right in the world.

"She put her hand to her throat as if she

were choking, and said:—'If it were not for you I should not be what I am.'

"'Good God!' I exclaimed, 'what do you mean?'

"'I mean,' said she, 'that when I was young and innocent——but why should I talk of that now?'

"I was confounded; for I thought she meant to accuse me of having led her from the path of virtue in some way.

"'Yes,' she continued, after a pause, 'you won my young, innocent heart, before I knew I had a heart; and after winning it you despised it. You let me go, just as if I was a worthless weed. I did not care what would become of me. I joined in every folly I was asked to join in. Poor Mary was gone, and I had no one to warn me. Oh! if I knew the world was so bad I might be able to take care of myself!'

"You can have no idea of the shock her words gave me. For the first time the thought occurred to me that in some degree I might be accountable for this poor girl's fall. I was so moved I could not help saying:

"'O Rose! I never despised you. On the contrary, I loved you better than my life.'

"Her whole face lighted up. I gazed at her with wonder. There was something startling in the transfiguration I beheld. Everything about her—her eyes, her lips, her blushes, her attitude—everything about her was 'pure womanly.'

"'And I have come here,' I continued, 'for no other purpose but to save you.'

"These words reminded her of what she really was, and the poor girl turned deadly pale. I thought she was fainting, and hastened to prevent her from falling.

"'Don't touch me,' she cried, holding out her arms to keep me off, 'oh! do not touch a thing like me.'

"There was something appalling in the change that had come over her. She appeared to have withered in an instant. I actually saw the wrinkles creeping over her face and forehead. She sank into a chair which I had placed near her. After considering for a moment I decided upon the course I should pursue.

"'Rose,' said I, 'here is my address. You know now you have a friend. And may God give you strength to turn back before it is too late.' I laid my card on a table near her, and withdrew.

"It was a moonlight night, and I spent an hour or two looking out on the waters of the great lake. I thought of Ireland, and of the sufferings of her children; in my desolation I thanked God that there was still something left me—that my heart could yet thrill with mingled love and pride and grief for that dear old land. Then I thought of the peaceful valley and my own home. That same moon looked mildly down upon them! I flung myself down by the shore of the great lake, far, far away, and for the first time since my great sorrow fell upon me, I burst into tears. Since that moment I have been an altered man. Life is no longer a burden to me. There is, to be sure, a shadow upon my path; but it is not the black one that rested on it so long. I dislike crowds, and hence I have exchanged the busy city for the lonesome prairie. But since Connor Shea's arrival I begin to think that I could enjoy the society of my *old* friends; and I am already longing to see my hermitage lighted up by poor Sally Cavanagh's bright looks. Connor and I are in deep plans for the future.

"But before I come to the end of my paper let me tell you the result of my interview with Rose Mulvany. I got a note from her, which I shall copy here:—

"'Never ask to see me again. I am not worthy. I could not bear it. But send some one else to take me away from this place. May God for ever bless you. Something tells me *that I am saved.*'

"I hastened to a good Irish priest, and told him the whole story. The result is that poor Rose Mulvany has been for the past twelve months an inmate of an industrial institution under the superintendence of the Sisters of Charity. I am slow to believe in complete reformation in cases of this kind; but my reverend friend assures me that it would be harder now to tempt Rose Mulvany from the path of virtue than if she had never left it. I wonder—but I shall not trouble you with my speculations, at least not now. How well I remember the evening I gave you that hurriedly-written chapter of my history! I expected to hear of your marriage from Connor. My dear friend, whatever disappointment you may have met with—whatever sorrow you may have to endure—be assured that the bitterest drop has not been poured into the cup so long as there is no *stain* upon the fair fame of the woman you loved."

"I believe him," exclaimed Brian, and he started up as if the thought stung him. "Even now that the struggle is over, and an impassable gulf between us, even now *that* thought would be the bitterest drop in the cup. How this poor fellow has suffered. And my poor friend Connor Shea! What a pang those few words about him would strike to the heart of his brave wife. Good God!" exclaimed Brian Purcell, as he put out one of the candles, "what selfish beings we are! How much we think of our own griefs, and how little of the griefs of others!"

The clock at the head of the stairs struck twelve, and Brian Purcell retired to rest.

PATRICK SHEEHAN.

My name is Patrick Sheehan,
  My years are thirty-four;
Tipperary is my native place,
  Not far from Galtymore:
I came of honest parents,
  But now they're lying low;
And many a pleasant day I spent
  In the Glen of Aherlow.

My father died; I closed his eyes
  Outside our cabin door;
The landlord and the sheriff too
  Were there the day before!
And then my loving mother,
  And sisters three also,
Were forced to go with broken hearts
  From the Glen of Aherlow.

For three long months, in search of work,
  I wandered far and near;
I went then to the poor-house,
  For to see my mother dear;
The news I heard nigh broke my heart;
  But still, in all my woe,
I bless the friends who made their graves
  In the Glen of Aherlow.

Bereft of home and kith and kin,
  With plenty all around,
I starved within my cabin,
  And slept upon the ground;
But cruel as my lot was,
  I ne'er did hardship know
'Till I joined the English army,
  Far away from Aherlow.

"Rouse up there," says the corporal,
  "You lazy Hirish hound;
Why don't you hear, you sleepy dog,
  The call 'to arms' sound?"
Alas, I had been dreaming
  Of days long, long ago;
I woke before Sebastopol,
  And not in Aherlow.

I groped to find my musket—
  How dark I thought the night!
O blessed God, it was not dark,
  It was the broad daylight!

And when I found that I was blind,
  My tears began to flow;
I longed for even a pauper's grave
  In the Glen of Aherlow.

O blessed Virgin Mary,
  Mine is a mournful tale;
A poor blind prisoner here I am,
  In Dublin's dreary jail;
Struck blind within the trenches,
  Where I never feared the foe;
And now I'll never see again
  My own sweet Aherlow!

THE IRISH PEASANT GIRL.

She lived beside the Anner,
  At the foot of Sliev-na-mon,
A gentle peasant girl,
  With mild eyes like the dawn;
Her lips were dewy rosebuds;
  Her teeth of pearls rare;
And a snow-drift 'neath a beechen bough
  Her neck and nut-brown hair.

How pleasant 'twas to meet her
  On Sunday, when the bell
Was filling with its mellow tones
  Lone wood and grassy dell!
And when at eve young maidens
  Strayed the river bank along,
The widow's brown-haired daughter
  Was loveliest of the throng.

O brave, brave Irish girls—
  We well may call you brave!—
Sure the least of all your perils
  Is the stormy ocean wave,
When ye leave your quiet valleys,
  And cross the Atlantic's foam,
To hoard your hard-won earnings
  For the helpless ones at home.

"Write word to my dear mother—
  Say, we'll meet with God above;
And tell my little brothers
  I send them all my love;
May the angels ever guard them,
  Is their dying sister's prayer"—
And folded in the letter
  Was a braid of nut-brown hair.

Ah, cold, and well-nigh callous,
  This weary heart has grown
For thy hapless fate, dear Ireland,
  And for sorrows of my own;
Yet a tear my eye will moisten,
  When by Anner side I stray,
For the lily of "the Mountain-foot"
  That withered far away.

DENIS FLORENCE MACCARTHY.

[Denis Florence MacCarthy, born 1817, died 1882. One of his finest and most spirit-stirring poems describes the glories of the Clan of Mac Caura, and Mr. MacCarthy can claim descent from the great Irish sept, of which he is the poet. To the *Nation* in its early days Mr. MacCarthy was a constant contributor, and some of his finest and best poems belong to that period. In 1850 the first collected edition of his works appeared, under the title *Ballads, Poems, and Lyrics*. In addition to the original pieces there were translations from most of the European languages, Mr. MacCarthy, like Mangan, Lady Wilde, and several other Irish singers, being a student of other literatures besides his own. In 1853 he gave further proof of both his poetic talents and linguistic attainments by publishing translations of Calderon's dramas, a work which received eulogies, not only from the judgment of his countrymen, but from the less partial estimates of English critics. In 1857 appeared a second collection of poems under the title *Under-Glimpses and other Poems*, and in the same year was also published the *Bell-founder and other Poems*. A prose work, *Shelley's Early Life from Original Sources* (1872), brought out some highly interesting facts in reference to the great English poet, especially as to that period of his youth when he for a while threw himself into the struggles of Ireland for the amelioration of her laws. "Waiting for the May" is one of Mr. MacCarthy's best known and most admired lyrics.[1] In the Centenary of Moore he was naturally chosen to take a leading part, and composed an ode which was fully worthy of the great occasion. Mr. MacCarthy has also edited an excellent eclection of Irish ballads.]

THE PILLAR TOWERS OF IRELAND.

The pillar towers of Ireland, how wondrously they stand
By the lakes and rushing rivers, through the valleys of our land!
In mystic file, through the isle, they lift their heads sublime,

[1] This poem was erroneously attributed to James Clarence Mangan by Samuel Lover, and was so printed in a part of the early impression of vol. iii. of the *Cabinet*.

These grey old pillar temples—these conquerors of time!

Beside these grey old pillars, how perishing and weak
The Roman's arch of triumph, and the temple of the Greek,
And the gold domes of Byzantium, and the pointed Gothic spires;
All are gone, one by one, but the temples of our sires!

The column, with its capital, is level with the dust,
And the proud halls of the mighty, and the calm homes of the just;
For the proudest works of man, as certainly, but slower,
Pass like the grass at the sharp scythe of the mower!

But the grass grows again, when, in majesty and mirth,
On the wing of the Spring comes the goddess of the Earth;
But for man, in this world, no spring-tide e'er returns
To the labours of his hands or the ashes of his urns!

Two favourites hath Time—the pyramids of Nile,
And the old mystic temples of our own dear isle;
As the breeze o'er the seas, where the halcyon has its nest,
Thus Time o'er Egypt's tombs and the temples of the West!

The names of their founders have vanished in the gloom,
Like the dry branch in the fire or the body in the tomb;
But to-day, in the ray, their shadows still they cast—
These temples of forgotten gods—these relics of the past!

Around these walls have wandered the Briton and the Dane—
The captives of Armorica, the cavaliers of Spain—
Phœnican and Milesian, and the plundering Norman peers—
And the swordsmen of brave Brian, and the chiefs of later years.

How many different rites have these grey old temples known!
To the mind, what dreams are written in these chronicles of stone!

What terror and what error, what gleams of love
    and truth,
Have flashed from these walls since the world was
    in its youth!
Here blazed the sacred fire, and when the sun was
    gone,
As a star from afar to the traveller it shone;
And the warm blood of the victim have these grey
    old temples drunk,
And the death-song of the Druid, and the matin
    of the Monk.

Here was placed the holy chalice that held the
    sacred wine,
And the gold cross from the altar, and the relics
    from the shrine,
And the mitre shining brighter with its diamonds
    than the East,
And the crozier of the Pontiff, and the vestments
    of the Priest!

Where blazed the sacred fire, rung out the vesper
    bell,—
Where the fugitive found shelter, became the her-
    mit's cell;
And hope hung out its symbol to the innocent and
    good,
For the Cross o'er the moss of the pointed summit
    stood!

There may it stand for ever, while this symbol
    doth impart
To the mind one glorious vision, or one proud throb
    to the heart;
While the breast needeth rest may these grey old
    temples last,
Bright prophets of the future, as preachers of the
    past!

THE CLAN OF MAC CAURA.[1]

Oh! bright are the names of the chieftains and
    sages,
That shine like the stars through the darkness of
    ages,
Whose deeds are inscribed on the pages of story,
There for ever to live in the sunshine of glory—
Heroes of history, phantoms of fable,
Charlemagne's champions, and Arthur's Round
    Table—
Oh! but they all a new lustre could borrow
From the glory that hangs round the name of Mac
    Caura!

Thy waves, Manzanares, wash many a shrine,
And proud are the castles that frown o'er the Rhine,
And stately the mansions whose pinnacles glance
Through the elms of Old England and vineyards
    of France;
Many have fallen, and many will fall—
Good men and brave men have dwelt in them all—
But as good and as brave men, in gladness and
    sorrow,
Have dwelt in the halls of the princely Mac Caura!

Montmorency, Medina, unheard was thy rank
By the dark-eyed Iberian and light-hearted Frank,
And your ancestors wandered, obscure and un-
    known,
By the smooth Guadalquivir, and sunny Garonne—
Ere Venice had wedded the sea, or enrolled
The name of a Doge in her proud "Book of Gold;"[2]
When her glory was all to come on like the morrow,
There were chieftains and kings of the clan of Mac
    Caura!

Proud should thy heart beat, descendant of Heber,[3]
Lofty thy head as the shrines of the Guebre,
Like *them* are the halls of thy forefathers shat-
    tered,
Like *theirs* is the wealth of thy palaces scattered.
Their fire is extinguished—*your* banner long
    furled—
But how proud were ye both in the dawn of the
    world!
And should both fade away, oh! what heart would
    not sorrow
O'er the towers of the Guebre—the name of Mac
    Caura!

What a moment of glory to cherish and dream on,
When far o'er the sea came the ships of Heremon,
With Heber, and Ir, and the Spanish patricians,
To free Inis-Fail from the spells of magicians.
Oh! reason had these for their quaking and pallor,
For what magic can equal the strong sword of
    valour?
Better than spells are the axe and the arrow,
When wielded or flung by the hand of Mac Caura![4]

From that hour a Mac Caura had reigned in his
    pride
O'er Desmond's green valleys and rivers so wide,
From thy waters, Lismore, to the torrents and rills

---

[1] Mac Carthy—Mac Cartha (the correct way of spelling the name in Roman characters)—is pronounced in Irish Mac Caura, the *th* or dotted *t* having in that language the soft sound of *h*.

[2] *Montmorency* and *Medina* are respectively at the head of the French and Spanish nobility.—The first Doge elected in Venice in 709. Voltaire considered the families whose names were inscribed in *The Book of Gold* at the founding of the city as entitled to the first place in European nobility.—*Burke's Commoners.*

[3] The Mac Carthys trace their origin to Heber Fionn, the oldest son of Milesius, King of Spain, through Oilioll Ollum, King of Munster, in the third century.—*Shrines of the Guebre*, the Round Towers.

[4] Heremon and Ir were also the sons of Milesius.—The people who were in possession of the country when the Milesians invaded it, were the Tuatha de Danaans, so called, says Keating, "from their skill in necromancy, of whom some were so famous as to be called gods."

That are leaping for ever down Brandon's brown
 hills;
The billows of Bantry, the meadows of Bear,
The wilds of Evaugh, and the groves of Glancare—
From the Shannon's soft shores to the banks of
 the Barrow—
All owned the proud sway of the princely Mac
 Caura!

In the house of Miodchuart,[1] by princes sur-
 rounded,
How noble his step when the trumpet was sounded,
And his clansmen bore proudly his broad shield
 before him,
And hung it on high in that bright palace o'er him;
On the left of the monarch the chieftain was seated,
And happy was he whom his proud glances
 greeted;
'Mid monarchs and chiefs at the great Feis of
 Tara—
Oh! none was to rival the princely Mac Caura!

To the halls of the Red Branch, when conquest
 was o'er,
The champions their rich spoils of victory bore,[2]
And the sword of the Briton, the shield of the
 Dane,
Flashed bright as the sun on the walls of Eamhain—
There Dathy and Niall bore trophies of war,
From the peaks of the Alps and the waves of the
 Loire:[3]
But no knight ever bore from the hills of Ivaragh
The breast-plate or axe of a conquered Mac Caura!

In chasing the red-deer what step was the fleetest,
In singing the love-song what voice was the
 sweetest—
What breast was the foremost in courting the
 danger—
What door was the widest to shelter the stranger—
In friendship the truest, in battle the bravest—
In revel the gayest, in council the gravest—
A hunter to-day, and a victor to-morrow?
Oh! who but a chief of the princely Mac Caura!

But, oh! proud Mac Caura, what anguish to
 touch on
The one fatal stain of thy princely escutcheon—
In thy story's bright garden the one spot of bleak-
 ness—
Through ages of valour the one hour of weakness!
Thou, the heir of a thousand chiefs, sceptred and
 royal—
Thou, to kneel to the Norman and swear to be
 loyal!
Oh! a long night of horror, and outrage, and
 sorrow,
Have we wept for thy treason, base Diarmid Mac
 Caura!

Oh! why, ere you thus to the foreigner pandered,
Did you not bravely call round your Emerald
 standard,
The chiefs of your house of Lough Lene and Clan
 Awley,
O'Donogh, MacPatrick, O'Driscoll, MacAwley,
O'Sullivan More from the towers of Dunkerron,
And O'Mahon the chieftain of green Ardinterran?
As the sling sends the stone, or the bent bow the
 arrow,
Every chief would have come at the call of Mac
 Caura!

Soon, soon, didst thou pay for that error in woe—[4]
Thy life to the Butler—thy crown to the foe—
Thy castles dismantled, and strewn on the sod—
And the homes of the weak, and the abbeys of God!
No more in thy halls is the wayfarer fed—
Nor the rich mead sent round, nor the soft heather
 spread—
Nor the *clairsech's* sweet notes, now in mirth, now
 in sorrow—
All, all have gone by, but the name of Mac Caura!

Mac Caura, the pride of thy house is gone by,
But its name cannot fade, and its fame cannot die—
Though the Arigideen,[5] with its silver waves,
 shine
Around no green forests or castles of thine—
Though the shrines that you founded no incense
 doth hallow,
Nor hymns float in peace down the echoing
 Allo[5]—
One treasure thou keepest—one hope for the
 morrow—
True hearts yet beat of the clan of Mac Caura!

THE SEASONS OF THE HEART.

The different hues that deck the earth
All in our bosoms have their birth—
'Tis not in blue or sunny skies,
'Tis in the heart the Summer lies!

---

[1] The house of *Miodchuart* was an apartment in the palace of Tara, where the provincial kings met for the despatch of public business, at the Feis (pronounced as one syllable), or parliament of Tara, which assembled then once in every three years: the ceremony alluded to is described in detail by Keating. See Petrie's "Tara."

[2] The house of the Red Branch was situated in the stately palace of Eamhain (or Emania), in Ulster; here the spoils taken from the foreign foe were hung up, and the chieftains who won them were called Knights of the Red Branch.

[3] Dathy was killed at the Alps by lightning, and Niall (his uncle and predecessor) by an arrow fired from the opposite side of the river by one of his own generals as he sat in his tent on the banks of the Loire in France.

[4] Diarmid Mac Carthy, King of Desmond, and Daniel O'Brien, King of Thomond, were the first of the Irish princes to swear fealty to Henry the Second.

[5] The *Arigdeen* means the little silver stream, and

The earth is bright if *that* be glad,
Dark is the earth if *that* be sad;
And thus I feel each weary day—
'Tis Winter all when thou'rt away!

In vain, upon her emerald car,
Comes Spring, "the maiden from afar,"
And scatters o'er the woods and fields
The liberal gifts that nature yields;
In vain the buds begin to grow,
In vain the crocus gilds the snow;
I feel no joy though earth be gay—
'Tis Winter all when thou'rt away!

And when the Summer, like a bride,
Comes down to earth in blushing pride,
And from that union sweet are born
The fragrant flowers and waving corn,
I hear the hum of birds and bees,
I view the hills and streams and trees,
Yet vain the thousand charms of May—
'Tis Winter all when thou'rt away!

And when the Autumn crowns the year,
And ripened hangs the golden ear,
And luscious fruits of ruddy hue
The bending boughs are glancing through,
When yellow leaves from sheltered nooks
Come forth and try the mountain brooks—
Even then I feel, as there I stray,
'Tis Winter all when thou'rt away!

And when the Winter comes at length,
With swaggering gait and giant strength,
And with his strong arms in a trice
Binds up the streams in chains of ice,
What need I sigh for pleasures gone—
The twilight eve, the rosy dawn?
My heart is changed as much as they—
'Tis Winter all when thou'rt away!

Even now, when Summer lends the scene
Its brightest gold, its purest green—
Whene'er I climb the mountain's breast,
With softest moss and heath-flowers dressed—
When now I hear the breeze that stirs
The golden bells that deck the furze—
Alas! ye all are vain, I say—
'Tis Winter all when thou'rt away!

But when thou comest back once more—
Though dark clouds hang and loud winds roar,
And mists obscure the nearest hills,
And dark and turbid roll the rills—
Such pleasures then my breast shall know,
That Summer's sun shall round me glow;
Then quick return, dear maid, I pray—
'Tis Winter all when thou'rt away!

Alto the echoing river. By these rivers and many others in the south of Ireland castles were erected and monasteries founded by the Mac Carthys.

CENTENARY ODE.

TO THE MEMORY OF THOMAS MOORE.[1]

Joy to Ierné! joy!
  This day a deathless crown is won,
  Her child of song, her glorious son,
  Her "Minstrel Boy"
Attains his century of fame,
  Completes the time-allotted zone,
And proudly with the world's acclaim
  Ascends the Lyric Throne.

Yes! Joy to her whose path so long,
  Slow journeying to her realm of rest.
O'er many a rugged mountain's crest,
He charmed with his enchanting song—
  Like his own princess in the tale,
When he who had her way beguiled
Through many a bleak and desert wild,
  Until she reached Cashmere's bright vale,
Had ceased those notes to play and sing,
  To which her heart responsive swelled,
She, looking up, in him beheld
  Her minstrel-lover and her king—
So Erin now—her journey well-nigh o'er—
Enraptured sees her Minstrel-King in Moore.

And round that throne whose light to-day
  O'er all the world is cast,
In words though weak, in hues though faint,
Congenial Fancy rise and paint
  The spirits of the past
  Who here their homage pay—
Those who his youthful Muse inspired,
Those who his early genius fired
  To emulate their lay:—
And as in some phantasmal glass
Let the immortal spirits pass,
Let each renew the inspiring strain,
And fire the poet's soul again.

. . . . .

  Oh! what dulcet notes are heard!
  Never bird,
  Soaring through the sunny air,
  Like a prayer
  Borne by angels' hands on high,
  So entranced the listening sky,
  As his song—
  Soft, pathetic, joyous, strong,
  Rising now in rapid flight,
  Out of sight
  Like a lark in its own light,

---

[1] We give some extracts from the fine-toned and beautiful Centenary Ode, written by D. F. Mac Carthy, and read by Dr. C. E. Tisdall at the Dublin celebration in 1879. Poems for the same occasion were also written by T. D. Sullivan, R. H. Stoddart, and Oliver Wendell Holmes. See *Thomas Moore the Poet, his Life and Works*. By A. J. Symington. (Blackie & Son. 1880.)—ED.

Now descending low and sweet
  To our feet,
Till the odours of the grass
  With the light notes, as they pass,
Blend and meet.
All that Erin's memory guards
  In her heart—
Deeds of heroes, songs of bards,
  Have their part.
Brian's glories re-appear,
Fionualla's song we hear,
Tara's walls resound again,
With a more inspirèd strain,
Rival rivers meet and join,
Stately Shannon blends with Boyne,
While, on high, the storm-winds cease,
Heralding the arch of peace.

 . . . . .

Glory to Moore, eternal be the glory
  That here we crown and consecrate to-day,
Glory to Moore, for he has sung our story
  In strains whose sweetness ne'er can pass away.

Glory to Moore, for he has sighed our sorrow
  In such a wail of melody divine,
That even from grief a passing joy we borrow,
  And linger long o'er each lamenting line.

Glory to Moore, that in his songs of gladness
  Which neither change nor time can e'er destroy,
Though mingled oft with some faint sigh of sadness,
  He sings his country's rapture and its joy.

What wit like his flings out electric flashes
  That make the numbers sparkle as they run—
Wit that revives dull history's Dead-sea ashes,
  And makes the ripe fruit glisten in the sun?

What fancy full of loveliness and lightness
  Has spread like his as at some dazzling feast,
The fruits and flowers, the beauty and the brightness,
  And all the golden glories of the East?

Perpetual blooms his bower of summer roses,
  No winter comes to turn his green leaves sere,
Beside his song-stream where the swan reposes
  The bulbul sings as by the Bendemeer.

But back returning from his flight with Peris,
  Above his native fields he sings his best,
Like to the lark whose rapture never wearies,
  When poised in air he singeth o'er his nest.

And so we rank him with the great departed,
  The kings of song who rule us from their urns,
The souls inspired, the natures noble hearted,
  And place him proudly by the side of Burns.

And as not only by the Calton Mountain,
  Is Scotland's bard remembered and revered,
But wheresoe'er, like some o'erflowing fountain
  Its hardy race a prosperous path has cleared,

There, 'mid the roar of newly-rising cities,
  His glorious name is heard on every tongue,
There, to the music of immortal ditties,
  His lays of love, his patriot songs are sung.

So not alone beside that Bay of beauty
  That guards the portals of his native town,
Where, like two watchful sentinels on duty,
  Howth and Killiney from their heights look down,—

But wheresoe'er the exiled race hath drifted,
  By what far sea, what mighty stream beside,
There shall to-day the poet's name be lifted,
  And Moore proclaimed its glory and its pride.

There shall his name be held in fond memento,
  There shall his songs resound for evermore,
Whether beside the golden Sacramento,
  Or where Niagara's thunder shakes the shore;—

For all that's bright indeed must fade and perish,
  And all that's sweet when sweetest not endure,
Before the world shall cease to love and cherish
  The wit and song, the name and fame of Moore.

MARTIN HAVERTY.

[Martin Haverty was born in Galway, in November, 1809. He studied in France; made the acquaintance of Campbell the poet, in Algiers, in 1834; wrote *Letters from Rome* in 1840; *Wanderings in Spain* in 1843; *An Account of the Aran Isles*, when the ethnological section of the British Association visited Ireland in 1857; and undertook the task of writing the *History of Ireland* at a time when an extraordinary impulse was given to the study of Irish history and antiquities by the labours of Petrie, Todd, O'Donovan, O'Curry, Gilbert, Wilde, Ferguson, Reeves, Meehan, O'Callaghan, and others, many of whom have since passed away, and the friendship of all of whom our author was fortunate enough to enjoy.

During a great part of his life he was connected with the daily press; succeeded Charles Mackay in 1845 as assistant editor of the

Morning Chronicle; was subsequently Irish correspondent to the *Daily News,* in succession to Daniel Owen Madden; and for a great many years was on the editorial staff of the *Dublin Freeman's Journal.* In 1864 he was appointed assistant librarian of the King's Inns Library, Dublin, an office which he continues to hold.

Mr. Haverty's *History of Ireland,* from which we quote, deserves the credit of being, as a rule, impartial—a eulogy, as we know, not too often deserved by Irish histories. The style is unambitious, clear, and terse.]

THE ELOPEMENT OF HUGH O'NEILL.

We have already made some mention of the marshal, Sir Henry Bagnal. This man hated the Irish with a rancour which bad men are known to feel towards those whom they have mortally injured. He had shed a great deal of their blood, obtained a great deal of their lands, and was the sworn enemy of the whole race. Sir Henry had a sister who was young and exceedingly beautiful. The wife of the Earl of Tyrone, daughter of Sir Hugh MacManus O'Donnell, had died, and the heart of the Irish chieftain was captivated by the beautiful English girl. His love was reciprocated, and he became in due form a suitor for her hand, but all his efforts to gain her brother's consent to their marriage were in vain. The story, indeed, is one which might seem to have been borrowed from some old romance, if we did not find it circumstantially detailed in the matter-of-fact documents of the State Paper Office. The Irish prince and the English maiden mutually plighted their vows, and O'Neill presented to the lady a gold chain worth £100; but the inexorable Sir Henry removed his sister from Newry to the house of Sir Patrick Barnwell, who was married to another of his sisters, and who lived about seven miles from Dublin. Thither the earl followed her. He was courteously received by Sir Patrick, and seems to have had many friends among the English. One of these, a gentleman named William Warren, acted as his confidant; and at a party at Barnwell's house the earl engaged the rest of the company in conversation while Warren rode off with the lady behind him, accompanied by two servants, and carried her safely to the residence of a friend at Drumcondra, near Dublin. Here O'Neill soon followed, and the Protestant Bishop of Meath, Thomas Jones, a Lancashire man, was easily induced to come and unite them in marriage the same evening. This elopement and marriage, which took place on the 3d of August, 1591, were made the subject of violent accusations against O'Neill. Sir Henry Bagnal was furious. 'I cannot but accurse myselfe and fortune,' he wrote to the lord-treasurer, 'that my bloude, which in my father and myselfe hath often been spilled in repressing this rebellious race, should nowe be mingled with so traiterous a stocke and kindred.' He charged the earl with having another wife living; but this point was cleared up, as O'Neill showed that this lady, who was his first wife, the daughter of Sir Brian MacFelim O'Neill, had been divorced previous to his marriage with the daughter of O'Donnell. Altogether, the government would appear to have viewed the conduct of O'Neill in this matter rather leniently; but Bagnal was henceforth his most implacable foe, and the circumstance was not without its influence on succeeding events.

[It is added, in a note, that the lady whose romantic marriage is here mentioned died in 1596, some years before the last scene of deadly strife between her brother and her husband.]

CHARLES GRAHAM HALPINE.

BORN 1829 — DIED 1868.

[Charles Graham Halpine was born in Oldcastle, Meath, in 1829. His father, the Rev. Nicholas J. Halpine, was an active journalist, being for a time editor of the *Dublin Evening Mail.* Young Halpine graduated in Trinity College, and then went to the English metropolis in search of literary work. Having become associated with the Young Ireland movement, he found that the United States would be a more congenial, and under the circumstances perhaps a safer abode. He there obtained abundant employment, and was a welcome contributor on most of the leading journals. He wrote for a time on the *Boston Post*, then became editor of a short-lived periodical entitled the *Carpet Bag;* and, in New York, contributed to the three leading journals—the *Herald*, the *Times*, and the *Tribune*.

When the civil war broke out he identified himself heart and soul with the Northern cause. Joining the army as lieutenant in the famous 69th Regiment, under Colonel Corcoran, he was promoted to be adjutant-general on the staff of General David Hunter, and afterwards of Major-general Halleck. He drew up the order by which the former commander enrolled the first regiment of negro soldiers, and was in consequence included in a proclamation of outlawry by the Southern authorities, which directed the immediate execution of his general and himself in case of capture. He retired, owing to ill health, from the army, and received due acknowledgment of his services by being raised by successive steps to the rank of brigadier-general. Halpine also took an active part in politics as one of the leaders of the Democratic party, and he honourably distinguished himself by his efforts to purge that body of the corruptions which had been fostered by Tammany Hall. His death was sudden and sad. A sufferer from sleeplessness, he had been for some time in the habit of taking soporifics, and he died on the night of August 3, 1868, from an overdose of chloroform.

The greater part of Halpine's poems appeared in the ephemeral pages of journalism, and were written for the hour. The verses by which he became best known were those written under the *nom de plume* of "Private Miles O'Reilly." A collected edition of his principal poems has been published in a handsome volume by Messrs. Harper Brothers, New York, under the editorship of Mr. R. B. Roosevelt.]

A VESPER HYMN.

The evening bells of Sabbath fill
  The dusky silence of the night,
And through our gathering gloom distil
  Sweet sparkles of immortal light;
  Such hours of peace as these requite
The labours of the weary week;
  When thus, with souls refreshed and bright,
Forgiveness of our sins we seek!

Oh! help us, Jesus, to conform
  Our spirits, thoughts, and lives to thine!
Beyond this earthly strife and storm,
  Oh! make Thy star of Love to shine!
When we are sinking in the brine
Of doubt and care—oh come, that we,
  As Peter did, may safe resign
Our sinking helplessness to thee!

Thy Godhood—whence all glory flows—
  Thou didst not scruple to abase,
To rescue from undying woes
  The sons of a rebellious race!
Who can, unmoved, unweeping, trace
Thy meek obedience to His will,
  Whose sole appointed means of grace
Thou didst, even to the Cross, fulfil!

Our wayward footsteps wander wide,
  Pursuing Joy's delusive rays;
And, in our hours of health and pride,
  Too oft from Thee our spirit strays;
But soon descend the darker days,
When youth and strength their lustre hide,
  And, journeying through a pathless maze,
We turn to our neglected Guide!

Lead back, oh Lord! thy wandering sheep—
  Oh, guide us gently to thy fold!
Instruct us all Thy laws to keep,
  And unto Thine our lives to mould!
For we are weak, and faith grows cold—
Nor ever sleep the Tempter's powers;
  Thou art our only stay and hold—
Through Thee alone can heaven be ours!

A darker shade, a denser gloom
  Descends on all the folded flowers,
While, silent as the voiceless tomb,
  Above them roll the midnight hours:
To-morrow's dawn, and their perfume
Again will fill their glowing bowers—
  Lord, after death so bid us bloom,
Where no frost chills, no tempest lowers!

NOT A STAR FROM THE FLAG SHALL FADE.

Och! a rare ould flag was the flag we bore,
  'Twas a bully ould flag, an' nice;
It had sthripes in plenty, an' shtars galore—
  'Twas the broth of a purty device.
Faix, we carried it South, an' we carried it far,
  An' around it our bivouacs made;
An' we swore by the shamrock that never a shtar
  From its azure field should fade.
    Ay, this was the oath, I tell you thrue,
    That was sworn in the souls of our Boys in Blue.

The fight it grows thick, an' our boys they fall,
   An' the shells like a banshee scream;
An' the flag—it is torn by many a ball,
   But to yield it we never dhream.
Though pierced by bullets, yet still it bears
   All the shtars in its tatthered field,
An' again the brigade, like to one man swears,
   "Not a shtar from the flag we yield!"
      'Twas the deep, hot oath, I tell you thrue,
      That lay close to the hearts of our Boys in
         Blue.

Shure, the fight it was won, afther many a year,
   But two-thirds of the boys who bore
That flag from their wives and sweethearts dear
   Returned to their homes no more.
They died by the bullet—disease had power,
   An' to death they were rudely tossed;
But the thought came warm in their dying hour,
   "Not a shtar from the flag is lost!"
      Then they said their pathers and aves
         through,
      An', like Irishmen, died—did our Boys in
         Blue.

But now they tell us some shtars are gone,
   Torn out by the rebel gale;
That the shtars we fought for, the states we won,
   Are still out of the Union's pale.
May their sowls in the dioul's hot kitchen glow
   Who sing such a lyin' shtrain;
By the dead in their graves, it shall not be so—
   They shall have what they died to gain!
      All the shtars in our flag shall still shine
         through
      The grass growing soft o'er our Dead in
         Blue!

IRISH ASTRONOMY.

A VERITABLE MYTH, TOUCHING THE CONSTELLATION OF
O'RYAN, IGNORANTLY AND FALSELY SPELLED ORION.

O'Ryan was a man of might
   Whin Ireland was a nation,
But poachin' was his heart's delight
   And constant occupation.
He had an ould militia gun,
   And sartin sure his aim was;
He gave the keepers many a run,
   And wouldn't mind the game laws.

St. Pathrick wanst was passin' by
   O'Ryan's little houldin',
And, as the saint felt wake and dhry,
   He thought he'd enther bould in.

"O'Ryan," says the saint, "avick!
   To praich at Thurles I'm goin',
So let me have a rasher quick,
   And a dhrop of Innishowen."

"No rasher will I cook for you
   While betther is to spare, sir,
But here's a jug of mountain dew,
   And there's a rattlin' hare, sir."
St. Pathrick he looked mighty sweet,
   And says he, "Good luck attind you,
And, when you're in your winding-sheet,
   It's up to heaven I'll sind you."

O'Ryan gave his pipe a whiff—
   "Them tidin's is transportin',
But may I ax your saintship if
   There's any kind of sportin'?"
St. Pathrick said, "A Lion's there,
   Two Bears, a Bull, and Cancer"—
"Bedad," says Mick, "the huntin's rare;
   St. Pathrick, I'm your man, sir."

So, to conclude my song aright,
   For fear I'd tire your patience,
You'll see O'Ryan any night
   Amid the constellations.
And Venus follows in his track
   Till Mars grows jealous raally,
But, faith, he fears the Irish knack
   Of handling the shillaly.

ADIEU.

Oh, heed him not, if rhymer prate
   Of parted love and endless woe;
   True love would scorn to babble so,
And grief is inarticulate,
   Or with a hoarse and broken flow
It rushes, murmuring, to its fate—
That ocean which, or soon or late,
   Receives the wreck of all we know,
   Or be it love, or be it hate.
Oh, heed him not. The spirit bowed
With grief sincere was ne'er so loud.

But if to say in simple praise
   That I will ne'er forget you, friends,
   Though at the earth's remotest ends
I pass my long unsolaced days;
   That, when the evening shade descends,
And high and bright the fagots blaze,
My faithful heart your forms shall raise,
   While memory the curtain rends
That time would drop o'er earlier days—
If this content you, 'tis sincere,
Though vouched by neither oath nor tear.

JOHN FRANCIS O'DONNELL.

BORN 1837 — DIED 1874.

[John Francis O'Donnell was born in Limerick in 1837. He was but fourteen years of age when he began to write verses, the vehicle for the offspring of his boyish pen being the *Kilkenny Journal*. After he had held some engagements on the provincial Irish press—having been among other things sub-editor of the *Tipperary Examiner*—he drifted to London; and, in 1860, we find him editing an Irish weekly called the *Universal News*. In 1861 he returned for a short time to Dublin, to fill a vacancy in the *Nation*. He was once again in London in the following year. It would be impossible to enumerate all the periodicals to which he contributed both prose and verse. He had a very ready and an extremely versatile pen. Among Irish journals he was a frequent contributor to the *Nation* and to the *Irish People* during its short existence. He also wrote in the *Lamp*;—a novel, entitled *Agents and Evictions*, originally appeared in that journal, and a lengthy poem well worthy of notice, entitled "The Christian Martyr." He wrote in the *Boston Pilot* and the *Dublin Review;* and for a while he was editor of the *Tablet*. His verses were always welcome to Charles Dickens, who was a helpful admirer of the poet; and a large number of his poems were published in *Chambers's Journal*. In 1871 he published *Memories of the Irish Franciscans*—a volume of verse suggested by the well-known and able work of the Rev. C. P. Meehan on the Franciscans. After years of literary drudgery, Mr. O'Donnell received an official appointment through the assistance of Lord O'Hagan; but he enjoyed his fortune for only a few months, and died in the May of 1874. He is buried in the Roman Catholic portion of Kensal Green Cemetery, London. It is a subject of great regret that his poems lie scattered over numberless periodicals, and under various *noms de plume*.]

WHERE!

A minute gone. She lingered here, and then
  Passed, with face backward turned, through
    yonder door;
The free fold of her garments' damask grain
  Fashioned a hieroglyph upon the floor,
  Then straightened, as it reached the corridor.

Down the long passages, I heard her feet
  Moving—a crepitating music slow—
And next her voice, an echo exquisite,
  But modulated in its tender flow—
  A harp through which the evening breezes blow.

Upon the table, there were books and flowers,
  And Indian trifles; a Mahratta blade
Whose ivory hilt sustained a cirque of towers,
  Wedded by the inexplicable braid
  On Vishnu's shrine at harvest full moon laid.

The curtains shook; a scarlet glamour crossed
  The stained wood and the white walls of the
    room—
Wavered, retreated, trembled, and was lost
  Between the statue's plinth, the console's gloom,
  And yon tall urn of yellow blossomed broom.

I see her face look backward at me yet,
  Just as she glided by the cypress chair;
Her happy eyes with happy tears are wet,
  And, over bust and shoulders, cool and fair,
  Stream the black coils of her abundant hair.

In what far past—in what abysm of time,
  Have I beheld that self-same look before?
There was no difference of hour or clime:
  A garment made a figure on a floor,
  Which straightened sweeping towards a corridor.

Rare trifles were around me, curtains blew,
  And worked their restless phantasms on a ceil;
A sidelong bird across a casement flew,
  Upon the table glittered graven steel,
  And a low voice thrilled me with soft appeal.

All things were there, as all things are, to-day,
  But where? I half remember, as a dream,
Such accidents, in epochs, long grown gray—
  Such glory, but with ever-narrowing beam,
  From which I'm severed by some shoreless
    stream.

Have I forgotten—is this flash of light,
  Which makes the brain and pulse together start,
Some ray reflected from the infinite
  Worlds, where I mayhap have left a heart—
  The Infinite of which I am a part?

Who shall unriddle it? Return, sweet wife,
  And with thy presence sanctify this pain;
Cling to my side, O faithful help of life!
  Lest, in the hour when night is on the wane,
  The destinies divide us two again.

TOMBS IN THE CHURCH OF MONTORIO, ON THE JANICULUM.

[Heic jacent O'Neallvs, Baro de Dvngannon, Magni Hugonis Fillvs, et O'Donnel, Comes De Tyrconnel, qvi contra hœreticos in Hybernia multos annos certervnt.—MDCVIII.]

All natural things in balance lie,
Adjustment fair of earth and sky,
And their belongings. Thunders bring
The red life from the heart of spring;
Thence summer, and the golden wane
  That comes with harvest, when each field,
Crimsoned with weeds, like fiery rain,
  Flames like a newly forgèd shield.
All things come true, in some dim sense,
Held good by absolute Providence.
Inquire not: Here you sleep at last—
  Sleeping, it may be face to face,
Right glorious leaders of our race,
Of faith profound, of purpose vast.

Around, above, this glittering dome,
Soars the majestic bulk of Rome;
This marble pave, this double cell
Enshrines you, and contents you well.
Better it were the twain should lie
  On some wild bluff of Donegal,
The sea below in mutiny,
  The terrible Heaven over all.
God wills and willed it shall not be.
Here is no rave of wind or sea.
Peace! incense, and the vesper psalm;
  The sob, the penitential groan;
  The lurid light, the dripping stone—
The earth's eternity of calm.

Sleep on, stern souls, 'twere wrong to shake
Your ashes—bid the dead awake,
To bitter welcome. Ireland lies
Under the heels of enemies.
So has she lain since that curst day
  That saw your good ship fly the Land;
Since Ulster's proud and strong array
  Dwindled to fragments, band by band.
And you two wept in leaving her
(Chased through the seas by Chichester).
Still buoyed with hope to find abroad
  Aid to prostrate our ancient foe,
  And to lay wall and rampart low,
And hear the saints in Heaven applaud.

It came not, and in regal Rome
Died the O'Donnell, sick for home,
Not all the pomp the city boasts
Consoled him for his native coasts.
Here Art's sublimed; but Nature there
  His heart, his passions satisfied;
  The forest depth, the delicate air
Were with his inmost soul allied.

So hoping, doubting went the days,
And tired at heart of time's delays,
He closed his eyes in Christ our Lord.
  No truer man had nobler birth,
  No braver soldier trod the earth,
With pitying or destroying sword.

And thou, O'Neill, Lord of Revolt,
Battle's impetuous thunderbolt,
Cliff-flinger, at whose name of might
The bronzed cheeks of the Pale turned white,
Dost thou lie here? And Ireland bleeds
  Her virgin life through every pore!
Great chief in unexampled deeds,
  We need thy smiting arm once more.
Rest, rest! the glory of thy life
Shines like tradition on the strife
Which Ireland wages hour by hour,
  Patient, yet daring for the best,
  And growing up, as worlds attest,
To freedom, majesty, and power.

GUESSES.

I know a maiden; she is dark and fair,
  With curvèd brows and eyes of hazel hue,
And mouth, a marvel, delicately rare,
  Rich with expression, ever quaint yet new.
O happy fancy! there she, leaning, sits,
  One little palm against her temples pressed,
  And all her tresses winking like brown elves;
The yellow fretted laurels toss in fits,
  The great laburnums droop in swoons of rest,
    The blowing woodbines murmur to themselves.

What does she think of, as the daylight floats
  Along the mignonetted window-sills,
And flame-like, overhead, with ruffled throats,
  The bright canaries twit their seeded bills?
What does she think of? Of the jasmine flower
That, like an odorous snowflake, opens slow,
  Or of the linnet on the topmost briar,
Or of the cloud that, fringed with summer shower,
  Floats up the river spaces, blue and low,
    And marged with lilies like a bank of fire?

Ah, sweet conception! enviable guest,
  Lodged in the pleasant palace of her brain,
Summoned a minute, at her rich behest,
  To wander fugitive the world again,
What does she think of? Of the dusty bridge,
  Spanning the mallow shadows in the heat,
    And porching in its hollow the cool wind;
Or of the poplar on the naked ridge:
  Or of the bee that, clogged with nectared feet,
    Hums in the gorgeous tulip-bell confined?

At times, her gentle brows are archly knit
  With tangled subtleties of gracious thought;
At times, the dimples round her mouth are lit
  By rosy twilights from some image caught.
What does she think of? Of the open book
  Whose pencilled leaves are fluttering on her knee;
Or of the broken fountain in the grass;
Or of the dumb and immemorial rook,
  Perched like a wingèd darkness on the tree,
    And watching the great clouds in silence pass?

I know not; myriad are the phantasies
  That trouble the still dreams of maidenhood,
And wonderful the radiant entities
  Shaped in the passion of her brain and blood.
O Fancy! through the realm of guesses fly,
  Unlock the rich abstraction of her heart
    (Her soul is second in the mystery):
Trail thy gold meshes thro' the summer sky;
  Question her tender breathings as they part,
    Tell me, Revealer, that she thinks of me.

ISAAC BUTT.

Born 1813 — Died 1879.

[In dealing with the late Chief-justice Whiteside we made the trite remark that the greatest part of the orator dies with himself. The words appear cold, formless, and prosaic which thrilled thousands to wild enthusiasm when they had the accessories of a fine presence, a sonorous voice, appropriate gesture, and extraneous but exciting circumstances. Of Isaac Butt this fact is truer than of the majority of orators; more true, especially, than of Whiteside. Whiteside's orations, apart from the force given to them by his great histrionic powers, smelt of the lamp; and thus in his spoken utterances we come across sentences which have all the polish of the careful writer in the closet. But the reader will look in vain through the speeches of Isaac Butt for passages of sustained beauty or of well-balanced sentences; and that default teaches us Butt's great merit. He was emphatically a man of ideas, not of words; filled with his subject, he forgot mere form; many of his sentences were unfinished, all of them rugged; and yet since O'Connell there was perhaps no Irish political orator who could so thoroughly convince and so deeply thrill Irish audiences. The secret was that the hearer could see every link as it was added to the chain of reasoning, and because the bursts of Isaac Butt came from a great heart and passionate conviction.

Isaac Butt was the son of a Protestant clergyman, the Rev. Robert Butt, and was born in Stranorlar, in the county of Donegal, in 1813. He entered Trinity College in 1832, and his course, both in his studies and in the College Historical Society, was brilliant. Of the famous debating body he was twice auditor and a gold medallist. Almost immediately after he had graduated he was elected Whately professor of political economy. In 1838 he was called to the bar. The reputation he had gained as a speaker in the mimic debates of the university followed him to the outside world, and, before he was long in his profession he was called to take part in important public proceedings. He made in the Mansion House, Dublin, in February, 1840, a very hot and strong Conservative speech—for Mr. Butt then belonged to the extreme Tory section—which created great enthusiasm; and, in the same year, he defended the old Dublin corporation before the House of Lords with such dexterity as to draw down the applause of several peers, and even to move the usually impassive Duke of Wellington. His professional advancement under such circumstances was naturally rapid; in six years after he was called to the bar he was made a Q.C., and for many years subsequently he was engaged in every important trial, political or otherwise, which took place in Ireland.

Besides the political triumphs already mentioned, the young barrister had the honour of meeting the redoubtable O'Connell himself in a pitched battle on the question of Repeal of the Union, in the Dublin Corporation, and the great Agitator paid a high compliment to the talents and the good feeling of his youthful opponent. It was inevitable under such circumstances that Butt should be drawn into politics, and in 1852 he was elected in the Conservative interest for Harwich. He next sought a constituency in his native country, and from 1852 to 1865 sate for Youghal. During this period his views had undergone some modification, and towards the close, he was little removed from a Liberal of the Palmerstonian school. In 1865 he was rejected by his old constituents, and for a while he was unheard of in politics; while at the Four

Courts, where he had been but rarely seen for years, he once more became a familiar figure. He took a prominent part in defending the Fenian prisoners, and thus rose to high popularity among the National party. This fact, together probably with his political experience in the past, led him to the thought of founding a new political party, and, having adopted Home Rule as a national platform, he devoted to it all his energies of pen and tongue and organization. The history of his action in that movement is too recent to be fully detailed, or perhaps impartially estimated. Suffice it to say that he was returned without opposition for the city of Limerick in September, 1871, and that for several sessions he was the undisputed leader of the Home Rule party. As time went on, younger and more ardent spirits proposed a policy more active than Mr. Butt was willing to sanction, and his last days were probably embittered by the sense of waning power. He died after a lingering illness in 1879. His death evoked a feeling of universal and deep sorrow, for the splendour of his talents, the genuineness of his nature, and above all, his simplicity and modesty, made him one of the most lovable of men.

Mr. Butt was a busy penman. He was among the founders and earliest contributors to the *Dublin University Magazine*. His stories in that journal were republished under the title *Chapters of College Romance*. The work is not equal to one's expectations. The stories are morbid, long-drawn out, and slovenly. His other most ambitious work is a *History of Italy from the Abdication of Napoleon I.* This book has many merits. It is impartial, clear in statement, unambitious in style; but on the other hand it is often bald, and wants compression and power of graphic description. He was more at home in the shorter works he from time to time produced on questions of the hour. A book of his on the land question is a marvel of analytic power. He was also a close student of metaphysics, and often spoke and wrote on the memory and theories of Bishop Berkeley, from whom he could boast collateral descent.]

ON LAND TENURE.

(FROM SPEECH IN HOUSE OF COMMONS, 1876.)

I have now brought down to 1866 the testimonies as to the state of feeling which exists between the landed proprietors and the occupants of the soil. However much we may regret that feeling, and desire to remove it, the legislature must deal with circumstances and with feelings as they exist. No such feeling exists in England, and therefore English gentlemen have difficulty in forming a correct opinion upon it; but I do not hesitate to say that there is a general desire on the part of the landed proprietors of Ireland to keep their tenants in a state of subjection to themselves. Remember this desire is not confined to those landlords who may be described as being cruel and hard, it is shared in by the landlords who would treat their tenants kindly and even aid them in distress. How was the object of the landlords accomplished? Simply by the power of notice to quit. I am speaking, of course, before the time the Land Bill became law. In a trial in which I was engaged I examined a gentleman who was believed to have a large number of notices to quit, but he denied it. I then asked him—"Did you not serve some last year?" "Yes," he replied, "but I do that every year—it is part of the management of my estate. I never intend to act upon a notice, but I want to be able to take any field or holding in case I should wish to do so, and, therefore, I give notice to quit each year." Yet this was a landlord of a humane and kindly character, who would not treat a tenant harshly. It is his desire to keep his tenants under his own power that so easily reconciles to his conscience the practice I have just alluded to. The Irish landlords think they can do much better for the tenant than he can for himself. I believe that a country in which you allow the mass of the population to be reduced to a state of serfdom never can be prosperous, never can be contented, and never can be peaceful. Bad landlords will abuse the power which a good landlord will only use for a beneficial purpose. The landlords who could serve notices to quit have two powers in their hands. They have the power of capricious eviction, and the power of arbitrarily raising the rents. While there are landlords in Ireland who would scorn to do either of these things, there were others who did them with a reckless cruelty which had not a parallel in history. I do not wish to dwell on the fearful scenes enacted between 1847 and 1852, but in a book of high authority, Mr. Ray's *Social Condition of Europe*, I find it stated that in one year, 1849, no fewer than 500,000 civil bill ejectments were served in Ireland; and I may add that I myself have seen whole districts desolated. Sir Matthew Barrington relates that immediately parliament passed the Poor Law, the landlords of Ireland began to clear their estates by notices to quit and by tumbling down houses. On many occasions the military were brought in to throw down houses, and hundreds of people were, to use an expressive phrase, thrown on the road, simply because the landlord wished to get rid of the superabundant population. Many measures, passed by statesmen with a most honest intention of doing good to Ireland, have produced results directly the reverse. This was because they were framed by men who had not the knowledge which can only be acquired by residence among the people, and by a long and intimate acquaintance with the circumstances. The case of the Poor Law was an instance of this, for it ought to have been foreseen that the giving of relief to the poor would lead to the very evil which followed. I will give one instance of what occurred. The matter came into a court of justice because the landlord, fortunately for justice, made some slight mistake in his proceedings. It was the case of an estate in the county of Meath, and there were on it twenty-seven families. It was admitted that their labour made the property rich and profitable, and that they never had been in arrear one half-year's rent during the thirty years that the landlord had been in possession of the estate. The landlord got embarrassed, and he sold the estate to a gentleman, who purchased it on condition that all the tenants should be evicted. The landlord concealed this circumstance from the tenants, and when he served them with notice to quit told them he did not intend to act upon it. Well, a jury of landlords gave to one of the evicted tenants the full value of the fee-simple of the land. Such things, it should be remembered, could not be done in England, for Henry VIII. got his parliament to pass an act that every landlord who pulled down a house should build it up again in six months, and in the reign of Queen Elizabeth another act was passed that gave a legal right of relief to every one who was born on the soil. If there had been a law of settlement in Ireland, many of the landlords who were now living on their estates would be in the workhouse to which they consigned their tenants.

But there was a still more grievous wrong—namely, the power of the landlord to confiscate the improvements of his tenants in Ireland. All the improvements of the soil—certainly all the improvements made up to a very recent period—were effected by the tenants. Yet there was nothing to prevent an unscrupulous landlord from confiscating these improvements, and, in point of fact, it was done over and over again. Lord Clarendon, I think it was, who spoke of it in the other house as a legalized robbery. It was to that state of things that the Land Act was applied. I believe that any friend to the Irish tenant would act very wrongly indeed if he spoke of the author of that act in other terms than those of profound respect, knowing, as I do, the difficulties he had to contend with and the prejudices he had to meet. I give him every credit for that act. At the same time, I regret to say, it has failed, from a reason which I foresaw,—as you leave to the landlords the power of eviction. In the circumstances of Ireland no device that the legislature can make can prevent them from converting that tremendous power into an instrument to render themselves absolute despots over their tenants. Still the act established a principle. It first legalized the Ulster tenant right. Now, what is the meaning of that? As property which was only protected by custom, and to which the tenant had no legal claim whatever, except in justice and in honour, was converted into a legal property, that is a very great principle as applied to Irish land.

I will now detain the house a few minutes by referring to some incidents which, I confess, have had effect on my own mind in reference to the value of giving security to tenants. One of the incidents is an old one, as old as the days of Arthur Young, who certainly described in a striking way what was the benefit of giving security to tenants. He says that a man with a wife and six children met Sir William Osborne in the county of Tipperary. The man could get no land, and Sir William Osborne gave him twelve acres of heathy land, and £4 to stock it with. Twelve years afterwards, when Young revisited Ireland, he went to see the man, and found him with twelve acres under full cultivation. Three other persons he found settled in the same way, and he says their industry had no bounds, nor was the day long enough for their energy. He says if you give tenants security, and let them be certain of enjoying the rewards of their labour, and treat them as Sir William Osborne did, there would be no better or more industrious farmers in the world. I have often thought of that, and have said that if there had been men like Sir William Osborne to give employment to those who have been evicted, and who took part in the Irish insurrection, there would not have been a better set of farmers in the kingdom. Now let me refer to another case. A Roman Catholic prelate, whom I can respect as much as a prelate of my own church, was examined before a committee of this house, and illustrated the advantages of giving security to the tenants. He describes how he one day saw a man enter into the occupation of some land. There was nothing but a barren heath, and he saw the man carrying on his back manure which he had brought from a road two miles distant. Two years after the prelate again passed that way, and he found corn growing on what had been heath, and a house built there. It had all been done by the man himself, and the simple cause, he had a lease, and was thus secure of his tenancy. The prelate then went to another man who had no lease, and who said:—"If I did the same as my neighbour has done my landlord would not only ask for an increase of rent upon my improvements, but also upon what I now hold." That is the sort of discouragement there is to industry all over Ireland, and it proceeds from the desire of the landlord not so much to extract money from the tenants—that is but an incident, but from the desire to keep the tenants in their power. Why, on some estates in Ireland they cannot marry, except with the consent of the landlord's agent, and at the risk of being evicted. I assure you that those rules still prevail on many estates in Ireland. Another rule which used to exist was that the tenant should not harbour a man at night. There is a story of one poor boy whose mother had been evicted from a farm, and who sought shelter with his uncle; the uncle would have let him in; but his neighbours said he must not, or the agent would evict them all. Therefore the boy was shut out, and the next morning was found lying at the door a lifeless corpse. The men who had refused him admittance were tried for murder, and were convicted of manslaughter, their defence being that they did not dare by the rules of their farms to give him shelter. Now no rights of property can give a man such dominion as that over his tenants, any more than property can give dominion over the thews and sinews of your servants. Now these evils can only be guarded against by taking away the arbitrary power of eviction, and allowing the tenant to hold his farm at a valued rent. The condition of every Irish estate was originally to give security of tenure. Your landlords have not done it. Your ancestors were placed there not to be lords over the people, but to settle and plant the country, and you are there still among the people whom you have neither conciliated nor subdued. There is not a landlord in Ireland who holds land except on trust for creating upon it a contented tenantry. I go upon the great principles of jurisprudence, which will allow no right of property to stand in the way of a general good. I go upon the principles established by the Irish Land Act, and I ask you, as you value the peace of Ireland, to carry those principles into full and beneficial effect. I will say nothing more about the peace of Ireland, or I shall be charged with making a stereotyped peroration. I have no official responsibility for the peace of Ireland, but I have the responsibility attaching to every man who takes ever so humble a part in public affairs, to promote peace and tranquillity. I have the anxiety which any man must feel who looks back on the ruin, desolation, and misery brought to many parts of Ireland by that civil war—for it was a civil war—which has raged between landlord and tenant since the days of the Cromwellian confiscations, and who regards with trembling the indications of a renewal of the war. I rejoice to say that those indications have at present come only from the landlords. I trust they will cease before they come from the tenants; but it is only by giving protection to these tenants that you can have security against a return to that state of things which every man of right feeling deplored.

BISHOP BERKELEY'S THEORY.[1]

I must now endeavour to place before you an outline of that celebrated speculation in which Berkeley is commonly supposed to have denied the reality of the external world. A very little thought will satisfy you that there is in his theory nothing very difficult to understand—may I venture to add, nothing very shocking to our notions of common sense. The reasonings of the theory of vision carried Berkeley on to his still more celebrated speculation of immaterialism. The first step in that speculation is the truth that all our ideas or perceptions exist in the mind, and are not external to it; the next is that which appeared established by the theory of vision, that these

---
[1] From Afternoon Lectures on Science and Art. Dublin, 1865.

ideas are not images or resemblances of anything external, but are impressions produced entirely within the mind itself. We know, indeed, that those perceptions are in our mind, and know also that they are caused by something external to our own mind. But that external cause may be something not bearing the remotest resemblance to the impression in the mind. Let these things be conceded, and, according to Berkeley's reasoning, all the evidence of a material world is gone. The impressions in our mind only tell us that there is some external force which produces them. But that force is the creative power of God—a power constantly exerted to produce upon the intellects which he has called into being impressions which he wills. The universe exists only in intellect and thought, or rather in the mind of the Great Creator, and his constant and never-ceasing action on the intellects which he has formed. The laws of nature are the laws by which God has ordained and regulated the course and order in which the impressions which he calls into being shall succeed one to the other in all created minds.

I am endeavouring to state the theory, not attempting to prove it, or even to bring before you the reasonings by which it has been sustained. I may, perhaps, say that it by no means implies any want of reality in those impressions which form to us the external or material world. On the contrary, it gives them an awful reality, in representing them as the direct agency of God upon our mind. That they would cease if God withdrew that agency takes nothing from the reality. The most inveterate believer in the existence of matter would scarcely say that it is beyond the power of Omnipotence to annihilate any portion of it. In Berkeley's theory, the annihilation would be produced simply by the withdrawal of the power which presented that impression to created minds. Berkeley literally understood the words, "In him we live, and move, and have our being," and saw in the Deity not merely the first cause that set all things in motion, then left them to themselves, but the supreme and ever-present Author of being, "who upholdeth all things by the word of his power."

I need scarcely say that such a theory is not to be answered by telling that if you do not turn away from danger, you will soon find the external world a reality. The laws in Berkeley's theory by which one impression follows another are just as inexorable and as binding as those by which materialists tell us that one physical effect follows another. In that theory all the phenomena of life and of the universe resolve themselves into the action of the Deity upon intellect, without the intervention of a senseless and inert mass which we call matter; but that agency is just as resistless and as regular as any of the laws which they who hold the contrary hypothesis can suppose the Creator to have impressed upon the physical nature of the material world.

Those who have thought most upon this subject will probably acquiesce in the observation that all we can say of Berkeley's theory is, that it presents fewer difficulties than any other that has ever attempted to solve the mystery of our existence. Those who would be little disposed to adopt the criticism of Byron, may probably not as promptly reject another, which, I believe, we owe to a popular periodical:—

"What is mind? It is no matter.
What is matter? Never mind."

If Berkeley had succeeded in showing our mental perceptions are not images of anything external, but signs and symbols which the Creator has ordained, it may be it is beyond our faculties, in our present state, to know the full meaning of those symbols. It is enough for us that they guide our conduct. All these speculations do little more than trace for us the limits of human knowledge. They are but the beating of the wings of the bird against the bars of its cage. Yet, after all, it is something to know the limit, and to feel that the bars are not realities of our existence, and that there are bright fields of air and light beyond to which we yet may flee away.

Shall I wander beyond the province of this lecture if I venture to suggest a view which has presented itself to my mind? It is, I think, impossible to reflect upon the nature of our own perceptions—impossible, certainly, to read the works of Berkeley—without receiving the conviction that our senses do not give us full information of the external world, even of the portion of it which we imagine to be cognizable by sense.

Reflecting upon these things, I have often been struck by a view which I do not remember to have seen in print, although it must have suggested itself to other minds. No one, I apprehend, will deny that if it had pleased God to create and sustain human beings without the endowment of sight, but with all our present intellectual faculties, our notions of the external world would be very different from those which we now entertain. Of all that vision conveys to us we should not only be wholly ignorant, but the remotest imagination could not enter our minds. In the case in which I suppose, sight would be a thing unthought of, unimagined, and unconceived. But have we any reason to believe that the senses with which we are now endowed, are all of which even the physical organization of our present frame is capable? May not that frame be capable of being endowed with some sense as remote from all our present conceptions as vision would be from those of a race who had been from creation blind—a sense which might alter and correct all our perceptions of the external world as completely as the gift of vision would enlighten and change the ideas formed of it by the blind? How unwise, then, and how rash is the judgment which would bring those things which appear to us the mysteries of religion, to the test of sense, while we can have no assurance that these senses give us full information, even of matters within the region of sense. It may be something as trifling as a minute film across the eye which prevents the development in our bodily senses of some power of which we have never dreamed; some power which would show us that statements which appear to our ignorance to contradict the evidence of our senses are only inconsistent with their imperfect testimony; a power, in the absence of which we are as incapable of taking in all that even sense can tell us of the external world as man admittedly would be in the absence of sight. We never can be certain that our senses convey to us all the knowledge as to the external world which our nature is fitted, even by this mode of information, to receive. Plurality of senses is, perhaps, given us to understand that it cannot be so. But all the probability is that they do not. In the few cases of persons born blind, who subsequently attained the faculty of sight, we are struck by the accounts they give of indescribable yearnings after something, which were satisfied by sight. No doubt this may have been produced by conversation about vision; but I cannot help thinking that it was produced by the existence in the mind of a mental faculty adapted to receive the ideas of sight—a faculty in the soul which sought its proper object.

Is it fanciful to say that all of us, in our communings with external nature, have felt these yearnings for a sense which would reveal to us something of which we now have strange and unrealized dreams? In the voice of the waves, in the moanings of the wind, who has not heard, if I may use the expression, something which sound did not convey? How often in the glories, the grandeur, or the gloom of scenery, have we felt that there was something which sight could not realize? Poets have in vain endeavoured to embody these vague feelings in words. Byron felt it when he wrote of—

"Those orbs of light,
So wildly, spiritually bright,
Who ever gazed upon their shining,
And turn'd to earth without repining,
Nor long'd for wings to flee away,
And mix with their eternal ray?"

The more philosophic Wordsworth has spoken of—

"Those obstinate questionings
Of sense and outward things,
Failings from us, vanishings;
Blank misgivings of a creature
Moving about in worlds not realized;
High instincts before which our mortal nature
Did tremble like a guilty thing surprised."

Is not this the feeling that "now we see through a glass darkly," the yearning for something for which our nature has capacities, by which we might realize all that we thus dimly feel, and know even as we are known?—

"Hence, in a season of calm weather,
Though inland far we be,
Our souls have sight of that immortal sea
Which brought us hither;
Can in a moment travel thither,
And see the children sport upon the shore,
And hear the mighty waters rolling evermore."

Is it unphilosophical to say that feelings like these are but the voice of our nature telling us that we have faculties that yearn for information from the external world which we might receive from senses yet unknown, and that a slight change in our organization might pour upon our perceptions a flood of light which would irradiate and glorify, and make intelligible them all, and show us that even in these forms which we supposed in our presumption that we fully comprehended, there are visions of beauty which no sense we now enjoy can realize, and which, therefore, our mind never framed—"good things which eye has not seen, nor ear heard, neither hath it entered into the heart of man to conceive."

. . . . . .

I now feel how inadequately I have been able to convey to you the interest which such a subject as I have chosen might well excite. I do not think, as I have said in the commencement, that I have been unduly influenced by feelings which naturally arise in my mind from even a remote relationship to Berkeley. Accident has given me other associations in connection with his name. More than thirty years have passed since I became familiar with the manse-house of Berkeley's see, when it was occupied by one who justly recalled the title of his predecessor in another great and good Bishop of Cloyne. It was from the lips of the great astronomer whose discovery of the parallax of the fixed stars made his name famous throughout Europe, that I first heard an explanation of Berkeley's theory, walking on the garden terrace which Berkeley's taste had formed. It was under the roof of the house in which he lived—I believe in the very room in which he studied—that a copy of his works was first placed in my hand; and I was invited to study the theory which denied the existence of the material world by one whose genius had done so much to explain its wonders. I have still a vivid remembrance of being brought by Bishop Brinkley to look at the jars of tar-water discovered at the roots of hedges in the palace gardens, which had been torn up in some improvements, in ignorance of the fact that the trees were planted by the hand of the author of *Siris*. The name of Berkeley recalls to me memories more sacred still:—

"The touch of a vanish'd hand,
The sound of a voice that is gone."

Yet I do not think that associations like these have led me astray in believing that the subject was one calculated to interest you; and even if this lecture is unworthy to close a series which, up to this day, has been brilliant and successful, I am not sure that you could carry away a last impression more suited to the objects of these meetings than that which must be left by the calm and lustrous dignity of Berkeley's character and mind. Within the range of subjects of these lectures I might easily have found topics more exciting and more popular—subjects which would have cost myself less time and thought in preparation; but I am not sure that I could have found any which would have conveyed a more useful or more attractive lesson. His single-minded love of truth, his large and sincere charity, his deep and reverential piety, his mild and gentle spirit of toleration—these are qualities which all of us may strive to imitate, although it is not given to us to ascend with him to those pure regions of contemplation, in which he saw the human intellect face to face with its Creator; and here, within sight of the university he adorned, and speaking on the soil of the land he loved, I may repeat with a deeper significance the words which, in another country, strangers inscribed upon his tomb. In the kindred feelings of love for our religion and our country all Irishmen may well feel proud that Berkeley lived—that he consecrated a mighty intellect to the defence of those immortal truths upon which are reposed our common hopes—and bequeathed to our common country the splendid inheritance of his genius, his virtue, and his fame:—

"Si Christianus fueris, si amans patriæ,
Utroque nomine gloriari potes Berkeleium vixisse."[1]

WILLIAM ALEXANDER—MRS. ALEXANDER.

[The Right Rev. William Alexander, D.D., Bishop of Derry and Raphoe, was born in Londonderry in April, 1824. His father was the Rev. Robert Alexander, rector of Aghadoey. He graduated in Brasenose College, Oxford, in 1847; and in the same year was ordained. After he had passed through various minor ecclesiastical appointments, he was made Dean of Emly in 1863; and in 1867, on the death of Dr. Higgin, was raised to the bishopric of Derry.

Though for many years past Dr. Alexander's muse has been silent, it was as a poet that he first became known in the intellectual world. One cannot read the productions of his youthful pen without deeply regretting that the heavy duties of his office, and his devotion to purely ecclesiastical literature, have weaned him so completely from his first literary love.

[1] The reader will find a notice of Bishop Berkeley, with extracts from his writings, in vol. i. p. 205 of the *Cabinet*.—ED.

It is equally to be regretted that his poems are not to be found collected in accessible form. The only volume in which his poetic writings have ever been bound together took the shape of *Specimens*, published in obedience to the demands of a special occasion, and, of course, now visible to the eye only of research.

Dr. Alexander, in 1853, wrote the ode in honour of the late Lord Derby's installation; and, in 1860, gained the Sacred Prize Poem with "The Waters of Babylon." In 1867 he was a candidate for the professorship of poetry in Oxford; he was defeated by Sir F. H. Doyle after a close contest.

Silent as a poet, Dr. Alexander is eminent as a pulpit orator; and there are few preachers of his Church who have such a power of poetic imagery and graceful expression. He is also a frequent contributor to ecclesiastic literature, the most noticeable of his works being *Witness of the Psalms to Christ and Christianity*, which formed the Bampton Lectures for 1876.

In 1849 Dr. Alexander married Miss Cecil Frances Humphreys, who has since acquired a very wide-spread reputation as an authoress of sacred songs. Her works—*Moral Songs, Hymns for Children*, and *Poems on Old Testament Subjects*—have passed through forty or fifty editions. We give the best known and most popular of her poems—"The Burial of Moses"—the sonorous rhythm of which rises to the height even of the great subject.

Mr. Robert Jocelyn Alexander, the son of those distinguished parents, has already given proof of inheriting their gifts. In 1873 he was the winner of the Newdigate Prize Poem —his subject being "The Last of the Red Indians." In 1877 he was equally successful with a Sacred Prize Poem, "Ismail;" and he has also gained the Chancellor's Prize Essay in prose—the subject being, "The Influence of the Schoolmen upon Modern Literature." This work displays great originality of thought, and traces in an ingenious and interesting way some of the notions we usually consider of most modern invention to the now mouldy writings of the forgotten scribes in the old monasteries.]

DEATH OF AN ARCTIC HERO.

BY BISHOP ALEXANDER.

At last an orange band,
Set in a dawn of ashen gray,
To things that winter in that dreadful land
Told like a prophet, of the sun at hand;
And the light flickered, like an angel's sword,
This way and that athwart the dark fiord;
  And strangely-coloured fires
Played round magnificent cathedral spires,
Gladly by winter of the glacier built
With fretted shafts, by summer glory-tipped,
And darkness was unmuffled and was ripped
Like crape from heaven's jewelled hilt.
Oh, those grand depths on depths that look like
  Fate,
Awfully calm and uncompassionate;
Those nights that are but clasps, or rather say,
Bridges of silver flung from day to day;
That vault which deepens up, and endeth never,
  That sea of starlit sky,
Broadening and brightening to infinity,
Where nothing trembles, suffers, weeps for ever.
But still the ships were fast in the ice-field,
And while the midnight Arctic sun outwheeled,
Thicker and thicker did Death's shadows fall
On the calm forehead of the Admiral.
  Oh, Admiral! thou hadst a shrine
    Of silver, not from any earthly mine,
    Of silver ice divine—
A sacrament, but not of bread and wine.
Thou hadst the Book, the stars, in whose broad
  skies
Are truths, and silences, and mysteries—
The love, which whoso loveth, never dies.
  Brave hearts! he cannot stay:
Only at home ye will be sure to say
How he hath wrought, and sought, and found—
  found what?
The bourne whence traveller returneth not!—
Ah, no! 'tis only that his spirit high
Hath gone upon a new discovery,
A marvellous passage on a sea unbounded,
Blown by God's gentle breath;
But that the white sail of his soul hath rounded
The promontory—Death!

. . . . .

How shall we bury him?
Where shall we leave the old man lying?
With music in the distance dying—dying,
Among the arches of the Abbey grand and dim,
There if we might, we would bury him;
And comrades of the sea should bear the pall;
And the great organ should let rise and fall
The requiem of Mozart, the Dead March in Saul—
  Then, silence all!
And yet far grandlier will we bury him.
Strike the ship-bell slowly—slowly—slowly!
Sailors! trail the colours half-mast high;
Leave him in the face of God most holy,
Underneath the vault of Arctic sky.
Let the long, long darkness wrap him round,
By the long sunlight be his forehead crown'd.
For cathedral panes ablaze with stories,
For the tapers in the nave and choir,

Give him lights auroral—give him glories,
Mingled of the rose and of the fire.
Let the wild winds, like chief mourners, walk,
Let the stars burn o'er his catafalque.
Hush! for the breeze, and the white fog's swathing
    sweep,
I cannot hear the simple service read,
Was it "earth to earth," the captain said,
Or "we commit his body to the deep,
Till seas give up their dead?"

BELOW AND ABOVE.

BY BISHOP ALEXANDER.

Down below, the wild November whistling
Through the beech's dome of burning red,
And the Autumn sprinkling penitential
Dust and ashes on the chestnut's head.

Down below, a pall of airy purple,
Darkly hanging from the mountain side,
And the sunset from his eyebrow staring
O'er the long roll of the leaden tide.

Up above, the tree with leaf unfading
By the everlasting river's brink,
And the sea of glass, beyond whose margin
Never yet the sun was known to sink.

Down below, the white wings of the sea-bird,
Dash'd across the furrows dark with mould,
Flitting with the memories of our childhood
Through the trees now waxen pale and old.

Down below, imaginations quivering
Through our human spirits like the wind,
Thoughts that toss like leaves about the woodland,
Hopes like sea-birds flash'd across the mind.

Up above, the host no man can number,
In white robes, a palm in every hand;
Each some work sublime for ever working,
In the spacious tracts of that great land.

Up above, the thoughts that know not anguish,
Tender care, sweet love for us below,
Noble pity free from anxious terror,
Larger love without a touch of woe.

Down below, a sad mysterious music,
Wailing through the woods and on the shore,
Burthen'd with a grand majestic secret
That keeps sweeping from us evermore.

Up above, a music that entwineth,
With eternal threads of golden sound,
The great poem of this strange existence,
All whose wondrous meaning hath been found.

Down below, the church to whose poor window
Glory by the autumnal trees is lent,
And a knot of worshippers in mourning,
Missing some one at the Sacrament.

Up above, the burst of Hallelujah,
And (without the sacramental mist
Wrapt around us like a sunlit halo)
The great vision of the face of Christ.

Down below, cold sunlight on the tombstones,
And the green wet turf with faded flowers;
Winter roses, once like young hopes burning,
Now beneath the ivy dripp'd with showers,

And the new-made grave within the churchyard,
And the white cap on that young face pale,
And the watcher, ever as it dusketh,
Rocking to and fro with that long wail.

Up above, a crown'd and happy spirit,
Like an infant in the eternal years,
Who shall grow in love and light for ever,
Order'd in his place among his peers.

O the sobbing of the winds of Autumn,
And the sunset streak of stormy gold,
And the poor heart, thinking in the churchyard,
"Night is coming, and the grave is cold."

O the pale, and plash'd, and sodden roses,
And the desolate heart that grave above,
And the white cap shaking as it darkens
Round that shrine of memory and love.

O the rest for ever, and the rapture,
And the hand that wipes the tears away;
And the golden homes beyond the sunset,
And the hope that watches o'er the clay!

THE BURIAL OF MOSES.

BY MRS. ALEXANDER.

By Nebo's lonely mountain, on this side Jordan's
    wave,
In a vale, in the land of Moab there lies a lonely
    grave;
And no man knows that sepulchre, and no man
    saw it e'er;
For, the angels of God upturned the sod, and laid
    the dead man there.

That was the grandest funeral that ever passed on
    earth;
But no man heard the trampling, or saw the train
    go forth—
Noiselessly, as the Daylight comes back when
    Night is done,
And the crimson streak on ocean's cheek grows
    into the great sun.

Noiselessly, as the spring-time her crown of verdure weaves,
And all the trees on all the hills open their thousand leaves;
So, without sound of music, or voice of them that
  wept,
Silently down from the mountain's crown, the
  great procession swept.

Perchance the bald old eagle, on gray Beth-Peor's
  height,
Out of his lonely eyrie, looked on the wondrous
  sight;
Perchance the lion stalking still shuns that hallowed spot,
For, beast and bird have seen and heard that
  which man knoweth not!

But when the Warrior dieth, his comrades in the
  war,
With arms reversed and muffled drum, follow his
  funeral car;
They show the banners taken, they tell his battles
  won,
And after him lead his masterless steed, while
  peals the minute-gun.

Amid the noblest of the land we lay the Sage to
  rest,
And give the Bard an honoured place, with costly
  marble drest,—
In the great minster transept, where lights like
  glories fall,
And the organ rings, and the sweet choir sings,
  along the emblazoned wall.

This was the truest warrior that ever buckled
  sword;
This the most gifted poet that ever breathed a
  word;
And never earth's philosopher traced with his
  golden pen,
On the deathless page, truths half so sage as he
  wrote down for men.

And had he not high honour,—the hill-side for a
  pall?
To lie in state, while angels wait, with stars for
  tapers tall?
And the dark rock-pines, like tossing plumes, over
  his bier to wave!
And God's own hand, in that lonely land, to lay
  him in the grave!

In that strange grave without a name,—whence
  his uncoffined clay
Shall break again, O wondrous thought! before
  the judgment-day,
And stand, with glory wrapt around, on the hills
  he never trod,
And speak of the strife that won our life, with the
  incarnate Son of God.

O lonely grave in Moab's land! O dark Beth-Peor's
  hill!
Speak to these curious hearts of ours, and teach
  them to be still.
God hath his mysteries of grace, ways that we
  cannot tell;
He hides them deep, like the hidden sleep of him
  he loved so well!

FRANCIS DAVIS.

[Francis Davis, "the Belfast Man," was born in Ballincollig, county Cork, on March 7, 1810. His father, formerly a respectable farmer, had through folly enlisted in the army, and his mother, descended from a Highland Scotch family, was a woman of great intellectual and moral strength. To her the boy owed the first development of his natural gifts, and in her he was to a great extent compensated for the loss of those social advantages caused by the unfortunate position of his other parent. In the deepest poverty she inspired her son with a love for noble thoughts in verse, and to her may be attributed that manly independence and truthful character which have distinguished Mr. Davis throughout his long life. Of this best of friends he was bereaved when but twelve years old, and was consigned by his father to the care of a rich but miserly relative, from whom he well earned board and shelter. In the meantime his father died, and the boy, unable longer to endure the hard treatment of his guardian, was received by a small farmer, who eked out a scanty subsistence by working at the loom. Francis, anxious to free himself from the galling dependence which he had endured, soon became a skilled weaver. He then settled in Belfast, and "as the weaver plied his shuttle, wove he too the mystic rhyme." The agitation for Catholic Emancipation provided the youthful poet with a theme for many songs and ballads, which were sung in the streets of Irish towns, and did undoubted service to the cause.

About 1830 Davis travelled through England and Scotland, earning his living by his trade as he went, and writing poems all the while, studying at the same time French, Greek, Latin, and Gaelic. During this period also he contributed to the *Nation* newspaper and to various periodicals, spending some years in Manchester. Returning to Belfast in 1845, he resumed his toil; but his fame had preceded him, and he left the loom to edit the *Belfastman's Journal*. He then engaged in literary work for a Belfast firm, also contributing to several magazines and journals. He was elected successively to the positions of librarian in the People's Institute and assistant registrar in Queen's College. His poetical works are *The Tablet of Shadows, The Lispings of the Lagan, Earlier and Later Leaves, or an Autumn Gathering*, and several love poems and patriotic songs.]

CASTE AND CREED.[1]

Come, man! your hand, a brother sings,
  Or silken be't or sergy;
The wars of nations leave to kings,
  And those of creeds to clergy;
And taste with us that grand sublime
  Which zests your every other,
By holding man, whate'er his clime,
    His caste or creed, a *brother!*
      May all who'd sow opposing views,
        Their harvests find tremendous,
      While, oh, from such, and from their dues,
        The Lord of love defend us!

What, though the waves should walk the air,
  Betwixt each earthly acre;
What, though each hill a differing pray'r
  Should offer to its Maker;
Do these make men the less akin,
  Or pleas for hate and slaughter?
If so, whate'er the weight of sin,
  It lies with hills and water!
    Ah, if, indeed, ye hold a creed,
      That Conscience calls a high one,
    Then hold it for your spirit's need,
      And not a scourge for my one!

We've fair—we're foul in every clime,
  In every creed and calling;
We've men to sport their chaff sublime
  O'er every feather's falling;
We've men of straw, of stick, of stone;
  We've soul whose savour such is

---

[1] By permission of the author.

If, loathing virtue—*blood* and *bone*,
  Adores the *ghost* on crutches!
    Ah, Virtue, ever in our throats,
      Much wear and tear attend thee!
    For wear thou wilt, as wear our coats,
      But, faith, 'tis worse to mend thee!

Still wherefore make the wordy moan
  O'er ills that mayn't be mended—
Where *will's* so weak that thousands groan
  In guilt they ne'er intended?
Our own poor mite of righteous ways,
  Let's hold from frost and ferment—
But not for crowds or stated days,
  Like Save-all's Sabbath garment!
    Let's clear our light to *show* the right—
      To aid in its extending;
    And loathe the bile would green the sight,
      O'er *any* Worth's ascending!

My *neighbour's* weal is weal to *me*,
  If reared not on my ruin!
And though for what I feel or be,
  He'd care no more than Bruin,
I'd say, *enjoy* your silken share—
  Yea! as I hope for Heaven;
For Coin and Care a wedded pair
  Are six times out of seven!
    Miss Fortune trips a painted porch,
      Too oft in slippery sandal,
    Where coldlier glares her gilded torch,
      Than Misery's farthing candle!

Then creeds and classes, To-or-Fro—
  Thy smile with each, my brother!
We must have sun, and shade, and snow—
  They'll *come* to aid each other!
Let matter, too, enjoy its grades,
  Nor deem it an unsound thing—
'Twere just as wise to measure blades,
  Because the world's a round thing!
    We *must* have low—we *must* have high,
      And *many* a niche between them;
    The *height* may be a tinselled lie—
      The *men* are what's within them!

And mark me, men, a day shall dawn
  When neither serge nor ermine,
Nor clime nor class shall make the man—
  Nor creed nor worth determine;
'Twill come—'twill come—and come to *stand*—
  The caste of LOVE-LIGHT STATURE,
When Love alone, where'er your land,
  Shall tell the *who*, and *what* you're!
    God send it soon, in peace—in might,
      God guide its rear and vanguard;
    Hurra for Love! for Light! for Right!
      The mind, and moral standard!

Then, brother man, if all agreed,
  Though live we mayn't to *see* such,

Let's tack this trifle to our creed,
 And chant a long "So *be* such!"
All knavish souls, or high or low,
 May conscience-cuffs distress them;
But honest hearts, where'er they grow,
 The King of Kingdoms bless them!
  May all who hold a sicklier thought,
   Hold *bitters*, too, to mend it;
  But bless, O Heaven, the better taught—
   Their teaching, Lord, defend it!

MY KALLAGH DHU ASTHORE.

Again the flowery feet of June
 Have tracked our cottage side;
And o'er the waves the timid moon
 Steals, smiling like a bride:
But what were June or flowers to me,
 Or waves, or moon, or more,
If evening came and brought not thee,
 My Kallagh dhu asthore!

Let others prize their lordly lands,
 And sceptres gemmed with blood;
More dear to me the honest hands
 That earn my babes their food:
And little reck we queens or kings
 When daily labour's o'er;
And by the evening embers sings
 My Kallagh dhu asthore!

And when he sings, his every song
 Is sacred freedom's own:
And like his voice his arm is strong,
 For labour nursed the bone:
And then his step, and such an eye!
 Ah, fancy! touch no more;
My spirit swims, in holy joy,
 O'er Kallagh dhu asthore!

His voice is firm, his knee is proud,
 When pomp's imperious tone
Would have the free-born spirit bowed,
 That right should bow alone;
For well does Kallagh know his due,
 Nor ever seeks he more;
Would Heaven mankind were all like you,
 My Kallagh dhu asthore!

And Kallagh is an Irishman
 In sinew, soul, or bone;
Not e'en the veins of old Slieveben
 Are purer than his own;
The wing of woe has swept our skies,
 The foreign foe our shore,
But stain or change thy race defies,
 My Kallagh dhu as'hore!

What wonder, then, each word he said
 Fell o'er my maiden day,
Like breathings o'er the cradle bed
 Where mothers kiss and pray;
Though dear your form, your cheek, and eye,
 I loved those virtues more,
Whose bloom nor ills nor years destroy,
 My Kallagh dhu asthore!

Oh could this heart, this throbbing thing,
 Be made a regal chair,
I'd rend its every swelling string,
 To seat you, Kallagh, there;
And oh, if honest worth alone
 The kingly bauble bore,
No slave wert thou, my blood, my bone,
 My Kallagh dhu asthore!

ONLY A FANCY.

Hast thou ever known a flower
 Which, when years had bustled by,
Flashed again upon thy dreamings—
 Dreaming 'neath a darker sky—
Till its phantom light and fragrance
 Forced a moisture from thine eye,
 As are those beloved faces,
 Filling long-deserted places
In thy wakening memory?

Heaven help me, I am weary—
 Ah, *how* weary can be known
To the Love that never sleepeth—
 The Almighty love alone—
As I climb my silent towers—
 Towers not of brick or stone—
 Towers whose aërial porches,
 Lit by Fancy's thousand torches,
Often flee beneath my moan!

Yet, I love my shadowy castles—
 Ah, they're all the world to me!
Where, if limbs be weak and shackled,
 All the soul is strong and free—
Free to build, and gild and glory,
 In her might a queen to be,
Even while her home, more lowly,
'Mongst the wreck of things unholy,
She can, downward looking, see!

Thus I walked a moonlight garden
 By my towers of the night,
With, at every side, a shadow
 On my left and on my right;
They were spirits, good and evil,
 One was dark and one was bright,
 As is soul in infant faces,
 Or as, in Day's death-embraces,
Blusheth heaven's feathery white!

There were flowers young and many,
　Glowing, glistening, here and there,
As when o'er the dews of summer,
　Morning floats her golden hair;
While one spirit urged my culling—
　'Twas the *dark* one, *not* the fair—
　　Till my full heart's solemn heavings,
　　Bounding hopes, and lame misgivings,
　Rose like voices on the air!

For, though beauties never, never,
　Burst the teeming earth like these,
They were mingled, good and evil—
　Body's health, and soul's disease,
Holding, in their fieriest splendour,
　What the fieriest truth might freeze;
　　So, I sighed, and whispered meekly:
　　"Nay, my eyes are dim and weakly,
　And I know not which *should* please!"

Then the fairer spirit caught me,
　And I wandered where she led,
While the *darker* followed, chiding,
　Though I knew not what she said;
Till a lake there gleamed beneath me,
　Like the round moon overhead;
　　Green its banks, and flower-besprinkled,
　　Then I sat, and songlets tinkled
　O'er each trefoil round us spread!

Leaves I wove in links together,
　Doing what I did not know,
Till the fairer spirit's fingers—
　Pencils—things of tinted snow—
Caught my wreath, and while they strewed it,
　"Little sweets," she murmured, "go,
　　Root along the coming hours,
　　Seeds are ye of many flowers,
　Which from out the winds shall grow!"

DION BOUCICAULT.

[Dion Boucicault was born in Dublin on December 26, 1822. He was brought up under the guardianship of Dr. Dionysius Lardner, whose life and writings we have noticed in vol. iii. Boucicault had scarcely reached his majority when he produced the play of *London Assurance*, which was brought out at Covent Garden in March, 1841. It was enormously successful, has since remained a stock piece on the stage, and is perhaps the best of all his works. From that time forward Mr. Boucicault has been constantly before the public, either as author, actor, or theatrical manager, and frequently in the combined character of the three. He has written upwards of fifty pieces. In most of these he has been indebted to some other author for his story, but that does not take away from him the merit of having used his materials with great skill. Most of his works are a singular mixture of merits and defects. He possesses unquestionably wit, skill in describing character, and marvellous ingenuity in stage effects. On the other hand, he depends for a great part of his success on the aid of the stage carpenter, and his plays, when they come to be read, appear very poor in comparison with the impression they produce on the stage. Among his chief pieces may be mentioned *London Assurance*, already referred to, the *Colleen Bawn*, the *Octoroon*, *Old Heads and Young Hearts*, *Janet Pride*, *The Corsican Brothers*, *Louis XI.*, and *The Shaughraun*. Since 1876 Mr. Boucicault has lived in New York, where he has brought out several pieces, some of which have appeared on the London stage.]

THE MAN OF FASHION IN THE COUNTRY.

(FROM "LONDON ASSURANCE.")

[Sir Harcourt Courtly is a London man of fashion: Charles is his son, a wild-going scapegrace: Max Harkaway is a country gentleman: Grace, his niece, is intended for Sir Harcourt: Meddle is a rural attorney, Dazzle a town adventurer, and Cool Sir Harcourt's servant.]

Enter MAX *and* SIR HARCOURT.

Max. Here we are at last. Now give ye welcome to Oak Hall, Sir Harcourt, heartily.

Sir H. (*Languidly.*) Cool, assist me. (*Cool takes off his furred cloak, gloves; gives him white gloves and a white handkerchief, then places a flower in his coat.*)

Max. Why, you require unpacking as carefully as my best bin of port. Well, now you are decanted, tell me what did you think of my park as we came along?

Sir H. That it would never come to an end. You said it was only a stone's throw from your infernal lodge to the house; why it's ten miles at least.

Max. I'll do it in ten minutes any day.

Sir H. Yes, in a steam-carriage. Cool, perfume my handkerchief.

Max. Don't do it. Don't! perfume in the country! why it's high treason in the very face of Nature; 'tis introducing the robbed to the robber. Here are the sweets from which your fulsome essences are pilfered, and libelled with their names,—don't insult them too.

Sir H. (To Meddle, who is by a rose-bush.) Oh! cull me a bouquet, my man!

Max. (Turning.) Ah, Meddle! how are you? This is Lawyer Meddle.

Sir H. Oh! I took him for one of your people.

Meddle. Ah! naturally—um—Sir Harcourt Courtly, I have the honour to congratulate—happy occasion approaches. Ahem! I have no hesitation in saying this *very* happy occasion approaches.

Sir H. Cool, is the conversation addressed towards me?

Cool. I believe so, Sir Harcourt.

Meddle. Oh, certainly! I was complimenting you.

Sir H. Sir, you are very good: the honour is undeserved; but I am only in the habit of receiving compliments from the fairsex. Men's admiration is so d——ably insipid. *(Crosses to Max, who is seated on a bench.)* If the future Lady Courtly be visible at so unfashionable an hour as this, I shall beg to be introduced.

Max. Visible! Ever since six this morning.—I'll warrant ye. Two to one she is at dinner.

Sir H. Dinner! Is it possible! Lady Courtly dine at half-past one P.M.!

Meddle. I rather prefer that hour to peck a little my——

Sir H. Dear me! who was addressing you?

Meddle. Oh! I beg pardon.

Max. Here, James! *(Calling.)*

Enter JAMES.

Tell Miss Grace to come here directly.

[*Exit James.*

Now prepare, Courtly, for, though I say it, she is—with the exception of my bay mare Kitty—the handsomest thing in the country. Considering she is a biped she is a wonder! Full of blood, sound wind and limb, plenty of bone, sweet coat, in fine condition, with a thorough-bred step, as dainty as a pet greyhound.

Sir H. Don't compare her to a horse.

Max. Well, I wouldn't, but she's almost as fine a creature,—close similarities.

Meddle. Oh, very fine creature! Close similarity amounting to identity.

Sir H. Good gracious, sir! What can a lawyer know about woman?

Meddle. Everything. The consistorial court is fine study of the character, and I have no hesitation in saying that I have examined more women than Jenks or——

Sir H. Oh, d—— Jenks!

Meddle. Sir, thank you.

Enter GRACE.

Grace. (Runs to him.) My dear uncle!

Max. Ah, Grace! you little jade, come here.

Sir H. (Eyeing her through his glass.) Oh, dear! she is a rural Venus! I'm astonished and delighted.

Max. Won't you kiss your old uncle? *(He kisses her.)*

Sir H. (Draws an agonizing face.) Oh!—ah—um!—*N'importe!* my privilege in embryo—hem! It's very tantalizing though.

Max. You are not glad to see me, you are not. *(Kissing her.)*

Sir H. Oh! no, no, *(aside)* that is too much. I shall do something horrible presently if this goes on. *(Aloud.)* I should be sorry to curtail any little ebullition of affection; but—ahem! May I be permitted?

Max. Of course you may. There, Grace, is Sir Harcourt, your husband that will be. Go to him, girl. *(She curtseys.)*

Sir H. Permit me to do homage to the charms, the presence of which have placed me in sight of paradise.

(Sir Harcourt and Grace retire.)

Enter DAZZLE.

Dazzle. Ah! old fellow, how are you? *(Crosses to him.)*

Max. I'm glad to see you! are you comfortably quartered yet, eh?

Dazzle. Splendidly quartered! What a place you've got here! Why it's a palace. Here, Hamilton.

Enter CHARLES COURTLY. COOL *sees him and looks astonished.*

Permit me to introduce my friend, Augustus Hamilton. *(Aside.)* Capital fellow! drinks like a sieve, and rides like a thunder-storm.

Max. (Crosses.) Sir, I'm devilish glad to see you. Here, Sir Harcourt, permit me to introduce to you—— (*Goes up stage to Sir Harcourt.*)

Courtly. The devil!

Dazzle. (*Aside.*) What's the matter?

Courtly. (*Aside.*) Why, that is my governor, by Jupiter!

Dazzle. (*Aside.*) What, old Whiskers! you don't say that!

Courtly. (*Aside.*) It is! what's to be done now?

Dazzle. Oh, I don't know.

Max. (*Advancing.*) Mr. Hamilton, Sir Harcourt Courtly—Sir Harcourt Courtly, Mr. Hamilton.

Sir H. (*Advancing.*) Hamilton! Good gracious! bless me—why, Charles, is it possible!—why, Max, that's my son!

Max. Your son!

Grace. Your son, Sir Harcourt! have you a son as old as that gentleman?

Sir H. No—that is—a—yes,—not by twenty years—a—Charles, why don't you answer me, sir?

Courtly. (*Aside to Dazzle.*) What shall I say?

Dazzle. (*Aside.*) Deny your identity.

Courtly. (*Aside.*) Capital!—(*Pause—they look at each other—aloud.*) What's the matter, sir?

Sir H. How came you down here, sir?

Courtly. By one of Newman's best fours—in twelve hours and a quarter.

Sir H. Isn't your name Charles Courtly?

Courtly. Not to my knowledge.

Sir H. Do you mean to say you are usually called Augustus Hamilton?

Courtly. Lamentable fact—and quite correct.

Dazzle. How very odd!

Sir H. Well, I never—Cool, is that my son?

Cool. No, sir—that is not Mr. Charles—but is *very* like him.

Max. I cannot understand all this. ⎰ (*Go up a*

Grace. (*Aside.*) I think I can. ⎱ *little.*)

Dazzle. (*Aside to Courtly.*) Give him a touch of the indignant.

Courtly. (*Crosses.*) Allow me to say what, Sir What-d'ye-call'em—Carthorse Hartly?

Dazzle. Sir Walker Cartly.

Sir H. Hartly, sir! Courtly, sir. Courtly!

Courtly. Well, Hartley, or Court-heart, or whatever your name may be, I say your conduct is—a—a—, and was it not for the presence of this lady, I should feel inclined—to—to——.

Sir H. No, no, that can't be my son,—he never would address me in that way.——Sir, your likeness to my son Charles is so astonishing, that it for a moment—the equilibrium of my etiquette—'pon my life I—permit me to request your pardon.

Meddle. Sir Harcourt, don't apologize, don't—bring an action. I'm witness.

Sir H. Some one take this man away. (*Meddle goes up the stage with Cool.*)

Enter JAMES.

James. Luncheon is on the table, sir.

Sir H. Miss Harkaway, I never swore before a lady in my life—except when I promised to love and cherish the late Lady Courtly, which I took care to preface with an apology, —I was compelled to the ceremony, and consequently not answerable for the language—but to that gentleman's identity I would have pledged—my hair.

Grace. (*Aside.*) If that security were called for, I suspect the answer would be—no effects.

[*Exit Sir Harcourt and Grace.*

Meddle. (*To Max.*) I have something very particular to communicate.

Max. Can't listen at present. [*Exit.*

Meddle. (*To Dazzle and Courtly.*) I can afford you information which I—

Dazzle. Oh, don't bother! ⎰

Courtly. Go to the devil! ⎱ [*Exeunt.*

Meddle. Now, I have no hesitation in saying that is the height of ingratitude. Oh—Mr. Cool—can you oblige me. (*Presents his account.*)

Cool. Why, what is all this?

Meddle. Small account *versus* you—to giving information concerning the last census of the population of Oldborough and vicinity, six-and-eightpence.

Cool. Oh, you mean to make me pay this, do you?

Meddle. Unconditionally.

Cool. Well, I have no objection—the charge is fair—but remember, I am a servant on board wages,—will you throw in a little advice gratis—if I give you the money.

Meddle. Ahem! I will.

Cool. A fellow has insulted me. I want to abuse him—what terms are actionable?

Meddle. You may call him anything you please, providing there are no witnesses.

Cool. Oh, may I? (*Looks round.*) Then—you rascally pettifogging scoundrel!

Meddle. Hallo! (*Retreats.*)

Cool. (*Following him.*) You mean—dirty—disgrace to your profession.

Meddle. Libel—slander——

Cool. (*Going up, turns.*) Aye, but where are your witnesses?

Meddle. Give me the costs— six-and-eight-pence.

Cool. I deny that you gave me information at all.

Meddle. You do?

Cool. Yes, where are your witnesses?
[*Exit.*

Meddle. Ah—damme! I'm done at last!
[*Exit.*

ORIGIN OF "THE SHAUGHRAUN."

A SKETCH FROM LIFE.

"George, it is five o'clock! Let us get away from the course before the crowd of carriages encumber the road. Recollect, we must reach Dublin by half-past six."

We were at Punchestown races, and I was announced to play the same evening in the "Colleen Bawn" at the Theatre Royal, Dublin.

"She can do it," said George D——, as he fondly patted the sleek coat of his mare, a splendid specimen of an Irish hunter, from whose quarters he had just slipped the rug. "I'll bet three pounds to one we are in College Green at six twenty."

"I'd like to take that, yer honour," said a low, sweet voice, that seemed to come from under the animal.

"Ha! is that yourself, Jack," said George, as he jumped into the dog-cart and gathered up the reins. "Do you think the mare cannot do it? You ought to know her better! She brought us down this morning in eighty-five minutes, and the whip never left the socket."

"Then she'll not go back in three hours this night, barrin' she goes by rail," said the man, rising from the stooping posture and standing back as he looked at the beast's near foreleg.

He was a lithe boy of some twenty years, dressed in a ragged scarlet coat, and an old black hunting cap, the cast-off suit of some whipper-in. One leg boasted a top-boot, on which a rusty spur was tied about his heel with a "taste of cord." On the other leg was the remainder of a Wellington boot. His breeches were like Joseph's coat of many colours; waistcoat and shirt he had none. The attire, pulled anyway about him, could not conceal one of those model shapes that Ireland alone contributes to the light cavalry of the English army. Broad in the shoulders, thin in the flank, his frame is what is vulgarly called "herring-gutted;" very long in the arms; the hips, when seen in profile, were broad, but narrow when seen in front; height, five-feet eight; weight, 150 pounds, and not an ounce of fat at that, all bone and sinew. Under a shock of brown hair a broad beaming face defied delineation, for the features were constantly on the move. A mouth vigorous, large, full of gleaming teeth, seemed shrewd and mischievous, over which two blue eyes, under long, black brows, were like limpid wells of good nature and fun.

"What's the matter with her leg, Jack?"

"Tisn't in the leg, yer honour, it's in the near fore fut. I watched her favourin' this whole day, and more betoken, it's hot as blazes round the coronet. I'm afeard, Master George, the crature has a touch o' the vickular."

"A touch of the navicular! Pooh! A touch of your grandmother! What do you know about it?"

"I know why the gintleman wants to get back to Dublin so airly, God bless him," he added, touching his ragged cap. "Wasn't I in the gallery of the Royal last Saturday, and I seen him fish the 'Colleen Bawn' out of the water. Whoo! It bates Banagher! Gorra, but I'd like to have a"— here he made a plunge at the earth, and turning what is called "a wheel," bounded lightly on his feet with a yell. The mare sprang on one side, and rose into the air, while George uttered a volley of imprecations upon my admirer's voluble athletics.

I threw the fellow half a sovereign, and the look of amazement and the parting gleam of gratitude that he shared between the coin and me was worth the money.

"Confound the fool!" said my companion, as the animal plunged forward. "I nearly broke a trace. So! Jenny, so! What's the matter with you?" The mare was cantering, and he tried to shape her down to a trot.

"That was a queer figure," said I.

"He is well known about here," replied George D——; "he's called Cantering Jack. There's not a fair or a race or a wedding, or any other public or private 'diversion,' at which Jack is not to be found. Two years ago he rode this mare for me. (So, Jenny.) She was entered for the —— stakes, a steeple-chase, and won me five hundred pounds. The scoundrel rides like a monkey, and has the light hand of a child."

"Why is he called Cantering Jack?"

"He lives under a hedge, and when he spies a carriage full of 'grandees,' Jack unstrings his fiddle, receives them with a wild dance, and will follow the carriage for miles, never failing to get sixpence sooner or later from the party. I have known him to run behind a dog-cart for twelve or fifteen miles, and never turn a hair or lose breath."

By this time we had left the main road to avoid the vehicles, and had entered a side lane by which George D—— assured me the distance to Dublin was nearly a mile shorter than by the highway. After pursuing these lanes for nearly twenty minutes, the mare that had never settled down to a square trot, began to show the cause of her uneasiness. George brought her to a standstill, and after resting her a minute, started her at a walk. There remained no doubt the animal was lame. He got down to examine the leg, while I held the reins. After a few moments he went a score of yards ahead, and asked me to drive her gently toward him. I did so, and he leaped up beside me.

"She has strained her fetlock; we must go quietly; this is very unfortunate."

I did not like to add my anxiety to his annoyance, so I held my tongue, and began to measure anxiously the distance to the theatre, and the dismal consequences of arriving late. The lord-lieutenant had given a "command" on that night, and that means he was coming in state, with his court, in gala uniform, and escorted by a troop of cavalry. On such occasions all Dublin turns out, and every available seat in the theatre is filled. I recollected the *j'ai failli attendre* of Louis XIV., and felt proportionately uncomfortable. The brave beast struggled with her pain, but at last, and rather suddenly, as if she had concealed its acuteness, she broke down to a walk. Darkness had set in, and the last milestone said sixteen miles still lay between us and the city. We were miles from the turnpike, where I might have picked up some conveyance, or found a good-natured party returning home, who would give me a lift. I looked at my watch—it wanted twelve minutes to six.

"Could I hire a horse from one of the farmers in the neighbourhood? Do you know where we are? Who lives near this place?"

"I have no idea," replied my companion, so dejectedly I had not the heart to exhibit my despair. Darkness was increasing, and the first drops of rain began to patter on the leaves above us. "I do not know where we are or what to do. I'm fairly at my wit's end."

The hedge that topped the bank skirting the road was divided above our heads, and a dark form bounded across the ditch, and Cantering Jack alighted beside us.

"Long life to your honours. I was afraid the craythur might not last. You are not angry, sir, bekase I kep an eye on ye," said he, apologizing to George for his presence.

"Don't stop to explain," he replied testily. "My friend must reach Dublin in fifty minutes. You know every foot of the road and every quadruped in the county. Can it be done? Can you 'beg, borrow, or steal' a horse that will carry him to town?"

Jack ran his fingers under his ragged cap to scratch his head.

"Well, to be sure," said he, after a moment's hesitation, "there's only one chance."

"Make it a certainty, Jack," I cried, "and I'll give you a five-pound note."

"I'll thry, anyway," said the boy; "take off her harness quick, while I'm off to see what's to be done;" and he disappeared in the gloom.

We stripped the mare and lighted the lamps of the dog-cart, and then, having no more to say nor else to do, we lighted cigars and waited.

The condemned felon on the morning of his execution, listening for the approaching footsteps of his executioner, never strained his ears more anxiously than we stretched ours. Hope wanted four footsteps. Fear dreaded two. Hark! Minute after minute passed and seemed like hours. Hark! patter! patter! brush! a pause—a gate swings opens and closes to.

"He has found a horse!" cried George. "If he had been alone he would have vaulted that gate and never stopped to open it. Here he comes!"

Up the lane he came, leading a horse by the forelock.

"Quick, now, for the love o' God. Slip the harness on him; gi' me the headstall; aisy wid them breechings, he is lively wid his heels."

While Jack and I clothed the horse, the mare standing patiently by and thankfully quiet, George D—— took out one of the lamps to light our labours.

"Good heavens, Jack! why I cannot be deceived. It is Mal"———

"Whisht, if ye plase, sir. I made an oath to meself I'd land his honour there in Dublin before Misther Lavey would dhrop the flag to the fiddlers, and begorra I'll be good as the word."

George stood agape as Jack ran the light dog-cart shafts over the flanks of the horse, who shivered as he was tucked in and buckled to. Seizing the reins, Jack leaped to the driver's seat, and I sprang up beside him.

"Whew!" he uttered a low whistle, and the

horse, with a snort and a plunge, went forward like a rocket. "Hould fast now," cried the lad, as the animal went at a headlong gallop down the lane, leaving George with the lamp in his hand—his pale face was the last thing I remember. For four or five miles we flew, swung around corners with the off-wheel in the air, speechless and almost breathless, guided by the light of the single lamp. We passed the gates of a park, at which a group of people were standing, some on horseback, some on foot. Their faces passed us like a flash. Another mile or two and Jack began to speak in a low voice to the horse. But the brute only shook his head, and the dog-cart quivered. Again the soft voice wheedled the horse, and his gallop relaxed to a canter.

"Ah, ye vagabone! ye ould thief o' the world! d'ye hear me talkin' to ye? Aisy, now, sure nobody wants to hurt the likes of ye. The Lord bless every bone in your skin."

The canter settled down to a trot as we mounted a hill, from the top of which we saw the gaslights of Dublin sparkling in the distance. Then I drew a breath. By the light of my cigar I looked at my watch—it wanted thirty-three minutes to seven—we had done between eleven and twelve miles in under forty minutes. The horse was now tolerably quiet, settled down to work.

"Now we are all right," said I, as we turned into the broad turnpike road, bordered by gas-lamps and tolerably clear of vehicles.

"Hould fast—he has never trod the stones nor seen a street; he's not aisy in his mind—look at his ears," whispered Jack; "don't spake, sir, if you please; I don't want him to know that any one else but meself is behind him."

Jack was right, and all his soft voice and light hand could do, he barely kept the startled animal in the roadway; for he swerved in fright from right to left, and back again, as the brilliant glare of the shops startled him.

"Surely it is some time since he was in shafts?" I whispered.

"Bedad, your honour may say that, for to-night is the first time he ever felt a collar on him."

Instinctively I gripped the rail, and I think I must have turned, if not white, at least drab. But the cigar I had been smoking slipped from my mouth, while I began to calculate the number of corners we had to turn, and the width of the streets through which we had to pass on our road to College Green.

A roadside public-house had attracted a few outside cars before its door. As we approached it I saw the reins were tightening, and Jack was using all his power; but the bit was fast jammed between the teeth of the brute.

"Can you stop her? I'll take one of those cars," I said, as coolly as I could.

"Never fear, sir; I'll dhrive ye all the way."

"No, Jack, I prefer to release you now."

"All right, your honour," and with a quick jerk he sawed the bit in the horse's mouth and pulled him upon his haunches. I leaped out and ran to his head. Jack was soon by my side.

"Hold on to him awhile, sir. I'll pick you a man that will rowl you up to the Royal;" and he ran up to the group of drivers drinking at the door. Presently one of them jumped on to his car and came down to where I stood.

"Now, Reilly, help me to get this harness off."

The two men unloosed the harness, while Jack drew a "taste of a rope" out of his pocket, and quick as thought had thrown it into the shape of a halter over the horse's head.

"Now, Reilly," said he, "get the dog-cart and harness undher the shed beyant, and keep them dry until Misther George D—— will send for it: d'ye hear now?"

Reilly, aghast, was looking at the horse which Cantering Jack held by the halter.

"Holy Moses!" cried the man, "what baste is that you have been dhrivin'? It is Malfac"——

"Howld yer dirty whisht, if ye want the gintleman to give ye five shillin's for takin' him to the Royal in sixteen minutes."

I handed Jack the five-pound note. He uttered a blessing and swung himself on the horse's back. A demivolte and a clash of hoofs, a smothered yell, a million sparks of fire, and the horse and man disappeared in the gloom.

"Well, to be sure! Oh, murdher!" ejaculated the man, looking with open mouth after Jack. "Well! well! Egorra! That bates the world."

Beyond such exclamations my driver uttered not a word during our rapid course through the city, and as I entered the theatre I heard the first bars of the overture to the "Colleen Bawn," mingled with the shouts of the audience greeting the lord-lieutenant and his party.

. . . .

That night I supped with the aides-decamps of the viceregal party. During the repast my ear caught these words—"I lay three to two Malefactor comes in first or second." The speaker was Lord A——, a celebrated sporting nobleman.

"As I went down to the races this morning," remarked one of the party, "I stopped at the farm, and saw Malefactor in his paddock. He looked in splendid condition, fit to run for a man's life."

"Yes," replied Lord A——, "I gave 1200 guineas for him last spring, and I think he is greatly improved."

"Are you fond of horses, Mr. B——?" he continued, turning quietly to me. "I should like to show you my nags. The farm where they are stabled is only about fifteen miles from the city; quite a pleasant drive."

"I shall feel quite delighted," I replied as unconcernedly as I could.

Lord A—— never dreamed I had done those fifteen miles behind his 1200 guinea horse; for the suspicion I entertained then became a certainty—that Malefactor had been stolen for the job by Cantering Jack.

Such is the personage—he still exists—that furnished me with the character of Conn, the hero of the "Shaughraun."

FRANCES BROWNE.

[Miss Browne is one of the most remarkable examples of the victories which perseverance and strength of will can achieve over great physical and social obstacles. She was born in Stranorlar, county Donegal, on January 16, 1816. An attack of small-pox deprived her of eyesight in infancy, but as she grew up she managed to teach herself and to get others to teach her, and she had at an early age intimate acquaintance with the chief masters of English literature. Her father was but a village postmaster, and she had to seek for a means of livelihood for herself. She began by sending a poem to the *Irish Penny Journal*, which was accepted. She next succeeded in obtaining admission to the *Athenæum*, *Hood's Magazine*, the *Keepsake*, and other periodicals. The editor of the first-named journal proved a warm friend of the struggling young poetess, and did much to call public attention to her works. In 1844 she ventured on the publication of a collection of her poems, under the title *The Star of Atteghei, the Vision of Schwartz, and other Poems*.

Miss Browne left Ireland in 1847, and has since resided either in Edinburgh or London. She has also written *Lyrics and Miscellaneous Poems*; *Legends of Ulster*; *The Ericksons*, a tale; *The Hidden Sin*, a novel (1866); and a sort of autobiography, entitled *My Share in the World* (1862). She enjoys a small pension from the civil list bestowed upon her by the late Sir Robert Peel. The poems of Miss Browne deserve attention altogether apart from the personal circumstances of the authoress. They are lucid in style, smooth in rhythm, and full of picturesque imagery.]

THE RETURNING JANISSARY.

There came a youth at dawn of day
From the Golden Gate of the proud Serai:—
He came with no gifts of warrior pride,
But the gleam of the good sword by his side,
  And an arm that well could wield;
But he came with a form of matchless mould—
Like that by the Delphian shrine of old—
And an eye in whose depth of brightness shone
The light by the Grecian sunset thrown
  On the dying Spartan's shield;—
For the days of his boyhood's bonds were o'er,
And he stood as a free-born Greek once more!

They brought him robes of the richest dyes,
And a shield like the moon in autumn skies,
A steed that grew by the Prophet's tomb,
And a helmet crown'd with a heron's plume,
  And the world's strong tempter—gold;
And they said—"Since thou turnest from the towers
Of honour's path and pleasure's bowers,
Go forth in the Spahi's conquering march—
And gold and glory requite thy search,
Till a warrior's death unfold
For thee the gates of Paradise,
And thy welcome beam'd by the Houris' eyes."—

"And where will the yearning memories sleep,
That have fill'd mine exiled years
With a voice of winds in the forest free,
With the sound of the old Ægean Sea,
Through echoing grove and green defile,
On the shores of that unforgotten isle
Which still the light of my mother's smile
  To her wanderer's memory wears—
And the voices ever sounding back
From my country's old triumphal track?

The faith that clings with a deathless hold
To the freedom and the fame of old,
Will they rest in a stranger's banner-shade,
   Though a conquering flag it be?
Will they joy with its myriad hosts to tread
   On a land that once was free?
Take back your gifts," the wanderer said—
   "And leave at last to me
That far land's love—for ye cannot part
His country from the exile's heart!"

They said—" Thine isle is a land of slaves;
It gives no galley to the waves—
No cry with the battle's onset blent—
No banner broad on its breezes sent—
   No name to the lists of fame;
Thy home still stands by its winding shore,
But thy place by the hearth is known no more;
The evening fire on that hearth shines on,
But the light of thy mother's smile is gone—
   For a stranger bears her name—
And, bright though her smile and glance may be,
They're not like those that grew dim for thee."—

" I know that my country's fame hath found
   No rest by her storied streams—
For cold is the chain for ages borne,
And deep is the track its weight hath worn!
The serf hath stood, in his fetters bound,
On hills that were freedom's battle-ground ;
And my name is a long-forgotten sound
   In the home of my thousand dreams ;—
For change hath passed o'er each household face,
And my mother's heart hath a resting-place
Where the years of her weary watch are past
For the step that so vainly comes at last.
But far there shines through the shadowy green
   Of the laurels bending there,
One beckoning light—'tis the glancing sheen
   Of a Grecian maiden's hair ;
Alas, for the clouds that rose between
   My gaze and one so fair !
Alas ! for many a morning ray
That passed from life's misty hills away !"

So spake the Greek, but the tempter said—
   "Why seek'st thou the flowers of summer fled ?—
The years that have made thy kindred strange
Have they not breathed with the breath of change
   On thine early chosen too?
They have bound the wealth of that flowing hair—
They have crossed the brow with a shade of care ;
For thy young and thy glad of heart hath grown
A matron, saddened in glance and tone—
   From whose undreaming view
Life's early lights have fallen—and thou
Art a long-forgotten vision now."

There rose a cloud in his clear dark eye,
   Like the mist of coming tears—

Yet it passed in silence, and there came
No after-voice from that perished dream :
But he said—" Is it so, my land ! Thou hast
No gift for thy wanderer but the past,
And a dream of a gathering trumpet's blast,
   And a charge of Grecian spears !
That bright dream's promise ne'er may be—
But the earth hath banners broad and free ;
There are gallant barks on the western wave—
And fields where a Greek may find a grave :
With a fearless arm, with a stainless brand,
   With a young brow I depart
To seek the hosts of some Christian land—
   But I go with an exile's heart.
Yet, oft when the stranger's fight is done,
And their shouts arise for the battle won,
This heart will dream what its joy might be
Were it won but for Greece and Liberty !"

THE LAST FRIENDS.[1]

I come to my country, but not with the hope
   That brightened my youth like the cloud-lighting bow,
For the vigour of soul, that seemed mighty to cope
   With time and with fortune, hath fled from me now;
And love, that illumined my wanderings of yore,
   Hath perished, and left but a weary regret
For the star that can rise on my midnight no more—
   But the hills of my country they welcome me yet !

The hue of their verdure was fresh with me still,
   When my path was afar by the Tanais' lone track ;
From the wide-spreading deserts and ruins, that fill
   The lands of old story, they summoned me back;
They rose on my dreams through the shades of the West,
   They breathed upon sands which the dew never wet,
For the echoes were hushed in the home I loved best—
   But I knew that the mountains would welcome me yet !

The dust of my kindred is scattered afar—
   They lie in the desert, the wild, and the wave ;
For serving the strangers through wandering and war,
   The isle of their memory could grant them no grave.

---

[1] One of the United Irishmen, who lately returned to his country after many years of exile, being asked what had induced him to revisit Ireland when all his friends were gone, answered: "I came back to see the mountains."

And I, I return with the memory of years,
  Whose hope rose so high, though in sorrow it set;
They have left on my soul but the trace of their
    tears—
  But our mountains remember their promises yet!

Oh, where are the brave hearts that bounded of old?
  And where are the faces my childhood hath seen?
For fair brows are furrowed, and hearts have grown
    cold,
  But our streams are still bright, and our hills
    are still green;
Ay, green as they rose to the eyes of my youth,
  When brothers in heart in their shadows we met;
And the hills have no memory of sorrow or death,
  For their summits are sacred to liberty yet!

Like ocean retiring, the morning mists now
  Roll back from the mountains that girdle our
    land;
And sunlight encircles each heath-covered brow,
  For which time hath no furrow and tyrants no
    brand;
Oh, thus let it be with the hearts of the isle—
  Efface the dark seal that oppression hath set;
Give back the lost glory again to the soil,
  For the hills of my country remember it yet!

WHAT HATH TIME TAKEN?

What hath Time taken? Stars, that shone
  On the early years of earth,
And the ancient hills they looked upon,
  Where a thousand streams had birth;
Forests that were the young world's dower;
  With their long unfading trees;
And the halls of wealth, and the thrones of power—
  He hath taken more than these.

He hath taken away the heart of youth,
  And its gladness, which hath been,
Like the summer sunshine o'er our path,
  Making the desert green;
The shrines of an early hope and love,
  And the flowers of every clime,
The wise, the beautiful, the brave,
  Thou hast taken from us, Time!

What hath Time left us? desolate
  Cities, and temples lone,
And the mighty works of genius, yet
  Glorious, when all are gone;
And the lights of memory, lingering long,
  As the eve on western seas—
Treasures of science, thought, and song—
  He hath left us more than these.

He hath left us a lesson of the past,
  In the shades of perished years;
He hath left us the heart's high places waste,
  And its rainbows fallen in tears.
But there's hope for the earth and her children still,
  Unwithered by woe or crime,
And a heritage of rest for all,
  Thou hast left us these, oh Time!

SIR GARNET JOSEPH WOLSELEY.

[Distinguished and remarkable as has been the career of Sir Garnet Wolseley, the notice of him in a literary work must necessarily be short, for his incursions into the domain of literature have been few and far between.

Sir Garnet Joseph Wolseley, K.C.B., G.C.M.G., is the son of Major G. J. Wolseley, and was born at Golden Bridge House, near Dublin, on June 4, 1833. He entered the army in 1852, and was engaged in that and the following year in the Burmese war. In the Crimean campaign he distinguished himself by almost reckless bravery; was wounded severely; and received the Legion of Honour and the order of the Medjidie. He next took part in suppressing the Indian mutiny, and was mentioned in despatches and raised to the rank of lieutenant-colonel. During the Chinese campaign he acted as quartermaster-general. When the expedition was organized to the Red River in 1870, Sir Garnet was given the chief command. The success with which he carried out the operations of this campaign established his reputation; and from that time forward he has been selected on such occasions as demanded great military skill and high qualities as a leader. He was the successful commander of the expedition against the King of Ashantee in 1873–74; and on his return to England received the thanks of parliament and a grant of £25,000; and the Corporation presented him with the freedom of the city of London, and a sword valued at one hundred guineas. He was soon afterwards sent to Natal to arrange some difficulties of administration and colonial defence; in 1878 he was made administrator of Cyprus; and in 1879 he was despatched again to South Africa, to succeed Lord Chelmsford in the command of the forces engaged in the Zulu war, which he soon brought to a successful termination.

Sir Garnet Wolseley has written a *Narrative of the War with China in 1860*, from which we give quotations; *The Soldier's Pocket-Book*, a work on field manœuvres; and he came forward in 1877 as the editor of a rather poor novel, styled *Marley Castle*. He has also written various articles in the magazines.]

SACK OF THE SUMMER PALACE.

(FROM "NARRATIVE OF THE WAR WITH CHINA.")

Upon the 7th of October, at daybreak, we fired twenty-one guns from the high earthen ramparts, near which we halted the evening before, and upon which we had kept large fires burning during the night. These measures were adopted for the purpose of intimating to our cavalry and the French the position we had taken up. A cavalry patrol, under an officer of the quartermaster-general's department, started, as soon as it became light, with orders to ascertain their position and communicate with the French, who were found to be at the Summer Palace, our cavalry being about two miles to their right. Sir Hope Grant, accompanied by Lord Elgin, rode thither in the course of the day for the purpose of seeing General Montauban, who said that as soon as he learned Sir Hope Grant's intention of marching upon Youen-ming-youen, he also made for that place, and fell in with our cavalry during his march, when both proceeded together until they reached the large village Hai-teen, which is situated close by the palace.

Our cavalry brigadier, naturally disliking the idea of getting his men entangled in a town of which he knew nothing, skirted it to the eastward, whilst the French proceeded direct through it and reached the palace gates. About twenty badly armed eunuchs made some pretence at resistance, but were quickly disposed of and the doors burst open, disclosing the sacred precincts of his majesty's residence to what a Chinaman would call the sacrilegious gaze of the barbarians. A mine of wealth and of everything curious in the empire lay as a prey before our French allies. Rooms filled with articles of *vertu*, both native and European, halls containing vases and jars of immense value, and houses stored with silks, satins, and embroidery, were open to them. Indiscriminate plunder and wanton destruction of all articles too heavy for removal commenced at once. When looting is once commenced by an army it is no easy matter to stop it. At such times human nature breaks down the ordinary trammels which discipline imposes, and the consequences are most demoralizing to the very best constituted army. Soldiers are nothing more than grown-up schoolboys. The wild moments of enjoyment passed in the pillage of a place live long in the soldier's memory. Although, perhaps, they did not gain sixpence by it, still they talk of such for years afterwards with pleasure. Such a time forms so marked a contrast with the ordinary routine of existence passed under the tight hand of discipline, that it becomes a remarkable event in life, and is remembered accordingly. I have often watched soldiers after the capture of a place wandering in parties of threes or fours through old ranges of buildings, in which the most sanguine even could scarcely hope to find anything worth having; yet every one of them bore about them that air of enjoyment which is unmistakable. Watch them approach a closed door; it is too much trouble to try the latch or handle, so Jack kicks it open. They enter, some one turns over a table, out of which tumbles perhaps some curious manuscripts. To the soldier these are simply waste paper, so he lights his pipe with them. Another happens to look round and sees his face represented in a mirror, which he at once resents as an insult by shying a foot-stool at it; whilst Bill, fancying that the "old gentleman" in the fine picture-frame upon the wall is making faces at him, rips up the canvas with his bayonet. Some fine statue of Venus is at once adorned with a moustache, and then used as an "Aunt Sally!" Cock-shots are taken at all remarkable objects, which, whilst occupying their intended positions, seem somehow or other to offend the veteran's eye, which dislikes the *in statu quo* of life, and studies the picturesque somewhat after the manner that Colonel Jebb recommends to all country gentlemen who are desirous of converting their mansions into defensible posts. The love of destruction is certainly inherent in man, and the more strictly men are prevented from indulging in it, so much the more keenly do they appear to relish it when the opportunity occurs. Such an explanation will alone satisfactorily account for the ruin and destruction of property which follows so quickly after the capture of any place; tables and chairs hurled from the windows, clocks smashed upon the pavement, and everything not breakable so injured as to be valueless henceforth.

Soldiers of every nation under heaven have peculiarities common to all of the trade, and the amusements which I have just described are amongst them. The French most certainly are no exception to the rule. If the reader will imagine some three thousand men, imbued with such principles, let loose into a city composed only of Museums and Wardour Streets, he may have some faint idea of what Youen-ming-youen looked like after it had been about twenty hours in possession of the French. The far-famed palaces of a line of monarchs claiming a celestial relationship, and in which the ambassador of an English king had been insulted with impunity, were littered with the *débris* of all that was highly prized in China. Topsy-turvy is the only expression in our language which at all describes its state. The ground around the French camp was covered with silks and clothing of all kinds, whilst the men ran hither and thither in search of further plunder, most of them, according to the practice usual with soldiers upon such occasions, being decked out in the most ridiculous-looking costumes they could find, of which there was no lack, as the well-stocked wardrobes of his imperial majesty abounded in such curious raiment. Some had dressed themselves in richly-embroidered gowns of women, and almost all had substituted the turned-up mandarin hat for their ordinary forage-cap. Officers and men seemed to have been seized with a temporary insanity; in body and soul they were absorbed in one pursuit, which was plunder, plunder. I stood by whilst one of the regiments was supposed to be parading; but although their fall in was sounded over and over again, I do not believe there was an average of ten men a company present. Plundering in this way bears its most evil fruit in an army; for if when it is once commenced an effort is made to stop it, the good men only obey; the bad soldiers continue to plunder, and become rich by their disobedience, whilst the good ones see the immediate effect of their steadiness is to keep them poor. I do not believe that it is attended with such demoralizing effects in a French army as it is in ours. The Frenchman is naturally a more thrifty being than the careless Britisher, who squanders his money in drinking, and "standing drink" to his comrades. Three days afterwards, when the French moved into their position before Pekin, they seemed to have regained their discipline, and their men were as steady under arms as if nothing had occurred to disturb the ordinary routine of their lives.

THE CITY OF NANKIN.

Nankin is but the shadow of its former self. Barely a tenth part of the houses once standing are now in existence.

Its walls are old, but massive, and are about 18 miles in circumference; but no more than a third of the inclosed space had ever been built upon, the other two-thirds being under tillage, or devoted to purposes of interment.

The walls are of brick, with the lower portion in many places of sandstone; they average from 40 to 60 feet in height, and are generally about 40 feet in thickness. The city is nearly triangular in shape, the apex being towards the river. A small range of hills stand within the city, extending down the western face, in some places abutting upon the walls. There are now six gates, each defended by a triple line of ramparts, which at those places are over 100 feet in thickness.

We were allowed to wander about the city unquestioned, the only difficulty ever experienced being at the gates, where the officers in charge occasionally stopped us, and put us to some annoyance in order to pass either in or out. Even Chinamen are not permitted to enter without a passport, which those employed as coolies, carrying in supplies, have sewed to the front of their jackets, so as to be visible at all times. Crowds of idlers invariably followed us, and the opprobrious epithet of *fan-qui* (foreign devil) was far more generally used than I expected to have found by a people professing to be our Christian brethren. When Kau-wan was asked how it was that the follower of the new dynasty persisted in retaining and using constantly the soubriquet which the imperialists had always had for the English, he said that these words were a sort of intonation natural to a Chinaman when he saw any foreigner; that, in fact, it was more an exclamation of astonishment than of intended rudeness. He hoped, however, that when all the people became more accustomed to our presence it would be entirely discontinued.

The Tartar quarter formed a regular fortified keep, resting upon the south-eastern face, or base of the triangle, in which the city had been originally laid out. The victorious Tartars when establishing their garrisons throughout the empire seemed to have carefully avoided placing them in the centres of cities, evidently preferring commanding positions somewhere along the original walls of the place, where they then constructed a small city for themselves, from which they domineered over the Chinese quarter. At Nankin all the buildings of the dominant race have been completely destroyed; their *débris* is now being used in the construction of the king's palaces, which are the only public works now in progress. Nankin is surrounded by gently sloping hills, which, towards the north-eastward, assume a rugged appearance, with pointed rocks and high cliffs showing themselves here and there. On some of these the rebels have constructed ridiculous outworks, which are incapable of defence if regularly attacked, and, if even cut off from communication with the garrison of the city, must surrender from want of water. To the north the ground between the city walls and the low slopes of the hills is mostly covered with water and deep marshes, which, strange to say, abound with pheasants. I have seen as many as thirty birds get up from a small piece of water-covered ground not more than fifty yards square.

WITH THE REBELS AT NANKIN.

All the rebel soldiers that we saw were badly armed, the universal weapon being a long bamboo with a pike on the top—a very small proportion having old muskets, matchlocks, or pistols; a few fowling-pieces and rifles. Every second man carried a huge flag, and some carried swords;—altogether it is impossible to imagine a more undisciplined or inefficient mob. Wherever they go they plunder and destroy. Civilization, and even animal life, seems to disappear before them, and their march may be tracked by the bodies of murdered peasants and the ruined habitations which they leave behind them. The country people, far and wide, fly from contact with them, transporting their little all to some place which they deem safer. On the banks of the river, beyond the territories thus laid waste, numbers of large straw-built villages are now to be seen, hastily thrown up by the unfortunate refugees, who endeavour to support life by fishing, or by any other local employment which they can obtain. In all such places as we had an opportunity of visiting the distress and misery of the inhabitants were beyond description. Large families were crowded together into low, small, tent-shaped wigwams, constructed of reeds, through the thin sides of which the cold wind whistled at every blast from the biting north. The denizens were clothed in rags of the most loathsome kind, and huddled together for the sake of warmth. The old looked cast down and unable to work from weakness, whilst that eager expression peculiar to starvation, never to be forgotten by those who have once witnessed it, was visible upon the emaciated features of the little children. With most it was a mere question of how many days' hunger they might drag on their weary lives, whilst even the very moments of many seemed already numbered. The rebel ranks are swelled in two ways: the first by the capture of unwilling men, and, secondly, by those who, being deprived of all they have in this world by the invading marauders, have, as their only alternative, either to starve or join their spoilers themselves. The destructive policy of the rebels in this way serves them well. As we steamed from Nankin up the river, how we desired that all those good people at home who wish the Tein-wanists well, and pray daily for their success, could but make a similar voyage, and thus have an opportunity of judging for themselves regarding the two rival powers who are struggling for mastery. When once you have passed clear from the last rebel outpost and got some distance within the still imperial territory, the contrast around could scarcely be believed without seeing it. The river which near the rebels is a great deserted highway, is there to be seen well-covered with trading craft; highly cultivated farms stretch down to the water's edge, whilst neatly built and snug-looking villages and hamlets are scattered along both banks.

In the neighbourhood of Hankow, where the blackened house-gables show the traveller that it also had one time shared in the misfortunes of Nankin, the work of rebuilding is going on steadily, and is likely to continue, as the exertions and the energy of the present viceroy inspire an ever-increasing confidence in those whom he governs. The local authorities laugh at the notion of the rebels taking the place whilst they have, as they assert, 30,000 men in arms there.

JOHN KEEGAN CASEY.

Born 1846 — Died 1870.

[John Keegan Casey was son of a peasant farmer of county Westmeath, and was born at Mount Dalton, a village close to Mullingar, the capital of that county, on August 22, 1846. In spite of unfavourable circumstances he devoted much of his time to study; and he was but sixteen when his first poem appeared in the *Nation*, under his well-known *nom-de-plume* of "Leo." He began life as a mercantile clerk; but after some time made literature his profession. In 1866 a first collection of the poems he had contributed to various journals was issued, under the title *A Wreath of Shamrocks*. The work was received with great favour in Ireland and America; and some London critics were fain to forget its political bias because of its literary merit.

In 1867 Casey was arrested for his connection with Fenianism; and the imprisonment through which he had to pass perhaps hurried his untimely end. In 1869 he published a second collection of his poems, under the title *The Rising of the Moon*. The *London Review* says of these poems, "Treason is put in a fascinating, tolerant, and intelligent shape. . . . Of course the Saxon comes in for it; but no Saxon could feel over-vexed at being railed at so eloquently in his own language." A sudden attack of hæmorrhage of the lungs brought Mr. Casey's promising life to a close, March 17, 1870, in his twenty-fourth year. The skill with which he had embodied popular feelings in his verse procured for him a high degree of popularity, and his funeral is said to have been attended by no less than 50,000 people.]

SONG OF GOLDEN-HEADED NIAMH.

AN OSSIANIC LAY.

Oh! come with me to Tirnan-og;
   There fruit and blossoms bend each tree,
Red sparkling wine and honey flow,
   And beauty smiles from sea to sea.
Your flowing locks will ne'er turn gray,
   No wrinkles on your forehead come,
Nor burning pain nor grim decay
     Across the threshold of your home.
       So haste away to Tirnan-og,
         My white steed waits in golden sheen;
       A diadem shall crown thy brow,
         And I will be thy bridal queen.

The feast is spread, within the hall
   Flash drinking cups with gold encrowned;
The harp leans lightly 'gainst the wall
   To strike for thee the welcome sound.
A hundred sword-blades for thy hand,
   A hundred of the swiftest steeds,
A hundred hounds, a matchless band
   Where'er the hunted quarry leads.
      So haste away to Tirnan-og, &c.

A hundred robes of precious silk,
   And gems from an enchanted mine,
A hundred kine of sweetest milk,
   And armour of the brightest shine.
And thou shalt wear that wondrous sword
   Of keenest edge, whose flash is death:
The summer wind will hear thy word,
   And gently pour its tender breath.
      So haste away to Tirnan-og, &c.

Young virgins, sweetest in the song,
   And beauteous as the morning sun,
Around thy noble steps will throng
   To make thy path a joyous one;
And heroes, in the combat stern,
   In speed and boldness unsurpassed,
Before whose prowess Fionn would learn
   To bow his haughty head at last.
      So haste away to Tirnan-og, &c.

O Oisin of the powerful hand!
   First in the chase, first in the war,
Over our sweet and glorious land
   Thy gallant deeds were borne afar.
Loch Leine is deep, but deeper still
   In Niamh's soul thy image dwells;
Then turn thee westward from this hill
   To where the sun-hued billow swells.
      Oh! haste away to Tirnan-og, &c.

MY CAILIN RUADH.

My fairy girl, my darling girl,
   If I were near thee now,
The sunlight of your eyes would chase
   The sorrow from my brow;
Your lips would whisper o'er and o'er
   The words so fond and true,
They whispered long and long ago,
   My gentle Cailin Ruadh.

No more by Inny's bank I sit,
   Or rove the meadows brown,
But count the weary hours away
   Pent in this dismal town;

I cannot breathe the pasture air,
  My father's homestead view,
Or see another face like thine,
  My gentle Cailin Ruadh.

Thy laugh was like the echo sent
  From Oonagh's crystal hall;
Thy eyes the moonlight's flashing glance
  Upon a waterfall;
Thy hair the amber clouds at eve,
  When lovers haste to woo;
Thy teeth Killarney's snowy pearls,
  My gentle Cailin Ruadh.

O sweetheart! I can see thee stand
  Beside the orchard stile,
The dawn upon thy regal brow,
  Upon thy mouth a smile;
The apple-bloom above thy head,
  Thy cheeks its glowing hue,
The sunflash in thy radiant eyes,
  My gentle Cailin Ruadh.

But drearily and wearily
  The snow is drifting by,
And drearily and wearily
  It bears my lonely sigh
Far from this lonely Connaught town,
  To Inny's wave of blue,
To the homestead in the fairy glen,
  And gentle Cailin Ruadh.

DONAL KENNY.

"Come, piper, play the 'Shaskan Reel,'
  Or else the 'Lasses on the heather,'
And, Mary, lay aside your wheel
  Until we dance once more together.
At fair and pattern oft before
  Of reels and jigs we've tripped full many;
But ne'er again this loved old floor
  Will feel the foot of Donal Kenny."

Softly she rose and took his hand,
  And softly glided through the measure,
While, clustering round, the village band
  Looked half in sorrow, half in pleasure.
Warm blessings flowed from every lip
  As ceased the dancers' airy motion:
O Blessed Virgin! guide the ship
  Which bears bold Donal o'er the ocean!

"Now God be with you all!" he sighed,
  Adown his face the bright tears flowing—
"God guard you well, *aric*," they cried,
  "Upon the strange path you are going."
So full his breast, he scarce could speak,
  With burning grasp the stretched hands taking,
He pressed a kiss on every cheek,
  And sobbed as if his heart was breaking.

"Boys, don't forget me when I'm gone,
  For sake of all the days passed over—
The days you spent on heath and bawn,
  With *Donal Ruadh*, the rattlin' rover.
Mary, *agra*, your soft brown eye
  Has willed my fate" (he whispered lowly);
"Another holds thy heart: good bye!
  Heaven grant you both its blessings holy!"

A kiss upon her brow of snow,
  A rush across the moonlit meadow,
Whose broom-clad hazels, trembling slow,
  The mossy boreen wrapped in shadow;
Away o'er Tully's bounding rill,
  And far beyond the Inny river;
One cheer on Carrick's rocky hill,
  And Donal Kenny's gone for ever.

* * *

The breezes whistled through the sails,
  O'er Galway Bay the ship was heaving,
And smothered groans and bursting wails
  Told all the grief and pain of leaving.
One form among that exiled band
  Of parting sorrow gave no token,
Still was his breath, and cold his hand;
  For Donal Kenny's heart was broken.

WILLIAM E. H. LECKY.

[Mr. Lecky has in a few years and by four works gained the right to be regarded as in the front rank of contemporary historians. His books have already attained to something like the position of classics on the subjects with which they deal, and the production of a new volume by him is now a literary event. This high position has been worthily won; the verdict passed originally by the periodical oracles of criticism has been confirmed by the reading public, and will be, in our opinion, endorsed by every one who devotes even a few hours to his fascinating volumes.

The record of his life up to the present is brief. William Edward Hartpole Lecky was born in the neighbourhood of Dublin on

March 26, 1838. He went through the usual course in Trinity College; graduated B.A. in 1859, and M.A. in 1863. His first work, *The Leaders of Public Opinion in Ireland*, was published anonymously in 1861. In this volume the great men who have at different times controlled Irish destinies are passed in review —Swift, Flood and Grattan, O'Connell; and their lives, characters, and influences are discussed with a fairness that is not too often the characteristic of Irish writers on Irish affairs. The work was not acknowledged till 1871–72 when a new edition was published. In 1865 appeared the *History of the Rise and Influence of the Spirit of Rationalism in Europe*. This work has already passed through several editions. The *History of European Morals from Augustus to Charlemagne* followed in 1869; and his latest work, published in 1878, are two volumes of *A History of England in the Eighteenth Century*.

All those works are characterized by the same qualities. A fine power of generalization is combined with a great mastery of detail: a glance at the foot-notes will suffice to show the vast extent of the author's reading. Mr. Lecky has to deal with most of the great moral and philosophical questions which divide the opinions of men; and though one may dissent, and some thinkers have strongly dissented, from his conclusions, no fair reader can deny that they have been arrived at after patient and calm investigation. Mr. Lecky's style is admirably adapted to his subject: clear, correct, simple, yet finished; and, though never ambitious, often truly eloquent.]

DUBLIN IN THE EIGHTEENTH CENTURY.

(FROM "HISTORY OF ENGLAND."[1])

What I have written may be sufficient to show that Irish life in the first half of the eighteenth century was not altogether the corrupt, frivolous, grotesque, and barbarous thing that it has been represented; that among many and glaring vices some real public spirit and intellectual energy may be discerned. It may be added that great improvements were at this time made in the material aspect of Dublin.

In the middle of the eighteenth century it was in dimensions and population the second city in the empire, containing, according to the most trustworthy accounts, between 100,000 and 120,000 inhabitants. Like most things in Ireland, it presented vivid contrasts, and strangers were equally struck with the crowds of beggars, the inferiority of the inns, the squalid wretchedness of the streets of the old town, and with the noble proportions of the new quarter, and the brilliant and hospitable society that inhabited it. The Liffey was spanned by four bridges, and another on a grander scale was undertaken in 1753. St. Stephen's Green was considered the largest square in Europe. The quays of Dublin were widely celebrated; but the chief boast of the city was the new Parliament House, which was built between 1729 and 1739 for the very moderate sum of £34,000, and was justly regarded as far superior in beauty to the Parliament House of Westminster. In the reigns of Elizabeth and of the early Stuarts the Irish Parliament met in the Castle under the eyes of the chief governor. It afterwards assembled at the Tholsel, in Chichester House, and during the erection of the Parliament House in two great rooms of the Foundling Hospital. The new edifice was chiefly built by the surveyor-general, Sir Edward Pearce, who was a member of the Irish Parliament, and it entitles him to a very high place among the architects of his time. In ecclesiastical architecture the city had nothing to boast of, for the churches, with one or two exceptions, were wholly devoid of beauty, and their monuments were clumsy, scanty, and mean; but the college, though it wanted the venerable charm of the English universities, spread in stately squares far beyond its original limits. The cheapness of its education and the prevailing distaste for industrial life which induced crowds of poor gentry to send their sons to the university, when they would have done far better to send them to the counter, contributed to support it, and in spite of great discouragement it appears on the whole to have escaped the torpor which had at this time fallen over the universities of England. It is said before the middle of the century to have contained about 700 students. A laboratory and anatomical theatre had been opened in 1710 and 1711. The range of instruction had been about the same time enlarged by the introduction of lectures on chemistry, anatomy, and botany, and a few years later by the foundation of new lectureships on oratory, history, natural and experimental philosophy. The library was assisted by grants from the Irish Parliament. It was

---

[1] This and the following extracts are made by permission of the author.

enriched by large collections of books and manuscripts bequeathed during the first half of the eighteenth century by Palliser, Archbishop of Cashel, by Gilbert, the vice-provost and professor of divinity, and by Stearn, the Bishop of Clogher, and its present noble reading-room was opened in 1732. Another library—comprising that which had once belonged to Stillingfleet—had been founded in Dublin by Bishop Marsh, and was incorporated by act of parliament in 1707.

The traces of recent civil war and the arrogance of a dominant minority were painfully apparent. The statue of William III. stood as the most conspicuous monument opposite the Parliament of Ireland. A bust of the same sovereign, bearing an insulting distich reflecting on the adherents of James, was annually painted by the corporation. The toast of "the glorious, pious, and immortal memory" was given on all public occasions by the viceroy. The walls of the House of Lords were hung with tapestry representing the siege of Derry and the battle of the Boyne. A standing order of the House of Commons excluded Catholics even from the gallery. The anniversaries of the Battle of Aghrim, of the Battle of the Boyne, of the Gunpowder Plot, and, above all, of the discovery of the rebellion of 1641, were always celebrated. On the last-named occasion the lord-lieutenant went in full state to Christ's Church, where a sermon on the rebellion was preached. At noon the great guns of the castle were fired. The church bells were rung, and the day concluded with bonfires and illuminations. Like London and Edinburgh, Dublin possessed many elements of disorder, and several men were killed and several others hamstrung or otherwise brutally injured in savage feuds between the Ormond and the Liberty boys, between the students of the university and the butchers around St. Patrick, between the butchers and the weavers, and between the butchers and the soldiers. As in most English towns, bull-baiting was a very popular amusement, and many riots grew out of the determination of the populace to bait cattle that were being brought to market. Occasionally, too, in seasons of great distress there were outbreaks against foreign goods, and shops containing them were sacked. The police of the town seems to have been very insufficient, but an important step was taken in the cause of order by the adoption in 1719 of a new system of lighting the streets after the model of London, which was extended to Cork and Limerick. Large lanterns were provided at the public expense to be lighted in the dark quarters of the moon from half an hour after sunset till two in the morning; in the other quarters of the moon, during which there had previously been no lights, whenever the moon was down or overshadowed. There was not much industrial life, but the linen trade was flourishing, a linen-hall was built in 1728, and there was also a considerable manufactory of tapestry and carpets.

Among the higher classes there are some traces of an immorality of a graver kind than the ordinary dissipation of Irish life. In the early Hanoverian period a wave of impiety broke over both islands, and great indignation and even consternation was excited in Ireland by the report that there existed in Dublin, among some men of fashion, a club called the "Blasters," or the "Hell-fire Club," resembling the Medmenham brotherhood which some years later became so celebrated in England. It was not of native growth, and is said to have derived its origin, or at least its character, from a painter named Peter Lens, who had lately come into the kingdom, and who was accused of the grossest blasphemy, of drinking the health of the devil, and of openly abjuring God. A committee of the House of Lords inquired into the matter in 1737, and presented a report offering a reward for the apprehension of Lens, and at the same time deploring a great and growing neglect of Divine worship, of religious education, and of the observance of Sunday, as well as an increase of idleness, luxury, profanity, gaming, and drinking. The existence of the Hell-fire Club has been doubted, and the charges against its members were certainly by no means established, but there can be little question that the report of the Lords' Committee was right in its censure of the morals of many of the upper classes. The first Lord Rosse was equally famous for his profligacy and for his wit; and in 1739 Lord Santry was arraigned and found guilty of murder by the House of Lords, for having killed a man in a drunken fray.

The number of carriages in proportion to the population of the city was unusually great. It is said that as many as 300 filled with gentlemen, sometimes assembled to meet the lord-lieutenant on his arrival from England. There were about 200 hackney-carriages and as many chairs, and it was noticed as a singularity of Dublin, which may be ascribed either to the wretched pavement or to the prevailing habits of ostentation, that ladies scarcely ever appeared on foot in the streets. They were famous for their grace in dancing, as the men were for their skill in swimming. The hospitality of the upper classes was notorious, and it was by no means destitute of brilliancy or grace. No one can look over the fugitive literature of Dublin in the first half of the eighteenth century without being struck with the very large amount of admirable witty and satirical poetry that was produced. The curse of absenteeism was little felt in Dublin, where the Parliament secured the presence of most of the aristocracy and of much of the talent of the country; and during the residence of the viceroy the influence of a court, and the weekly balls in the winter time at the castle, contributed to the sparkling, showy character of Dublin society. Dorset, Devonshire, and Chesterfield were especially famous for the munificence of their hospitality, and the unnatural restriction of the spheres of political and industrial enterprise had thrown the energies of the upper classes to an unhealthy degree into the cultivation of social habits.

On the whole, however, the difference between society in Dublin and in London was probably much less than has been supposed. Mrs. Delany, who moved much in both, and whose charming letters furnish some of the best pictures of Irish life in the first half of the eighteenth century, writing from Dublin in 1731, says: "As for the generality of people that I meet with here, they are much the same as in England—a mixture of good and bad. All that I have met with behave themselves very decently according to their rank; now and then an oddity breaks out, but never so extraordinary but that I can match them in England. There is a heartiness among them that is more like Cornwall than any I have known, and great sociableness." Arthur Young, nearly half a century later, when drawing the dark picture I have already quoted of the reckless and dissipated character of the Irish squireens, took care to qualify it by adding that "there are great numbers of the principal people residing in Ireland who are as liberal in their ideas as any people in Europe," and that "a man may go into a vast variety of families which he will find actuated by no other principles than those of the most cultivated politeness and the most liberal urbanity. The ostentatious profusion of dishes and multiplication of servants at Irish entertainments which appeared so strange to English travellers, and which had undoubtedly bad moral effects, were merely the natural result of the economical condition of the country, which made both food and labour extremely cheap. Another difference which was perhaps more significant was the greater mixture of professions and ranks; and the social position of artists and actors was perceptibly higher than in England. Handel was at once received with an enthusiastic cordiality, and Elrington, one of the best Irish actors of his day, refused an extremely advantageous offer from London in 1729, chiefly on the ground that in his own country there was not a gentleman's house to which he was not a welcome visitor.

Booksellers were numerous; and the house of Faulkner, the friend and publisher of Swift, was for many years a centre of literary society. For the most part, however, they were not occupied with native productions, but were employed in fabricating cheap editions of English books. As the act of Anne for the protection of literary property did not extend to Ireland, this proceeding was legal, the most prominent English books were usually reprinted in Dublin, and great numbers of these reprints passed to the colonies. It is an amusing fact that when Richardson endeavoured to prevent the piracy by sending over for sale a large number of copies of *Pamela* immediately on its publication, he was accused of having scandalously invaded the legitimate profits of the Dublin printers. *The Dublin News-letter*, which seems to have been the first local newspaper, was published as early as 1685. *Pue's Occurrences*, which obtained a much greater popularity, appeared in 1703, and there were several other papers before the middle of the century.

The taste for music was stronger and more general than the taste for literature. There was a public garden for musical entertainments after the model of Vauxhall; a music-hall, founded in 1741; a considerable society of amateur musicians, who cultivated the art and sang for charities; a musical academy, established in 1755, and presided over by Lord Mornington. Foreign artists were always warmly welcomed. Dubourg, the violinist, the favourite pupil of Geminiani, came to Dublin in 1728, and resided there for many years. Handel, as we have seen, first brought out his *Messiah* in Dublin. Roubillac, at a time when he was hardly known in England, executed busts for the university. Geminiani came to Dublin about 1763. Garrick acted "Hamlet" in Dublin before he attempted it in

England. There were two theatres, and a great, and indeed extravagant, passion for good acting. Among the dramatists of the seventeenth century Congreve and Farquhar were both Irish by education, and the second, at least, was Irish by birth. Among the Irish actors and actresses who attained to great eminence on the English stage during the eighteenth century we find Wilkes, who was the contemporary and almost the equal of Betterton; Macklin, the first considerable reviver of Shakspere; Barry, who was pronounced to be the best lover on the stage; Mrs. Woffington, the president of the Beefsteak Club; Mrs. Bellamy, whose memoirs are still read; as well as Elrington, Sheridan, and Mrs. Jordan. The Dublin theatres underwent many strange vicissitudes which it is not necessary here to record, but it may be mentioned as a curious trait of manners that when Sheridan had for a time reformed the chief theatre it was warmly patronized by the Protestant clergy. "There have been sometimes," he stated, "more than thirty clergymen in the pit at a time, many of them deans or doctors of divinity, though formerly perhaps none of that order had ever entered the doors, unless a few who skulked in the gallery disguised." In 1701 the fall of a gallery in the theatre during the representation of *The Libertine*, one of the most grossly immoral of the plays of Shadwell, had produced for a time a religious panic, and the play was for twenty years banished from the stage; but in general there appears to have been little or nothing of that puritanical feeling on the subject which was general in Scotland, and which in the present century became almost equally general among the clergy of Ireland.

INFLUENCE OF THE ELDER PITT.

(FROM "HISTORY OF ENGLAND.")

Pitt made large demands upon the self-sacrifice and resolution of the nation, but in this respect he was never disappointed. England under his guidance was almost wholly unlike the England of Walpole and Pelham. Its relaxed energies were braced anew. The thick crust of selfishness, corruption, and effeminacy was broken, and an emulation of heroism and enterprise was displayed. Foreign nations cordially recognized the greatness of the change. "England," said Frederick, "had long been in labour, but had at last produced a man;" and long years after Pitt had been removed from office, it was observed that the mere mention of the probability of his returning to power was sufficient to quell the boasts of the French. At the same time he never appears to have been regarded in France with the intensity of hatred which was bestowed upon his son. The magnanimous and generous features of his character, and the somewhat theatrical nature of his greatness, in some degree dazzled even his enemies; and it is remarkable that one of the most eloquent eulogies of Chatham is from a Frenchman, the Abbé Raynal.

The intellectual and moral qualities that constitute a great war minister and a great home minister are so very different that they have hardly ever been united in the same man. In judging the influence of Pitt on home politics we must remember how short a time he was in power and in health. During the last years of George II., when his authority was so great, the energies of the nation were absorbed in the war; nor did he ever attain in home politics the authority which was willingly conceded him in military administration. In the succeeding reign he was either in opposition, or, being in office, was prostrated by illness. His proposals were seldom or never carried into effect, or even fully elaborated. They were like the unfinished sketches of a great artist, or like beacon-lights kindled in the darkness to mark out a path for his successors. That he possessed the qualities of a great home or peace minister can hardly be alleged. In matters of finance and on questions of commercial policy he was extremely ignorant. We look in vain in his career for any great signs of administrative or constructive talent, and he was eminently deficient in the tact, the moderation, and the temper that are requisite for party management. Yet even in this sphere he exercised a profound, and on the whole a salutary influence. The most remarkable characteristic of his home policy was the great prominence he gave to the moral side of legislation, or, in other words, the skill with which he acted upon the higher enthusiasms of the people. In his conception of politics the supreme end of legislation is to inspire the nation with a lofty spirit of patriotism, courage, and enterprise; to enlist its nobler qualities habitually in the national service, and to make the legislature a faithful reflex of its sentiments. No preceding statesman showed so full a confidence in the people. It was thus that, by arming the Jacobite clans, he attracted to national channels the martial enthusiasm of Scotland, which had been so often in the service of the Stuarts. It was thus that he proposed, and at last carried out, the scheme of a national militia, and but for the opposition of his colleagues he would have extended it to Scotland. It was thus that he supported, though without success, the measure which was brought forward by Pratt in 1758 to extend the operation of the Habeas Corpus Act, which applied only to those who were detained on some criminal charge, to all who were confined under any pretence whatever. In the following reign he was the first conspicuous statesman who raised the banner of parliamentary reform, and it was characteristic of him that he based his proposal not on the common ground of the irregularities or anomalies of the legislature, but on the ground that the strong patriotic spirit that animated the country was not adequately represented in it; that corrupt or personal motives had lowered its tone, and that an infusion of the popular element was necessary to reinvigorate it.

It was in the same spirit that he attempted in his latter days to break down the system of party government, under the belief that it diverted the energies of politicians from national objects; and to withdraw the government of India from the East India Company, under the belief that so great a territory should not remain in the hands of a mercantile company, or be governed on merely commercial principles, but should be thoroughly incorporated in the British Empire. No one who follows his career can doubt that, had he been in power at the time of the American troubles, he could have conciliated the colonies; and it was during the later ministry of Pitt that the first steps were taken towards the introduction of a better government into Ireland. He never could have conducted party government with the tact of Walpole; he never could have framed, like Burke, a great measure of economical reform, or have presided, like Peel, over a great revolution of the commercial system; but no minister had a greater power of making a sluggish people brave, or a slavish people free, or a discontented people loyal.

Although he cannot be said to have carried a single definite measure increasing the power of the people, or diminishing the corrupt influence of the crown or of the aristocracy, it may be said, without a paradox, that he did more for the popular cause than any statesman since the generation that effected the Revolution. With very little parliamentary connection, and with no favour from royalty, he became, by the force of his abilities, and by the unbounded popularity which he enjoyed, the foremost man of the nation. In him the people for the first time felt their power. He was essentially their representative, and he gloried in avowing it. He declared, even before the privy council, that he had been called to office by the voice of the people, and that he considered himself accountable to them alone. The great towns, and especially London, constantly and warmly supported him; and though his popularity was sometimes for a short time eclipsed, it was incomparably greater than that of any previous statesman. In our day such popularity, united with such abilities, would have enabled a statesman to defy all opposition. In the days of Pitt it was not so, and he soon found himself incapable of conducting government without the assistance of the borough patronage of the aristocracy, or of resisting the hostility of the crown. But although he was not omnipotent in politics, the voice of the people at least made him so powerful that no government was stable when he opposed it, and that all parties sought to win him to their side. This was a new fact in parliamentary history, and it marks a great step in the progress of democracy.

His influence was also very great in raising the moral tone of public life. His transparent and somewhat ostentatious purity formed a striking contrast to the prevailing spirit of English politics, and the power and persistence with which he appealed on every occasion to the higher and unselfish motives infused a new moral energy into the nation. The political materialism of the school of Walpole perished under his influence, and his career was an important element in a great change which was passing over England. Under the influence of many adverse causes the standard of morals had been greatly depressed since the restoration; and in the early Hanoverian period the nation had sunk into a condition of moral apathy rarely paralleled in its history. But from about the middle of the eighteenth century a reforming spirit was once more abroad, and a steady movement of moral ascent may be detected. The influence of Pitt in politics and the influence of Wesley and his followers in religion, were the earliest and most important agencies in effecting it. It was assisted in another department by the example of George III., who introduced an improved tone into fashionable life, and it was reflected in the smaller sphere of public amusements in the Shaksperian revival of Garrick. In most respects Pitt and Wesley were, it is true, extremely unlike. The animating principles of the latter are to be found in doctrines that are most distinctively Christian, and especially in that aspect of Christian teaching which is most fitted to humble men. Pitt was a man of pure morals, unchallenged orthodoxy, and of a certain lofty piety, but yet his character was essentially of the Roman type, in which patriotism and magnanimity and well-directed pride are the first of virtues; and the sentences of the Latin poets and the examples of the age of the Scipios, which in a letter to a bishop he once called "the apostolic age of patriotism," appear to have left the deepest impression on his mind. But with all these differences there was a real analogy and an intimate relation between the work of these two men. The religious and political notions prevailing in the early Hanoverian period were closely connected. The theological conception which looked upon religion as a kind of adjunct to the police-force, which dwelt almost exclusively on the prudence of embracing it and on the advantages it could confer, and which regarded all spirituality and all strong emotions as fanaticism, corresponded very faithfully to that political system under which corruption was regarded as the natural instrument, and the maintenance of material interests as the supreme end of government; while the higher motives of political action were systematically ridiculed and discouraged. By Wesley in the sphere of religion, by Pitt in the sphere of politics, the tone of thought and feeling was changed, and this is perhaps the aspect of the career of Pitt which possesses the most abiding interest and importance. The standard of political honour was perceptibly raised. It was felt that enthusiasm, disinterestedness, and self-sacrifice had their place in politics; and although there was afterwards, for short periods, extreme corruption, public opinion never acquiesced in it again.

It was a singular fortune that produced, in so brief a period, from the ranks of the Whig party, one of the greatest peace ministers and the greatest war minister of England, and it would be difficult to find two nearly contemporary statesmen of the same party and of equal eminence, who in character and policy were more directly opposed than Walpole and Pitt. Each was in many respects immeasurably superior to the other, and in some respects they will hardly admit of comparison. We can scarcely, for example, compare a speaker who was simply a clear, shrewd, and forcible debater without polish of manner or elevation of language, with an orator who surpassed Chesterfield in grace, while he equalled Demosthenes in power. In his private life Walpole, though a man of great kindness of nature, was notoriously lax and immoral, while Pitt was without reproach; but we must remember that the first was full of constitutional vigour, while the second was a confirmed invalid. In public integrity there was, I think, less real difference between them than is usually imagined. There is no proof that Walpole ever dishonestly appropriated public money. Both statesmen received large rewards for their services, and these rewards in kind and in amount were nearly the same. The factious conduct of Walpole during the administration of Stanhope may be fairly balanced by the conduct of Pitt towards Walpole, and afterwards towards Newcastle. Pitt, however, was entirely free from nepotism, while Walpole bestowed vast public revenues upon his sons. Walpole hated everything theatrical and declamatory. He had too little dignity for the position he occupied, and in his best days he was more liked than respected. Pitt was always in some degree an actor. His want of social freedom greatly impaired his success as a party leader, and he inspired more awe than any other English politician. The ability of the one was shown chiefly in averting, that of the other in meeting, danger. A cautious wisdom predominated in the first, an enterprising greatness in the second. The first dealt almost exclusively with material interests, and sought only to allay strong passions. The second delighted in evoking, appealing to, and directing the most fiery enthusiasms. The first was incomparably superior in his knowledge of finance; the second in his management of war. The first loved peace, and made England very prosperous; the second loved war and surrounded his country with glory.

The influence of the two men on political morals was, as we have seen, directly opposite. With much quiet patriotism Walpole had none of the loftiness of character of Pitt, and was entirely incapable of the traits of splendid magnanimity and disinterestedness which were so conspicuous in the latter. Though he did not originate, he accepted, systematized, and extended parliamentary corruption; his personal integrity, though probably very real, was never above suspicion, and his ridicule of all who professed high political principles contributed very much to lower the prevailing tone. It was reserved for Pitt to break the spell of corruption, and he did more than any other English statesman to ennoble public life and to raise the character of public men.

CHARACTER OF MARCUS AURELIUS.

(FROM "HISTORY OF EUROPEAN MORALS.")

It was a saying of Plutarch that stoicism, which sometimes exercised a prejudicial and hardening influence upon characters that were by nature stern and unbending, proved peculiarly useful as a cordial to those which were naturally gentle and yielding. Of this truth we can have no better illustration than is furnished by the life and writings of Marcus Aurelius, the last and most perfect representative of Roman stoicism. A simple, child-like, and eminently affectionate disposition, with little strength of intellect or perhaps originally of will, much more inclined to meditation, speculation, solitude, or friendship, than to active and public life, with a profound aversion to the pomp of royalty and with a rather strong natural leaning to pedantry, he had embraced the fortifying philosophy of Zeno in its best form, and that philosophy made him perhaps as nearly a perfectly virtuous man as has ever appeared upon our world. Tried by the chequered events of a reign of nineteen years, presiding over a society that was profoundly corrupt, and over a city that was notorious for its license, the perfection of his character awed even calumny to silence, and the spontaneous sentiment of his people proclaimed him rather a god than a man. Very few men have ever lived concerning whose inner life we can speak so confidently. His *Meditations*, which form one of the most impressive, form also one of the truest books in the whole range of religious literature. They consist of rude fragmentary notes without literary skill or arrangement, written for the most part in hasty, broken, and sometimes almost unintelligible sentences amid the turmoil of a camp, and recording, in accents of the most penetrating sincerity, the struggles, doubts, and aims of a soul of which, to employ one of his own images, it may be truly said that it possessed the purity of a star which needs no veil to hide its nakedness. The undisputed master of the whole civilized world, he set before him as models such men as Thrasea and Helvidius, as Cato and Brutus, and he made it his aim to realize the conception of a free state in which all citizens are equal, and of a royalty which makes it its first duty to respect the liberty of the citizens. His life was passed in unremitting activity. For nearly twelve years he was absent with armies in the distant provinces of the empire; and although his political capacity has been much and perhaps justly questioned, it is impossible to deny the unwearied zeal with which he discharged the duties of his great position. Yet few men have ever carried farther the virtue of little things, the delicate moral tact and the minute scruples which, though often exhibited by women and by secluded religionists, very rarely survive much contact with active life. The solicitude with which he endeavoured to persuade two jealous rhetoricians to abstain during their debates from retorts that might destroy their friendship, the careful gratitude with which, in a camp in Hungary, he recalled every moral obligation he could trace even to the most obscure of his tutors, his anxiety to avoid all pedantry and mannerism in his conduct, and to repel every voluptuous imagination from his mind, his deep sense of the obligation of purity, his laborious efforts to correct a habit of drowsiness into which he had fallen, and his self-reproval when he had yielded to it, become all, I think, inexpressibly touching, when we remember that they were exhibited by one who was the supreme ruler of the civilized globe, and who was continually engaged in the direction of the most gigantic interests. But that which is especially remarkable in Marcus Aurelius is the complete absence of fanaticism in his philanthropy. Despotic monarchs sincerely anxious to improve mankind are naturally led to endeavour, by acts of legislation, to force society into the paths which they believe to be good, and such men, acting under such motives, have sometimes been the scourges of mankind. Philip II. and Isabella the Catholic inflicted more suffering in obedience to their consciences than Nero and Domitian in obedience to their lusts. But Marcus Aurelius steadily resisted the temptation. "Never hope," he once wrote, "to realize Plato's republic. Let it be sufficient that you have in some slight degree ameliorated mankind, and do not think that amelioration a matter of small importance. Who can change the opinions of men? and without a change of sentiments what can you make but reluctant slaves and hypocrites?" He promulgated many laws inspired by a spirit of the purest benevolence. He mitigated the gladiatorial shows. He treated with invariable deference the senate, which was the last bulwark of political freedom. He endowed many chairs of philosophy which were intended to diffuse knowledge and moral teaching through the people. He endeavoured by the example of his court to correct the extravagances of luxury that were prevalent, and he exhibited in his own career a perfect model of an active and conscientious administrator; but he made no rash efforts to force the people by stringent laws out of the natural channel of their lives. Of the corruption of his subjects he was keenly sensible, and he bore it with a mournful but gentle patience. We may trace in this respect the milder spirit of those Greek teachers who had diverged from stoicism, but it was especially from the stoical doctrine that all vice springs from ignorance that he derived his rule of life, and this doctrine, to which he repeatedly recurred, imparted to all his judgments a sad but tender charity. "Men were made for men; correct them, then, or support them." "If they do ill, it is evidently in spite of themselves and through ignorance." "Correct them if you can; if not, remember that patience was given you to exercise it in their behalf." "It would be shameful for a physician to deem it strange that a man was suffering from fever." "The immortal gods consent for countless ages to endure without anger, and even to surround with blessings, so many and such wicked men; but thou who hast so short a time to live, art thou already weary, and that when thou art thyself wicked!" "It is involuntarily that the soul is deprived of justice, and temperance, and goodness, and all other virtues. Continually remember this; the thought will make you more gentle to all mankind." "It is right that man should love those who have offended him. He will do so when he remembers that all men are his relations, and that it is through ignorance and involuntarily that they sin—and then we all die so soon."

The character of the virtue of Marcus Aurelius, though exhibiting the softening influence of the Greek spirit which in his time pervaded the empire, was in its essentials strictly Roman. Though full of reverential gratitude to Providence, we do not find in him that intense humility and that deep and subtle religious feeling which were the principles of Hebrew virtue, and which have given the Jewish writers so great an ascendency over the hearts of men. Though borne naturally and instinctively to goodness, his *Meditations* do not display the keen æsthetical sense of the beauty of virtue which was the leading motive of Greek morals, and which the writings of Plotinus afterwards made very familiar to the Roman world. Like most of the best Romans, the principle of his virtue was the sense of duty, the conviction of the existence of a law of nature to which it is the aim and purpose of our being to conform. Of secondary motives he appears to have been little sensible. The belief in a superintending Providence was the strongest of his religious convictions, but even that was occasionally overcast. On the subject of a future world his mind floated in a desponding doubt. The desire for posthumous fame he deemed it his duty systematically to mortify. While most writers of his school regarded death chiefly as the end of sorrows, and dwelt upon it in order to dispel its terrors, in Marcus Aurelius it is chiefly represented as the last great demonstration of the vanity of earthly things. Seldom, indeed, has such active and unrelaxing virtue been united with so little enthusiasm, and been cheered by so little illusion of success. "There is but one thing," he wrote, "of real value—to cultivate truth and justice, and to live without anger in the midst of lying and unjust men."

The command he had acquired over his feelings was so great that it was said of him that his countenance was never known to betray either elation or despondency. We, however, who have before us the records of his inner life, can have no difficulty in detecting the deep melancholy that overshadowed his mind, and his closing years were darkened by many and various sorrows. His wife, whom he dearly loved and deeply honoured, and who, if we may believe the court scandals that are reported by historians, was not worthy of his affection, had preceded him to the tomb. His only surviving son had already displayed the vicious tendencies that afterwards made him one of the worst of rulers. The philosophers who had instructed him in his youth, and to whom he had clung with an affectionate friendship, had one by one disappeared, and no new race had arisen to supply their place. After a long reign of self-denying virtue, he saw the decadence of the empire continually more apparent. The stoical school was rapidly fading before the passion for oriental superstitions. The barbarians, repelled for a time, were again menacing the frontiers, and it was not difficult to foresee their future triumph. The mass of the people had become too inert and too corrupt for any efforts to regenerate them. A fearful pestilence, followed by many minor calamities, had fallen upon the land and spread misery and panic through many provinces. In the midst of these calamities the emperor was struck down with a mortal illness, which he bore with the placid courage he had always displayed, exhibiting in almost the last words he uttered his forgetfulness of self and his constant anxiety for the condition of his people. Shortly before his death he dismissed his attendants, and, after one last interview, his son, and he died as he long had lived, alone. —Thus sank to rest in clouds and darkness the purest and gentlest spirit of all the pagan world, the most perfect model of the later Stoics. In him the hardness, asperity, and arrogance of the sect had altogether disappeared, while the affectation its paradoxes tended to produce was greatly mitigated. Without fanaticism, superstition, or illusion, his whole life was regulated by a simple and unwavering sense of duty. The contemplative and emotional virtues which stoicism had long depressed, had regained their place, but the active virtues had not yet declined. The virtues of the hero were still deeply honoured, but gentleness and tenderness had acquired a new prominence in the ideal type.

BARTHOLOMEW SIMMONS.

[Bartholomew Simmons was born in the earlier years of the century at Kilworth, co. Cork, the scenery of which is very faithfully and effectively described in his poems. He early obtained an appointment in the Excise Office, London, which he held until his death on July 21, 1850. For a considerable number of years he contributed poems to several of the leading magazines and annuals, which met with wide-spread approval. A writer in *Blackwood's Magazine*, where many of his effusions made their first appearance, speaks of him in the following terms:— "Simmons, on the theme of Napoleon, excels all our great poets. Byron's lines on that subject are bad; Scott's poor; Wordsworth's weak; Lockhart and Simmons may be bracketed as equal; theirs are good, rich, and strong;" and the following poems from his pen will show that by his early death Ireland lost one of the most promising poets who were ever born on her soil.]

NAPOLEON'S LAST LOOK.

What of the night, ho! Watcher there
    Upon the armed deck,
That holds within its thunderous lair
    The last of empire's wreck—
E'en him whose capture now the chain
    From captive earth shall smite;
Ho! rock'd upon the moaning main,
    Watcher, what of the night?

"The stars are waning fast—the curl
    Of morning's coming breeze,
Far in the north begins to furl
    Night's vapour from the seas.
Her every shred of canvas spread,
    The proud ship plunges free,
While bears afar with stormy head
    Cape Ushant on our lee."

At that last word, as trumpet-stirr'd,
    Forth in the dawning gray
A silent man made to the deck
    His solitary way.
And leaning o'er the poop, he gazed
    Till on his straining view,
That cloud-like speck of land, upraised,
    Distinct, but slowly grew.

Well may he look until his frame
    Maddens to marble there;
He risked Renown's all-grasping game,
    Dominion or despair—
And lost—and lo! in vapour furled,
    The last of that loved France,
For which his prowess cursed the world,
    Is dwindling from his glance.

He lives, perchance, the past again,
    From the fierce hour when first
On the astounded hearts of men
    His meteor-presence burst—

When blood-besotted Anarchy
　Sank quelled amid the roar
Of thy far-sweeping musketry,
　Eventful Thermidor!

Again he grasps the victor-crown
　Marengo's carnage yields—
Or bursts o'er Lodi, beating down
　Bavaria's thousand shields—
Then turning from the battle-sod,
　Assumes the Consul's palm—
Or seizes giant-empire's rod
　In solemn Notre-Dame.

And darker thoughts oppress him now—
　Her ill-requited love,
Whose faith as beauteous as her brow
　Brought blessings from above—
Her trampled heart—his darkening star—
　The cry of outraged Man—
And white-lipped Rout, and Wolfish War,
　Loud thundering on his van.

Rave on, thou far-resounding Deep,
　Whose billows round him roll!
Thou'rt calmness to the storms that sweep
　This moment o'er his soul.
Black chaos swims before him, spread
　With trophy-shaping bones;
The council-strife, the battle-dead,
　Rent charters, cloven thrones.

Yet, proud One! could the loftiest day
　Of thy transcendent power,
Match with the soul-compelling sway
　Which, in this dreadful hour,
Aids thee to hide, beneath the show
　Of calmest lip and eye,
The hell that wars and works below—
　The quenchless thirst to die?

The white dawn crimson'd into morn—
　The morning flashed to day—
And the sun followed glory-born,
　Rejoicing on his way—
And still o'er ocean's kindling flood
　That muser cast his view,
While round him awed and silent stood
　His fate's devoted few.

O! for the sulphureous eve of June,
　When down that Belgian hill
His bristling Guards' superb platoon
　He led unbroken still!
Now would he pause, and quit their side
　Upon destruction's marge,
Nor king-like share with desperate pride
　Their vainly glorious charge?

No—gladly forward he would dash
　Amid that onset on,
Where blazing-shot and sabre-crash
　Pealed o'er his empire gone—
There, 'neath his vanquished eagles tost,
　Should close his grand career,
Girt by his heaped and slaughtered host,
　He lived—for fetters *here!*

Enough—in moontide's yellow light
　Cape Ushant melts away—
Even as his kingdom's shattered might
　Shall utterly decay—
Save when his spirit-shaking story,
　In years remotely dim,
Warms some pale minstrel with its glory
　To raise the song to Him.

THE FLIGHT TO CYPRUS.

De Vere has loos'd from Ascalon—Judea's holy
　gale,
Fresh with the spikenard's evening scent, is rust-
　ling in his sail;
A victor he to Normandy ploughs homeward through
　the brine,
Herald and harp shall laud him long for deeds in
　Palestine.

How gallantly, as night comes down, upon the
　Syrian seas,
The *Bel-Marie* all canvas crowds to catch the
　springing breeze.
A prosperous course be hers!—the spears above
　her poop that gleam
Have flash'd ere now, like stars, I trow, on Siloa's
　solemn stream.

Precious the freight that proud bark bears—the
　ransom and the spoil
Reap'd from Mahound's blaspheming crew on many
　a field of toil;
Large lustrous cups—Kathay's bright robes—the
　diamond's living rays—
Carpets from Tyre, whose costly fire for kings
　alone should blaze;

And worth them all, that Fairest One, whose
　tresses' sunny twine,
Far down unroll'd, outshames the gold of tawny
　India's mine;
When storm'd the Cross round Gaza's fosse, all
　bright but faithless, she
Fled from her Emir-spouse, De Vere's light para-
　mour to be.

And now, when sultry day is done, her languid
　brow to cool,
Soft couch'd upon the curtain'd deck reclines the
　Beautiful;

Voluptuous in repose, as she who, 'mid the Ægean
    Isles,
Rose radiant from the frowning deep, she dazzled
    into smiles.

Fast by that lady's pillow sits the passionate De
    Vere,
Now dimming with his doating kiss the glory of
    her hair;
Or watching till their sleepy lids her eyes' blue
    languish veil—
Or murmuring on her lips of rose fond love's un-
    tiring tale.

Yet restless all is her repose, no solace can she
    find;
The press of canvas overhead hoarse-groaning in
    the wind—
The cordage-strain — the whistling shrouds—De
    Vere's devoted words—
All things, or soft or sullen, now disturb her spirit's
    chords.

"In vain thy love would lull my ear, thou flatter-
    ing knight, for whom
I faithless fled my lord and land!—methinks that,
    through the gloom,
Some fearsome Genii's mighty wings are shadow-
    ing my soul,
Black as the clouds and waters now that round
    about us roll."

"Ah, cheer thee, sweet — 'tis but the rude and
    restless billows' heaving,
That frets thy frame of tenderest mould with
    weariness and grieving;
'Twill vanish soon: when mounts the moon at
    midnight from the sea,
Sweet Cyprus, with its rosy rocks high shining on
    our lee,

"Shall see us anchor'd—if the truth our Moorish
    pilot tell,
Who, since we weigh'd, has steer'd for us so steadily
    and well.
E'en now I go to track below our bearings by the
    chart;—
With freight like thee can I be free from wistful-
    ness of heart?"

De Vere is gone. His silent crew, from all the
    decks above,
Descend, lest even a murmur mar the slumbers of
    his Love;
Yon aged Moor, who, spectre-like, still at the
    rudder stands,
Yon stripling, station'd at the prow, are all the
    watching bands.

Pavilion-screen'd, from her soft couch how oft
    that lady bright
Raised like an evening star her head, and look'd
    upon the night,
Praying the tardy moon to rise—and through the
    shadows dim,
Encountering but that spectral form beside the
    rudder grim.

The moon at last!—blood-red and round, she
    wheeleth up the wave,
Soaring and whitening like a soul ascending from
    the grave;
Then riseth too the Beauty-brow'd, and quits with
    gentlest motion
Her tent's festoons,—two rival Moons at once upon
    the ocean!

O Queen of Quiet—thou who winn'st our adoration
    still,
As when a wondering world bow'd down on thine
    Ephesian hill!—
Stainless thyself, impart thy calm and purifying
    grace,
To her, the stain'd one, watching thee with her
    resplendent face!

The breeze has dropp'd—the soundless sails are
    flagging one by one;
While in his cabin still De Vere the parchment
    pores upon;
Sudden a shriek—a broken groan, his ear have
    smitten—hark!
That laughing yell!—sure fiends from hell are
    hailing to the Bark!

He gains the deck—the spot where last idolatrous
    he stood,
Is cross'd by some dark horrid thing—a narrow
    creeping flood;
Great Heaven forbid!—but where's the heart from
    whence it gush'd?—for now
The decks contain no form but that stone-stiff be-
    side the prow.

Stone-stiff—half life, half death—it stands with
    hideous terror dumb,
And bristling hair, and striving still for words
    that will not come:
Speak thou—speak thou, who from the prow kept
    watch along the water,
And kill thy lord with one dread word of Gaza's
    glorious daughter!

He told at last, that as he turn'd, what time the
    breeze had died,
To rouse his mates—far at the stern, the lady he
    espied,
Sky-musing there: and by the helm, with eyes
    coal-blazing—Him,
The Evil One, in semblance of their Moorish
    pilot grim,

Who stole to her, before that boy could cross him-
    self for grace,
His turban doff'd, then touch'd her arm, and stared
    her in the face—
That furnace-stare!—her scorch'd head droop'd—
    a flash—at once she fell
Prone at his feet, who instantly sprang with her
    down to hell!

Where olive-groves their shadows fling from Cy-
    prus' musky shore,
The *Bel-Marie* high stranded lies, to plough the
    waves no more;
And day by day, far, far away, in Rouen's aisles
    I ween,
Down-broken, like that stately bark, a mournful
    monk is seen.

EARL CAIRNS.

[The career of Lord Cairns is one of the most remarkable of any man even among the brilliant band who have risen to the same great height. His life has been an unbroken series of triumphs; and even those who have no love for his politics cannot deny that those triumphs have been legitimately earned. Lord Cairns owes his success to the sheer force of great abilities.

Hugh M'Calmont Cairns was born on December 27, 1819, and is the son of William Cairns, Esq., of Cultra, county Down. He was educated at Trinity College, Dublin, where he had a distinguished undergraduate career, obtaining first class in classics. He graduated B.A. in 1838. In January, 1844, he was called to the English bar at the Middle Temple.

Before long he became one of the most largely employed barristers in the courts of equity; and while still a stuff-gownsman could boast of a larger practice than the majority of those at the inner bar. In 1856 he was made a queen's counsel and a bencher of Lincoln's Inn. He had meantime entered upon another and more important career, having been elected Conservative member for Belfast in 1852, and the time soon came when this position placed the highest gifts of the legal profession at his disposal. In February, 1858, he was made solicitor-general in the administration of Lord Derby. Promotion to office so high after but fourteen years' practice at the bar was almost unprecedented; but the comments of the profession and the press were unanimously favourable.

The new solicitor-general soon proved the wisdom of Lord Derby's choice. The successful lawyer is frequently a terrible parliamentary failure; but the part Sir Hugh Cairns took in the great debate on Lord Ellenborough's censure of Lord Canning's proclamation proved his right to a place in the front rank of parliamentary orators. His fame as a speaker was established; and from this time forward he was recognized as one of the great debaters, who, if they cannot sway divisions—which no orator almost ever does in a representative assembly —can excite the enthusiasm of friends and the dread of foes.

Lord Derby's resignation in December, 1858, deprived Sir Hugh Cairns of office. When his chief returned to power in June, 1866, he became attorney-general. This post he did not long hold, accepting in the October following a lord-justiceship of appeal. In February, 1867, he was raised to the peerage as Baron Cairns of Garmoyle in the county of Antrim; and just about a year afterwards (February, 1868) he became Lord-chancellor of England. After the retirement of the ministry in 1868 he assumed for a while the responsible position of leader of the Conservative party in the House of Peers. When the Conservatives returned to office in February, 1874, he resumed his place of lord-chancellor. In September, 1878, he was still further advanced, attaining the honour of an earldom—a dignity that has not been reached by some of the most brilliant of his predecessors.

The style of Lord Cairns's eloquence is chaste. He rarely soars to high flights, and he is deficient in humour. His great merit is perfect lucidity of expression, so that his arguments are always presented as if they formed tightly-bound links in an unbroken chain of reasoning.]

ON THE OUDE PROCLAMATION.

[In the course of the session of 1858, when the Derby-Disraeli government was in power, Lord Ellenborough, who was president of the Board of Control, got his party into trouble by his treatment of Lord Canning, then Governor-general of India. Lord Canning had issued a proclamation to the people of Oude, making considerable changes in the tenure of land there, and Lord Ellenborough, before he received the full text of the document, wrote a despatch strongly denouncing it. A storm was raised in the House of Commons, and several motions of censure on the ministry were proposed. Lord (then Sir Hugh) Cairns as solicitor-general made, in the speech from which we give the following extract, one of the ablest defences of the government.]

A judgment upon that proclamation may be formed by having recourse to a very trite dilemma. Either it is right, or it is wrong. If it is right, and if the principles which it enunciates are principles just and politic, the government, beyond all doubt, was wrong in censuring it at all, and still more wrong in making that censure public. But if, upon the other hand, the principles which are embodied in that proclamation are neither consistent with justice nor in conformity with sound policy, then I challenge the right hon. gentleman to show upon what good grounds he calls upon the house to censure the condemnation of that which in itself is contrary to justice and to policy.

Now let me ask, to whom was this proclamation intended to be addressed? Not to the sepoys of India. They were mutineers in the strictest sense of the word. They had eaten our bread and received our pay. They were our sworn subjects, bound to us by every tie of allegiance and fidelity. They threw off that allegiance and rebelled. In the course of that rebellion they committed acts of murder, deeds of cruelty and treachery, cold-blooded, wilful, and deliberate. They were—or, at all events, many of them were—persons whose hands were stained by crimes of the deepest dye. Under these circumstances their lives and property were sacrificed by their crimes. But it was not to them, but to the king and people of Oude, this proclamation of Lord Canning was addressed. What says Mr. Edmonstone, the secretary to the chief commissioner of Oude? He states in the nineteenth paragraph that the proclamation was addressed to the chiefs and inhabitants of Oude, and not to the mutineers. But what was the kingdom of Oude? Our relations with it were relations of conquest, and not of allegiance. I know it has been said that Oude had voluntarily become incorporated with our dominions—that its people had willingly come into our allegiance, and that the hostilities in Oude were rebellion and not war. Sir, these assertions I deny, and my denial is capable of easy proof. I do not now desire to enter into the merits of the question of the annexation of that kingdom. That is a question which never has been, and in all probability never will be, discussed in this house as fully as it might deserve. In speaking of the subject I will only say that the strongest feeling by which I was impressed upon reading the papers connected with it—and I have read them carefully—was the hope that history may be as lenient to us with regard to that transaction as we have been to ourselves. But, declining to open up that large question, I shall proceed to deal with facts about which there can be no dispute. In the year 1856 the treaty which the East India Company asserted was the treaty regulating our relations with the King of Oude, was a treaty made in 1801, which contained a clause guaranteeing to the vizier, his heirs and successors, the possession of their territories, together with the free exercise of their authority within their dominions. In the year 1856, however, the East India Company, considering that the kingdom of Oude was misgoverned, deemed that the misgovernment conferred upon them the right, I do not say whether justly or unjustly, to annex that territory to our possessions in India. How did they carry the right into effect? Substantially by means of conquest. A commissioner was sent to Oude. A body of British troops crossed the Ganges. A treaty was presented to the king, who refused to sign the treaty; and he was consequently dethroned, his palace taken possession of, his property sold, his ministers either made prisoners or held to bail.

I do not say whether this was right or wrong—I will assume it to be right. But I still confidently ask whether the case of Oude was one of voluntary submission or of simple conquest and annexation? My answer to the question is that our relations with Oude were relations of conquest. All that was done there was done under protest, and that protest continued until the sepoy revolt broke out. The people of Oude, which was under forced submission, taking advantage of that rebellion, made war against England—war, I admit, stained by bloody and barbarous crimes, but still war. By the valour of our troops poured into the country, the skill and energy of our commander-in-chief—and, I cheerfully and gratefully add, by the skill and energy of

Lord Canning—by the heroism almost unparalleled of small handfuls of men, ay, and women, who maintained their position in the country until our troops arrived—by all these means the contest in India has resulted in decisive and, I trust, a lasting victory.

But now we are victorious, let me ask what is the policy which as victors we ought to pursue? I am prepared to declare what that policy should be upon the broad grounds of justice. But first let me examine the question upon the narrower grounds of prudence and self-interest. Do you mean to hold Oude? If so, how do you propose to effect that object? Is it by the aid of a standing army? You may achieve your end in that way, but its attainment will cost you dear. Do you desire the willing and cheerful submission of the people of Oude? How can you procure that submission? Is it not an important element in the question to gain the good-will of the landowners of that country? A child could answer that question. Which of two things do you do, let me ask—provoke hostility or conciliate good-will by taking from them that which they hold dearer than their lives? Let us go a step further. Do you desire to put down the mutiny of the sepoys? Of course you do. Then it follows naturally that you must also desire to prevent the sepoys from taking refuge and obtaining support in neighbouring states. Where is it most likely that they would obtain that support which would enable them again to make head against us? In the kingdom of Oude. If we have the people of Oude in our favour they will assist us in beating down and delivering up those sepoys who may take refuge in their country; but if you alienate the feelings of that people the consequence is easy to foresee; you will throw them into the arms of the sepoys—they will combine with the sepoys, and you will have in that distant and separate territory to crush and to subdue, not merely the natives of the territory, but also the sepoys, who will certainly assemble there. Therefore, I say, upon the lowest ground of self-interest and policy it is for the advantage of this country to conciliate the affections of the people of Oude.

But I desire to rest the case on broader grounds than these. Whatever other nations may do, England ought not to retrograde from those laws of war which civilization has introduced. How, then, upon the principles of justice and the practice of civilized nations, which this country is bound to observe, ought we to treat the property of a conquered people? My proposition is this—you make war with kings and governments, but not with individuals. If in the course of war individuals commit crimes, they put themselves beyond the pale of that rule; but, except as to such cases, every individual is entitled to protection of life and property from the victorious nation. You might as well confiscate the lives of the conquered as their property.

. . . .

Sir, I have gone through the right hon. gentleman's charges against the government, which are reduced to the charge of writing and the charge of publishing the despatch. The charge for publishing it has fallen to the ground. The charge of writing it depends upon the higher and broader question of the policy of the proclamation. On this question, sir, the right hon. gentleman and myself are at direct and positive issue. He appeals to the house to be silent—I appeal to the house not to be silent. I appeal to them on behalf of the dearest interests of this country and of India—on behalf of 5,000,000 of people—who may be misguided, misgoverned, and even barbarous, but who are men with like passions, feelings, perceptions, and prejudices as ourselves. I appeal to the house in the cause of humanity and justice. I make that appeal to the British House of Commons, to which that appeal never has been, and never will be, made in vain. Do not let this go forth as a matter of doubt, or as a matter to be slurred over by a captious and catching motion, prepared by a cabal to embarrass and displace a ministry. Tell it out by your vote, in terms neither vague nor indistinct, to the people of India, that you desire submission and not spoliation—that the war we wage is the war of nations, and not the war of freebooters—that England knows how to make war and conquer, but also knows how to treat those who are conquered—that she offers to those who are conquered, and who submit to her arms, that protection for their lives and property which will be the best earnest to them of the mildness of the rule which the fate of battles has assigned to them.

Sir, if ever there was a time at which it was necessary that our policy with regard to India should be clear and distinct, it is the present. We are upon the point of transferring the government of India from the Company to the Queen. In the course of the discussions in this house upon the subject of our past government of that country some confessions have been made, which you may rely on it have not escaped the attention of the people of India. There was a confession made by the right hon. gentleman, the member for Radnor (Sir G. C. Lewis), which I heard, I must say, with respectful amazement. The right hon. gentleman, the then chancellor of the exchequer, the minister of the crown, who was advocating the bill which was introduced into parliament to transfer the government of India to the queen, was speaking of the past government of that country. It is true he was speaking of the government prior to the year 1784, but at a time when not the most insignificant parts of our acquisitions in India were made. The right hon. gentleman said:—"I do most confidently maintain that no civilized government ever existed on the face of this earth which was more corrupt, more perfidious, and more rapacious than the government of the East India Company from the years 1765 to 1784."

Sir, in this sentiment I, for one, do not concur; but, at all events, let there be no mistake with respect to our future government. Let us tell the people of India that we are not ashamed to confess that we offer them mercy and justice, and not spoliation; that the war which we wage against them is a war consistent with mercy and justice, and not for the sake of plunder, and that no faction and no intrigue will tempt the House of Commons even for a moment to lay themselves open to suspicion that the dynasty we are about to introduce into India is to be a dynasty of reckless, ruthless, and indiscriminate confiscation.

THE EMPRESS OF INDIA.[1]

Upon a subject of this kind there is, in a country like ours, a higher authority to appeal to with regard to the views and wishes of the people than petitions. I have always understood that it was one of the advantages of a country possessing representative institutions that the views of the people of the country could be ascertained through the mouths of the representatives of the people. It so happens that this bill has passed the ordeal of the representative assembly before it has come to your lordships.

The noble earl (Earl Grey) who spoke the other night near me dealt with this difficulty

[1] Extract from speech on the Royal Titles Bill, April 3, 1876.

in a very singular way. He said it was quite true that this bill had passed the House of Commons by a large majority, but that a great number of those who voted for it did so with great reluctance. The noble earl is one to whom we look for instruction upon all matters of parliamentary and constitutional practice; but it is a dangerous doctrine for this house to hold or listen to, that we are so to regard the votes in the House of Commons. I know what your lordships would think if, after your lordships had arrived at a decision, some person in the House of Commons—not some novice, but some one experienced in public life, some *vir pietate gravis*—should rise in his place and say, "It is quite true in voting they were discharging a great public function, but in reality their votes were not given on any principle of that kind, but on another principle, and from other motives, with reluctance and against their judgment and conscience." If the noble earl's observations do not amount to that, I am at a loss to know what they do mean. There is one other observation I may make with regard to the majority of which the noble earl spoke so lightly. It might be said that the majority supporting the government were bound by the bond which usually attaches them to the government; but, my lords, that ground is entirely cut away from under the noble earl, because it so happens that the majority which carried this bill was, if I mistake not, something like double the ordinary majority by which the government is supported.

This being the evidence which we have of the feeling of the country, the noble earl (the Earl of Shaftesbury) asks your lordships to carry to the foot of the throne a statement which, under these circumstances, appears to me to be both violent and unjustified. He proposes, in effect, that your lordships should inform her most gracious majesty that the title of Empress—even if assumed for India, even if used for India—is a title which will not be in accordance with the loyal feelings of her majesty's subjects. That is, he proposes absolutely and unreservedly to state to the crown —after the House of Commons has stated its opinion—not what is the opinion of this house, but what is the opinion of the people of this country. I must say that if anything could be imagined which is an usurpation of the powers of a representative body, it is for this house to go out of its way to express, not our own opinion, but something which we undertake to say is the opinion of the people of this country. But, my lords, have we any evidence that the title of Empress is a title which will, in the opinion of the people of this country, properly express the power of the throne in India? I think we have some evidence on that point. I believe that at the time this controversy was raised there were large numbers of people in this country who were under the impression that her majesty was already Empress of India. I recollect, at the time of her majesty's gracious speech from the throne, receiving a communication from a keen observer of the public history of this country, which stated that the government were under a misapprehension on this matter; that in 1858 the queen had become Empress of India, and that was her title at the present moment. My lords, I believe that this was really the opinion and belief of a large number of people at the commencement of this year. The noble earl ridicules the references that have been made to school-books and almanacs, and I know that a good deal of contempt was thrown upon any reference to authorities of that kind. But I must say for myself that I think that the public man who throws contempt upon the school-books of the nation may be a man of very keen wit and of a very sharp tongue, but he is not a man of a very great deal of common sense. When I find that in school-books and in almanacs, circulating through the country by hundreds of thousands, and circulating for years, the style given to the queen with regard to India is Empress of India, and that no voice has ever been heard against it, I consider that is very cogent evidence that there is nothing in that title, providing it does not affect the English title, which is objectionable to the feelings of the people of this country. If your lordships will take up one of those depositories of information, which I never open without amazement and admiration—I mean one of those books which contain a statement of the titles and histories of your lordships—you will find, I think, this one which I hold in my hand is about the oldest established in this country—that the title of the queen is thus described, "Victoria, Queen of the United Kingdom of Great Britain and Ireland, and of the Colonies and Dependencies thereof, Empress of India." It has, so far as I know, never occurred to any person to protest against the title thus given as repulsive to English feelings.

I have anxiously endeavoured to discover what were the arguments upon which it was stated that the title of the Queen of England would be interfered with by the title of the Empress of India, and I do not desire to overlook any one of them. The first argument that is used is what I may term the social argument. I think it was the noble duke who spoke the other night (the Duke of Somerset) who said that, of course, the title would be used in England, and that it would be used not merely by the sovereign, but by other members of the royal family. That argument is very shortly answered. I will read to your lordships what was stated on these points by the prime minister. He said:—

"The noble lord who has just addressed us has put the case very fairly before us. He gives myself and colleagues credit for being sincere in the statements we have made, and feels that we have given honest advice to the sovereign—and that advice, I am bound to say, has been received with the utmost sympathy—namely, that the title which her majesty has been advised, for great reasons of state, to assume, shall be exercised absolutely and solely in India when it is required, and that on becoming Empress of India she does not seek to be in any way Empress of England, but will be content with the old style and title of Queen of the United Kingdom. To all purposes, in fact, her majesty would govern the United Kingdom as she has always governed it."

As to the members of the royal family, he said, "The advice which the government gave to the crown, and which was received with sympathy, was that no change should be made in, if I may use the term, the courtesy titles of the royal family. That appears to me to terminate this point."

But the noble duke (the Duke of Somerset) had another string to his bow on this part of the question. He said—"But suppose you provide for the sovereign exercising the title in the way you say, you must look at the other side. What will people do after the bill is passed even with these limitations? It is said that the moment we pass this bill no country will take up the title of Empress, and that it will in the course of time become the ordinary title of the crown." Now, I want the noble duke who used that argument to contrast it with another which fell from him in the same speech. He said the people in this country disliked the title of Empress—that they would not have it under any circumstances. Now, if that is the case, how does the noble duke establish his first proposition —that the moment the title is adopted every person will be eager and ready to use it? I must submit to the noble duke that it is not customary for well-balanced reasoning minds to lay down two antagonistic propositions destructive of each other in the same speech.

My lords, reference has been made in the debate to the ancient history of France. I do not wish to enter into a controversy on the subject, but there is one part of it which I think may be usefully referred to in answer to the argument of the noble earl near me (Earl Granville). My lords, I believe I am right in stating that during the French monarchy, and down to the termination of the reign of Louis Philippe—a time during which, if there was ever any people attached to the title of king it was the French people—it was the rule of the French government that oriental potentates in diplomatic intercourse with France should be addressed—and the sovereign of France in diplomatic intercourse with those potentates should style himself—Emperor. I have copies of several such documents, during the reign of Louis Philippe, and I have never heard that the practice led to any general introduction of the title of Emperor of France.

I now come to the argument with regard to the royal style in public documents. In answer to a question the other night, I said, speaking in general terms, and without referring to any definite form of proclamation, that where it was necessary to use the whole of the royal style, the whole of the royal style should, as a rule, be used. The documents in question I believe may be generally classified as commissions, patents, writs, and possibly charters. It is not from the perusal of documents of that kind that the greatest amount of public information is obtained; but any difficulty which might arise from the new title being used in such cases will be avoided. The bill authorizes her majesty to make such addition to the royal style and titles as she may think fit. In that respect it follows the measures connected with the union with Ireland in the year 1801. A proclamation was on that occasion issued by the sovereign defining the new title then introduced, and stating that it was to be used so far as convenient on all proper occasions. But the proclamation at the same time provided that on all coinage, as well as stamps, dies, and instruments of that kind, the old style and title should continue to be used. Well, my lords, I have to state that it is the intention of the government that the proclamation to be issued by her majesty under this bill shall comply literally with the engagements which have been given to the House of Commons, and that it will provide in a manner analogous to the proclamation of 1801—that upon all writs, commissions, patents, and charters intended to operate within the United Kingdom, the royal style shall continue as it is, without any addition.

There is another, and I believe it is the last argument that has been advanced. It is said that the new title of Empress of India will overshadow the title of Queen of England. My lords, that appears to me to be not an argument, but a mere figure of speech. It is difficult to answer a figure of speech; and I am at a loss to conceive how the great title of Queen of England, unchanged and unaltered and sacred in this country, and beloved by every subject of the crown, can possibly be overshadowed by the addition of a title apposite and appropriate to and only to be used in India. But, my lords, to my mind there will be much in the juxtaposition of those two titles that will appear to the people of India to be both significant and appropriate. There will appear in that juxtaposition to be not an obscuring shadow, but a beneficent lustre, and the light, in my opinion, will not fall from the Empress upon the Queen, but from the Queen upon the Empress. My lords, the sovereign of this country is in substance and in fact the Empress of India, but she is Empress of India because she is Queen of England. India does not possess in herself that capacity for self-government which we enjoy; but Providence has fortunately placed her under the power of this country—a power which, while in its action upon India it is paramount, is at the same time in its exercise checked and controlled by all the limits and responsibilities of constitutional government. My lords, it is the twofold aspect of this paramount power—its aspect of origin and limit on the one hand, and its aspect of incidence and action on the other—that the pre-eminent fitness of this twofold title is to be found. And, my lords, when this measure goes forth to India, bearing—as I trust it will bear—to the chiefs and people of that great world the assurance that their destinies and interests are indissolubly united with those of this empire, it will serve to remind them at the same time that the sovereign who claims their submission and allegiance is not only, and not primarily, Empress of India, but that her first, her greatest, her most grateful title is that of Queen of England.

JOSIAS LESLIE PORTER.

[In our notice of the late Dr. Cooke we referred to the excellent memoir of him from the pen of his son-in-law Dr. Porter, who is himself well entitled to a place among the literary names of his native country.

Josias Leslie Porter was born on October 4, 1823, at Burt, county Donegal. He received his earliest instruction in the house of the Rev. S. Craig, of Crossroads, county Derry; and, like many Ulster young men of that day, entered the university of Glasgow, where he graduated B.A. in 1842, and M.A. in the following year. He then began his theological training in the University of Edinburgh, where he was one of the pupils of Dr. Chalmers, and afterwards studied at the Free Church College there. Having been ordained in 1846, he was first employed in pastoral work in Newcastle. His next sphere was as a missionary to the Jews at Damascus; and before proceeding to this distant scene of labour he married in 1849 the youngest daughter of Dr. Henry Cooke. He remained in the East for eight years, during which time he travelled extensively through Palestine, Syria, Egypt, Asia Minor, and Greece. After his return home he was appointed in 1860 to the professorship of biblical criticism in the Assembly's College, Belfast. In 1864 the University of Edinburgh conferred on him the honorary degree of D.D., and the University of Glasgow that of LL.D. In 1875 he was chosen moderator of the General Assembly of the Irish Presbyterian Church. When the Board of Commissioners of Intermediate Education in Ireland was brought into existence in 1878, Dr. Porter was naturally pointed out as the fittest representative of his co-religionists at the board, and in the same year he was made assistant-commissioner. In 1879 he was raised to the still higher position of president of Queen's College, Belfast.

Dr. Porter has written a large number of separate works, besides being a constant contributor to the higher class of periodicals. He has described his oriental experiences in three books: *Five Years in Damascus* (1855), *Handbook for Syria and Palestine* (1856), and *The Giant Cities of Bashan* (1865). He has written some volumes of biblical criticism: *The Pentateuch and the Gospels*, and a *Reply to Colenso on the Pentateuch*. He is also the author of numerous articles in Smith's *Dictionary of the Bible*, Kitto's *Cyclopædia of Biblical Literature*, the American *Bibliotheca Sacra*, the *Encyclopædia Britannica*, and of a considerable number of pamphlets.]

LYDDA.

(FROM "THE GIANT CITIES OF BASHAN."[1])

The sun was already low in the west when we entered the broad avenue-like road that leads to Lydda. It was a beautiful evening—the sky cloudless, the atmosphere transparent as crystal. The sunbeams fell slanting on the dense foliage of the orange and apricot trees, here gilding the topmost leaves, and yonder shooting in lines of gold through the openings. The sea-breeze was just setting in. Now it played among the rustling branches of the tall palms, and now it seemed to come down for a moment and breathe its balmy breath in our faces. The road, covered deeply with red sand, is lined with orchards in which we saw orange, lemon, peach, pomegranate, and carub trees, intermixed with the palm, walnut, and sycamore; and the whole inclosed by huge hedges of cactus, whose luscious fruit, clinging quaintly to the sides of the great thick leaves, was now almost ripe. An easy walk of three-quarters of an hour brought us to *Ludd*, the modern as well as the more ancient name of the apostolic Lydda (1 Chron. viii. 12). I have often been sadly disappointed on approaching an old Bible city, which fancy had somehow decked in the choicest beauties of nature and art, but which reality transformed into mud hovels on a rocky hill-side. It was not so with Lydda. Even now, though its glory is gone, Lydda has an imposing look. It is embowered in verdure. Olive groves encircle it, and stretch far out over the surrounding plain, and their dusky hue is relieved here and there by the brighter foliage of the apricot and mulberry; while, near the houses, vines are seen creeping over garden walls and clambering up the great gnarled trunks and branches of the walnut trees.

The village stands on a gentle eminence, and

---

[1] By permission of the author.

high above its terraced roofs rise the splendid ruins of England's patron saint. Lydda, tradition says, was the native place of St. George; and England's chivalrous king, the lion-hearted Richard, built in his honour this noble church, the ruins of which now form the chief attraction of Ludd. The walls and part of the groined roof of the chancel still remain, and also one lofty pointed arch, with its massive clustered columns and white marble capitals, rich in carving and fret-work.

We climbed to the top of the crumbling wall, and there sat down to read the story of Peter's visit to this place (Acts ix. 32-39). The whole village was in full view, and the great plain around it. Peter was away on one of his missionary tours in the hill country of Samaria, "and he came down also to the saints which dwelt at Lydda." He *came down* through the defiles of those mountains, and across that broad rich plain of Sharon, or "Saron," and up the gentle ascent to this old town. The saints met him as he entered, and told him of the sufferings of poor paralytic Eneas; and the scene then enacted at his bedside was such as the people had never before witnessed. "Peter said unto him, Eneas, Jesus Christ maketh thee whole; arise and make thy bed. And he arose immediately." As the words reached his ears, divine power operated on his body. The wondrous tidings sped from mouth to mouth, from group to group, from town to country. All eagerly inquired; some probably at first doubted, but when they saw the healed paralytic, faith triumphed, and "all that dwelt in Lydda and Saron turned to the Lord." The joyful news soon found its way to Joppa, ten miles distant; and then the mourning friends of the charitable Tabitha despatched quick messengers to tell Peter of her death, half hoping that even she might not be beyond the reach of his power. Peter delayed not, but set out across that western plain on another journey of mercy.

As we looked from our commanding position over that wide landscape, we could not but admit that there was a charm in it independent of all its hallowed associations. It was one of those views which, like a picture by Claude, never pass from the memory. On the north lay the vast plain of Sharon, variegated with green meadows and yellow cornfields; for, though only the end of April, the fields were "already white to the harvest." In the far distance we could just distinguish the pale blue summits of Carmel. On the east the view was bounded by the long range of the mountains of Israel, their rounded tops now tinged with the ruddy evening light; and the deep purple shadows of their ravines throwing out in bold relief the old ruined cities and modern villages that crown nearly all the projecting cliffs. On the south a swell in the plain concealed Philistia; but that swell was clothed with the orchards of Ramleh, whose tapering minarets and tall white tower shoot up from the midst of the dense foliage. On the west, beyond the gardens, there was first a stretch of brown sandy plain; then a narrow dark belt traced by the orange groves of Joppa; and then the Mediterranean, gleaming like a mirror of burnished gold beneath the setting sun.

On Monday morning, before the sun had yet risen over Judah's hills, we were all in the saddle, following a gay trooper, bristling with arms, along the broad sandy road to Philistia. Selim, our new companion, was to fill the double post of guide and guard: and he was admirably qualified for office; for he knew the name of every village, fountain, and wady between Ramleh and Gaza; and he was on terms of close friendship with all the bandits in the province. Our route was at first dreary enough, traversing bleak downs of brown sand, over which a few flocks of sheep and goats followed their shepherds, apparently bound for better pastures. But the morning, as usual, was bright and beautiful, the air fresh and exhilarating, and Selim full of tales of border raids, and old traditions about Samson and Jalûd (Goliath); so we got on cheerily. An hour's ride brought us to the top of the swell which separates Sharon from Philistia. The latter plain now opened up before us, rolling away to the southern horizon in graceful undulations, clothed with a rich mantle of green and gold—harvest-field and pasture-land. Ruins were visible everywhere; but the villages were few, small, and far between. The distant hill-sides were more thickly studded with them; and Selim told us that though, like the old Danites, the people lived there for security, their possessions and crops were chiefly in the plain.

THE DRUSES.

(FROM "THE GIANT CITIES OF BASHAN.")

The Druses are a remarkable people. Their religion is a mystery; their manners are simple and patriarchal; their union and courage are proverbial; and though small in number they form the most powerful party in Syria. Whenever danger threatens, or whenever they find it expedient to resist the demands or exactions of the Porte, they congregate in the Haurân, and no force has ever been found sufficient to dislodge or subdue them. Here they defied Ibrahim Pasha, and destroyed the flower of the Egyptian army; here they have once and again defeated the Turkish troops, and driven them back with disgrace to the very walls of Damascus. Physically they are the finest race in Western Asia—tall, stalwart, hardy mountaineers. Accustomed from childhood to vigorous exercise, and trained in athletic sports and the use of arms, they form a body of brave and daring "irregulars," such as the world could scarcely match. But the grand secret of their power is their union. They act together as one man. Brotherly union in peace and war, in prosperity and adversity, is the chief article of their religious creed. As regards religion, they are divided into two classes, the *Initiated* and the *Ignorant*. With the former the rites, ceremonies, and doctrines remain a profound secret. The holy books are preserved and read by them alone. They assemble in chapels every Thursday evening, refusing admission to all others. What they do then and there is unknown; but there is reason to believe that these meetings are quite as much of a political as a religious character.

The Druse sheikhs form a hereditary nobility, and preserve with great tenacity all the pride and state of their order. They receive and entertain travellers with profuse hospitality, and no compensation in money can be offered to them. To strangers, under ordinary circumstances, they are obliging, communicative, and faithful. In time of peace they are industrious and courteous; but in war they are noted alike for daring courage and unsparing ferocity. When among this strange and primitive people in Bashan, I felt at once that I was out of the beaten track of tourists, where one can pitch his tent, picket his horses, cook his provisions, and march again, caring for nobody, and nobody caring for him. Here all is different. We are among a people of patriarchal manners and genuine patriarchal hospitality. We were looked on and treated as welcome guests. We could not pass town or village without being entreated to accept hospitality. "Will not my lord descend while his servants prepare a little food?" is the urgent language of every village sheikh. The coffee is always on the hearth; a kid or lamb—representative of the old "fatted calf"—is at hand, and can be "got ready" with all the despatch of ancient days. Food for servants, "provender" for horses, accommodation for all, are given as matters of course. In travelling through Bashan one fancies himself carried back to the days when the patriarchs sat in their tent-doors, ready to welcome every visitor and hail every passer-by.

. . . .

On one of the southern peaks of the mountain range, some two thousand feet above the vale of Kerioth, stands the town of Hebrân. Its shattered walls and houses looked exceedingly picturesque, as we wound up a deep ravine, shooting out far overhead from among the tufted foliage of the evergreen oak. Our little cavalcade was seen approaching, and ere we reached the brow of the hill the whole population had come out to meet and welcome us. The sheikh, a noble-looking young Druse, had already sent a man to bring a kid from the nearest flock to make a feast for us, and we saw him bounding away through an opening in the forest. He returned in half an hour with the kid on his shoulder. We assured the hospitable sheikh that it was impossible for us to remain. Our servants were already far away over the plain, and we had a long journey before us. He would listen to no excuse. The feast *must* be prepared. "My lord could not pass by his servant's house without honouring him by eating a morsel of bread, and partaking of the kid which is being made ready. The sun is high; the day is long; rest for a time under my roof; eat and drink, and then pass on in peace." There was so much of the true spirit of patriarchal hospitality here, so much that recalled to mind scenes in the life of Abraham (Gen. xviii. 2), and Manoah (Judges xiii. 15), and other Scripture celebrities, that we found it hard to refuse. Time pressed, however, and we were reluctantly compelled to leave before the kid was served.

EASTERN POLITENESS.

(FROM "HAND-BOOK FOR SYRIA AND PALESTINE.")

The inhabitants of Syria and Palestine form a most interesting study. Their dress, their manners and customs, and their language, are all primitive. No European nation, with the exception perhaps of the Spaniards, bears the least resemblance to them. Like Spain, too, the best specimens of humanity are here found among the lower classes. The farther we go from the contaminated atmosphere of government offices, the more successful shall we be in our search after honesty, industry, and genuine patriarchal hospitality—the great, almost the only unadulterated virtue of the Arab. They are illiterate, of course, and extremely ignorant of all Frank inventions; but still there is a native dignity in their address and deportment, which will both please and astonish those who have seen the awkward vulgarity of the lower classes in some more favoured lands. Whether we enter the tent of the Bedawy or the cottage of the *fellah*, we are received and welcomed with an ease and courtesy that would not disgrace a palace. The modes of salutation are very formal—perhaps some would call them verbose and even tedious. One is apt to imagine, on hearing the long series of reiterated inquiries after the health, happiness, and prosperity of the visitor who drops in, and the evasive replies given, that there is surely some hidden grief, some secret malady, which his politeness would fain conceal, but which the heartfelt sympathy of the host constrains him to search into. It is disappointing to discover, as every one will in time discover, that this is all form; and that the "thousand and one" *keif keifaks?* and *keif khâtěraks?* and *keif hâl sâhhětaks?* and *in-shallah mabsûts?* and the equally numerous, but not very satisfactory responses of, *Ullah ynsallěmak*, *Ullah yusallem khâtěrak*, *Ullah gahfâzak*, *Ullah yutawwel 'umrak*—are all phrases which mean nothing, so far as the feelings of those who use them are concerned. Still there is something pleasing in these inquiries, compliments, and good wishes, empty though they be. The gestures used in salutation are also graceful, if a little complicated. The touching of the heart, the lips, and the forehead with the right hand, seems to say that each one thus saluted is cherished in the heart, praised with the lips, and esteemed with the intellect. When peculiar deference and respect are intended to be shown, the right hand is first lowered almost to the ground, as a proof that the individual would honour your very feet, or the soil you tread. A still greater deference is implied in kissing the hand; and the greatest of all is kissing the feet. These latter, however, it is just as dignified for travellers firmly, but courteously, to resist. Another remark may be made on a curious custom which universally prevails in Syria. An Arab when eating, whether in the house or by the wayside, however poor and scanty may be his fare, never neglects to invite the visitor, or passing wayfarer, to join him. And this is not always an empty compliment; indeed there are few Arabs who will not feel honoured by the traveller's tasting their humble fare. The invitation, however, is generally declined by a set courteous phrase. The word of invitation is invariably *tefuddhel*, the multifarious meaning of which I can only interpret by the Italian *favorisca*. The complimentary declinature is, *Ullah yezid fudhlak*, "May God increase your bounty." In passing his house, too, in company with a stranger, the Arab will always invite him in by the same *tefuddhel*; and in presenting coffee, sherbet, fruit, or any other delicacy, the same word is used—in fact, with the exception of *bakhshish*, it is the most common and expressive word in the Arabic language.

In making purchases from an Arab his politeness is almost amazing. When the price is asked he replies, "Whatever you please, my lord." When pressed for a more definite answer, he says, "Take it without money." One cannot but remember under such circumstances, Abraham's treaty with the sons of Heth for the cave of Machpelah (Gen. xxiii.). Our feelings of romance, however, are somewhat damped when we find that the price ultimately demanded is four or five times the value of the article. An Arab always tells you that his house is yours, his property is yours, he himself is your slave; that he loves you with all his heart, would defend you with his life, &c. &c. This all sounds very pretty, but it will be just as well not to rely too much on it for fear of disappointment. Nothing, however, is lost by politeness; and so one may seem to believe all that is said, and even utter an occasional *Ullah yutawwel 'umrak ya sidy*, "May God prolong your life, O my lord!" by way of showing gratitude. The Arabs are most profuse in the use of titles. Every beggar will address his fellow with "O my lord," *ya sidy* (pronounced *seedy*), or "Your excellency," *jěnâbak*; while the traveller is generally *saadatak*, "Your highness." It has been too often the practice of Englishmen to "manage" their Arab servants and muleteers by bullying and browbeating; but this is a great mistake. Insolent *dragomen* generally resort to such practices to sustain their temporary tyranny. I need not say that such conduct is beneath the dignity of an English gentleman. Unvarying courtesy, accompanied with as unvarying *firmness*, will gain the desired object far more effectually. This is especially the case with the Bedawin, who can often be persuaded by a kind word when they could not be driven by a rod of iron. At the same time any approach to undue familiarity should be immediately checked; the permission of such familiarity will be attributed by the Arab to weakness of character, perhaps in some cases to fear, of which he will not be slow to take advantage when occasion offers. To know one's place and keep it, and to know one's rights and insist on obtaining them, are all-important qualifications in Syria as elsewhere.

ALFRED PERCEVAL GRAVES.

[Alfred Perceval Graves is the son of Dr. Graves, the Bishop of Limerick, and was born in Dublin in 1846. He was educated at Trinity College, obtaining double-first honours in classics and English. He graduated in 1870, after entering the Home Office, where he became private secretary to Mr. Winterbotham, then under-secretary in that department, whose premature decease, it may be remembered, caused some years ago so much regret among all parties. Mr. Graves is now one of Her Majesty's inspectors of schools.

Brought up amid scholastic surroundings, Mr. Graves began at an early age to write. His first literary production appeared in the *Dublin University Magazine* when he was but sixteen or seventeen years of age. He employed himself at this time for the most part in giving poetic translations from the Greek and Latin classics. Mr. Graves has also contributed to *Fraser*, the *Spectator*, *Punch*, and several other periodicals. The first collection of his poems was published in 1872, under the title *Songs of Killarney*. The work was received with a chorus of praise from the journals—literary and political, English, Irish, and Scotch, and, it may be added, American. The book consists for the most part of Irish songs and ballads. The aim of the poet has been to express the humour and pathos of the Irish character, and, further, to make the expression of these passions take the simplicity of form in which the Irish people would themselves clothe them. Our first two quotations are from this collection, and we think the book as a whole shows that the author has attained remarkable success in his object. These poems are full of genuine Irish humour, which is delicate and graceful, and utterly free, it need scarcely be said, from the buffoonery that has been made to pass as characteristically Irish. There is also true natural melody in the verses, and the sentiment is pure and healthy.

Mr. Graves is also the joint author of a successful work on school management, entitled the *Elementary School Manager*. Another volume of his poems, under the title *Irish Songs and Ballads*, is in the press, from which we make our remaining quotations.]

IRISH SPINNING-WHEEL SONG.[1]

Show me a sight
Bates for delight
An ould Irish wheel wid a young Irish girl at it.
O! No!
Nothin' you'll show
Aqnals her sittin' and takin' a twirl at it.

Look at her there,
Night in her hair—
The blue ray of day from her eye laughin' out on us!
Faix, an' a foot,
Perfect of cut,
Peepin' to put an end to all doubt in us

That there's a sight
Bates for delight
An ould Irish wheel wid a young Irish girl at it.
O! No!
Nothin' you'll show
Aqnals her sittin' an' takin' a twirl at it.

How the lamb's wool
Turns coarse an' dull
By them soft, beautiful, weeshy, white hands of her,
Down goes her heel,
Roun' runs the reel,
Purrin' wid pleasure to take the commands of her.

Then show me a sight
Bates for delight
An ould Irish wheel wid a young Irish girl at it.

[1] This and the following pieces are quoted by the author's permission.

O! No!
    Nothin' you'll show
Aquals her sittin' an' takin' a twirl at it.

    Talk of Three Fates,
      Seated on seats,
Spinnin' and shearin' away till they've done for me.
    You may want three
      For your massacree,
But one fate for me, boys, and only the one for me.

    And
      Isn't that fate,
      Pictured complate,
An ould Irish wheel wid a young Irish girl at it?
      O! No!
      Nothin' you'll show,
Aquals her sittin' an' takin' a twirl at it.

IRISH LULLABY.

I'd rock my own sweet childie to rest in a cradle
    of gold on a bough of the willow,
To the *shoheen ho* of the wind of the west and the
    sho hoo lo of the soft sea billow.
    Sleep, baby dear,
    Sleep without fear,
Mother is here beside your pillow.

I'd put my own sweet childie to sleep in a silver
    boat on the beautiful river,
Where a *shoheen* whisper the white cascades, and
    a *sho hoo lo* the green flags shiver.
    Sleep, baby dear,
    Sleep without fear,
Mother is here with you for ever.

Sho hoo lo! to the rise and fall of mother's bosom
    'tis sleep has bound you,
And O, my child, what cozier nest for rosier rest
    could love have found you?
    Sleep, baby dear,
    Sleep without fear,
Mother's two arms are clasped around you.

FATHER O'FLYNN.

Of priests we can offer a charmin' variety,
    Far renowned for larnin' and piety;
Still, I'd advance ye widout impropriety,
    Father O'Flynn as the flower of them all.
      Here's a health to you, Father O'Flynn,
      Slainté, and slainté, and slainté agin;
        Powerfullest preacher, and
        Tinderest teacher, and
      Kindliest creature in ould Donegal.

Don't talk of your Provost and Fellows of Trinity,
Famous for ever at Greek and Latinity,
Faix and the divels and all at Divinity,
    Father O'Flynn 'd make hares of them all!
      Come, I vinture to give ye my word,
      Never the likes of his logic was heard,
        Down from mythology
        Into thayology,
    Troth! and conchology if he'd the call.
      Here's a health to you, Father O'Flynn, &c.

Och! Father O'Flynn you've the wonderful way
    wid you,
All the ould sinners are wishful to pray wid you,
All the young childer are wild for to play wid you,
    You've such a way wid you, Father avick!
      Still, for all you've so gentle a soul,
      Gad, you've your flock in the grandest control;
        Checking the crazy ones,
        Coaxin' onaisy ones,
    Liftin' the lazy ones on wid the stick.
      Here's a health to you, Father O'Flynn, &c.

And though quite avoidin' all foolish frivolity,
Still at all seasons of innocent jollity,
Where was the play-boy could claim an equality
    At comicality, Father, wid you?
      Once the Bishop looked grave at your jest,
      Till this remark set him off wid the rest:
        "Is it lave gaiety
        All to the laity?
    Cannot the clargy be Irishmen too?"
      Here's a health to you, Father O'Flynn,
      Slainté, and slainté, and slainté agin;
        Powerfullest preacher, and
        Tinderest teacher, and
      Kindliest creature in ould Donegal.

LOVE'S WISHES.

Would I were Erin's apple-blossom o'er you,
    Or Erin's rose in all its beauty blown,
To drop my richest petals down before you,
    Within the garden where you walk alone;
In hope you'd turn and pluck a little posy,
    With loving fingers through my foliage pressed,
And kiss it close and set it blushing rosy
    To sigh out all its sweetness on your breast.

Would I might take the pigeon's flight towards you,
    And perch beside your window-pane above,
And murmur how my heart of hearts it hoards you,
    O hundred thousand treasures of my love;
In hope you'd stretch your slender hand and take
    me,
And smooth my wildly-fluttering wings to rest,
And lift me to your loving lips and make me
    My bower of blisses in your loving breast.

THE BANKS OF THE DAISIES.

When first I saw young Molly
   Stretched beneath the holly,
Fast asleep, forenint her sheep, one dreamy summer's day,
   With daisies laughing round her,
   Hand and foot I bound her,
Then kissed her on her blooming cheek, and softly stole away.

But, as with blushes burning
   Tip-toe I was turning,
From sleep she starts, and on me darts a dreadful lightning ray;
   My foolish flowery fetters
   Scornfully she scatters,
And like a winter sunbeam she coldly sweeps away.

But Love, young Love, comes stooping
   O'er my daisies drooping,
And oh! each flower with fairy power the rosy boy renews;
   Then twines each charming cluster
   In links of starry lustre,
And with the chain enchanting my colleen proud pursues.

   And soon I met young Molly
   Musing melancholy,
With downcast eyes and starting sighs, along the meadow bank;
   And oh! her swelling bosom
   Was wreathed with daisy blossom,
Like stars in summer heaven, as in my arms she sank.

I ONCE LOVED A BOY.

I once loved a boy, and a bold Irish boy,
   Far away in the hills of the West;
Ah! the love of that boy was my jewel of joy,
   And I built him a bower in my breast,
      In my breast;
   And I built him a bower in my breast.

I once loved a boy, and I trusted him true,
   And I built him a bower in my breast;
But away, wirrasthrue! the rover he flew,
   And robbed my poor heart of its rest,
      Of its rest;
   And robbed my poor heart of its rest.

The spring-time returns, and the sweet speckled thrush
   Murmurs soft to his mate on her nest,
But for ever there's fallen a sorrowful hush
   O'er the bower that I built in my breast,
      In my breast;
   O'er the desolate bower in my breast.

IRISH LAMENTATION TO THE ULSTER GOLL.

Cold, dark, and dumb lies my boy on his bed;
Cold, dark, and silent the night dews are shed,
Hot, swift, and fierce fall my tears for the dead!

His footsteps lay light in the dew of the dawn,
As the straight, slender track of the young mountain fawn;
But I'll ne'er again follow them over the lawn!

His modest cheek blushed with the sun's rising ray,
And he shone in his strength like the sun at midday;
But a cloud of black darkness has hid him away!

And that cloud of black darkness shall cling to the skies,
And never, ah! never, shall I see him arise,
Lost warmth of my bosom, lost light of my eyes!

THOMAS N. BURKE.

[The Rev. Thomas N. Burke—or, to use the popular name by which he is usually called among his co-religionists, "Father Tom Burke"—was born in the picturesque old town of Galway in 1830. At an early age he determined to devote himself to the priesthood, and when he was seventeen years old he went to Italy to pass through the necessary years of study and novitiate. After a period of five years spent in this preparation he was sent to England, and there was ordained a priest of the Dominican order of friars. After four years of missionary work in Gloucestershire, he was sent to his native land to found a house at Tallaght, county Dublin, in connection with his order. He remained for about seven years in Ireland, and then again he was ordered to Italy, becoming superior of the monastery of Irish Dominicans at San Clemente, Rome.

The death of Cardinal Wiseman in 1865 drew Dr. Manning from Italy, and Father Burke was selected to succeed him as the English preacher during the Lenten services in the church of Santa Maria del Popolo in Rome. It will be known that those services used to be attended by large and critical audiences, the congregation consisting often in great part of Protestant tourists whom the feasts of the holy season attracted to the Eternal City, and the office of preacher was accordingly bestowed only on those who were regarded as the ablest exponents of the Roman Catholic creed. Having held this distinguished position for five years in succession, Father Burke once more returned to Ireland. In the next few years, and indeed for many years before, he was the most popular and the most frequent preacher in Ireland, and the competition for his services was consequently keen. Whenever a church was to be opened, or an orphanage to be built, or a school to be rescued from debt, Father Burke was asked to speak; and those incessant though flattering demands upon him resulted more than once in breaking down a not very robust physical system.

In 1872 he had perhaps his greatest triumph. Despatched on a religious mission to the United States, he happened to arrive there at the moment when Mr. Froude was engaged in his famous anti-Irish crusade. Father Burke was forced into the controversy, and delivered a series of lectures in reply to the attacks of the English historian. Those lectures, as well as many of his sermons, have been republished in volume form. As is so often the case, much of the effectiveness of the speaker is lost in the printed addresses. Father Burke can only be appreciated by being heard, and even a cool head can scarcely avoid being carried away by his rush of brilliant imagery, sonorous language, and broad mirth. He has the advantage, also, of great powers of acting, and his voice, though not musical, is managed with consummate skill.]

A NATION'S HISTORY.[1]

The most precious—the grandest—inheritance of any people, is that people's history. All that forms the national character of a people, their tone of thought, their devotion, their love, their sympathies, their antipathies, their language—all this is found in their history, as the effect is found in its cause, as the autumn speaks of the spring. And the philosopher who wishes to analyse a people's character and to account for it—to account for the national desires, hopes, aspirations, for the strong sympathies or antipathies that sway a people—must go back to the deep recesses of their history; and there, in ages long gone by, will he find the seeds that produced the fruit that he attempts to account for. And he will find that the nation of to-day is but the child and offspring of the nation of bygone ages; for it is written truly, that "the child is father of the man." When, therefore, we come to consider the desires of nations, we find that every people is most strongly desirous to preserve its history, even as every man is anxious to preserve the record of his life; for history is the record of a people's life. Hence it is that, in the libraries of the more ancient nations, we find the earliest histories of the primeval races of mankind written upon the durable vellum, the imperishable asbestos, or sometimes deeply carved, in mystic and forgotten characters, on the granite stone or pictured rock, showing the desire of the people to preserve their history, which is to preserve the memory of them, just as the old man dying said, "Lord, keep my memory green!"

But, besides these more direct and documentary evidences, the history of every nation is enshrined in the national traditions, in the national music and song; much more, it is written in the public buildings that cover the face of the land. These, silent and in ruins, tell most eloquently their tale. To-day "the stone may be crumbled, the wall decayed;" the clustering ivy may, perhaps, uphold the tottering ruin to which it clung in the days of its strength; but

"The sorrows, the joys of which once they were part,
 Still round them, like visions of yesterday, throng."

They are the voices of the past; they are the voices of ages long gone by. They rear their venerable and beautiful gray heads high over the land they adorn; and they tell us the tale of the glory or of the shame, of the strength or of the weakness, of the prosperity or of the adversity of the nation to which they belong. This is the volume which we are about to open; this is the voice which we are about to

[1] From a lecture on the "History of Ireland as told in her Ruins."

call forth from their gray and ivied ruins that cover the green bosom of Ireland; we are about to go back up the highways of history, and, as it were, to breast and to stem the stream of time, to-day, taking our start from the present hour in Ireland. What have we here? It is a stately church—rivalling—perhaps surpassing—in its glory the grandeur of bygone times. We behold the solid buttresses, the massive wall, the high tower, the graceful spire piercing the clouds, and upholding, high towards heaven, the symbol of man's redemption, the glorious sign of the cross. We see in the stone windows the massive tracery, so solid, so strong, and so delicate. What does this tell us? Here is this church, so grand, yet so fresh and new and clean from the mason's hand. What does it tell us? It tells us of a race that has never decayed; it tells us of a people that have never lost their faith nor their love; it tells us of a nation as strong in its energy for every highest and holiest purpose, to-day, as it was in the ages that are past and gone for ever.

THE CURSE OF IGNORANCE.[1]

Now, first of all, consider that the greatest misfortune that Almighty God can let fall upon any man is the curse of utter ignorance, or want of education. The Holy Ghost, in the Scriptures, expressly tells us that this absence of knowledge, this absence of instruction and education, is the greatest curse that can fall upon a man; because it not only unfits him for his duties to God, and for the fellowship of the elect of God, and for every godlike and eternal purpose, but it also unfits him for the society of his human kind; and, therefore, the Scripture says so emphatically—"Man, when he was in honour" (that is to say, created in honour), "lost his knowledge." He had no knowledge. What followed? He was compared to senseless beasts, and made like to them. What is it that distinguishes man from the brute? Is it the strength of limb? No! Is it gracefulness of form? No! Is it acute sensations—a sense of superior sight, or a more intense and acute sense of hearing? No! In all these things many of the beasts that roam the forest exceed us. We have not the swiftness of the stag; we have not the strength of the lion; we have not the beautiful grace of the antelope of the desert; we have not the power to soar into the upper air, like the eagle, who lifts himself upon strong pinions and gazes on the sun. We have not the keen sense of sight of many animals, nor the keen sense of hearing of others. In what, then, lies the difference and the superiority of man? Oh, my dear friends, it lies in the intelligence that can know, and the heart which, guided by that intelligence, is influenced to love for intellectual motives, and in the will, which is supposed to preserve its freedom, by acting under the dominion of that enlightened intellect and mind. For, mark you, it is not the mere power of knowing that distinguishes man from the brutes, and brings him to the perfection of his nature. It is the actual presence of knowledge. It is not the mere power of loving that distinguishes man from the lower creatures. No. For if that love be excited by mere sensuality, by the mere appeal to the senses, it is not the high human love of man, but it is the mere lust of desire and passion of the brute. It is not the will that distinguishes man in the nobility of his nature from the brute; but it is the will, preserving its freedom, keeping itself free from the slavery and dominion of brute passions, and answering quickly—heroically—to every dictate of the high, and holy, and enlightened intelligence that is in man. What follows from this? It follows that if you deprive him of intelligence or knowledge, if you leave him in utter ignorance and withdraw education, you thereby starve, and, as far as you can, annihilate the very highest portion of the soul of man; you thereby dwarf all his spiritual powers; you thereby leave that soul, which was created to grow, and to wax strong, and to be developed by knowledge—you leave it in the imbecility and the helplessness of its natural, intellectual, and spiritual infancy. What follows from this? It follows that the uneducated, uninstructed, ignorant, dwarfed individual is incapable of influencing the affections of the heart with any of the higher motives of love. It follows that if that heart of man is ever to love it will not love upon the dictate of the intelligence, guiding it to an intellectual object, but, like the brute beast of the field, it will seek the gratification of all its desires upon the mere brutal, corporeal evidence of its senses. What follows, moreover? It follows that the will which was created by the Almighty God in freedom, and which, by the very composition of man's nature, was destined to exercise that freedom under the dictate of intelligence, is now left without its

[1] From a lecture on "Catholic Education."

proper ruler, an intelligent, instructed intellect; and, therefore, in the uninstructed man the allegiance of the will—and its dominion—is transferred to the passions, desires, depraved inclinations of man's lower nature. And so we see that in the purely and utterly uninstructed man there can be no loftiness of thought, no real purity of affection, nor can there be any real intellectual action of the will of man. Therefore, I conclude that the greatest curse Almighty God can let fall upon a man is the curse of utter ignorance, unfitting him thereby for every purpose of God and every purpose of society.

First then, my dear friends, I assert that want of education, or ignorance, unfits a man for his position, no matter how humble it be, in this world and in society. For all human society exists amongst men, and not amongst inferior animals, because of the existence in men of intelligence. All human society or intercourse is based upon intellectual communication, thought meeting thought; intellectual sympathy corresponding with the sympathy of others. But the man who is utterly uninstructed; the man who has never been taught to write or to read; the man who has never been taught to exercise any act of his intelligence; the poor, neglected child that we see about our streets—growing up without receiving any word of instruction—grows up, rises to manhood, utterly unfit to communicate with his fellowmen, for he is utterly unprepared for that intercommunion of intelligence and intellect which is the function of society. What follows? He cannot be an obedient citizen, because he cannot even apprehend in his mind the idea of law. He cannot be a prosperous citizen, because he can never turn to any kind of labour which would require the slightest mental effort. In other words, he cannot labour as a man. He is condemned by his intellectual imbecility to labour merely with his hands. Mere brute force distinguishes his labour; and the moment you reduce a man to the degree and amount of mere corporeal strength, the moment you remove from his labour the application of intellect, that moment he is put in competition with the beasts; and they are stronger than he; therefore he is inferior to them. Take the utterly uninstructed man; he it is that is the enemy of society. He cannot meet his fellowmen in any kind of intellectual intercommunion. He is shut out from all that the past tells him in the history of the world; from all the high present interests that are pressing around him; from all his future he is shut out by his utter destitution of all religious education as well as civil. What follows from this? Isolated as he is—flung back upon his solitary self—no humanizing touch; no gentle impulse; no softening remembrance even of sorrow or trouble; no aspiration for something better than the present moment; no remorse for sin; no consolation in pain; no relief in affliction; nothing of all this remains to him: an isolated, solitary man, such as you or I might be, if in one moment, by God's visitation, all that we have ever learned should be wiped out of our minds; all our past lost to us; all the hopes of the future cut off from us;—such is the ignorant man; and such society recognizes him to be. If there be a man who makes the state, and the government of the state, to tremble, it is the thoroughly uninstructed and uneducated man; it is the class neglected in early youth, and cast aside; and utterly uninstructed and undeveloped in their souls, in their hearts, and in their intellects. It is this class that, from time to time, comes to the surface, in some wild revolution, swarming forth in the streets of London, or the streets of Paris, or in the streets of the great continental cities of Europe; swarming forth, no one knows from whence; coming forth from their cellars; coming forth from out the dark places of the city; with fury unreasoning in their eyes, and the cries of demons upon their lips. These are the men that have dyed their hands red in the best blood of Europe, whether it came from the throne or the altar. It is the thoroughly uninstructed, uneducated, neglected child of society that rises in God's vengeance against the world and the society that neglected him, and pays them lack with bitter interest for the neglect of his soul in his early youth.

NATIONAL MUSIC.[1]

What shall we say of the power of music in stirring up all the nobler emotions of man? The soldier arrives after his forced march, tired, upon the battle-field. He hopes for a few hours' rest before he is called upon to put forth all his strength. The bugle sounds in the morning, and this poor and unrested man is obliged to stand to his arms all day, and face death in a thousand forms. The tug of

---

[1] From a lecture on "The National Music of Ireland."

war lasts the whole day long. Now retreating, now advancing, every nerve is braced up, every emotion excited in him, until at length nature appears to yield, and the tired warrior seems unable to wield his sword another hour. But the national music strikes up; the bugle and the trumpets send forth their sounds in some grand national strain! Then, with the clash of the cymbal all the fire is aroused in the man. Drooping, fainting, perhaps wounded as he is, he springs to his arms again. Every nobler emotion of valour and patriotism is raised within him; to the sound of this music, to the inspiration of this national song, he rushes to the front of the battle, and sweeps his enemy from the field.

Thus, when we consider the nature of music, the philosophy of music, do we find that it is of all other appeals to the senses the most spiritual; that it is of all other appeals to the soul the most powerful; that it operates not as much by the mode of reflection, as in exciting the memory and the imagination, causing the spirit and the affections of men to rise to nobler efforts, and to thrill with sublime emotions and influences. And, therefore, I say it is, of all other sciences, the most noble and the most godlike, and the grandest that can be cultivated by man on this earth.

And now, as it is with individuals, so it is with nations. As the individual expresses his sense of pain by the discordant cry which he utters; as the individual expresses the joy of his soul by the clear voice of natural music; so, also, every nation has its own tradition of music, and its own national melody and song. Wherever we find a nation with a clear, distinct, sweet, and emphatic tradition of national music, coming down from sire to son, from generation to generation, from the remotest centuries—there have we evidence of a people strong in character, well marked in their national disposition—there have we evidence of a most ancient civilization. But wherever, on the other hand, you find a people light and frivolous—not capable of deep emotions in religion—not deeply interested in their native land, and painfully affected by her fortunes—a people easily losing their nationality, or national feeling, and easily mingling with strangers, and amalgamating with them—there you will be sure to find a people with scarcely any tradition of national melody that would deserve to be classed amongst the songs of the nations. Now, amongst these nations, Ireland—that most ancient and holy island in the western sea—claims, and deservedly, upon the record of history, the first and grandest pre-eminence among all peoples. I do not deny to other nations high musical excellence. I will not even say that, in this our day, we are not surpassed by the music of Germany, by the music of Italy, or the music of England. Germany for purity of style, for depth of expression, for the argument of song, surpasses all the nations to-day. Italy is acknowledged to be the queen of that lighter, more pleasing, more sparkling, and, to me, more pleasant style of music. In her own style of music England is supposed to be superior to Italy, and, perhaps, equal to Germany. But, great as are the musical attainments of these great peoples, there is not one of these nations, or any other nation, that can point back to such national melody, to such a body of national music, as the Irish. Remember that I am not speaking now of the laboured composition of some great master; I am not speaking now of a wonderful mass, written by one man; or a great oratorio, written by another—works that appeal to the ear refined and attuned by education; works that delight the critic. I am speaking of the song that lives in the hearts and voices of all the people; I am speaking of the national songs you will hear from the husbandman, in the field, following the plough; from the old woman, singing to the infant on her knee; from the milkmaid, coming from the milking; from the shoemaker at his work, or the blacksmith at the forge, while he is shoeing the horse. This is the true song of the nation; this is the true national melody, that is handed down, in a kind of traditional way, from the remotest ages; until, in the more civilized and cultivated time, it is interpreted into written music; and then the world discovers, for the first time, a most beautiful melody in the music that has been murmured in the glens and mountain valleys of the country for hundreds and thousands of years. Italy has no such song. Great as the Italians are as masters, they have no popularly received tradition of music. The Italian peasant—(I have lived amongst them for years)—the Italian peasant, while working in the vineyard, has no music except two or three high notes of a most melancholy character, commencing upon a high dominant and ending in a semitone. The peasants of Tuscany and of Campagna, when, after their day's work, they meet in the summer's evenings to have a dance, have no music; only a girl takes a tambourine and beats upon it, marking time, and they dance to that, but they have no music. So with other countries. But go to Ireland; listen to the old woman as she rocks herself in her chair, and pulls down the hank of flax for the spinning; listen to the girl coming home from the field with the can of milk on her head; and what do you hear?—the most magnificent melody of music. Go to the country merry-makings and you will be sure to find the old fiddler, or old white-headed piper, an infinite source of the brightest and most sparkling music.

How are we to account for this? We must seek the cause of it in the remotest history. It is a historical fact that the maritime or sea-coast people of the north and west of Europe were, from time immemorial, addicted to song. We know, for instance, that in the remotest ages, the kings of our sea-girt island, when they went forth upon their warlike forays, were always accompanied by their harper, or minstrel, who animated them to deeds of heroic bravery. Even when the Danes came sweeping down in their galleys upon the Irish coast, high on the prow of every war-boat sat the *scald*, or poet—white-haired, heroic, wrinkled with time—the historian of all their national wisdom and their national prowess. And when they approached their enemy, sweeping with their long oars through the waves, he rose in the hour of battle, and poured forth his soul in song, and fired every warrior to the highest and most heroic deeds. Thus it was in Ireland, when Nial of the Nine Hostages swept down upon the coast of France, and took St. Patrick (then a youth) prisoner; the first sounds that greeted the captive's ear were the strains of our old Irish harper, celebrating in a language he knew not the glories and victories of heroes long departed.

WILLIAM FRANCIS BUTLER.

[Major W. F. Butler is a native of the county Tipperary, where he was born in 1838. At twenty years of age he was appointed to an ensigncy in the 69th Regiment, and rose rapidly, becoming captain in 1872; major, 1874; and deputy-adjutant-quartermaster-general, head quarter-staff, 1876. He served with distinction on the Red River expedition, and acted as special commissioner to the Saskatchewan Territories in 1870 and 1871. While in command of the West Akim native forces during the Ashantee war, he was honourably mentioned in several despatches of Sir Garnet Wolseley. In 1874 he received the order of companionship of the Bath. While in North America he collected materials for his two well-known works, *The Great Lone Land* and *The Wild North Land*. *Akinfoo, the History of a Failure*, gives a very vivid account of an attempt made by Major Butler to induce some of the natives to join with the English troops in an attack upon Coomassie, which endeavour did not prove successful. All his works are characterized by a picturesque, and occasionally highly eloquent style. He becomes particularly captivating when describing startling adventures or depicting beautiful natural scenery. Major Butler married, in June, 1877, Miss Elizabeth Thompson, the well-known painter.]

A VIEW OF THE PRAIRIE.

(FROM "THE WILD NORTH LAND.")

On the 27th of April I set out from Hudson's Hope to cross the portage of ten miles, which avoids the Great Cañon at the farther end of which the Peace River becomes navigable for a canoe.

We crossed the river once more at the scene of our accident two days previously; but this time, warned by experience, a large canoe was taken, and we passed safely over to the north shore. It took some time to hunt up the horses, and mid-day had come before we finally got clear of the Hope of Hudson.

The portage trail curved up a steep hill of 800 or 900 feet; then on through sandy flats and by small swamps, until, at some eight or nine miles from the Hope of Hudson, the outer spurs of the mountains begin to flank us on either side. To the north a conspicuous ridge, called the Buffalo's Head, rises abruptly from the plain, some 3000 feet above the pass; its rock summit promised a wide view of mountain ranges on one side, and of the great valley of the Peace River on the other. It stood alone, the easternmost of all the ranges, and the Cañon of the Peace River flowed round it upon two sides, south and west.

Months before, at the forks of the Athabasca River, a man who had once wandered into these wilds told me, in reply to a question of mine, that there was one spot near the mouth of the Peace River Pass which commanded a wide range of mountain and prairie. It was the Buffalo's Head.

Nine hundred miles had carried me now to that spot. The afternoon was clear and fine; the great range had not a cloud to darken the glare of the sun upon its sheen of snow; and the pure cool air came over the forest trees fresh from the thousand billows of this sea of mountains. The two men went on to the portage end; I gave them my horse, and, turning at right angles into a wood, made my way towards the foot of the Buffalo's Head.

Thick with brulé and tangled forest lay the base of the mountain; but this once passed, the steep sides became clear of forest, and there rose abruptly before me a mass of yellow grass and soft-blue anemones. Less than an hour's hard climbing brought me to the summit, and I was a thousand times repaid for the labour of the ascent.

I stood on the bare rocks which formed the frontlet of the Buffalo's Head. Below, the pines of a vast forest looked like the toy-trees which children set up when Noah is put forth to watch the animals emerging from his ark, and where everything is in perfect order, save and except that perverse pig, who will insist on lying upon his side in consequence of a fractured leg, and who must either be eliminated from the procession altogether, or put in such close contact to Mrs. Noah, for the sake of her support, as to detract very much from the solemnity of the whole procession.

Alas, how futile is it to endeavour to describe such a view! Not more wooden are the ark animals of our childhood than the words in which man would clothe the images of that higher nature which the Almighty has graven into the shapes of lovely mountains! Put down your wooden woods bit by bit; throw in colour here, a little shade there, touch it up with sky and cloud, cast about it that perfume of blossom or breeze, and in Heaven's name what does it come to after all? Can the eye wander away, away, away until it is lost in blue distance as a lark is lost in blue heaven, but the sight still drinks the beauty of the landscape, though the source of the beauty be unseen, as the source of the music which falls from the azure depths of sky.

That river coming out broad and glittering from the dark mountains, and vanishing into yon profound chasm with a roar which reaches up even here—billowy seas of peaks and mountains beyond number away there to south and west—that huge half dome which lifts itself above all others sharp and clear cut against the older dome of heaven! Turn east, look out into that plain—that endless plain where the pine-trees are dwarfed to spear-grass and the prairie to a meadow-patch—what do you see? Nothing, poor blind reader, nothing, for the blind is leading the blind; and all this boundless range of river and plain, ridge and prairie, rocky precipice and snow-capped sierra, is as much above my poor power of words, as He who built this mighty nature is higher still than all.

Ah, my friend, my reader! Let us come down from this mountain-top to our own small level again. We will upset you in an ice-rapid; Kalder will fire at you; we will be wrecked; we will have no food; we will hunt the moose and do anything and everything, you like,—but we cannot put in words the things that we see from these lonely mountain-tops when we climb them in the sheen of evening. When you go into your church, and the organ rolls and the solemn chant floats through the lofty aisles, you do not ask your neighbour to talk to you and tell you what it is like. If he should do anything of the kind the beadle takes him and puts him out of doors, and then the policeman takes him and puts him indoors, and he is punished for his atrocious conduct; and yet you expect me to tell you about this church, whose pillars are the mountains, whose roof is the heaven itself, whose music comes from the harp-strings which the earth has laid over her bosom, which we call pine-trees; and from which the hand of the Unseen draws forth a ceaseless symphony rolling ever around the world.

MY SHIPMATES.

(FROM "THE GREAT LONE LAND.")

A trip across the Atlantic is now-a-days a very ordinary business; in fact, it is no longer a voyage—it is a run, you may almost count its duration to within four hours; and as for fine weather, blue skies, and calm seas, if they come, you may be thankful for them, but don't expect them, and you won't add a sense of disappointment to one of discomfort. Some experience of the Atlantic enables me to affirm that north or south of 35° north and south latitude there exists no such thing as pleasant sailing.

But the usual run of weather, time, and tide outside the ship is not more alike in its characteristics than the usual run of passenger one meets inside. There is the man who has never been sea-sick in his life, and there is the man who has never felt well upon board ship, but who, nevertheless, both manage to consume about fifty meals of solid food in ten days. There is the nautical landsman who tells you that he has been eighteen times across the Atlantic and four times round the Cape of Good Hope, and who is generally such a bore upon marine questions that it is a subject of infinite regret that he should not be performing a fifth voyage round that distant and interesting promontory. Early in the voyage, owing to his superior sailing qualities, he has been able to cultivate a close intimacy with the captain of the ship; but this intimacy has been on the decline for some days, and, as he has committed the unpardonable error of differing in opinion with the captain upon a subject connected with the general direction and termination of the Gulf Stream, he begins to fall quickly in the estimation of that potentate. Then there is the relict of the late Major Fusby, of the Fusiliers, going to or returning from England. Mrs. Fusby has a predilection for port-negus and the first Burmese war, in which campaign her late husband received a wound of such a vital description (he died just twenty-two years later), that it has enabled her to provide, at the expense of a grateful nation, for three youthful Fusbies, who now serve their country in various parts of the world. She does not suffer from sea-sickness, but occasionally undergoes periods of nervous depression which require the administration of the stimulant already referred to. It is a singular fact that the present voyage is strangely illustrative of remarkable events in the life of the late Fusby; there has not been a sail or a porpoise in sight that has not called up some reminiscence of the early career of the major; indeed, even the somewhat unusual appearance of an iceberg has been turned to account as suggestive of the intense suffering undergone by the major during the period of his wound, owing to the scarcity of the article ice in tropical countries. Then on deck we have the inevitable old sailor who is perpetually engaged in scraping the vestiges of paint from your favourite seat, and who, having arrived at the completion of his monotonous task after four days' incessant labour, is found on the morning of the fifth engaged in smearing the paint-denuded place of rest with a vilely glutinous compound peculiar to ship-board. He never looks directly at you as you approach, with book and rug, the desired spot, but you can tell by the leer in his eye and the roll of the quid in his immense mouth that the old villain knows all about the discomfort he is causing you, and you fancy you can detect a chuckle as you turn away in a vain quest for a quiet cosy spot. Then there is the captain himself, that most mighty despot. What king ever wielded such power, what czar or kaiser had ever such obedience yielded to their decrees? This man, who on shore is nothing, is here on his deck a very pope; he is infallible. Canute could not stay the tide, but our sea-king regulates the sun. Charles V. could not make half a dozen clocks go in unison, but Captain Smith can make it twelve o'clock any time he pleases; nay, more, when the sun has made it twelve o'clock no tongue of bell or sound of clock can proclaim time's decree until it has been ratified by the fiat of the captain; and even in his misfortunes what grandeur, what absence of excuse or crimination of others in the hour of his disaster!

FIRST SIGHT OF THE ROCKY MOUNTAINS.

(FROM "THE GREAT LONE LAND.")

It was near sunset when we rode by the lonely shores of the Gull Lake, whose frozen surface stretched beyond the horizon to the north. Before us, at a distance of some ten miles, lay the abrupt line of the Three Medicine Hills, from whose gorges the first view of the great range of the Rocky Mountains was destined to burst upon my sight. But not on this day was I to behold that long-looked-for vision. Night came quickly down upon the silent wilderness; and it was long after dark when we made our camps by the bank of the Pas-co-pee, or Blindman's River, and turned adrift the weary horses to graze in a well-grassed meadow lying in one of the curves of the river. We had ridden more than sixty miles that day.

About midnight a heavy storm of snow burst upon us, and daybreak revealed the whole camp buried deep in snow. As I threw back the blankets from my head (one always lies covered up completely), the wet, cold mass struck chillily upon my face. The snow was wet and sticky, and therefore things were much more wretched than if the temperature had been lower; but the hot tea made matters seem brighter, and about breakfast-time the snow ceased to fall, and the clouds began to clear away. Packing our wet blankets together, we set out for the Three Medicine Hills, through whose defiles our course lay; the snow was deep in the narrow valleys, making travelling slower and more laborious than before. It was mid-day when, having rounded the highest of the three hills, we entered a narrow gorge fringed with a fire-ravaged forest. This gorge wound through the hills, preventing a far-reaching view ahead; but at length its western termination was reached, and there lay before me a sight to be long remembered. The great chain of the Rocky Mountains rose their snow-clad sierras in endless succession. Climbing one of the eminences, I gained a vantage-point on the summit from which some bygone fire had swept the trees. Then, looking west, I beheld the great range in unclouded glory. The snow had cleared the atmosphere, the sky was coldly bright. An immense plain stretched from my feet to the mountain—a plain so vast that every object of hill and wood and lake lay dwarfed into one continuous level, and at the back of this level, beyond the pines and the lakes and the river-courses, rose the giant range, solid, impassable, silent—a mighty barrier rising midst an immense land, standing sentinel over the plains and prairies of America, over the measureless solitudes of this Great Lone Land. Here at last lay the Rocky Mountains.

Leaving behind the Medicine Hills, we descended into the plain and held our way until sunset towards the west. It was a calm and beautiful evening; far-away objects stood out sharp and distinct in the pure atmosphere of these elevated regions. For some hours we had lost sight of the mountains, but shortly before sunset the summit of a long ridge was gained, and they burst suddenly into view in greater magnificence than at mid-day. Telling my men to go on and make the camp at the Medicine River, I rode through some fire-wasted forest to a lofty grass-covered height which the declining sun was bathing in floods of glory. I cannot hope to put into the compass of words the scene which lay rolled beneath from this sunset-lighted eminence; for, as I looked over the immense plain and watched the slow descent of the evening sun upon the frosted crest of these lone mountains, it seemed as if the varied scenes of my long journey had woven themselves into the landscape, filling with the music of memory the earth, the sky, and the mighty panorama of mountains. Here at length lay the barrier to my onward wanderings, here lay the boundary to that 4000 miles of unceasing travel which had carried me by so many varied scenes so far into the lone land; and other thoughts were not wanting. The peaks on which I gazed were no pigmies; they stood the culminating monarchs of the mighty range of the Rocky Mountains. From the estuary of the Mackenzie to the Lake of Mexico no point of the American continent reaches nigher to the skies. That eternal crust of snow seeks in summer widely-severed oceans. The Mackenzie, the Columbia, and the Saskatchewan spring from the peaks whose teeth-like summits lie grouped from this spot into the compass of a single glance. The clouds that cast their moisture upon this long line of upheaven rocks seek again the ocean which gave them birth in its far-separated divisions of Atlantic, Pacific, and Arctic. The sun sank slowly behind the range, and darkness began to fall on the immense plain, but aloft on the topmost edge the pure white of the jagged crest-line glowed for an instant in many-coloured silver, and then the lonely peaks grew dark and dim.

As thus I watched from the silent hill-top this great mountain-chain, whose summits slept in the glory of the sunset, it seemed no stretch of fancy which made the red man place his paradise beyond their golden peaks. The "Mountains of the Setting Sun," the "Bridge of the World," thus he has named them, and beyond them the soul first catches a glimpse of that mystical land where the tents are pitched midst everlasting verdure and countless herds and the music of ceaseless streams.

AN AFRICAN QUEEN.

(FROM "AKIM-FOO.")

On the day following my arrival, Queen Amaquon came to visit me. She brought with her a large bevy of the ugliest women I had ever seen. The dress of the queen and the court at Swaidroo was peculiar. Queen Amaquon wore a necklace of beads, a stick, and a scant silk cloth; her ladies were attired in a costume which, for simplicity and economy, I can safely recommend to the talented authoress of that charming book, "How to Dress on Fifteen Pounds a Year," since it might almost be achieved on as many pence. Nearly all the ladies had babies on their backs; there were no men. Here and there in the crowd one occasionally saw a woman with the peculiar eye and eyelash of the better-looking Akims—an eye which I have nowhere else noted on the coast or in the interior.

I was introduced in turn to the queen's daughters, to her "fetish woman," a large wild-eyed lassie, and to several other ladies of rank and quality. As the ceremony was gone through, the lady presented stepped up into the hut, and shook hands with me as I lay on my couch; and it not unfrequently happened that the baby on the bustle at her back, looking out under her elbow and beholding a white man in such close proximity, would howl in terror at the sight.

At first but a limited number of women came into the inner yard of my hut, and the queen alone entered the hut itself; but as the interview went on the outsiders grew bolder, and at last the yard and opposite hut were filled to overflowing.

But the event of the day was the statement of the queen's illness. I had tried to turn her mind to war. I had spoken of the warlike deeds of a former queen of Akim—of how, sword in hand, she had led her soldiers against the Ashantis at Dodowa, saying, "Osay has driven me from my kingdom because he thinks I am weak; but though I am a woman he shall see I have the heart of a man;" but the effort was useless.

"That was all true," she said; but the point which grieved her most was this illness under which she suffered, and on which she wanted my opinion.

Now I was sufficiently ill myself to make the diagnosis of an old lady's ailment by no means an attractive pastime. I doubt if at any time I should have entered into such a question with the slightest interest. Nevertheless, the situation was not without novelty, and African fever was not so totally depressing as to shut out the ridiculous aspect of finding myself Physician Extraordinary to Her Majesty Queen Amaquon of Akim. Seated on a low stool she began the statement of her case. There is no necessity to enter now into the symptoms. They consisted of the usual number of pains, in the usual number of places, at the usual number of hours; but their cause and cure?—ah, that was the question.

"Did I consider," asked the queen, "these symptoms could have had their origin in poison? She had visited Cape Coast Castle four years before this time, and ever since her return had suffered from this ailment. Perhaps she had been poisoned by the people of the Coast?"

I inquired "if she had consumed much rum during that visit to the coast? Rum was a subtle poison." The soft impeachment of having tippled freely was as freely admitted; but it was a mistake to suppose that rum could harm anybody. "Surely, among the medicines which I carried, I must have some drug which would restore her to health."

Now my stock of drugs was not a large one. The specifics in use against fever were precious, they could not be spared.

Had I any more? Yes—a bottle of spirit of sal volatile. Her majesty bent her nose to the bottle, and the tent shook with her oft-repeated sneezes.

The whole court was in a commotion. The fetish woman demanded a smell; the royal daughters grew bolder; the ladies pressed in from without, and the queen declared, when sneezing left her at liberty to articulate, that she felt immensely relieved. It was some time before order could be fully restored.

The heat meantime became stifling, and the press of women seemed to threaten suffocation. "Tell Queen Amaquon," I said to the interpreter, "that to-morrow I will see her again. Meanwhile I have to cure myself." With difficulty I got rid of the lot.

A FOREST SCENE IN AFRICA.

(FROM "AKIM-FOO.")

Morning. A dense white steam fills the forest; the eye cannot follow the great gray tree-trunks more than half-way to their summits; there is the ceaseless drip of rain-drops on the broad-leaved undergrowth, and a clammy cold clings to the air; there is, the natives say, "a bad smoke" out to-day, and yet, long before mid-forenoon this smoke has vanished, and the fiery sun has come out—the clammy chill has changed to suffocating damp heat.

Mid-day. The great sun blazes in sullen fury down upon the silent forest, but the fierce rays fall only in nets of gold on the great gray stems which raise their buttressed trunks 100 feet without a branch, and then fork in massive limbs whose every length would make a forest tree. One hundred feet higher still the waving surface of this ocean of foliage lies outspread before the glare of day—a vast sea of tree-tops whose waves ripple in a middle region seemingly set between earth and heaven.

Evening. There is the splash of water upon the topmost trees; the rain hisses down in ceaseless dreariness, and the roll of the thunder crashes loud and long over the reverberating forest.

But, though the hours may pass as they will, and sunlight, fog, and lightning ring their changes over this sea, still all unchanged, set in an eternity of sombre gloom, rests this huge equatorial forest. The day and the night are the same to it; noiseless rivers steal along under dense layers of tangled foliage; huge poisonous fruits fall down from lofty close-set trees, and lie beneath the undergrowth, emitting noisome odours; great orchids hang over the pathway, spiral creepers, hundreds of feet in length, twisted like huge serpents, cling from tree to tree; and far down below the mass of foliage, amidst these tangled and twisted evergreens, beneath the shadow of the great gray tree-trunks, man moves as though he slowly picked his way at the bottom of some mighty ocean.

This forest of Akim and Ashanti is the only forest I have ever seen which defies man; you could not clear it, for the reason that long before you could cut it down a new forest would have arisen. During six months there is continuous rain; during four months more, heavy tropical storms occur almost daily; for five or six weeks the weather is dry; but all the twelve months through the heat is very great, hence there is produced on the Gold Coast a vegetation such as one sees nowhere else on the globe.

So vast is this vegetable kingdom that the animal world sickens and dies out before it—this immense forest holds scarcely a living creature. For months I have trodden its labyrinths, and seen only a diminutive deer, a gray monkey, and a few serpents. How little we knew in England of the true nature of this forest! "It will burn," wrote one wise man to a daily paper. "Take plenty of petroleum oil, pour it over the forest, and then set fire to it."

"I know tropical forests well," wrote another, "the underbush will burn when the dry weather comes, as it does in Burmah and Tenasserim. Then you will be able to march through it with ease."

But, alas! the African forest is always green, always wet, always fire-proof.

There is a lighter opening in the forest gloom ahead—all at once the trees end abruptly, and low, mud-walled houses, thatched with reeds, appear before us. The forest treads upon the very skirts of the croom—there is no cleared space, save where the houses stand, these houses form little clusters of huts, each cluster having a tiny square yard in the centre, upon which all the huts open; by-paths lead out at the corners into the street, which is usually broad, clean, and adorned with a fetish tree, beneath which the gossip of the place is carried on. The women are nearly always engaged in household work; the men are always idle, sometimes gambling with sticks, sometimes with old cards, seldom doing any useful labour.

"Why do you not clear the forest for some distance all around your croom?" I have asked the people of a village, "and plant the open space with corn and plantains?" "It would be no use," they have answered, "other people would come and take our grain and fruit. We could not refuse them, so we go three or four miles off, and make our gardens there, and then it is too far for people to go to look for food."

So closely does this forest hem in the crooms, that if it were possible to walk along the tops of the trees, one would look right down into the huts from the edge of the clearing; but often the croom stands upon a knoll, or sloping hill, and the surrounding forest looks somewhat less impending.

TIMOTHY DANIEL SULLIVAN.

[Timothy D. Sullivan was born in May, 1827, in Bantry, co. Cork. At an early age he gave indications of a strong tendency towards literature; and the *Nation* gladly accepted the poetic contributions which were sent to it from the then unknown contributor. In 1855 he entered on a permanent engagement; and from that day till the present, when he is its proprietor and editor, he has maintained his association with that journal.

For many years Mr. Sullivan, with a modesty not too common, was content to publish his poems without any further indication of their origin than his initials; and the outside public had no means of knowing that many of the finest and most effective articles in the *Nation* also came from his pen.

Mr. Sullivan has written a historical poem of some length entitled "Dunboy," in which the memorable siege of Dunboy is told with great spirit. He is best known, however, by his songs, some of which have received that truest stamp of such poetry—they have been caught up by the popular ear, and have become familiar as household words in the many countries in which the Irish race has settled down. In 1876 he became editor of the *Nation* on the retirement of his brother, Mr. A. M. Sullivan, M.P.

Mr. Sullivan's poems are comprised in two volumes, one entitled *Poems, by T. D. Sullivan*, the other *Green Leaves, a Volume of Irish Verses*. The most popular perhaps among his lyrical compositions are "Thiggin Thu?" "God save Ireland," "The Little Wife," and "Our own Green Isle." Many of his poems are of a serious character; but another class of Mr. Sullivan's numerous admirers will perhaps be disposed to turn to those verses in which he gives free play to the high powers of genuine humour which he possesses.]

O'NEILL IN ROME.

Where yellow Tiber's waters flow,
  Within the seven-hilled city's bound,
An aged chief, with footsteps slow,
  Moves sadly o'er the storied ground:
Or, from his palace window panes,
  Looks out upon the matchless dome,
The ruins grand, the glorious fanes,
  That stud the soil of holy Rome.
    But, oh! for Ireland, far away—
      For Ireland in the western sea!
    The chieftain's heart is there to-day;
      And there, in truth, he fain would be.

On every side the sweet bells ring,
  And faithful people bend in pray'r;
Sweet hymns, that angel choirs might sing,
  And loud hosannas fill the air.
His place is with the princely crowd,
  Amidst the noblest and the best;
His large white head is lowly bowed;
  His hands are clasped before his breast.
    But, oh! for Ireland, far away—
      For Ireland, dear, with all her ills—
    For mass in fair Tyrone, to-day,
      Amid the circling Irish hills!

Kind friends are round him—pious freres,
  And pastors of Christ's mystic fold;
The holy Pope, 'mid many cares,
  For him has blessings, honours, gold;
Grave fathers, speaking words of balm,
  Bid him forget the bygone strife,
And spend, resigned in holy calm,
  The years that close a noble life.
    But, oh! for Ireland! there again,
      The grand old chieftain fain would be;
    'Midst glittering spears, on hill or plain,
      To charge for Faith and Liberty!

His fellow-exiles—men who bore,
  With him, the brunt of many a fight—
Talk past and future chances o'er,
  Around his table grouped at night.
While speeds each tale of grief or glee,
  With tears their furrowed cheeks are wet;
And oft they rise and vow to see
  A glorious day in Ireland yet.
    And, oh! for Ireland o'er the main—
      For Ireland where they yet shall be,
    Since Irish braves, in France and Spain,
      Have steel and gold to set her free.

He sits, abstracted, by the board;
  Old scenes are pictured in his brain—
Benburb! Armagh! the Yellow Ford!—
  He fights and wins them o'er again.
Again he sees fierce Bagnal fall;
  Sees craven Essex basely yield;
Meets armoured Segrave, gaunt and tall,
  And leaves him lifeless on the field.
    But, oh! for Ireland—there once more
      To rouse the true men of the land;
    And proudly bear, from shore to shore,
      The banner of the "Blood-red Hand!"

And, when the wine within him plays,
  Bold, hopeful words the chief will speak;
He draws his shining sword, and says—
  "The King of England deems me weak!
Ah, would the Englishman were nigh
  That hates me most—my deadliest foe—
To cross his sword with mine, and try
  If this right arm be weak or no!"
    But, oh! for Ireland, where good swords
      And valiant arms are needed most,
    To fall on England's cruel hordes,
      And sweep them from the Irish coast!

Years come and go; but, while they roll,
  His limbs grow weak, his eyes grow dim;
The hopes die out that buoyed his soul;
  War's mighty game is closed for him.
Before him, from the earth have passed
  Friends, kinsmen, comrades true and brave;

And well he knows he nears, at last,
   His place of rest—a foreign grave!
   But, oh! for Ireland, far away—
   For Irish love and holy zeal;
   Oh! for a grave in Irish clay,
     To wrap the heart of Hugh O'Neill!

THE LITTLE WIFE.

Frown not, my love! ah, let me chase
   Away the shade of care that lies
To-night so darkly on your face,
   And mist-like o'er your manly eyes.
Ah, let me try the winning ways
   You said were mine—the angel art
To pour at once ten thousand rays
   Of dancing sunlight on your heart!
     My love, my life!
      Your little wife
   Must bid these gloomy thoughts depart.

When love was young and hopes were bright,
   I thought, 'midst all our dreams of bliss,
That clouds might come like these to-night,
   And hours of sorrow such as this.
And, then, I said, my task shall be
   To soothe his heart so fond and true,
And he who loves me thus, shall see
   How much his little wife can do.
     My heart, my life,
      Your little wife
   Must bid you dream those dreams anew.

Then let me lift those locks that fall
   So wildly o'er your lofty brow,
And smooth, with fingers soft and small,
   The veins that cord your temples now.
How oft, when ached your wearied head,
   From manly care, or thought divine,
You've held me to your heart, and said
   You wanted love so deep as mine!
     My own, my life!
      Your little wife,
   That love is all her life's design.

And here it is—a love as wild
   As e'er defied the world's control;
The fondness of a tearful child,
   The passion of a woman's soul,
All mingled in my breast for thee,
   In one hot tide—I cannot speak:
But feel my throbbing heart, and see
   Its brightness in my burning cheek—
     My love, my life!
      Your little wife
   Must cheer you, or her heart will break.

Ah, now the breast I found so cold,
   Grows warm within my close embrace;

And smiles as sweet as those of old
   Are stealing softly o'er your face;
And far within your brightening eyes
   My image, true and clear, I see;
Each shade of care and sorrow flies,
   And leaves your heart again to me—
     My love, my life!
      Your little wife
   Its joy and light must ever be.

SONG FROM THE BACKWOODS.

Deep in Canadian woods we've met,
   From one bright island flown;
Great is the land we tread, but yet
   Our hearts are with our own.
And ere we leave this shanty small,
   While fades the autumn day,
     We'll toast old Ireland!
     Dear Old Ireland!
     Ireland, boys, hurra!

We've heard her faults a hundred times,
   The new ones and the old,
In songs and sermons, rants and rhymes,
   Enlarged some fifty-fold.
But take them all, the great and small,
   And this we've got to say:—
     Here's dear old Ireland!
     Good old Ireland!
     Ireland, boys, hurra!

We know that brave and good men tried
   To snap her rusty chain,
That patriots suffered, martyrs died,
   And all, 'tis said, in vain;
But no, boys, no! a glance will show
   How far they've won their way—
     Here's good old Ireland!
     Loved old Ireland!
     Ireland, boys, hurra!

We've seen the wedding and the wake,
   The patron and the fair;
The stuff they take, the fun they make,
   And the heads they break down there,
With a loud "hurroo" and a "pillalu,"
   And a thundering "clear the way!"—
     Here's gay old Ireland!
     Dear old Ireland!
     Ireland, boys, hurra!

And well we know in the cool gray eves,
   When the hard day's work is o'er,
How soft and sweet are the words that greet
   The friends who meet once more;
With "Mary machree!" and "My Pat! 'tis he!"
And "My own heart night and day!"

Ah, fond old Ireland!
  Dear old Ireland!
    Ireland, boys, hurra!

And happy and bright are the groups that pass
  From their peaceful homes, for miles
O'er fields, and roads, and hills, to mass,
  When Sunday morning smiles!
And deep the zeal their true hearts feel
  When low they kneel and pray.
    Oh, dear old Ireland!
    Blest old Ireland!
    Ireland, boys, hurra!

But deep in Canadian woods we've met,
  And we never may see again
The dear old isle where our hearts are set,
  And our first fond hopes remain!
But come, fill up another cup,
  And with every sup let's say—
    Here's loved old Ireland!
    Good old Ireland!
    Ireland, boys, hurra!

TO MY BROTHER.

Though Fate will permit us no longer
  To struggle through life side by side,
Let our love grow purer and stronger,
  However our hearts may be tried.
We are parted—it may be for ever—
  But, though we be far from each other,
One bond that no distance can sever
  Shall always connect us, my Brother.

And oft, when my prospects look dreary,
  When those I have trusted deceive,
When I sink, disappointed and weary,
  And scarcely know what to believe;
When the dark clouds of life gather o'er me,
  One star shall outshine every other,
And the long, rugged pathway before me
  Grow bright with the love of my Brother.

How oft does some sweet recollection,
  From various occasions, arise,
That touches the chords of affection,
  And brings a hot dew to my eyes.
How oft does some incident waken
  The thoughts I could share with no other;
And my heart, like a chamber forsaken,
  Re-echo my wish for my Brother.

As barks that the tempests have driven
  And tossed far apart on the main,
Steer on by the beacons of Heaven,
  And meet in one harbour again;
Even so, if the storms of existence
  Have parted us here from each other,
Let us steer to that light in the distance,
  And meet in that haven, my Brother.

DONAL OF BEARA.

(FROM "DUNBOY.")

Brave Donal! foes and traitors knew
His spirit high, and feared it too;
While young or old, the poorest man,
Matron or maid, amongst his clan,
Whose cause was good, whose claim was just,
In his true heart might safely trust,
And ask from his superior might
Support and succour for the right.
Strong-boned, but spare of flesh was he,
Fit for brave toils by land and sea;
Tall, straight, and lithe, his stately form
Seemed well inured to sun and storm.
His face was thin, his light brown hair
Half hid a forehead smooth and fair;
Fast came his thoughts whene'er he spoke,
From his blue eyes quick flashes broke;
But while he mused, or walked alone,
His features took another tone,
And slow of step he moved along,
Like one inwrapt in love or song.
Yet ever in that manly breast
The passion ruling all the rest,
The source to which his thoughts returned,
The central fire that in him burned,
By all life's forces fed and fanned,
Was love of his dear native land.
Fit chieftain he his clan to sway
From that tall castle by the bay,
Whose firm and well-embattled front
Seemed built to bear war's fiercest brunt,
Yet whose broad halls were warm and bright
With music, laughter, love, and light,
Whose strong walls held a quiet nook
Where stood the Cross and holy Book,
Where bended knees and reverent feet
  By night and day the flooring trod,
Whence many a prayer, in accents sweet,
  Went through the turrets up to God.

Stern Donal! many a care and pain
Tried that great soul, that brilliant brain;
Rude shocks of war, and subtler art,
Broke vainly on that gallant heart,
  And only proved, when all was done,
A patriot pure and true till death,
A hero to his latest breath
  Was Beara's prince, O'Sullivan.

THE FARMER'S SON.

Where'er are scattered the Irish nation,
  In foreign lands or on Irish ground,
In every calling, and rank, and station,
  Good men and true will be always found;

But 'midst their masses, and ranks, and classes,
   When noble work must be dared and done,
No heart's more ready, no hand's more steady,
   Than the heart and hand of a farmer's son.

His homely garb has not fashion's graces,
   But it wraps a frame that is lithe and strong;
His brawny hand may show labour's traces,
   But 'tis honest toil that does no man wrong.
For generous greeting, for social meeting,
   For genial mirth, or for harmless fun,
'Midst high or low men, 'midst friends or foemen,
   Oh, where's the match for a farmer's son?

Some other men may have words more flowing
   To prove and plead for dear Ireland's cause,
And others, too, may have ways more knowing
   To win her smiles and her fond applause;
But when her story is crowned with glory,
   Howe'er the battle was fought and won,
In front to gain it, and still maintain it,
   You'll find most surely a farmer's son.

A LETTER.

From Miss Bessie Green, residing at Kingstown, to Miss Lizzie Malone, in the County Tipperary.

My dear little Liz, here's a letter at last,
   And to make it a long one I mean to try:
We are staying at Kingstown these three weeks past,
   Papa and Mamma, and Charlie, and I.
And oh, it's so lovely, with bands and boats,
   And the ocean grand, and the mantling wave,
With robes à la *Watteau*, and braided coats,
   And naval officers, brown and brave.
      And its oh-hi-ho, and yo-heave-yo,
         And starboard topsail, and helm-a-lee,
      (You'll note, dearest Liz, I am coming to know
         A lot about ships and the deep blue sea).

For Charlie is coaching me every day:
   He shows me the yachts that have just come in,
And he tells all about them,—but, oh, by the way,
   Do you know who is here?—why, that tall Miss Glynn.
I saw her last night near the fort, my dear,
   In a rather fantastic and light costume,
Just as the *Connaught* came round the pier,
   With her foresail set on her stern jib-boom.
      And it's oh-hi-ho for a weatherly craft,
         For a three-reefed shroud and a whispering breeze,
      For flowing binnacles fore and aft,
         And a backstay cleaving the foaming seas!

You know the regatta will soon take place,
   The people are fast filling in for it too,
And the fashion runs all upon muslin and lace,
   With under-jupes flounced in the style *Frou-Frou*.
In a pale blue silk will I dress for the day,
   With guipure trimming, and bows behind;
And then from a rock I shall look on the bay
   While the yachts tack up on a quarterly wind.
      And it's yo-heave-yo for the snow-white sail
         While the starboard scuppers are floating free,
      While the marlin' spike bends in the fresh'ning gale,
         And the crosstree groans in the plunging sea!

Come up, dearest Liz, to the pleasant sea air;
   Papa and Mamma will be glad if you do;
You will see the new styles in dress, bonnets, and hair,
   See some beauties perhaps, and of frights not a few.
And I, dearest Liz, will be happy indeed
   To teach you the whole of my nautical lore;
I'll give you my Cooper and Marryatt to read,
   And Charlie will tell you a hundred times more.
      And it's oh-hi-ho, and yo-heave-yo,
         And a life on the ocean wave for me,
      As out on the shining deep we go
         With mainyard furled and helm-a-lee!

YOU AND I.

I know what will happen, sweet,
   When you and I are one—
Calm and bright and very fleet
   All our days will run:
Fond and kind our words will be,
   Mixed no more with sighs;
Thoughts too fine for words we'll see
   Within each other's eyes.

Sweet, when you and I are one
   Earth will bloom anew,
Brighter then the stars and sun,
   Softer then the dew;
Sweeter scents will then arise
   From the fields and flowers;
Holier calm will fill the skies
   In the midnight hours.

Music now unheard, unknown,
   Then will reach our ears,
Not a plaint in any tone,
   Not a hint of tears;
In a round of bliss complete
   All our days will run—
That is what will happen, sweet,
   When you and I are one.

ALEXANDER MARTIN SULLIVAN.

[Alexander Martin Sullivan was born in Bantry in 1830—three years later than his brother the poet. Destined for other pursuits, he at an early age discovered that his true vocation was journalism, and in 1853, having made the acquaintance of Gavan Duffy, he began to contribute to the *Nation*. Two years after, Duffy, as has been told in his memoir, threw up in despair Irish journalism and Irish politics, and Mr. Sullivan succeeded to the then not promising heritage of editing the *Nation*. He held that position for upwards of twenty years, and throughout that lengthened period his pen was constantly active in defence of the Nationalist side in politics. His post, as well as his natural disposition and talents, threw him into political warfare, and there has been no movement of importance in Irish politics for the last quarter of a century in which he has not taken a prominent part. Possessed of great oratorical powers, gifted with an eloquence ready, spontaneous, and brilliant, his aid was eagerly sought, and his friendship or hostility was an important factor in the political struggles of his time. In 1857 he took a short vacation, paying a visit to the United States, and he has left a record of his impressions in a volume entitled *A Visit to the Valley of Wyoming*. In 1868 he came, like most National Irish journalists, into collision with the authorities, and having been indicted on two charges in connection with the processions in memory of the three Fenians executed at Manchester, he was convicted on one of the charges, and sent to prison. During his incarceration he learned that the corporation of Dublin had determined to give the most significant mark of its respect by nominating him to the position of lord-mayor; but he refused the flattering proposal. He in like manner would not accept a subscription which had been collected as a testimonial to him on his release, and insisted on devoting the £300 already gathered to the fund for erecting the statue to Henry Grattan, which now stands in College Green, Dublin.

In 1874 Mr. Sullivan entered on a new career. He was started for Louth in opposition to an important member of the Liberal administration—Mr. Chichester Fortescue (now Lord Carlingford)—and was returned. He had some time previously made up his mind to seek in the profession of the lawyer another sphere of action. In 1876 he was admitted to the Irish bar, and in 1877 he joined the bar of England, receiving the unusual honour of a "special call" to the Inner Temple. He had in 1876, as has been mentioned in the preceding notice, resigned his connection with the *Nation*.

For the last few years Mr. Sullivan's career has been chiefly connected with England. He was not long in the house when he established his right to occupy there the same prominent position to which his talents had previously raised him in the assemblies of his own country; and, though he belongs to a party not very acceptable to the British parliament, he has succeeded in placing himself in the ranks of those speakers whose voices control divisions. Mr. Sullivan has published several works. Of these, one of the most popular was an Irish history called *The Story of Ireland*, which had a very large sale. His best known work, however, is *New Ireland*. This book has had a marvellous success; it has been received with equal favour by the English, the Scotch, and the Irish press, and it has passed in a short period through a large number of editions.]

"FORTY-EIGHT."

(FROM "NEW IRELAND."[1])

John Mitchel—the first man who, since Robert Emmet perished on the scaffold in 1803, preached an Irish insurrection and the total severance of Ireland from the British Crown—was the son of the Rev. John Mitchel, Unitarian minister of Dungiven, county Derry. He was born in 1815, and was educated at Trinity College, Dublin. Like many another Trinity student he early became a contributor to the *Nation* newspaper; and in 1845, on the death of Thomas Davis, accepted an editorial position on that journal, in conjunction with Charles Gavan Duffy and Thomas Darcy M'Gee. The stern Unitarian Ulsterman soon developed a decided bent in favour of what half a century before would

---

[1] By permission of the author.

be called "French principles." He was republican and revolutionary. At all events, during the scenes of the famine period he quite drew away from the policy advocated by his colleagues, and eventually called upon the Irish Confederation to declare for a war of independence. He it was who revived the "Separatist" or revolutionary party in Irish politics. From 1803 up to 1845 no such party had any recognized or visible existence. There was, beyond question, disaffection in the country, a constantly maintained protest against, or passive resistance to, the existing state of things; but no one dreamed of a political aim beyond Repeal of the Union as a constitutional object to be attained by constitutional means. The era of revolt and rebellion seemed gone for ever. John Mitchel, however, thrust utterly aside the doctrines of loyalty and legality. He declared that constitutionalism was demoralizing the country. By "blood and iron" alone could Ireland be saved.

These violent doctrines were abhorrent to Smith O'Brien, and indeed to nearly every one of the Confederation leaders. O'Brien declared that either he or Mitchel must quit the organization. The question was publicly debated for two days at full meetings, and on the 5th of February, 1848, the "war" party were utterly outvoted, and retired from the Confederation. Seven days afterwards John Mitchel, as if rendered desperate by this reprehension of his doctrines, started a weekly newspaper called the *United Irishman*, to openly preach his policy of insurrection.

He was regarded as a madman. Young Irelanders and Old Irelanders alike laughed in derision or shouted in anger at this proceeding. But events were now near, which, all unforeseen as they were by Mitchel and by his opponents, were destined to put the desperate game completely into his hands.

The third number of the new journal had barely appeared when news of the French revolution burst on an astonished world. It set Ireland in a blaze. Each day added to the excitement. Every post brought tidings of some popular rising, invariably crowned with victory. Every bulletin, whether from Paris, Berlin, or Vienna, told the same story, preached, as it were, the same lesson: barricades in the streets, overthrow of the government, triumph of the people. It may be doubted if the *United Irishman* would have lived through a third month but for this astounding turn of affairs. Now its every utterance was rapturously hailed by a wildly excited multitude. What need to trace what may be easily understood—Ireland was irresistibly swept into the vortex of revolution. The popular leaders, who a month previously had publicly defeated Mitchel's pleadings for war, now caught the prevalent passion. Struck by the events they beheld, and the examples set on every side, they verily believed that Ireland had but to "go and do likewise," and the boon of national liberty would be conceded by England, probably without a blow.

Confederate "clubs" now sprang up all over the country, and arming and drilling were openly carried on. Mitchel's journal week by week laboured with fierce energy to hurry the conflict. The editor addressed letters through its pages to Lord Clarendon, the Irish Viceroy, styling him "Her Majesty's Executioner General and General Butcher of Ireland." He published instructions as to street warfare; noted the "Berlin system," and the "Milanese system," and the "Viennese system;" highly praised molten lead, crockeryware, broken bottles, and even cold vitriol, as good things for citizens, male or female, to fling from windows and housetops on hostile troops operating below. Of course Mitchel knew that this could not possibly be tolerated. His calculation was that the government must indeed seize him, but that before he could be struck down and his paper be suppressed he would have rendered revolution inevitable.

The Confederation leaders had indeed embraced the idea of an armed struggle, yet the divergence of principles between them and the Mitchel party was wide almost as ever. They seemed marching together on the one road, yet it was hardly so. For a long time O'Brien and his friends held to a hope that eventually concession and arrangement between the government and Ireland would avert collision. Mitchel, on the other hand, feared nothing more than compromise of any kind. They would fain proceed soberly upon the model of Washington and the colonies; he was for following the example of Louis Blanc and the boulevards of Paris. The ideal struggle of their plans, if struggle there must be, was a well-prepared and carefully-ordered appeal to arms,[1] and so they would wait till autumn, when the harvest would be gathered in.

---

[1] A private letter written from his cell in Newgate Prison by Gavan Duffy to O'Brien in the week preceding the outbreak, and found in O'Brien's portmanteau after his arrest, brings out very curiously these views:—

"I am glad to learn you are about to commence a series of meetings in Munster. There is no half-way house for

"Rose-water revolutionists," Mitchel scornfully called them. "Fools, idiots," exclaimed one of his lieutenants; "they will wait till muskets are showered down to them from heaven, and angels sent to pull the triggers."

Behind all this argument for preparation and delay there undoubtedly existed what may be called the "conservative" ideas and principles, which some of the leading Confederates entertained. O'Brien stormed against "the Reds," as he called the more desperate and impatient men. They, on the other hand, denounced him as an "aristocrat" at heart, and a man whose weakness would be the ruin of the whole enterprise. Speaking with myself years afterwards, he referred bitterly to the reproaches cast upon him, for his alleged "punctiliousness" and excessive alarm as to anti-social excesses. "I was ready to give my life in a fair fight for a nation's rights," said he; "but I was not willing to head a *jacquerie*."

But if the whilom Young Irelanders were thus split into two sections, led respectively by O'Brien and Mitchel, there was a third party to be taken into account, the O'Connellite Repealers. These were as hostile to the revolutionists—both "rose-water" and "vitriol"—as were the life-long partisans of imperial rule. On the occasion of a public banquet given to O'Brien, Meagher, and Mitchel, in the city of Limerick, in March, 1848, an O'Connellite mob surrounded the hall and dispersed the company in a scene of riot and bloodshed. The immediate cause of this astonishing proceeding was an attack on the memory of O'Connell in Mitchel's paper, the dead tribune having been contumeliously referred to for his "degrading and demoralizing moral force doctrines."

One important class in Ireland - a class long accustomed to move with or head the people—throughout all this time set themselves invincibly against the contemplated insurrection: the Catholic clergy. They had from the first, as a body, regarded the Young Irelanders with suspicion. They fancied they saw in this movement too much that was akin to the work of the Continental revolutionists, and

greatly as they disliked the domination of England, they would prefer it a thousand times to such "liberty" as the Carbonari would proclaim. At this time, in 1848, the power of the Catholic priests was unbroken, was stronger than ever. The famine scenes, in which their love for the people was attested by heroism and self-sacrifice such as the world had never seen surpassed, had given them an influence which none could question or withstand. Their antagonism was fatal to the movement—more surely and infallibly fatal to it than all the power of the British crown.

Lord Clarendon, though fully aware that the war-policy Young Irelanders were comparatively weak in numbers, evidently judged that an outbreak once begun might have an alarming development. He determined to strike quickly and strike hard. On the 21st of March O'Brien, Meagher, and Mitchel were arrested, the first two charged with seditious speeches, Mitchel with seditious writings. The prosecutions against O'Brien and Meagher on this indictment failed through disagreement of the juries. As to Mitchel, before his trial by the ordinary course of procedure for sedition could be held, the government passed through parliament a new law called the "Treason Felony Act," which gave greater facilities for dealing with such offences. On the 22d of May he was arraigned under the new act in Green Street Court-house, Dublin, and on the 26th was found guilty.

The Mitchelite party had determined and avowed that his conviction—any attempt to remove him from Dublin as a convict—should be the signal for a rising, and now the event had befallen. There can be no question that had they carried out their resolution a desperate and bloody conflict would have ensued. Mitchel possessed in a remarkable degree the power of inspiring personal attachment and devotion; and there were thousands of men in Dublin who would have given their lives to rescue him. The government were aware of this, and occupied themselves in preparations for an outbreak in the metropolis. The Confederation leaders, however, who considered that any resort to arms before the autumn would be disastrous, strained every energy in dissuading the Mitchelites from the contemplated course of action. The whole of the day previous to the conviction was spent in private negotiations, interviews, arguments, and appeals. This labour was prolonged far into the night, and it was only an hour or two before morning dawned on the 27th of May,

---

you; you will be the head of the movement, loyally obeyed; and the revolution will be conducted with order and clemency, or the mere anarchists will prevail with the people, and our revolution will be a bloody chaos. You have at present Lafayette's place as painted by Lamartine, and I believe have fallen into Lafayette's error of not using it to all its effect and in all its resources. I am well aware that you do not desire to lead or influence others; but I believe with Lamartine that that feeling, which is a high civic virtue, is a vice in revolutions."

1848, that Dublin was saved from the horrors of a sanguinary struggle.

The friends of Mitchel never concealed their displeasure at the countermand thus effected by the O'Brien party, and prophesied that the opportunity for a successful commencement of the national struggle had been blindly and culpably sacrificed. The consent of the Dublin clubs to abandon the rescue or rising on this occasion was obtained, however, only on the solemn undertaking of the Confederation chiefs that in the second week of August the standard of insurrection would absolutely be unfurled.

A rumour that some such dissuasion was being attempted—that Smith O'Brien and his friends were opposed to the intended conflict —spread through Dublin late on the evening of the 26th of May, and painful uncertainty and apprehension agitated the city next morning. The government, though well informed through spies of everything that was passing, took measures in preparation for all possible eventualities. Mitchel was sentenced to fourteen years' transportation beyond the seas. The court was densely crowded with his personal and political friends and former fellow-students of Trinity College. He heard the sentence with composure, and then a silence as if of the tomb fell on the throng as it was seen he was about to speak. He addressed the court in defiant tones. "My lords," said he, "I knew I was setting my life on that cast. The course which I have opened is only commenced. The Roman who saw his hand burning to ashes before the tyrant promised that three hundred should follow out his enterprise. Can I not promise for one—for two—for three—aye, for hundreds?" As he uttered these closing words he pointed first to John Martin, then to Devin Reilly, next to Thomas Francis Meagher, and so on to the throng of associates whom he saw crowding the galleries. A thundering cry rang through the building, "Promise for me, Mitchel! Promise for me!" and a rush was made to embrace him ere they should see him no more. The officers in wild dismay thought it meant a rescue. Arms were drawn; bugles in the street outside sounded the alarm; troops hurried up. A number of police flung themselves on Mitchel, tore him from the embrace of his excited friends, and hurried him through the wicket that leads from the dock to the cells beneath. It may be pronounced that in that moment the Irish insurrectionary movement of 1848 was put down.

At an early hour that morning the war-sloop *Shearwater* was drawn close to the north wall jetty at Dublin quay. There she lay, with fires lighted and steam up, waiting the freight that was being prepared for her in Green Street Court-house. Scarcely had Mitchel been removed from the dock than he was heavily manacled, strong chains passing from his wrists to his ankles. Thus fettered he was hurried into a police-van waiting outside the gateway, surrounded by dragoons with sabres drawn. At a signal the cavalcade dashed off, and skilfully making a detour of the city so as to avoid the streets wherein hostile crowds might have been assembled or barricades erected, they reached the *Shearwater* at the wharf. Mitchel was carried on board, and had scarcely touched the deck when the paddles were put in motion, the steamer swiftly sped to sea, and in a few hours the hills of Ireland had faded from view.

The news of his conviction and sentence, the astounding intelligence that he was really gone, burst like a thunderclap on the clubs throughout the provinces. A cry of rage went up, and the Confederation chiefs were fiercely denounced for what was called their fatal cowardice. Confidence in their determination vanished. Unfortunately, from this date forward there was for them no retreating. They now flung themselves into the provinces, traversing the counties from east to west, addressing meetings, inspecting club organizations, inquiring as to armament, and exhorting the people to be ready for the fray. Of course the government was not either inattentive or inactive. Troops were poured into the country; barracks were improvised, garrisons strengthened, gunboats moved into the rivers, flying camps established; every military disposition was made for encountering the insurrection.

In all their calculations the Confederate leaders had reckoned upon two months for preparation, which would bring them to the middle of August. By no legal process of arrest or prosecution known to them could their conviction be effected in a shorter space of time. Never once did they take into contemplation the possibility (and to men dealing with so terrible a problem it ought to have been an obvious contingency) that the government would dispense with the slow and tedious forms of ordinary procedure, and grasp them quickly with avenging hand. While O'Brien and Dillon and Meagher, O'Gorman and M'Gee, were scattered through the country, arranging for the rising, lo! the news reached Dublin one day in the last week of July that the previous evening the government had passed through parliament a bill for suspending the *Habeas Corpus* act. That night proclamations were issued for the arrest of the Confederate leaders, and considerable rewards were offered for their apprehension.

This news found O'Brien at Ballinkeele, in Wexford county. He moved rapidly from thence through Kilkenny into Tipperary, for the purpose of gathering, in the latter county, a considerable force with which to march upon Kilkenny city—this having been selected as the spot whence a provisional government was to issue its manifesto, calling Ireland to arms. Before any such purpose could be effected, he found himself surrounded by flying detachments of military and police. Between some of these and a body of the peasantry, who had assembled to escort him at the village of Ballingary, a conflict ensued, the result of which showed him the utter hopelessness of the attempted rising, and in fact suppressed it there and then. As the people were gathering in thousands—and they would have assembled in numbers more than sufficient to have defeated any force that could then have been brought against him—the Catholic clergy appeared upon the scene. They rushed amidst the multitude, imploring them to desist from such an enterprise, pointing out the unpreparedness of the country, and demonstrating the too palpable fact that the government were in a position to quench in blood any insurrectionary movement. "Where are your arms?" they said;—there were no arms. "Where is your commissariat?"—the multitude were absolutely without food. "Where are your artillery, your cavalry? Where are your leaders, your generals, your officers? What is your plan of campaign? Mr. O'Brien and Mr. Dillon are noble-minded men; but they are not men of military qualification. Are you not rushing to certain destruction?" These exhortations, poured forth with a vehemence almost indescribable, had a profound effect. The gathering thousands melted slowly away, and O'Brien, dismayed, astounded, and sick at heart, found himself at the head, not of 50,000 stalwart Tipperary men, armed and equipped for a national struggle, but a few hundred half-clad and wholly unarmed peasantry. Scarcely had they set forth when they encountered one of the police detachments. A skirmish took place. The police retreated into a substantially built farmhouse close by, which, situated as it was, they could have held against ten times their own force of military men without artillery. The attempt of the peasantry to storm it was disastrous, as O'Brien forbade imperatively the execution of the only resort which could have compelled its evacuation. Three of his subordinates had brought up loads of hay and straw to fire the building. It was the house of a widow, whose five children were at the moment within. She rushed to the rebel chief, flung herself on her knees, and asked him if he was going to stain his name and cause by an act so barbarous as the destruction of her little ones. O'Brien immediately ordered the combustibles to be thrown aside, although a deadly fusilade from the police force within was at the moment decimating his followers. These, disgusted with a tenderness of feeling which they considered out of place on such an occasion, abandoned the siege of the building, and dispersed homewards. Ere the evening fell, O'Brien, accompanied by two or three faithful adherents, was a fugitive in the defiles of the Kilnamanagh mountains. No better success awaited his subordinates elsewhere. In May they had prevented a rising; now they found the country would not rise at their call.

Soon after Mitchel's transportation, Duffy was arrested in Dublin, and on the 28th of July armed police broke into the *Nation* office, seized the number of the paper being then printed, smashed up the types, and carried off to the Castle all the documents they could find. Throughout the country arrests and seizures of arms were made on all hands. Every day the *Hue and Cry* contained new proclamations and new lists of fugitives personally described. There was no longer any question of resistance. Never was collapse more complete. The fatal war-fever that came in a day vanished almost as rapidly. Suddenly every one appeared astounded at the madness of what had been contemplated; but somehow very few seemed to have perceived it a month before.

Throughout the remaining months of the year Ireland was given over to the gloomy scenes of special commissions, state trials, and death-sentences. Of the leaders or prominent actors in this abortive insurrection, O'Brien, Meagher, MacManus, Martin, and O'Doherty were convicted; Dillon, O'Gorman, and Doheny succeeded in accomplishing their escape to America. O'Brien, Meagher, and MacManus, with one of their devoted companions in danger,

Patrick O'Donoghue by name, having been convicted of high treason, were sentenced to death; but by authority of a specially passed act of parliament, the barbarous penalty of hanging, disembowelling, and quartering, to which they were formally adjudged, was commuted into transportation beyond the seas for life. Duffy was thrice brought to trial; but although the crown made desperate efforts to effect his conviction, the prosecution each time broke down, baffled by the splendid abilities of the defence conducted by Mr. Isaac Butt, Q.C.

Eventually the proceedings against him were abandoned. Of less important participators numbers were convicted, and hundreds fled the country never to return. "Forty-eight" cost Ireland dearly—not alone in the sacrifice of some of her best and noblest sons, led to imolate themselves in such desperate enterprise as revolution, but in the terrible reaction, the prostration, the terrorism, the disorganization that ensued. Through many a long and dreary year the country suffered for the delirium of that time.

PATRICK WESTON JOYCE.

[Patrick Weston Joyce was born in 1827 in the village of Ballyorgan, county Limerick. He was educated at private schools. In 1845 he entered the service of the Commissioners of National Education, under whom he held several successive posts till 1860, when he was placed at the head of the Central National Model Schools, Dublin. He was next raised to the position of a professor in the commissioners' training department for teachers—a post he still holds. While he was thus climbing the ladder of promotion in his department he found time to enter and graduate in Trinity College, of which he became a B.A. in 1861, an M.A. in 1865, and LL.D. in 1870.

Dr. Joyce's first work was suggested by his own occupation. *A Handbook of School Management and Methods of Teaching*, published in 1863, has passed through many editions, and continues to be universally used by the teachers of Irish National Schools. He was elected a member of the Royal Irish Academy in 1863, and two years afterwards he put at the disposition of that body the results of his investigations into the laws by which the Irish names of places were formed. The series of papers in which he developed his ideas were received with favour by Petrie, Todd, and other leading Irish scholars. Thus encouraged, Dr. Joyce continued his investigations, and in 1869 he published his work on the *Origin and History of Irish Names of Places*. This is a fascinating volume, full of quaint stories, curious information, most interesting analysis of the superstitions and history hidden in the names by which localities are known. The success of the book was immediate, a second edition being called for within a few months. In 1875 came a "Second Series," and the book, now consisting of two volumes, is unique of its kind; for in no other country in Europe have place-names been subjected to the same detailed scientific analysis, and the results given in a readable form.

In 1872 was issued *Ancient Irish Music*, a collection of one hundred Irish airs hitherto unpublished, with historical and illustrative text. The work contained, besides, several songs, some of them by Dr. Joyce himself, others by his brother Robert Dwyer Joyce. In 1879 appeared *Old Celtic Romances*, a series of eleven of the ancient bardic tales of Ireland, translated into plain homely English from the Gaelic manuscripts of the Royal Irish Academy and Trinity College, Dublin—a work which, like the *Irish Names of Places*, has been very favourably reviewed, and is already an established success. Dr. Joyce is, besides, author of *How to Prepare for Civil Service Competition*, and *A School Irish Grammar*.]

FAIRIES AND THE NAMES OF PLACES.[1]

Most of the different kinds of fairies, so well known at the present day to those acquainted with the Irish peasantry, have also been commemorated in local names. A few of those I will here briefly mention, but the subject deserves more space than I can afford.

The Pooka—Irish *phca*—is an odd mixture of merriment and malignity; his exploits form

---

[1] The above extract is from the chapter on "Fairies, Demons, Goblins, and Ghosts," in the first series of the *Origin and History of Irish Names of Places*.

the subject of innumerable legendary narratives; and every literary tourist who visits our island seems to consider it a duty to record some new story of this capricious goblin. Under the name of Puck he will be recognized as the "merry wanderer of the night," who boasts that he can "put a girdle round about the earth in forty minutes;" and the genius of Shakspere has conferred on him a kind of immortality he never expected.

There are many places all over Ireland where the Pooka is still well remembered, and where, though he has himself forsaken his haunts, he has left his name to attest his former reign of terror. One of the best known is Pollaphuca in Wicklow, a wild chasm where the Liffey falls over a ledge of rocks into a deep pool, to which the name properly belongs, signifying the pool or hole of the Pooka. There are three townlands in Clare, and several other places in different parts of the country, with the same name; they are generally wild lonely dells, caves, chasms in rocks on the sea-shore, or pools in deep glens like that in Wicklow—all places of a lonely character, suitable haunts for this mysterious sprite. The original name of Puckstown in the parish of Mosstown in Louth, and probably of Puckstown near Artaine in Dublin, was Pollaphuca, of which the present name is an incorrect translation. Boheraphuca (*boher*, a road), four miles north of Roscrea in Tipperary, must have been a dangerous place to pass at night in days of old. Carrigaphooca (the Pooka's rock), two miles west of Macroom, where, on the top of a rock overhanging the Sullane, stand the ruins of the M'Carthy's castle, is well known as the place whence Daniel O'Rourke began his adventurous voyage to the moon on the back of an eagle; and here for many a generation the Pooka held his "ancient solitary reign," and played pranks which the peasantry will relate with minute detail.

About half-way between Kilfinane in Limerick, and Mitchelstown in Cork, the bridge of Ahaphuca crosses the Ounageeragh river at the junction of its two chief branches, and on the boundary of the two counties. Before the erection of the bridge this was a place of evil repute, and not without good reason, for on stormy winter nights many a traveller was swept off by the flood in attempting to cross the dangerous ford; these fatalities were all attributed to the malice of the goblin that haunted the place; and the name—the Pooka's ford—still reminds us of his deeds of darkness.

He is often found lurking in raths and lisses; and accordingly there are many old forts through the country called Lissaphuca and Rathpooka, which have, in some cases, given names to townlands. In the parish of Kilcolman, in Kerry, are two townlands called Rathpoge on the ordnance map, and Rathpooke in other authorities—evidently *Rathpuca*, the Pooka's rath. Sometimes his name is shortened to *pook*, or *puck*; as, for instance, in Castlepook, the goblin's castle, a black, square, stern-looking old tower near Doneraile in Cork, in a dreary spot at the foot of the Ballyhoura hills, as fit a place for a pooka as could be conceived. This form is also found in the name of the great moat of Cloghpook in Queen's county (written Cloyth-an-puka in a rental book of the Earl of Kildare, A.D. 1518), the stone or stone fortress of the Pooka; and according to O'Donovan, the name of Ploopluck near Naas in Kildare is a corruption—a very vile one indeed—of the same name. . . . .

Fairies are not the only supernatural beings let loose on the world by night; there are ghosts, phantoms, and demons of various kinds; and the name of many a place still tells the dreaded scenes nightly enacted there. The word *dealbh* (dalliv), a shape or image (*delb*, effigies, Zeuss, 10) is often applied to a ghost. The townland of Killernagallive in the parish of Templebredon, Tipperary, took its name from an old churchyard, where the dead must have rested unquietly in their graves; for the name is a corruption of *Cillin-na-adealbh*, the little church of the phantoms. So also Drumnanaliv in Monaghan, and Clondallow in King's county, the ridge and the meadow of the spectres. And in some of the central counties, certain clusters of thorn bushes, which have the reputation of being haunted, are called by the name of Dullowbush (*dullow*, i.e. *dealbh*), i.e. the phantom bush.

There is a hideous kind of hobgoblin generally met with in churchyards, called a *dullaghan*, who can take off and put on his head at will—in fact you generally meet him with that member in his pocket, under his arm, or absent altogether; or if you have the fortune to light on a number of them you may see them amusing themselves by flinging their heads at one another, or kicking them for footballs. Ballindollaghan in the parish of Baslick, Roscommon, must be a horrible place to live in, if the dullaghan that gave it the name ever shows himself now to the inhabitants.

Every one knows that a ghost without a head is very usual, not only in Ireland, but all over the world; and a little lake in the parish of Donaghmore in Donegal, four miles south of Stranorlar, is still called Lough Gillagancan, the headless man's lake, from having been haunted by one of these visitants. But I suppose it is only in Ireland you could meet with a ghost without a shirt. Several of these tasteless fellows must have at some former period roamed nightly at large in some of the northern counties, where there are certain small lakes, which are now called Lough Gillaganleny, the lake of the shirtless fellow: one, for instance, two miles east of the northern extremity of Lough Eask, near the town of Donegal; and another in the parish of Rossinver in Leitrim, five miles from Manorhamilton (*gilla*, a fellow; *gan*, without; *leiné*, a shirt).

CONNLA OF THE GOLDEN HAIR AND THE FAIRY MAIDEN.[1]

Connla of the Golden Hair was the son of Conn the Hundred-fighter.[2] One day as he stood with his father on the royal Hill of Usna,[3] he saw a lady a little way off, very beautiful, and dressed in strange attire. She approached the spot where he stood; and when she was near, he spoke to her, and asked who she was, and from what place she had come.

The lady replied, "I have come from the Land of the Living[4]—a land where there is neither death nor old age, nor any breach of law. The inhabitants of earth call us Aes-shee,[5] for we have our dwellings within large, pleasant, green hills. We pass our time very pleasantly in feasting and harmless amusements, never growing old; and we have no quarrels or contentions."

The king and his company marvelled very much; for though they heard this conversation, no one saw the lady except Connla alone.

"Who is this thou art talking to, my son?" said the king.

And anon she answered for the youth, "Connla is speaking with a lovely, noble-born young lady, who will never die, and who will never grow old. I love Connla of the Golden Hair, and I have come to bring him with me to Moy-mell, the plain of never-ending pleasure. On the day that he comes with me he shall be made king, and he shall reign for ever in Fairyland, without weeping and without sorrow. Come with me, O gentle Connla of the ruddy cheek, the fair, freckled neck, and the golden hair! Come with me, beloved Connla, and thou shalt retain the comeliness and dignity of thy form, free from the wrinkles of old age, till the awful day of judgment."

Thy flowing golden hair, thy comely face,
Thy tall majestic form of peerless grace,
That show thee sprung from Conn's exalted race.

King Conn the Hundred-fighter being much troubled, called then on his druid[6] Coran, to put forth his power against the witchery of the banshee:—"O Coran of the mystic arts and of the mighty incantations, here is a contest such as I have never been engaged in since I was made king at Tara—a contest with an invisible lady, who is beguiling my son to Fairyland by her baleful charms. Her cunning is beyond my skill, and I am not able to withstand her power; and if thou, Coran, help not, my son will be taken away from me by

---

[1] This is the shortest of the *Old Celtic Romances* by Dr. Joyce. It has been translated from the "Book of the Dun Cow," a manuscript which was transcribed A.D. 1100, now in the Royal Irish Academy, Dublin. The story is one of the most ancient illustrations to be found of the wide-spread Irish superstition that fairies sometimes take away mortals to their enchanted palaces. ED.

[2] Conn Ced-cathach or Conn the Fighter of a Hundred (not Conn of the Hundred Battles, as the name is generally translated) was King of Ireland from A.D. 123 to 158.

[3] The Hill of Usna, in the parish of Conry, in Westmeath, one of the royal residences of Ireland.

[4] The ancient Irish had a sort of dim vague belief that there was a land where people were always youthful, and free from care and trouble, suffered no disease and lived for ever. This country they called by various names: —*Tir-na-mbeo*, the land of the ever-living; *Tir-na-nóg*, the land of the ever-youthful; *Moy-mell*, the plain of pleasure, &c. It had its own inhabitants—fairies, but mortals were sometimes brought there; and while they lived in it were gifted with the everlasting youth and beauty of the fairy people themselves, and partook of their pleasures. As to the exact place where Tirnanoge was situated, the references are shadowy and variable, but they often place it far out in the Atlantic Ocean, as far as the eye can reach from the high cliffs of the western coast.

[5] The fairies were also supposed to live in palaces in the interior of pleasant green hills, and they were hence called Aes-shee or Deena-shee, *i.e.* people of the *shee* or fairy hills; and hence also the word *banshee*, *i.e.* a woman (*bean*) of the fairy hills. Tirnanoge was often regarded as identical with these bright subterranean palaces. In my boyhood days the peasantry believed that the great limestone cavern near Mitchelstown in the county Cork, was one of the entrances to Tirnanoge.

[6] The ancient Irish druids do not appear to have been *priests* in any sense of the word. They were, in popular estimation, men of knowledge and power—"men of science," as they were often designated; they knew the arts of healing and divination, and they were skilled above all in magic. In fact, the Irish druids were magicians, neither more nor less; and hence the Gaelic word for "druidical" is almost always applied where we should use the word "magical"—to spells, incantations, metamorphoses, &c.

the wiles and witchery of a woman from the fairy hills."

Coran the druid then came forward, and began to chant against the voice of the lady. And his power was greater than hers for that time, so that she was forced to retire.

As she was going away she threw an apple to Connla, who straightway lost sight of her; and the king and his people no longer heard her voice.

The king and the prince returned with their company to the palace; and Connla remained for a whole month without tasting food or drink except the apple. And though he ate of it each day, it was never lessened, but was as whole and perfect in the end as at the beginning. Moreover, when they offered him aught else to eat or drink he refused it; for while he had his apple he did not deem any other food worthy to be tasted. And he began to be very moody and sorrowful, thinking of the lovely fairy maiden.

At the end of the month, as Connla stood by his father's side among the nobles, on the Plain of Arcomin, he saw the lady approaching him from the west. And when she had come near, she addressed him in this manner:— "A glorious seat, indeed, has Connla among wretched, short-lived mortals, awaiting the dreadful stroke of death! But now, the ever-youthful people of Moy-mell, who never feel age, and who fear not death, seeing thee day by day among thy friends, in the assemblies of thy fatherland, love thee with a strange love, and they will make thee king over them if thou wilt come with me."

When the king heard the words of the lady, he commanded his people to call the druid again to him, saying,—"Bring my druid Coran to me; for I see that the fairy lady has this day regained the power of her voice."

At this the lady said, "Valiant Conn, fighter of a hundred, the faith of the druids has come to little honour among the upright, mighty, numberless people of this land. When the righteous law shall be restored, it will seal up the lips of the false black demon; and his druids shall no longer have power to work their guileful spells."

Now the king observed, and marvelled greatly, that whenever the lady was present his son never spoke one word to any one, even though they addressed him many times. And when the lady had ceased to speak, the king said, "Connla, my son, has thy mind been moved by the words of the lady?"

Connla spake then, and replied, "Father, I am very unhappy; for though I love my people beyond all, I am filled with sadness on account of this lady!"

When Connla had said this, the maiden again addressed him, and chanted these words in a very sweet voice:—

> A land of youth, a land of rest,
> A land from sorrow free;
> It lies far off in the golden west,
> On the verge of the azure sea.
> A swift canoe of crystal bright,
> That never met mortal view—
> We shall reach the land ere fall of night,
> In that strong and swift canoe;
> We shall reach the strand
> Of that sunny land,
> From druids and demons free;
> The land of rest,
> In the golden west,
> On the verge of the azure sea!

A pleasant land of winding vales, bright streams, and verdurous plains,
Where summer all the live-long year in changeless splendour reigns;
A peaceful land of calm delight, of everlasting bloom;
Old age and death we never know, no sickness, care, or gloom;
> The land of youth,
> Of love and truth,
> From pain and sorrow free,
> The land of rest,
> In the golden west,
> On the verge of the azure sea!

There are strange delights for mortal men in that island of the west;
The sun comes down each evening in its lovely vales to rest;
> And though far and dim
> On the ocean's rim
> It seems to mortal view,
> We shall reach its halls
> Ere the evening falls,
> In my strong and swift canoe;
> And evermore
> That verdant shore
> Our happy home shall be;
> The land of rest,
> In the golden west,
> On the verge of the azure sea!

It will guard thee, gentle Connla of the flowing golden hair,
It will guard thee from the druids, from the demons of the air,
My crystal boat will guard thee, till we reach that western shore,
When thou and I in joy and love shall live for evermore!
> From the druid's incantation,
> From his black and deadly snare,
> From the withering imprecation
> Of the demon of the air,

It will guard thee, gentle Connla of the flowing golden hair;
My crystal boat shall guard thee, till we reach that silver strand
Where thou shalt reign in endless joy, the king of the Fairyland!¹

When the maiden had ended her chant, Connla suddenly walked away from his father's side, and sprang into the curragh, the gleaming, straight-gliding, strong, crystal canoe. The king and his people saw them afar off, and dimly moving away over the bright sea towards the sunset. They gazed sadly after them, till they lost sight of the canoe over the utmost verge; and no one can tell whither they went, for Connla was never again seen in his native land.

ROBERT DWYER JOYCE.

[Robert Dwyer Joyce, brother of the preceding, was born in 1830, in the village of Glenosheen, county Limerick. He entered the service of the Commissioners of National Education. In 1857 he became a student at the Queen's College, Cork, graduated with science honours, and took the degree of M.D. in 1865.

In the following year he emigrated to the United States, and settled in Boston, where he still resides. The Irish population had been already familiar with his name through his writings in the National press; and from the year of his arrival to the present day he has had an extensive and lucrative practice as a medical man. During his residence in Cork he had been a frequent contributor to the poetical columns of the *Nation*, and he had also written a number of articles on Irish literature in several other periodicals.

Dr. Joyce's first book was a volume of *Ballads, Romances, and Songs*. This was published in Dublin in 1861, and is the only one of his works which has been brought out in Ireland. In 1868 appeared his *Legends of the Wars in Ireland*, a number of prose stories, founded on traditions preserved by the peasantry of the northern counties of Ireland. This was followed in 1871 by another volume of the same kind, *Irish Fireside Tales*. His next work, *Ballads of Irish Chivalry* (1872), includes most of the pieces in his first work, but contains many others of greater power, the results of more careful elaboration and of a more mature judgment. In 1876 appeared the finest and most successful of his poems. This is *Deirdrè*, a free poetical version of one of the old romances of Ireland, *The Fate of the Children of Usna*. The story is told in heroic rhyming verse, and the character of Deirdrè, the heroine, is one of the most beautiful and most attractive in the poetic literature of our country. The poem was at once received with unanimous eulogy in America, and the judgment of critical periodicals in England and Ireland have fully confirmed the favourable verdict.

Dr. Joyce's latest work—*Blanid*—published in 1879, is not yet well known in Europe, but it is fully equal in merit to *Deirdrè*. The author has pursued the same plan of weaving into a poetic story a tragedy of real life in the old days. The period described is the first century of the Christian era, when the Red Branch Knights flourished; and the basis of the tale is an ancient Irish tragedy, the death of the great champion Curoi, king of South Munster, and of his captive, the "bloom-bright Blanid." The poem bears some resemblance in its construction to Tennyson's *Princess;* and the short lyrics which are interspersed contain, like those in the great work of the poet-laureate, beautiful fancies in exquisitely melodious verse.]

NAISI RECEIVES HIS SWORD

(FROM "DEIRDRÈ.")

[Naisi the Usnanian prince, whilst waiting to attack the Fomorian pirates, receives a mighty sword from the sea-god Mananan. The pirates with their king Tale are defeated and slain, their galleys are captured, and in them Naisi with Deirdrè and their companions sail for Alba or Scotland.]

Now in the lonely hour when with her ray
The moon o'er ocean trailed a shimmering way
That the bright Spirit-folk to heaven might take,
A voice struck Naisi's ear and bade him wake.

---

¹ This is an expansion, rather than a translation, of the original, which is very short, and in some places very obscure.

Sudden he woke and wondering, to behold,
Beneath the couch's furs and cloth of gold,
His wife beside him wrapt in sleep serene,
And 'mid the pillows, in the moony sheen,
His little boy with wild eyes weird and bright
Laughing and crowing loud in huge delight,
With dimpled arms outstretched all silvered o'er
By moonbeams from the calm tent's open door,
As if some godlike Presence none could see
With kindly wiles there woke his infant glee!
There Naisi looked, and filled with sudden awe
A mighty sword beside its scabbard saw
Stuck two good span-lengths in the grassy earth,
And bright as though the moon had given it birth
And cast it flashing down to where it stood
Within the tent-door, glorying in her flood
Of silver light. Then back in calm repose
The strong babe sank, and, wildered, Naisi rose
And bent above the weapon, marvelling
If mortal hand ere forged so fair a thing,
And as with curious eyes the hero gazed
On the gold hilt that bright with diamonds blazed,
A spirit voice through his whole being ran,
That seemed to say, "The gift of Mananan!
Take it, and fear not!" Then with eager hand
He grasped the hilt, and plucked the dazzling
  brand
From the soft earth, and from the tent withdrew
Into the light, and looked with wonder new
On the great blade whereon was pictured
All shapes that live and move in Ocean's bed.
Long time he gazed upon its mimic sea,
Then whirled the weapon round full joyously
O'er his proud head in circles of bright flame
That made the night breeze whistle as it came.

He stood and paused; stole softly to the tent;
Donned his strong garb of war, and musing went
Down the smooth hill-side to the glassy sound,
And halted on the shore and gazed around
On rugged isle and smooth white-tented hill,
And moonlit shore, that lay all cold and still,
Sleeping as though they ne'er would wake again
To life and morning and the sea-lark's strain.
And, as he looked, a breeze blew on his face,
Perfumed with scents from all the lovely race
Of flowers that blossom by the windy sea,—
The fragrant pink, the wild anemone,
The armed thistle ere its head grows old
And the winds blow its beard across the wold,
The foxglove, heather, and sweet-smelling
  thyme,—
Yea, all the flowers, from north to southland
  clime
That meet the morn with smiles, their odours
  sent,
With the fresh salty smell of ocean blent,
On that strange breeze that, waxing momently,
Fulfilled the hero with wild ecstasy
Of heart and brain, as though his footsteps fell
In heaven 'mid meadows of sweet asphodel!
And now, as stronger still the breeze blew by,
The sound's clear water caught the hero's eye:
Moveless it gleamed, with not one wave to show
That o'er its surface that weird breeze could blow.
Whereat great wonder filled him. To a tree,
That grew behind on the declivity
Of the green height, he turned: no motion there
Of branch or leaf;—not even his own dark hair
Was lifted by the marvellous wind. Around
Again the hero turned, and with a bound
Of his strong heart, and tingling cheeks all warm
From the fresh blood, beheld the giant form
Of a huge warrior, clad in sea-green mail,
Standing upon the shore. The flowing sail
Of a great bark appeared his cloak; the spray
That dances with the morning winds at play,
Topmost o'er all the woods on Seraba's elm,
Seemed the tall plume that waved above his helm,
While like a spire he stood, upon the sand
His long spear resting, towering from his hand
As a great larch's shaft in Ara's dell.
Silent he stood, the while his glances fell
On the Fomorian gate. A shadow vast
Betimes he seemed, wherethro' the moonbeams
  passed
With shimmering glow, or in his mantle caught,
Or linkèd mail, to Naisi's vision brought
Strange shifting shapes of all the things that be,
Living or dead, within the crystal sea!

THE EXPLOITS OF CUROI.

(FROM "BLANID.")

[The princes form a league to attack the stronghold of the king of Mana and carry off his beautiful daughter Blanid. The place is defended by a mighty wheel "set in ages long gone by by Mananan the ruler of the sea," which stirred the waters of the fosse into a torrent no "living wight could pass." By the help of his magic spear Curoi destroys the terrible monsters, and strikes the "magic engine still as a frozen mill-wheel." Mana is captured, and Blanid carried off.]

There many a man's dim closing eye was cast
  In wonder at the strange Knight's glittering
    form,
His spear-shaft sloped, like a tall galley's mast
  Bent slantwise by the buffets of the storm,
As with grim frowning brows and footsteps fast
  Along the breach with heroes' heart-blood warm,
'Mid showers of bolts and darts, like Crom the
    God
Of Thunder, toward the magic wheel he trod.

Now paused he for a space and looked, when, lo!
  Between him and the fosse erstwhile so near,

There spread a stricken war-field, where the glow
  Fell lurid upon broken sword and spear;
And from a reedy marsh a javelin's throw
  Upon his right crept forth a thing of fear,
A serpent vast, with crested head, and coils
Would crush ten battle chargers. Like the spoils

Of a great city gleamed his spotted back
  As from the trembling reeds his volumes rolled,
Wide spread, approaching o'er the tangled wrack
  Of battle, his bright head now flashing gold,
Now red, now green, now sapphire. On his track
  The hero stood in wrath, and with firm hold
Raised high the spear that from his right hand sped
Down crashing through the monster's burnished head.

As he plucked forth his spear and still strode on,
  Out from behind a heap of slain there rose
A dreadful beast with eyes that gleamed and shone
  In fury, like the eyes of one of those
Twin Dragons of the strife that ever run
  Beside the feet of Bava when she goes
From the bright Mount of Monad with the brand
Of war far flaring in her armed hand.

So flashed the beast's wild eyes, while o'er the dead
  He rushed to meet his foe; as he drew nigh
Uprose the glittering shaft and spear-point dread
  And then shot forth, and 'mid the fire-bright eye
Pierced him through brain and body, on the bed
  Of war transfixing him; then rising high
The hero loosed his spear, and 'mid the slain
Left him still writhing, and strode forth again.

And, as he went, there rose at every rood
  Some monster dire his onward course to stay
To the dread wheel, but through the demon brood
  He fearless broke, until before him lay
A river whirling by of streaming blood.
  Shouting he plunged therein, and made his way
Up the far bank, and raising high his spear
Strode onward still across that field of fear.

Then rose from off the blood-stained fern a shape
  Tall, threatening, with a crown upon his head,
Bright clad in gold and brass from heel to nape
  Of sturdy neck, and with a mantle red
Wind-blown, that let the dazzling flashes 'scape
  Of the strong mail, as now with onward tread
He strode, and raised his giant arm in wrath,
To the great wheel to stop the hero's path;—

The hero who, now pausing, looked, and there
  Under the crown saw his dead father's face
Approaching with fell frowning, ghastly stare
  Against him: yet no whit the hero's pace

Was checked thereat;—on high his spear he bare
  And pierced the Phantom's breast, and all the place
Was empty now, and by the fosse's marge
He felt the mortal arrows smite his targe.

Then stood he like a tower and poised his spear;
  And lightning-like the fateful weapon flung,
And lodged it in the wheel's loud-roaring gear,
  Firm fixed in the huge plank whereon 'twas hung;—
No more the fosse whirled round with tide of fear,
  No more the magic engine thundering rung:
Still as a frozen mill-wheel now it lay,
And through the last breach open was the way.

No minstrel's tongue, or taught in heaven or hell,
  Whate'er of pearls of price his harp adorn,
Howe'er his fingers touch the strings, could tell
  The great deeds done upon that far-famed morn;
How amid heaps of slain the old King fell,
  How to the wood the Bloom-bright One forlorn
And her fair maids were brought forth from the hold,
With all the treasures of bright gems and gold.

THE BLACKSMITH OF LIMERICK.

(FROM "BALLADS OF IRISH CHIVALRY.")

He grasped his ponderous hammer, he could not stand it more,
To hear the bomb-shells bursting, and thundering battle's roar;
He said, "The breach they're mounting, the Dutchman's murdering crew—
I'll try my hammer on their heads, and see what *that* can do!

"Now, swarthy Ned and Moran, make up that iron well,
'Tis Sarsfield's horse that wants the shoes, so mind not shot or shell."
"Ah, sure," cried both, "the horse can wait—for Sarsfield's on the wall,
And where you go, we'll follow, with you to stand or fall!"

The blacksmith raised his hammer, and rushed into the street.
His 'prentice boys behind him, the ruthless foe to meet—
High on the breach of Limerick, with dauntless hearts they stood,
Where bomb-shells burst, and shot fell thick, and redly ran the blood.

"Now look you, brown-haired Moran, and mark you, swarthy Ned,
This day we'll prove the thickness of many a Dutchman's head!

Hurrah! upon their bloody path they're mounting gallantly;
And now the first that tops the breach, leave him
 to this and me!"

The first that gained the rampart, he was a captain brave,—
A captain of the grenadiers, with blood-stained
 dirk and glaive;
He pointed, and he parried, but it was all in vain,
For fast through skull and helmet the hammer
 found his brain!

The next that topped the rampart, he was a colonel
 bold,
Bright, through the dust of battle, his helmet
 flashed with gold.
"Gold is no match for iron," the doughty blacksmith said,
As with that ponderous hammer he cracked his
 foeman's head.

"Hurrah for gallant Limerick!" black Ned and
 Moran cried,
As on the Dutchmen's leaden heads their hammers
 well they plied.
A bomb-shell burst between them—one fell with-
 out a groan,
One leaped into the lurid air, and down the
 breach was thrown.

"Brave smith! brave smith!" cried Sarsfield,
 "beware the treacherous mine!
Brave smith! brave smith! fall backward, or surely
 death is thine!"
The smith sprang up the rampart, and leaped the
 blood-stained wall,
As high into the shuddering air went foemen,
 breach, and all!

Up, like a red volcano, they thundered wild and
 high,—
Spear, gun, and shattered standard, and foemen
 through the sky;
And dark and bloody was the shower that round
 the blacksmith fell;—

He thought upon his 'prentice boys—they were
 avenged well.

On foemen and defenders a silence gathered down;
'Twas broken by a triumph shout that shook the
 ancient town,
As out its heroes sallied, and bravely charged and
 slew,
And taught King William and his men what Irish
 hearts could do!

Down rushed the swarthy blacksmith unto the
 river side;
He hammered on the foe's pontoon to sink it in
 the tide;
The timber it was tough and strong, it took no
 crack or strain;
"Mavrone! 'twon't break," the blacksmith roared;
 "I'll try their heads again!"

He rushed upon the flying ranks—his hammer
 ne'er was slack,
For in through blood and bone it crashed, through
 helmet and through jack;
He's ta'en a Holland captain, beside the red pontoon,
And "Wait you here," he boldly cries; "I'll send
 you back full soon!

"Dost see this gory hammer? It cracked some
 skulls to-day,
And yours 'twill crack if you don't stand and list
 to what I say:—
Here! take it to your cursèd king, and tell him
 softly too,
'Twould be acquainted with *his* skull, if he were
 here, not you!"

The blacksmith sought his smithy, and blew his
 bellows strong;
He shod the steed of Sarsfield, but o'er it sang no
 song.
"Ochone! my boys are dead," he cried; "their
 loss I'll long deplore,
But comfort's in my heart—their graves are red
 with foreign gore!"

WILLIAM JOHN FITZPATRICK.

[Mr. Fitzpatrick has been perhaps the most industrious student of our day into the careers of illustrious Irishmen, and is one of our best authorities on the social life of the past in our country.

William John Fitzpatrick was born on August 31, 1830, and was educated at Clongowes Wood College. His first work of any importance was *The Life, Times, and Correspondence of Dr. Doyle* (1861). This was followed by a biography of Lord Cloncurry, and a work in defence of Lady Morgan, entitled *The Friends, Foes, and Adventures of Lady Morgan*, to which there came a sequel, *Lady Morgan, her Career, Literary and Personal. Anecdotal Memoirs of Archbishop*

Whately next appeared; and this was followed by *Lord Edward Fitzgerald and his Betrayers* (1869). In 1870 Mr. Fitzpatrick produced a very interesting work under the title of *Ireland before the Union*, and this was succeeded by a volume of even greater historical value, entitled *The Sham Squire and the Informers of 1798*. The description of this remarkable figure in the history of Ireland is brought out clearly, and the whole story is a striking picture of the state of society at the troubled period immediately before and after the Act of Union. In 1873 a volume of pleasant gossip under the title of *Irish Wits and Worthies, including Dr. Lanigan*, was published; and the most recent production of Mr. Fitzpatrick's pen has been a biography of his famous compatriot Charles Lever. He has also written *Historical Discoveries of the Days of Tone and Emmet*, and has been a frequent contributor to periodical literature. He is an honorary Doctor of Laws, a member of the Royal Irish Academy, and of the Royal Dublin Society.]

ANECDOTES OF KEOGH, THE IRISH MASSILLON.

(FROM "IRISH WITS AND WORTHIES."[1])

That love of hospitable and convivial pleasure characteristic of the old school of Irish priesthood, and which our historian sought to vindicate against the aspersions of Giraldus Cambrensis, was not only illustrated in Lanigan's own idiosyncracy, but in that of his friend, the Rev. M. B. Keogh, as well. The latter was hospitable to a fault, and would almost coin his heart into gold to give away; while legitimate creditors, as is often the fashion with literary men, were invariably left unpaid. A merchant to whom Mr. Keogh was indebted, knowing that he would have no chance of a settlement if directly applied for, appealed to him with the representation that, as he was in great difficulties, a pecuniary loan would be specially acceptable. The preacher replied that he could not give it just then, but if the applicant would come and dine with him on the following Sunday he would try meanwhile to make out the loan for him somehow or another. The money was duly produced, and the merchant, full of expressions of gratitude, reminding him of his old claim, returned the overplus to Father Keogh, who henceforth regarded him with feelings not altogether paternal.

As a natural consequence of the perverse principle which he cultivated, Father Keogh was constantly in debt and difficulties. One day, when disrobing after delivering a charity sermon in Whitefriar Street Chapel, where a vast crowd had congregated to hear him surpass himself, two bailiffs stalked into the sacristy, and placing him in a covered car drove off in triumph. Dr. Spratt good-naturedly accompanied his friend, and as they neared the sheriff's prison one of the officers, pulling out a pistol, said: "Father Keogh, I know your popularity, and in case you appeal to the mob, I draw the trigger." The idol of the people submitted to his fate with the desperate resignation he had so often inculcated in his sermons, and turning to Dr. Spratt said: "My dear friend, I am arrested at the suit evidently of B——, the coach-maker. Go to him and arrange it." The good priest did as requested, and returned to the prison with a receipt in full, which he considered equivalent to an order for the liberation of his friend. But the document proved futile; it turned out that Mr. Keogh was arrested at the suit of an utterly different creditor, and the glee of the coach-maker, who never expected to be paid, was only equalled by Mr. Keogh's dismay.[2]

The late Rev. J. Lalor, P.P. of Athy, the former coadjutor of Father Keogh at Baldoyle, used to tell that his curates, as they could never get one farthing from him, were generally most shabbily clad, and tried to console themselves by the reflection that in this respect they resembled our Lord's disciples, who were sent without scrip or staff. Mr. Lalor, at last losing patience, reefed the knee of his small-clothes, and furnished with this startling argument waited upon the pastor and claimed the price of a new one. "My dear fellow," was the reply, "I have not a farthing in the world; but if you go into that dressing-room yonder you may take your choice of four."

The late Dr. M——l was in the habit of paying Father Keogh, when in delicate health, a visit every Wednesday, and remaining to dine with him. One evening the doctor drank more than freely, and advised no end of draughts of less palatable flavour. When taking leave, Mr. Keogh placed a crumpled paper in his hand. The doctor's knock was

---

[1] By permission of the author.

[2] This, and several other anecdotes which follow, were communicated by the late Very Rev. Dr. Spratt, 6th January, 1871. Dr. Spratt died, universally regretted, 27th May, 1871.

heard betimes next morning. "I called," said he, "to represent a slight mistake. Only fancy, you gave me an old permit instead of a note." The reply was cool: "You cannot carry more than a certain amount of whisky without a permit; I saw that you had exceeded the proper quantum." Father Michael Keogh's powers of sarcasm, often most capriciously and dyspeptically exercised, were withering. A priest who had formerly been a Jesuit was lionized at a dinner where Mr. Keogh was present. "I think, sir," he exclaimed from the end of the table, "you were a Jesuit, but have since left the order." A stiff bow was the reply. "Judas was also in the society of Jesus," proceeded his tormentor, "but he took the cord and died a Franciscan."

But Fr. Keogh's forte, after pulpit oratory, was rare powers of histrionic mimicry. He was once invited by the late good though eccentric pastor of Duleek to preach a charity sermon. After delivering a powerful appeal, which melted many of the audience to tears, Father Keogh proceeded to read aloud some papers, containing parochial announcements, which the parish priest had placed in his hands for that purpose. But the most illiterate member of the assembled flock at once perceived that Mr. Keogh, by his tone and gesture, was mimicking the peculiarities of their primitive pastor. The latter was not slow in recognizing his own portrait, and starting up from a seat of honour which he occupied beneath the pulpit, exclaimed: "You Dublin jackeen, was it for this I invited you to Duleek?"

How an ecclesiastic, whose brow when engaged in delivering a divine message seemed not unsuited for the mitre, could sometimes suffer the cap and bells to usurp its place can be accounted for in no other way than that vagaries of this sort formed part of the eccentricity of his high genius. He had a keen eye to detect the weaknesses or absurdities of his neighbour, but was utterly blind to his own. In hearing these anecdotes of this remarkable Irishman—which are now told publicly for the first time—it is difficult to associate them with one whose prestige was of the most brilliant and exalted character. Since Dean Kirwan preached, there had not appeared a more irresistible or impressive pulpit orator. Hundreds of Protestants daily attended his controversial sermons; and we have heard them say that it was a rare treat to hear Father Keogh answering in the evening the polemical propositions enunciated from the pulpit by the Rev. Mortimer O'Sullivan in the morning. He was entitled to the receipts taken at some of these evening sermons. Father Murphy, his prior, handed him on one of these occasions £2, 10s. "I viewed the congregation," said Mr. Keogh, "and there was more than £4, 10s. present." "Granted," replied his superior, "but you owe me £2 for ten years, and I had no other means of getting paid." "Those who know me," observed Dr. Willis, in a communication to the author, "are aware that I never was given to weeping, especially in my younger days; but I do declare that during a course of Lenten sermons in Church Street, Keogh had every one of the congregation in tears, including myself, whom he had so often previously, in private, convulsed with laughter."

The old magazine from which an extract has been already culled opens with an elaborate sketch of the Rev. M. B. Keogh: "The practice of extemporary preaching, so judiciously encouraged or enforced by the Church of Rome," it states, "is admirably calculated to call forth the powers and the resources of such a mind as Mr. Keogh's. He is evidently of a quick and ardent temperament, swayed by sudden impulse, and often, in the hurrying moment of excitement, carried beyond himself by a species of inspiration. To tie down such a man to his notes would be to extinguish half his enthusiasm; it would be a sort of intellectual sacrilege—an insult to the majesty of genius." Mr. Keogh's success as a preacher was not due to commanding appearance, for, like Curran's, it seems to have been far from prepossessing. He had the same powers of mind and eye as Curran, who was wont to observe that it cost him half-an-hour longer to reach the hearts of the jury than it would have taken a less repulsive-featured man with the same arguments. "See him in the season of Lent," observes a contemporary critic, "for, probably, the fortieth time, standing unrobed before the unornamented altar, without text, form, or genuflexion, starting solemnly but abruptly upon his subject. Mark the extending of his arm, the penetrating glance of his kindled eye; hear his deep, mellow, and impressive tones; listen to his rich, impassioned, spirit-stirring diction, and then say, if you can, that you feel the absence of fine features, courtly manners, or commanding stature." And yet we are not aware that the sermons of this great orator exist in any accessible form. Nor is the loss, perhaps, as great as might at first sight be supposed. As in the case of Dean Kirwan—whose printed sermons are unworthy of his high reputation—the great effect of Father Keogh's pulpit oratory seems, on *post mortem* examination, due rather to the manner than the matter. Dr. Spratt, having got a discourse of his reported, presented him with the proof-sheets for correction; but, although accurately taken down, Mr. Keogh would not believe that he had delivered it in that form, and, filled with disgust, tore up the sheets and irrevocably cancelled the sermon.

Mr. Keogh, during his hours of relaxation, exhibited all the exuberance of a liberated school-boy on the playground. A gentleman, who we fear played cards rather for profit than pleasure, having one evening at Raheny pocketed pool after pool with complacent rapacity, at last, having secured an unusually large "hawl," suddenly stood up and declared it was time to leave. Keogh, with the utmost good humour, replied that it was too early to break up, and that he should give his host and friends an opportunity of retrieving their losses. But the man of lucre, with pleasant banter, extricated himself from the playful, "collaring" of his friends; and just as he had reached the hall, Fr. Keogh caught him in his muscular grip, and, turning him upside down, the entire contents of his pockets fell in a loud avalanche to the ground. The money was gathered up, the gamester returned, and the play continued with varying success until a later hour. This anecdote was told by the butler of the house, who at least was a considerable gainer by the incident.

"An idle brain is the devil's workshop," was an apothegm of his own concoction, which his audience heard him utter more than once. Two other favourite expressions of his were, "tinselled vanity" and "feathered foppery," and he declared inextinguishable war against both. Like Curran, Moore, and other great contemporaries, Mr. Keogh's origin was humble. He never shrank from avowing it manfully, and, we rather think, used those avowals as physic to purge the pride engendered by public adulation. The father of the Irish Massillon was a coffin-maker in Cook Street.[1] A friend asked him one day, "How is your father?" "Oh," replied Keogh with a very long visage, "I left him working for death!"

Nevertheless, the sire saw the son down; and his death occurred under the following circumstances. In attempting to attain an almost celestial degree of perfection as deliverer of divine messages, he sank from Scylla into the jaws of Charybdis. Somewhat erroneously supposing that his articulation was not quite as distinct as formerly, he desired a dentist to pull out all his front teeth, and to insert a false set in their room. Dental science was not then in its prime—the cure proved far worse than the disease. The clumsy tusks which had been substituted for nature's teeth obstructed rather than facilitated the flow of his oratory; but, still worse, they refused to perform the office of mastication. Dyspepsia, with a hundred other ills, were fostered in this way, and Mr. Keogh rapidly sank beneath their sapping influence. One of his last letters, written from his father's house in Cook Street, where he died, was addressed to Dr. Spratt, begging his prayers. But, like Curran—whose physican remarked to him, a day or two before his death, that he seemed to cough with greater difficulty, and was greeted with the reply: "That is very strange, for I have been practising all night"—Keogh also had his joke at that solemn hour. A priest, famous for following the fox-hounds, having paid him a visit, Keogh in a voice hardly audible muttered, "Ah, Father John, you were always in at the death." Mr. Keogh did not long survive his friend Dr. Lanigan. He died 9th September, 1831, aged forty-three years. A tablet to his memory, inscribed with a very eulogistic epitaph, is erected in the Roman Catholic Church, Baldoyle; but his remains repose in the vaults of SS. Michael and John, Exchange Street, Dublin.

FINGLAS CHURCHYARD.

(FROM "IRISH WITS AND WORTHIES.")

Forgetting present sorrows in the contemplation of the past, Dr. Lanigan loved to wander through picturesque fields, fertile with bright memories, and to moralize on the mutability of human happiness and fame. Young was never so happy as when wandering solitary through a churchyard, and courting thoughts of gloom. Lanigan was also given to the society of the dead; but he derived more than thoughts of gloom from the associa-

---

[1] Mr. Keogh worked at the trade for a time himself. He used to say, that when people faulted coffins, because of unsightly knots in the wood, he would reply: "Oh, I can hide them with an angel or two." Father Keogh inherited his talent from his mother, who kept a school. He was such an apt scholar, that the usual period for theological study was considerably abridged in his favour.

tion. The old graveyard of Finglas, the happy asylum for the poor sufferers who at last died in Dr. Harty's so-called asylum, lay close by. To this rural cemetery, where Lanigan himself was destined ere long to sleep, he often bent his course, and mused among the graves of priests and prelates, apostles and apostates,[1] knights and patriots, madmen and sages, and the rude forefathers of the hamlet. Here judges rest—judged according to their works —among the graves of some whose larcenies earned early death; commanders, too, skilled in killing—at last laid low themselves;[2] and shepherds sleep with the flock whom for forty years they had guarded with unsleeping vigilance.[3] The good had passed away, but other losses were more legitimately deplored by Dr. Lanigan. He bemoaned the loss of that valuable memoir of St. Canice, which, as Usher records, had long been preserved within Finglas Abbey; and the old stone cross, defaced by the iconoclastic hands of Cromwell's soldiers, received, we may be assured, a tear of sympathy.

Beneath the dark shelter of the yews planted by Canice's own hand, he thought of the terrible consequences which, Cambrensis tells us, pursued the English archers who sacrilegiously despoiled them to make bows. Sometimes the old man found himself in Donsoghly Castle— at other times in Drumcondra churchyard, where Grose and Gandon—both names dear to Ireland—sleep; and one day at this time a black hearse, nodding its white plumes, might be seen wending its way thither, and inclosing the mortal part of a gifted young poet, Thomas Furlong, to whom Lanigan had often shown considerate attention when a reader at the Royal Dublin Society. Previous to his death in 1827 Lanigan occasionally met him at Finglas, which the poet had often visited, and under the signature of "The Hermit in Ireland," contributed some sparkling descriptions of its many sports to *The London and Dublin Magazine* for 1825. It is rather remarkable that, like Lanigan, Furlong was fond of wanderings and ponderings in the very district to which his body was consigned; and his poem, "Upon Drumcondra-road I strolled," will long live.[4] Another Finglas brooder about this time was the once noisy Watty Cox, now retired from the storm of politics. He outlived Lanigan by a few years, and received the last sacraments from the pastor of Finglas. —The atmosphere of Finglas was holy and wholesome. Anciently a rural bishopric, the *Annals of the Four Masters* record the deaths of many of its abbots and prelates. In the year 1860, during some excavations at Finglas, a coffin was discovered containing the remains of a bishop in remarkable preservation as if embalmed. The hand still grasped the crozier, and even the episcopal ring still shone upon the finger. The mitre and vestments were also in comparatively good preservation. A medical gentleman in the neighbourhood, more curious than reverential, anxious to ascertain whether any process of embalmment had been pursued, disinterred the remains, and removed a portion of the face. The rector (who is by law custodian of the churchyard) very properly threatened legal proceedings, and compelled the gentleman in question to replace the body and close the grave. . . .

Pastoral peace filled the place, broken only by the melodious chirping of birds, the distant tinkle of the sheep-bell, or the gentle murmur of the river, which, as Jocelyn tells us, St. Patrick crossed after performing several miracles at Finglas. At eventide, 'tis true, an important and somewhat noisy visitor regularly came, presenting in its rapid, red, panoramic progress down the village hill a not uninteresting object. A merry bugle, raising distant echoes, announces the advent of the Antrim Royal Mail, its passengers from "the Black North" white with dust, and dashed by horses' foam, but with countenances joyously radiant at the prospect of a long and tedious journey soon ending, and "the honest welcome frank and free" of expectant friends in Dublin. The champing horses pause for a moment before a shebeen to allow some weary traveller to wash the dust out of his throat; the *boccagh* receives his alms, and mutters "God-speed!" the guard cries "All right!" sees that the priming in his blunderbuss is safe; and away they go again, now hid from view by interposing trees, while anon the scarlet and gold of the guard peep out rapidly here and there among the interstices of their branches. The clatter of the horses' hoofs gradually dies away, and the neighbourhood once more relapses into a repose which the buzzing of the drone alone disturbs.

---

[1] The Rev. Samuel Mason, a Roman Catholic priest, having read his recantation in Christ Church before Sir H. Sydney, received, in 1567, the living of Finglas; but, dying in the following year, was buried in this churchyard.

[2] Baron Pocklington is interred here; also Colonel Bridges, Captain Flower, and others, whose military services are duly enumerated.

[3] One stone over Father Benson records that for forty years he was the zealous pastor of Finglas.

[4] A notice of Thomas Furlong will be found in the *Cabinet*, vol. ii. p. 221.—ED.

EARL OF DUFFERIN.

[It has often been remarked that the British government has found its best administrators in Irishmen, and Lord Dufferin is certainly a remarkable example in favour of the truth of this proposition. It has been given to him so successfully to conduct the government of one of the greatest British dependencies as to depart from it amid the regrets of all parties and creeds, though in that dependency party and creed are marked by peculiar acrimony. It has also been his fortune to be contended for by rival politicians at home, and to be offered a high and difficult office by the chief of the party to which he has always been opposed.

The Right Hon. Frederick Temple Blackwood, Earl of Dufferin, is son of the fourth Baron Dufferin, and was born in 1826. His mother—whose romantic history we have already referred to[1]—was the granddaughter of Richard Brinsley Sheridan, and thus he is one more of the long list of Sheridans who have proved that wit can run in families. He was educated at Eton, and Christ Church, Oxford, but did not take a degree. He was still a minor when, in 1841, he succeeded to his father's title. His first entrance into official life was one of those small honorary offices attached to the court, and his first literary production was a narrative of a visit he made to Ireland during 1846-7, under the title of *Narrative of a Journey from Oxford to Skibbereen during the Year of the Irish Famine*. In February, 1855, he formed one of the numerous train which accompanied Lord John Russell to Vienna. In 1860 appeared the first work which drew particular attention to his name. It proved the possession of those great gifts of humorous observation which are now everywhere known to characterize him. He had in the previous year made a voyage in his yacht to Iceland, and an account of his stay in that island appeared in *Letters from High Latitudes*. This book bubbles over with fun, and a description of an Icelandic dinner-party, which we quote, can be read by few, we think, without aching sides.

In 1860 Lord Dufferin made what may be called his first real *entrée* into official life. He was in that year sent to Syria as British commissioner, for the purpose of inquiring into cruelties which had been practised by Turkish officials on the Christian population. He pursued his investigations with relentless vigilance, and administered condign punishment to the most notable malefactors. The home authorities were thoroughly satisfied by his action, and he was made a K.C.B. In 1864 he became for a while under-secretary for India; and during the year 1866 he acted as under-secretary for war.

When Mr. Gladstone was raised to power in 1868 Lord Dufferin was made chancellor of the Duchy of Lancaster—an office with undefined duties, which constituted him—as he wittily described it—"maid of all work" to the ministry. In 1872 he was appointed Governor-general of Canada. Never, as we have already said, was there a more successful ruler. The Orangeman and the Roman Catholic, the Conservative and Radical, alike bent under the influence of his clear judgment, his impartial action, his pleasant manners, and bewitching tongue. The speeches which he made have been collected into volume form by more than one enterprising publisher, and they can be read with an amount of pleasure which is rare when one peruses in print spoken addresses. Their chief characteristics are a lofty tone of feeling, bright wit, and, occasionally, great eloquence. On his retirement from the Canadian governorship he was chosen by Lord Beaconsfield as British ambassador at the court of St. Petersburg,—an office of great splendour, and, perhaps, greater difficulty.

Besides the works above mentioned, Lord Dufferin has written several books on the questions that chiefly disturb his native country. Their titles are, *Irish Emigration and the Tenure of Land in Ireland, Mr. Mill's Plan for the Pacification of Ireland Examined*, and *Contributions to an Inquiry into the State of Ireland*. Lord Dufferin has had a true helpmate in his wife during his brilliant career. She also is the member of an historic Irish family, being daughter of the late Captain Archibald Rowan Hamilton. His lordship was made an Earl of the United Kingdom in 1871, has been president of the Geographical Society, and is an honorary LL.D. of Harvard University.]

---

[1] See *Cabinet*, vol. iii. p. 235.

AN ICELANDIC DINNER.

(FROM "LETTERS FROM HIGH LATITUDES.")

Yesterday—no—the day before—in fact I forget the date of the day—I don't believe it had one—all I know is, I have not been in bed since,—we dined at the Governor's;—though dinner is too modest a term to apply to the entertainment.

The invitation was for four o'clock, and at half-past three we pulled ashore in the gig; I, innocent that I was, in a well-fitting white waistcoat.

The Government House, like all the others, is built of wood, on the top of a hillock; the only accession of dignity it can boast being a little bit of mangy kitchen-garden that hangs down in front to the road, like a soiled apron. There was no lock, handle, bell, or knocker to the door, but immediately on our approach a servant presented himself, and ushered us into the room where Count Trampe was waiting to welcome us. After having been presented to his wife we proceeded to shake hands with the other guests, most of whom I already knew; and I was glad to find that, at all events in Iceland, people do not consider it necessary to pass the ten minutes which precede the announcement of dinner as if they had assembled to assist at the opening of their entertainer's will, instead of his oysters. The company consisted of the chief dignitaries of the island, including the bishop, the chief-justice, &c. &c., some of them in uniform, and all with holiday faces. As soon as the door was opened Count Trampe tucked me under his arm—two other gentlemen did the same to my two companions—and we streamed into the dining-room. The table was very prettily arranged with flowers, plate, and a forest of glasses. Fitzgerald and I were placed on either side of our host, the other guests, in due order, beyond. On my left sat the rector, and opposite, next to Fitz, the chief physician of the island. Then began a series of transactions of which I have no distinct recollection; in fact, the events of the next five hours recur to me in as great disarray as reappear the vestiges of a country that has been disfigured by some deluge. . . .

I gather, then, from evidence—internal and otherwise—that the dinner was excellent, and that we were helped in Benjamite proportions; but as before the soup was finished I was already hard at work hob-nobbing with my two neighbours, it is not to be expected I should remember the bill of fare.

With the peculiar manners used in Scandinavian skoal-drinking I was already well acquainted. In the nice conduct of a wine-glass I knew that I excelled, and having an hereditary horror of heel-taps, I prepared with a firm heart to respond to the friendly provocations of my host. I only wish you could have seen how his kind face beamed with approval when I chinked my first bumper against his, and having emptied it at a draught, turned it towards him bottom upwards with the orthodox twist. Soon, however, things began to look more serious even than I had expected. I knew well that to refuse a toast, or to half empty your glass, was considered churlish. I had come determined to accept my host's hospitality as cordially as it was offered. I was willing, at a pinch, to *payer de ma personne;* should he not be content with seeing me *at* his table, I was ready, if need were, to remain *under* it! but at the rate we were then going it seemed probable this consummation would take place before the second course: so, after having exchanged a dozen rounds of sherry and champagne with my two neighbours, I pretended not to observe that my glass had been refilled; and, like the sea-captain, who, slipping from between his two opponents, left them to blaze away at each other the long night through,—withdrew from the combat. But it would not do; with untasted bumpers and dejected faces they politely waited until I should give the signal for a renewal of *hostilities,* as they well deserved to be called. Then there came over me a horrid, wicked feeling. What if I should endeavour to floor the Governor, and so literally turn the tables on him! It is true I had lived for five-and-twenty years without touching wine,—but was not I my great-grandfather's great-grandson, and an Irish peer to boot! Were there not traditions, too, on the other side of the house, of casks of claret brought up into the dining-room, the door locked, and the key thrown out of the window? With such antecedents to sustain me, I ought to be able to hold my own against the staunchest toper in Iceland! So, with a devil glittering in my left eye, I winked defiance right and left, and away we went at it again for another five-and-forty minutes. At last their fire slackened: I had partially quelled both the Governor and the rector, and still survived. It is true I did not feel comfortable; but it was in the neighbourhood of my

waistcoat, not my head, I suffered. "I am not well, but I will not out," I soliloquized, with Lepidus[1]—"δός μοι τό πτερόν," I would have added, had I dared. Still the neck of the banquet was broken—Fitzgerald's chair was not yet empty,—could we hold out perhaps a quarter of an hour longer our reputation was established; guess then my horror, when the Icelandic doctor, shouting his favourite dogma by way of battle cry, "Si trigintis guttis, morbum curare velis, erras," gave the signal for an unexpected onslaught, and the twenty guests poured down on me in succession. I really thought I should have run away from the house; but the true family blood, I suppose, began to show itself, and with a calmness almost frightful, I received them one by one.

After this began the public toasts.

Although up to this time I had kept a certain portion of my wits about me, the subsequent hours of the entertainment became henceforth developed in a dreamy mystery. I can perfectly recall the look of the sheaf of glasses that stood before me, six in number; I could draw the pattern of each: I remember feeling a lazy wonder they should always be full, though I did nothing but empty them,—and at last solved the phenomenon by concluding I had become a kind of Danaid, whose punishment, not whose sentence, had been reversed: then suddenly I felt as if I were disembodied,—a distant spectator of my own performances, and of the feast at which my person remained seated. The voices of my host, of the rector, of the chief-justice, became thin and low, as though they reached me through a whispering tube; and when I rose to speak it was as to an audience in another sphere, and in a language of another state of being: yet, however unintelligible to myself, I must have been in some sort understood, for at the end of each sentence cheers, faint as the roar of waters on a far-off strand, floated towards me; and if I am to believe a report of the proceedings subsequently shown us, I must have become polyglot in my cups. According to that report it seems the Governor threw off (I wonder he did not do something else), with the queen's health in French, to which I responded in the same language. Then the rector, in English, proposed my health,—under the circumstances a cruel mockery,—but to which, ill as I was, I responded very gallantly by drinking to the *beaux yeux* of the Countess. Then somebody else drank success to Great Britain, and I see it was followed by really a very learned discourse by Lord D. in honour of the ancient Icelanders; during which he alluded to their discovery of America, and Columbus' visit. Then came a couple of speeches in Icelandic, after which the bishop, in a magnificent Latin oration of some twenty minutes, a second time proposes my health; to which, utterly at my wits' end, I had the audacity to reply in the same language. As it is fit so great an effort of oratory should not perish, I send you some of its choicest specimens:—

"Viri illustres," I began, "insolitus ut sum ad publicum loquendum, ego propero respondere ad complimentum quod recte reverendus prelaticus mihi fecit, in proponendo meam salutem: et supplico vos credere quod multum gratificatus et flattificatus sum honore tam distincto.

"Bibere, viri illustres, res est, quæ in omnibus terris, 'domum venit ad hominum negotia et pectora:'[2] (1) requirit 'haustum longum, haustum fortem, et haustum omnes simul:' (2) ut canit poeta, 'unum tactum Naturæ totum orbem facit consanguineum,' (3) et hominis natura est—bibere (4).

"Viri illustres, alterum est sentimentum equaliter universale: terra communis super quam septentrionales et meridionales, eâdem enthusiasmâ convenire possunt: est necesse quod id nominarem? Ad pulchrum sexum devotio!

"'Amor regit palatium, castra, lucum:' (5) Dubito sub quo capite vestram jucundam civitatem numerare debeam. Palatium? non regem! castra? non milites! lucum? non ullam arborem habetis! Tamen Cupido vos dominat haud aliter quam alios,—et virginum Islandarum pulchritudo per omnes regiones cognita est.

"Bibamus salutem earum, et confusionem ad omnes bacularios: speramus quod eæ caræ et benedictæ creaturæ invenient tot maritos quot velint,—quòd geminos quottanis habeant, et quod earum filiæ, maternum exemplum

---

[1] Antony and Cleopatra.

[2] As the happiness of these quotations seemed to produce a very pleasing effect on my auditors, I subjoin a translation of them for the benefit of the unlearned:—
1. "Comes home to men's business and bosoms."—*Paterfamilias, Times.*
2. "A long pull, a strong pull, and a pull all together."—*Nelson at the Nile.*
3. "One touch of nature makes the whole world kin."—*Jeremy Bentham.*
4. Apothegm by the late Lord Mountcoffeehouse.
5. "Love rules the court, the camp, the grove."—*Venerable Bede.*

sequentes, gentem Islandicam perpetuent in sæcula sæculorum."

The last words mechanically rolled out, in the same "ore rotundo" with which the poor old Dean of Christchurch used to finish his Gloria, &c., in the cathedral.

Then followed more speeches,—a great chinking of glasses,—a Babel of conversation,—a kind of dance round the table, where we successively gave each alternate hand, as in the last figure of the Lancers,—a hearty embrace from the Governor,—and finally—silence, daylight, and fresh air, as we stumbled forth into the street.

ON IRISHMEN AS RULERS.[1]

Gentlemen,—I hardly know in what terms I am to reply to the address I have just listened to, so signal is the honour which you have conferred upon me. That a whole province, as large, as important, as flourishing as many a European kingdom, should erect into an embassy the mayors of its cities,—the delegates of its urban and rural municipalities,—and despatch them on a journey of several hundred miles, to convey to a humble individual like myself an expression of the personal goodwill of the constituencies they represent, is a circumstance unparalleled in the history of Canada, or of any other colony. To stand as I now do in the presence of so many distinguished persons, who have put themselves to great personal inconvenience on my account, only adds to my embarrassment. And yet, gentlemen, I cannot pretend not to be delighted with such a genuine demonstration of regard on the part of the large-hearted inhabitants of the great province in whose name you have addressed me; for, quite apart from the personal gratification I experience, you are teaching all future administrators of our affairs a lesson which you may be sure they will gladly lay to heart, since it will show them with how rich a reward you are ready to pay whatever slight exertions it may be within their power to make on your behalf. And when in the history of your Dominion could such a proof of your generosity be more opportunely shown? A few weeks ago the heart of every man and woman in Canada was profoundly moved by the intelligence, not only that the government of Great Britain was about to send out as England's representative to this country one of the most promising among the younger generation of our public men, but that the queen herself was about to intrust to the keeping of the people of Canada her own daughter. If you desired any illustration of the respect, the affection, the confidence with which you are regarded by your fellow-subjects and by your sovereign at home, what greater proof could you require than this, or what more gratifying, more delicate, more touching recognition could have rewarded your never-failing love and devotion for the mother country and its ruler? But though parliament and the citizens of Canada may well be proud of the confidence thus reposed in them, believe me when I tell you that, quite apart from these especial considerations, you may well be congratulated on the happy choice which has been made in the person of Lord Lorne for the future Governor-general of Canada. It has been my good fortune to be connected all my life long with his family by ties of the closest personal friendship. Himself I have known, I may say, almost from his boyhood, and a more conscientious, high-minded, or better qualified viceroy could not have been selected. Brought up under exceptionally fortunate conditions, it is needless to say he has profited to the utmost by the advantages placed within his reach, many of which will have fitted him in an especial degree for his present post. His public school and college education, his experience of the House of Commons, his large personal acquaintance with the representatives of all that is most distinguished in the intellectual world of the United States, his literary and artistic tastes, his foreign travel, will all combine to render him intelligently sympathetic with every phase and aspect of your national life. Above all, he comes of a good Whig stock—that is to say, of a family whose prominence in history is founded upon the sacrifices they have made in the cause of constitutional liberty. When a couple of a man's ancestors have perished on the scaffold as martyrs in the cause of political and religious freedom, you may be sure there is little likelihood of their descendant seeking to encroach, when acting as the representative of the crown, upon the privileges of parliament or the independence of the people.

As for your future princess, it would not become me to enlarge upon her merits—she will soon be amongst you, taking all hearts by storm by the grace, the suavity, the sweet simplicity of her manners, life, and conversation. Gentle-

---

[1] A speech to the municipalities of Ontario, delivered at Quebec, Sept. 5, 1878, in reply to their joint address.

men, if ever there was a lady who in her earliest youth had formed a high ideal of what a noble life should be—if ever there was a human being who tried to make the most of the opportunities within her reach, and to create for herself, in spite of every possible trammel and impediment, a useful career and occasions of benefiting her fellow-creatures, it is the Princess Louise, whose unpretending exertions in a hundred different directions to be of service to her country and generation have already won for her an extraordinary amount of popularity at home. When to this you add an artistic genius of the highest order, and innumerable other personal gifts and accomplishments, combined with manners so gentle, so unpretending, as to put every one who comes within reach of her influence at perfect ease, you cannot fail to understand that England is not merely sending you a royal princess of majestic lineage, but a good and noble woman, in whom the humblest settler or mechanic in Canada will find an intelligent and sympathetic friend. Indeed, gentlemen, I hardly know which pleases me most, the thought that the superintendence of your destinies is to be confided to persons so worthy of the trust, or that a dear friend of my own like Lord Lorne, and a personage for whom I entertain such respectful admiration as I do for the Princess Louise, should commence their future labours in the midst of a community so indulgent, so friendly, so ready to take the will for the deed, so generous in their recognition of any effort to serve them, as you have proved yourselves to be.

And yet, alas! gentlemen, pleasant and agreeable as is the prospect for you and them, we must acknowlegde there is one drawback to the picture. Lord Lorne has, as I have said, a multitude of merits, but even spots will be discovered on the sun, and unfortunately an irreparable, and, as I may call it, a congenital defect attaches to this appointment. Lord Lorne is not an Irishman! It is not his fault—he did the best he could for himself—he came as near the right thing as possible by being born a Celtic Highlander. There is no doubt the world is best administered by Irishmen. Things never went better with us either at home or abroad than when Lord Palmerston ruled Great Britain—Lord Mayo governed India—Lord Monck directed the destinies of Canada —and the Robinsons, the Kennedys, the Laffans, the Callaghans, the Gores, the Hennesys, administered the affairs of our Australian colonies and West Indian possessions. Have not even the French at last made the same discovery in the person of Marshal MacMahon? But still we must be generous, and it is right Scotchmen should have a turn. After all, Scotland only got her name because she was conquered by the Irish—and if the real truth were known, it is probable the house of Inverary owes most of its glory to an Irish origin. Nay, I will go a step further—I would even let the poor Englishman take an occasional turn at the helm—if for no better reason than to make him aware how much better we manage the business. But you have not come to that yet, and though you have been a little spoiled by having been given three Irish governor-generals in succession, I am sure you will find that your new viceroy's personal and acquired qualifications will more than counterbalance his ethnological disadvantages.

And now, gentlemen, I must bid you farewell. Never shall I forget the welcome you extended to me in every town and hamlet of Ontario when I first came amongst you. It was in travelling through your beautiful province I first learned to appreciate and understand the nature and character of your destinies. It was there I first learned to believe in Canada, and from that day to this my faith has never wavered. Nay, the further I extended my travels through the other provinces the more deeply my initial impressions were confirmed; but it was amongst you they were first engendered, and it is with your smiling happy hamlets my brightest reminiscences are intertwined. And what transaction could better illustrate the mighty changes your energies have wrought than the one in which we are at this moment engaged? Standing, as we do, upon this lofty platform, surrounded by those antique and historical fortifications, so closely connected with the infant fortunes of the colony, one cannot help contrasting the present scene with others of an analogous character which have been frequently enacted upon the very spot. The early Governors of Canada have often received in Quebec deputies from the very districts from which each of you have come, but in those days the sites now occupied by your prosperous towns, the fields you till, the rose-clad bowers, and trim lawns where your children sport in peace, were then dense wildernesses of primeval forest, and those who came from thence on an errand here were merciless savages, seeking the presence of the viceroy either to threaten war and vengeance, or at best to proffer a treacherous and uncertain peace. Now, little could Montmagny, or Tracy, or Vaudreuil, or Frontenac, have ever imagined on such occasions that for the lank dusky forms of the Iroquois or Ottawa emissaries, would one day be substituted the beaming countenances and burly proportions of English-speaking mayors and aldermen and reeves. And now, gentlemen, again good-bye. I cannot tell you how deeply I regret that Lady Dufferin should not be present to share the gratification I have experienced by your visit. Tell your friends at home how deeply I have been moved by this last and signal proof of their good-will, that their kindness shall never be forgotten, and that as long as I live it will be one of the chief ambitions of my life to render them faithful and effectual service.

A PLEA FOR TOLERATION.[1]

Gentlemen,—Few things could have given me greater pleasure than to receive such an address as that which you have presented to me. I recollect the friendly reception you gave me on my first arrival, and I rejoice at this opportunity of bidding you farewell. I am well aware of the useful nature of the task you have set yourselves, and of the broad and liberal spirit in which you execute it, and it is, therefore, to you, and through you to the rest of our Irish fellow-countrymen in Canada, that I feel irresistibly compelled to convey one last and parting entreaty. No one can have watched the recent course of events without having observed, almost with feelings of terror, the unaccountable exacerbation and recrudescence of those party feuds and religious animosities from which for many a long day we have been comparatively free. Now, gentlemen, this is a most serious matter; its import cannot be exaggerated; and I would beseech you and every Canadian in the land who exercises any influence amid the circle of his acquaintance—nay, every Canadian woman, whether mother, wife, sister, or daughter, to strain every nerve, to exert every faculty they possess, to stifle and eradicate this hateful and abominable root of bitterness from amongst us. Gentlemen, I have had a terrible experience in these matters. I have seen one of the greatest and most prosperous towns of Ireland —the city of Belfast—helplessly given over for an entire week into the hands of two contending religious factions. I have gone into the hospital and beheld the dead bodies of young men in the prime of life lying stark and cold upon the hospital floor—the delicate forms of innocent women writhing in agony upon the hospital beds—and every one of these struck down by an unknown bullet— by those with whom they had no personal quarrel—towards whom they felt no animosity, and from whom, had they encountered them in the intercourse of ordinary life, they would have probably received every mark of kindness and good-will. But where these tragedies occurred—senseless and wicked as were the occasions which produced them— there had long existed between the contending parties traditions of animosity and ill-will and the memory of ancient grievances; but what can be more Cain-like, more insane, than to import into this country—unsullied as it is by any evil record of civil strife—a stainless paradise, fresh and bright from the hands of its Maker,—where all have been freely admitted upon equal terms—the blood-thirsty strife and brutal quarrels of the Old World? Divided as you are into various powerful religious communities, none of whom are entitled to claim either pre-eminence or ascendency over the other, but each of which reckons amongst its adherents enormous masses of the population, what hopes can you have except in mutual forbearance and a generous liberality of sentiment? Why, your very existence depends upon the disappearance of these ancient feuds. Be wise, therefore, in time, I say, while it is still time, for it is the property of these hateful quarrels to feed on their own excesses; if once engendered they widen their bloody circuit from year to year, till they engulf the entire community in internecine strife. Unhappily, it is not by legislation or statutory restrictions, or even by the interference of the armed executive, that the evil can be effectually and radically remedied. Such alternatives, even when successful at the time— I am not alluding to anything that has taken place in Canada, but to my Irish experiences —are apt to leave a sense of injustice and of a partial administration of the law rankling in the minds of one or other of the parties; but surely when reinforced by such obvious considerations of self-preservation as those I have indicated, the public opinion of the community at large ought to be sufficient to repress the evil. Believe me, if you desire to avert an impending calamity, it is the duty of

---

[1] A speech to the Irish Protestant Benevolent Society, Toronto, Sept. 25, 1878, in reply to an address read by Captain M'Master.

every human being amongst you—Protestant and Catholic, Orangeman and Union man—to consider with regard to all these matters what is the real duty they owe to God, their country, and each other. And now, gentlemen, I have done. I trust that nothing I have said has wounded the susceptibilities of any of those who have listened to me. God knows I have had but one thought in addressing these observations to you, and that is to make the best use of this exceptional occasion, and to take the utmost advantage of the good-will with which I know you regard me, in order to effect an object upon which your own happiness and the happiness of future generations so greatly depend.

JOHN CASHEL HOEY.

[John Cashel Hoey was born in Dundalk, county Louth, in 1828, and is the eldest son of Mr. Cashel F. Hoey of that town, and some time of Charleston, South Carolina. He was one of the many young men of literary ability who were attracted by the Young Ireland movement, and he gave in his adhesion to the party just on the eve of the outbreak of 1848. When, in the following year, the suppressed *Nation* was revived by Sir C. G. Duffy, Mr. Hoey became chief of the staff. Subsequently he was joint proprietor, and when Sir Charles went to Australia, under the circumstances narrated in his memoir, Mr. Hoey occupied the editorial chair. In 1858 he disposed of his interest in the paper to Mr. A. M. Sullivan and left Ireland. He was called to the English bar in 1861.

In his new home Mr. Hoey followed still the literary calling, and in 1865 he became connected with a remarkable man, and a periodical which exercises considerable sway over certain religious and political schools of thought. Mr. W. G. Ward was at that period editor of the *Dublin Review*, and Mr. Hoey became his associate in this work, and so remained until 1879, when the quarterly passed under a different directorate. Mr. Hoey had meantime entered on an official career, having been for some years a member of the Board of Advice in London for the colony of Victoria. For a time, also, he held the position of secretary to the agent-general for the colony in England. In 1874 he transferred his services to the New Zealand office, holding the same position to the agent-general; and in 1879 he again returned to the Victorian ministry, and still holds the office of secretary there. Mr. Hoey is a knight of the orders of Malta, Este, Pius IX., Francis I., and La Caridad. He married in 1858 Frances, widow of Mr. Adam Murray Stewart.

Mr. Hoey has republished a few of his more remarkable essays, but the large majority of them lie hidden in the pages of the *Dublin Review*. This is to be regretted, for there is scarcely a periodical writer of our time who treats contemporary politics with a more vigorous pen. His essays abound in brilliant passages; sometimes the reader is startled by a bit of picturesque description or striking portraiture, and the sarcasm has the virtue and the fault of being relentless.]

ORIGIN OF O'CONNELL.[1]

Its very seclusion and wildness made Kerry a fit cradle for a great native leader. The spirit of liberty dwells in "the liberal air of the iced mountain top," and the cadences of ocean have a spell and a lesson for him who is born to move masses of men by the sound of his voice. The waves taught him their music, and early filled his mind with the sense of their vastness and freedom. He loved to speak of them as breaking on the cliffs of Kerry after rolling for three thousand miles from the grim shores of Labrador. The "kingdom of Kerry," as it was the fancy of its people to call it, had remained from its very picturesque and unprofitable remoteness the most Celtic region of Munster. There can hardly have been a drop of Norman or of Saxon blood in Daniel O'Connell's veins. He was a Celt of the Celts, of a type which becomes more and more rare—that in which black hair, luxuriant and full of curl, is combined with an eye of gray or blue; with features small, but fine, yet in the nose leaving room for amendment; with lips plastic, nervous, of remarkable mobility and variety of expres-

[1] This and following extract by permission of the author.

sion; with a skull curiously round; with a figure graceful, lithe, yet of well-strung muscles, capable of great endurance. It is a type which some Irish ethnologists suppose, not without reason, to be of Spanish origin; and there were two very remarkable Irishmen of the same period who were fine examples of its form. One was General Clarke, Duc de Feltre, French minister of war throughout, and indeed before, Napoleon's reign, and who was also for some time Governor-general of Prussia; the other, not built on so grand a scale, was Thomas Moore, the poet. Nature gave to Mr. O'Connell a frame as perfect and commanding as ever was developed of this rare type; a voice of unparalleled volume and range; ever-buoyant energy, unfatiguing perseverance, a quick wit, a sound and capacious understanding, craft bred and stimulated by the sense of oppression, courage easily flaming to headlong wrath at the hurt to pride of withheld right; every talent that every great orator has possessed (some in excess), with, most of all, the talent of speaking in the strain of its own sympathies to every audience, from the highest and most accomplished to the lowest and most ignorant; and to these last he often spoke of his best, and he loved to speak best of all. In Kerry there still remained, a hundred years ago, there even yet remains, more that tells of what Celtic and Catholic Ireland was like than in any other district of the south. Many of the native gentry, elsewhere banished and erased, or reduced to become traders in the towns built by their ancestors and tenants on their own estates, in Kerry held some little-coveted fragment of ancient property on sufferance, and maintained at least the show among their people of the old tribal order. Of the Irish titles which are still borne by the heads of Celtic septs, by far the greater number were transmitted in Kerry, or in neighbouring districts of Cork and Limerick, "where the king's writ did not run." There or thereabouts, in the wild south-west, dwelt a hundred years ago, and there are still to be seen, representatives of The O'Donoghue of the Glens (near kinsmen of the O'Connells), O'Grady of Killballyowen, MacGillicuddy of the Reeks, The O'Donovan, The O'Driscoll—and two titles which, though only dating from the period of the Pale, told of traditions hardly less dear to the Irish memory and imagination, the Knight of Glin and the Knight of Kerry, scions of that illustrious house which for many a hundred years accepted for its motto the reproach that it was more Irish than the Irish themselves. Five years before O'Connell's birth died the last MacCarthy More, greatest of the Kerry toparchs, and lineal descendant of that Florence MacCarthy who, as Sir William Herbert once said, "was a man infinitely adored in Munster:" and now Kerry was about to give birth to a man destined to be infinitely adored throughout Ireland. Kerry still spoke the Irish tongue, and it was the tongue that Daniel O'Connell learned on his nurse's knee. Such was the soil from which he sprung, and he was racy of it. . . . .

It is very difficult to apply the standard of historical criticism to Mr. O'Connell's character and career without at least seeming to speak in a strain of hyperbole. Lord Lytton, in those lines of singular power and felicity which describe him in the act of addressing a monster meeting, raises the image of the great Athenian orator as the fitting illustration of his marvellous mind-compelling power and majestic energy and ease of speech. But even his enemies would have said that Demosthenes was not his perfect parallel; that he had all the craft of Ulysses, and, when he pleased, the tongue of Thersites as well. In our modern days the son of a Corsican notary, immediately after the most all-levelling revolution the world has as yet witnessed, implanted a worship of himself in the heart of the French nation, surpassing in its self-sacrificing devotion all the loyalty ever lavished on its bravest and holiest kings. But Napoleon was a great soldier, and empires are the natural estate of conquerors, and from a very early age he had the whole power of the government of France to work out his purposes. O'Connell had the whole power of the government which conquered Napoleon, wielded at last by the soldier who gave him his final defeat, opposed to him at every point, and from the beginning to the end of his great achievement; and his method was to try if it were possible to make the same use of peace as a means of victory that soldiers make of war. He led his people out of bondage not less ignominious than the Egyptian, through a probation that may fitly be compared, even in point of time, with that of the Sinaitic desert, and, on the whole, with perhaps a better behaviour on the part of those who followed him; yet he was not visibly, awfully, raised and inspired by the living God, face to face, as Moses was. His career is unique. From its commencement to its close he carried the whole apparatus of his power within his head. His sceptre and sword was the gift of speech; and he spoke to and for the most impoverished, neglected, and uncultivated people in all Christendom.

THE COAST OF CLARE.

(FROM THE "DUBLIN REVIEW.")

The state of Ireland throughout the autumn and winter which have passed may be likened to a day such as often comes on its western coast, when the one season is passing into the other, and all the elements seem to be mingled in the weather. Overhead masses of cloud, gaunt and vast, career across a sky at one moment muffled in gloomy vapour fringed with fire, at another so blue, so lofty, and so clear, that the pale light of the moon and the strong ray of the northern star aid in its atmosphere the labouring flame which strives almost in vain to assert the realm of day. He who hears the ocean break, when in those days the indefatigable sou'-wester hurls wave after wave against the mountain scarp of the coast of Clare, will not find much of melancholy in the music with which the Atlantic first hails the shores of Ireland—but a sound like the cheering of many men in the stress of some great labour, with now and then an undertone of joyous melody, felt as it were through the sphere, when a tall billow, which has made its boisterous way from Labrador, sinks to sudden rest on velvet sand under the echoing dome of some stalactite-incrusted cave. But when the tide ebbs at the same hour that the sun is setting in this climacteric of the year, then the cloud-compelling wind pauses for a while, and the peace which falls upon land and sea is, in the variety of its beauty, the depth of its serenity, and the extent of its horizon, peculiar to the place and of its genius. The broad golden track that marks the line of the sunset on the waters, visibly connects earth and sky. Nowhere does the sun sink in such an aureole of light and such a canopy of colour, with such a glow of longing ardour, and such a lingering pomp of promise. Nowhere in our latitudes are clouds to be seen of such strange shapes and such vivid colours — violet, vermilion and purple, and crimson and azure and orange, and the white of the dove's down, and the tender green of young leaves. Weary ocean makes a truce with land, and seems to have changed its hue for that of the invincible verdure, which gleams through every fissure of the scarred rocks and mantles the stalwart battlements of the bay. Already the dawning moonlight falls softly on the venerable cone of that Round Tower on Scattery's holy isle, where Christ was worshipped first in the far west; and bleaches the sails of the Boston-bound emigrant-ship rushing swiftly over the bar on the flood of the Shannon.

MRS. CASHEL HOEY.

[Mrs. Cashel Hoey, wife of the author whose life and extracts precede this, is known as one of the most fertile, and at the same time most accomplished female writers of our time. She is the eldest daughter of Mr. Charles B. Johnston, and Charlotte Shaw his wife, and was born at Bushy Park, co. Dublin, the seat of Sir Robert Shaw, Bart., in 1830. She was married, firstly, in 1846 to Mr. Adam Murray Stewart, of Cromleich, co. Dublin, and secondly, in 1858 to Mr. John Cashel Hoey.

Mrs. Hoey is a constant contributor to high-class periodical literature, being perhaps at her best in such writings as a critic. She has written, besides, the following works:— *A House of Cards, Falsely True, Out of Court, The Blossoming of an Aloe, A Golden Sorrow,* *Griffith's Double, All or Nothing;* and two volumes of her collected stories have also appeared. She has also translated a number of works from the French, including *Pictorial Life in Japan, The Government of M. Thiers,* &c.

Our extract is taken from *No Sign*—one of her shorter tales—in our opinion the most powerful thing she has written.]

A TERRIBLE INTERVIEW.[1]

[Dominick Daly is in jail on a charge of murdering his wife. The crime has really been committed by Kate Farrell, a woman by

[1] By permission of the authoress.

whom Daly is loved. The following passage describes an interview in the jail between the two.]

"Person to see you; governor's order," or some such words, met the prisoner's ear, as he sprang to his feet in a moment. The next, the prison official had slammed and locked the door, and he and his visitor were alone. Another, and the woman had flung herself upon him, not into his arms—for he did not make any movement—but, with her own clasped tightly round him, had forced him back into the chair from which he had risen, and was kneeling beside him, still holding him in that frantic grasp.

"Dominick! Dominick!"

"Katharine! Great heavens! You here!"

They were almost the same words that he had said to her the last time she had come unexpectedly into his presence; but the voice in which he said them was not like his voice, and his face was like a spectre's. She shifted the clasp of her arms, and raised them to his shoulders; she pressed her face against his rigid breast, and ground her teeth together with a shivering moan.

His arms were free now, but he did not move them; he did not put her from him, or draw her to him; he sat perfectly still, as if the touch of her had turned him to stone. Her face was quite hidden, the brow and eyes were squeezed against his rough coat, and she caught the cloth in her teeth, while she fought with a strong convulsive agony, and put it over her.

"I'm here, I'm here, at last. I wasn't able to come sooner, for my strength played me false, and left me; but it's come back, darling, and I'm here. I'm strong again; I'm strong *enough* for what I have to do."—Again she shivered, and ground her teeth, and hid her face yet more closely against his rigid breast. And still he did not move, but he shut his eyes fast, and breathed like a tired runner.

"And what's that, Katharine?"

She looked up, strained her head back, saw his face distinctly, loosed her hold of him, and sunk on the floor, gazing awe-stricken at him. Her face was thin and white, her almost colourless eyes were dim, but there looked out of them a terrible despair.

"'*What's that?*' he asks me. To tell you the truth—all the truth—and then to tell it to *them*, and take you out of this."

He pushed his chair back beyond her reach as she sat huddled on the floor, and spoke, but without looking at her.

"I know the truth, not all of it, but enough —all I want to know. For God's sake, tell me nothing, and go, go!"

"You *know!* What do you mean?" Her voice almost died away with some terror, with some sickening anguish, stronger than that which had rent her soul when she came into the prison room. "You can't know. Why don't you look at me, Dominick? Why won't you touch me? Why don't you kiss me?" She raised herself to a kneeling attitude, and dragged herself a few inches along the ground towards him; but he stopped her with an outstretched hand.

"Come no nearer me," he said; "you are my wife's murderess." He spoke in the lowest whisper, and with his gaze upon the door.

"O God! And I did it for your sake!"

After this there is a silence, and the two look in each other's faces, as two lost souls might look. Then the woman begins to speak, low and rapidly; and as she speaks, she sinks back into her former attitude, but tears off her bonnet, and clutches the masses of her thick red hair, which have fallen on her neck, and pulls at them wildly.

"I did it for your sake. I had been thinking about it, about how it could be done, ever since that night when Father John O'Connor spoke to you—the same night that you told me she wanted you to send her a new cure. It was that night you vexed me to the soul; for you pitied her, and would not grudge her the life that was no good to her, and was standing between you and me. And after that you vexed me sorer and sorer; for you sent her cures, and I thought they were like to do with her, for she grew no worse; and the time was creeping on, and the priest was watching you and me. And then came the strong and heavy hand of him upon me, and he said I must go—go away to a strange place, and leave you, after all the pains it cost me to come where you were, and to stay where you were. I must go, and you must stay, and be no nearer to me than in the beginning, when I *could* have lived without you, Dominick Daly. And then I thought how little good her life was to herself, and how much harm to us, and how easily it might be ended, if only *I* could get some way of sending her a cure.

"The **way** of getting the—stuff came to my mind **readily.** I had only to get back to Athboyle, **for ever so short a** time, and Sam Sullivan would not watch what I was doing in the shop so close but that I could get something that would not hurt her much, but would put her out of your way and mine."

He listened, after a fruitless attempt to stop her, with a fascinated eagerness, but with growing horror and avoidance, as the words came more and more coherently from her livid lips.

"I swear—I could swear it if it were the last word I had to speak in this world—I never thought that she would have anything to suffer. I knew nothing about—about poison that tortured. I believed that poison only put people to sleep for ever; and when I got at it, through Dr. Mangan's leaving his keys about, it was laudanum I was looking for; but when I found the powder I had no other notion but that it would be all the same, only easier to get it sent to her somehow. But I never could think of a way of sending it, and I carried it about in my pocket day after day, until that day I went to see you at Grange's, and you went out to speak to some one, and left me in the room with the letter you had just written to her, and the cure you were sending to her. I read the letter, and I saw the opportunity. Who was to know? She would just take the powder you were sending her, and some of mine in it, and she would go to sleep for ever; and we would be quit of her, and happy, happy, happy, ever after."

She rocked herself from side to side, pulling at her hair, and he listened, appalled.

"You stayed away a good while, and I made up the powder; and when we went out you put it in the post; and the next I heard of it was the news that she was dead, and you were taken —you, as innocent as the daylight, Dominick, my darling. And, first, I nearly died with the fright, and the helplessness; but then I saw that there was something for me to do, and I did it."

She paused, and checked the swaying of her body. Her hands hung in the heavy loops of her red hair. Something like a smile came for a moment into her face.

"I got into *the place*—the horrid place at Kilkevin; it was close to my new school-house —and I picked acquaintance with the servants, and I set fire to the laboratory. I went very near to saving myself and you that time."

"Stop, stop; for God's sake, stop!" said Daly, hoarsely. "What's the use?"

"Very near to saving myself and you," she went on, as if he had not spoken, knitting her brows into a frown; "but fate was against me. And then I fell sick. I don't know any more, until two days ago, and then I got well enough to come here."

"Why did you come? Oh, why did you come?"

"He asks me!" she said again. "He asks me! I came for the same reason that made me do everything else that I have done; because I love you, and I must take you out of this now."

Was she mad? Had the crime turned her brain? or rather had she committed the crime because her brain was already turned? In his mind, weary, although strained to the utmost pitch of excitement, he asked himself these questions. He was awake to the imminent need of making her comprehend the full truth as regarded him and his determination; and he conquered the horror of speaking to her, a great horror, though the ruined wreck of the old guilty love floated somewhere on the surging waves of his troubled mind all the while. They would have little time, and there was much to say.

So Daly rose, and lifted her from the floor. As his hand closed round her arm she kissed it quickly, roughly; but he did not heed the action. He placed her in the chair beside the table, and picked up her bonnet.

"Put this on," he said; "you haven't long to stay here; and now you are here, there's a great deal to be said. I prayed God that you might not come, but prayers of mine are not likely to get far on their way to heaven. I prayed that I might never see you again"— she started—"for your sake and my own. I hoped you were safe out of harm's way, when I knew it was you that did it."

"How did you know?"

"I knew it from the first moment. I knew it because I remembered that night, and the feeling that came over me, like a warning, when you wished the sick woman dead. I knew *because I deserved it*—not *how* you did it, but that you had done it, and what the end must be."

"Yes, the end is easy to see," she said. "It would have come quicker if I could have stood, or walked, or been carried here, before to-day. But you'll forgive me for that, won't you? I wanted to tell you all, before I should tell the others."

"What others?"

"The gentlemen; and get you out of this. It's all over, and it seems a long, long time since I had the notion that we might be quit of her, and harm could never come to you. How should I have dreamed that harm could come, when your own letter seemed to make it secure?"

His glance turned to the letter as he had written it out from memory. It lay close beside her hand at that moment.

"It seems a long time since then; everything is lost and gone. That was before the shock, before I knew they had suspected you and taken you. But since, I have come to my right mind again, and can tell it all clear out. Some of the harm can be undone."

"None of the harm can ever be undone," said Daly. "Listen to me now, for time is precious, and try with all your might to understand every word that I am saying to you."

"I understand, I understand." Once more she began to rock herself from side to side, and to twist her fingers as if in pain.

"You must do nothing of what you intended to do. You cannot take me out of this, or out of what is to come, by anything that you can do or say. Hush! do not interrupt me by one single word!"

The woman obeyed him; she was cowed by the power and the command in him which she had never seen before, and she was too true a woman not to recognize them, with something like faint, far-off, admiration, even thus, and now.

"You must go away, and stay away; you must never make a sign. Everything that can be done for my defence will be done; the gentlemen are seeing to that. I shall have a fight made for me; it will fail, but not through the fault of my friends, God bless and reward them! But you must never be heard of again in any way or anything relating to me."

She looked at him, in sheer blank astonishment, quiet now.

"Until the trial? Do you mean that? But when I tell them, there will be no trial."

"You shall never tell them."

In an instant she started from her seat, and rushed towards the door. But he caught her, and held her, while she struggled with him fiercely, trying to tear away the folds of her shawl, with which he had covered her mouth.

"Let me go! let me go!" she gasped faintly; "am I to kill her and you too?"

"You surely *will* kill me if you don't obey me."

Still she struggled, until he repeated this several times; at length she yielded, exhausted, and feebly muttering, "Go on, then, tell me what I am to do," sank down before the table, with her arms spread out upon it, and her face hidden. He spoke from thenceforth with perfect composure.

"There will be a trial, and I shall be defended. I have told the gentlemen that I am not guilty, and they believe me. I have told them the truth; there was nothing but soda in the powder I put in the letter, and the letter was intended to prevent my poor wife from finding out that I was putting a harmless cheat upon her. The doctor would have told her that I was, if she had let him see the medicine *as I sent it*. My defence will be the simple truth, and that the poison that killed her got mixed with the harmless powder in some way which I cannot explain. That defence will be quite useless, because there will be the letter—they'll believe their reading of it, and not mine; and there will be the motive" —he paused, and a shiver passed over him— "the motive, which can so easily be proved against me."

"Aye, aye," she murmured, "there was a motive, only it was mine, not yours; it was mine, like the crime."

"No," he said, sorrowfully, "it was ours; and I am the guiltier. It was a terrible day for you when you saw me first."

"My curse—no, no, my blessing be upon that day!" murmured the woman.

"Curses or blessings upon it are all one now. I am not going to give it either. All that is gone for ever, like the time that is gone. What we have got now is very short. That letter—there's a copy of it under your arm this minute—and the motive, the talk about you and me—the talk that I might have hindered, had I been an honest man, and so saved you from all the rest—and the evidence, will hang me, if all the counsellors in the kingdom were on my side."

She lifted her face, and turned it, hardly to be recognized in its mask of livid fear, towards him. His meaning was breaking upon her.

"Hang you! When I did it! When I shall tell them that I did it!"

"You shall never tell them. This is what I have to say to you. I have known from the first that you did it, and there is no turn which you could have given to circumstances, that I have not been prepared for. Did you think, that you were coming here to confess your crime to me, your tempter and your fellow-sinner?"

"No, no, my lover; oh, Dominick, my lover!"

"Did you think, I say, that you were coming here to confess it, because you and I too are utterly beaten, and then to go and tell it to the world and take the penalty of it, letting me go free? Free to what? Did you, in your womanish folly, when the madness of murder had passed away from you, think such a thing as that?"

Scorn of her, horror of her, pity too, were in his voice and in his face, and also the power which forced her to reply with the truth.

"I did. I think so now. It shall be so."

"It shall not be so. You shall not tell that truth, and before we part for the last time in this world you shall swear to me, your lover, as you called me, the only oath I want from you—that you will never tell it till your death is near to you, nearer than mine to me to-day, or for many days to come. You shall swear this to me, if you don't want to know that the blackest despair of all comes to me from you, blacker despair than jury or judge could sentence me to, if I had ten lives for them to take from me. Listen to me, Katharine," the vehemence of his tone changed to a solemn earnestness; "by the living God, who shall be our judge, if you do not swear that oath to me, or, having sworn it, if you do not keep it, I will go into the dock and plead guilty."

"And what good would that do you," she stammered, "if I was there, and told them the truth?"

"Which I would swear was a lie. Who would believe your word against mine, do you think? I would tell them: here is a girl whom I have deceived, an innocent girl, with a good character, and respectable people to swear to it, and I, a married man, made love to her, and tempted her, and promised to marry her when I should be free. And she loved me, and trusted me, and now she wants to die for me. D'ye think they'd believe your story, when I'd tell them mine from the dock, with the letter, and the remains of the powder, and the evidence to back it; and nothing to back yours but the love of a villain like me to account for your tremendous lie, and the old belief that there's nothing a woman won't do for her lover, to make them think mine the truth? There would not be a chance for you. There's not a man from Donegal to Cape Clear would believe your story, or doubt mine. So, if you want to hang me, as surely as if you put the rope round my neck with your own arms——"

"And what else have I done?" she moaned.

"Go and tell your story. At least it would make a quick end. There's little trouble with a murderer who pleads 'Guilty,' and tells them all they want to know from the dock. It will have the same ending, anyhow, as I believe, but there are my chances in a trial. Great or small, there's always some chance, and God is above all. Who knows, he may have mercy upon me, if mercy it would be. Tell your story, and you destroy my chance; you are the minister of his justice to me. Anyhow, I have told you what *I* will do. Make up your mind —there's very little time, we shall be interrupted soon—what you will do."

"I will swear, and keep my oath."

She stood up, trembling, but her face was calmer, less death-like, and she touched a crucifix upon the table—"I swear to obey you in this; but, but, the chances, there are chances?"

"I have said, there are chances. I don't count upon them; don't you count upon them either. You have no more to do with this, or with me. You have only to go away, and to keep silence, in any case, and to—to repent."

His voice faltered, and his eyes dropped from her face. She laughed.

"That's all!" she said. "In any case, whether you are saved from the punishment of my act, or whether you suffer for it, I—I who did it, wicked as it was, devil as I am, for your sake, and because I could not live without you, I have only to go away, and keep silence, and repent. I must obey you, for you are stronger than I am, and you have beaten me by your threat, because I never thought of what you could do, only of what I could do myself; and now I know you would keep your word, so you have conquered me. It's done with. It's over; but I'll tell you, at least, what was in my miserable mind. It was, that when I had told the truth, when you knew that my wretched ignorance had never taken in the notion that the death she had to die could be a hard one, or the most distant dread that it could harm you;—an awful fool, Dominick, a miserable fool;—when I was going to give myself up to my righteous doom, and you were going to be cleared of suspicion, you would tell me that you forgave me, because it was all for your sake; that you would let me rest for one moment in your arms again; that you would say to me, 'I loved you once.'"

She made the slightest possible movement, as if to approach him, but he stepped back. She went on rapidly—"That can't be now—you have beaten me. You know better than I, and your ingenuity would make anything that I could do useless. The punishment must come to me in its worst shape. You told me once that you would die for me, Dominick, and I believed you; but you, you could live for me yet; there are those chances you spoke of, you know. There's that one gleam in all this black, dreadful night!"

She drew a little nearer; a wild light came into her eyes, her white cheeks were streaked with crimson. Her hands fluttered like leaves, and her gown stirred with the trembling of her knees.

"I will repent, I will repent, if the chances are for you; and, and, if you will give me a chance then, Dominick, my darling, my lover—I love you—how shall it be, since you have beaten me, and I cannot die for you, if the chances are for you?"

She clasped her hands, and stretched them towards him. A terrible yearning, half madness, half memory, all anguish, was in her beautiful, dreadful face. He recoiled still farther, and answered her thus:—

"Woman, if the chances were for me, I would rather be hanged twice over than see your face again."

She uttered a sharp cry, like that of an animal caught in a trap. The next instant the step of the jailer sounded on the flags outside. She drew her shawl around her, she lowered her veil, and she said, between her shut teeth, as the key turned in the lock—

"I shall never repent. You never loved me, and the past is a lie."

The prison official had brought Daly's dinner.

"I am ready to go now," said Katharine Farrell, with perfect composure. "Perhaps you will kindly take me to the gate."

She passed through the door without another word, and stood in the passage until the man joined her.

WILLIAM GORMAN WILLS.

[It has been the good fortune of Mr. Wills to have written several plays which have the double merit of being acceptable on the public stage and at the same time readable in the closet. To a knowledge of theatrical effect he joins much poetic fancy, graceful and sometimes highly vigorous diction, and a fine eye to telling dramatic situation.

William Gorman Wills was born in 1828 in county Kilkenny. Sent to Trinity College, he passed through the entire undergraduate course, but did not trouble himself to take a degree—a piece of neglect which doubtless led to many gloomy prognostications of an unfortunate and unprosperous future. The first love of Mr. Wills, as of so many *littérateurs*, was art, and he devoted himself for many years with great assiduity to portrait-painting. In this branch of artistic effort he has attained considerable distinction, and in recent years—for he has never wholly forgotten his pencil while busy with his pen—he has had, among several other distinguished sitters, the Princess Louise.

The *Man o' Airlie* was the first drama of Mr. Wills which attracted a large amount of public attention. This work—produced at the Princess's Theatre, 1866—is a striking picture of the degradation and misery brought on a great poetic genius by drink, and some of the soliloquies and scenes are deeply moving. *Hinko*—brought out at the Queen's Theatre in 1871—is, in our opinion, the best of the dramatist's plays, full of splendid situations, of clever character-drawing, and of stately language. It was not, however, suitable for the English public in its present temper, and did not prove particularly popular. *Charles the First*, on the other hand, was one of the most successful plays put on the stage in this generation. Brought out at the Lyceum (1872), it gave Mr. Irving a most popular part, and it had—exclusive of revivals—a run of two hundred nights. *Eugene Aram*, produced in the same theatre, and with Mr. Irving again in the chief *rôle*, also had a lengthened run. In addition to the plays mentioned, Mr. Wills has also written *Mary Queen o' Scots*—in which the beautiful and hapless Mrs. Rousby made one of her last public appearances; *Jane Shore*, an historical drama—produced at the Princess's Theatre in 1876, where it ran for five consecutive months; *England in the Days of Charles II.*—founded on Scott's *Peveril of the Peak*, and not a wholly undeserved failure; *Olivia*, in which the Vicar of Wakefield's daughter has her familiar story once more told in poetic and touching language; *Nell Gwynne*, and *Ninon*.

Mr. Wills is also the author of many novels; of these the best known are *Notice to Quit* and the *Wife's Evidence*, both of which have been republished in America.]

THE QUEEN AND CROMWELL.

(FROM "CHARLES THE FIRST.")

Whitehall Palace. CROMWELL *discovered seated.*

Cromwell. On me and on my children!
So said the voice last night! A lying dream!
This blood—this blood on me and on my children?
It is my wont to feel more heartiness
When face to face with action. But this deed
Doth wrap itself in doubt and fearfulness.
Do I well to confront him at this hour,
Even when yon scaffold waiteth for its victim,
And his pale face doth look like martyrdom?
I will not. Out upon my sinking heart!
The standard-bearer fainteth, and my followers
Grow slack. I'll hie me to them,—
And yet, if by the granting him his life
He abdicate—no shifts—he abdicate!
Then—then this offer of the Prince of Wales—
This young Charles Stuart—he is in our absolute power,
As he doth promise if we spare his father.
Why if he come—I had not thought of that,—
Both son and father given to our hands:
Then have we scotched the snake!

Enter an Attendant, who hands CROMWELL *a letter.*

Cromwell (reads the letter). "Declines to see me!"
Well—well—
"*His last hour disturb'd!*" It shall be thy last hour.
"*As touching the Prince of Wales' noble
Offering of himself for me. Look back
On my past life, and thou art answer'd!*"
Past life! full of deceit and subtle courage.
"*I pardon thee and all mine enemies,
And may Heaven pardon them!*"
What now doth stay to send away this patch
On our new garment?
England! one hour—gray tyranny is dead!
And in this hand thy future destiny.

Enter the Queen.

Madam, my daughter hardly did prevail
That I should grant you this last interview.
It must be brief and private, or I warn you
I cannot answer for your safe return.

Queen (aside). Sainte Vierge, aidez moi! This is the man who holds
My husband's life within his hands. Ah! could I—
Sainte Marie, inspirez moi, mettez votre force dans mes prières.
I see him as the drowning swimmer sees
The distant headland he can never reach.
Sir, do not go. I wish to speak to you.

Cromwell. Madam, I wait.

Queen. Oh, sir! the angels wait and watch your purpose;
Unwritten history pauses for your deed,
To set your name within a shining annal,
Or else to brand it on her foulest page!

Cromwell. Madam, 'tis not for me to answer you.
And for unwritten history—thou nor I
Can brief it in our cause; 'twill speak the truth!
England condemns the king! and he shall die!

Queen. Oh, pity! pity! Hast a human heart?
How canst thou look on me so cruelly?
I look for pity on thy stubborn cheek
As I might place a mirror to dead lips
To find one stain of breath.
The brightest jewel ever set in crown
Were worthless to the glisten of one tear
Upon thy lid—one faint hope-star of mercy.
Be merciful! A queen doth kneel to thee.

Cromwell. Not to me! Nor am I now
A whit more moved because thou art a queen!

Queen. I am no queen; but a poor stricken woman,
On whom this dreadful hour is closing in.
(*Chimes the half hour.*)
Dost hear the clock? Each second quivering on
Is full of horror for both thee and me.
Endless remorse *thy* doom, and sorrow mine.

Cromwell. Madam, no more. I shall have no remorse
For an unhappy duty well perform'd.

Queen. Thou call'st it duty; but all heaven and earth
Shall raise one outraged cry, and call it murder;
It shall be written right across the clouds
In characters of blood till Heaven hath judged it.

Cromwell. Nay, you forget: the righteous cause doth prosper.
If this be crime, the hand of Heaven not in it,
Then had thy husband flourish'd; on our side
God's heavy judgment fallen, shame and slaughter!

Queen. God speaketh not in thunder when he judges,
But in the dying moans of those we treasure,
And in the silence of our broken hearts!
Thou hast a daughter, and her cheek is pale;
Her days do balance between life and death,
Whether they wither or abide with thee.
Let him be cruel who hath none to love;
But let that father tremble who shall dare
Widow another's home! She loves the king.
Take now his sacred life, and hie thee home.
Smile on her, call her to thee, she will linger.
Ask for thy welcome, she will give it thee!
A shudder as she meets thee at the door;
A cry as thou wouldst think to touch her lips;
A sickening at thy guilty hand's caress!
The haunting of a mute reproach shall dwell
For ever in her eyes till they both be dead!

Cromwell (moved). Silence! You speak you know not what. No more!
Thou voice within, why dost thou seem so far?
Shine out, thou fiery pillar! Bring me up
From the dead wilderness—
  Queen. Oh! yield not to that voice, hearken to mercy,
And I will join my prayers to thine henceforth
That thy Elizabeth may live for thee.
  Cromwell. Madam, I came here with intent of mercy,
And with a hope of life.
  Queen. Of life!—of life!
  Cromwell. I offer'd him his life—he scorn'd my offer!
  Queen. No—no—he shall not. I am somewhat faint;
The hope thou showest striketh me like lightning.
Life! didst thou say his life? Ask anything.
  Cromwell. If he would abdicate and quit the kingdom.
  Queen. And he shall do it. I will answer for it.
Give me but breathing-time to move him, sir.
  Cromwell. Stay, madam. If we spare your husband's life
Your son has offer'd to submit his person
Into our hands, and set his sign and seal
To any proposition we demand.
  Queen. Thou strikest a fountain for me in the rock,
And ere my lips can touch it, it is dry!
My husband first must abdicate, and then my son.—
What was the answer of the king to thee?
  Cromwell. He doth refuse our mercy, and elects
To carry to his death the name of king.
  Queen. When all was lost at Newark, and thy king
Was bought and sold by his own countrymen,
'Twas thou who with a fawning cozenage
Lured thy good master to undo himself,
To doubt where all his hope was to confide,
And blindly trust where every step was fatal!
'Twas thou, when the repenting Parliament
Were fain for reconcilement, brought thy soldiers—
Thou (jealous stickler for the Commons' rights)
Arrested every true man in the house,
And packed the benches with thy regicides!
  Cromwell. What, madam, is the purpose of this railing?
  Queen. Thou think'st to make the mother a decoy,
And, holding the lost father in thy grip,
Secure the son who yet may punish thee!
  (*Chimes.*—*Three-quarters.*)
  Cromwell. Madam, the clock! say, what dost thou intend?
  Queen. To choke my sighs, to hide each bitter tear,
To keep a calm and steadfast countenance,
To mask my anguish from his majesty.
  Cromwell. So! it were well; and then—
  Queen. Then we will both be faithful to ourselves,
Even unto death!
  Cromwell. Will you not, madam, use your influence!
  Queen. Never! My husband, sir, shall die a king!
  Cromwell. Thou shadow of a king, then art thou doom'd! I wash my hands of it.
  (*Aside.*) What melancholy doth ravin on my heart!
Thou child of many prayers, Elizabeth!—
I'll to the General's. Fairfax relents,
That will not I. My hand is on the plough;
I will not look behind.   [*Exit Cromwell.*

WILLIAM ARTHUR.

[The Rev. William Arthur, author of one of our most popular biographies, was born in Ireland in 1819. He received his education at Hoxton College, and in 1839 went to India, where he was engaged for some years in missionary labour. In 1847 he published *A Mission to the Mysore*, which was favourably received, a critic in *Bentley's Miscellany* declaring "the whole work so enlivened by anecdotes and descriptions of men and things that the attention to it never for a moment flags. Macaulay himself never wrote a chapter more worthy of a Christian statesman's perusal than is the seventh chapter of this volume, entitled 'India, what is it ?'" In 1851 the death of the well-known Mr. Samuel Budgett of Bristol suggested to Mr. Arthur the idea of a work "wherein an actual and a remarkable life is traced in relation to *commerce*—a familiar book for the busy, to which men from the counting-house or the shop might turn, and for which they might possibly be the better here and hereafter." Accordingly in 1852 *The Successful Merchant* appeared, and the immediate popularity which it attained amply justified the idea of the author. Some eighty-four or eighty-five thousand copies have now (1880) been issued in England, besides translations into French, Dutch, German, and Welsh, and it has proved one of the most interesting and useful works which have appeared for many years, written in a singularly lively and happy manner. *The Tongue of Fire, or the True Power of Christianity*—a volume on the Christian life—was issued in 1856, and of this book upwards of twenty editions have been sold in England, besides translations into French, Italian, Welsh, Kafir, and other languages. In 1860 he published *Italy in Transition*, a work which, says the *Athenæum*, derives its chief value from having appeared at the proper time. *The Pope, the King, and the People*, a history of the Vatican Council, appeared in 1878. Mr. Arthur is also the author of a number of pamphlets on miscellaneous subjects. Since 1848 he has held the office of secretary to the Methodist Missionary Society, and was also for some years president of the Methodist College at Belfast.]

COMMERCIAL BIOGRAPHY.

(FROM "THE SUCCESSFUL MERCHANT."[1])

"Who would ever think of writing the life of the moiling pelf-worm, who works and wriggles through the dust, thinking of nothing but making his way?" True, who would? But who would think of writing the life of the common-place soldier, who wheels to right or left, loads, presents, fires, and fixes bayonet? or of the scribbler who palms a book upon the world? or of the spouter who perpetrates dull speeches? The ignoble is ignoble in any sphere; the great is great in any. Commerce, like other spheres, has had its marvellous men; and, to the moralist, no class he could handle would afford such innumerable points on which important light might be shed upon life's actual ways, wherein the plodding and the practical are ever tempted to sell truth and integrity for gold. But from them the literati seem to have turned away. *The* TERRA INCOGNITA *of the learned is ordinary life*. The *Chronicles of the Stock Exchange*, the *History of Banking*, the *Bankers' Magazine*, and some prints devoted to economical questions, all show that literature has at length set out to explore that region of reputed desert.

For business men, as a class, literature has done little. They can lay their hands on few books that are not likely to estrange them from their avocations just in proportion as they charm them. The young men of any other profession, beside the dry study of principles, may at the same time relax their minds and rouse up all their professional aspirations by the lives of some who have trodden the very path on which they are starting, and found it the way to eminence. Not so the young merchant, of whatever grade. For the lives of the great he must go out of his own line and perhaps learn to despise it, when he might have learned its value and had all his views ennobled. Thus many business men dread books, just as literary men dread business. The two things have been at enmity. The literatus has looked down on the man of figures and facts, with counting-house taste and cash-box imagination. The merchant has looked down on the man of lofty ideas and light pockets, redundant in sentiment but lacking in common sense. You can hardly ever find a business man who has any just notion of the mercantile value of genius, or a literary man who has any appreciation of business. How seldom does a millionaire take any pains to encourage letters; or a scholar care to analyze the life of a merchant, whatever mental power he may have displayed, whatever impulse he may have given to the improvement of international or internal relations, whatever influence he may have exerted on the history of a kingdom. Consequently, little light has been shed into the recesses of commerce from higher spheres. Men of business have been left to form their own codes of morals, with a millionth part of the criticism, from the erudite, on the moral correctness of this principle and of that mode of transaction, that has been spent on the letter *h*, the Greek article, or the digamma. The politics of commerce are now, per force, a favourite study; but the *morality of purchase and sale*, the effect of business upon character, the relation which art, science, and literature bear to commerce, are points on which business men are little indebted to those whose calling it is to instruct. Had it been otherwise, the mercantile class might have been great gainers, in enlarged views, in refined pleasure, in appreciation of the efforts and the utility of the higher orders of mind, and also in clear views of the moral principles of trade.

But more attention to practical life, on the part of literary men, would be as rich in benefit to themselves as to men in business.

---

[1] By permission of the author.

In handling that subject, they would grow wiser, and would impart more wisdom. They would have an endless variety of theme. They would discover that fictitious characters were no more necessary to furnish interest, pleasure, amusement, surprise, and sadness, than fictitious landscapes are necessary to furnish mountain, forest, water, and sky. They would constantly find moral problems, which might engage the most subtle dialectitians, and yet would interest the stock-jobber and the shopman. . . .

I have now to tell you of a genuine son of English commerce: not of one who, like Gresham, was by birth a prince of the blood in the empire of trade; but of one who, beginning in the ranks, fought his way up to eminence: not of one who took his stand among the archers of speculation, and, drawing his bow at their brilliant target, chanced to strike the gold; but of one who rose by sheer dint of working, systematizing, and extending his own legitimate business: not of one who accumulated by the simple power of retention—getting, griping, holding, and never giving; but of one who was as apt to scatter as to increase: not of one in whom early influence and education had combined the polish of aristocratic circles with the pursuits of commercial life; but of one who was, to the last, the keen, bustling, downright man of business: not of one who was so absorbed in trade that he never had a spare thought or a spare moment for recreation, friendship, the interests of others, the culture of his mind, or the care of his soul; but of one who, while passionately earnest in business, had always a heart for a friend, a hand for the poor, an hour for good works, a relish for a book, and a lively solicitude for the things that never pass away: not of one who amassed and left behind him a fortune, making a wonder in itself; but of one who did not care to die rich: not of one who moved in the high walks of cosmopolitan philanthropy; but of one whose work was wrought near his own door, among the colliers and the lane-side cots of a poor and unpolished neighbourhood.

POSITION AND MIND.

(FROM "THE SUCCESSFUL MERCHANT.")

There are two things which, to look upon, are very uncomely. The one, a man who has risen in the world, and as he rose has improved his attire, improved his abode, improved his fare, improved his furniture, improved his children, improved his servants, improved his circle of friends, but has never improved his mind. There it is, the same mind precisely in fine broadcloth and "velvet hat," that it was in fustian and paper cap; the same mind with a carriage and pair, that it was with heavy clogs; the same mind with silver services and champagne and venison, that it was with pewter and cheese and ale; the same mind with daughters that can play Handel and read Racine, that it would have been with daughters who never touched a key or opened a grammar; the same mind with circles of educated friends, who value his sense and worth despite the remnants of the outlandish, as it was with friends whose talk was in dialect of other days and all on themes intimate to the village.

Now, that kind of spectacle is beyond doubt most particularly uncomely. You never see it without feeling your temper a little tried. In the name of common sense and common propriety, why did not the man, when he saw that Providence was lifting him up in society, take a little pains to fit himself for his new position, as he did to fit everything about him for it? He would not furnish his fine house with the same articles which sufficed for his original dwelling. The house must needs have seemly furniture; and it should also have a seemly master. Three-legged stools and plain deal tables would look quaint beside damasks and mirrors and chandeliers; but do not queer rough accents and vulgar phrases look quite as odd there? Do then, if rising in life, take a little pains; not to make yourself an accomplished man in letters or in etiquette,—that is out of the question now, and it is not the thing for you to run after even if hope of overtaking it remained; but, take a little pains to rub off all offensive roughnesses which have been left by early neglect, and which abridge your influence and usefulness in your new sphere. But, remember, young lady at the grand piano, you are not to blush for the ill-ordered grammar of papa. He is of a great deal more consideration in the world than you will ever be. You will never rise above the level to which his brave arm carries you, and had it not been for his talent and worth you would not have been at that piano, but maybap at a spinning-jenny. Honour him as he deserves, and all sensible men will honour you. See that you use well the valuable fruits which his labours have obtained for you.

But uncomely as is the spectacle of a man whose mind is behind his circumstances, there is another spectacle quite as uncomely and far more provoking. A young man whom Providence has plainly designed to serve his generation by following some useful business, has taken it into his head to be a man of parts and a hero-hunter. He has some notion of the new books and of the great men who are just now agoing. He is deep in Warren, thinks well of Macaulay, patronizes Carlyle, has an opinion on Chateaubriand and Alexander Dumas, knows that Tennyson is poet-laureate, and kneels down to Dickens. He is versed in the parliamentary orators, balances Disraeli and Derby most nicely, is at home on the merits of the great preachers, and, above all things, his talk smells of science. He often hears Professor Polysmatter, Professor Panprattle, and Professor Poluphloisbos, who lecture on æsthetics, megalosauri, metempsychosis, and several other things with brave names; he, therefore, talks of elements, strata, developments, oxygen, carbonic acid, and the vital principle. He is very "intellectual," and, in business, very good for nothing. He makes a great figure in discussion, but a poor figure in work. He sneers at his neighbour, who has not "two ideas;" but his neighbour has a quiet consciousness that with his one idea he manages to get on better than Polysmatter with his profusion of ideas. He wonders how his neighbour has so little taste; his neighbour wonders how he has so little sense. He is surprised that his neighbour does not buy more books and hear more professors; his neighbour wonders how he can be constantly running after everything but his business. He thinks his neighbour not at all fit to converse with men of education; his neighbour sees that men of education never laugh at him, while they always laugh at Polysmatter.

Now, this Polysmatter is ridiculous even beside the good man who is untutored amid glittering affluence. You may regret that the latter has not been awake to the duty of self-improvement; but you cannot despise him. He has not missed his way. He is no abortion. He has done his work. He has elevated a family. He has set an example of energy. He has filled up in the movement of society the full place of a workman. As he stands there in his homeliness, even though you were as fastidious as Beau Nash, you prefer him ten thousand times to an imposture of a man, who, being called to labour at an honest trade, betakes himself to dandyfying his intellect.

"But," cries Polysmatter, "a man ought to improve his mind." To be sure he ought; but do you call that kind of work improving the mind—turning it away from the task God has set before it, giving it a disrelish for plain and serviceable duty, habituating it to sips and scents and whiffs and glimpses and passing tones of every sort of glossy, pretty, jingling smatter, and thus unfitting it for all sober thought and real knowledge, all deep search after truth, all earnest application to duty. Improve your mind, indeed! You are leading it, poor mind, a most ruinous course; you are spoiling its taste, spoiling its digestion, relaxing its muscles, enfeebling its joints and sinews, and making it fit neither for books nor business—a sheer wreck of dissipation. You are just doing with your mind what a man would do with his body, if, under pretext of improving it, he set to and learned the names of all the most celebrated pastry-cooks, made acquaintance with all the tastiest dishes, all the richest wines, all the best spicery, and fed himself with scraps of dainty confectionery and scents of perfumery. He might be a great connoisseur, might have a deal to say, and might enjoy the thing for a while; but his poor body would soon be unfit for any purpose for which God ever sent a man into the world. This is quite the case with the mind of a man who, having little time to read, sets up for a *savant*, and runs about tasting literary confectionery, instead of taking some substantial food, eating it, digesting it, absorbing it into his own frame, and deriving from it both vivacity and force.

Many who pretend to be improving their mind are not only dissipating it, but debasing it. Improving it! what do they introduce to it by way of improving it, forsooth? Fiction, nonsense, trifle, trash, intrigue, the vices in court dress. If their mind is to be improved by that, it must be bad indeed. No, no; it is idle to say that the things which many read are read from any view to improvement. Such things are read from sheer badness of heart, from the love of evil excitement, from the impulse of the great tempter. For one man who reads novels from anything like a literary aim, there are a thousand who read them just because they stimulate low passions.

Yes, you ought to improve your mind; but then, take care you do not set up for a man of parts. From that day your mind is in a lost case—as lost as a garden plot in which you attempted to grow cereals, vegetables, flowers, shrubs, and forest trees all in one crop. If you want to improve your mind, do what Samuel Budgett did. Feel that you know little; be content that others should see that; ask questions which show your ignorance; set about reading something solid, —something which will enable you better to understand man, the earth, the sky, the Bible. Learn your own tongue. Learn your own world. Know not only its continents, but its nooks; not only its nations, but its tribes; not only its great systems, but its sects. Learn history, ancient, modern, ecclesiastical, —any branch of it; for all tell of man and of Providence. Learn poetry; fix some of it, however little, in your memory. A few good pieces made thoroughly your own, will insensibly refine your taste, elevate your conceptions, and improve your mode of expression. Learn, in fact, anything that is real, solid, useful; but *learn* it. Do not taste and smell; eat. Do not perfume your raiment with the scent of knowledge; what you know, know it, and be the better. Be content to know little. Be content to add to your knowledge slowly. Be content to be unnoticed when Polysmatter is passing for a prodigy, and to hold your peace when Poluphloisbos is rolling forth cataracts of erudition.

SIR WILLIAM THOMSON.

[Highly distinguished and most useful as has been the career of Sir William Thomson, it can receive but brief notice in a work on literature. His domain has been science; and his numerous works deal with subjects which are "caviare to the general."

Sir William Thomson was born in Belfast in 1824, but at an early age removed to Glasgow, his father having been appointed to the professorship of mathematics in the university of that city. Brought up amid scientific surroundings, Thomson was ready for a collegiate career at an age when most boys are most deeply interested in the mysteries of marble-playing; for he was but thirteen when he entered Glasgow University. He afterwards went to St. Peter's College, Cambridge, and graduated there in 1845. In the following year he became professor of natural philosophy in Glasgow University—a position he still holds.

It would not be within our scope to enumerate his contributions to science; it will suffice to say that in more than one department he has made discoveries or inventions which amount to a scientific revolution. His most remarkable achievements have been in connection with submarine telegraphy. It is to him, more perhaps than to any other scientist of our time, that we owe the system of cables that now join together all the countries of the world. In 1866 he obtained a just recognition of his services, when, on the completion of the Atlantic cable in that year, he received the honour of knighthood. He is the inventor of a number of instruments besides, which by their extraordinary delicacy and accuracy have enabled observations to be made with regard to atmospheric electricity which were impossible before. His discoveries as to the nature of heat also display a power of scientific investigation and generalization, which place him among the highest scientific intellects of our time.

Sir William Thomson has of course received all the honours which can be conferred by universities or scientific associations. He is an LL.D. of the three universities of Dublin, Cambridge, and Edinburgh, and a D.C.L. of Oxford—is also a fellow of the London and Edinburgh Royal Societies; and in 1871 was president of the British Association at its meeting at Edinburgh. It is from his address on this occasion that our quotation is taken.]

THE ORIGIN OF LIFE.

(FROM ADDRESS TO THE BRITISH ASSOCIATION.)

The essence of science, as is well illustrated by astronomy and cosmical physics, consists in inferring antecedent conditions, and anticipating future evolutions, from phenomena which have actually come under observation. In biology the difficulties of successfully acting up to this ideal are prodigious. The earnest naturalists of the present day are, however, not appalled or paralyzed by them, and are struggling boldly and laboriously to pass out of the mere "natural history stage" of their study, and bring zoology within the range of natural philosophy. A very ancient speculation, still clung to by many naturalists (so much so that I have a choice of modern terms to quote in expressing it), supposes that, under meteorological conditions very different from the present, dead matter may have run together or crystallized or fermented into "germs of life," or "organic cells," or "protoplasm." But science brings a vast mass of inductive evidence against this hypothesis of spontaneous generation, as you have heard from my predecessor in the presidential chair. Careful enough scrutiny has, in every case up to the present day, discovered life as antecedent to life. Dead matter cannot become living without coming under the influence of matter previously alive. This seems to me as sure a teaching of science as the law of gravitation. I utterly repudiate, as opposed to all philosophical uniformitarianism, the assumption of "different meteorological conditions"—that is to say, somewhat different vicissitudes of temperature, pressure, moisture, gaseous atmosphere—to produce or to permit that to take place by force or motion of dead matter alone, which is a direct contravention of what seems to us biological law. I am prepared for the answer, "Our code of biological law is an expression of our ignorance as well as of our knowledge." And I say yes: search for spontaneous generation out of inorganic materials; let any one not satisfied with the purely negative testimony, of which we have now so much against it, throw himself into the inquiry. Such investigations as those of Pasteur, Pouchet, and Bastian are among the most interesting and momentous in the whole range of natural history, and their results, whether positive or negative, must richly reward the most careful and laborious experimenting. I confess to being deeply impressed by the evidence put before us by Professor Huxley, and I am ready to adopt, as an article of scientific faith, true through all space and through all time, that life proceeds from life, and from nothing but life.

How, then, did life originate on the earth? Tracing the physical history of the earth backwards, on strict dynamical principles, we are brought to a red-hot melted globe on which no life could exist. Hence when the earth was first fit for life there was no living thing on it. There were rocks solid and disintegrated, water, air all round, warmed and illuminated by a brilliant sun, ready to become a garden. Did grass and trees and flowers spring into existence, in all the fulness of ripe beauty, by a fiat of Creative Power? or did vegetation, growing up from seed sown, spread and multiply over the whole earth? Science is bound, by the everlasting law of honour, to face fearlessly every problem which can fairly be presented to it. If a probable solution, consistent with the ordinary course of nature, can be found, we must not invoke an abnormal act of Creative Power. When a lava stream flows down the sides of Vesuvius or Etna it quickly cools and becomes solid; and after a few weeks or years it teems with vegetable and animal life, which for it originated by the transport of seed and ova and by the migration of individual living creatures. When a volcanic island springs up from the sea, and after a few years is found clothed with vegetation, we do not hesitate to assume that seed has been wafted to it through the air, or floated to it on rafts. Is it not possible, and if possible, is it not probable, that the beginning of vegetable life on the earth is to be similarly explained? Every year thousands, probably millions, of fragments of solid matter fall upon the earth—whence came these fragments? What is the previous history of any one of them? Was it created in the beginning of time an amorphous mass? This idea is so unacceptable that, tacitly or explicitly, all men discard it. It is often assumed that all, and it is certain that some, meteoric stones are fragments which had been broken off from greater masses and launched free into space. It is as sure that collisions must occur between great masses moving through space as it is that ships, steered without intelligence directed to prevent collision, could not cross and recross the Atlantic for thousands of years with immunity from collisions. When two great masses come into collision in space it is certain that a large part of each is melted; but it seems also quite certain that in many cases a large quantity of débris must be shot forth in all directions, much of which may have experienced no greater violence than individual pieces of rock experience in a land-slip or in blasting by gunpowder. Should the time when this earth comes into collision with another body, comparable in dimensions to itself, be when it is still clothed as at present with vegetation, many great and small fragments carrying seed and living plants and animals would undoubtedly be scattered through space. Hence, and because we all confidently believe that there are at present, and have been from time immemorial, many worlds of life besides our own, we must regard it as probable in the highest degree that there are countless seed-bearing meteoric stones moving about through space. If at the present instant no life existed upon this earth, one such stone falling upon it might, by what we blindly call *natural* causes, lead to its becoming covered with vegetation. I am fully conscious of the many scientific objections which may be urged against this hypothesis; but I believe them to be all answerable. I have already taxed your patience too severely to allow me to think of discussing any of them on the present occasion. The hypothesis that life originated on this earth through moss-grown fragments from the ruins of another world may seem wild and visionary; all I maintain is that it is not unscientific.

From the earth stocked with such vegetation as it could receive meteorically, to the earth teeming with all the endless variety of plants and animals which now inhabit it, the step is prodigious; yet, according to the doctrine of continuity, most ably laid before the Association by a predecessor in this chair (Mr. Grove), all creatures now living on earth have proceeded by orderly evolution from some such origin. Darwin concludes his great work on *The Origin of Species* with the following words:—" It is interesting to contemplate an entangled bank clothed with many plants of many kinds, with birds singing on the bushes, with various insects flitting about, and with worms crawling through the damp earth, and to reflect that these elaborately-constructed forms, so different from each other, and dependent on each other in so complex a manner, have all been produced by laws acting around us." . . . "There is grandeur in this view of life with its several powers, having been originally breathed by the Creator into a few forms or into one; and that, whilst this planet has gone cycling on according to the fixed law of gravity, from so simple a beginning endless forms, most beautiful and most wonderful, have been and are being evolved." With the feeling expressed in these two sentences I most cordially sympathize. I have omitted two sentences which come between them, describing briefly the hypothesis of "the origin of species by natural selection," because I have always felt that this hypothesis does not contain the true theory of evolution, if evolution there has been, in biology. Sir John Herschel, in expressing a favourable judgment on the hypothesis of zoological evolution (with, however, some reservation in respect to the origin of man), objected to the doctrine of natural selection, that it was too like the Laputan method of making books, and that it did not sufficiently take into account a continually guiding and controlling intelligence. This seems to me a most valuable and instructive criticism. I feel profoundly convinced that the argument of design has been greatly too much lost sight of in recent zoological speculations. Reaction against the frivolities of teleology, such as are to be found, not rarely, in the notes of the learned commentators on Paley's *Natural Theology*, has, I believe, had a temporary effect in turning attention from the solid and irrefragable argument so well put forward in that excellent old book. But overpoweringly strong proofs of intelligent and benevolent design lie all round us; and if ever perplexities, whether metaphysical or scientific, turn us away from them for a time, they come back upon us with irresistible force, showing to us through Nature the influence of a free-will, and teaching us that all living beings depend on one ever-acting Creator and Ruler.

JOHN TODHUNTER.

[Mr. Todhunter has written some remarkable poems. Many of them were originally contributed to *Kottabos*, a periodical started some years ago in connection with the Dublin University, which, although it has fostered the unhappy inclination for dabbling in Greek and Latin verse, one of the relics of a barbarous system of education, has done much to inspire the poetic talent of Ireland. The poems are published in a volume entitled *Laurella and other Poems*. These verses show very high poetic power, rich, powerful imagination, picturesqueness, and vigour of language, and considerable control over the mysteries of rhyme. "Laurella," the first and longest poem in the volume, is a rendering into verse of one of the prettiest of the tales of Paul Heyse, one of the best known German romancists of our time. The story is brightly and in some parts finely retold.

But Mr. Todhunter has sufficient originality of his own not to seek for the incidents of his story in another writer. A more remarkable poem is "The Daughter of Hippocrates." In this, too, the poet sought for his story in another author, for the poem is founded, as he himself acknowledges, on a legend as told by Leigh Hunt in the *Indicator*. The legend, however, as is generally known, is much older than Leigh Hunt, and has attracted the attention of many poetic minds. It is, in fact, also the subject of "The Lady of the Land," in Mr. Morris's *Earthly Paradise*. The tale is of a fair woman concealed in the shape of a loathsome snake, who, through a kiss from the mortal lips of the man she loves, is restored to the original beauty of the human form. Some of the scenes are described with extraordinary force. The volume also contains a number of lyrics, many joyous, many sad, and nearly all full of real poetic inspiration and melody.

Mr. Todhunter was born in Dublin on 29th December, 1839. He entered Trinity College in 1862, took the degree of M.B. in 1867, and of M.D. in 1871. He obtained the gold medal of the Philosophical Society for composition, and the vice-chancellor's prize for English verse three times. He practised medicine for some years in Dublin, but has now devoted himself wholly to the literary calling. He has also written *Alcestes, a Dramatic Poem*, and has in preparation a volume entitled *A Study of Shelley*.]

THE DAUGHTER OF HIPPOCRATES.

(EXTRACT.[1])

       Then
Gaultier was left alone.
      There he stood,
The chivalrous passion tingling through his blood,
Yet half-faint, agonizing on the tense
Of expectation. By all gates of sense
The scene infixed itself upon his soul.
In an eternal present glowed the whole
Charmed garden in the hush of high mid-noon;
The feverous hum of bees and creaking tune
Of myriad crickets thronging through the grass
Boomed in his ears; but all things seemed to pass
In the dim background of his mind.
       Then came
A sudden rustling, and those eyes of flame
Burnt at his very feet. It was too late
For flight—he sickened in the grasp of fate;

And a cold shiver stirred his rising hair.
Trembling, yet with a heart that bayed despair,
He gazed upon the cruel-fangèd jaws
That fawned around him, making gentle pause
As though to win his pity.
       Awed he spake:
"In the name of God, what art thou?"
       Then the snake
Answered him in a human voice—none less
Appalling for its feminine slenderness:
"Hast thou not heard of me?"
       He made essay,
With dry and tuneless tongue, to stammer, "Yea,
Thou art—*the fearful Thing of Cos!*"
       Again
The monster spoke, writhing as if in pain,
And its voice shook: "I am that loathly thing."
Then it was dumb; but every lurid ring
Swelled with a passionate grief, which seemed at last
To tear itself a way, as fierce and fast
Words followed words: "Ay, thou hast heard my tale—
Thy ears have heard; but how shall I assail
With this chill tongue thy heart? How shall my woe
Plead there in sacred human guise? Yet O
Believe, believe, I was not always barred
By this dread prison from my kind's regard!
Not always was I thus—a thing to flee!—
Teach the clear eyes of thy just soul to see
Beneath this husk of hideousness a form
That hath moved men to love—a bosom warm
With more than woman's tenderness—a heart
Where passions, pent for centuries, ache to start
Into wild life. O dost thou long for love?
How *I* could love thee—with a strength above
All that thy dreams—— nay, woe is me, I rave!—
Love hissed upon this tongue moves loathing! Brave
As thou art proved, that were a dream too dread.
Yet mercy, mercy! Since thou hast not fled,
Save me—be pitiful! Ah, was ever fate
More piteous than mine, whom Dian's hate—
Think of it—tortures thus, age after age?
That tale is true; my father was the sage
Hippocrates! How measure you the years
That have remoulded nature since his tears
Fell, unavailing as his prayers, for me?
Since the fierce gods, in vengeful cruelty
Cursing the issues of my mortal breath,
Bound me to hateful life! No nearer death
For aging all the long, long century through,
I cast my slough, my hideous youth renew—
Ah, think, think, think of it, and save me! O
Salve with a moment's pang this age-long woe!
Cancel this curse of Dian—laid on me
Until ——" Her keen eyes sparkled horribly,
Her jaws dilating as she raised her crest
At once eagerly upward to his breast.
"O gentle youth, kiss me upon the mouth!"

---

[1] By permission of the author.

Shuddering, he started back—a deadly drouth
Parching his tongue, and all his flesh a-creep
With a damp chill. The serpent seemed to weep,
For twice he heard a piteous inward groan;
Then down she grovelled, with a sobbing moan,
Upon the ground; a wailing smote his ears,
As when a woman weeps, and warm large tears
Sprang in her eyes, and bathed her loathsome
    cheek.
Gaultier was moved, and said: "What boots to
    speak,
O Lady—if thou lady art indeed—
Of curse of that false goddess, whom our creed
Holds for a devil? 'Tis a thing of naught.
I cannot kiss thee!" At the sickening thought
Such charnel savours to his palate rose
As presage oft a swoon, and death drew close,
With icy fingers clutching at his heart.
    .   .   .   .   .
              Then, lifting higher
Her crested strength, she spoke again: "This
    curse
A thing of naught! O what a cloud perverse
Hangs in the heaven of thy fair sympathy!
I tell thee 'twas my sin, though none in thee,
That I denied this goddess. I was made
The hated thing I am because I paid
No worship at her altars. Hated? Lo!
So past all hate, that thou, who seest my woe,
In pitiless loathing wilt redungeon me
Where love and joy, like wailing spectres, flee
My passion's clasp; where on the iron door
Wan hopes beat out their lives for evermore!
O foulness, foulness, with what mortal blight
Thou nipp'st my womanhood's grace. Thy gorgon
    sight
Chills men to marble gods, whom beauty's tale
Had found refreshing rivers. Hence with that
    pale
And comfortless face of thine!—for my despair
Has dreadful promptings, which this moment tear
My breast like tigers. Hence I charge thee—fly!
Fair as thou art, I would not have thee die;
But misery breeds fell brood—a tyrant thought
Shakes all my feeble soul, long overwrought
With passion self-represt, and I could well—
Nay go! I *will* not harm thee."
                   Then she fell
A-weeping in contorted agony;
And Gaultier, filled with wonder thus to see
Her sorrowing rage for cruelty confest,
Felt such a fascination in his breast
As a man feels when hideous temptings rise
To an abhorrèd sin. He kept his eyes
Fixed on her writhing neck, and clutched his
    sword,
Ready to strike.
            But now she turned her tow'rd
Her palace, with a passionate shriek of "Go!"
Then Gaultier spoke again: "How can I know

Thou dost not lure me to some dreadful doom—
Death—or a death-in-life of spell-bound gloom,
With thee, for ages in this charmèd isle?
I pity thee—yet—I fear thy serpent guile."
  Thereat she slowly rose, swelling her height
Like a majestic wave; serener light
Gleamed in her eyes, and in her voice awoke
A grand and mournful music as she spoke:
"O green and happy woods, breathing like sleep
In quiet sunshine! Living things that creep,
Or run, or fly amid these glades in peace!
O earth! O sea! O heavens, that never cease
Your gentle ministry, witness my truth!
Must every word that melts man's heart to ruth,
Move grim suspicion and the fear of lies?
O powers of nature, grand benignities
Of all this dumb creation! must the clay
That shades our delicate lamp from the fierce day
Of boundless life, lie on us like a mound
Of graveyard earth, that shuts us from the sound
Of all the kindly world, smothers our pale
And struggling lips, and makes our feeble wail
Come strangely to men's ears, like a ghost's cry?
My voice appals? Alas! 'tis one deep sigh
To be made lovely by one loving act;
Yet he who hears leagues me in horrid pact
With nether powers of ill. Farewell, thou fair
Dream of a man, who comest, like despair,
To torture me in happy human shape.
Man's faith is not like woman's—nought can
    'scape
His sceptic fears—not faith itself—farewell!
Thy doubts did ice the tender founts that swell
Here in my breast a moment; but once more
They gush as warm as tears. My passion's o'er—
I blame thee not. Farewell, and happy be;
But in thy distant world remember me!"
                    Gaultier's dread
Changing, chameleon-fashion, as her mood
Took tenderer lights, had grown less deadly-hued,
Shot through with pity's colours. All his powers,
Like stripling soldiers whom the first stern hours
Of battle veterans make, now burnt to dare
That final grip with danger which did scare
The vanward fancy; like a captain now,
Who stares across the field with resolute brow
He rallied them, as with a trumpet-call
Sounding to desperate charge. "Stand I or fall,
O Christ," he murmured, "whom the wormy
    grave
Held three days in its womb, us men to save
From our corruptions, I will follow thee
Even to the death! Shed now thy blood in me,
To save this soul and mine!" Aloud he spake,
And shuddering closed his eyes: "I'll kiss thee,
    snake!"
And held his lips out, thinking on his name
Who cast, when she besought Him in her shame,
Seven devils out of Mary Magdalen;
And with the cross he signed himself.

                        O then
In his blind agony he seemed to sink
In a cold sea of horror. He must drink
The cup of loathing to the very lees.
He felt the kiss approaching by degrees—
That venomous toad-mouth, with its clammy chill;
Now!—now!—
            It came at last. A sudden thrill
Ran through his frame. A soft mouth fast and
        warm
Was prest on his—about his neck an arm
Clung rapturously. He looked, and, O surprise!
O transport! gazed into the sweetest eyes
That ever made a heaven for mortal man.
It was too vast revulsion—faint and wan,
He sank upon the ground.

"HITHER, O LOVE!"

Hither, O love! Come hither
  On pinions of young delight,
Ere the bloom of the morning wither,
  While the dew lies bright;
The meadows their balm are breathing,
Day bends o'er the limpid lake,
All nature her beauties wreathing
    For thy sweet sake!

O joy is the mate of morning,
  And love is the child of light,
And youth is the time for scorning
    The bonds of night!
Then come—while the world lies jaded,
The elves of the woodland wake,
And dawn keeps her fields unfaded
    For thy sweet sake!

CHORALE.

Where shall Freedom's banner wave?
Where shall be the glorious grave
Of the world-redeeming brave?

Not in fanes that once were holy,
Cities proud, or hamlets lowly;
Not in plots 'mid sheltering trees,
Pleasant haunts of lovers' ease.

But where lightnings flash and glare,
Burning poison from the air;
And the eagle laughs aloud
In the glooming thunder-cloud;
Where the free winds come and go,
Where sweet waters rise and flow,
On mountain-peaks where first the day
Sets his feet that make no stay;

There, clear-shining like a star,
O'er the clouds beheld from far,—
On her fortress, once the grave
Of the world-redeeming brave,
There shall Freedom's banner wave!

LOST.

I wandered from my mother's side
  In the fragrant paths of morn;
Naked, weary, and forlorn,
I fainted in the hot noontide.

For I had met a maiden wild,
  Singing of love and love's delight;
And with her song she me beguiled,
  And her soft arms and bosom white.

I followed fast, I followed far,
  And ever her song flowed blithe and free;
"Where Love's own flowery meadows are,
  There shall our golden dwelling be!"

I followed far, I followed fast,
  And oft she paused, and cried, "O here!"
But where I came no flower would last,
  And Joy lay cold upon his bier.

I wandered on, I wandered wide,
  Alas! she fleeted with the morn;
Weary, weeping, and forlorn,
  She left me in the fierce noontide.

FOUND.

Naked, bleeding, and forlorn,
  I wandered on the mountain-side;
To hide my wounds from shame and scorn,
  I made a garment of my pride.

Till there came a tyrant gray,
  He stript and chained me with disgrace,
He led me by the public way,
  And sold me in the market-place.

To many masters was I bound,
  And many a grievous load I bore;
But in the toil my flesh grew sound,
  And from my limbs the chains I tore.

I ran to seek my mother's cot,
  And I found Love singing there,
And round it many a pleasant plot,
  And shadowy streams and gardens fair.

Like virgin gold the thatch I see,
  Like virgin gold the doorway sweet;
And in the blissful noon each tree
  A ladder for the angel's feet.

ROSA MULHOLLAND.

[Miss Rosa Mulholland was born in Belfast, and is the daughter of the late Joseph S. Mulholland, M.D., of that city. Her family on both sides is purely Irish. After the death of her father she spent some years in a remote mountainous part of the west of Ireland; and the picturesque scenery and primitive people by whom she was surrounded doubtless did a good deal towards developing literary longings and talents. Her first idea was to be an artist, and when only fifteen she ventured to send a set of comic pictures to *Punch*, which were, however, rejected. Her next attempt was in another direction, and was more successful. She sent a poem of twenty-two stanzas called "Irene" to the *Cornhill Magazine*, which was accepted. It was also accompanied by an illustration by Millais. The great artist was kind enough to offer his assistance to Miss Mulholland in the pursuit of her artistic studies; but she was unable to remain in London.

After this her success was rapid. She found an earnest friend in Charles Dickens, who pressed her to write a serial story for *All the Year Round*, and he himself chose the title "Hester's History." While the tale was proceeding he frequently expressed his gratification with it, and it was afterwards republished in volume form by Messrs. Chapman and Hall. It is from this tale our extract is taken. Dickens also selected Miss Mulholland's story "The Late Miss Hollingford" (published originally in *All the Year Round*), to be coupled with his own "No Thoroughfare" in a volume of the Tauchnitz Collection.

Miss Mulholland has also written *Dunmara, The Wicked Woods of Toberevvil, Elder-gowan, Puck and Blossom, The Little Flower-seekers, Five Little Farmers, The First Christmas for our Dear Little Ones, Prince and Saviour; Holy Childhood;* and a large number of short stories and poems in *All the Year Round* and other magazines, to which her name has not been attached.]

THE PURSUIT OF A REBEL.[1]

[The scene of the incident is the north of Ireland; the time, the year 1798.]

Lady Helen Munro might live with her ears full of cotton wool, and Miss Janet Golden might toss her head at having her horses turned on the road when going out for an evening's amusement; but there were fierce doings making a hot progress through the country, the perpetrators of which were but little concerned for the convenience of fair ladies.

Dire tidings did the daily post now bring to the peaceful fishing village that had sat gratefully for so many hundred years in the lap of its fertile glens at the feet of its bountiful bay. A hostile soldiery, utterly unchecked in their terrible license, scoured the land. The flower of the population was melting off the mountain-sides; dales and hamlets were giving up their strength and pride to the prison, the torture, and the gibbet. Even already in our glens the wail of desolation had arisen among the cottages. Sir Archie Munro, in anguish for his people, strove in vain to shield them from the horrors of the times. Day by day one disappeared and another disappeared from among the hearty glensmen. Frantic tales of distress came flying to the castle. The servants clenched their hands and cursed over their work. Miss Madge sat up in her solitude and wept herself nearly blind. Lady Helen went into hysterics at every fresh piece of news. Miss Golden blanched, and was silent for a while, but refused to believe one half the stories; and Hester sat up in her tower with her needle trembling in her fingers; for the stitching and ornamenting, the embroidering and flouncing, had all to go on the same, just as if a rain of blood had not begun to fall over the land.

Miss Golden began to think that it had been better she had taken Sir Archie's advice and returned to England; but she was, as she had said, not a coward, and she made up her mind, bravely enough, to see the worst to its end. Lady Helen lamented sorely that she should have been the means of bringing her darling Janet to so miserable a country. Yet, in the same breath, her ladyship quarrelled with her son, because he proposed for the women of the household a prudent retreat to England or France till such time as these miseries should be over. No, why should they go flying over the world, to hide themselves, as if they were a set of rebels? She believed that Archie made the most of things. They could not become so bad as he seemed to expect. She would not set off

---

[1] By permission of the authoress.

on a journey in such times, to be dragged out of her coach and shot. She would just lie by on the cosiest couch in her drawing-room, with the most interesting novel she could lay hands upon; and let no one come telling her frightful stories till this panic should have subsided, and the world have come to its senses!

One day a terrible cry arose throughout the glens, rolled along the valley, rang through the mountains. The name of a man, a rebel, hunted by the soldiers, was shouted from rock to rock, — was muttered in prayers by tongues that quivered and clove to the mouth with terror. This man was the joy and pride of his friends, foremost among the favourites of the lowly glenspeople. They hunted him in the morning, and they hunted him in the evening, and days went past, and even his own kinsfolk had no clue to his hiding-place; and a month went past. A stray goat had given him milk, and the heath had given him its berries; but these resources having failed, he was at last driven by starvation from his lair. Pallid, shivering, his clothing saturated with the damps of the dripping cavern in which he had lain, tottering upon his feet with the weakness of hunger, fearing to meet the form of a man lest an enemy should make him his prey, or to draw near a dwelling lest destruction should come with him over the threshold of a fellow-creature; sick and desolate, he found himself driven by the very scourge of approaching death to creep down a little lower on the mountain side, were it even to warm his shivering limbs by the sides of the wandering kine, or to crave a handful of meal out of a roving beggar's wallet.

No such comfort for the hunted rebel. The soldiers espied his meagre stooping form creeping along under the shelter of the whinbushes and heathery knolls. It would have been difficult for eyes less practised in manhunting to recognize the stalwart youth who had fled to the hills from the bayonet, in the bent shuddering creature who sought shelter from the bonnie braes that had carried his feet with pride. But these soldiers were right skilful at their work.

The game was scented; the cry was up. Oh that a jovial sun should ever look down upon such a piteous scene! A brave son of the mountains, hunted like a fox to the death among those mountains, the pure love of mother-land being his crime. But then Lady Helen said he was very much to blame. He had been right well off in his cottage in the glens. Why need he take to troubling himself about the misery of his country? And certainly it was most inconsiderate of him to throw her ladyship into hysterics on her sofa.

The chase lasted long, for the rebel knew the secrets of his hills. But bloodhounds will not be balked when they have once scented blood, neither would our brave soldiers miss their prey. Yet, notwithstanding, when it was late in the afternoon this rebel, having been started some seven times since morning, gave them the slip, and was lost sight of in the neighbourhood of the castle.

The cook had just sent up an afternoon cup of tea to the several bed-rooms of the ladies. The red setting sun was warming up the comfortable haunts of the kitchen, pantries, housekeeper's room, and the various closets and passages of the servants' quarters. Several of the servants were gathered together in a passage discussing in whispers the latest news of the rebel hunt. Pretty Polly, Lady Helen's maid, was pale and red-eyed, struggling to put in her word between recurring agonies of tears. But then the rebel in question was her lover. When last she had seen him he had been handsome and stout, bringing her a bunch of gay ribbons from the fair. Now he was a shadow, a spectre of starvation, with a price upon his head, and bayonets lying in wait for him at every point from which the blessed wind could blow. Good God! who was this here amongst them?

Pat the butler had opened a back-door of the premises, leading into a thick grove, into which evening shadows were already creeping. A flying phantom, somewhat like a galvanized skeleton, had leaped past him through the doorway, clasped its hands in his face, and sped on further into the castle.

Poor Polly sank in a little pale heap in her corner, and was a trouble to no one till such time as people had leisure to look to her, unasked. It was the best thing she could have done in the interests of her lover, for had she been conscious of what followed, her shrieks or her moans might have betrayed him. The other servants fell back on each side as our rebel dashed amongst them. No one spoke, but they signed to him to pass up the stairs. And up the stairs he fled.

"To the tower!" some one whispered. What tower, and where? Poor rebel dashed blindly onward, upward, beat the doors right and left with his feeble hands, burst over Miss Madge's threshold in the end, and precipitated himself into the middle of her floor; stood in her very presence, quivering, suppliant.

The Honourable Madge was at her afternoon cup of tea. A cup of tea was a thing that had always comforted her greatly, and was the only medicine she found soothing during the sorrows of these times. She was seated on a settee in the corner of her room, with a table drawn up before her; a table on which were placed a tray, an ancient silver tea-pot, some thin bread and butter in a dish, some sweet winter apples, and a tea-cup with its saucer. And Miss Madge's feet were on a footstool. Nothing could be more comfortable and placid than the appearance which she presented amongst these kindly-looking arrangements.

The settee on which Miss Madge was sitting was long and low, and was placed in a corner with its back to the wall. It was covered very amply with chintz of a large pattern, Chinese pagodas on an amber ground, mandarins seated apparently upon tea-chests, presenting roses to languishing ladies with curled-up toes and very arched eyebrows. And the settee was draped down to the ground with a garniture of that flouncing well known to be so dear to the Honourable Madge's heart.

Now if the Honourable Madge were mad, as had sometimes been whispered, most certain it is that she kept her madness for the amusement of her friends. On such an emergency as this she was found to be exceedingly sane.

"My friend! my friend!" cried Miss Madge, clapping her mittens, and upsetting her tea-cup into the lap of her yellow silk dress. But that was nothing even to Miss Madge at such a moment. She whirled up the flounce of her settee with prompt hands.

"Get under!" she cried, in a frantic whisper. "Crawl! Get in and lie close. In, in!" And she pushed him in and packed him away till there was not a vestige of him to be seen. "Now, God's mercy be with you, and keep as still as if you were dead!"

"And it may be that mocking will be catching," muttered Madge to herself, as she cleared up the signs of her own confusion, "for I think death would have little to do but close your eyes!"

Down on her knees she went, drying up the spilt tea. She arranged her little tray; she drew her table nearer to her couch. She spread out her silken skirts, and picked up a novel, which she placed open in her lap to hide the tea-stains. She was sipping her tea with her eyes upon her book, when the door was a second time thrown open, and a gentleman, an officer in the king's service, appeared.

I say a gentleman, for this officer had been bred to some of the habits of a gentleman, though he had a taste for rebel blood. And he was a little taken aback when he saw a simple-looking lady with astonished eyes raised at his intrusion, with her innocent cup of tea, dropping sideways in amazement from its mincing hold in her genteelly arranged fingers, and with her fashionable novel on her knees.

"I beg pardon," he began, "you are surprised—the fact is ——"

"Oh, pray, don't apologize!" said the Honourable Madge, making violently graceful efforts to overcome a ladylike surprise and bashfulness, very creditable to any spinster on such an occasion. "It is I who should apologize for my stupidity. You have the advantage of me truly, though I have no doubt you are quite familiar to me if my memory were not so bad. To what do I owe the pleasure of such a charmingly unceremonious visit? Pray have a cup of tea, I always do of an afternoon. So refreshing! A cup of tea with such a book as this delightful Evelina in one's hand, I call it a luxury, nothing less. And really, ha, ha! do you know I get so ridiculously absorbed in a story, ha, ha! I actually thought when I looked up that you were the hero, walking into the room."

And she reached down an ornamental cup and saucer of precious china, which was sitting most conveniently on a bracket above her head, poured some fragrant tea from her little silver pot, enriched it delightfully with thick cream and glistening sugar, and presented it with her sweetest smile to her gallant guest, as she was pleased to call him.

Now this soldier had heard tell that Miss Madge was a little "cracked." She was not a lovely woman, and her sweetness and her winningness were not much after his taste. However, her cup of tea was tempting, and the soldier was fatigued. He drank and he apologized.

"The fact is, madam," he said, "we have been searching for a rebel, supposed to have taken refuge in the castle."

Miss Madge gave a piercing little scream, and her cup fell with a crash upon the tray.

"Ah, ah!" she shrieked, "they will be the death of me, those rebels! Oh, sir, be so good as not to go till you tell me. A rebel in the castle! Ah, my sad fate, a rebel! Promise me that you will search, or I shall not sleep a wink. Not a wink for a month!"

And the Honourable Madge's eyes began to roll, and her nostrils to quiver, and she began to flutter up and down in her seat. She had observed these ominous workings in Lady Helen on sundry occasions, and a hint was never lost upon Miss Madge. The officer made her rapid protestations as to his activity, and terrified at the prospect of approaching hysterics, rang the bell violently, bowed, and retired.—But Polly mounted guard over her lover that evening in a very retired corner of the castle. And he was nursed and fattened unknown to master or mistress; unknown to any but the servants, Hester, and Miss Madge. And when he was able to go forth he went in search of better fortune.

JANUARIUS A. MACGAHAN.

Born 1845 — Died 1878.

[Januarius Aloysius MacGahan was born in 1845, in the state of Ohio. His father was a native of the north of Ireland, and his mother, American by birth, was Irish by descent. He began life as a commercial clerk, but soon managed to save sufficient money to take a tour in Europe. He was studying law in Brussels when he made the acquaintance of Dr. Hosmer, then the European agent of the *New York Herald*. He was engaged as special correspondent during the Franco-German war, which had just begun; and the proofs he then gave of graphic descriptive powers and daring led to a permanent engagement. Some time after the close of the Franco-German war came the Russian expedition to Khiva, and MacGahan was selected to represent the *Herald*. The Russian authorities had forbidden any correspondents to accompany the army; and MacGahan had to travel twenty-nine days through the desert, accompanied by only a few attendants, and pursued all the time by a regiment of Cossacks. He ultimately arrived at General Kaufmann's headquarters. This was perhaps one of the most remarkable achievements ever accomplished by a special correspondent.

His next mission for the *Herald* was to the scene of the Carlist war, and on his return from Spain he was sent on the expedition to the North Pole, which, under the command of Captain (now Sir Allen) Young, was despatched by Mr. James Gordon Bennett in search of the North-west Passage. In 1877 his connection with the *Herald* ceased. When the reports of the Turkish atrocities in Bulgaria arrived in England, MacGahan was sent by the *Daily News* to make investigations on the spot. The letters which he wrote produced a marvellous effect, and for a while formed the most important factor in the creation of English opinion on the Eastern question. MacGahan afterwards went through all the fatigues and dangers of the war between Russia and Turkey. He had by this time become one of the best known journalists in the world, and everybody looked forward to his having a bright and prosperous career. Those hopes were illusory; for, just as the treaty of San Stefano was in negotiation and the war and its dangers were past, MacGahan sickened and died of fever, in Constantinople, June 9, 1878.

He wrote two books—*Campaigning on the Oxus* and *Under the Northern Lights*. The first describes his journey to Khiva, and is one of the most brilliant descriptions of adventure ever written. The book at once met with great and well-deserved success, and has now taken its place as a standard work of travel. *Under the Northern Lights* tells MacGahan's Arctic experiences; and the work contains many passages of great eloquence. But the best of his work was given to journals; and scattered in the columns of the *Herald* and the *Daily News* are numerous vivid descriptions of remarkable scenes, which unfortunately remain uncollected.]

THE RUSSIAN OFFICER.

(FROM "CAMPAIGNING ON THE OXUS."[1])

Andrei Alexandrovitch comes of one of the oldest families of Russia. This is saying a good deal, for some of these old Russian families can trace their genealogy back to the eighth century, when they were reigning houses of the then disjointed Muscovite people.

[1] By permission of Messrs. Sampson Low, Marston, & Co.

In this long descent of a thousand years Andrei's family has degenerated little; and many of them still retain that physical strength and power of endurance which made their ancestors kings. It is no uncommon thing to find among them, as among many other families of rank, a man who will break a five-franc piece with his fingers with as great apparent ease as if it were lead. The relatives of Andrei retain all their ancient pride of race; and no Hohenzollern glories more proudly in his ancient lineage.

The parents of Andrei Alexandrovitch have a large estate in the environs of Kharkoff, were formerly the owners of several hundred serfs, and are very rich. Andrei's father served with distinction in the wars of Napoleon, attained a high rank, and won several decorations. He not unnaturally wished his son to follow in the same honourable career; and he easily obtained for Andrei, who was a handsome boy, admission into the *corps des pages* in the imperial household at a very early age. Here Andrei was petted by the ladies, and patted on the head by a grand-duke, or sometimes even by the emperor. He learned to dance, sing, and fence; to return compliment for compliment and sarcasm for sarcasm, and all the other accomplishments which are supposed to win the favour of ladies and distinction among men. Having, after a time, entered the military school, he in due course graduated as an ensign, and entered the Guard.

Now the Guard is the rock on which every Russian splits. Everybody in Russia enters the Guard. It is the fashionable thing to do. You will not find a man with the least pretension to respectability who has not been at some time or other in this favoured corps. It is the *corps d'élite* of the empire, and is the centre of all that wild whirl of dissipation, of extravagance, and folly for which St. Petersburg is so famous. It requires a cooler head and a more phlegmatic disposition than most Russian young gentlemen possess to steer through this vortex of dissipation without suffering financial ruin; and the Guard, it may be safely asserted, is responsible for three-fourths of the wrecked careers of which there are so many in Russian society. This fact does not seem to produce any warning influence on anxious parents; and it produces far less, of course, upon their hopeful sons just entering upon their career. In spite of the hundreds of examples before them, parents exhaust every effort to obtain admission for their sons into the Guard, and look upon a commission in that corps as the most brilliant and desirable start in life. As to the young men themselves, they all evince that faculty for imitation, and that lamentable want of originality, which have been always regarded as the peculiar characteristics of sheep.

Andrei Alexandrovitch proves no exception to the rule. Three years of life in the Guards suffices to ruin him. In that time he has managed to squander his fortune and his credit, and to get himself, besides, head over ears in debt. He is obliged to leave the Guard, because he can pay his way there no longer, and falls back into a regiment of the line.

Andrei now passes a certain time in what may be called a transition state; dodging his creditors, "doing" landlords and restaurant proprietors, and generally living from hand to mouth by the aid of his wits and his skill in card-playing. But this cannot go on for ever; and Andrei Alexandrovitch at last finds himself compelled to choose one of three different courses. He may marry the daughter of a rich tradesman, and so re-establish his fortunes; he may try his chance in a civil profession; or he may go to Turkistan.

Andrei Alexandrovitch feels no liking just yet for the quiet joys of conjugal existence; he has no taste for a civil career; while in Turkistan there is the still attractive *abandon* of a soldier's life, with double pay and double chance of promotion. For Turkistan has now taken the place of the Caucasus as the refuge of men like Andrei, ruined in fortune, but still hopeful of the future. So Andrei bids adieu to his friends in St. Petersburg, reaches Kazala, and is immediately sent forward to take part in the siege operations against Ak-Mesdjid.

On the day of his arrival he finds everything prepared for an assault, and immediately volunteers to lead the forlorn hope. His bravery wins him a decoration and two grades, and fortune once more seems to smile upon him. But Andrei Alexandrovitch possesses the faculty of defeating his own fortunes faster than a hundred fairy godmothers could mend them.

One morning he takes a walk outside the town, to visit the kibitka of a young lady of the Kirghiz race, whose charms have some attraction for him. In the kibitka he finds his brother officer, Stefan Ivanovitch. Now Stefan Ivanovitch is one of the few men for whom Andrei has no love. Already they have had more than one quarrel in their cups and over the card-table; and Andrei, whose pugnacious disposition is notorious, has been advised by more than one friend to avoid meeting Stefan as much as possible. Andrei had promised to obey the suggestion; but, of course, a meeting so unexpected and in such peculiar circumstances could only end in a duel. The duel comes off, and Stefan receives a bullet through the heart at the first shot. Andrei is brought before a court-martial and reduced to the ranks; for in the Russian army an officer may be, and often is, reduced to the rank of a common soldier. Thus Andrei not only loses all that he had won in Turkistan, but something more.

In Central Asia, however, where more or less fighting is always going on, a brave officer does not long remain without an opportunity of distinguishing himself. After two or three years Andrei rises to his old rank and gains two or three decorations more. Meantime the Russians have been advancing in Turkistan, and General Tchernaieff has sat down before the walls of Tashkent. Here Andrei has another opportunity of distinguishing himself, and he takes advantage of it in the following manner:—

In the course of the siege operations he becomes involved in a quarrel with a brother officer, who throws some imputation on his courage. Andrei, without any more ado, proposes to his assailant that they should together make an assault on the walls. Without any orders, the two officers draw up their men in line and rush to the assault. There is a wide and deep ditch to cross, the walls are about thirty feet high, no breach has been battered, and the soldiers have no ladders. The result may easily be imagined. One half of the men are left in the ditch; the other half retreat with difficulty from the impossible and absurd enterprise, under a terrible fire from the walls; Andrei Alexandrovitch himself receives three wounds, and has to be carried off the field by his men; whilst his opponent is left amongst the dead. For this little feat he is once again reduced to the ranks.

During the next few years he has but few opportunities of distinguishing himself; so he leads a listless, careless, vagabond sort of life, which is, in Central Asia, not without its charms. He spends nearly every day in the same round of smoking, drinking vodka, and playing cards, varied only by an occasional hunt for tigers.

Andrei Alexandrovitch was one of the first men who addressed me when I reached General Kaufmann's army; and the acquaintance, thus begun, rapidly ripened into intimacy, and even friendship. At this time, after twenty years' service, he has attained the elevated rank of ensign. This disparity between his age and rank does not, however, strike you as unbecoming; for the fellow seems to have the gift of perpetual youth. Though now close upon forty, he looks scarcely more than twenty, despite the wild, reckless life he has led.

I found him to be the best of good fellows, and generous to a fault. Utterly careless as to the future, he would spend one morning the £20 he had won at cards the night before on a breakfast to his brother officers, and next day borrow money to buy tea and sugar for himself and barley for his horse. Brave as a lion, he would lead a forlorn hope, start on a three months' march across the desert, or go on parade with equal coolness and indifference, and with about the same amount of preparation. In fact, he had entered on the Khiva campaign with only three days' supply of provisions.

Andrei Alexandrovitch is a good linguist, but by no fault of his. When he was a child, he had English, French, and German governesses; and he thus learned these languages as he had learned his own, without study or application. He has now spent several years in Turkistan, yet he knows scarcely a word of the Tartar language. Whatever he knows of military affairs—and he knows a great deal—he has learned, not from books, but from actual experience. He has literary talent, too, of no mean order, and can coin French verses with a facility which is remarkable.

After the Khivan campaign he received two decorations, the Saint Vladimir and the Saint Anne. He was offered promotion, likewise, but this he refused. "You see," said he to me, "the difference between the pay of an ensign and that of a lieutenant is so small that it is not an object. At my age I would just as soon be one as the other. It is not everybody either that can be an ensign at thirty-eight."

"I think I would prefer the promotion to the decoration," I observed. "Ah! there you would be wrong. I have a respected maternal relative who, when she hears I have won the Vladimir—the highest order, you know, next to Saint George—will probably come down with twenty thousand roubles." "How long do you think that will last you when you get it?" I ask. "Why, a year or two, perhaps. No use in having money unless you spend it, and get something for it, you know."

Andrei Alexandrovitch is a slightly exaggerated type of the Russian officer in Turkistan—I might say of a large class of officers throughout the entire empire. They have not all been reduced to the ranks several times, and they are not all ensigns at forty; but the career of each of them is parallel to that of Andrei Alexandrovitch in every other particular. They have all been in the Guard; they have all squandered their fortunes in it; they have all followed faithfully in the beaten track of their predecessors. All are careless of the future, determined to make the most of the present; and all lead the same easy, indifferent, vagabond kind of life. They pass most of their time in playing cards; the mania of the Russians of all classes, indeed, for play is most excessive. I have seen them sit down and play for forty-eight hours, scarcely ever rising from the table during the whole time. I had thought only savages could evince such a passion for gaming; and the truth is, this passion among the Russians is a relic of barbarism which still clings to them.

They never study; and they no more bother their heads about the future operations of the army, or even the orders for the morrow, than does one of their own soldiers. In most armies on a campaign like the present the officers would all know and discuss the plan of operations, the movements about to be made, and what would be required for their execution. They would all have maps and all the information to be obtained regarding the route over which they were marching.

This was not the case with the Russians. They neither knew nor cared what were the movements to be made, nor their chances of success. Of the orders for the morrow, the preparation that might be required for their execution, they knew nothing. None of them, except, of course, two or three of the staff, had maps; and none of them even knew how far it was to the next well. They simply obey orders, no matter what they are; and the possibility of executing an order is a thing they never discuss.

Although all good linguists, there were not three officers in the whole of Kaufmann's detachment that knew the language of the country.

It is not to be supposed from this that the Russians are poor officers. They are as brave as lions; and there is not one among them that would hesitate to lead a forlorn hope, or that would not walk up to certain death with as much coolness as to dinner. They obey orders with a kind of blind, unreasoning heroism, that is only equalled by that of their own soldiers. Generous, kindly, pleasant fellows withal, ever ready to offer you their hospitality or do you a favour, they are sure to win your affection and esteem.

The Russian officers have very strong likes and dislikes. For the Americans and the French they have feelings of the utmost friendliness. They speak, by preference, the French language; love French literature and French music; and they endeavour to imitate French ways of living. And their sympathies in the last war were altogether with France. The Germans they detest as cordially as they like the French; and, indeed, a Frenchman hates the German with a hatred scarcely more bitter than that of the Russian, civilian or soldier. The origin of this hatred must be sought in the time of Peter the Great. When that monarch determined to introduce western civilization into his empire, he had, of course, to cast about among foreigners for the men to carry out this purpose. He naturally selected Germany, as the country nearest to him, and Germans were chosen to fill the highest offices in the state, civil and military. The jealousy thus created still lasts; for many of the descendants of the Germans—although they are now, of course, thorough Russians—still occupy foremost places in the country. And thus it is that Russia is filled with hatred for Germany, that has been so often her most steadfast friend; and with love for France, that has been in past times her greatest enemy. The feelings of the Russian officers towards the English are very different. They look upon the English, if not with liking, at least with a good deal of respect; but none the less anticipate a time when the collision of Russian and English interests may bring Russian and English armies into conflict. But into such a contest they would bring no feeling of national and ineradicable hate. And just as Russian and English officers, during the days of truce at the Crimea, smoked cigarettes, and exchanged friendly and courteous conversation with each other, so Russian officers would fight with Englishmen without any great personal grudge, but, on the contrary, with a chivalric feeling of respect and esteem.

MISS CASEY (E. OWENS BLACKBURNE).

[Elizabeth Casey is another example of the strength of will and tenacity of purpose by which women have so often shown their ability to overcome apparently insurmountable obstacles.

Elizabeth Owens Blackburne Casey was born on May 10, 1848, in Slane, county Meath. When about eleven years of age she lost her sight; an operation failed to restore vision, and for many years she had to endure all the physical and mental suffering that blindness inflicts. The late Sir William Wilde succeeded where another physician had failed, and Miss Casey had the happiness of recovering her sight. Her circumstances naturally prevented her from receiving any regular education; but when about eighteen she set to work at instructing herself, and in the examinations for women took first medal and a certificate.

She had from an early age written for her own amusement; but it was not till 1869 that she sent a story to a periodical. The editor accepted the manuscript, and so Miss Casey was started in literary life.

In the latter end of 1873 she determined to embark on the vast and often cruel ocean of London literary life; and after a period of hard struggle succeeded in obtaining for herself a recognized position. Miss Casey has contributed to many newspapers and periodicals, but she is best known as a novelist. She is the author of the following serial stories:— *The Love that loves Alway; Aunt Delia's Heir; The Glen of Silver Birches; In the Vale of Honey; Shadows in the Sunlight; A Modern Parrhasius; A Woman Scorned; The Way Women Love; A Chronicle of Barham*, which appeared in *The Quiver* for 1878; and *Molly Carew*. She has also written *Illustrious Irishwomen*, an excellent work, on which we have had occasionally to draw; and a collection of her fugitive stories, under the title *A Bunch of Shamrocks*, was published in 1879.

Miss Casey is most at home in describing Irish peasant life, which she understands thoroughly; and many of the scenes she paints remind one of Carleton. She has also great power in imagining picturesque and dramatic delineations; and her plots are skilfully woven. She is generally known to the public as Miss Owens Blackburne—a portion of her name which she has adopted as a *nom de plume*.]

BIDDY BRADY'S BANSHEE.

(FROM "A BUNCH OF SHAMROCKS."[1])

"Arrah, thin!—an' did yeh nivir hear tell av 'Biddy Brady's Banshee!' Shure, iviry wan for three parishes roun' was talkin' about it! Bedad, it was th' grandest piece av fun ivir happened in th' place, and only jist t' mintion it t' ould Biddy Brady is like shakin' a red rag at a bull! It's she that gets mad av yeh ask her av she ivir seen a banshee!

"Yis! alannah machree, I'll tell yeh the story. Shure no wan knows it betther nor meself, for wasn't I there th' day Father Connor found out all about it, so here it's for yeh!

"Well—four years ago whin ould Paddy Brady was dyin'—he died av an indigestion av th' lung, ma'am—at laist, that's what th' docthor sed, but ould Rosy Finnegan, that's a very knowledgable ould woman, sez that it wasn't that at all, but a demur in his back,[2] or aither that or a fallin' av his breastbone, an' sure it's as like as not that Rosy was right, for sure she's been raisin' breastbones for th' last thirty years.[3] An' th' sorra much docthors knows afther all! Throth, ma'am, it's my belief, an' Biddy Brady's too, that poor Paddy—God rest his sowl this blessed day!—'ud be here alive an' hearty now, av th' docthor had only let ould Rosy Finnegan clap a plasther av ivy laves an' goose-grase an th' small av his back! But no! bedad! Docthor Joyce wouldn't, an' so among them poor Paddy Brady was kilt all out!

"Ah! Yis. Th' docthors, wid ther new-fangled ways, don't like people t' be cured so aisy. That's about th' thruth av it; but, faix! it's many and many's th' fine cure I seen done an a sore eye wid th' nine blessed dawks from th' whitethorn be th' Holy Well there beyant pinted at it, in th' name av th' Blessed Thrinity! Ay, faix! many's th' wan; an many's th'

---

[1] By permission of the authoress.
[2] "Demur in the back"—*i.e.* lumbago.
[3] "Falling of the breastbone." This imaginary complaint is cured in the following manner:—Some oil is burned in a cup, and the air exhausted, and the upturned cup placed over the region of the heart, whilst the operator mutters some prayers. Not long ago a man died in the north of Ireland who had amassed a considerable sum of money by "raising the breastbone."

child bewitched be th' fairies, and wastin' away, that I seen th' charm bruk be feedin' the crathur wid milk from goats that fed an' a fairy mountain. But there's no use in tellin' that t' th' docthors; they're too consaited, an' consait's a bad thing in any dacint Christian, lettin' alone docthors.

"Och! Here I am now discoorsin' out av me—but, shure! it's no wondher, for it's not iviry day I get a lady like yerself t' listen t' me—an' I'm forgettin' all about ould Biddy Brady's banshee! Well, I was tellin' yeh, ma'am, that ould Paddy Brady—the heavens be his bed this blessed day, for th' sorra dacinter nabour ivir dhrew th' breath av life, though I'm his mother's third-cousin that sez it!—yis, ould Paddy Brady died, lavin' Biddy wid a fine big lump av a boy av nineteen. He was six fut high, wid a fine healthy face as roun' an' as red as th' sun in a fog an th' top av th' mountain over there, an' a fine thick head av carroty hair an him. I dunno whether yeh know it or not, ma'am, but ould Biddy and Paddy nivir had but th' wan child—boy nor girl, nor any soort—an' shure, what d'ye think but Biddy always kep gommochin' afther him, an' thratin' him like a child, and he nineteen years av age!

"I was at poor ould Paddy's wake—his sowl to glory—an' Biddy was sittin' in th' middle av the flure, wid her cloak on, an' a little new shawl pinned over her cap, an' a white pockethandkercher in her hand, an' she rockin' herself backwards and forwards, an' she takin' up th' keen now an' agin. Now I don't care much for ould Biddy Brady, but I'll say this much for her, ma'am, that a nicer-behaved woman at a husband's wake I nivir seen. The corpse, too, was laid out beautiful. It was waked in the kitchen, and bekase th' bed was fixed in th' wall av the room Tom Doolan, th' boccaty[1] carpenter, lint two nine-feet planks, that wor covered wid sheets, an' did beautiful, an' th' inds av them that stuck out med sates for some av the nabours. Ay, indeed, an' it was on that very sate that Christy Brady, ould Biddy's son, ma'am, was sittin' beside Judy Blake, not that he was givin' her much discoorse; he was too well behaved t' talk much at his ould father's wake; that wouldn't be right behaviour.

"'Biddy, acushla,' sez I to her, 'it's you that ought t' be th' proud woman, t' have such a fine boy as Christy t' look afther th' bit av land for yeh.'

"'Yis, Peggy darlint, so I am,' sez she, fouldin' up her pockethandkercher jist like a lady, an' sittin' up very straight, 'but I'm thinkin' it's not this dirty bit av land that Christy'll be mindin'!'

"'Arrah, no!' sez I, an' we all looked at her.

"'Bekase,' sez she, tuckin' her cloak roun' her, as grand as yeh plaze, 'Christy's goin' t' be a gintleman, he's goin' t' be a priest! I can tell yez all we're not th' common soort av people yez always thought we war.'

"'Och! poor ould Biddy,' sez Rosy Finnegan t' me in a whisper, 'she was always quare, but she's goin' aff av her head intirely wid the loss av poor ould Paddy.'

"'Throth, Biddy,' sez Tom Doolan, that lint th' planks, 'no wan in th' parish cud ivir even anythin' t' you or yours but th' hoighth av daciney an' behaviour.'

"'We've more nor behaviour, I can tell yeh, Tom Doolan,' sez ould Biddy, wid a shake av her head, 'it's grandheur we have. It's a banshee we have follyin' th' family. Take that now!'

"'It's as thrue as you're sittin' there, Tom,' sez Christy, all av a suddint from the corner, 'me and me mother and me poor father—God rest his sowl—heard it three nights runnin' afore me father died.'

"'Bedad he did,' sez Biddy; 'the first night I heerd it I thought I heerd somethin' scrapin' or tappin' at th' windy, so I wint over an' opened it, an' there, in th' light av the moon I seen a little ould woman dhressed all in red. Well, th' minit she seen me she gev a schreech an' run away down by th' boreen. "Christy, alannah," sez I, "it's a banshee." "Thrue for you, mother," sez he, "so it is," an' wid that he run out afther it, an' was a good two hours lookin' about, but th' sorra bit av it he cud see.'

"'An' did ye see it agin, Biddy?' sez Tom Doolan.

"'Yis, agrah, yis,' sez Biddy Brady, 'twict it kem an' gev th' same schreech. So I med Christy rub his fingers wid a bit av the blessed candle, an' gev him the holy wather to sprinkle her wid—but not a bit av her cud he find.'

"'Bedad I'll ketch her yet,' sez Christy, 'av any wan does. I'm determined not t' have her comin' and disturbin' me pace a'thout knowin' th' raison why.'

"'Arrah, Christy,' sez ould Rosy Finnegan, 'shure it's aisy seein' what brought th' banshee—shure it kem for yer poor father, God be good t' him. But bedad, Biddy, it's a great

---

[1] Lame.

day for yeh t' have a banshee followin' th' family.'

"'It's only people whose aunt's sisthers wor kings and queens, that does have banshees in th' family,' sez Tom Doolan; and mind yeh, ma'am, Tom has a power av larnin', and can say Latin again' Father Connor, for Tom wanst used to sarve Mass; 'but I don't rimimber,' sez he, 'any king av the name av Brady, nor a queen nayther. There was a King O'Tool, that was made into a church be raison iv a charm St. Kevin put an him; an' there was the Queen av Sheeby—but I'm not right shure that she was pure Irish.'

"'Not she,' sez Pat Gaffney, 'she cudn't be more than half Irish. Sure "sheeby" is only th' half av "shebeen."'

"'Throth, yer right there, Pat,' sez Tom Doolan; 'but let me think—there was King Solomon.'

"'No, asthore machree, no,' sez Biddy Brady. 'It wasn't King Solomon, for I wanst heerd Father O'Connor tell that he wanted t' cut a baby in two halves, an' th' nerra a dacint Brady id ivir think av doin' such an onchristian thing. No, agrah, it wasn't King Solomon that was th' first av th' Bradys.'

"'I know who it was,' sez Pat Gaffney; 'it was Brian Boru. Shure, Brian Boru and Brady is as like as two pays.'

"'Holy Saint Dinnis! look at th' corpse!' screeches out Rosy Finnegan; 'it's risin' up from th' dead t' say that it's thrue about Brian Boru!'

"Faix, ma'am, we all schreeched, an' no wondher, for th' corpse stood up nearly sthraight, an' med a dash out at poor ould Biddy that was sittin', as I tould yeh, ma'am, right in the middle av th' flure.

"But, shure, it didn't come t' life at all; it was only Christy Brady an' little Judy Blake that laned too heavy on the ind av th' plank th' wor sittin' on, an' thin th' other ind wint np an' threwn out th' corpse.

"Well, ma'am, poor ould Paddy Brady—God rest his sowl—was berried th' next Sunday—that was th' next day—an' poor ould Biddy was near half dead from not gettin' over th' fright av the corpse flyin' at her.

"'Throth, I'm afeard,' sez she, 'that it's wantin' th' rites I'll be meself afore long; an' maybe it's a saucer av snuff an me buzzom an' two mould candles at me head ye'll see afore th' year is out. It was a mortial bad sign for th' corpse t' make a grab at me.'

"'Well,' sez I, 'there is some thruth in that. An' are ye in airnest, Biddy, about makin' Christy a priest?'

"'Och, bedad I am, he's a gintleman born; I know that from the banshee, the Lord betchune uz an' all harm. So he must be eddicated like wan.'

"About a fortnight afther ould Paddy was berried, I was doin' a bit av washin' wan day, whin who comes in but ould Biddy Brady.

"'God save yeh, kindly,' sez she, comin' in.

"'Amin; th' same t' you, Biddy,' sez I; 'yer welcome, acushla! sit down.'

"'Peggy,' sez she, an' she sittin' an the settle-bed be th' side av th' harth, 'I'm in desp'rate throuble intirely.'

"'Arrah, what about,' sez I, 'shure it's not about poor Paddy—God be good t' him—for he always minded his duty an' confession, an' ye have that little red heifer t' give Father Connor for masses for his sowl.'

"'No, Peggy, it's not about Paddy—God rest him—I'm aisy in me mind about him, for a red heifer is as much as cud be expected from a poor widda woman, an' I'm thinkin' maybe they'll throw in th' good blood av th' Bradys. But it's about the banshee.'

"'Saints above!' sez I, 'an' did it come agin?'

"'Come!' she sez, 'och! bedad it did! Nine times it kem, and nine times Christy follied it wid the holy wather, but th' sorra bit cud he ketch it.'

"'Bedad! it's quare all out,' sez I.

"'Begorra, it is!' sez she; 'so I jist wint up an' towld Father Connor about it—it's he that's the dacint priest!—an' t' night, Peggy, he's goin' t' watch an' see if he can't say a charm agin t' banshee. An' I'm not t' tell Christy,' he sez; 'an' I want yeh t' come up an' be there, Peggy, acushla, av it comes.'

"'Troth, I will,' sez I.

"'An' what d'ye think,' sez she, 'but Christy, that I hardly ivir let out av me sight an' was rarin' up t' be a credit t' th' blood av th' Bradys, he sez now that he won't be a priest, but that he'll git marrid! Troth! me hart's near bruk between him an' th' banshee, only it's such a dacint thing t' have in th' family.'

"Well, ma'am, I wint up t' ould Biddy Brady's that evenin', and it was a Christmas Eve. Christy was there, an' he not knowin' a word about Father Connor. We had some punch, and th' sorra word we sed about the banshee. Meself was thinkin' it wasn't comin' at all; or that, maybe, the nine times was th charm; a' that somewan was t' die afther that —whin, all av a suddint, me blood run cowld wid hearin' a schreech roun' be th' boreen!

Ould Biddy got all av a thrimble, an' began sayin' her bades as fast as she cud, for there was schreech after schreech until th' kem t' th' very doore.

"'Gi' me the holy wather, mother!' sez Christy, takin' it an' makin' a run at the doore. But jist as he opened it, who walks in but Father Connor an' little Judy Blake.

"Och! bedad! it's thrue as yer there, ma'am. It nivir was a banshee at all; only little Judy Blake, wid her mother's ould red cloak roun' her, an' her arms all bare an' white. An' th' whole raison av it was that Biddy Brady kep such a sharp eye after her big lump av a son that he had no other way av coortin' Judy Blake. So he tould Father Connor afore us all, an' Father Connor gave thim a sermon about frightenin' people.

"'Och! yer rivirence! an' isn't it too bad,' sez Biddy, 'an he cut out for a priest! He looks that ginteel av a Sunda' whin he's shaved an' has his clane shirt an, that he locks th' very moral av yerself, yer rivirence!'

"'No, Biddy,' sez his rivirence; 'I don't think that Christy's cut out for a priest. Shure a priest 'ud nivir think av runnin' afther th' girls.'

"'Thrue, for yer rivirence,' sez Biddy.

"'Now, Biddy,' sez Father Connor, 'yeh must make it up wid th' two young people, for at this blessed Christmas time yeh must forgive and forgit.'

"So, ma'am, there was a great laugh at them all in th' chapel-yard, afther mass on Christmas Day. An' at last Biddy used t' get mad whin anythin' was sed, for shure she didn't like t' be chated out av her grandheur. But no wan in th' parish can help laughin' whin anywan talks about 'Biddy Brady's Banshee.'"

JOHN BOYLE O'REILLY.

[Mr. O'Reilly holds at the present moment the post of chief editor of the *Boston Pilot*. Before reaching the repose of the editorial chair he had to pass through a career of adventure and danger. He was one of those who took part in the Fenian movement; and being tried and convicted, he was sentenced to transportation to Western Australia. Thence he escaped amid circumstances of daring and peril; and finally he found shelter in the United States.

His voyage across the ocean suggested a number of poems which he published under the title of *Songs from the Southern Seas*. The verses are partly descriptive and partly lyrical. The descriptive contain many passages of picturesque detail, and have an undercurrent of dry humour and reckless pathos that recall the style of Bret Harte. Mr. O'Reilly is known as an able and vigorous journalist.]

CHUNDER ALI'S WIFE.

"I am poor," said Chunder Ali, while the Mandarin above him
Frowned in supercilious anger at the dog who dared to speak;
"I am friendless and a Hindoo: such a one meets few to love him
Here in China, where the Hindoo finds the truth alone is weak.
I have naught to buy your justice; were I wise, I had not striven.
Speak your judgment;" and he crossed his arms and bent his quivering face.
Heard he then the unjust sentence: all his goods and gold were given
To another, and he stood alone, a beggar in the place.
And the man who bought the judgment looked in triumph and derision
At the cheated Hindoo merchant, as he rubbed his hands and smiled
At the whispered gratulations of his friends, and at the vision
Of the more than queenly dower for Ahmeer, his only child.
Fair Ahmeer, who of God's creatures was the only one who loved him,
She, the diamond of his treasures, the one lamb within his fold,
She whose voice, like her dead mother's, was the only power that moved him,—
She would praise the skill that gained her all this Hindoo's silk and gold.
And the old man thanked Confucius, and the judge, and him who pleaded.——
But why falls this sudden silence? why does each one hold his breath?
Every eye turns on the Hindoo, who before was all unheeded,

And in wond'ring expectation all the court grows
    still as death.
Not alone stood Chunder Ali; by his side Ahmeer
    was standing,
And his brown hand rested lightly on her shoulder
    as he smiled
At the sweet young face turned toward him.
    Then the father's voice commanding
Fiercely bade his daughter to him from the dog
    whose touch defiled.
But she moved not, and she looked not at at her
    father or the others
As she answered, with her eyes upon the Hin-
    doo's noble face:
"Nay, my father, he defiles not; this kind arm
    above all others
Is my choosing, and for ever by his side shall be
    my place.
When you knew not, his dear hand had given
    many a sweet love-token,
He had gathered all my heartstrings and had
    bound them round his life;
Yet you tell me he defiles me: nay, my father,
    you have spoken
In your anger, and not knowing I was Chunder
    Ali's wife."

MY NATIVE LAND.

It chanced to me upon a time to sail
Across the Southern Ocean to and fro;
And, landing at fair isles, by stream and vale
Of sensuous blessing did we ofttimes go.
And months of dreamy joys, like joys in sleep,
Or like a clear, calm stream o'er mossy stone,
Unnoted passed our hearts with voiceless sweep,
And left us yearning still for lands unknown.

And when we found one,—for 'tis soon to find
In thousand-isled Cathay another isle,—
For one short noon its treasures filled the mind,
And then again we yearned, and ceased to smile.
And so it was, from isle to isle we passed,
Like wanton bees or boys on flowers or lips;
And when that all was tasted, then at last
We thirsted still for draughts instead of sips.

I learned from this there is no Southern land
Can fill with love the hearts of Northern men.
Sick minds need change; but, when in health
    they stand
'Neath foreign skies, their love flies home *agen*.
And thus with me it was: the yearning turned
From laden airs of cinnamon away,
And stretched far westward, while the full heart
    burned
With love for Ireland, looking on Cathay!

My first dear love, all dearer for thy grief!
My land, that has no peer in all the sea

For verdure, vale or river, flower or leaf,—
If first to no man else, thou'rt first to me.
New loves may come with duties, but the first
Is deepest yet,—the mother's breath and smiles:
Like that kind face and breast where I was nursed
Is my poor land, the Niobe of isles.

MY MOTHER'S MEMORY.

There is one bright star in heaven
    Ever shining in my night;
God to me one guide has given,
    Like the sailor's beacon-light,
Set on every shoal of danger,
    Sending out its warning ray
To the home-bound weary stranger
    Looking for the land-locked bay.

In my farthest, wildest wand'rings
    I have turned me to that love,
As a diver, 'neath the water,
    Turns to watch the light above.

UNSPOKEN WORDS.

The kindly words that rise within the heart
And thrill it with their sympathetic tone,
But die ere spoken, fail to play their part
And claim a merit that is not their own.
The kindly word unspoken is a sin—
A sin that wraps itself in purest guise,
And tells the heart that, doubting, looks within,
That not in speech, but thought, the virtue lies.

But 'tis not so: another heart may thirst
For that kind word, as Hagar in the wild—
Poor banished Hagar—prayed a well might burst
From out the sand, to save her parching child.
And loving eyes that cannot see the mind
Will watch the expected movement of the lip:
Ah! can ye let its cutting silence wind
Around that heart and scathe it like a whip?

Unspoken words like treasures in the mine
Are valueless until we give them birth.
Like unfound gold their hidden beauties shine
Which God has made to bless and gild the earth.
How sad 'twould be to see a master's hand
Strike glorious notes upon a voiceless lute—
But oh, what pain when at God's own command
A heart-string thrills with kindness, but is mute!

Then hide it not, the music of the soul,
Dear sympathy expressed with kindly voice,
But let it like a shining river roll
To deserts dry—to hearts that would rejoice.
Oh! let the symphony of kindly words
Sound for the poor, the friendless, and the weak,
And He will bless you. He who struck these chords
Will strike another when in turn you seek.

JOHN PEYTLAND MAHAFFY.

[Mr. Mahaffy is one of the alumni of Trinity College, Dublin, who have proved the current falsehood that our national university contrasts unfavourably with the sister universities in literary production. The large number of subjects on which he has written show to some extent that extraordinary variety of knowledge for which he is remarkable.

John Peytland Mahaffy was born on February 26, 1839, at Chafonnaire, near Vevay, in Switzerland. He was brought up in Germany, and received his early education from his parents. In 1856 he entered Trinity College, Dublin, and, after a highly successful undergraduate course, obtained a fellowship in 1864. He was appointed precentor of the college chapel in 1867, and his love and knowledge of music have enabled him to introduce great reforms in the choir. In 1871 he became professor of ancient history in the University, a post he still holds; and in 1873 he was the Donnellan lecturer. His interest in ancient and modern Greece has been recognized by the King of the Greeks, who in 1877 conferred upon him the "Gold Cross of the Order of the Saviour."

Mr. Mahaffy's first work was a translation of Kuno Fischer's well-known work on the great German philosopher, which appeared in 1866 under the title *Commentary on Kant*. In 1868 were published *Twelve Lectures on Primitive Civilization*; in 1871, *Kant's Critical Philosophy for English Readers*; and in the same year, *Prolegomena to Ancient History*. A subject perhaps less recondite, and certainly more popular, was discussed in *Social Life in Greece from Homer to Menander*, a work which has already passed through several editions. A book on *Greek Antiquities* followed in 1876, and in the same year appeared the work *Rambles and Studies in Greece*, from which our quotations are taken. Mr. Mahaffy is, besides, a constant contributor to periodical literature.]

THOUGHTS ON NEARING GREECE.[1]

A voyage to Greece does not at first sight seem a great undertaking. We all go to and fro to Italy as we used to go to France. A trip to Rome, or even to Naples, is now an Easter holiday affair. And is not Greece very close to Italy on the map? What signifies the narrow sea that divides them? This is what a man might say who only considered geography, and did not regard the teaching of history. For the student of history cannot look upon these two peninsulas without being struck with the fact that they are, historically speaking, turned back to back; that while the face of Italy is turned westward, and looks towards France and Spain, and across to us, the face of Greece looks eastward, towards Asia Minor and towards Egypt. Every great city in Italy, except Venice, approaches or borders the Western Sea—Genoa, Pisa, Florence, Rome, Naples.

All the older history of Rome, its development, its glories, lie on the west of the Apennines. When you cross them you come to what is called the back of Italy; and you feel in that dull country, and that straight coast line, you are separated from the beauty and charm of real Italy. Contrariwise, in Greece, the whole weight and dignity of its history gravitate towards the eastern coast. All its great cities—Athens, Thebes, Corinth, Argos, Sparta—are on that side. Their nearest neighbours were the coast cities of Asia Minor and the Cyclades, but the western coasts were to them harbourless and strange. If you pass Cape Malea, they said, then forget your home.

So it happens that the coasts of Italy and Greece, which look so near, are outlying and out-of-the-way parts of the countries to which they belong; and if you want to go straight from real Italy to real Greece, the longest way is that from Brindisi to Corfu, for you must still journey from Naples to Brindisi, and from Corfu to Athens. The shortest way is to take ship at Naples, and to be carried round Italy and round Greece from the centres of culture on the west of Italy to the centres of culture (such as they are) on the east of Greece. But this is no trifling passage. When the ship has left the coasts of Calabria, and steers into the open sea, you feel that you have at last left the west of Europe, and are setting sail for the Eastern Seas. And I may anticipate for a moment here, and say that even now the face of Athens is turned, as of old, to the east. Her trade and her communications

---

[1] By permission of the author.

are through the Levant. Her intercourse is with Constantinople and Smyrna, and Syra, and Alexandria, to which a man may sail almost any day in the week. You can only sail to Italy—I had almost said to Europe—on Saturdays, and upon an occasional Thursday.

This curious parallel between ancient and modern geographical attitudes in Greece is, no doubt, greatly due to the now bygone Turkish rule. In addition to other contrasts, Mohammedan rule and eastern jealousy—long unknown in Western Europe—first jarred upon the traveller when he touched the coasts of Greece; and this dependency was once really part of a great Asiatic empire, where all the interests and communications gravitated eastward, and away from the Christian and better civilized West. The revolution which expelled the Turks was unable to root out the ideas which their subjects had learned; and so, in spite of Greek hatred of the Turk, his influence still lives through Greece in a thousand ways.

MARATHON.

The plain of Marathon, as everybody knows, is a long crescent-shaped strip of land by the shore, surrounded by an amphitheatre of hills, which may be crossed conveniently in three places, but most easily towards the south-west, along the road which we travelled, and which leads directly to Athens. When the Athenians marched through this broad and easy passage, they found that the Persians had landed at the northern extremity of the plain—I suppose because the water was there sufficiently deep to let them land conveniently. Most of the shore, as you proceed southward, is lined on the seaboard by swamps. The Greek army must have marched northwards, along the spurs of Pentelicus, and taken up their position near the north of the plain. There was evidently much danger that the Persians should force a passage through the village of Marathon, towards the north-west. Had they done this, they might have rounded Pentelicus, and descended the main plain of Attica, from the valley below Dekeleia. Perhaps, however, this pass was then defended by an outlying fort, or by some defences at Marathon itself. The site of the battle is absolutely fixed by the great mound, upon which was placed a lion, which has been carried off, no one knows when or whither.

This mound is exactly an English mile from the steep slope of one of the hills, and about half a mile from the sea at present; nor was there, when I saw it, any difficulty in walking right to the shore, though a river flows out there, which shows, by its sedgy banks and lofty reeds, a tendency to create a marshy tract in rainy weather. But the mound is so placed that, if it marks the centre of the battle, the Athenians must have faced nearly north, and, if they faced the sea eastward, as is commonly stated, this mound must mark the conflict on their left wing. The mound is very large—I suppose thirty feet high, altogether of clay, so far as we could see, and bears traces of having been frequently ransacked in search of antiquities.

Like almost every view in Greece, the prospect from this mound is full of beauty and variety—everywhere broken outlines, everywhere patches of blue sea, everywhere silence and solitude. Byron is so much out of fashion now, and so much more talked about than read—though even that notice of him is fast disappearing—that I will venture to remind the reader of the splendid things he has said of Greece, and especially of this very plain of Marathon. He was carried away by his enthusiasm to fancy a great future possible for the country, and to believe that its desolation and the low condition of the inhabitants were simply the result of Turkish tyranny, and not of many natural causes, conspiring for twenty centuries. He paints the Greek brigand or pirate as many others have painted the "noble savage," with the omission of all his meaner vices. But, in spite of all these faults, who is there who has felt as he the affecting aspects of this beautiful land—the tomb of ancient glory—the home of ancient wisdom—the mother of science, of art, of philosophy, of politics—the champion of liberty—the envy of the Persian and the Roman—the teacher, even still, of modern Europe? It is surely a great loss to our generation, and a bad sign of its culture, that the love of more modern poets has weaned them from the study of one not less great in most respects, but far greater in one at least—in that burning enthusiasm for a national cause, in that red-hot passion for liberty which, even when misapplied, or wasted upon unworthy objects, is ever one of the noblest and most stirring instincts of higher man.

But Byron may well be excused for raving about the liberty of the Greeks, for truly their old conflict at Marathon, where a few thousand ill-disciplined men repulsed a larger number of still worse disciplined Orientals, without any recondite tactics—perhaps even without any very extraordinary heroism— how is it that this conflict has maintained a celebrity which has not been equalled by all the great battles of the world, from that day down to our own? The courage of the Greeks, as I have elsewhere shown, was not of the first order. Herodotus praises the Athenians in this very battle for being the first Greeks that dared to look the Persians in the face. Their generals all through history seem never to feel sure of victory, and always endeavour to harangue their soldiers into a fury. Instead of advising coolness, they specially incite to rage—ὀργῇ πρεσμίξωμεν, says one of them in Thucydides—as if any man not in this state would be sure to estimate the danger fully, and run away. It is, indeed, true that the ancient battles were hand to hand, and therefore parallel to our charges of bayonets, which are said to be very seldom carried out by two opposing lines, as one of them almost always gives way before the actual collision takes place. This must often have taken place in Greek battles, for, at Amphipolis, Brasidas in a battle lost seven men; at a battle at Corinth, mentioned by Xenophon—an important battle, too—the slain amounted to eight; and these battles were fought before the days when whole armies were composed of mercenaries, who spared one another, as Ordericus Vitalis says, "for the love of God, and out of good feeling for the fraternity of arms." So, then, the loss of 192 Athenians, including some distinguished men, was rather a severe one. As to the loss of the Persians, I so totally disbelieve the Greek accounts of such things, that it is better to pass it by in silence.

Perhaps most readers will be astonished to hear of the Athenian army as undisciplined, and of the science of war as undeveloped, in those times. Yet I firmly believe this was so. The accounts of battles by almost all the historians are so utterly vague, and so childishly conventional, that it is evident these gentlemen were not only quite ignorant of the science of war, but could not easily find anyone to explain it to them. We know that the Spartans—the most admired of all Greek warriors—were chiefly so admired because they devised the system of subordinating officers to one another within the same detachment, like our gradation from colonel to corporal. So orders were passed down from officer to officer, instead of being bawled out by a herald to a whole army. But this superiority of the Spartans, who were really disciplined, and went into battle coolly, like brave men, certainly did not extend to strategy, but was merely a question of better drill. As soon as any real strategist met them they were helpless. Thus Iphicrates, when he devised Wellington's plan of meeting their attacking column in line, and using missiles, succeeded against them, even without firearms. Thus Epaminondas, when he devised Napoleon's plan of massing troops on a single point, while keeping his enemy's line occupied, defeated them without any considerable struggle. As for that general's great battle of Mantinea, which seems really to have been introduced by some complicated strategical movements, it is a mere hopeless jumble in our historians. But these men were in the distant future when the battle of Marathon was being fought.

Yet what signifies all this criticism? In spite of all scepticism, in spite of all contempt, the battle of Marathon, whether badly or well fought, and the troops at Marathon, whether well or ill trained, will ever be more famous than any other battle or army, however important or gigantic its dimensions. Even in this very war the battles of Salamis and Plataea were vastly more important and more hotly contested. The losses were greater, the results were more enduring, yet thousands have heard of Marathon to whom the other names are unknown. So much for literary ability—so much for the power of talking well about one's deeds. Marathon was fought by Athenians; the Athenians eclipsed the other Greeks as far as the other Greeks eclipsed the rest of the world, in literary power. This battle became the literary property of the city, hymned by poet, cited by orator, told by aged nurse, lisped by stammering infant; and so it has taken its position, above all criticism, as one of the great decisive battles which assured the liberty of the West against Oriental despotism.

THE ACROPOLIS OF ATHENS AND THE ROCK OF CASHEL.

It was my good fortune, a few months after I had seen the Acropolis, to visit a ruin in Ireland which, to my great surprise, bore many curious resemblances to it—I mean the Rock of Cashel. Both were strongholds of religion—honoured and hallowed above all other places in their respective countries—both were covered with buildings of various dates, each representing their peculiar ages and styles in art. And as the Greeks, I suppose for effect's sake, have varied the posture of their temples, so that the sun illumines them at different moments, the old Irish have varied the orientation of their churches, that the sun might rise directly over against the east window on the anniversary of the patron saint. There is at Cashel the great Cathedral—in loftiness and grandeur the Parthenon of the place; there is the smaller and more beautiful Cormac's Chapel, the holiest of all, like the Erechtheum of Athens. Again, the great sanctuary upon the Rock of Cashel was surrounded by a cluster of other abbeys about its base, which were founded there by pious men on account of the greatness and holiness of the archiepiscopal seat. Of these one remains, like the Theseum at Athens, eclipsed by the splendour of the Acropolis.

The prospect from the Irish sanctuary has, indeed, endless contrasts to that from the Pagan stronghold, but they are suggestive contrasts, and such as are not without a certain harmony. The plains around both are framed by mountains, of which the Irish are probably the more picturesque; and if the light upon the Greek hills is the fairest, the native colour of the Irish is infinitely more rich. So, again, the soil of Attica is light and sandy, whereas the Golden Vale of Tipperary is among the richest in the world. But who would not choose the historic treasures of the former in preference to the bucolic value of the latter? Still, both places were the noblest homes, each in their own country, of religions which civilized, humanized, and exalted the human race; and if the Irish Acropolis is left in dim obscurity by the historical splendour of the Parthenon, on the other hand, the gods of the Athenian stronghold have faded out before the moral greatness of the faith preached upon the Rock of Cashel.

RICHARD DOWLING.

[Richard Dowling was born in Clonmel on the 3d of June, 1846, and is the son of Mr. David Jeremiah Dowling of that town. He was sent to schools in Clonmel, Waterford, and Limerick. At first he was intended for the legal profession; then a business career was considered more suitable, and with that view he was placed in the office of his uncle Mr. William Downey; but, finally, Dowling found his true vocation, and became a literary man.

His first engagement was on the staff of the Dublin *Nation*. He then became editor of a comic periodical—*Zozimus*—to which he contributed a number of humorous essays; and afterwards he was the chief spirit in another enterprise of the same kind—*Ireland's Eye*. In 1874 he emigrated to London—the maelstrom which nearly always drags towards it the best literary talent of Ireland and Scotland. He was engaged as a contributor to the *Illustrated Sporting and Dramatic News*. Among other sketches, he published in that journal "Mr. Andrew O'Rourke's Ramblings." *Yorick*, a comic paper, which he started and edited, had a brief existence of six months, and it was not till 1879 that Mr. Dowling may be said to have had his first great success. In that year Messrs. Tinsley Brothers published *The Mystery of Killard*. This work had been written in 1875-6, but the author sought then in vain for a publisher. It was, immediately after its appearance, hailed as one of the most striking romances of the year. The central idea of the work—the abnormal nature of a deaf-mute, which leads him to hate his own child because that child can hear and speak—is one of the most original in literature, and there is an atmosphere of weirdness about the whole story which deeply impresses the imagination, and lifts one to regions undreamed of by the ordinary three-volume novelist. Many of the scenes, too, show high powers of dramatic conception, and are worked out with great vigour of language.

Mr. Dowling has just published a second three-volume novel, entitled *The Weird Sisters;* he is the author of *On Babies and Ladders*, one of the late John Camden Hotten's Shilling Books of Humour; and has, besides, done that heterogeneous work of leader-writer, versifier, and descriptive correspondent, which falls to the lot of the journalist in our day.]

THE DEAF-MUTE CASTS OFF HIS SON.

(FROM "THE MYSTERY OF KILLARD."[1])

[David Lane is a deaf-mute who lives alone with his son on a wild island connected with the mainland by means of a rope bridge thrown across the intervening channel. His father and mother had been deaf-mutes like himself, but his son he suspects of being able to hear and speak. The attempts he makes to penetrate this mystery, and the results, are described in the following passage.]

When, on that August morning, Lane's son left his sleeping chamber in the hut, he found his father busily engaged preparing breakfast. The spirits of the boy seemed utterly crushed; the father was dull and gloomy, with a lowering danger in his eyes, but his actions were as kind as usual. He helped his son liberally to food, and pressed him to eat more when the boy appeared satisfied. But he did not kiss him, or fondle him, as was his custom. The boy's eyes were full of tears, and he could hardly swallow the potatoes and fish. He rarely looked at his father, and when their glances chanced to meet, the latter dropped his and frowned.

As soon as breakfast was finished the father cleared the table. Then, turning to the boy, he made signs to him, and the son taking a basket, went out, crossed the island, and descended slowly and heedlessly the precipitous path leading to the ledge. Here he drew in the hand-lines, removed the fish, and rebaited the hooks. Having gathered the fish into the basket, he sat down and fixed his eyes wearily on the sea.

Meanwhile the father had taken the gun out of its hiding-place under the bed, examined it carefully at the nipple, and placed it against the inner edge of the door jamb. When this was done he stood outside the door, so as to command a view of the head of the path leading to the ledge, folded his arms, set his teeth, knit his brow, and waited.

The sky was serene and blue, not a cloud broke the infinite expanse. The light was cool and gracious, the air fresh and invigorating. The sea-fowl had by this time passed out far from shore, and their shrill dreary notes no longer floated above the dull low murmur of the swells two hundred and fifty feet below.

The boy was long, much longer than usual, but David Lane never moved a muscle. His attitude and his features remained as fixed as though a withering vapour from the pole had frozen him as he stood. The expression of his countenance was that of one awaiting fate rather than one expecting a foe, but it was tragic. Tragic with a dire resolution, and far down under the resolution a wild appalling grief. It was not the face of a man who thought. There was no trace of succession of ideas; but it seemed as though his mind, like his body, was frozen into one unalterable attitude; as though one picture were burned against that path, and nothing could displace it.

At length, above the level of the island, appeared the boy's head.

No muscle of the father moved. He remained rigid.

The shoulders and bust of the boy rose into view, then the arms and basket he carried.

Still David Lane never stirred.

The figure of the child emerged completely, and he took one pace in the direction of the hut.

Instantly, as though the vitality of a thousand men had been flung upon him, the father sprang into the hut, seized the gun, lifted it to his shoulder, and aiming at the chimney-place, fired.

The explosion was terrific, for the charge was large and the chamber small, and, in the calm of the morning, it seemed as though the Bishop's Island had been riven from summit to base.

Upon the instant he fired, quick as the flash itself, the man spun round on his heel and looked at the door. No smoke had reached it. The smoke lay huddled in blue waves near the fireplace.

Then Lane folded his arms swiftly across his breast, knit his brows, and, setting his teeth, stood inside the door confronting fate, as he had awaited it without.

In a second the boy bounded into the open, pale and awe-stricken. His eyes were wild with terror. He had lost his hat and his basket, and his hair waved hither and thither as if blown by a wind. When he saw his father standing safe before him, the expression changed electrically, and with a low moan of relief he stretched forth his arms and sank to the ground.

The father sprang back, as though the nether realms gaped at his feet, and with a wild shrill yell of despair threw his hands towards heaven, and with his upturned eyes and outstretched

---

[1] By permission of the author.

arms seemed to clamour for annihilation. While the father remained thus, the boy lay motionless on the ground. His arms were doubled under him, and his knees drawn up; his face deadly pale, his lips blue, his eyes open but rayless.

In a few moments the father's arms dropped, the expression of his face altered, and his eyes fell upon the prostrate form in the doorway. Stepping hastily forward, he sprang over the child, and, having reached the open air, strode several times up and down the island, through the white warm sunshine and fragrant dewy air. Then he returned to the doorway and looked in.

The position of the figure had not changed in the least. Again David Lane turned away, and dashed hither and thither blindly. Once more he paused at the doorway. The boy had not moved. A sudden fear seemed to seize upon the father. He leaped into the hut, stooped near the fireplace, and examined the wall. Presently, with his fingers he picked something out from between two of the stones. Holding this to the light, he examined it carefully. Yes, it was the chief portion of the leaden bullet. It broke in two as he turned it in his hand, and showed in the interior an old seam. That was the cut through which the hand-line had passed.[1] A look of angry perplexity now passed over his face, and his eyes turned once more to the ground, near the doorway.

Not a muscle had stirred; not a fold of the clothes had been displaced. Frowning heavily, as if he suspected a trick, the father crossed the room, stooped, and catching the child at the waist, lifted him. The head, and arms, and lower limbs, hung down limp and nerveless.

A spasm of horror passed over the features of the father, and he shook the child once, twice, thrice, without effect. Then lifting him higher, he carried him across the little chamber, and placed him on the bed where the boy's mother had died. He put a pillow under his son's head, drew down his limbs, and crossed the long arms over the breast. When this was done he sat down as far off as he could, and regarded the bed with a rigid expressionless air.

In a little while a light shot into his eyes. He rose, kindled a candle, and held the flame opposite the open lips. He had seen this done in Killard during the cholera years. The yellow flame, pale and sickly in the blaze of the August morning, flicked and waved regularly. The child breathed. He flung the candle down, and resumed his old position.

He had seen death and sleep; these were the only forms of human unconsciousness with which he was familiar. But here was something which was more deep than sleep, less profound than death. What could it be? Was the boy ever to wake? If sleep, which is less powerful than this, lasts a night time, how long will this last? A week or a month?

Death lasts for ever, and sleep for a night; when will this be over, and what is the end to be—deeper or lighter sleep, death or waking?

Whichever it was, doubts that had haunted his mind for a long time were now made certainties. He had seen sea-fowl, which had been invisible, rise and fly away in terror at the firing of a gun, yet, unless he were quite close, and could feel the concussion, he could not tell a gun had been fired.

Tom the Fool had told him it was possible to know at a great distance that a gun had been fired, and that the knowledge came, not through the eyes or sense of touch, but through the ears. Nothing came to him through the ears. They were like fingers, they possessed feeling, nothing more.

Tom had told him the firing of a gun could be known through the ears farther off than anything else.

Accordingly, to make sure above all doubt, he had bought the gun. He had fired that gun, and his son knew he had fired that gun, although he could not know it by the sense of touch, or by the sight of smoke, for he had fired so that the boy could see no smoke. Therefore the boy got messages through his ears.

But his father had married a wife who got no messages through the ears; he had married a wife like himself in this respect; here was his boy now unlike him. His father had told him the gold could not be kept by any one who could send or receive news by the ears, hence he had married a wife like him, David, and he himself one like himself.

The women never knew of the gold, and could not tell anyone; his father had told him, and made him promise to marry a wife such as she that had died of the cholera, and to communicate the secret only to a son, and to a son who could neither know nor make known through the ears. Everyone else was to be kept in darkness; for if once the secret of

---

[1] A fishing-sinker had been used for a bullet.

the gold came to be known it would be useless to them, and they would all perhaps be slain, for his own father did not know the penalty.

Now here was the traitor, come in the person of his own boy. The boy he loved with all his heart and soul. Here was a traitor in his own house; one who, as soon as he knew of the secret, would send it abroad, and betray his own father unto death.

Yes, this son for whom he would freely have died, could not, on account of his accursed ears, help betraying his father. He would do it as a matter of certainty, as soon as he knew. Here, lying before him, was the only being on earth he cared for, and this being would hurl his own father to destruction on the very first opportunity. This boy would turn his own father off the Bishop's, tear up the island, and give his father to the police, not because of any want of affection, but because he was cursed with ears that felt and could send messages to other ears!

Monster! Hideous, unnatural child! Mysterious curse! Away! Away! Away! There is infinite malignity of terror in your presence!

The boy's eyelids trembled. With a weary sigh he sat up and yawned, and smiled at his father. His eyes looked a little dull. He had forgotten what had passed.

When David Lane saw the boy return to consciousness and smile upon him, the look of angry dread gave place to one of frantic yearning. It seemed as though he strove with his eyes to draw his child back into his own nature. His heart hungered to absorb him; but he made no sign. His arms lay clasped upon his knees; his head was thrust forward, his figure motionless; but the agony of love betrayed was in his eyes.

There was no indignation now against his child. The worst possible certainty had been reached. If by any perversity of nature intelligible to himself he feared betrayal at the hands of his son, there might have been a struggle between indignation and love, and, for a time at least, love might have triumphed. But it was not his boy opposed him, but fate, in a form he could not understand. The son, by no fault of his own, but by the power of some curse, had been endowed by fate with an ability which he could not fail to exert for his father's destruction.

This boy, his own child, the idol of his life, his own flesh and blood, was the vessel of some spirit of wrath with power to work his destruction through mysterious and infallible agencies against which neither he nor the boy could strive with hope of success. His son was the flesh of his flesh, but the spirit of his ruin!

By this time the boy had realized all, and covered his face, and was weeping.

David Lane caught him by the shoulder and led him forth, flung the loop over the hook, and prepared the meshes for crossing the chasm. When this was done he made signs to the boy.

The latter turned pale with terror. The father repeated the signs calmly, without a trace of passion.

The boy appealed to him with outstretched hands.

Lane pointed to the mainland, and made a swift, decided gesture.

The child flung himself down moaning, and seized his father's knees and clasped them, and rested his pale tear-stained cheek against them in piteous supplication.

The deaf-mute never moved. His resolution was taken inexorably. Nothing could shake him. He raised his son gently, set him on his feet, and turning his back on him went towards the hut. In a few minutes he came back; the boy was gone.

Raising the rope he shook it free of the hook, and the island was cast off into isolation, and he into the rayless solitude of a life without a single love, a single hope, a single ambition, a single fear, save the one guilty one, not his own, but which seemed part of himself, born with his nature and laid upon him anew when first his father communicated the secret to him, and named the precautions and possible penalties in case of discovery.

When the rope once more hung idly down the dim deep cleft, Lane went into his own sleeping room. Something bright lying on the floor attracted his attention. He stooped and looked. It was his boy's clasp-knife. A sudden fury of sorrow seized him and shook him. His breath came short, his chest heaved, he bellowed aloud like a stricken beast. His blood-shot eyes ran fiercely round the place seeking something. Suddenly they stopped, riveted by the sight of the gun lying in a corner. He clutched it by the barrel as though he would drive the sides together, and with a hoarse yell dashed into the sunlight, sprang to the brink of the cliff facing the ocean, and swinging the weapon swiftly twice over his head, let it go, sending it far out into the sunlit air. With a sudden plunge it shot downward and disappeared for ever.

He looked awhile as if to give it time to reach the water, then clutching his head in both his hands, tottered to his own chamber and threw himself heavily on the earthen floor, his arms and legs spread wide and his powerful hands digging into the hard ground until they were covered with blood.

[The child was found on the top of the cliff and taken care of by kind friends, under whose fostering care he soon found his voice.]

ARTHUR O'SHAUGHNESSY.

[Arthur O'Shaughnessy has too much originality to be called the literary child of any author or period; but he is unquestionably the creation of a school of poetry which has arisen within the last quarter of a century, and which has elicited for some of its qualities the highest admiration, and for others the deepest antipathy. The most notable member of this school is Mr. Swinburne. Apart from the subject matter of poets of this school, one of their chief characteristics is their great mastery of exquisite melody, and their Hellenic worship of beauty in nature and art.

Arthur O'Shaughnessy was born in 1846. On his father's side he belongs to the Galway branch of the O'Shaughnessy family, the several divisions of which in Galway, Clare, and Limerick are supposed to have a common descent from Lieut.-col. William O'Shaughnessy, son of Sir Dermot O'Shaughnessy the second. His mother was of English royalist descent.

An Epic of Women and other Poems was Mr. O'Shaughnessy's first work,—a volume which, we may remark by the way, is now almost out of print, and which has a considerable bibliographical interest on account of a symbolical title-page and curious designs by Mr. J. T. Nettleship, a friend of the poet and author of *An Essay on Robert Browning*, and other works. In the *Epic* the most notable poem is perhaps "Creation," verses which caused such division of opinion in the ranks of rival critics as to be read among what we may call the *pièces judicatoires* in a literary libel trial which attracted some attention a few years ago. Other well-known poems in the volume are "The Daughter of Herodias" and "Cleopatra." But that which obtained immediate popularity, has been quoted everywhere, and is a particular favourite in America, is the exquisite lyric entitled "The Fountain of Tears." Two of the *Lays of France* (1873) are founded on the lyrics of Marie de France; but the greater part are original. Of these the most characteristic are "The Lay of the Two Lovers" and "Chaitivel," in the latter of which, best known, are the splendid lines which describe "The Farewell of Sattazine to her dead lover Pharamond." *Music and Moonlight* (1874) contains some of the choicest of Mr. O'Shaughnessy's lyrics. Of these the most widely known is the "Outcry," a passionate love-dream. Very remarkable also are "Song of a Shrine," "Song of the Holy Spirit," and "Supreme Summer." The last is distinctly one of the best of the poet's productions. Mr. O'Shaughnessy was a frequent contributor to periodical literature, and many of his poems, although not yet collected, have been taken up by the public. Amongst these we may mention the "Song of a Fellow-worker." A new volume is in preparation.

His genius was to a considerable extent inspired by French influence, he being an intimate friend of the majority of contemporary French poets, Victor Hugo among the rest. Though not living in France he wrote to French journals, more especially to *Le Livre*, and he was one of the chief contributors to the once well-known *La République des Lettres*. In 1873 he married the daughter of Westland Marston, the dramatist. This lady had a great deal of the literary talent of the family, and with her husband published in 1874 *Toyland*, a series of stories about toys. She died in 1879. Her husband's death followed, January 30, 1881.]

SUPREME SUMMER.[1]

O heart full of song in the sweet song-weather,
A voice fills each bower, a wing shakes each tree,
Come forth, O winged singer, on song's fairest feather,
And make a sweet fame of my love and of me.

---

[1] This and following extracts are by permission of the author.

The blithe world shall ever have fair loving leisure,
   And long is the summer for bird and for bee;
But too short the summer and too keen the pleasure
   Of me kissing her and of her kissing me.

Songs shall not cease of the hills and the heather;
   Songs shall not fail of the land and the sea:
But, O heart, if you sing not while we are together,
   What man shall remember my love or me?

Some million of summers hath been and not known her,
   Hath known and forgotten loves less fair than she;
But one summer knew her, and grew glad to own her,
   And made her its flower, and gave her to me.

And she and I, loving, on earth seem to sever
   Some part of the great blue from heaven each day:
I know that the heaven and the earth are for ever,
   But that which we take shall with us pass away.

And that which she gives me shall be for no lover
   In any new love-time, the world's lasting while;
The world, when it loses, shall never recover
   The gold of her hair nor the sun of her smile.

A tree grows in heaven, where no season blanches
   Or stays the new fruit through the long golden clime;
My love reaches up, takes a fruit from its branches,
   And gives it to me to be mine for all time.

What care I for other fruits, fed with new fire,
   Plucked down by new lovers in fair future line?
The fruit that I have is the thing I desire,
   To live of and die of—the sweet she makes mine.

And she and I, loving, are king of one summer,
   And queen of one summer to gather and glean:
The world is for us what no fair future comer
   Shall find it or dream it could ever have been.

The earth, as we lie on its bosom, seems pressing
   A heart up to bear us and mix with our heart;
The blue, as we wonder, drops down a great blessing
   That soothes us and fills us and makes the tears start.

The summer is full of strange hundredth-year flowers,
   That breathe all their lives the warm air of our love,
And never shall know a love other than ours
   Till once more some phœnix-star flowers above.

The silver cloud passing is friend of our loving;
   The sea, never knowing this year from last year,
Is thick with fair words, between roaring and soughing,
   For her and me only to gather and hear.

Yea, the life that we lead now is better and sweeter,
   I think, than shall be in the world by and bye;
For those days, be they longer or fewer or fleeter,
   I will not exchange on the day that I die.

I shall die when the rose-tree about and above me
   Her red kissing mouth seems hath kissed summer through:
I shall die on the day that she ceases to love me—
   But that will not be till the day she dies too.

Then, fall on us, dead leaves of our dear roses,
   And, ruins of summer, fall on us ere long,
And hide us away where our dead year reposes;
   Let all that we leave in the world be—a song.

And, O song that I sing now while we are together,
   Go, sing to some new year of women and men,
How I and she loved in the long loving weather,
   And ask if they love on as we two loved then.

SONG.

In the long enchanted weather,
When lovers came together,
And fields were bright with blossoming,
   And hearts were light with song;

When the poet lay for hours
In a dream among the flowers,
And heard a soft voice murmuring
   His love's name all day long;

Or for hours stood beholding
The summer time unfolding
Its casket of rich jewelries,
   And boundless wealth outpoured;

Saw the precious-looking roses
Its glowing hand uncloses,
The pearls of dew and emeralds
   Spread over grass and sward;

When he heard besides the singing,
Mysterious voices ringing
With clear unearthly ecstasies
   Through earth and sky and air;

Then he wondered for whose pleasure
Some king made all that treasure—
That bauble of the universe,
   At whose feet it was laid:

Yea, for what celestial leman,
Bright saint or crownèd demon,

Chimed all the tender harmonies
  Of that rich serenade.

But his heart constrained him, sinking
Back to its sweetest thinking,
His lady all to celebrate
  And tell her beauty's worth;

And he sought at length what tender
Love-verses he should send her:
Oh, the love within him overflowed,
  And seemed to fill the earth!

So he took, in his emotion,
A murmur from the ocean;
He took a plaintive whispering
  Of sadness from the wind;

And a piteous way of sighing
From the leaves when they were dying,
And the music of the nightingales
  With all his own combined;

Yea, he stole indeed some phrases
Of mystic hymns of praises,
The heaven itself is perfecting
  Out of the earthly things;

And with these he did so fashion
The poem of his passion,
The lady still is listening,
  And still the poet sings!

SONG.

Has summer come without the rose,
  Or left the bird behind?
Is the blue changed above thee,
  O world! or am I blind?
Will you change every flower that grows,
  Or only change this spot,
Where she who said, I love thee,
  Now says, I love thee not?

The skies seemed true above thee,
  The rose true on the tree;
The bird seemed true the summer through,
  But all proved false to me.
World! is there one good thing in you,
  Life, love, or death—or what?
Since lips that sang, I love thee,
  Have said, I love thee not?

I think the sun's kiss will scarce fall
  Into one flower's gold cup;
I think the bird will miss me,
  And give the summer up.
O sweet place! desolate in tall
  Wild grass, have you forgot

How her lips loved to kiss me,
  Now that they kiss me not?

Be false or fair above me,
  Come back with any face,
Summer!—do I care what you do?
  You cannot change one place—
The grass, the leaves, the earth, the dew,
  The grave I make the spot—
Here, where she used to love me,
  Here, where she loves me not.

THE FOUNTAIN OF TEARS.

If you go over desert and mountain,
  Far into the country of sorrow,
  To-day and to-night and to-morrow,
And maybe for months and for years;
  You shall come, with a heart that is bursting
  For trouble and toiling and thirsting,
You shall certainly come to the fountain
  At length,—To the Fountain of Tears.

Very peaceful the place is, and solely
  For piteous lamenting and sighing,
  And those who come living or dying
Alike from their hopes and their fears;
  Full of cypress-like shadows the place is,
  And statues that cover their faces:
But out of the gloom springs the holy
  And beautiful Fountain of Tears.

And it flows and it flows with a motion
  So gentle and lovely and listless,
  And murmurs a tune so resistless
To him who hath suffered and hears—
  You shall surely—without a word spoken,
  Kneel down there and know your heart broken,
And yield to the long curb'd emotion
  That day by the Fountain of Tears.

For it grows and it grows, as though leaping
  Up higher the more one is thinking;
  And ever its tunes go on sinking
More poignantly into the ears:
  Yea, so blessèd and good seems that fountain,
  Reached after dry desert and mountain,
You shall fall down at length in your weeping
  And bathe your sad face in the tears.

Then, alas! while you lie there a season,
  And sob between living and dying,
  And give up the land you were trying
To find mid your hopes and your fears;
  —O the world shall come up and pass o'er you;
  Strong men shall not stay to care for you,
Nor wonder indeed for what reason
  Your way should seem harder than theirs.

But perhaps, while you lie, never lifting
   Your cheek from the wet leaves it presses,
  Nor caring to raise your wet tresses
And look how the cold world appears,—
   O perhaps the mere silences round you—
  All things in that place grief hath found you,
Yea, e'en to the clouds o'er you drifting,
May soothe you somewhat through your tears.

You may feel, when a falling leaf brushes
   Your face, as though some one had kissed you;
  Or think at least some one who missed you
Hath sent you a thought,—if that cheers;
   Or a bird's little song, faint and broken,
  May pass for a tender word spoken:
—Enough, while around you there rushes
That life-drowning torrent of tears.

And the tears shall flow faster and faster,
   Brim over, and baffle resistance,
  And roll down bleared roads to each distance
Of past desolation and years;
   Till they cover the place of each sorrow,
  And leave you no Past and no morrow:
For what man is able to master
And stem the great Fountain of Tears?

But the floods of the tears meet and gather;
   The sound of them all grows like thunder:
  —O into what bosom, I wonder,
Is poured the whole sorrow of years?
   For Eternity only seems keeping
  Account of the great human weeping:
May God then, the Maker and Father—
May He find a place for the tears!

HON. LEWIS WINGFIELD.

[The Hon. Lewis Wingfield was born on February 25, 1842. He was educated at Eton and Bonn, and was originally intended for the diplomatic service. He preferred, however, to adopt the stage as a profession; and having appeared in various provincial companies, made his début at the Haymarket as Laertes in *Hamlet*, and Minerva in the burlesque of *Ixion*. But he soon abandoned the stage, and entered as an art-student in the academy at Antwerp, at the same time studying surgery in the hospital of St. Elizabeth in the same city. He finished his studies in painting in Paris, under Couture, in 1870, and obtained his diploma as a surgeon. When the Franco-German war broke out he went to the German side as a medical man, and was present at the battles of Woerth and Wissembourg. He returned to Paris in time for the first siege, and was employed during those trying days as head-assistant surgeon in the American hospital, and correspondent of the *Daily Telegraph*.

Mr. Wingfield was also present during the commune and the second siege of the French metropolis, and during this period he was the special correspondent of the *Times*. Meanwhile he had not been idle with his brush; one of his pictures was bought by the French government, and hangs in the town-hall at Orleans. In 1876 Mr. Wingfield entered on a new career, publishing a novel under the title *Slippery Ground*. At the end of 1877 appeared *Lady Grizel*, a story dealing with the history of George III., which created a considerable amount of attention. Still more marked was the success of *My Lords of Strogue*—a tale dealing with Irish affairs at the period of the Union. This work has received great and deserved praise, and is marked by eloquence and high powers of graphic description. Mr. Wingfield's latest work is a novel which deals with prison life. Inspired by the idea that the books published on this subject by ex-convicts contained gross exaggerations and misrepresentations, he entered on a series of original investigations, receiving special facilities from the Home Office.]

STROGUE ABBEY.

(FROM "MY LORDS OF STROGUE."[1])

The home of the Glandores on Dublin Bay is a unique place, perched on rising ground, shaded by fine old timber. Originally an ecclesiastical establishment, it was turned into a fortress by Sir Amorey Crosbie in 1177, and has been altered and gutted, and rebuilt, with here a wing and here a bay, and there a winding staircase, or mysterious recess, to suit the whim of each succeeding owner, till it has swelled into a stunted honey-comb of meandering suites of rooms, whose geography puzzles a stranger on his first visit there.

[1] By permission of the author.

The only portions of it which remain intact are (as may be seen by the great thickness of the walls) the hall, a long, low, narrow space, panelled in black oak and ceiled in squares; the huge kitchen, where meat might be roasted for an army; and the dungeons below ground. The remaining rooms (many of them like monkish cells) are of every shape and pattern, alike only in having heavy casement frames set with diamond panes, enormous obstinate doors, which creak and moan, declining to close or open unless violently coerced, and worm-eaten floors that slope in every freak of crooked line except the normal horizontal one. Indeed, the varied levels of the bedroom floor (there is but one story) are so wildly erratic, that a visitor, who wakes for the first time in one of the pigeon-holes that open one on the other, like the alleys of a rabbit warren, clings instinctively to his bed-clothes as people do at sea, and, on second thoughts, is seized with a new panic lest the house be about to fall—an idle fear, as my lady is fond of showing; for the cyclopean rafters, that were laid in their places by the crumbled monks, are hard and black as iron, so seasoned by sea-air that they will possibly stand good so long as Ireland remains above the water. A gloomier abode than this it is scarce possible to picture; for the window-sashes are of exceeding clumsiness, the ornamentation of a ponderous flamboyancy in which all styles are twisted, without regard for canons, into curls and scrolls; and yet there is a blunt cosiness about the ensemble which seems to say, "Here at least you are safe. If Dublin Bay were full of hostile ships, the adjacent land teeming with the enemy in arms, they might batter on for ever. They might beat at our portals till the last trump should summon them to more important business, but our panels would never budge."

On approaching the Abbey by the avenue you are not aware of it—so masked is it by trees and ivy—till a sharp turn brings you upon a gravelled quadrangle, three sides of which are closed in by walls, while the fourth is marked out by a row of statues (white nymphs with pitchers), whose background is the chameleon sea. Directly facing these figures —at the opposite end of the square, that is— a short wide flight of steps, and a low terrace paved with coloured marbles, lead to the front entrance. The left side of the quadrangle is the "Young Men's Wing," sacred to whips and fishing-tackle, pierced by separate little doors for convenience on hunting mornings—two sets of separate chambers, in fact, which may be entered without passing through the hall; and above them is the armoury, a neglected museum of rusty swords and matchlocks, an eyrie of ghosts and goblins, which is never disturbed by household broom. The right side is bounded by a close-clipped ivied wall, pierced by an archway which gives access to the stables and the kennels, ended by a mouldering turret, converted long since into a water-tower.

The grand hall, low and dark as it is with sable oak and stiff limnings of dead Crosbies, occupies the whole length and width of the central portion of the house, or rather of the narrow band which joins the two side blocks together. You may learn, by looking at the time-discoloured map which hangs over its sculptured mantelpiece, that the ground-plan of the Abbey is shaped like the letter H, whose left limb forms the young men's wing, the offices, and dining-room; whose right limb is made up of my lady's bedroom, the staircase vestibule, and the reception saloons; while the grand hall, or portrait gallery, reproduces the connecting bar. Five steps, with a curiously-carved banister, lead out of the grand hall at either end; that to the left opening into the dining-room—a finely-proportioned chamber, panelled from floor to ceiling, with trophies of rusty armour breaking its sombre richness; that to the right communicating with my lady's bedroom, painted apple-green with arabesques of gold, which is chiefly remarkable for luxuriously-cushioned window-seats, from whence a fine view may be obtained of the operations in the stable-yard. The late lord used to sip his chocolate here in brocaded morning-gown and nightcap, haranguing his whipper-in and bullying the horse-boys, or tossing scraps to favourite hounds as they were trotted by for his inspection; and my lady has continued the practice through her widowhood, for it gratifies her vanity, as chatelaine, to watch the numberless grooms and lackeys, the feudal array of servants and retainers. An odd nest for a lady, no doubt; but the countess chooses to inhabit it, she says, till her son brings home a bride, for the late lord sent for Italian workmen to decorate it according to her taste, and in it she will remain till the hour for abdication shall arrive.

A second door, at right angles to my lady's, opens from the hall on to the staircase with its heraldic flight of beasts; beyond this is the chintz drawing-room, a cheery pale-tinted chamber which Doreen has taken to herself as a boudoir, although it is practically no better than a passage-room leading to the tapestried saloons. She likes it for its brightness, and because it looks out on the garden front, known as "Miss Wolfe's Plot," a little square fenced in at one end by the hall, on the further side by the dining-room, while at the other end there is a tall gilt grille of florid design, through which you may wander, if it pleases you, into the pleasaunce. This small quaint inclosure is Doreen's favourite haunt. She has laid it out with her own hands in strange devices of pebbles and clipped box, with a crazy sundial for a centre, and sits there for hours with needlework that advances not, dreaming sombrely, and sighing now and then, as her eyes travel along the cut beech hedges, smooth leafy walls, which spread inland in vistas beyond the golden gate, like the arms of some giant star-fish. These hedges are the most remarkable things about a very remarkable abode. They are each of them half-a-mile long, thirty-six feet high, and twelve feet thick, perforated at intervals by arches; and they form together a series of triangular spaces sheltered from sea-blasts, in which flourish such a wealth of roses as is a marvel to all comers.

Obese, old-fashioned roses, as big as your fist, hang in cataracts from tottering posts which once were orchard trees; large pink blossoms or bunches of small white ones, whose perfume weighs down the air; balls of glorious colour, which, when a rare breeze shakes them, shower their sweet petals in a lazy swirl upon the grass, whence Doreen gleans and harvests them for winter, with cunning condiments, in jars. From time to time the perfume varies, as the wind sets E. or W., from that of Araby the blest to one of the salt sea—a tarry, seaweedy, nautico-piratical odour, with a strong dash of brine in it, which seems wafted upward from below to remind the dwellers in the Abbey of their long line of corsair ancestors.

The most sumptuous of all the apartments is undoubtedly the tapestried saloon, nicknamed by wags my lady's presence-chamber; for there, looking out upon the roses, she loves to sit erect surrounded by ghostly Crosbies whose mighty deeds are recorded on the walls, portrayed by the most skilful hands upon miracles of Gobelin manufacture. Mr. Curran often wondered, as he played cribbage with the chatelaine, whether those deeds were fabulous; for if not, he reflected, judging the present by the past—then were the mighty grievously come down. Here was Sir Amorey alone on a spotty horse, trouncing a whole army with his doughty sword. There was Sir Teague at the head of his Kernes, making short work of the French at Agincourt. Further on, the first earl—prince of salt-water thieves, with a vanquished Desmond grimacing underneath his heel. How different were these from the present and last Glandores, whose lives were filled up to overflowing with wine and with debauchery; whose sins lacked the picturesque wickedness of these defunct seafaring murderers. Then, perceiving the countess's eye fixed on him, her crony would feel guilty for his unflattering reflections, and rapidly pursue the game; for my lady as she aged grew just the least bit garrulous, and as he loved not the aristocracy as such, it was afflicting to listen to long-winded dissertations upon the family magnificence, which he declared she invented as she went along. He was never tired though, when he could snatch a rare holiday from his professional labours, of exploring the dungeons and chimney recesses and awful holes and crannies. He it was who ferretted out the long lost secret way beneath the sea from the water-tower to Ireland's Eye; and bitterly he repented later that he had not kept that discovery to himself; for by means of it he might have brought about the vanishing of many of the proscribed, instead of—but we travel on too fast.

ENNISHOWEN.

(FROM "MY LORDS OF STROGUE.")

Shane and Doreen arrived by and by at the summit of a hill-crest, from which the northern half of the promontory lay spread like a map before them. Just below was a white speck—the village of Carndonagh—beyond, a row of lakes, tiny mirrors set in the hill-flank—on either side the jagged lines of Loughs Foyle and Swilly, varied with many a peaked headland and jutting point and shelving bay scooped out of the living rock. In front, a flat stretch on which cloud-shadows were playing hide-and-seek—a bopeep dance of subtly-chequered tones; and away still farther, looming through the mist, the bluffs of Malin Head, the extreme limit, to the north, of Ireland. As they looked the mists melted in eddying swirls of gold, unveiling an expanse of immense and lonely sea, dotted with fairy islets strewn in a ravelled fringe—the long span of the blue-green Atlantic, marked with a line of white where it seethed and moaned and lashed without ceasing against the foot of the beetling cliff.

"What a lovely spot!" Doreen exclaimed, as she sniffed the brisk breeze; "how wild—how desolate—how weirdly fair! . Not the vestige of a dwelling as far as eye can reach—except that speck below us."

Unpoetic Shane had been busy counting the wild-fowl, watching the hawks, marking the sublime slow wheeling of a pair of eagles far away in ether heavenward. At the call of his cousin he brought his thoughts down to earth, and cried out:—

"By the Hokey! a nice coast for the French to land upon. I wish them joy of it if they try. If they do we shall be in the thick of it, for look! You can just discern Glas-aitch-é—that dot in the sea, no bigger than a pin's point—between Dunaff and Malin. A fleet would have to pass close by us that was making either for Lough Swilly or Lough Foyle. But come—a canter down the hill, and we will see what we can get to eat. This sharp air gives one a plaguy appetite!"

Doreen spoke truly, for Ennishowen is weirdly fair. The atmosphere of winter gave the desolation she had passed through a special charm. The ponderous banks of rolling steel-gray clouds, which had only just been conquered by a battling sun, gave a ghastly beauty to its wildness. Dun and steel-gray, sage-green and russet-brown, with here and there a bit of genuine colour—a vivid tuft of the Osmunda fern. Such chromatic attributes were well in harmony with the intense stillness, broken only by the rustle now and then of whirring wings, or the sharp boom of the frightened bittern. But beyond Carndonagh the face of nature changed—or would have if it had been summer—for bleak elevated moorland and iron gorge vary but little with the season, whilst lower-lying districts are more privileged. During the warm months the track between Carndonagh and Malin is like a garden—an oasis of rich, damp, dewy verdure from the ever-dripping vapours of the Atlantic—an expanse of emerald mead saturated with the moisture of the ocean. Every bush and bank breaks forth in myriad flowers. Each tarn is edged with blossom, each path is tricked with glory. It is as if Persephone had here passed through the granite-bound gates of hell, and had dropped her garland at its portals. White starry water-lilies clothe the lakelets. The bells of the fuschia-hedges glow red from beneath a burden of honeysuckle and dog-roses; orange-lilies and sheets of yellow iris cast ruddy reflections into the streams, while purple heather and patches of wild heartsease vie with each other in a friendly struggle to mask the wealth of green.

Strabagy Bay cuts deep into the peninsula. A rider must skirt its edge with patience, rewarded now and again by some vision of surprise, as he finds himself at a turn in the pathway on the summit of a precipice 1200 feet above the water, or in a sheltered cove where waves of *céladon* and malachite plash upon a tawny bed. At one point, if the tide happens to be in, he must sit and await its ebb; for the only passage is by a ford across the sand, which is dangerous to the stranger at high water. Not so to the dwellers in this latitude, for they speed like monkeys along the overhanging crags, or like the waddling penguins and sea-parrots that are padding yonder crannies with the softest down from off their breasts for the behoof of a yet unborn brood.

Towards Malin Head the ground rises gradually from a shingly beach till it breaks off abruptly to seaward in a sheer wall of quartz and granite—a vast frowning face, vexed by centuries of tempest, battered by perennial storms, comforted by the clinging embrace of vegetation, red and russet heath of every shade, delicate ferns drooping from cracks and fissures, hoary lichens, velvet mosses, warm-tinted cranesbill; from out of which peeps here and there the glitter of a point of spar, a stain of metal or of clay, a sparkling vein of ore. The white-crested swell which never sleeps laps round its foot in curdled foam; for the bosom of the Atlantic is ever breathing—heaving in arterial throws below, however calm it may seem upon the surface. Away down through the crystal water you can detect the blackened base resting on a bank of weed—dense, slippery citrine hair, swinging in twilit masses slowly to and fro, as if humming to itself under the surface, of the march of time, whose hurry affects it not; for what have human cares, human soul-travail, human agony, to do with this enchanted spot, which is, as it were, just without the threshold of the world? The winter waves, which dash high above the bluffs in spray, have fretted, by a perseverance of many decades, a series of caverns half-submerged; viscous arcades, where strange winged creatures lurk that hate the light; beasts that, hanging like some villanous fruit in clusters, blink with purblind eyes at the fishes which dart in and out, fragments of the sunshine they abhor; at the invading shoals of seals, which gambol and turn in clumsy sport, with a glint of white bellies as they roll, and a shower of prismatic gems.

In June the salmon arrive in schools, led each by a solemn pioneer, who knows his own special river; and then the fisher-folk are busy. So are the seals, whose appetite is dainty. Yet the hardy storm-children of Ennishowen love the seals although they eat their fish—for their coats are warm and soft to wear; their oil gives light through the long winter evenings for weaving off stuff and net-mending. There is a superstition which accounts for their views as to the seals; for they believe them to be animated by the souls of deceased maiden-aunts. It is only fair in the inevitable equalization of earthly matter that our maiden-aunts should taste of our good things, and that we in our turn should live on theirs.

A mile from the shore—at Swilly's mouth—stands Glas-aitch-é Island, a mere rock, a hundred feet above sea-level, crowned by an antique fortress, which was modernized and rendered habitable by a caprice of the late lord. At the period which now occupies us it consisted of a dwelling rising sheer from the rock on three sides; its rough walls pierced by small windows, and topped by a watch-tower, on which was an iron beacon-basket. The fourth side looked upon a little garden, where, protected by low scrub and chronically asthmatic trees, a few flowers grew unkempt—planted there by my lady when she first visited the place as mistress. On this side, too, was a little creek which served as harbour for the boats—a great many boats of every sort and size; for the only amusement at Glas-aitch-é was boating, with a cast for a salmon or a codling now and again, and an occasional shot at a seal or cormorant.

MISS LAFFAN.

[Miss Laffan is to some extent the precursor of a new school in Irish fiction. The Irishman always witty, good-humoured, and blundering, was almost annihilated by the stern realism of Carleton, who painted him as he too often is—sad, broodiug, and amid unhappy surroundings. But Carleton wrote only of the very poor, and his realism, though sometimes unsparing enough, was usually sympathetic. Miss Laffan draws most of her pictures from the middle classes; and she cannot be accused as a rule of too much sympathy with the people she describes. Even her admirers cannot acquit her of overdrawing occasionally; for she is a satirist, and satire can rarely keep within the modesty of nature; but, on the other hand, she deserves the highest praise for the courage and the remarkable skill with which she has exposed some of the shams and the narrowness that deface the society of Ireland as of every other country. Her writings in this respect mark unquestionably a new era in Irish literature.

Her first work was *Hogan, M.P.* In this her satire is perhaps seen in its most crude, and, to some minds, most repellent form. The central figure is a loud-mouthed and insincere demagogue; and this character is sustained with great force and fidelity. An important feature of the book is the discussions that take place in the conversations between the characters on the so-called "burning questions" of Irish politics; and these discussions reveal a penetrating sense of the real issues and the genuine opinions of people that are especially remarkable in an authoress. The fault of the book is that those debates are interpolated, so to speak—and do not (as in the case say of Miss Keary's *Castle Daly*) arise naturally out of the incidents of the story. *The Hon. Miss Ferrard* is written in a milder key, and on a pleasanter theme; for it deals chiefly with the wayward loves of two Celtic natures; and there are passages descriptive of nature full of picturesqueness, and conversations and situations of deep romantic charm. *Flitters, Tutters, and the Counsellor*—from which our extracts are taken—is a work of quite a different character from any Miss Laffan had yet produced. It is a study of Arab life in Dublin, full of human pathos, and, let us hope, though intended to be relentlessly realistic, not wholly free from exaggeration. This short story is perhaps the most successful Miss Laffan has written, and fully deserves the unanimous praise which it has received. In *Christy Carew*—which is the last book the authoress has produced—she is back once again among the middle classes of Dublin, and her biting satire of some of the meannesses of metropolitan life cannot be read without much amusement and without a certain degree of sadness.]

THREE DUBLIN ARABS.

(FROM " FLITTERS, TATTERS, AND THE COUNSELLOR.")

Ladies first. Flitters, aged eleven, sucking the tail of a red herring, as a member of the weaker and gentler sex first demands our attention. She is older and doubly stronger than either Tatters or the Counsellor, who are seated beside her on the wall of the river, sharing with her the occupation of watching the operations of a mud-barge at work some dozen yards out in the water. Of the genus street Arab Flitters is a fair type. Barefooted, of course, though, were it not for the pink lining that shows now and again between her toes, one might doubt that fact—bareheaded, too, with a tangled, tufted, matted shock of hair that has never known other comb save that ten-toothed one provided by nature, and which, indeed, Flitters uses with a frequency of terrible suggestiveness.

The face consists mainly of eyes and mouth; this last-named feature is enormously wide, so wide that there seemed some foundation for a remark of the Counsellor's, made in the days of their early acquaintance before time and friendship had softened down to his unaccustomed eyes the asperities of Flitters' appearance, and which remark was to the effect that only for her ears her mouth would have gone round her head. The Counsellor was not so named without cause, for his tongue stopped at nothing. This mouth was furnished with a set of white, even teeth, which glistened when Flitters vouchsafed a smile, and gleamed like tusks when she was enraged, which she was often, for Flitters had a short temper and a very independent disposition. The eyes, close set, under overhanging, thick brows, were of a dark brown, with a lurid light in their depths. She was tall for her age, lank of limb, and active as a cat: with her tawny skin and dark eyes one might have taken her for a foreigner, were it not for the intense nationalism of the short nose and retreating chin, and the mellifluousness of the Townsend Street brogue that issued from between the white teeth.

For attire she had a *princesse robe*, a cast-off perhaps of some dweller in the fashionable squares. This garment was very short in front, and disproportionately long behind, and had a bagginess as to waist and chest that suggested an arbitrary curtailment of the skirt. Viewed from a distance it seemed to have a great many pocket-holes, but on closer inspection these resolved themselves into holes without the pockets; underneath this was another old dress, much more ancient and ragged. However, as it was summer weather, Flitters felt no inconvenience from the airiness of her attire. Indeed, to look at her now with her back against a crate of cabbages which was waiting its turn to take its place on board the Glasgow steamer, one would think she had not a care in the world. She was sitting upon one foot, the other was extended over the quay wall, and the sun shone full in her eyes, and gilded the blond curls of Tatters, who, half lying, half sitting close beside her, was musingly listening to the conversation of the Counsellor. Tatters was about six years old, small and infantine of look, but with a world of guile in his far-apart blue eyes. He could smoke and chew, drink and steal, and was altogether a finished young reprobate. He wore a funny, old jerry hat, without any brim, and with the crown pinched out, doubtless with a view to its harmonizing with the rest of his attire, the most prominent portion of which was undoubtedly the shirt. The front part of this seemed not to reach much below his breastbone; but whether to make amends for this shortcoming, or to cover deficiencies in the corduroy trousers, the hinder part hung down mid-thighs at the back. One leg of the corduroys was completely split up, and flapped loosely in front, like a lug-sail in a calm. His jacket, which was a marvel of raggedness, was buttoned up tight; and seated, hugging both his knees with his hands, he looked a wonderfully small piece of goods. He had an interesting, sweet, little face; his little black nose was prettily formed; a red cherry of a mouth showed in the surrounding dirt, and gave vent to the oaths and curses of which his speech was mainly composed in an agreeable little treble pipe.

The Counsellor, or Hoppy, for he had two names, the second derived from a personal deformity which affected his gait, was nine years old, but might have been ninety, for the *Welt-kunst* his wrinkled, pock-marked countenance portrayed. He had small, bright, black eyes, and a sharp, inquisitive nose. A keen, ready intelligence seemed to exude from every feature. He was the ruling spirit of the trio. Tatters' manner to him was undisguisedly deferential, and Flitters only maintained her individuality at the expense of a bullying ostentation of superior age and strength. They were all three orphans. Flitters' father had run off to America a year before;—her mother was dead. Tatters was a foundling, whose nurse had turned him loose on the streets when she found no more money forthcoming for his maintenance, and the Counsellor's antecedents were wrapped in complete obscurity. He sometimes alluded mistily to a grandmother living in Bull Lane; but he was one of those people who seem all-sufficient in themselves, and for whom one feels instinctively, and at the first glance, that no one could or ought to be responsible. He had on a man's coat, one tail of which had been removed—by force, plainly, for a good piece of the back had gone with it, giving him an odd look of a sparrow which a cat has clawed a pawful of feathers out of. He had on a great felt hat of the kind known as billycock, which overshadowed well his small, knowing face. He wore shoes of very doubtful fit or comfort, but still shoes, and thus distinguishing him from his companions, who, to borrow a phrase from their own picturesque dialect, were both "on the road."

It may be asked whence they received their names. Hoppy knew of none but his nickname; his grandmother's name was Cassidy, which he did not scruple to appropriate if occasion required it. Flitters remembered to have been called Eliza once, and her father's name was Byrne; but nicknames in the Arab class are more common than names, which, indeed, are practically useful only to people who have a fixed habitation—a luxury these creatures know nothing of. . .

Flitters could not read. The Counsellor possessed all the education as well as most of the brains of the party. Nevertheless, Flitters was its chief support. She sang in the streets. The Counsellor played the Jew's harp, or castanets, and sometimes sang duets with her, while Tatters stood by, looking hungry and watching for halfpence. They had other resources as well: coal-stealing along the wharfs, or sometimes sifting cinders on the waste grounds about the outskirts of the city, to sell afterwards; messages to run for workmen—a very uncertain and precarious resource, as no one ever employed them twice. Altogether, their lives were at least replete with that element so much coveted by people whose every want and comfort is supplied—to wit, excitement.

THE DEATH OF "FLITTERS."

["Flitters" has just been entertained by Mrs. Kelly, wife of Hugh Kelly, who had been a friend of her mother's, and who now remains alone kind to her of all people in the world. Flitters has left Mrs. Kelly's house, and this is what follows.]

She drew up and stopped on seeing a sudden rush of people down a side lane. Following them with her eyes, she saw two men who had just come out of a low groggery in the lane, rolling over each other in the mud, clutching and struggling for the upper hand.

A fight clearly: Flitters forgot all the world beside, flew down the lane, and in a few minutes reached the ring that was rapidly forming round the combatants.

Two great draymen, one half drunk and encumbered with his frieze coat; the other, in his shirt sleeves, wholly drunk and in a fury of rage. They staggered to their feet, striking and kicking like wild horses. Flitters was staring open-mouthed at the man in the big coat. She knew him, but she was so dazed with excitement, that, for an instant, her recollection was puzzled—Hugh Kelly. The name flashed before her in an instant—her friend's husband; and the next moment Flitters, seeing he was at a disadvantage in the fight, had thrown herself headlong between the combatants. Which of them struck her, or how it was, she alone knew; but the next moment the two men were dragged apart by the horrified bystanders, and she fell senseless, her head crashing against the stone step of the door.

Tatters and the Counsellor, meantime, had grown impatient, and had left the rendezvous to wander up and down in search of their partner. They knew the street, but not the house, and as the pair, angry and discontented, turned into it, they beheld in the centre of a crowd a stretcher borne by four policemen, and on it lying Flitters, quiet and silent as a stone.

Tatters fell back against the wall and gasped with terror, grief, and rage. What had happened? was she hurt, or had she "done anything?" To do anything that could bring them within the pale of the law meant five years in a reformatory. Magistrates are only too glad to clear the streets of such creatures, knowing that, however costly the reformatory system may be, it is a saving in the long run. But the recipients of the bounty are rarely in accord with this opinion; and if Flitters was to be "quodded" for that period, it meant starvation to Tatters at least. The Counsellor might be able to make out a living for himself, but Tatters would inevitably be reduced to breaking a lamp or demanding alms of a poor-law guardian, either a preparatory step to following his friend.

The Counsellor, meantime, uttered a wide-mouthed howl, and flinging himself into the throng, proclaimed himself her brother, and demanded at large the history of the calamity. From twenty voices he heard twenty stories, each widely differing from the others. This much at least he knew, she was being carried to the hospital; and the two draymen who had "killed" her were in custody.

He rushed back to Tatters, whom he found now the centre of a group of sympathizing women, who were bidding him not to cry, and trying to obtain his address from him. Tatters, in all his grief, did not for an instant lose his self-possession, or forget his mendacity, and was in the middle of a pathetic family history when the Counsellor arrived.

"Who hot her?" he sobbed.

"'Twas Hugh Kelly: no, 'twas Slattery," replied another; "bud when she comes to she'll 'dentify him, if so be sh's raelly kilt. Don' ye remember when Bill Casey got six months for murderin his mother-in-law wid the poker; he an' his brother was in it, an' they were both had up to hospital for the old wan to choose which done it. She'll have to 'dentify Kelly whenever she comes to."

The Counsellor listened so far, his sharp ears selecting all the salient points out of the babel, for everybody had rushed out into the street to enjoy the excitement. Then he seized Tatters, and started with him in pursuit of the cortége.

They followed it to the hospital, and waited until nearly seven o'clock to hear the report of the doctors.

. . . .

Two o'clock was the hour at which the poor senseless body was to recover its understanding and human intelligence. Long before even mid-day Tatters and the Counsellor might have been seen skulking about the precincts of the hospital. They saw a pale, sickly woman, with a tiny infant in her arms, go up the huge granite steps of the door, and beg in vain for admittance. After a short interview with the portress sister she crept away again, sobbing despairingly.

Perhaps it was as well for Hugh Kelly's wife that the Counsellor did not guess her bootless errand.

It was a beautiful day. A hot sun beat on the roofs, the granite steps of the great portico glistened with a dazzling sheen, and the huge plate-glass windows were wide open, like so many mouths gasping for air.

Tatters and the Counsellor went down a back lane—the same where the former had changed his toilette the preceding day, and lay down to pass the anxious hours as best they could.

The Counsellor's expedition in search of evidence had been absolutely useless. No one had seen the blow. Some were positive it was Slattery; others equally positive it was Hugh Kelly's foot that had given the fatal kick. His only hope lay now in the chance of Flitters being able to identify the criminal. He lay quite still, biting his fingers, and fidgeting with impatience for the hour of admittance to chime on the steeple clock near by. Tatters was quieter; he had made up his mind for the worst, and lay still in the sun-heat, mechanically tracing figures in the soft white dust of the path, or plucking idly at the blades of grass that struggled for a dusty existence in the stone-bordering beside him.

One o'clock struck; but the Counsellor was so busy counting the chimes that preceded the hour-stroke, that he did not see a cab roll by, with a policeman seated on the box, and two more inside in company with two big rough-coated men. An outside car followed, with some men in plain clothes seated on it.

They all passed up the great, white, hot steps, and through the door into a wide long hall, so cool, so clean, and fragrant of flowers, that it felt like heaven itself after the sweltering heat and dust without. They stood still, waiting for orders. The prisoners, stunned and soddened-looking, hardly raised their eyes from the tesselated floor. At last a timid, pretty nun appeared, and, drooping her eyes, murmured something to one of the men in plain clothes, at which the whole troop set themselves in motion, and followed her up a great carved oak staircase through fresh wide halls with deep windows full of cool green ferns, into a ward where, on one white bed among many others, some tenanted, some empty, lay Flitters, her dark eyes half closed, and her wild hair streaming back on the snowy pillow.

The sun-stained face had been sponged with vinegar and water, and looked strangely colourless and pinched. The dark violet circles round the eyes and mouth were most significant of all. The reverend mother stood with a grave, anxious face at the head of the bed; and, as the men in plain clothes prepared their writing materials, the beads of her great rosary slipped through her fingers one by one.

She knew well what the identification meant—starvation and ruin to the man's wife and little children.

Flitters, dying, half dead as she was, knew this too. She could see the figures going and coming against the white painted wall before her; she could hear drowsily the sounds of life and stir without in the air that streamed through the open casements, and now and again black spots, like flies, passed before her eyes. She knew Hugh Kelly had struck her, and that he was there waiting for her to say so, in order to be marched back to prison till the assizes came on; and his wife, her friend, and the tiny baby that had lain in her lap the day before, were to starve. Flitters curled her lip at the idea.

Then Slattery, a big black-headed, burly man, was made to stand up before the bed, with his hat on as he had it when the offence was committed. The usual questions were put. Flitters answered clearly, "No, that was not the man." With a sigh of relief, and a look of thankfulness, he moved to one side, and Hugh Kelly, with every trace of colour faded from his red face, and with lips that trembled, though he bit them, tried to make his eyes meet the great burning light of Flitters', as she stared resolutely at him.

"No!" she said, in an emphatic, though broken tone, "that's not him, either."

Every one started, and, most of all, Hugh Kelly himself. Flitters repeated in a fainter voice, what she had said. Positively sure, on her oath, and all the rest of it. She knew she was dying, and didn't care; he never laid a finger on her.

Then she broke down, and could say no more. Her eyes closed, and she seemed to fall back into the stupor from which she had been just roused. Further questioning was declared to be as impossible as it was useless, and, baffled and wondering, the ministers of justice withdrew.

They gave her some restoratives, and, after a while, she sank into a restless stupor.

As soon as two chimed, the impatient Counsellor jumped up, and taking Tatters by the hand, presented himself at the door. They were put into the waiting-room; after an hour's impatient detention there the door opened and admitted the reverend mother.

She led the way through the vast painted halls up the carved staircase, past niches whence great white statues held out hands that expressed pity or benediction; windows filled with cool green ferns, or bright, sweet-smelling flowers, through the open sashes of which currents of warm balmy air came pouring in. They stepped on soft, thick matting, or polished slippery oak. Everything seemed large and magnificent to their unaccustomed eyes, and the Mother Superior's black trailing cloak gave her the proportions of a goddess.

At last they reached Flitters' bedside; two nuns were beside her, and held up the pillow which the child's head rested on, that she might breathe more easily, for she was gasping pitifully now. Her eyes rested a moment on the faces of her partners, and she signed Tatters to draw nearer to her. He obeyed, passing up the side of the bed opposite to that where the two sisters were. He was crying, and laid his grubby little hand on hers.

The Counsellor pushed rapidly behind him. "Flitters," he said, "did ye 'dentify Hugh Kelly, eh?"

Flitters did not reply; she was looking beseechingly at the reverend mother; she, wondering and compassionating, took the place of the other nuns, who moved away down to the foot-rail of the bed, and bent her handsome, kind face over the dying form.

Flitters held out her hand, holding that of Tatters in it, and looked again from him to the Mother Superior's face.

She now understood, and, with tears in her eyes, took the dirty little paw from Flitters.

"Don't fear, my poor child, I will take care of him, and God, who cares for the desolate——"

Flitters' face seemed to lighten for an instant, somehow, and she turned her deep eyes to the Counsellor.

"D'ye hear me?" he repeated; "did ye 'dentify him, Hugh Kelly, ye know?"

He spoke in a loud, quick voice, for he saw that all light and understanding was fast fading from her face.

She heard him, though. The great eyes opened wide once more, and met the Counsellor's with all the old light and fire glowing in their depths. With a supreme effort she caught back, as it were, one fleeting breath.

"Ye lie," she gasped, "he nev—er laid a finger"——

The word died upon her lips; and, as it did, the fierce, defiant look faded from her face into a gentle smile, that remained there when the nun's white hands had closed the eyes for ever.

EDWARD DOWDEN.

[Edward Dowden was born in Cork, on May 3, 1843. He entered Trinity College in 1859. During his undergraduate career he chiefly devoted his attention to the study of mental science, and obtained the highest collegiate distinctions attainable in this subject. His fellow-students gave the perhaps not less valuable testimony to his mastery of this branch of study by electing him president of the University Philosophical Society twice in succession. In 1867 he became professor of English literature.

Mr. Dowden has been a frequent contributor to all the high-class magazines: the *Contemporary*, *Fortnightly*, *Westminster*, *Fraser*, and *Cornhill*. His first work was published in 1875—*Shakspere, his Mind and Art, a Critical Study*. This is a very remarkable contribution to the literature of the great English dramatist, and has already taken rank among the standard works on the subject. It is now in its fourth edition, and has been translated into German and Russian. A volume of *Poems*, which appeared in 1876, was received with great favour by the leading critical journals, and has passed that Rubicon of poets—a second edition. *Studies in Literature* (1875) contained a number of suggestive criticisms on the chief literary masters of our time—the most remarkable perhaps being that on George Eliot. Mr. Dowden has, besides, contributed a *Shakspere Primer* to the "Literature Primers" edited by the well-known historian Mr. J. R. Green, and he was chosen to contribute *Southey* to the series of "English Men of Letters," in course of publication under the guidance of Mr. John Morley.]

THE GROWTH OF SHAKSPERE'S MIND AND ART.[1]

Now we proceed to observe, in some few of its stages of progress, the growth of that organism. Shakspere in 1590, Shakspere in 1600, and Shakspere in 1610, was one and the same living entity; but the adolescent Shakspere differed from the adult, and again from Shakspere in the supremacy of his ripened manhood, as much as the slender stem, graceful and pliant, spreading its first leaves to the sunshine of May, differs from the moving expanse of greenery visible a century later, which is hard to comprehend and probe with the eye in its infinite details, multitudinous and yet one, receiving through its sensitive surfaces the gifts of light and dew, of noonday and of night, grasping the earth with inextricable living knots, not unpossessed of haunts of shadow and secrecy, instinct with ample mysterious murmurs,—the tree which has a history, and bears in wrinkled bark and wrenched bough memorials of time and change, of hardship, and drought, and storm. The poet Gray in a well-known passage invented a piece of beautiful mythology, according to which the infant Shakspere is represented as receiving gifts from the great Dispensatress:—

"Far from the sun and summer gale
In thy green lap was Nature's darling laid,
What time, where lucid Avon strayed,
To him the mighty mother did unveil
Her awful face; the dauntless child
Stretched forth his little arms and smiled;
This pencil take, she said, whose colours clear
Richly paint the vernal year,
Thine too these golden keys, immortal Boy!
This can unlock the gates of Joy,
Of Horror that, and thrilling Fears,
Or ope the sacred fount of sympathetic tears."

But the mighty mother, more studious of the welfare of her charge, in fact gave her gifts only as they could be used. Those keys she did not intrust to Shakspere until, by manifold experience, by consolidating of intellect, imagination, and passions, and by the growth of self-control, he had become fitted to confront the dreadful, actual presences of human anguish and of human joy.

Everything takes up its place more rightly in a spacious world, accurately observed, than in the narrow world of the mere idealist. In bare acquisition of observed fact Shakspere marvellously increased from year to year. He grew in wisdom and in knowledge (such an admission does not wrong the divinity of genius), not less but more than other men. Quite a little library exists illustrating the minute acquaintance of Shakspere with this branch of information, and with that: *The Legal Acquirements of Shakspere; Shakspere's Knowledge and Use of the Bible; Shakspere's*

[1] By permission of the author.

Delineations of Insanity; The Rural Life of Shakspere; Shakspere's Garden; The Ornithology of Shakspere; The Insects mentioned by Shakspere; and such like. Conjectural inquiry, which attempts to determine whether Shakspere was an attorney's clerk or whether he was a soldier, whether Shakspere was ever in Italy, or whether he was in Germany, or whether he was in Scotland,—inquiry such as this may lead to no very certain result with respect to the particular matter in question. But one thing which such special critical studies as these establish is the enormous receptivity of the poet. This vast and varied mass of information he assimilated and made his own. And such store of information came to Shakspere only by the way, as an addition to the more important possession of knowledge about human character and human life which forms the proper body of fact needful for dramatic art. In proportion as an animal is of great size, the masses of nutriment which he procures are large. "The Arctic whale gulps in whole shoals of acephalæ and molluscs."

But it was not alone or chiefly through mass of acquisition that Shakspere became great. He was not merely a centre for the drifting capital of knowledge. Each faculty expanded and became more energetic, while at the same time the structural arrangement of the man's whole nature became more complex and involved. His power of thought increased steadily as years went by, both in sure grasp of the known, and in brooding intensity of gaze upon the unknown. His emotions, instead of losing their energy and subtlety as youth deepened into manhood, instead of becoming dulled and crusted over by contact with the world, became (as is the case with all the greatest men and women) by contact with the world swifter and of more ample volume. As Shakspere penetrated farther and farther into the actual facts of our life, he found in those facts more to rouse and kindle and sustain the heart; he discovered more awful and mysterious darkness, and also more intense and lovelier light. And it is clearly ascertainable from his plays and poems that Shakspere's *will* grew with advancing age, beyond measure, calmer and more strong. Each formidable temptation he succeeded, before he was done with it, in subduing, at least so far as to preclude a fatal result. In the end he obtained a serene and indefeasible possession of himself. He still remained, indeed, baffled before the mystery of life and death; but he had gained vigour to cope with fate; and could "accept all things not understood." And during these years, while each faculty was augmenting its proper life, the vital play of one faculty into and through the other became more swift, subtle, and penetrating. In Shakspere's earlier writings we can observe him setting his wit to work, or his fancy to work; now he is clever and intellectual, and again he is tender and enthusiastic. But in his latter style imagination and thought, wisdom, and mirth, and charity, experience and surmise, play into and through one another, until frequently the significance of a passage becomes obscured by its manifold vitality. The murmur of an embryo thought or feeling already obscurely mingles with the murmurs of the parent life in which it is enveloped.

Now what does this extraordinary growth imply? It implies capacity for obtaining the materials of growth; in this case materials for the growth of intellect, of imagination, of the will, of the emotions.

It means, therefore, capacity of seeing many facts, of meditating, of feeling deeply, and of controlling such feeling. It implies the avoidance of injuries which interfere with growth, escape from the enemies which bring life to a sudden end, and therefore strength, and skill, and prudence in dealing with the world. It implies a power in the organism of fitting its movements to meet the numerous external co-existences and sequences. In a word, we are brought back once again to Shakspere's resolute fidelity to fact. By virtue of this his life became a success, as far as success is permitted to such a creature as man in such a world as the present.

THE SINGER.

"That was the thrush's last good-night," I thought,
And heard the soft descent of summer rain
In the drooped garden leaves; but hush! again
The perfect iterance,—freer than unsought
Odours of violets dim in woodland ways,
Deeper than coilèd waters laid a-dream
Below mossed ledges of a shadowy stream,
And faultless as blown roses in June days.
Full-throated singer! art thou thus anew
Voiceful to hear how round thyself alone
The enrichèd silence drops for thy delight
More soft than snow, more sweet than honey-dew?
Now cease: the last faint western streak is gone,
Stir not the blissful quiet of the night.

MARGARET STOKES.

[It is one among the many hopeful signs of our times that the enthusiasm for the study of Ireland's remote past, which is practically a new phenomenon in Irish literature, has passed from the ranks of men to those of women. Equally encouraging is it to see the love of archæological study pass from one generation to another.

Miss Stokes, it will be known, has a hereditary right to deal with Celtic archæology. Her father, who finds a place in vol. iii., attained, as we have said, great distinction as an Irish scholar; and his daughter has worthily pursued the same path of study. Her chief work is *Early Christian Architecture in Ireland*. This is a remarkably able book. It is written in a clear and pleasant style; the facts are skilfully grouped, and the authoress shows a complete mastery of her subject. Miss Stokes has also edited *Christian Inscriptions in the Irish Language*.]

THE NORTHMEN IN IRELAND.

(FROM "EARLY CHRISTIAN ARCHITECTURE.")

Pugin has observed in his essay on the "Revival of Christian Architecture" that "the history of architecture is the history of the world;" therefore in tracing the origin and growth of new forms in this art, we may expect to find a parallel stream in the course of events which mark the career of the race to whom it belongs. Where any decided innovation occurs in the architecture of any country, it seems probable that some revolution in its history may be found to account for the phenomenon. Hitherto the churches of Ireland, in their humble proportions and symmetrical simplicity, were the natural offspring, not only, as Dr. Petrie has beautifully expressed it, "of a religion not made for the rich, but for the poor and lowly;" they were also the result of choice and adherence to a primitive national system. Even after the introduction of the ornamental style termed Irish Romanesque, we find that there was no material departure from the simple ground-plan and small dimensions of the earlier churches of the horizontal lintel. The church-system of Ireland continued to be, as it had always been, one that entailed the erection of a number of small buildings, either grouped together as at Glendalough, or thickly scattered over the face of the country; and at the time of transition to Romanesque there was no corresponding change in the ecclesiastical system of the country.

When the group of humble dwellings which formed the monasteries and schools of Ireland is seen at the foot of the lofty tower whose masonry rarely seems to correspond in date with the buildings that surround it, and which does not, as elsewhere, seem a component and accessory part of the whole pile that formed the feudal abbey, we cannot but feel that some new condition in the history of the Irish Church must have arisen to account for the apparition of these bold and lofty structures. And here we may take up the thread of the history where we left it, at the close of the period of steady progress from the fifth to the end of the eighth century, when the language of Ireland was being developed and her schools were the most frequented in Northern Europe. In the beginning of the ninth century a new state of things was ushered in, and a change took place in the hitherto unmolested condition of the Church. Ireland became the battlefield of the first struggle between paganism and Christianity in Western Europe; and the result of the effort then made in defence of her faith is marked in the ecclesiastical architecture of the country by the apparently simultaneous erection of a number of lofty towers, rising in strength of "defence and faithfulness of watch" before the doorways of those churches most liable to be attacked. For seven centuries Christianity had steadily advanced in Western Europe. At first silent and unseen, we feel how wondrously it grew, until, in the reign of Charlemagne, it became an instrument in the hands of one whose mission was to strengthen his borders against the heathen, and to establish a Christian monarchy.

Dense as is the obscurity in which the cause of the wanderings and ravages of the Scandinavian Vikings is enveloped, yet the result of the investigations hitherto made upon the subject is, that they were in a great measure consequent on the conquests of Charlemagne in the north of Germany, and on the barrier which he thereby—as well as by the introduction of Christianity—set to their onward march. It can scarcely be attributed to accident that with the gradual strengthening of the Frankish dominion the hordes of Northmen descended on the British Islands in ever-increasing numbers. The policy of Charlemagne in his invasion of Saxony, A.D. 772, and the energy by which he succeeded in driving his enemies beyond the Elbe and to the German Ocean, were manifestly directed and intensified by religious zeal. The Saxons were still heathens, and the first attack made by the Frankish king was on the fortress of Eresbourg, where stood the temple of Irminsul, the great idol of the nation.

We read that he laid waste their temples, and their idols were broken in pieces. "He built monasteries and churches, founded bishoprics, and filled Saxony with priests and missionaries. For some years previously the countries between the Elbe, Upper Saxony, the German Ocean, and the Baltic, had been devastated by the Frankish army, the population flying into Denmark and the north, and the war of Charlemagne," writes Mr. Haliday, "was now a crusade. Its object was alike to conquer and convert. The military and religious habits were united in his camp, which was the scene of martial exercises, solemn processions, and public prayers; and the clergy who crowded round his standard participated in the objects and results of his victories." The war thus entered upon leads us to that point in the history of the Western Church when the religion of Christ is first met by a mighty revulsion arising in the mingled grandeur and gloom of all that is great and all that is false in the spirit of ancient heathenism, when the flood, driven backwards into the northern seas, first heaved its mighty volume of resistant waters, and broke in a great wave upon the Irish shore.

However it may appear from ancient authorities that for some centuries before the Scandinavians had occasionally infested the southern shores of Europe, yet in the added light that is cast by the Irish annals upon the subject we perceive that from this date their piratical incursions afford evidence not before met with of preconcerted plan and insistent energy; and these events in the reign of Charlemagne may lead us to discover what was the strong impulse that thus tended in some measure to condense and concentrate their desultory warfare. Impelled by some strong, overmastering passion, these hordes of northern warriors held on from year to year their avenging march; and such was the fury of their arms that even now, after a lapse of a thousand years, their deeds are held in appalling remembrance throughout Europe, not only in every city on the sea-shore or on the river, but even in the peasant traditions of the smallest inland village. "Wheresoever," says Mr. Laing, "this people from beyond the pale and influence of the old Roman Empire and of the later Church empire of Rome, either settled, mingled, or marauded, they have left permanent traces in society of their laws, institutions, character, and spirit. Pagan and barbarian as they were, they seemed to have carried with them something more natural, something more suitable to the social wants of man, than the laws and institutions formed under the Roman power."

But when all has been said that can be for the invigorating influence of their energy and the enkindling spark they are held to have borne with them of a free social existence, in which men might have a voice in their government and in the enactment of their laws, it must still be borne in mind that at the period when Ireland was the scene of this struggle, and indeed for two centuries later, the faith of these Northmen was idolatry, and there is no proof that they possessed the knowledge of letters. In contemplating the history of a period which left, as it did, such important traces in the ecclesiastical architecture of North-western Europe, we may pause to consider the two forms of faith that now met face to face in battle. In both these systems we find belief in the immortality of the soul, but the latter is merely based on faith in the potency for good or ill of the embodied forces of nature. "The primary characteristic of this old northland mythology," says Carlyle, is the "impersonation" and "earnest simple recognition of the workings of physical nature, as a thing wholly miraculous, stupendous, and divine"—the recognition of such forces as personal agencies, gods and demons; and in this faith the main result attained was the belief in an inexorable and inflexible destiny which it is useless trying to bend or soften, and that the one thing needful for a man was to be brave. Odin stands the central figure of this Scandinavian religion; Frigga, Faeya, and Thor attend with a number of minor deities, and throughout the whole mythology vestiges of ancient and general tradition are to be found. Oracles, divinations, auspices, presages, and lots formed parts of their system. The Christianity by which this religion was confronted may be also said to have preserved vestiges of ancient heathenism; but if we contemplate it in the only fair way to look at any form of faith—that is, as revealed to us by its representative men and through the medium of their mind—we behold it as the handmaid of original investigation and discovery. The teachers of Ireland, from the eighth to the tenth century, declared the spherical form of the earth, and the summer solstice in the northern hemispheres, while her astronomers had well-nigh anticipated the theory of Copernicus. We find these ecclesiastics upholding Greek learning and philosophic speculation, asserting the freedom of the will, even at this early date, and still clinging fast to that faith which, more than a century before, had given us the Hymn of Patrick, with its passionate and absorbing devotion to Christ; while in the fearless denunciations of sin poured forth by Columbanus and Kilian upon the rulers in whose power they lay, we see the courageous faith of men ready to lay down their lives in the cause of that moral purity which is involved in our religion.

JUSTIN McCARTHY.

[Men of letters do not often receive in Great Britain recognition in the shape of political honours. This fully accounts for the general satisfaction with which the return to parliament of a *littérateur* like Mr. McCarthy was received; but the popularity of the event was due still more to the feeling that the new member had won his way in literature by brilliant work, and that he bears his honours with the modesty of genuine ability.

Justin McCarthy was born in Cork in November, 1830. He had the advantage of an excellent education. In 1853 he went to Liverpool, which was then—perhaps owing to the fact that an Irishman was the owner of a leading paper in the city—a favourite hunting-ground of Irish journalists, and retained his connection with one of the newspapers till 1860. In that year he obtained a London engagement, being employed by the *Morning Star* as a member of its reporting staff. In the autumn of the same year he obtained another and more congenial situation on the same journal, being appointed foreign editor; and in 1864 he received further and well-merited recognition of his talents by being raised to the position of chief editor. In 1868 he resigned this post, and went to the United States. Here he found a public ready to welcome him; for he was well known, both through his own writings and as the conductor of a journal that had been unswerving in its friendship to the United States. His pen was eagerly sought for; but though he wrote a good deal, he chiefly employed himself in lecturing, and performed the remarkable feat of visiting nearly every town in the Union.

On his return to England, Mr. McCarthy was offered an engagement as a leader-writer on the *Daily News*—a position he still holds.

It will be seen from this sketch that Mr. McCarthy has had a sufficiently active life as a mere journalist; but he has found time besides to write a number of works which have made his name familiar throughout the whole English world. His first novel, *The Waterdale Neighbours*, was published in 1867. To this have succeeded *My Enemy's Daughter* (1869); *Lady Judith* (1871); *A Fair Saxon* (1873)—a work in which, we may mention *en passant*, the Anglo-Irish difficulty is discussed in a very good-tempered, and, indeed, it may be said, charming fashion, for the disputants are a beautiful Englishwoman and an Irish lover; *Linley Rochford* (1874); *Dear Lady Disdain*, (1875); *Miss Misanthrope* (1877); and *Donna Quixote* (1880). The qualities which distinguish all those works are a graceful, elegant, transparent style; keen insight into character, especially female character; and a satire which, though it can occasionally be sharp, is never absolutely cruel.

Mr. McCarthy's most successful work is in a different line from any of its predecessors. It is *A History of our own Times* (4 vols. 1879). Those volumes—written in lucid and vigorous English, free from party spirit, and abounding in picturesque description and striking portraits—have been eagerly read by all parties; and have passed through a large number of editions in a very short time. Mr. McCarthy is also the author of a volume of essays entitled *Con Amore*. Having, at the general election in 1874, refused two offers to stand for Irish constituencies, he in 1879 stood for county Longford and was returned without opposition. He was again returned for this county at the general election in 1880. His long acquaintance with politics, sound and moderate judgment, and graceful eloquence, will, it is hoped, procure for him in the House of Commons the same eminent position he enjoys in literature.]

THE AFGHAN TRAGEDY.

(FROM "A HISTORY OF OUR OWN TIMES."[1])

We conquered Dost Mahomed and dethroned him. He made a bold and brilliant, sometimes even a splendid resistance. We took Ghuznee by blowing up one of its gates with bags of powder, and thus admitting the rush of a storming party. It was defended by one of the sons of Dost Mahomed, who became our prisoner. We took Jellalabad, which was defended by Akbar Khan, another of Dost Mahomed's sons, whose name came afterwards to have a hateful sound in all English ears. As we approached Cabul, Dost Mahomed abandoned his capital and fled with a few horsemen across the Indus. Shah Soojah entered Cabul accompanied by the British officers. It was to have been a triumphal entry. The hearts of those who believed in his cause must have sunk within them when they saw how the Shah was received by the people who, Lord Auckland was assured, were so devoted to him. The city received him in sullen silence. Few of its people condescended even to turn out to see him as he passed. The vast majority stayed away and disdained even to look at him. One would have thought that the least observant eye must have seen that his throne could not last a moment longer than the time during which the strength of Britain was willing to support it. The British army, however, withdrew, leaving only a contingent of some 8000 men, besides the Shah's own hirelings, to maintain him for the present. Sir W. Macnaghten seems to have really believed that the work was done, and that Shah Soojah was as safe on his throne as Queen Victoria. He was destined to be very soon and very cruelly undeceived.

Dost Mahomed made more than one effort to regain his place. He invaded Shah Soojah's dominions, and met the combined forces of the Shah and their English ally in more than one battle. On November 2, 1840, he won the admiration of the English themselves by the brilliant stand he made against them. With his Afghan horse he drove our cavalry before him, and forced them to seek the shelter of the British guns. The native troopers would not stand against him; they fled and left their English officers, who vainly tried to rally them. In this battle of Purwandurrah victory might not unreasonably have been claimed for Dost Mahomed. He won at least his part of the battle. No tongues have praised him louder than those of English historians. But Dost Mahomed had the wisdom of a statesman as well as the genius of a soldier. He knew well that he could not hold out against the strength of England. A savage or semi-barbarous chieftain is easily puffed up by a seeming triumph over a great power, and is led to his destruction by the vain hope that he can hold out against it to the last. Dost Mahomed had no such ignorant and idle notion. Perhaps he knew well enough too that time was wholly on his side; that he had only to wait and see the sovereignty of Shah Soojah tumble into pieces. The evening after his brilliant exploit in the field Dost Mahomed rode quietly up to the quarters of Sir W. Macnaghten, met the envoy, who was returning from an evening ride, and to Macnaghten's utter amazement announced himself as Dost Mahomed, tendered to the envoy the sword that had flashed so splendidly across the field of the previous day's fight, and surrendered himself a prisoner. His sword was returned; he was treated with all honour; and a few days afterwards he was sent to India, where a residence and a revenue were assigned to him.

But the withdrawal of Dost Mahomed from the scene did nothing to secure the reign of the unfortunate Shah Soojah. The Shah was hated on his own account. He was regarded as a traitor who had sold his country to the foreigners. Insurrections began to be chronic. They were going on in the very midst of Cabul itself. Sir W. Macnaghten was warned of danger, but seemed to take no heed. Some fatal blindness appears to have suddenly fallen on the eyes of our people in Cabul. On November 2, 1841, an insurrection broke out. Sir Alexander Burnes lived in the city itself; Sir W. Macnaghten and the military commander, Major-general Elphinstone, were in cantonments at some little distance. The insurrection might have been put down in the first instance with hardly the need even of Napoleon's famous "whiff of grapeshot." But

---

[1] By permission of the author.

It was allowed to grow up without attempt at control. Sir Alexander Burnes could not be got to believe that it was anything serious even when a fanatical and furious mob were besieging his own house. The fanatics were especially bitter against Burnes, because they believed that he had been guilty of treachery. They accused him of having pretended to be the friend of Dost Mahomed, deceived him, and brought the English into the country. How entirely innocent of this charge Burnes was we all now know; but it would be idle to deny that there was much in the external aspect of events to excuse such a suspicion in the mind of an infuriated Afghan. To the last Burnes refused to believe that he was in danger. He had always been a friend to the Afghans, he said, and he could have nothing to fear. It was true. He had always been the sincere friend of the Afghans. It was his misfortune, and the heavy fault of his superiors, that he had been made to appear as an enemy of the Afghans. He had now to pay a heavy penalty for the errors and wrongdoing of others. He harangued the raging mob, and endeavoured to bring them to reason. He does not seem to have understood up to the very last moment that by reminding them that he was Alexander Burnes, their old friend, he was only giving them a new reason for demanding his life. He was murdered in the tumult. He and his brother and all those with him were hacked to pieces with Afghan knives. He was only in his thirty-seventh year when he was murdered. He was the first victim of the policy which had resolved to intervene in the affairs of Afghanistan. Fate seldom showed with more strange and bitter malice her proverbial irony than when she made him the first victim of the policy adopted in despite of his best advice and his strongest warnings.

The murder of Burnes was not a climax; it was only a beginning. The English troops were quartered in cantonments outside the city, and at some little distance from it. These cantonments were in any case of real difficulty practically indefensible. The popular monarch, the darling of his people, whom we had restored to his throne, was in the Balla Hissar, or citadel of Cabul. From the moment when the insurrection broke out he may be regarded as a prisoner or a besieged man there. He was as utterly unable to help our people as they were to help him. The whole country threw itself into insurrection against him and us. The Afghans attacked the cantonments and actually compelled the English to abandon the forts in which all our commissariat was stored. We were thus threatened with famine even if we could resist the enemy in arms. We were strangely unfortunate in our civil and military leaders. Sir W. Macnaghten was a man of high character and good purpose, but he was weak and credulous. The commander, General Elphinstone, was old, infirm, tortured by disease, broken down both in mind and body, incapable of forming a purpose of his own, or of holding to one suggested by anybody else. His second in command was a far stronger and abler man, but unhappily the two could never agree. "They were both of them," says Sir J. W. Kaye, "brave men. In any other situation, though the physical infirmities of the one, and the cankered vanity, the dogmatical perverseness of the other, might have in some measure detracted from their efficiency as military commanders, I believe they would have exhibited sufficient courage and constancy to rescue an army from utter destruction, and the British name from indelible reproach. But in the Cabul cantonments they were miserably out of place. They seem to have been sent there, by superhuman intervention, to work out the utter ruin and prostration of an unholy policy by ordinary human means." One fact must be mentioned by an English historian; one which an English historian has happily not often to record. It is certain that an officer in our service entered into negotiations for the murder of the insurgent chiefs who were our worst enemies. It is more than probable that he believed in doing so he was acting as Sir W. Macnaghten would have had him do. Sir W. Macnaghten was innocent of any complicity in such a plot, and was incapable of it. But the negotiations were opened and carried on in his name.

A new figure appeared on the scene, a dark and a fierce apparition. This was Akbar Khan, the favourite son of Dost Mahomed. He was a daring, a clever, an unscrupulous young man. From the moment when he entered Cabul he became the real leader of the insurrection against Shah Soojah and us. Macnaghten, persuaded by the military commander that the position of things was hopeless, consented to enter into negotiations with Akbar Khan. Before the arrival of the latter the chiefs of the insurrection had offered us terms which made the ears of our envoy tingle. Such terms had not often been even suggested to British soldiers before. They were simply unconditional surrender. Macnaghten indignantly rejected them. Everything went wrong with him, however. We were beaten again and again by the Afghans. Our officers never faltered in their duty; but the melancholy truth has to be told that the men, most of whom were Asiatics, at last began to lose heart and would not fight the enemy. So the envoy was compelled to enter into terms with Akbar Khan and the other chiefs. Akbar Khan received him at first with contemptuous insolence—as a haughty conqueror receives some ignoble and humiliated adversary. It was agreed that the British troops should quit Afghanistan at once; that Dost Mahomed and his family should be sent back to Afghanistan; that on his return the unfortunate Shah Soojah should be allowed to take himself off to India or where he would; and that some British officers should be left at Cabul as hostages for the fulfilment of the conditions.

The evacuation did not take place at once, although the fierce winter was setting in, and the snow was falling heavily, ominously. Macnaghten seems to have had still some lingering hopes that something would turn up to relieve him from the shame of quitting the country; and it must be owned that he does not seem to have had any intention of carrying out the terms of the agreement if by any chance he could escape from them. On both sides there were dallyings and delays. At last Akbar Khan made a new and startling proposition to our envoy. It was that they two should enter into a secret treaty, should unite their arms against the other chiefs, and should keep Shah Soojah on the throne as nominal king, with Akbar Khan as his vizier. Macnaghten caught at the proposals. He had entered into terms of negotiation with the Afghan chiefs together; he now consented to enter into a secret treaty with one of the chiefs to turn their joint arms against the others. It would be idle and shameful to attempt to defend such a policy. We can only excuse it by considering the terrible circumstances of Macnaghten's position; the manner in which his nerves and moral fibre had been shaken and shattered by calamities; and his doubts whether he could place any reliance on the promises of the chiefs. He had apparently sunk into that condition of mind which Macaulay tells us that Clive adopted so readily in his dealings with Asiatics, and under the influence of which men, naturally honourable and high-minded, come to believe that it is right to act treacherously with those whom we believe to be treacherous. All this is but excuse, and rather poor excuse. When it has all been said and thought of, we must still be glad to believe that there are not many Englishmen who would, under any circumstances, have consented even to give a hearing to the proposals of Akbar Khan.

Whatever Macnaghten's error, it was dearly expiated. He went out at noon next day to confer with Akbar Khan on the banks of the neighbouring river. Three of his officers were with him. Akbar Khan was ominously surrounded by friends and retainers. These kept pressing round the unfortunate envoy. Some remonstrance was made by one of the English officers, but Akbar Khan said it was of no consequence, as they were all in the secret. Not many words were spoken; the expected conference had hardly begun when a signal was given or an order issued by Akbar Khan, and the envoy and the officers were suddenly seized from behind. A scene of wild confusion followed, in which hardly anything is clear and certain but the one most horrible incident. The envoy struggled with Akbar Khan, who had himself seized Macnaghten; Akbar Khan drew from his belt one of a pair of pistols which Macnaghten had presented to him a short time before, and shot him through the body. The fanatics who were crowding round hacked the body to pieces with their knives. Of the three officers one was killed on the spot; the other two were forced to mount Afghan horses and carried away as prisoners.

At first this horrid deed of treachery and blood shows like that to which Clearchus and his companions, the chiefs of the famous ten thousand Greeks, fell victims at the hands of Tissaphernes, the Persian satrap. But it seems certain that the treachery of Akbar, base as it was, did not contemplate more than the seizure of the envoy and his officers. There were jealousies and disputes among the chiefs of the insurrection. One of them in especial had got his mind filled with the conviction, inspired no doubt by the unfortunate and unparalleled negotiation already mentioned, that the envoy had offered a price for his head. Akbar Khan was accused by him of being a secret friend of the envoy and the English. Akbar Khan's father was a captive in the hands of the English, and it may have been thought that on his account and for personal purposes Akbar was favouring the envoy and even intriguing with him. Akbar offered to prove his sincerity by making the envoy a captive and handing him over to the chiefs. This was the treacherous plot which he strove to carry out by entering into the secret negotiations with the easily-deluded envoy. On the fatal day the latter resisted and struggled; Akbar Khan heard a cry of alarm that the English soldiers were coming out of cantonments to rescue the envoy; and, wild with passion, he suddenly drew his pistol and fired. This was the statement made again and again by Akbar Khan himself. It does not seem an improbable explanation for what otherwise looks a murder as stupid and purposeless as it was brutal. The explanation does not much relieve the darkness of Akbar Khan's character. It is given here as history, not as exculpation. There is not the slightest reason to suppose that Akbar Khan would have shrunk from any treachery or any cruelty which served his purpose. His own explanation of his purpose in this instance shows a degree of treachery which could hardly be surpassed even in the East. But it is well to bear in mind that the suspicion of perfidy under which the English envoy laboured, and which was the main impulse of Akbar Khan's movement, had evidence enough to support it in the eyes of suspicious enemies; and that poor Macnaghten would not have been murdered had he not consented to meet Akbar Khan and treat with him on a proposition to which an English official should never have listened.

A terrible agony of suspense followed among the little English force in the cantonments. The military chiefs afterwards stated that they did not know until the following day that any calamity had befallen the envoy. But a keen suspicion ran through the cantonments that some fearful deed had been done. No step was taken to avenge the death of Macnaghten even when it became known that his hacked and mangled body had been exhibited in triumph all through the streets and bazaars of Cabul. A paralysis seemed to have fallen over the councils of our military chiefs. On December 24, 1841, came a letter from one of the officers seized by Akbar Khan, accompanying proposals for a treaty from the Afghan chiefs. It is hard now to understand how any English officers could have consented to enter into terms with the murderers of Macnaghten before his mangled body could well have ceased to bleed. It is strange that it did not occur to most of them that there was an alternative; that they were not ordered by fate to accept whatever the conquerors chose to offer. We can all see the difficulty of their position. General Elphinstone and his second in command, Brigadier Shelton, were convinced that it would be equally impossible to stay where they were or to cut their way through the Afghans. But it might have occurred to many that they were nevertheless not bound to treat with the Afghans. They might have remembered the famous answer of the father in Corneille's immortal drama, who is asked what his son could have done but yield in the face of such odds, and exclaims in generous passion that he could have died. One English officer of mark did counsel his superiors in this spirit. This was Major Eldred Pottinger, whose skill and courage in the defence of Herat we have already mentioned. Pottinger was for cutting their way through all enemies and difficulties as far as they could, and then occupying the ground with their dead bodies. But his advice was hardly taken into consideration. It was determined to treat with the Afghans; and treating with the Afghans now meant accepting any terms the Afghans chose to impose on their fallen enemies. In the negotiations that went on some written documents were exchanged. One of these, drawn up by the English negotiators, contains a short sentence which we believe to be absolutely unique in the history of British dealings with armed enemies. It is an appeal to the Afghan conquerors not to be too hard upon the vanquished; not to break the bruised reed. "In friendship, kindness and consideration are necessary, not overpowering the weak with sufferings!" In friendship!—we appealed to the friendship of Macnaghten's murderers; to the friendship, in any case, of the man whose father we had dethroned and driven into exile. Not overpowering the weak with sufferings! The weak were the English! One might fancy he was reading the plaintive and piteous appeal of some forlorn and feeble tribe of helpless half-breeds for the mercy of arrogant and mastering rulers. "Suffolk's imperious tongue is stern and rough," says one in Shakespeare's pages when he is bidden to ask for consideration at the hands of captors whom he is no longer able to resist. The tongue with which the English force at Cabul addressed the Afghans was not imperious or stern or rough. It was bated, mild, and plaintive. Only the other day, it would seem, these men had blown up the gates of Ghuznee and rushed through the dense smoke and the falling ruins to attack the enemy hand to hand. Only the other day our envoy had received in surrender the bright sword of Dost

Mahomed. Now the same men who had seen these things could only plead for a little gentleness of consideration, and had no thought of resistance, and did not any longer seem to know how to die.

We accepted the terms of treaty offered to us. Nothing else could be done by men who were not prepared to adopt the advice of the heroic father in Corneille. The English were at once to take themselves out of Afghanistan, giving up all their guns except six, which they were allowed to retain for their necessary defence in their mournful journey home; they were to leave behind all the treasure, and to guarantee the payment of something additional for the safe conduct of the poor little army to Peshawur or to Jellalabad; and they were to hand over six officers as hostages for the due fulfilment of the conditions. It is of course understood that the conditions included the immediate release of Dost Mahomed and his family and their return to Afghanistan. When these should return the six hostages were to be released. Only one concession had been obtained from the conquerors. It was at first demanded that some of the married ladies should be left as hostages; but on the urgent representations of the English officers this condition was waived—at least for the moment. When the treaty was signed, the officers who had been seized when Macnaghten was murdered were released.

It is worth mentioning that these officers were not badly treated by Akbar Khan while they were in his power. On the contrary, he had to make strenuous efforts, and did make them in good faith, to save them from being murdered by bands of his fanatical followers. One of the officers has himself described the almost desperate efforts which Akbar Khan had to make to save him from the fury of the mob, who thronged thirsting for the blood of the Englishman up to the very stirrup of their young chief. "Akbar Khan," says this officer, "at length drew his sword and laid about him right manfully" in defence of his prisoner. When, however, he had got the latter into a place of safety, the impetuous young Afghan chief could not restrain a sneer at his captive and the cause his captive represented. Turning to the English officer, he said more than once, "in a tone of triumphant derision," some words such as these: "So you are the man who came here to seize my country?" It must be owned that the condition of things gave bitter meaning to the taunt, if they did not actually excuse it. At a later period of this melancholy story it is told by Lady Sale that crowds of the fanatical Ghilzyes were endeavouring to persuade Akbar Khan to slaughter all the English, and that when he tried to pacify them they said that when Burnes came into the country they entreated Akbar Khan's father to have Burnes killed, or he would go back to Hindostan, and on some future day return and bring an army with him, "to take our country from us;" and all the calamities had come upon them because Dost Mahomed would not take their advice. Akbar Khan either was or pretended to be moderate. He might indeed safely put on an air of magnanimity. His enemies were doomed. It needed no command from him to decree their destruction.

The withdrawal from Cabul began. It was the heart of a cruel winter. The English had to make their way through the awful pass of Koord Cabul. This stupendous gorge runs for some five miles between mountain ranges so narrow, lofty, and grim, that in the winter season the rays of the sun can hardly pierce its darkness even at the noontide. Down the centre dashed a precipitous mountain torrent so fiercely that the stern frost of that terrible time could not stay its course. The snow lay in masses on the ground; the rocks and stones that raised their heads above the snow in the way of the unfortunate travellers were slippery with frost. Soon the white snow began to be stained and splashed with blood. Fearful as this Koord Cabul Pass was, it was only a degree worse than the road which for two whole days the English had to traverse to reach it. The army which set out from Cabul numbered more than four thousand fighting men, of whom Europeans, it should be said, formed but a small proportion; and some twelve thousand camp-followers of all kinds. There were also many women and children. Lady Macnaghten, widow of the murdered envoy; Lady Sale, whose gallant husband was holding Jellalabad at the near end of the Khyber Pass towards the Indian frontier; Mrs. Sturt, her daughter, soon to be widowed by the death of her young husband; Mrs. Trevor and her seven children, and many other pitiable fugitives. The winter journey would have been cruel and dangerous enough in time of peace; but this journey had to be accomplished in the midst of something far worse than common war. At every step of the road, every opening of the rocks, the unhappy crowd of confused and heterogeneous fugitives were beset by bands of savage fanatics, who with their long guns and long knives were murdering all they could reach. It was all the way a confused constant battle against a guerilla enemy of the most furious and merciless temper, who were perfectly familiar with the ground, and could rush forward and retire exactly as suited their tactics. The English soldiers, weary, weak and crippled by frost, could make but a poor fight against the savage Afghans. "It was no longer," says Sir J. W. Kaye, "a retreating army; it was a rabble in chaotic flight." Men, women, and children, horses, ponies, camels, the wounded, the dying, the dead, all crowded together in almost inextricable confusion among the snow and amid the relentless enemies. "The massacre"—to quote again from Sir J. W. Kaye—"was fearful in this Koord Cabul Pass. Three thousand men are said to have fallen under the fire of the enemy, or to have dropped down paralysed and exhausted to be slaughtered by the Afghan knives. And amidst these fearful scenes of carnage, through a shower of matchlock balls, rode English ladies on horseback or in camel panniers, sometimes vainly endeavouring to keep their children beneath their eyes, and losing them in the confusion and bewilderment of the desolating march."

Was it for this, then, that our troops had been induced to capitulate? Was this the safe-conduct which the Afghan chiefs had promised in return for their accepting the ignominious conditions imposed on them? Some of the chiefs did exert themselves to their utmost to protect the unfortunate English. It is not certain what the real wish of Akbar Khan may have been. He protested that he had no power to restrain the hordes of fanatical Ghilzyes whose own immediate chiefs had not authority enough to keep them from murdering the English whenever they got a chance. The force of some few hundred horsemen whom Akbar Khan had with him were utterly incapable, he declared, of maintaining order among such a mass of infuriated and lawless savages. Akbar Khan constantly appeared on the scene during this journey of terror. At every opening or break of the long straggling flight he and his little band of followers showed themselves on the horizon; trying still to protect the English from utter ruin, as he declared; come to gloat over their misery and to see that it was surely accomplished, some of the unhappy English were ready to believe. Yet his presence was something that seemed to give a hope of protection. Akbar Khan at length startled the English by a proposal that the women and children who were with the army should be handed over to his custody to be conveyed by him in safety to Peshawur. There was nothing better to be done. The only modification of his request, or command, that could be obtained was that the husbands of the married ladies should accompany their wives. With this agreement the women and children were handed over to the care of this dreaded enemy, and Lady Macnaghten had to undergo the agony of a personal interview with the man whose own hand had killed her husband. Few scenes in poetry or romance can surely be more thrilling with emotion than such a meeting as this must have been. Akbar Khan was kindly in his language, and declared to the unhappy widow that he would give his right arm to undo, if it were possible, the deed that he had done.

The women and children and the married men whose wives were among this party were taken from the unfortunate army and placed under the care of Akbar Khan. As events turned out this proved a fortunate thing for them. But in any case it was the best thing that could be done. Not one of these women and children could have lived through the horrors of the journey which lay before the remnant of what had once been a British force. The march was resumed; new horrors set in; new heaps of corpses stained the snow; and then Akbar Khan presented himself with a fresh proposition. In the treaty made at Cabul between the English authorities and the Afghan chiefs there was an article which stipulated that "the English force at Jellalabad shall march from Peshawur before the Cabul army arrives, and shall not delay on the road." Akbar Khan was especially anxious to get rid of the little army at Jellalabad at the near end of the Khyber Pass. He desired above all things that it should be on the march home to India; either that it might be out of his way, or that he might have a chance of destroying it on its way. It was in great measure as a security for its moving that he desired to have the women and children under his care. It is not likely that he meant any harm to the women and children; it must be remembered that his father and many of the women of his family were under the control of the British government as prisoners in Hindostan. But he fancied that if he had the English women in his hands the army at Jellalabad could not refuse to obey the condition set down in the article of the treaty. Now that he had the women in his power, however, he demanded other guarantees with openly acknowledged purpose of keeping these latter until Jellalabad should have been evacuated. He demanded that General Elphinstone, the commander, with his second in command, and also one other officer, should hand themselves over to him as hostages. He promised if this were done to exert himself more than before to restrain the fanatical tribes, and also to provide the army in the Koord Cabul Pass with provisions. There was nothing for it but to submit; and the English general himself became, with the women and children, a captive in the hands of the inexorable enemy.

Then the march of the army, without a general, went on again. Soon it became the story of a general without an army; before very long there was neither general nor army. It is idle to lengthen a tale of mere horrors. The straggling remnant of an army entered the Jugdulluk Pass—a dark, steep, narrow, ascending path between crags. The miserable toilers found that the fanatical, implacable tribes had barricaded the pass. All was over. The army of Cabul was finally extinguished in that barricaded pass. It was a trap; the British were taken in it. A few more fugitives escaped from the scene of actual slaughter, and were on the road to Jellalabad, where Sale and his little army were holding their own. When they were within sixteen miles of Jellalabad the number was reduced to six. Of these six, five were killed by straggling marauders on the way. One man alone reached Jellalabad to tell the tale. Literally one man, Dr. Brydon, came to Jellalabad out of a moving host which had numbered in all some sixteen thousand when it set out on its march. The curious eye will search through history or fiction in vain for any picture more thrilling with the suggestions of an awful catastrophe than that of this solitary survivor, faint and reeling on his jaded horse, as he appeared under the walls of Jellalabad, to bear the tidings of our Thermopylæ of pain and shame.

EDMUND JOHN ARMSTRONG.

BORN 1841 — DIED 1865.

[Edmund John Armstrong was born in Dublin on the 23d July, 1841. As a child he showed remarkable precocity, and began to write poetry while still a boy. He entered Trinity College in 1859, and commenced his College career with a series of brilliant successes; but from a neglected cold and excessive physical exertion he ruptured a blood-vessel in the lung in the spring of 1860, and was obliged to betake himself for rest to the Channel Islands. His health being restored, he made a long pedestrian tour in France in 1862, during which he collected the material for *The Prisoner of Mount St. Michael*, a poem which has been highly praised by the *Edinburgh Review*, both for the treatment of the story and the remarkable ease and power of the blank verse. In the same year he returned to Dublin, and, recommencing his University studies, and entering the intellectual societies of the College, won much distinction as an essayist, and in 1864 was awarded the gold medal for composition in the Historical Society, and elected president of the Philosophical Society. In the winter of 1864, a severe congestion having attacked the lung which had been so seriously injured by the accident of 1860, he was unable to shake it off, and died on the 24th February, 1865. A selection from his poems was published in the autumn of 1865, as a memorial of him, by the Historical and Philosophical Societies and several eminent friends, and was well received by the press, and warmly praised by some of the most distinguished writers of the day. He was also the author of *Ovoca, an Idyllic Poem*, and other poetical works, a second edition of which, with his *Life and Letters*, and *Essays and Sketches*, was published in London in 1877.

A life thus brief can only be spoken of as to its promise: there can be little doubt that Armstrong, if granted greater length of days, might have attained to high poetic excellence. He had a bright fancy, keen sensibility, and, as has been said already, a command of easy and flowing blank verse which was remarkable in one so young.]

MARY OF CLORAH.[1]

In the dewy April weather,
When the tufts were on the heather
And the feathery larch was green,

---

[1] This and the following extracts are by permission of the author's representatives.

Mary, like the young Aurora,
Shone amid the woods of Clorah;
  Pride was in her stately mien.

O, her laugh was like the runnel
Bubbling in its pebbly channel
  'Mid the glistening moss and fern;
But it hushed the stock-dove sighing,
And it set the cuckoo flying,
  And it scared the lonely hern.

She was all alone, sweet Mary,
Tripping like a winsome fairy
  Through the woods at break of morn,
Laughing to herself, and singing
Rustic snatches that went ringing
  Through the glens like laughs of scorn.

When a year had fled, the weather
Was as fair, as fresh the heather,
  And the feathery larch as green;
But no pride was left in Mary,
And the laughing winsome fairy
  Was no more what she had been.

O'er her little babe her laughter
Burst in fits, but sighs came after;
  Through her mirth was breathed a sigh.
Now she kissed her infant wildly,
Now she looked upon it mildly
  Through the tears that dimmed her eye.

Then she murmured, "Baby mine,
Would my soul were calm as thine!
  Sleep, my darling little boy;
Sleep, the winds about thee moaning;
Sleep, nor heed thy mother groaning;
  Sleep, my own, my only joy.

"Ah, methinks thine eyes of blue
Are more loving, deep, and true,
  Closed beneath those silken lashes,
Than the smiling eyes that hold
My spirit with their glances bold,—
  Tempest-gleams and lightning-flashes!

"Would that I had never strayed,
Wayward, in the greenwood shade,
  Singing at the break of morn!
Those dear eyes had never dazed me,
Those sweet words had never mazed me—
  Would I never had been born!

"Then I saw him, as a dream,
Standing by the brawling stream,
  And I felt a sudden shiver
Seize me as I gazed on him—
He was fishing by the brim
  Of the roaring mountain river.

"Then he turned, and took the breath
From my breast that shook beneath
  Those steadfast eyes; he smiled, and then

I was bold, and broke the spell,
And passed on proudly . . . well, ah! well,
  I learned to love that smile again!

"Ah me, I *never* broke the spell!
My love is more than I can tell;
  It burns, it scorches . . . yet I know
This should not be: my babe, I wrong
Thy father, but I am not strong—
  Worn weaker by this hidden woe.

"I never broke my marriage vows;
Thy father is my wedded spouse;
  And if my heart be with another,
God knows I've striven, howe'er in vain,
Though baffled by the blissful pain,
  I've striven this wrongful love to smother.

"Thy sweet eyes open, baby mine;
And from their depths of violet shine
  Such lustres pure of trustful love,
I am rebuked. I dare not dwell
In fancy on the baleful spell
  That turns me false to thee, sweet dove.

"Well I love thee, little child,
Soothing with thy glances mild
  All my trouble. Thou wilt be
My help, my angel; thou wilt make
Thy father kind for thy sweet sake,
  And charm away his cruelty."

Laughing lightly, lightly sighing
O'er the babe all calmly lying
  In her arms, she showered kisses
On its tender mouth and brows;
And she felt a lover's vows
  Were not worth a mother's blisses.

Then a step within the wood
Stilled the beating of her blood,
  And she clasped her infant tight:
In a dark tempestuous mood
The man she loved before her stood,
  And her face and lips grew white.

A man of noble gait was he,
As fair a lord as you might see:
  And his frown became him well
When she rose and turned away,
And took the homeward path that lay
  Among the wild-flowers of the dell.

He strode on with passion pale,
And her limbs began to fail
  When he touched her trembling arm.
Then she uttered a low cry:
But he, "Have comfort; it is I,
  Mary; I never meant you harm.

"I loved you with all truth; my love
Is registered in Heaven above;
  I would have made you wife, I swore,

And I have never broken vows . . .
Ha! there's a sadness on your brows—
I never saw that gloom before.

"Ah me! you loved me, then? O, why
Did you not trust me? I would die
 To save those saddened eyes from tears.
Your doubts have made a young man old.
Such love as mine may not be told,
 Nor will it fade with lapse of years."

She broke in weeping, "Woe is me!
They said you died in Italy . . .
 My mother almost starved" . . . then, wild
With love and the keen agony
Of duty, sobbing bitterly,
 Fled moaning, "O my child, my child!"

Long stood he there in silent woe;
And when the sun was dipping low
 Behind the larches of the glen,
He knelt and wept—then passed away
For ever. Never from that day
 He lingered in those woods again.

A JOURNEY IN WOE.

(FROM "THE PRISONER OF MOUNT ST. MICHAEL.")

PREAMBLE.—The narrator of the following history perished on the scaffold on the morning on which he penned its closing lines. He sketched it hurriedly, under the influence of agonizing passions and still more agonizing fears, during the three days previous to his death, while awaiting the summons of the executioner in the solitude of the condemned cell. The victim of the treachery of her whom he loved, his mind is for a time wholly unable to realize her duplicity, and he would fain convince himself of her purity by believing that he is the dupe of an illusion. As the hours roll on, and as he recapitulates one by one the incidents of his history, he begins to apprehend more clearly the character of the woman who has destroyed him; and at the last, after a great struggle, he learns to pardon her, looking back upon the past as from another world, and accepting his destiny as a blessing rather than a curse. . . .

The gloomy superstitions and the peculiar habits of the Bretons have been made familiar to the public through the works of MM. de la Villemarqué and Souvestre. The prisoner, a Breton by birth, but a man of good parentage and average education, appears to have retained throughout his life the dark, romantic tone of thought which essentially distinguishes the native of Brittany even at the present day. The Breton character, with its deep passions and its habitual melancholy, its superstitious terrors and its strong religious bias, exhibits itself in his thought and actions, and gives a colour to his expressions, written down hastily in the intervals of despair and hope, which seem to have possessed him alternately during the closing hours of his life.

The woods were wrapt in midnight when I rose,
And staggered—where I knew not. Chains of lead
Pressed on my spirit, and the chill of woe
Made mute my tongue, and only a low wail,
Such sound of wordless pain as ever flows
Around the eddying darkness and the fires
Of Tophet from the spirits of the fallen,
Gushed from my lone and desolated heart.
Anon I found my wavering course had strayed,
Unguided by the broken helm of will,
To the wet strand left naked by the sea.
A dark thought seized my brain and sent its
 shock
Through all the stagnant courses of my blood.
I knew the quicksands of St. Michael's bay,
The cheating tombs that swallow up alive
So many souls—what if they sank with me,
And buried me for ever with my curse?
No trace would tell it to the prying world;
The tide of morn would wash my tracks away,
Leaving the image of the ebbing wave;
So would my memory fade from lips of men.
The impulse mastered me. I trod the beach
With clenched teeth and hands. My pulses beat
In tumult with the might of my resolve.
My feet were treading on the skirts of Death
Ere terror stayed them. God, I thank Thee now!
Thou madest my curse a blessing. Better here,
Far better here to die a felon's death
(If so be I may grasp the gift, and go
Washed white in deep repentance) than to have
 plunged
In the abyss in madness, whence to meet
Thy face in shame that cannot hide or die!
I bless Thee, Father: Thou art wise and good.

Snatched from the grave by Him who girds our
 lives
With power as the round ocean rings the lands,
I wandered through the night till the East grew
 pale
And quenched the whitening stars. Then by the
 sea
I communed with my lonely soul, and said:
"I am not weak, to offer thus my cheek
To the smiter, and then turn aside and mourn;
Nor yet so strong as to forbear revenge,
To sheathe the dagger in its silken sheath
When I might sate its hungry edge. The way
Divides in twain—to slay or to be slain.
To die—I dare not. I will rise, and turn,
And front the waste, alone with my despair;
So perish, if I perish." Wrestling thus,
A quick resolve flashed on me, blinding me—
To fly those woods to be for ever haunted
By terrible suggestions, which might swoop
Upon me, unaware, or weak with doubt,
And drive my feet to evil. Wherefore there
I bade my shores farewell.
 From day to day
I wandered, with a sense of dullest pain
Around, before, above me—like a ghost
That clings to him whose hands with guilt are red,
The vampire of his soul. Through Normandy

I wandered, aimless, hopeless, seeking rest,
Not caring much to find it. All the vales,
The bosomed vales sprinkled with buds and bells,
The snowy blossoms of the orchard-fields,
The quiet loveliness of copse and grange,
Wore a cold glare of beauty to my eyes.
I strayed amid the Valleys of the Vire
Four weary days, and revelled in my woe,
Fevering a heavy heart with drink and song—
The songs of Basselin fragrant of the vine,
Which with a fascinated zest I sung,
Draining the bowl in passionate despair,
And laughing loud and long with wassailers
Who knew not of the canker-worm within.
The contrast filled me with a fierce delight;
But soon I tasted of the bitter dregs,
And wallowed in the dust of crumbled hopes
Once more, in agony of shame. Inflamed
By self-contempt, and goaded by the sting
Of penitence, I journeyed on afoot,
Not recking whither, till I saw the spires
Of moonlit Caen piercing the starry heaven;
And there I bode three dismal nights and days,
Nursing my grief and changing words with none.

   On through the blossomed valleys wearily
I dragged my solitary way, and passed
The blue, the slumbering Seine, from bank to bank,
To the great Haven, with its crowded marts
And labour-ringing quays. The Orient
Breathed on the ocean with his panting steeds,
And the tall ships, with canvas broad unfurled,
Moved swanlike on the wave. A dull desire
To leave the sunny land, which now was dark
With my soul's gloom, possessed me, and I sailed
To the white cliffs of Albion. Isle of peace,
Thou hadst no peace for me! My memory flies
O'er that sad waste of exile; for the fields,
The dewy woods, the gardens, and the halls
Of that fair land, brought no delicious calm
To hush the tempest of my soul; but, sad
And sullen as a fallen spirit allowed
To pass within the jewelled gates of Heaven
And view the glories that no more are his,
So in the land that once I longed to know
I moved contentless. No, much dearer seems
The bleak bare coast of Erin, where I mused
Beside the deep Atlantic many days,
Dreaming of Brittany, poring on the waves,
Whose deep-voiced thunder numbed my sharper
   pain,
Scourging the bases of the crags with surf,
And sweeping the long caverns with a roll
Of booming guns. I sat from dawn till eve
Watching the grand confusion, till it sank
Into my spirit with a sense of rest,
An influence of peace from tumult born,
As light from darkness, as the calm blue heaven
From clouds of tempest, as the even pulse
From fever. Then I yearned for my own land,
And, weak and pale with suffering, viewed once
   more
Thy vines and orchards, O beloved France!

PILGRIMS.

Wild blows the tempest on their brows
   Lit by the dying sunset's fire;
While round the brave ship's keel and o'er the bows
The thundering billows break. And, as a lyre
Struck by a maniac writhes with storms of sound,
Wherein the moan of some low melody
Is crushed in that tumultuous agony
That sweeps and whirls around;
So, in the roar and hiss of the vexed sea,
And 'mid the flapping of the tattered sails,
The thousand voices of the ruthless gales
Are blended with the sigh of murmured prayer,
The long low plaint of sorrow and of care—
The sound of prayer upon the storm-blown sea,
The sound of prayer amid the thunder's roll,
'Mid the howl of the tempest, the pale-flashing
   gleam
Of the waters that coil o'er the decks black and
   riven,
While hither and thither through chink and
   through seam
The foam of the green leaping billows is driven.
A moment their forms are aglow in the flash
Of the red, lurid bolt; then the vibrating crash
Of the echoing thunder above and below
Shakes the folds of the darkness; they reel to
   and fro
From the crest to the trough of the flickering
   wave,
Where the waters are curved like the crags of a
   cave
That drip with red brine in the vapours of gold
From the doors of the sunrise in hurricane rolled.
   The sea-birds are screaming,
   The lightning is gleaming,
The billows are whirling voluminously;
   Like snakes in fierce battle
    They twist and they fold,
   Amid the loud rattle
    Of ocean and sky,
While the terrible bell of the thunder is tolled
And the fiends of the storm ride by;
Till the buffeting blast
Is hushed to a whisper at last;
And the sun in his splendour and majesty
Looks down on the deep's aerial blue;
And the soft low cry of the white scamew,
And the plash of the ripple around the keel,
Like a girl's rich laughter, lightly steal
O'er those true hearts by troubles riven;
And a song of praise goes up to Heaven.

GEORGE FRANCIS ARMSTRONG.

[Mr. G. F. Armstrong was born in Dublin county in May, 1845, and educated at Trinity College. Returning from a tour in Normandy, whither he had accompanied his brother Edmund, he gained, in 1864, the highest distinctions in English verse. In 1866 the gold medal for composition was awarded to him in the Historical Society; and in the following year his essays won the gold medal of the Philosophical Society, of which he was twice elected president. *Poems, Lyrical and Dramatic*, appeared in 1869, and in 1870 *Ugone*, a tragedy, which had been suggested by his travels and residence in Italy. In the following year he was appointed Professor of History and English Literature in Queen's College, Cork. In 1872 he was presented with the degree of M.A. in Dublin University, revisited Italy and Switzerland, and published the first part of *The Tragedy of Israel*, "King Saul," together with new editions of his former works. In 1874 appeared "King David," and in 1876 "King Solomon," the second and final parts of *The Tragedy of Israel*. In 1877 he brought out the *Life, Letters*, and *Essays* of his brother, and a new edition of the *Poems* of the latter, the first edition having appeared under his editorship in 1865.

All these works have received an equally favourable reception from the chief organs of criticism. *Ugone*—from which we quote—in particular displays a dramatic vigour, poetic passion, and pathos, which speak for the possession of the true poetic inspiration.]

UGONE'S LAST HOURS.

[The ruin of Ugone's father and the downfall of his house have been brought about by the machinations of Count Teodulfo and his natural son and *soi-disant* nephew, Count Rocco. The deaths of his father and mother have left Ugone guardian and sole support of his younger brother Francesco, a precocious but delicate boy, and his sister Cecilia, a beautiful girl just emerging from childhood. Ugone, a noble and gifted youth, who endeavours to combine the pursuit of art with the humble toil by which he is forced to earn his bread, resides from necessity chiefly at Milan, while Francesco and Cecilia live with an old domestic in a decayed villa on the shores of Lago Maggiore, which their father had contrived to buy back before his death out of the remnant of his broken fortunes. At Milan Ugone is taken by the hand by an English nobleman, to whose daughter, the lady Adelaide, he becomes affianced. Returning in high hope and joyful expectation to the villa by the lake, Ugone witnesses the blight of Francesco's noble though boyish love for the worldly-minded and fickle Marina, and finds Cecilia in the arms of Count Rocco. He restrains his anger to save his sister from more dishonour. Count Rocco manages with crafty devices to alienate him temporarily from Adelaide by causing doubts of her fidelity to be sown in his mind; and he prevails upon Cecilia to fly to him. He seduces her, and in her shame and despair she drowns herself in the lake. Ugone is present when her body is discovered; and when it is brought home he swears that he will avenge her. He finds Rocco in a wood by the lake side, pursues him, and kills him. He has been followed by Francesco (lately risen from a bed of sickness), who suspects his purpose; and, as he enters his boat to fly, Francesco jumps in along with him, and insists on accompanying him. They cross the lake to Baveno, and arrive at night at Domo D'Ossola, where the following scene opens.]

Night. A room in an Inn at Domo D'Ossola. Lightning and thunder at frequent intervals. UGONE *asleep on a couch.* FRANCESCO *sitting watching.*

Fran. Poor fallen king of men, my own Ugone,
Thou on whose shoulder I have laid my head
How many a time, when tears o'erran my face,
And the child's heart within me ached for grief,
Touched by the world's indefinite agonies,
Liest thou thus?... O, blind my eyes, great Heaven!
I cannot watch the dear belovèd face,
And think upon his ruin.... Brother, brother...
I cannot call thee "brother".. wreck of glory,
My pride that is my shame, my loathèd love,
I cling to thee as the lorn widow clings
To the dead ghastly flesh that was her lord's;
She loves the body for the soul it held,
As I thee love for thy wrecked majesty,
Though horrible as that... sleep on, sleep on.
                              (*Thunder heard.*)
... The thunder's come at last; I felt its coming.
As we drew near the village, all the road
Smelt as of sulphur—something in the soil
Drawn by the sultry air. Footsore, and weak
Nigh unto death, I longed for rain and storm.
If there be any in pursuit, he'll steal

Beyond them with the tempest. But the night
Will find not life within *my* wasted frame.
I know that death is near, so cool, so cool
My temples now, so clear, so clear mine eye.
Not far the end. If all were well with him,
I were content to perish.
  Ugone (awaking).   Air, air, air! (*Leaps up.*)
Get to thy grave!—what dost thou, with thy
    worms
Crawling about thee, *here?* Avaunt, I say.
I cannot slay a dead man . . . come not nigh! . . .
Open the door—(*Beats the door*)—open the door,
    I say!
  Fran. Help me, great God, to help him!
  Ugone.   How the light
Flashes across—broad day from blakest night,
Midday to midnight—and the thunder breaks,
Rolling athwart the mountain-peaks that leap
Livid, amid the lightnings, out of gloom!
How can the miserable spirit brook
The horror of such tempest? . . . Are you near,
Francesco?
  Fran. Ay, Ugone, I am near.
  Ugone. Speak to me, then, dear lad, for God's
    sake, speak.
The night will drive me mad. Have you slept
    since?
  Fran. Not yet, Ugone.
  Ugone.   Sleep not yet, not yet.
Watch with me, if you still can pity me.
Speak!—sing! sing! . . . have you any mirthful
    song?
Sing, lad, and mock the tempest—sing, I say.
  Fran. I cannot sing; my heart's too icy cold.
  Ugone. I bid you do it; why should you not
    obey?
  Fran. What shall I sing you?
  Ugone.   Ah, some jovial thing,
Some bacchanalian, merry, devilish song,
Such as doth trample fear, sorrow, and care.
Music can sweep the worlds from heaven, and
    frame
New heavens, new earth for us.
  Fran.   Ah me, I cannot;
There's grief in music's solace; old songs hold
Sweet childhood's days within their arms . . . *they*
    throng
All in upon me. . . . ah, the early times! . . .
Ugone, O Ugone.
  Ugone.   Horrible!
Why will you plague me still? The whole long
    day
Scarce have you spoken word to me. You sigh,
You shudder like a girl, your eyes grow moist,
You stand aloof and will not touch my flesh;
When we sat down to sup, you set your chair
Afar from me, and would not taste the bread
I served you; when you droopt upon the road,
And twice I took you on my back for help,
You would not rest your arms against my neck,

Nor lean your head to mine, but hung as dead,
Cold, frigid, loveless. Why have you come here?
  Fran. Because I love you, brother.
  Ugone.   Love me, love me? . . .
You love me, lad . . . you love me . . . love me—
    ay? . . .
O, whisper it close, close . . . you—*love* me, lad?
Just now I seemed to stand amid the worlds
Alone, cut off from God, abhorred of men . . .
It is not so; *you* love me, though God hates!
  Fran. O, I do love you. Come you near,
    Ugone.
I'll kiss your brow though blood drip o'er its
    white;
I'll kiss your cheek; I'll kiss your stained hands.
They shall not take me from you. Ay, your deed
Is my deed; nought shall separate our souls.
If you are guilty, I am guilty too;
If they slay you, me also must they slay;
If your name's black with sin, so shall be mine;
If you are thrust to Darkness, by your side
I'll enter; you shall know no loneliness;
Fire shall not sever our true brothers' hearts,
Our loves will make Hell Heaven.
  Ugone.   O, Francesco,
Let us away, away into night.
Dread you the storm without? . . . I'll not be cruel.
Sleep, take your rest until the morrow dawn.
Poor lad, I'll watch the doors with steady eye,
And none shall harm you. . . . Nay, then on
    my breast
Pillow your head, as when a little child
You nestled here. . . . O, sleep is swift to steal
Light from the weary eyes. Rest, rest, my boy.
. . . It comes; let gentle dreams come in with it.
Lie there, poor lamb.
  Fran.   I drift away, away.
I cannot watch, Ugone. Sleep doth blind
Mine eyes like dust, and stops mine ears like wool.
                        (*Sleeps.*)
  Ugone. Rest till the dawn.
        (*Lays him gently on the couch.*)
. . . Is dawn still far away?
Sleep is a hell; I'll woo it not again—
Rather annihilation than such sleep!
I'd rather hear the tempest howl like that,
And feel the lightning drench me with its fire,
Than go into the caverns of black sleep
And see such sights again. . . . Ay, howl and roar;
Though all earth's thunders break, I'll grapple
    them
Better worst truth than Fancy's hellish lies;
There's mercy in the touch of Nature's hands,
The Mind knows none. . . . *He* hears not any
    storm,
The lightnings gleam along his livid eyes
And force no wink. Man, is it well with thee?
Is thy sleep weird as mine? Have I done well
Or ill to thee? I meant nor ill nor well . . .
If thou hadst used another way with me,

I had not struck. Ay, dost thou curse me for it,
Or mock me in exultant liberty? . . .
I have read tales of those who shed men's blood,
And shuddered at their names: am I as they?
I from the world have cast a devil out—
I am no murderer! . . . I've marvelled oft
How felt the slayer, when the deed was o'er.
Even as the bride after her bridal-day,
When forth she comes and the world looks at her—
All's strange; she is abashed; she fears men's eyes;
There's a new life around her; there's a chill
Creeping of awe at mystic presences
Felt through and through her, and a silent calm
As of a sabbath's early morn when all
Labour hath rest, and skies are grey with cloud,
Though the birds sing at times, and light is mild.
So seemed it as I sped across the lake
At first, and the wind kissed me on the brows,
And as by dusty roads we walked awhile,
All silent, resting at the wayside inn
To eat and drink, and speaking yet no word.
My heart was like a soldier's after battle—
Still, sad a little, thankful, and at peace—
Till sleep o'erthrew me . . . then the fantasies,
Then the black pit of fear! . . . If this be rest,
What shall be *life?* . . . What marvel if the brain,
Finding no peace in sleep, should many times

Flatter the hand to quench it with swift death!
I will not brook another sleep like that,
Which throws its net about to drag me down . . .
Francesco, wake again! . . . Will no one come
And lay a cool pure hand across my brow?
What ailed thee, Adelaide, in all my woe,
That thou didst bring no help?—thou, false as
he! . . .
Furnace of roaring fire to left, to right,
Horror of death, torment of guilt! . . . wake,
wake! . . .
Dear human voice, O, speak to me once more!
I shall go mad in all this loneliness . . .
Francesco, wake!
  Fran. (*Awaking.*)   I think you called me,
    brother?
  Ugone. Arise! . . . my God! . . . arise . . .
    we must away . . .
Into the night, into the storm, away . . .
Tarry not . . . they are swift upon our track . . .
I stifle in this fire.
  Fran. (*Rising.*) A little sleep . . .
A little rest, my brother! Surely dawn
Is not yet come . . .
  Ugone. No more of it, no more . . .
  (*Clutches him*). On, while my purpose holds,
    O, on, Francesco!   [*Exeunt.*

STANDISH O'GRADY.

[A more intimate knowledge of the earlier Celtic legends which has been gained during the last quarter of a century, while it has inspired the poetry of Dr. Dwyer Joyce, has led to the production of a remarkable work in prose by Standish O'Grady. In his history of early Irish life, the old poems, the old traditions, the old chronicles acquire new life, and the entire story is told with an enthusiasm and poetic fervour that make the book a work *sui generis.*

Mr. O'Grady's only publications up to the present are the *History of Ireland*, vols. i. and ii. In these volumes the author purports to give a picture of the ethnic civilization of Ireland by the relation of the history of Cuculain, who flourished about the period of the incarnation, and of the other leading contemporary characters. His authorities are, besides the Annals and the Brehon laws, the immense mass of published and unpublished bardic literature dealing with that period and the heroes who then flourished.

The record of Mr. O'Grady's life is brief.

He was born in Ireland on Sept. 18th, 1846. He is the son of the Rev. Thomas O'Grady, rector of the parish of Magourney, county Cork, who was son of Lieutenant James O'Grady, second brother of Standish O'Grady, first Viscount Guillamore. He was educated at Tipperary grammar-school and Trinity College, Dublin, where he gained a classical scholarship. He was called to the Irish bar in 1873.]

FIGHT OF CUCULAIN AND FARDIA.

(FROM "HISTORY OF IRELAND."[1])

[Queen Meave at the head of an army drawn from Meath, Leinster, Connaught, and Munster, invades Ulster, the territory of the Ultonians or Red Branch Knights (Gaelicé, Crave Rue). The Ultonians, suffering from a supernatural visitation, do not resist, Cuculain alone bars her progress. Under a compact the

[1] By permission of the author.

forces of Queen Meave undertake not to cross the Avon Dia until Cuculain is subdued in single combat. After slaying many warriors he is at last confronted by an olden friend Fardia. Love for Queen Meave's daughter, and the expectation that Cuculain will retire before him voluntarily, are the inducements which lead Fardia to oppose his friend. Also he has given a promise to that effect while intoxicated at a banquet. Until he sees him Cuculain believes that Fardia is warring in Espán (Spain).]

Then a milder mood came over the mind of Cuculain, and he remembered his friends who were with Meave, and how they had received him coming, and he recalled the firm friendship of Lewy Mac Neesh, and, especially, he thought of Fardia, the son of Daman, now warring among the Clanna Goedil in Espán, and, as he thought on these things, lo! the dawn trembling through the forest, and the hoar-frost glittering on the grass.

Then started forth Cuculain, and he drew from the chariot the venison which he had cooked, and ate thereof, and drank his last draught of ale, making a gurgle in his strong, bare throat, and his strength revived in him. Nevertheless, his countenance was hollow and wan, dull were his splendid eyes, and there was a wound in his hand and in his leg and in his left side, and his noble breast was mangled, and all his body black with dried gore.

Then he tore away the iron-work from his chariot, and filled the broken centre and upper rim of his shield, strapping it tightly with the leathern reins, and with the colg that was by his side he hewed down a young fir-tree, and shore away the crackling branches, and cut off the top. After this he brake off the steel peak of the chariot, and sunk it into the rough spear tree, and bound it firmly to the wood. Then arose Cuculain, the unconquerable, striding through the forest, and he wondered which of the great champions of Meave should be brought against him that day; and when he came out into the open, he beheld the whole south country filled with a vast multitude, as it had been the Æneach of Taylteen or the great Feis of Tara when the authority of the Ard-Rie is supreme, and all the tribes of Erin gather together with their kings. But he saw not at first who was the champion that had come out against him, and he advanced through the willows, and came to the edge of the ford, and looked across, and he saw Fardia, son of Daman, of the Fir-bolgs, and Fardia looked upon Cuculain, and Cuculain looked upon Fardia.

Then Cuculain blushed, and his neck and face above, and his temples waxed fiery red, and then again paler than the white flower of the thorn, and his under jaw fell, and he stood like one stupefied; but Fardia held his shield unmoved, with his spears resting on the ground, and beneath the heavy cath-barr his brows stronger than brass.

But Cuculain sent forth a voice hoarse and untuned, and said: " Is it Fardia Mac Daman of the Fir-bolgs, for there is a mist before my eyes?"

But Fardia answered not.

Then said Cuculain: "Art thou come out to meet me in arms to-day, seeking to slay me?"

And Fardia answered sternly: "Go back, O Cuculain, to thy own people, and cease to bar the gates of the north against our host, and I shall not slay thee or dishonour thee; but if thou remainest, I shall slay thee here at the ford. Therefore, I bid thee go back into the province."

But Cuculain answered him, and his voice became like the voice of a young girl, or the accents of one seeking an alms:—" And is it thou alone of all this great host that has come out against thy friend, seeking to slay me or dishonour me. There are the battle-standards of all the warrior tribes of Erin, save only the Ultonians; the banners of the children of Ith and Heber, all the far-spreading clans of Heremon, the children of Amargin and Brega, of Donn and Biela, and the Desie of Temair; there are the warlike clans of the Fomoroh, and the remnant of the people of Partholán, the Clanna Nemedh, from the great harbour southwards, the children of Orba, the Ernai, and the Osree, the Gamaradians, and the clan Dega. Could no champion be sought out of this great host that covers the green plains of Conaul Murthemney to the limits of the furthest hills to come out against me, but that thou alone shouldest stand forth against thy friend? Persist not, O son of Daman, but retire, and I will meet three champions instead of one from this day forward. We parted with mutual gifts and with tears, why does thy spear now thirst after my blood, and why dost thou seek to dishonour me?"

And Fardia made answer: "Other champions by their prowess bear away many gifts, why should I ever have my hands empty? Bright as the sun is the brooch of Meave, which she has given me, the Royal Brooch of Cruhane, emblem of sovereignty among the Gæil. Gems glitter along the rim. Like a level sunbeam in the forest is the shining *de'g*[1] of it. I shall have honour while I live, and my clan after me shall be glorious to the end of time. Therefore prepare for battle, O son of Sualtam; I remember thee not at all, or as one whom years since I met and straight again forgot. Therefore, prepare thyself for battle, or I shall slay thee off thy guard."

And Cuculain said: "O Fardia, I believe thee not. Full well dost thou remember. Beneath the same rug we slept, and sat together at the feast, and side by side we went into the red battle. Together we consumed cities, and drave away captives. Together we practised feats of arms before the warrior-queen,[2] grieving when either got any hurt. Together we kept back the streaming foe in the day of disaster, when the battle-torrent roared over us, either guarding the other more than himself."

Then beneath his lowering brows the hot tears burst forth from the eyes of the son of Daman, and fell continuously from his beard, and he answered with a voice most stern, but that held within it a piteous tone, like a vessel in which the careless eye sees not the hidden flaw, but at a touch, lo, it is broken, so sounded the stern voice of the warrior.

"Go back now, O Cuculain, to thy pleasant Dûn—Dûn Dalgan upon the sea. Go back now, for I would not slay thee, and rule over Murthemney and the rough headland of thy sires, and Meave will not waste thy territory or injure aught that is thine. And care no more for the Red Branch, for they have forsaken thee, and given thee over to destruction, who have conspired against thee, trusting in thy great heart that thou wouldst be slain on the marches of the province, holding the gates of the north against thy foes, for Hound is thy name, and Royal Hound thy nature. Therefore go back, O Cuculain, and save thy young life; return now to thy infant son and thy sweet bride. Go back, O Cuculain, for sweet is life, the life of the warrior, and very dark and sorrowful and empty is the grave."

"I will not go back, O Fardia Mac Daman, but here on the marches, while there is blood in my veins, and while reason, like a king rebelled against but unsubdued, holds the sovereignty of my mind, shall I contest the borders of thy nation, though forsaken and alone. My people have indeed abandoned me, and conspired for my destruction; but there is no power in Erin to dissolve my knightship to the son of Nessa, and my kinship with the Crave Rue. Though they hate me, yet cannot I eject this love out of my heart. And not the kings only and the might of the Crave Rue, but the women and the young children of Ulla are under my protection, and all the unwarlike tribes, and this the sacred soil of Ulla upon which I stand. And this, too, well I know, that no power in the earth or in the air can keep the Red Branch my foe for ever, and that loud and deep will be their sorrow when the red pyre flames beneath me. And seek not to terrify me with death, O son of Daman, of yore, too, our minds did not agree, for dark and sorrowful death is not but a passage to the land of the ever young, the Tiernanóg. There shall I see the Tuatha face to face, and there the heroic sons of Milith and himself, a mighty shade, and there all the noblest of the earth. There hatred and scorn are not known, nor the rupturing of friendships, but sweet love rules over all."

"Go back, O Cuculain, go back now again, for I would not slay thee. Think no more of the son of Nessa and the Red Branch, than whom the race of Milith hath produced nought fiercer or more baleful. Rooted out and cast down shall be the Red Branch in this foray, whether thou, O Cuculain, survivest or art slain. Go back, O son of Sualtam, return to thy own Dûn. Once, indeed, thou wast obedient to me and served me, and polished my armour, and tied up my spears, submissive to my commands. Therefore go back; add not thy blood to the bloody stream."

"Revilest thou my nation, O son of Daman. Talk no more now, but prepare thyself for battle and for death. I will not obey thee or retire before thee, nor shalt thou at all dishonour me, as thou hast most foully dishonoured thyself. This, indeed, I well know, that I shall be slain at the ford when my strength has passed away, or my mind is overthrown; but by thee, O son of Daman, I shall not meet my death. Once, indeed, I was subservient to thee, because I was younger than thee. Therefore was I then as a servant unto thee, but not now; and which of us twain shall die I know, and it is thou, O Fardia, son of Daman."

Therewith then they fought, and Cuculain had no weapon save only his colg, for the gæ

---

[1] The spear of the brooch: the brooches were of great size.

[2] Skathah, queen of Skye, at whose court they resided in boyhood.

bolg, the rude spear which he had fashioned, he dropped upon the shore, and Fardia discharged his javelins at the same time, for he was ambidexter, and quick as lightning Cuculain avoided them, and they stuck trembling in the thither bank, and swift to right and left Cuculain severed the leathern thongs, rushing forward. Then drew Fardia his mighty sword, that made a flaming crescent as it flashed, most bright and terrible, and rushed headlong upon Cuculain, and they met in the midst of the ford. But straightway there arose a spray and a mist from the trampling of the heroes, and through the mist their forms moved hugely, like two giants of the Fomoroh contending in a storm. But the war-demons, too contended around them fighting, the Bocanahs and Bananahs, the wild people of the glens, and the demons of the air, and the fiercer and more bloodthirsty of the Tuatha[1] De Danan, and screeched in the clamour of the warriors, the clash of the shields and the clatter of *land* and meeting *colg*.[2] But the warriors of Meave turned pale, and the war-steeds broke loose, and flew through the plain with the war-cars, and the women and camp-followers brake forth and fled, and the upper water of the divine stream gathered together for fear, and reared itself aloft like a steed that has seen a spectre, with jags of torn water and tossing foam. But Cuculain was red all over, like a garment raised out of the dyeing-vat, and Fardia's great sword made havoc in his unarmoured flesh. Three times Cuculain closed with the Fir-bolg, seeking to get within the ponderous shield, and three times the son of Daman cast him off, as the cliffs of Eyrus cast off a foaming billow of the great sea; but when the fourth time he was rushing on like a storm, he heard as it were the voice of Læg,[3] the son of Riangowra, taunting and insulting him; and himself he saw, standing in the river ford on the left, for he was accustomed to revile Cuculain. Yet this time, too, the Fir-bolg cast him off, and advanced upon Cuculain to slay him. Then stepped back Cuculain quickly, and the men of Meave shouted, for Cuculain's shield was falling to pieces. But again rushed forward the hound of Ulla, stooping, with the gæ bolg in his hand, using it like a spearman in the battle, and he drave Fardia through the ford and upon the hither bank, pressing against the shield, but Fardia himself, too, retreated back. But when the Fir-bolgs saw what was done they feared mightily for their champion, and they raised a sudden howl of lamentation and rage, and rushed forward, breaking through the guards. Which, when Fergus Mac Roy beheld, he sprang down from his chariot, shouting dreadfully, and put his hand into the hollow of his shield, and took out his battle-stone, and smote Imchall, the son of Dega, with the battle-stone upon the head, and he fell rushing forward amongst the first. But Cormac Conlingas and Mainey Lamgarf ran thither with the queen's spearmen restraining the Fir-bolgs.

But, meantime, Cuculain lifted suddenly the gæ bolg above his head, and plunged it into Fardia; and it passed through the upper rim of the brazen shield, and through the strong bones of his breast beneath his beard, and he fell backward with a crash, and grasped with outstretched hands at the ground, and his spirit went out of him, and he died.

But Cuculain plucked out the spear and stood above him, panting, as a hound pants returning from the chase, and the war-demons passed out of him, and he looked upon Fardia, and a great sorrow overwhelmed him, and he lamented and moaned over Fardia, joining his voice to the howl of the people of Fardia, the great-hearted children of Mac Erc, and he took off the cath-barr from the head of Fardia, and unwound his yellow hair, tress after bright tress, most beautiful, shedding many tears, and he opened the battle-dress and took out the queen's brooch—that for which his friend had come to slay him—and he cursed the lifeless metal, and cast it from him into the air, southwards over the host, and men saw it no more.

MRS. J. H. RIDDELL.

[Charlotte Eliza Lawson Cowan, author of so many popular novels, is the youngest child of James Cowan of Barn Cottage, Carrickfergus, county Antrim, where she was born. At an early age she began to use her pen as a writer of fiction, and in 1858 published

---

[1] Supernatural beings.
[2] *Land*=sword; *colg*=a short dagger-like weapon.
[3] This was a vision of his absent friend and charioteer seen by the excited and distraught mind of Cuculain.

The Moors and the Fens. In 1860 *Too Much Alone* appeared, which was very favourably received by the critical press. It is a thoroughly good novel, with a well conceived and well wrought-out story; and from its ability a successful career was predicted for the writer. After this, volume succeeded volume in rapid succession, until Mrs. Riddell is now the author of about twenty different novels, the reception of which by the press and the reading public has justified the early anticipations of her success in this field of literature. In 1857 Miss Cowan married J. H. Riddell, grandson of Luke Riddell, Esq., Winson Green House, Staffordshire. Her earlier works had appeared under the pseudonym of "F. G. Trafford," but after the appearance of *George Geith of Fen Court* in 1864—a story which fully established her literary reputation, and which the *Athenæum* called an "excellent novel, powerfully and carefully written"—she has used her marital name. Besides those above mentioned, we may notice what are considered as among the best of Mrs. Riddell's works—*City and Suburb* (1861), *Maxwell Drewitt* (1865), *Phemie Keller* (1866), *Far above Rubies* (1867), *A Life's Assize* (1870) —from which we quote; *Mortomley's Estate* (1874), *Above Suspicion* (1875), and a very readable novel entitled *Her Mother's Darling* (1877). In 1867 Mrs. Riddell became co-proprietor and editor of the *St. James's Magazine*, and she has also contributed to the pages of *Once a Week* (in which appeared *The Race for Wealth*), *Illustrated London News*, *London Society*, &c. &c.]

NOT PROVEN.

(FROM "A LIFE'S ASSIZE."[1])

[Andrew Hardell, having murdered Kenneth Challerson in self-defence, has been placed on his trial for the crime in Dumfries. He has pleaded "not guilty" to the charge, and Mr. Dunbar, his counsel, has just finished his address to the jury.]

After him came the judge.

Every point in the prisoner's favour was rehearsed; every sentence repeated which could bear on his innocence; "but," added Lord Glanlorn—

"Confound him!" thought Mr. Dunbar; "there he goes again;" while the advocate-depute adjusted his wig and pulled up his gown, and smiled to himself at the sound of that ominous conjunction.

Word upon word, line upon line, the judge piled up against the prisoner. He showed how every presumption in the case went to support the idea of his guilt. They had the evidence of two witnesses to the fact of a button being missing from the prisoner's coat. There was no reason to doubt the truthfulness of Euphemia Stewart's testimony, and she distinctly swore that not merely a button was gone, but also that a piece of cloth had gone with it. The jury would bear in mind that no such rent had been discovered in any coat worn by the prisoner, but he would not have them place too much importance on this circumstance, since the question involved really was, had the prisoner three suits of tweed or only two? He had ample time and opportunity for disposing of one suit between the hour of his leaving New Abbey and that of his arrival at Kirkcudbright. He had a lonely shore; the darkness of night; the absence of any company; all in his favour. One circumstance, however, that looked like innocence, must not be overlooked, namely, that he had not changed his original route, but went straight forward to Kirkcudbright, as though no murder had been committed. On the other hand, the jury would bear in mind they had not in this case to deal with a criminal of the ordinary type, but with a highly-educated and clever man, possessed evidently of a mind capable of weighing consequences and calculating possibilities; and this consideration, also, should have considerable weight with them in deciding the exact amount of credence which they ought to attach to the evidence of the witness Anthony Hardell.

He (the judge) did not consider that witness had given his evidence in a satisfactory manner. He was evidently biassed by his friendship for the accused. He was labouring under considerable excitement, and had fenced off important questions with more cleverness than straightforwardness.

If the jury believed the bulk of the evidence which had been that day given, they could scarcely fail to arrive at the conclusion that the prisoner had first betrayed the confidence of a man who trusted too much in his honour, and then murdered that man.

Whether the blow were dealt in passion or in cool blood, whether it terminated a quarrel or were given treacherously, was not the matter for them to consider.

The real question for them to decide was whe-

---

[1] By permission of the authoress.

ther Kenneth Challerson was murdered, and, if so, whether the panel were his murderer.

And Lord Glauloru looked as though he thought the jury ought to deliver their verdict without leaving the box.

The jury, however, apparently arrived at a different conclusion, for after a little whispering among themselves, and putting together of heads, they retired to consult.

Then came a time, when, like Agag, the prisoner said to himself, "Surely the bitterness of death is past."

He knew it had all gone against him; already he seemed to be like one clean forgotten, one for whom the world's pleasures and prizes were but as the memory of a dream.

What he might have done—oh, God! what he might have done, but for this awful misfortune. He saw himself a successful preacher, a happy husband, the father of children, a respected and useful member of society—that was the might-have-been of his life—and this was the reality.

A felon's dock in a far country—with the evening shadows stealing down—not a friendly face near him, and fifteen men in an adjoining room deciding whether or not he should hang by the neck till he was dead.

He sat in the dock, with his hands clasped, and his head bowed—his eyes were so misty with tears that he could not see the scene distinctly—but he had a confused memory afterwards of observing the judges leave the bench, and perceiving the counsel break up into knots and talking with the sheriffs and such of the spectators as had seats assigned to them in the boxes near the bench.

He knew they were speaking about him. Well—well, let the future bring what it might, he thought vaguely, it could never bring an hour of such intense misery—such utter loneliness as that. He was an interesting speculation to those people, nothing more. He felt very bitter against them all—unjustly bitter, for there were many there who, even believing him guilty, pitied him exceedingly.

After a minute or two his own advocate came over to speak to him,—told him not to despair yet,—to keep up for a little while longer.

Then he too went away, and the darkness deepened. Candles were brought into court —dips that guttered down and made long wicks—and soon after the judges returned and resumed their seats, and the jury trooped back into their places, and there was a great silence for a moment.

Instinctively the prisoner rose to meet his doom. The faces of the jury looked in the fitful light, pale and stern and just—inexorably just. You might have heard a pin drop in court when, in answer to the judge's question, the foreman said—

"We find a verdict of NOT PROVEN."

Of what happened after that, Andrew Hardell had no clear recollection. He remembered that the judge said something to him, but of what nature he never could tell. He knew that one of the men who had sat guarding him allowed him to pass out on the side farthest from the trap-door through which he had ascended from the subterranean passage. He felt the cool air blowing on his forehead, and he saw a way cleared for him by the people, who closed up again and followed him out into the street.

There was only one man to wish him joy.

"Thank the Lord!" said a voice in his ear; and turning, he saw the face of the waiter from the "King's Arms."

"Take me to some place where I can be quiet," Andrew petitioned, "where nobody will know me;" and thus entreated, the man, under cover of the darkness, led him hurriedly along Buccleugh Street, and down the steps into the lane below, where not a soul was stirring.

"Ye'll be in need of something to eat," said the man, and Andrew thankfully yielded himself to such friendly guidance.

There was only a single feeling uppermost in his mind as he hurried along guided by David Johnstoun, and that was a wondering thankfulness at his deliverance.

As to the future, he was too bewildered to think of it. He was free—the trial was over —the danger past. As to the actual meaning of the verdict he had not yet quite grasped it.

He was spent, and he wanted rest. He was confused, and he needed time to collect his thoughts. He was faint, and he required food. He never could accurately remember what he felt while he walked through the twilight up the narrow streets, except that he was very glad.

He had not yet realized the nature of his hurt; it was not mortal, he knew, and that was then enough for him to comprehend.

Out of the darkness they turned into an inn of the commoner description, where, around a blazing fire, a number of men were gathered drinking and smoking.

A comely, middle-aged woman was in the act of supplying one of her customers with another "noggin" of whisky, when David beckoned and spoke to her in a low tone.

Instantly she bent her eyes on his companion with a look of curious inquiry, then, without a word, led the way up a narrow staircase and into a bed-room on the first floor.

"Ye'll be quiet enough here," she said, setting the candlestick she carried down on a small round table, and again favouring Andrew Hardell with the same look of irrepressible curiosity she had honoured him with below. "And ye wad like something till eat—what will ye please to have?"

"I will come down wi' ye and see to that," David Johnstoun hurriedly interposed. "Will ye sit, Mr. Hardell, and rest yourself a-bit?" and the pair departed from the room, leaving Andrew alone.

Then all at once there fell upon him such a sense of desolation as I might never hope to put into words; the comprehension of his position dropped down into his heart as a stone drops down into a well, troubling the waters at the bottom.—He was not innocent—he knew that; and the sentence pronounced declared as much.

Not proven—ay, not proven in law—but there was not a creature in court—not an inhabitant of Dumfries—not even the waiter from the "King's Arms," the only friend who had stopped to congratulate him—that believed he was other than guilty.

They had hurried him through the kitchen that he might not be recognized. They had brought him up to this room, not that he might physically be more comfortable, but that mentally he should escape annoyance.

He looked round the apartment, in which no fire blazed cheerfully, which was only lighted by a solitary dip, and contrasted its cold dreariness with the warmth and coziness of the kitchen below.

He glanced at the bed placed in one corner, at the chest of drawers near the door, at the small round three-legged table where the candle was guttering down and making for itself a long wick with a cross of blackness at the top of the flame; he surveyed the empty grate and the strip of matting, and then his eye, still wandering round the room, fell on the looking-glass. Moved by a sudden impulse, he took up the light, and holding it close to the mirror, beheld his own reflection.

He looked at himself with a bitter smile. He had been, if not handsome, at least well-favoured. His had been that sort of face which mothers bless as "bonnie," and women admire for its frank, fearless, honest comeliness. He had never boasted chiselled features, nor dreamy, poetic speaking eyes. He had not been beautiful as a dream. In his best days no person could have said of him that he looked as though he had stepped down from the canvas of one of the old masters to walk amongst men—but yet he had been something more than passable, and he had been young.

Now he seemed young no longer; since he stood before a free man, another sculptor than nature had taken chisel and mallet in hand to alter her work. His face was worn, his cheek hollow. There was a drawn expression about his mouth; his eyes were sunk; he had lines across his forehead; his hair was thin, and streaks of gray appeared amidst the brown; his clothes hung upon him, and the hand which held the candlestick looked, reflected in the glass, like the hand of a skeleton.

The beauty of his youth was gone, and the hope of his youth with it.

JOHN T. GILBERT.

[There are few men, even among the many laborious and brilliant Celtic scholars of the last quarter of a century, who have done more towards the elucidation of Irish history than Mr. John T. Gilbert. He has written the first book on the metropolis of Ireland which could make even a pretence to the dignity of a history; he has told the stories of the various Irish viceroys; and his republication of several old manuscripts has thrown quite a new light on some of the most important and most eagerly discussed passages in Irish annals.

Mr. Gilbert's chief work is his *History of Dublin* (3 vols. 1854-9). For this he was presented with the gold medal of the Royal Irish Academy—perhaps the highest literary honour that can be conferred by any body in Ireland. The work is full of the most interesting and varied matter. "As illustrating the wide range of subjects treated of," justly observed the president of the Academy in presenting Mr. Gilbert with the medal for his work, "under their respective localities, I may cite the account of the tribe of Mac

Gillamocholmog (vol. i. p. 230) traced through unpublished Gaelic and Anglo-Irish records from the remote origin of the family to its extinction in the fifteenth century; while, as a specimen of the work in a totally different department, I may refer to the history of Crow Street Theatre, as giving the only accurate details hitherto published of that once-noted establishment, verified by original documents never before printed, from the autograph of Richard Brinsley Sheridan and other dramatic celebrities."

The *History of the Viceroys of Ireland* (1865), like its predecessor, contains an enormous amount of fresh information. The work displays a great and even astonishing width of acquaintance with all the sources—whether printed or in MS.—of Irish history, and the author has the tact, which is not always a gift with laborious investigators, of weaving his facts into a connected and readable story. The book, dealing with the chief rulers of Ireland, really comes to be a history of the country since the Anglo-Norman invasion; and thus the work has a large historical sweep, as well as a series of most interesting studies into the characters and careers of some highly picturesque figures in the annals of Ireland.

The other labours in which Mr. Gilbert has been engaged consist principally of the re-publication of old Irish documents. In 1870 he edited *Historic and Municipal Documents of Ireland, A.D. 1172-1320*, which was published in the government series of "Chronicles and Memorials." He also superintended the production of *Facsimiles of National MSS. of Ireland*—a large folio with coloured plates, which is considered the finest publication of its class ever issued by government. A yet more important work is a *Contemporary History of Affairs in Ireland, 1641-52* (6 vols. 4to). This book brings documents to light which for the first time presents the Irish view of the momentous period of the Roman Catholic rising, and goes far towards superseding the statements hitherto current in English histories.

Mr. Gilbert, who is a native of Dublin, was secretary of the Public Record Office of Ireland till that office was abolished, when government awarded him a special pension for his services. He is at present engaged in editing for government the *National MSS. of Ireland*, and in examining and reporting on the manuscripts in collections in Ireland for the Royal Commission on Historical MS. He is a Fellow of the Society of Antiquaries of London, honorary librarian of the Royal Irish Academy, and honorary secretary of the Irish Archæological and Celtic Society for the publication of Materials for the History of Ireland.]

THE LIMITS OF THE PALE.

(FROM "HISTORY OF THE VICEROYS OF IRELAND."[1])

Before the commencement of the fifteenth century so much of the English settlement had been regained by the Irish, that even in Leinster only the four shires of Dublin, Meath, Kildare, and Louth partially acknowledged the jurisdiction of the crown of England. The great lords of the Anglo-Norman descent, as the Earls of Kildare, of Desmond, and of Ormonde, absorbed their revenues in their own districts, where they administered justice, jealously excluding the king's officials. Some of the chief branches of the Anglo-Norman families repudiated the authority of England, and confederated with the Irish; but, when it suited their ends, they asserted rights under English law, and seldom failed to obtain charters of pardon through the interest of their influential kinsmen. "These English rebels," says a viceregal despatch, "style themselves men of noble blood and idelmen, whereas, in truth, they are strong marauders." The enactments against such secessionists remained inoperative, as royal officers would not incur the perils of essaying to carry them into effect.

The "Statute of Kilkenny" was promulgated in several successive parliaments, but the settlers found the strict application of its provisions more prejudicial to themselves than the natives. The King of England was thus fain to accede to petitions in which the commonalties of his towns declared their inability to pay taxes, and that they should be ruined or famished, unless authorized to trade and make purchases from the Irish. Numerous applications were also made by the settlers for permission to send out their children to be fostered among the Irish; and we have on record the official concession to a memorial from some liege English praying that an Irish minstrel might be allowed to sojourn among them, notwithstanding the express prohibition under the "Statute of Kilkenny." Governmental licenses were also frequently issued for holding parleys with the Irish. These negotia-

---

[1] By permission of the author.

tions were usually held on the borders, the respective parties coming to the appointed place with a few attendants, while their troops were drawn up within call. The borders formed the resort of bodies of mercenary native light-armed foot soldiery, styled "kerns" and battle-axe men, called *gallocclach*, or *galloglasses*, who, living by war, were ever ready to accept service from either Irish or colonists who secured them payment and maintenance. Beyond the wasted and desolated "marches," or borders, lay the Irish territories, almost inaccessible through woods and narrow defiles, rendered impassable with peculiar art in times of war. Within these and other defences were the habitations, and the cultivated lands which supplied the septs with stores of corn and provender for their large herds of cattle. The rights of the chief, sub-chiefs, and families of each sept were regulated under the Brehon code, which, with minute precision, laid down rules for adjudicating on almost every variety of dispute, encroachment, or breach of law. Although the main attribute of the head of a clan was that of unfailing vigour and prowess in arms, to defend his territory against both foreigners and encroaching Irish, there were other duties deemed scarcely secondary. Such were the improvement of the land, the observance of strict justice, the liberal support of religious establishments, under the patronage of the saints of the tribe; implicit obedience to the decrees of the hereditary Brehons or judges, and the maintenance of the endowments made of old for the support of their learned men and chroniclers. Their intimate relations with Scotland, and frequent pilgrimages to France, Spain, and Italy, rendered the chiefs and their families conversant with the affairs of the Continent, with which constant communication was maintained by their clergy and ecclesiastical students. The internal condition of the settlement, and the manifold injustices perpetrated by the officials of the colonial government on those under their control, tended to repel, rather than attract, the independent Irish towards the English system as then administered. Many of the judges and chief legal officials of the colony were illiterate and ignorant of law, obtained their appointments by purchase, and leased them to deputies, who promoted and encouraged litigation, with the object of accumulating fees. Commissioners of Oyer and Terminer were multiplied, before whom persons were constantly summoned by irresponsible non-residents, to such an extent that no man could tell when he might be indicted or outlawed, or if a process had issued to eject him from his property. The king's officers often seized lands and appropriated their rents, so long as legal subterfuges enabled them to baffle the claims of the rightful proprietors; and thus agriculture and improvements were impeded. Ecclesiastics, lords, and gentlemen were not unfrequently cast into jail by officers of the crown on unfounded charges, without indictment or process, and detained in durance till compelled by rigorous treatment to purchase their liberation. The agricultural settlers and landholders were harassed by troops of armed "kerns" and mounted "idelmen," who levied distresses, maltreated and chained those who resisted, and held forcible possession of the farmer's goods till redeemed with money. The troops engaged for the defence of the colonists became little less oppressive than enemies. Under the name of "livere," or liverey, the soldiery took, without payment, victuals for themselves and provender for their horses, and exacted weekly money payments, designated "coygnes." It was not unusual for a soldier having a billet for six or more horses to keep only three, but to exact provender for the entire number, and on a single billet the same trooper commonly demanded and took "livery" in several parts of a county. The constables of royal castles, and the purveyors of the households of the viceroys, seldom paid for what they took, and for the purpose of obtaining bribes to release their seizure they made exactions much more frequently than needed. These grievances, wrote the prelates, lords, and commons to the King of England, have reduced your loyal subjects in Ireland to "a state of distraction and impoverishment, and caused them even to hate their lives." Most of the king's manors, customs, and other sources of revenue having been granted or sold to individuals, but little came to the treasury of the fees, fines, and crown profits, which previously had defrayed part of the expenses of the colonial government. These reduced finances were nearly exhausted by pensions and annuities, paid to propitiate the chiefs of the border Irish, and to secure the settlement against their inroads. Various good towns and hamlets of the colony were destroyed, while several royal castles and fortresses became ruinous, as those in charge of them embezzled the rents and profits allocated for their maintenance, repairs, and garrisons.

EARL OF DUNRAVEN.

[The fourth Earl of Dunraven and Mount-Earl was born in 1841. Before his father's death, while Viscount Adare, he devoted himself very considerably to literary pursuits, and gained a good deal of the experience afforded by the discharge of the varied and adventurous duties of special correspondent. In this capacity he served the *Daily Telegraph* throughout the Abyssinian campaign and the Franco-German war, and his letters contained some of the most graphic descriptions that appeared even in that journal of graphic writing during these exciting periods. He afterwards made a tour through the less frequented parts of the United States, and the result of his observations was given to the world in a book entitled *The Great Divide*, a work which abounds in brilliant descriptions, and which received almost universally favourable criticism. He succeeded to the title in 1871. During the last few years he has taken a prominent part in the debates in the House of Lords, and he is probably one of those marked out for office in future Liberal administrations.]

CANOE TRAVELLING.

(FROM "THE GREAT DIVIDE.")

Among all the modes of progression hitherto invented by restless man, there is not one that can compare in respect of comfort and luxury with travelling in a birch-bark canoe. It is the poetry of progression. Along the bottom of the boat are laid blankets and bedding; a sort of wicker-work screen is sloped against the middle thwart, affording a delicious support to the back; and indolently, in your shirt sleeves if the day be warm, or well covered with a blanket if it is chilly, you sit or lie on this most luxurious of couches, and are propelled at a rapid rate over the smooth surface of a lake or down the swift current of some stream. If you want exercise, you can take a paddle yourself. If you prefer to be inactive, you can lie still and placidly survey the scenery, rising occasionally to have a shot at a wild duck; at intervals reading, smoking, and sleeping. Sleep indeed you will enjoy most luxuriously, for the rapid bounding motion of the canoe as she leaps forward at every impulse of the crew, the sharp quick beat of the paddles on the water, and the roll of their shafts against the gunwale, with the continuous hiss and ripple of the stream cleft by the curving prow, combine to make a more soothing soporific than all the fabrications of poppy and mandragora that can be found in the pharmacopœia of civilization.

Dreamily you lie side by side—you and your friend—lazily gazing at the pine-covered shores and wooded islands of some unknown lake, the open book unheeded on your knee; the half-smoked pipe drops into your lap; your head sinks gently back; and you wander into dreamland, to awake presently and find yourself sweeping round the curve of some majestic river, whose shores are blazing with the rich crimson, brown, and gold of the maple and other hard-wood trees in their autumn dress.

Presently the current quickens. The best man shifts his place from the stern to the bow, and stands ready with his long-handled paddle to twist the frail boat out of reach of hidden rocks. The men's faces glow with excitement. Quicker and quicker flows the stream, breaking into little rapids, foaming round rocks, and rising in tumbling waves over the shallows. At a word from the bowman the crew redouble their efforts, the paddle-shafts crash against the gunwale, the spray flies beneath the bending blades. The canoe shakes and quivers through all its fibres, leaping bodily at every stroke.

Before you is a seething mass of foam, its whiteness broken by horrid black rocks, one touch against whose jagged sides would rip the canoe into tatters and hurl you into eternity. Your ears are full of the roar of waters; waves leap up in all directions, as the river, maddened at obstruction, hurls itself through some narrow gorge. The bowman stands erect to take one look in silence, noting in that critical instant the line of deepest water; then bending to his work, with sharp, short words of command to the steersman, he directs the boat. The canoe seems to pitch headlong into space. Whack! comes a great wave over the bow; crash! comes another over the side. The bowman, his figure stooped, and his knees planted firmly against the side, stands, with paddle poised in both hands, screaming to the crew to paddle hard; and the crew cheer and shout with excitement in return. You, too, get wild, and feel inclined to yell defiance to the roaring hissing flood that madly dashes you from side to side. After the first plunge you are in a bewildering whirl of waters. The shore seems to fly past you. Crash! You are right on that rock, and (I don't care who you are) you will feel your heart jump into your mouth, and you will catch the side with a grip that leaves a mark on your fingers afterwards. No! With a shriek of command to the steersman, and a plunge of his paddle, the bowman wrenches the canoe out of its course. Another stroke or two, another plunge forward, and with a loud exulting yell from the bowman, who flourishes his paddle round his head, you pitch headlong down the final leap, and with a grunt of relief from the straining crew glide rapidly into still water.

Through the calm gloaming, through the lovely hours of moonlit night you glide, if the stream is favourable and the current safe; the crew of *Metis*, or French half-breeds, asleep, wrapped in their white capotes, all but the steersman, who nods over his paddle and croons to himself some old Normandy or Breton song. Or, landing in the evening, you struggle back from the romance of leaf tints and sunset glows to the delicious savouriness of a stew, composed of fat pork, partridges, potatoes, onions, fish, and lumps of dough; and having ballasted yourself with this compound, and smoked the digestive pipe, sleep on sweet pine-tops till you're *levéed* by the steersman in the morning, when you pursue your way, not miserable and cross, as you would be at home after such a mess of pottage, but bright, happy, and cheerful; capable of enjoying to the full the glories of the daybreak, watching the watery diamonds from the paddle-blades flashing in the sun, and listening to the echoing notes of *A la claire fontaine*, or some other French-Canadian song.

A CITY IN THE GREAT WEST.

(FROM "THE GREAT DIVIDE.")

Virginia City. Good Lord! What a name for the place! We had looked forward to it during the journey as to a sort of haven of rest, a lap of luxury; a Capua in which to forget our woes and weariness; an Elysium where we might be washed, clean-shirted, rubbed, shampooed, barbered, curled, cooled, and cocktailed. Not a bit of it! Not a sign of Capua about the place! There might have been laps, but there was no luxury. A street of straggling shanties, a bank, a blacksmith's shop, a few dry-goods stores, and bar-rooms, constitute the main attractions of the "city." A gentleman had informed me that Virginia *city* contained brown stone-front houses and paved streets, equal, he guessed, to any Eastern *town*. How that man did lie in his Wellingtons! The whole place was a delusion and a snare. One of the party was especially mortified, for he had been provided with a letter of introduction to some ladies, from whose society he anticipated great pleasure; but when he came to inquire, he found, to his intense disgust, that they were in Virginia City, *Nevada*, "ten thousand miles away!" However, we soon became reconciled to our fate. We found the little inn very clean and comfortable; we dined on deer, antelope, and bear meat, a fact which raised hopes of hunting in our bosoms; and the people were exceedingly civil, kind, obliging, and anxious to assist strangers in any possible way, as, so far as my experience goes of America, and indeed of all countries, they invariably are as soon as you get off the regular lines of travel.

Virginia City is situated on Alder Gulch. It is surrounded by a dreary country, resembling the more desolate parts of Cumberland, and consisting of interminable waves of steep low hills, covered with short, withered grass. I went out for a walk on the afternoon of our arrival, and was most disagreeably impressed. I could not get to the top of anything, and consequently could obtain no extended view. I kept continually climbing to the summit of grassy hills, only to find other hills, grassier and higher, surrounding me on all sides. The wind swept howling down the combes, and whistled shrilly in the short wiry herbage; large masses of ragged-edged black clouds were piled up against a leaden sky; not a sign of man or beast was to be seen. It began to snow heavily, and I was glad to turn my back to the storm and scud for home.

Alder Gulch produced at one time some of the richest placer workings of the continent. It was discovered in 1863, and about thirty millions of dollars' worth of gold have been won from it. Of late years very little has been done, and at present the industrious Chinaman alone pursues the business of re-washing the old dirt heaps, and making money where any one else would starve. In truth, he is a great washerwoman is your Chinaman, equally successful with rotten quartz and dirty shirts. Alder Gulch is about twelve miles in length, and half a mile broad. It is closed at the head by a remarkable limestone ridge, the highest point of which is known as "Old Baldy Mountain," and it leads into the Jefferson Fork of the Missouri. Along the sides of the valley may be seen many patches of black basalt, and the bottom is covered entirely by drift, composed of material weather and water worn out of metamorphic rocks, the fragments varying in size from large boulders to fine sand and gravel. In this drift the float gold is found. In Montana the deposits of the precious metal generally occur in metamorphic rocks, belonging probably to the Huronian or Laurentian series. These are clearly stratified, not unfrequently intercalated with bands of clay or sand, and underlie the whole country, forming beds of great thickness, very massive and close-grained in their lower layers, but growing softer and looser in texture towards the surface. The superimposed formations, carboniferous limestones and others, appear to have been almost wholly removed by erosion. In this part of Montana, indeed, the forces of erosion must have acted with great vigour for a long period of time. The general character of the country where placer mines exist may be said to be a series of deep gulches, frequently dry in the height of summer, but carrying foaming torrents after heavy rains and in snow-melting time, leading at right angles into a principal valley, and combining to form a little river, or, as it would be locally called, a creek. This principal stream courses in a broad valley through the mountains for perhaps 60, 80, or 100 miles, and at every two or three miles of its progress receives the waters of a little tributary torrent, tearing through the strata in deep cañons for ten or twelve miles, and searching the very vitals of the hills. Down these gulches, cañons, and valleys are carried the yellow specks torn from their quartz and felspar cradles, hurried downward by the melting snow, and battered into powder by falling boulders and grinding rocks, till they sink in beds of worthless sand and mud, there to lie in peace for ages amid the solitudes of primeval forest and eternal snow. Some fine day there comes along a dirty, dishevelled, tobacco-chewing fellow—"fossicker," as they would say in Australia, "prospector," as he would be called in the States. Impelled by a love of adventure, a passion for excitement, a hatred of "the town and its narrow ways," and of all and any of the steady wage-getting occupations of life, he braves summer's heat and winter's cold, thirst and starvation, hostile Indians and jealous whites; perhaps paddling a tiny birch-bark canoe over unmapped, unheard-of lakes, away to the far and misty North, or driving before him over the plains and prairies of a more genial clime his donkey or Indian pony, laden with the few necessaries that supply all the wants of his precarious life—a little flour, some tea and sugar tied up in a rag, a battered frying-pan and tin cup, a shovel, axe, and rusty gun. Through untrodden wastes he wanders, self-dependent and alone, thinking of the great spree he had the last time he was in "settlements," and dreaming of what a good time he will enjoy when he gets back rich with the value of some lucky find, till chance directs him to the Gulch. After a rapid but keen survey, he thinks it is a likely-looking place, capsizes the pack off his pony, leans lazily upon his shovel, spits, and finally concludes to take a sample of the dirt. Listlessly, but with what delicacy of manipulation he handles the shovel, spilling over its edges the water and lighter mud! See the look of interest that wakens up his emotionless face as the residue of sediment becomes less and less! Still more tenderly he moves the circling pan, stooping anxiously to scan the few remaining grains of fine sand. A minute speck of yellow glitters in the sun; with another dexterous turn of the wrist, two or three more golden grains are exposed to view. He catches his breath; his eyes glisten; his heart beats. Hurrah! He has found the colour! and "a d——d good colour too." It is all over with your primeval forest now; not all the Indians this side of Halifax or the other place could keep men out of that gulch. In a short time claims are staked, tents erected, shanties built, and "Roaring Camp" is in full blast with all its rowdyism, its shooting, gambling, drinking, and blaspheming, and its under-current of charity, which never will be credited by those who value substance less than shadows, and think more of words than deeds.

Although the float gold undoubtedly had its origin in the metamorphic rocks through which the streams have cut their way, yet, strange as it may appear, the exceptions where paying lodes have been found at the head of rich placer mines are extremely rare. No discoveries of any value have been made in the rocks towards the head of Alder Gulch, from which the tons of gold-dust, panned out from the bed of the stream, must have come. It would appear as though the upper portions of the strata contained all the metal, and the inferior layers were either very lean or entirely destitute of ore. The lodes throughout all this section have a general north-east and south-west strike, and dip nearly west at an angle of fifty or sixty degrees. The matrix is felspar and quartz, exhibiting various degrees of hardness in texture, and occurring generally in gneiss. The trend of the whole metamorphic series is about north-west and south-east.

There was nothing to interest us in Virginia City, or in the neighbourhood. The chances of good sport appeared on inquiry to be very doubtful, and so, as soon as we had rested ourselves, we decided, after a council of war, to go to Fort Ellis, and have a week's hunting in that locality, while we were waiting for Wynne, who *ought* to have joined us long ago.

CHARLES ANDERSON READ.

BORN 1841 — DIED 1878.

[Charles Anderson Read was born on 10th November, 1841, at Kilsella House, near Sligo. Misfortune compelled the removal of the family to Hilltown, near Newry, where Mr. Read, senior, obtained the appointment of schoolmaster. It was intended that Charles should be prepared for the Church, but this project had to be abandoned, and at an early age he was, much to his regret, apprenticed to a merchant in Rathfriland. He made good use of his leisure hours, however, continued his study of Latin, and, under the instruction of his mother, acquired a knowledge of Irish. He also attempted original composition, and when only about fifteen he contributed verses to the local journals. The business in which he was engaged changed hands; the new proprietor offered him the position of acting partner, which he accepted; and subsequently he became the sole proprietor. For a short time success appeared to crown his adventure, and he married in 1862. But although he could act firmly enough when another person's interest was involved, he could not act so firmly when only his own safety was at stake. He gave assistance and credit to every one who appeared to be in difficulty, and only a year after his marriage he was obliged to close his doors. He gave everything he possessed to his creditors, and in the course of a few years, by dint of hard work and much personal privation, he paid their demands in full with interest.

On the failure of his business he made his way to London, where he obtained an engagement in the publishing office of Mr. James Henderson,[1] the proprietor of several popular periodicals. He retained his connection with this establishment till the end. His widow writes: "After his office hours, and only then, he followed his favourite pursuit of literature, not at that time, as formerly, for amusement, but of stern necessity." In this manner he produced numerous sketches, poems, short tales, and nine novels, the most notable of the latter being *Love's Service*, which appeared in the *Dublin University Magazine*. Indeed, it is his best novel, although less known than his *Aileen Aroon*, or *Savourneen Dheelish*, of which the *London Review* said: "We are presented with a view of agrarian crime in its most revolting aspect, and there is no false glamour thrown around any of the characters. Many of the incidents are highly dramatic, while the dialogue is bright and forcible." In 1873 he became so ill that he took a voyage to Australia. He returned apparently restored to health, and resumed work with as much energy as ever, although he could scarcely be said to have ceased work, for during the voyage out and home he completed two tales and a metrical version of the Psalms of David. A series of stories from the classics for the young appeared in rapid succession in *Young Folks*, a periodical circulating over 100,000 copies weekly, and we can scarcely overestimate the educational influence which must

---

[1] In after years this gentleman persuaded Mr. Read to undertake a voyage to Australia in the hope that it might check the fatal disease (consumption) which had attacked him, and made all necessary arrangements to enable him to do so in comfort.

have been exercised upon such a mass of readers by the representation in a popular form of the adventures of "Achilles," "Odysseus," "Hercules," and "Jason."

During his last two years he was engaged in the most grateful task he had ever undertaken, namely, the production of *The Cabinet of Irish Literature*. With all the enthusiastic admiration of his country, its people, and its literature, which is characteristic of Irishmen, he regarded this work as one which ought to have appeared long ago; he believed that it would prove of the deepest interest to his countrymen, enabling them to realize the long roll of brilliant poets, orators, and prose writers which was their heritage, and he took it up reverently. One of his chief aims was to show how many of those authors who hold a first place in "English literature" belonged to his country.

Knowing that his time here was to be brief, he worked arduously, craving only for strength to complete this book. There is no more pathetic incident in literary biography than the appeal he made to his medical adviser when, a few weeks before the end came, feeling himself extremely feeble, he put the question: "Can I live for six months, so that I may finish this book?" The doctor (a faithful friend) felt it to be his duty to say, "I am afraid not;" and the answer was received in silence. He turned quietly to the duties of the day, setting his house in order, diligently utilizing every moment of strength, writing with his own hand when he was able to sit up, and at other times dictating to his wife. It was during this period that the poem "Beyond the River" was composed; it was found by Mrs. Read in his desk after his death, and it was evidently inspired by his thoughts of her. He died at his residence, Thornton Heath, Surrey, on 23d January, 1878.

The sorrow which is felt for his early death is in large measure relieved by the remembrance of how much he achieved; but there will always linger in the minds of those who knew him well a regret that he had not lived longer. Imaginative, and yet possessed of what is called common-sense to a remarkable degree,—prudent, and yet generous to a fault in helping those who were unfortunate,—he earned and deserved the respect of all with whom he came in contact.[1]]

---

[1] For this sketch of the life of Mr. Read we are indebted to the pen of Mr. Charles Gibbon, author of *Robin Gray*, and other well-known novels.

AN IRISH MISTAKE.[2]

"I cannot reach Sligo now before dark; that's certain," I muttered, as I hoisted my knapsack an inch or two higher, and began to cover the ground at my best rate. "However, the sooner I get there the better."

Presently I reached a spot where four roads met, and while I stood doubtful which to take a gig driven by some one singing in a loud key overtook me. At sight of my lonely figure the gig was halted suddenly, and the driver ceased his song.

"Ah, thin, may I ask, is your honour goin' my way?" said a full round voice. "It's myself that's mighty fond of company o' nights about here."

"I don't know what *your* way may be," I replied. "I wish to go to Sligo."

"Ah! thin, an' it's that same Sligo, the weary be on it, that I'd be afther goin' to myself," answered the driver. "But your honour looks tired—manin' no offince—an' perhaps you'd take a lift in the gig?"

"Thank you; I will take a lift," I replied, as I stepped forward and sprang quickly to the seat. "The truth is, I feel rather tired, as you say."

"An' has your honour walked far?" asked the driver, as the gig rolled on towards the town.

"I've walked from Ballina since morning," I replied quietly.

"From Ballina! There, now, the Lord save us!" cried the man, as he half turned in his seat and gazed at me in astonishment. "Why, that's a day's work for the best horse in the masther's stables."

"Your master must keep good horses, if I may judge by the one before us," I answered.

"The best in all the county, your honour, though I say it. There isn't a gossoon in the three baronies but knows that."

"Your master's a bit of a sportsman, then?"

"Yes, your honour; an' if he'd stick to that, it's himself'd be the best-liked man from Ballina to Ballyshannon. You wouldn't find a better rider or a warmer heart in a day's march. But thim politics has been his ruin with the people."

"Oh, ah! I have heard that Sligo is rather a hot place during elections," I replied. "But surely the people don't turn upon their friends at such a time?"

---

[2] Quoted by permission of the Messrs. Chambers.

"They'd turn upon their own father, if he wint agin them," replied the driver solemnly. "See now, here I am, drivin' the masther's own gig to town just be way of a blin', ye see, while he's got to slip down the strame in Jimmy Sheridan's bit of a boat. Ah, thim politics, thim politics!"

"Oh, then, there's an election about to take place, I presume?"

"Thrue for ye, your honour, thrue for ye," replied the man dolefully. "There nivir was such a ruction in Sligo before, in the mimiry of man. Two lawyers a-fightin' like divils to see who's to be mimbir."

"Then I'm just in time to see the fun."

"Fun, your honour?" echoed the man. "It's not meself that 'id object to a bit of a scrimmage now an' agin. But it's murther your honour 'll see before it's all over, or my name isn't Michael O'Connor. Whist now! Did ye hear nothin' behin' that hedge there?"

At this moment we were about the middle of a rather lonesome stretch of the road, one side of which was bounded by a high thin hedge. The dusk of the evening was fast giving way to the gloom of night.

"I—ah—yes, surely there is something moving there," I replied. "It's some animal, most likely."

"Down in the sate! down, for your life!" cried the driver, as in his terror he brought the horse to a halt. "I——"

His speech was cut short by a couple of loud reports. A lance-like line of fire gushed from the hedge, and one, if not two, bullets whizzed close past my ear.

As I sprang to my feet in the gig, the driver slid down to the mat, and lay there in a heap, moaning. "Are you hurt?" I asked, as I strove to get the reins out of his palsied hands.

"I'm kilt, kilt intirely!" he moaned.

"Aisy now, aisy there, your honour!" cried a voice from behind the hedge just as I had gained the reins. "It's all a mistake, your honour, all a mistake!"

"Give the mare the whip! give the mare the whip!" cried the driver, as he strove to crawl under the seat; "we'll all be murthered!"

Instead of taking his advice, however, I held the mare steady, while a man pressed through the thin hedge and stood before us, a yet smoking gun on his shoulder.

"What's the meaning of this?" I asked coolly, for the new-comer's coolness affected me. "Did you want to murder a person you never saw before?"

"I'm raale downright sorry, your honour," replied the man, in just such a tone as he might have used had he trod upon my toe by accident; "but ye see you're in Wolff O'Neil's gig, an' I took ye for him.—Where's that fellow Michael?"

As he said this the man prodded the driver with the end of his gun, while I—I actually laughed outright at the strangeness of the affair.

"Go away with ye, go away!" moaned the driver. "Murther! thaves! murther!"

"Get up with ye, an' take the reins, you gomeril you," said the man, as he gave Michael another prod that brought him half out. "You're as big a coward as my old granny's pet calf. Get up, an' take the reins, or I'll——"

"Oh, don't; there, don't say nothin', for the love of heaven," cried the driver, as he scrambled into his seat again and took the reins in his shaking hands. "I'll do anythin' ye till me, on'y put that gun away."

"There," replied the man, as he lowered the gun till its mouth pointed to the ground; "will that plase ye? Now, tell me where's Squire O'Neil?"

"He's in the town be this," replied the driver. "O thim politics, thim politics!"

"Hum; so he's managed to get past us, after all. Well, tell him from me, Captain Rock, that if he votes for the sarjint to-morrow, it's an ounce of lead out of this he'll be after trying to digest. Now mind."

"I'll tell him, captain, dear! I'll tell him," replied the driver, as he fingered the reins and whip nervously. "But mayn't we go on now? mayn't we go on?"

"Yis, whiniver the gentleman plases," replied the man. "An' I'm raale sorry, as I told your honour, I'm raale sorry at the mistake."

"Well, I'm pleased, not sorry," I replied, laughing, "for if you'd hit me it wouldn't have been at all pleasant. But let me advise you to make sure of your man next time before firing. Good-night."

"Good-night, your honour, good-night," cried the man, as Michael gave the mare the whip, and sent her along at the top of her speed to the now fast-nearing lights of the town. In less than a quarter of an hour we had dashed through the streets and halted opposite a large hotel. Here Michael found his master, as he expected; and here I put up for the night, very much to the astonishment of every one. Soon after my arrival I asked to be shown to my room; but it was one o'clock in the morning before the other guests ceased their noise and allowed me to go to sleep. Next day I slept rather late, and might have slept even later, but that I was rudely shaken out of a pleasant dream by a wild howl, as of a thousand demons just let loose. Starting up quickly, and looking out on the street, I saw that it was filled with a fierce-looking crowd, out of whose many mouths had proceeded the yell that wakened me. Dragging on my clothes I rushed down to the coffee-room. There I learned that the people outside had just accompanied Squire O'Neil back from the polling-place, where he had been the first to vote for "the sarjint." Now that this fact had become generally known, they were clamorous that he should be sent out to them, "to tear him limb from limb." Presently, while their cries rose loud and long, the squire entered the room—a tall, military-looking man, with a little of a horsey tone, nose like a hawk, eyes dark, yet glowing like fire.

"They don't seem over-fond of me, I see," he said with a smile, as he bowed to those in the room, and advanced to one of the windows and coolly opened it. Waving his hand, the crowd became instantly silent.

"Now, don't be in a hurry, gentlemen," he said, in a clear voice that must have been distinctly heard by every one. "You shall have the honour of my company so soon as my horse can be harnessed, I assure you."

"Eh, what! what does he mean?" I asked of a person next me. "Surely he will not venture out among these howling fiends?"

"That is just what he is going to do," replied my companion. "There is no use talking to him. He has given orders for the mare and gig to be got ready, and it's as much as any one's life is worth to try to stop him. Wolff by name, and wolf by nature; he's enraged at having to steal down here last night like a thief. Ah, there the fun begins! Look out!"

As my companion spoke he griped me by the arm, and dragged me close against a space between two windows. Next moment a shower of stones crashed through the windows, leaving not a single inch of glass unbroken. Then, at longer or shorter intervals, volley followed volley, till the floor of the room was completely covered with road metal and broken glass. Presently there was a lull in the storm, and the crowd became all at once as silent as the grave. In the hush I could distinctly hear the grating sound of the opening of some big door almost under us. I looked inquiringly at my companion.

"It's the entry doors being opened to let the wolf out," he said in reply. "Ah! there he is."

I glanced out of the window, and saw the squire alone in his gig, a smile on his face, his whole bearing as cool and unconcerned as if there was not a single enemy within a thousand miles. Then I heard the great doors clang to, and as they did so the crowd gave vent to a howl of delighted rage.

At the first appearance of the squire in his gig the people had swayed back, and left an open space in front of the hotel. Now they seemed about to close in on him, and one man in the front stooped to lift a stone. Quick as lightning the hand of the squire went to his breast, and just as the man stood upright to throw, I heard the sharp crack of a pistol. The man uttered a wild shriek of pain, clapped his hands to his cheeks, and plunged into the crowd. The bullet had entered at one cheek and gone out at the other, after tearing away a few teeth in its passage. The man was the very person who had made the mistake in shooting at me over-night.

"A near nick that for our friend," said the squire in his clear voice, while the crowd swayed back a pace or two. "But the next will be nearer still, and I've nearly half-a-dozen still left. Now, will any of you oblige me by stooping to lift a stone?"

He paused and glanced round, while every man in the crowd held his breath and stood still as a statue.

"No? you won't oblige me?" he said presently, with a sneer. Then fierce as if charging in some world-famous battle: "Out of my way, you scoundrels! Faugh-a-ballagh!"

At the word he jerked the reins slightly, and the mare moved forward at a trot, with head erect and bearing as proud as if she knew a conquerer sat behind her. Then, in utter silence, the crowd swayed to right and left leaving a wide alley, down which the squire drove as gaily as if the whole thing were some pleasant show. When he had disappeared the crowd closed to again, utterly crestfallen. Then for a short time the whole air was filled with their chattering one to another, like the humming of innumerable bees; and presently without a shout, and without a single stone being thrown, the great mass melted away.

Next morning, at an early hour, I left Sligo

as fast as a covered conveyance could carry me. I did not care to wait for the slower means of escape by foot, fearful that next time a mistake was made with me the shooting might possibly be better than it was at first.

BEYOND THE RIVER.

Weep no more about my bed;
Weep no more, be comfortèd.
That which pale and cold you see,
Once was mine, but is not me:
Kiss no more that thing of clay,
  That as garment once I wore;
Foul, I fling it far away,
  That it soil my soul no more—
That no more it close me in
With its bands of grief and sin.

Weep no more about my bed;
Weep no more, be comfortèd.
That which you to earth convey,
Weeping, wailing on the way,
Is but as an empty shell,
  As a cage whence bird is flown,
As a hut where one did dwell
  Ever full of pain and moan,
As a mask that mocks and jeers
'Fore a face all filled with tears.

Weep no more about my bed;
Weep no more, be comfortèd.
Now at last I live in truth,
Now I feel unfading youth,
Now the world's dark ways are clear,
  Now the weary wonder dies,
Now your little doubts appear
  Mists that fail to vail the skies;—
Now your knowledge, skill, and strength,
Childish toys appear at length.

Weep no more about my bed;
Weep no more, be comfortèd.
He you weep you may not see,
But he stands beside your knee:
He who lov'd you loves you still,—
  Loves you with a treble pow'r,—
Loves you with a mightier will,
  Growing, growing every hour.
He you clasped in arms of clay
Tends you closely day by day.

Weep no more about my bed;
Weep no more, be comfortèd.
Where I am ye soon will come;
This, this only is our home.
I am only gone before,
  Just a moment's little space;
Soon upon this painless shore
  Ye shall see me face to face;
Then will smile, and wonder why
Ye should weep that I should die.

LIST OF THE AUTHORS,

SELECTIONS FROM WHOSE WRITINGS ARE GIVEN IN THIS WORK.

Author	vol.	page
Abernethy, John,	i.	101
Alexander, Bishop,	iv.	170
Alexander, Mrs.,	iv.	170
Allingham, William,	iv.	137
Anster, John,	iii.	201
Armstrong, Edmund John,	iv.	312
Armstrong, George Francis,	iv.	316
Arthur, William,	iv.	200
Banim, John,	ii.	300
Banim, Michael,	iii.	249
Barber, Mrs.	i.	227
Barrett, Eaton Stannard,	ii.	172
Barry, Ludovick,	i.	20
Berkeley, Bishop,	i.	205
Bickerstaff, Isaac,	ii.	50
Blackburne, E. Owens,	iv.	277
Blessington, Countess of,	ii.	317
Boucicault, Dion,	iv.	176
Boyle, John, Earl of Cork,	i.	213
Boyle, Hon. Robert,	i.	64
Boyle, Roger, Earl of Orrery,	i.	54
Boyse, Samuel,	i.	187
Brady, Nicholas,	i.	86
Brooke, Charlotte,	i.	234
Brooke, Henry,	i.	310
Browne, Frances,	iv.	182
Burgh, Walter Hussey,	ii.	15
Burgoyne, General,	i.	328
Burke, Edmund,	ii.	18
Burke, Thomas N.,	iv.	213
Burton, Richard Francis,	iv.	93
Bushe, Charles Kendal,	ii.	248
Butler, William Archer,	iii.	175
Butler, William Francis,	iv.	218
Butt, Isaac,	iv.	164
Cairns, Earl,	iv.	201
Callanan, James Joseph,	ii.	233
Carleton, William,	iii.	213
Casey, E. O. B.,	iv.	277
Casey, John Keegan,	iv.	188
Castlereagh, Lord,	ii.	169
Centlivre, Mrs. Susanna,	i.	117
Cherry, Andrew,	ii.	123
Chesney, General,	iii.	231
Clarke, Adam,	ii.	226
Cobbe, Frances Power,	iv.	121
Concanen, Matthew,	i.	202
Congreve, William,	i.	149
Cooke, Henry,	iii.	177
Coyne, Joseph Stirling,	iii.	292
Croker, John Wilson,	iii.	103
Croker, Thomas Crofton,	iii.	137
Croly, George,	iii.	122
Crowe, Eyre Evans,	iii.	247
Cunningham, John,	i.	245
Curran, John Philpot,	ii.	143
D'Alton, John,	iii.	211
Darley, George,	iii.	38
Davis, Francis,	iv.	173
Davis, Thomas Osborne,	iii.	289
Delacour, James,	i.	206
Delany, Patrick,	i.	252
Denham, Sir John,	i.	36
Dermody, Thomas,	ii.	58
De Vere, Sir Aubrey,	ii.	331
De Vere, Aubrey T.,	iv.	40
Dodwell, Henry,	i.	78
Dowden, Edward,	iv.	301
Dowling, Richard,	iv.	285
Downing, Ellen,	iv.	145
Doyle, James Warren,	ii.	242
Drennan, William,	ii.	140
Drummond, Wm. Hamilton,	iii.	165
Dufferin, Earl of,	iv.	245
Dufferin, Lady,	iii.	285
Duffet, Thomas,	i.	89
Duffy, Sir Charles Gavan,	iv.	108
Dugan, Maurice,	i.	47
Dunraven, Earl of,	iv.	327
Edgeworth, Maria,	ii.	254
Emmet, Robert,	ii.	60
Farquhar, George,	i.	71
Father Mathew,	iii.	117
Father Prout,	iii.	302
Father Tom Burke,	iv.	213
Ferguson, Sir Samuel,	iv.	58
Fitzgerald, Maurice,	i.	29
Fitzpatrick, William John,	iv.	240
Flecknoe, Richard,	i.	52
Flood, Henry,	ii.	1
Francis, Philip,	i.	242
Francis, Sir Philip,	ii.	130
Fraser, John D.,	iii.	132
French, Nicholas,	i.	42
Furlong, Thomas,	ii.	221
Gentleman, Francis,	i.	317
Gilbert, John T.,	iv.	324
Godkin, James,	iv.	19
Goldsmith, Oliver,	i.	264
Grattan, Henry,	ii.	170
Grattan, Thomas Colley,	iii.	189
Graves, Alfred Perceval,	iv.	211
Grierson, Mrs. Constantia,	i.	148
Griffin, Gerald,	iii.	58
Hall, Mrs. S. C.,	iv.	34
Halpine, Charles Graham,	iv.	150
Hamilton, Count,	i.	93
Hamilton, Sir Wm. Rowan,	iii.	279
Havard, William,	i.	208
Haverty, Martin,	iv.	158
Hickey, William,	iii.	282
Higgins, Matthew James,	iii.	296
Hoey, John Cashel,	iv.	251
Hoey, Mrs. Cashel,	iv.	253
Irwin, Thomas Caulfield,	iv.	90
Jacob Omnium,	iii.	296
Jameson, Mrs.,	iii.	102
Jephson, Robert,	ii.	69
Johnstone, Charles,	ii.	46
Jones, Henry,	i.	248
Joyce, Patrick Weston,	iv.	233
Joyce, Robert Dwyer,	iv.	237
Junius,	ii.	130
Kavanagh, Julia,	iv.	113
Keary, Annie,	iv.	132
Keating, Geoffry,	i.	1
Keegan, John,	iii.	94
Keightley, Thomas,	iii.	236
Kelly, Eva Mary,	iv.	145
Kelly, Hugh,	i.	289
Kennedy, Patrick,	iii.	314
Kenney, James,	ii.	312
Kickham, Charles Joseph,	iv.	148
King, Dr. William,	i.	126
Kirwan, Richard,	ii.	95
Kirwan, Walter Blake,	ii.	64
Knowles, James Sheridan,	iii.	151
Laffan, Miss,	iv.	290
Lanigan, John,	ii.	104
Lardner, Dionysius,	iii.	134
Leadbeater, Mary,	ii.	208
Lecky, William E. H.,	iv.	180
Le Fanu, Joseph Sheridan,	iv.	44
Leland, Thomas,	i.	305
Lever, Charles,	iv.	1
Londonderry, Marquis of,	iii.	52
Lover, Samuel,	iii.	262
Lysaght, Edward,	ii.	87
MacCarthy, Denis Florence,	iv.	154
McCarthy, Justin,	iv.	305
M'Clure, Sir Robert,	iii.	317
MacDaire, Teige,	i.	9
MacDonnell, John,	i.	218
MacFirbis, Duald,	i.	48
MacGahan, J. A.,	iv.	273
M'Gee, Thomas D'Arcy,	iv.	71
M'Hale, Archbishop,	iv.	14
Macklin, Charles,	ii.	8
Madden, Daniel Owen,	iii.	205
Madden, Samuel,	i.	224
Magee, William Connor,	iv.	99
Maginn, William,	ii.	285
Magrath, Andrew,	i.	326
Maguire, John Francis,	iii.	324
Mahaffy, J. P.,	iv.	252
Mahony, Francis Sylvester,	iii.	302
Malone, Edmund,	ii.	119

LIST OF THE AUTHORS.

Name	vol.	page
Mangan, James Clarence,	iii.	70
Marsden, William,	ii.	229
Martin Doyle,	iii.	282
Mathew, Rev. Theobald,	iii.	117
Maturin, Charles Robert,	ii.	200
Maxwell, William Hamilton,	iii.	106
Meagher, Thomas Francis,	iv.	54
Miles O'Reilly,	iv.	159
Miller, George,	ii.	309
Millikin, Richard Alfred,	ii.	128
Mitchel, John,	iii.	320
Molesworth, Robert Viscount,	i.	114
Molloy, Charles,	i.	221
Molyneux, William,	i.	57
Monk, Hon. Mrs.,	i.	80
Moore, Thomas,	iii.	1
Morgan, Lady,	iii.	26
Mulholland, Rosa,	iv.	270
Murphy, Arthur,	ii.	79
Napier, Lieut.-gen. Sir C. J.,	iii.	97
Napier, Sir Joseph,	iv.	17
Napier, Sir Wm. Francis P.,	iii.	126
Norton, Hon. Mrs. Caroline,	iv.	26
Nugent, Gerald,	i.	8
O'Brien, William Smith,	iii.	275
O'Carolan, Turlough,	i.	156
O'Clery, Michael,	i.	10
O'Connell, Daniel,	ii.	200
O'Curry, Eugene,	iii.	171
O'Donnell, John Francis,	iv.	102
O'Donovan, John,	iii.	258
O'Flaherty, Roderic,	i.	89
O'Flanagan, James Roderick,	iv.	97
O'Grady, Standish,	iv.	318
O'Hara, Kane,	i.	303
O'Keefe, John,	ii.	215
O'Neachtan, John,	i.	131
O'Reilly, John Boyle,	iv.	280
O'Shaughnessy, Arthur,	iv.	289
Ogle, Hon. George,	ii.	100
Orr, James,	ii.	165
Otway, Cæsar,	ii.	329
Parnell, Thomas,	i.	108
Petrie, George,	iii.	167
Pilkington, Mrs. Laetitia,	i.	209
Plunket, Wm. Conyngham,	iii.	15
Porter, J. L.,	iv.	207
Prendergast, John Patrick,	iv.	24
Read, Charles A.,	iv.	330
Reid, Mayne,	iv.	140
Riddell, Mrs. J. H.,	iv.	321
Roche, James,	iii.	46
Roscommon, Earl of,	i.	61
Russell, William Howard,	iv.	104
Ryves, Elizabeth,	ii.	36
Savage, Marmion W.,	iv.	51
Shee, Sir Martin Archer,	iii.	40
Shell, Richard Lalor,	iii.	79
Sheridan, Frances,	i.	258
Sheridan, Richard Brinsley,	ii.	101
Sheridan, Thomas,	i.	320
Simmons, Bartholomew,	iv.	198
Sloane, Sir Hans,	i.	102
Southerne, Thomas,	i.	196
Speranza,	iv.	79
Stanihurst, Richard,	i.	18
Steele, Sir Richard,	i.	134
Sterne, Laurence,	i.	229
Stokes, Margaret,	iv.	303
Stokes, William,	iii.	322
Strangford, Viscount,	iii.	114
Sullivan, A. M.,	iv.	223
Sullivan, T. D.,	iv.	223
Swift, Jonathan,	i.	166
Tate, Nahum,	i.	82
Taylor, Meadows,	iv.	84
Tennent, Sir James Emerson,	iii.	288
Thompson, William,	iii.	149
Thomson, Sir William,	iv.	264
Tighe, Mrs. Mary,	ii.	116
Todd, James Henthorn,	iii.	311
Todhunter, John,	iv.	266
Toland, John,	i.	103
Tone, Theobald Wolfe,	ii.	39
Torrens, William M'Cullagh,	iv.	75
Trench, Archbishop,	iv.	22
Tyndall, John,	iv.	126
Usher, Archbishop,	i.	23
Walker, Joseph Cooper,	ii.	74
Waller, John Francis,	iv.	123
Walsh, Edward, M.D.,	ii.	212
Walsh, Edward,	iii.	145
Walsh, John Edward,	iv.	31
Ward, Owen,	i.	15
Ware, Sir James,	i.	30
Wellington, Arthur, Duke of,	iii.	41
Whiteside, James,	iv.	64
Wilde, Lady,	iv.	79
Wilde, Richard Henry,	ii.	334
Williams, Richard Dalton,	iv.	117
Wills, James,	iii.	208
Wills, William Gorman,	iv.	258
Wilson, John Crawford,	iv.	130
Wingfield, Hon. Lewis,	iv.	292
Wiseman, Cardinal,	iii.	240
Wolfe, Charles,	ii.	107
Wolseley, Sir Garnet Joseph,	iv.	184

THE END.

LONDON: BLACKIE AND SON; DUBLIN, GLASGOW, AND EDINBURGH.

www.ingramcontent.com/pod-product-compliance
Lightning Source LLC
Chambersburg PA
CBHW020321240426
43673CB00039B/883